THE USES OF TRADITION

THE USES OF TRADITION

JEWISH CONTINUITY IN THE MODERN ERA

EDITED BY

JACK WERTHEIMER

THE JEWISH THEOLOGICAL SEMINARY
OF AMERICA
NEW YORK AND JERUSALEM

DISTRIBUTED BY HARVARD UNIVERSITY PRESS
CAMBRIDGE, MASSACHUSETTS AND LONDON

Library of Congress Cataloging-in-Publication Data
The Uses of Tradition : Jewish continuity in the modern era / edited by Jack Wertheimer.
p. cm.
Includes bibliographical references and index.
ISBN 0-674-93157-2 (cloth)—ISBN 0-674-93158-0 (paper)
1. Judaism—History—Modern period. 1750– 2. Judaism—20th century. 3. Judaism—Customs and practices—History—20th century. 4. Orthodox Judaism—History. 5. Jews—Cultural assimilation. 6. Jewish way of life. 7. Judaism—United States. I. Wertheimer, Jack.
BM195.U83 1993
296'.09'03—dc20 92-33133

Contents

PART II
The Retrieval of Tradition in
Modern Jewish Culture / 187

PART III
The Reappropriation of Tradition in Contemporary Judaism / 327

CONCLUSION
When Modern Jews Appropriate From the Tradition: A Symposium / 463

Foreword

In the closing decades of the twentieth century, movements throughout the world have challenged the supremacy of modern Western culture and have called for a return to traditional ways—especially religious teachings. Groups long regarded as peripheral, as fossils of a discarded past, have demonstrated remarkable resilience and a capacity to mobilize masses to battle against the ills of modern society. In the United States, for example, the traditional wings of American Protestantism, Catholicism, and Judaism manifest new-found strength. Suddenly these factions are more vocal, and seemingly more compelling, than their liberal counterparts. Religious traditionalists proudly broadcast their new appeal, while their liberal counterparts struggle to fill church and synagogue pews. The waning decades of the century are an age of triumphalism for religious and cultural traditionalists.

Within the American Jewish community, the romance with modernity has faded, especially among Jews preoccupied with their own survival as a distinctive group. One contributing factor has been the Holocaust, which has shattered the confidence Jews long entertained in the benign, and even protective, qualities of modern culture. The failure of enlightened Western culture to inoculate Europeans against murderously rabid anti-Semitism has shaken the faith of Jews, a population that previously had been unusually enamored of modernity. Disillusionment also stems from the failure of modern culture, particularly in the United States, to provide a coherent identity and communal anchor. In response to the openness and amorphousness of American culture, some Jews—like other Americans—have seized upon religious and cultural traditionalism, hoping to find secure mooring in a bewildering and rapidly changing world.

The quest for an authentic Judaism grounded in hallowed traditions has spurred some Jews to go back to the sources of their religion. Every branch of American Judaism has been reinvigorated by a movement of return (*teshuvah*). Not accidentally, some of the most attractive programs of the past two decades have selectively retrieved traditional forms—the *ḥavurah* among those in quest of community, New Moon and other women's rituals in feminist circles, Kabbalah for the mystically inclined, and midrash among those seeking older modes of interpretation to address current sensibilities. Traditional ways retain a powerful allure even for Jews fully at home in the modern world.

To date, most interpretations of the modern Jewish experience have scanted the role of traditionalism and favored the theme of modernization. By virtually all accounts, dynamic transformations, if not convulsive ruptures, were the hallmarks of Jewish modernity: Jews created new types of communities, restructured their economic activities, embraced unprecedented social opportunities, related to governments and gentile neighbors in new ways, reformed their religion, and reconceived the nature of Judaism and Jewish culture. In short, most historical works focus on Jews who broke with their past in order to live in the modern world.

The Uses of Tradition differs from these accounts because it is concerned primarily with THE PERSISTENCE OF TRADITION in modern Jewish life. The essays in this volume seek to understand the Jews who have resisted change or managed to evade the powerful impress of modern culture in order to maintain a degree of fidelity to the traditions of the past. By emphasizing continuity rather than change, these essays do not ignore the profound impact of modernization upon all facets of Jewish life. Indeed, several essays reveal the extent to which even the most traditional Jews created radically new ideologies and patterns of religious observance as they waged warfare against modernity. Still, this book is predominantly concerned with the way Jews have appropriated traditional aspects of their religion and culture to sustain them in the modern world.

In order to encompass the range of such acts of reappropriation, no single definition of tradition has been imposed upon contributors. In some cases, "tradition" is used as the antithesis of "modernization";

hence, when groups challenge modern modes of thinking or practices and seek to preserve or retrieve earlier ways, they are labeled as traditional. In other cases, "tradition" is defined more narrowly as "that which is handed down"—that is, any beliefs or practices which bring the past into the present. The specific content of these transmitted beliefs and practices is less important than their origination in the past or whether they are old or new traditions. Most often, the essays in this volume refer to traditions that are specific and normative: values, modes of thinking, interpretations, behaviors, and rituals are retrieved from the past to play a role in the lives of modern Jews. Such varying definitions reflect the diversity of scholarly opinion on the proper uses of the term "tradition." Fortunately, several of the essays in this volume directly address both this confusion over terminology as well as the social significance of the term "tradition" for modern Jews.[1]

The opening section of the book considers the relationship between various modern forms of religious orthodoxy and earlier expressions of Judaism. The so-called ultra-Orthodox and Ḥaredi sectors of Jewish society both in Eastern Europe and Israel receive greatest attention here because they claim to be the true heirs to traditional Judaism. Several essays aim to clarify DISCONTINUITIES between these varieties of Judaism and the traditional Judaisms of the past. Equally important, they examine the strategies employed by different types of orthodox Jews to reinterpret tradition—sometimes in a radical fashion—in order to withstand the onslaughts of modernity. By so doing, these essays introduce the broader theme of the book, namely how Jews in the modern world have employed [the] tradition selectively to forge a Judaism that can thrive in the modern world.

The book's early essays also examine the response of Jewish elites—particularly rabbinic figures—to the disintegration of traditional Jewish society. Spanning Jewish societies as disparate as those of North Africa and the Soviet Union, central Europe and the state of Israel, these essays shed light on the efforts of religious elites to halt the corrosive effects of modernization: To what extent could rabbis shield the Jewish masses

[1] See especially the statements in the conclusion of this book and the earlier essays of Charles S. Liebman and Arnold M. Eisen for discussions of the terminology and references to some of the major books and essays that reflect on the uses of the term "tradition." A good brief analysis of how social scientists employ the term appears in Lenore Eve Weissler, "Making Judaism Meaningful: Ambivalence and Tradition in a Havurah Community." (Dissertation: University of Pennsylvania, 1982), pp. 23-30.

from change? And how did they shore up the collapsing boundaries of religious communities under siege? The essays in Part I analyze the varieties of Orthodoxy designed to combat and retard the process of change.

The book's second section consists of historical essays on nineteenth- and early twentieth-century efforts to retrieve selectively aspects of traditional religion and culture. The unifying motif of these essays is the repeated efforts of modern Jews to retrieve the past—sometimes through selective reappropriation and other times by reinvention of the past—in order to maintain some relationship with a traditional religion and culture that no longer existed. This process of reinvention expressed itself in the unprecedented emphasis on heretofore insignificant holidays, such as Hanukkah; the nostalgic evocation of a destroyed Jewish culture through literature and art; and the reinterpretation and mythologizing of the Jewish historical past to address modern sensibilities and yearnings. These essays illustrate how modern Jews have creatively retrieved aspects of their past, even though they no longer lived within the enchanted circle of tradition. The act of retrieval has proven necessary to validate their distinctly modern lives by grounding them in an "authentic" tradition.

In the book's concluding section, several social scientists and historians of religion and Jewish thought reflect on contemporary efforts to reappropriate aspects of tradition. To some extent, such acts of reappropriation express a need to legitimize novel religious behaviors and beliefs: earlier models and modes of interpretation are invoked to justify distinctly modern approaches. The appropriation of the past, however, is also symptomatic of a yearning for rootedness and authenticity. The reappropriation of traditions thereby reflects a new respect for the ways of the ancients and at least a partial disillusionment with modernity.

By analyzing the persistence of tradition among modern Jews, this book seeks to redress an imbalance in Jewish historiography. Works on Jewish history lavish disproportionate attention on modernizers, often a small and unrepresentative elite, whereas the role of traditionalists often receives scant attention. This is most dramatically evident in historical works on the Jews of eastern Europe and Muslim lands, where the vanguard of revolutionaries and modernizers are accorded central importance; the vast majority of Jews whose culture and religion remained firmly traditional until well into the twentieth century are relegated to the periphery. The essays in this volume, by contrast, emphasize the struggle of traditionalists to maintain their communities' ways despite the transformations wrought by modernization.

An examination of the relationship of Jewish modernists to tradition also opens new avenues for exploration. Even the most radically innovative ideologies have retrieved aspects of traditional religion and culture—at times to mask their revolutionary aims in traditional rhetoric, at other times to fashion new solutions by recasting earlier forms, and at still other times in order to satisfy a longing for authenticity. Students of religion and Jewish society may profitably study the diverse ways in which modern Jews reappropriate traditional religion and culture with an eye to clarifying the limits of such acts of reappropriation: How extensively can tradition be reinterpreted before it is subverted? At what point is creative reinvention an act of betrayal? And how effectively can the SELECTIVE borrowing from tradition sustain a religious community? The essays in this volume shed light on these larger questions as they explore how modern Jews have reclaimed aspects of their tradition and how religious and cultural traditions continue to make claims on modern Jews.

Acknowledgments

Most contributions to this volume were first presented at the Henry N. Rapaport Memorial Conference held in November 1989 at the Jewish Theological Seminary of America. That conference was funded by an endowment established in memory of Henry N. Rapaport, a distinguished attorney who served on the board of the Jewish Theological Seminary and as president of the United Synagogue of America. We are indebted to Mrs. Selma Rapaport Pressman and her family, who have made it possible for JTS to present public programs of distinction, including two Rapaport Conferences, during the past decade.

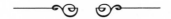

Throughout the years of conference planning and manuscript editing, I have benefited from the warm support of colleagues at the Jewish Theological Seminary of America. I particularly thank Chancellor Ismar Schorsch for providing me with the exciting opportunity to organize the Rapaport Conference and for his generously offered counsel and encouragement as the project unfolded. Dr. John Ruskay, Vice Chancellor for Public Affairs, participated actively in shaping the conference and book. He and Professor Ivan Marcus, who recently became Provost, attended to the myriad details attendant to the publication of a book. Professor Marcus was also generous in offering help with a variety of editorial matters. In conceptualizing the theme of the Rapaport conference, I was assisted by a hard-working committee of colleagues—Dr. John Ruskay and Professors Neil Gillman, David Kraemer, and David Roskies, with the latter playing a critical role in alerting us to the far-ranging implications of the topic. Renee Gutman participated actively in our deliberations and insured the smooth running of the Rapaport conference.

As the manuscript neared completion, I benefited greatly from the help of Jean Highland, publications consultant to the Seminary. Her sound advice has steered me through several complex ventures and has tempered my impatience when the publication process seemed interminable. Peter T. Daniels, the book's copyeditor, lavished meticulous attention to detail on the manuscript as he struggled to achieve consistency in the writing of twenty-one different authors. Timothy Hanssen performed superbly as a research and administrative assistant.

Finally, my sincere thanks to the score of colleagues who entrusted their work to me for publication in this volume. They have patiently endured much delayed gratification until they could finally see their work in print. I am especially indebted to Arnold M. Eisen, Harvey E. Goldberg, Jenna Weissman Joselit, and Stuart Schoenfeld for graciously agreeing on short notice to write essays that were not part of the conference in order to fill major gaps. I thank all the contributors listed in the table of contents for investing their creativity and energy in a common inquiry into the uses of Jewish tradition in the modern era.

Contributors

RICHARD I. COHEN, Senior Lecturer in Modern Jewish History at the Hebrew University of Jerusalem. He is the author of *The Burden of Conscience: French-Jewish Leadership During the Holocaust* (1987) and editor of *Vision and Conflict in the Holy Land* (1985). He has also edited and contributed to Raymond-Raoul Lambert, *Carnet d'un Temoin (1940-1943)* (1985); *The French Revolution and Its Impact* (in Hebrew, 1991); and served as guest symposium editor of "Art and Its Uses: The Visual Image and Modern Jewish Society," *Studies in Contemporary Jewry,* 1990. He is currently at work on a book of essays on the interrelationship between Jewish art and Jewish social history in the modern period and on a history of modern Jewish biographies.

ARNOLD M. EISEN. Associate Professor of Religious Studies and Aaron-Roland Fellow at Stanford University. He is a scholar of modern Jewish thought and practice, and he is the author of *The Chosen People in America: A Study in Jewish Religious Ideology* (1983) and *Galut: Modern Jewish Reflection on Homelessness and Homecoming* (1986). His current projects include a study of modern Jewish attitudes toward ritual observance and the self-identity of contemporary Jews.

DAVID ELLENSON. Anna Grancell Professor of Jewish Religious Thought at Hebrew Union College – Jewish Institute of Religion in Los Angeles. He is the author of *Tradition in Transition: Orthodoxy, Halakha, and the Boundaries of Modern Jewish Identity* and *Rabbi Esriel Hildesheimer and the Creation of a Modern Jewish Orthodoxy.* He is currently working on a volume tentatively entitled *Responsa Literature of the Nineteenth and Twentieth Centuries.* In addition, he is writing another book, *Major Trends in Modern Judaism.*

DAVID E. FISHMAN. Assistant Professor of Jewish History at the Jewish Theological Seminary of America, and Research Associate at the YIVO Institute for Jewish Research. He has published studies on the religious, intellectual, and cultural history of east European Jewry and is currently writing a book on Byelorussian Jewry in the era of Catherine the Great. He has translated the Warsaw Ghetto writings of Rabbi Shimon Huberband, *Kiddush Hashem,* and is editor-in-chief of *YIVO Bletter.* He directs a joint program in Jewish studies between the Seminary, YIVO, and the Russian State University of the Humanities in Moscow.

MENACHEM FRIEDMAN. Associate Professor of Sociology at Bar Ilan University. He is the author of *Ḥevrah ve-dat: Ha-ortodoqsia ha-lo-ṣionit be-eretz yisraʾel, 1918–1936* (Society and Religion: The Non-Zionist Orthodox in Eretz-Israel, 1918–1936) and is coauthor of a pamphlet entitled *The Ḥaredim in Israel: Who are They And What Do They Want?*

HARVEY E. GOLDBERG. Professor in the Department of Sociology and Anthropology at the Hebrew University of Jerusalem. His research interests are in the Jewish communities of the Middle East, and he writes on ethnicity in Israeli society. He has edited a collection entitled *Judaism Viewed from Within and from Without: Anthropological Studies,* a volume designed to show the relevance of anthropology to Judaic studies. Most recently he has published *Jewish Life in Muslim Libya: Rivals and Relatives.*

JAY M. HARRIS. Harris K. Weston Associate Professor of the Humanities at Harvard University. He is the author of *Nachman Krochmal: Guiding the Perplexed of the Modern Age.* He is currently at work on a book devoted to the history of Jewish legal exegesis and its place in Jewish culture throughout the ages.

BARRY W. HOLTZ. Codirector of the Melton Research Center at the Jewish Theological Seminary of America and Associate Professor in the Seminary's Department of Jewish Education. He is the author of *Finding Our Way: Jewish Texts and the Lives We Lead Today* and is the editor of *Back to the Sources: Reading the Classic Jewish Texts.*

PAULA E. HYMAN. Lucy Moses Professor of Modern Jewish History at Yale University, where she also chairs the Program in Judaic Studies. Her study of the accommodation of village Jews to the political, economic, and cultural features of modern France has recently been published as *The Emancipation of the Jews of Alsace: Acculturation and Tradition in the Nineteenth Century.* She is also the author of *From Dreyfus to Vichy: The Remaking of French Jewry, 1906-1939* and *The Jewish Woman in America* (with Charlotte Baum and Sonya Michel) and coeditor (with Steven M. Cohen) of *The Jewish Family: Myths and Reality.* She is currently working on a book of lectures on the topic "Gender and Assimilation: Roles and Representation of Women in Modern Jewish History."

JENNA WEISSMAN JOSELIT. Senior Research Scholar at the Center for Jewish Studies of the City University of New York Graduate Center. She is the author of *Our Gang: Jewish Crime and the New York Jewish Community* and *New York's Jewish Jews: The Orthodox Community of the Interwar Years,* and, most recently, she is coeditor with Susan Braunstein of *Getting Comfortable in New York: The American Jewish Home, 1880-1950.* She is currently writing a social history of American Jewish domestic culture.

LAWRENCE KAPLAN. Associate Professor of Rabbinics and Jewish Philosophy in the Department of Jewish Studies of McGill University. He is a specialist in both medieval and modern Jewish thought and has published numerous articles in popular and scholarly journals. He received a special commendation from the National Jewish Book Council for his translation from the Hebrew of Rabbi Joseph Soloveitchik's monograph, *Halakhic Man.* He recently both coedited and contributed to two volumes of essays, *The Thought of Moses Maimonides* and a forthcoming book on the thought of Rabbi Abraham I. Kook. He is currently completing a monograph on the thought of Rabbi Joseph Soloveitchik.

CHARLES S. LIEBMAN. Professor of Political Studies at Bar Ilan University and author of books and articles dealing with American Judaism, Israel–Diaspora relations, and religion and politics in Israeli society. His most recent books include *Civil Religion in Israel,* coauthored with Eliezer Don-Yehiya, and *Two Worlds of Judaism: The Israeli and American Experiences,* coauthored with Steven M. Cohen.

SHULAMIT S. MAGNUS. Acting Assistant Professor of History, Department of History, Stanford University. Her areas of research include modern German Jewry, Jewish women's history, and gender in Jewish history. She is currently at work on *Cologne: Jewish Emancipation in a German City, 1798–1871* as well as an analysis of the memoirs of Pauline Wengeroff (*Memoiren einer Grossmutter*).

IVAN G. MARCUS. Professor of Jewish History and Provost at the Jewish Theological Seminary of America. He is the author of *Piety and Society: The Jewish Pietists of Medieval Germany* and is completing a monograph on a Jewish child's cultural initiation into elementary schooling in medieval Europe, as well as a new critical edition and English translation of *Sefer Ḥasidim.*

PAUL MENDES-FLOHR. Professor of Modern Jewish Thought at the Hebrew University of Jerusalem. His research interests include modern Jewish intellectual history, with particular emphasis on central Europe. He has edited some twenty-five books and has written four, including *Divided Passions: Jewish Intellectuals and the Experience of Modernity* (1991) and *From Mysticism to Dialogue: Martin Buber and the Transformation of German Social Thought* (1990). He is currently working on a cultural biography of Franz Rosenzweig.

MICHAEL A. MEYER. Professor of Jewish History at Hebrew Union College – Jewish Institute of Religion in Cincinnati. Among the books he has published are *The Origins of the Modern Jews, Ideas of Jewish History, Response to Modernity,* and *Jewish Identity in the Modern World.* His research interests are focused in the areas of modern Jewish religious and intellectual history and Jewish historiography. He is currently the general editor and one of the contributors to a projected four-volume history of modern German Jewry, to appear in 1995 under the auspices of the Leo Baeck Institute.

JOSEPH REIMER. Assistant Professor in the Hornstein Program in Jewish Communal Service at Brandeis University. A scholar in the field of moral development and education, Dr. Reimer is the author of *Promoting Moral Growth: From Piaget to Kohlberg.* He is currently writing a book on the synagogue as an educational institution.

DAVID G. ROSKIES. Professor of Jewish Literature at the Jewish Theological Seminary of America. He is cofounder and editor of *Prooftexts: A Journal of Jewish Literary History.* His book *Against the Apocalypse: Responses to Catastrophe in Modern Jewish Culture* received the Ralph Waldo Emerson Prize from Phi Beta Kappa. A companion volume, *The Literature of Destruction,* was published in 1989. The present essay was written in tandem with two of his forthcoming books: *The Dybbuk and Other Writings by S. Ansky* and *The Lost Art of Yiddish Storytelling.*

STUART SCHOENFELD. Associate Professor of Sociology and Jewish Studies at Glendon College, York University in Toronto. He is the author of numerous articles, including a series of studies of bar and bat mitzvah as rituals of identification in contemporary Jewish life. He is presently chair of the Research Network in Jewish Education.

MICHAEL K. SILBER. Lecturer in the Department of Jewish History and the Director of the Rosenfeld Research Project on the History of the Jews of Hungary and the Habsburg Empire at the Hebrew University of Jerusalem. He has recently edited *Jews in the Hungarian Economy, 1760-1945.*

JACK WERTHEIMER. Holds the Joseph and Martha Mendelson Chair in American Jewish History at the Jewish Theological Seminary of America, where he also directs the Joseph and Miriam Ratner Center for the Study of Conservative Judaism. He is the author of *Unwelcome Strangers: East European Jews in Imperial Germany* and is completing a book on the transformation of American Judaism in the second half of the twentieth century. He is also the editor of *The American Synagogue: A Sanctuary Transformed* and *The Modern Jewish Experience: A Reader's Guide.*

PART I

The Confrontation of Traditionalists With Modernity

David Ellenson's opening essay announces the overarching theme of this section when he claims that "a religious tradition stands in conjunction with, not separate from, the world in which it exists." The six essays in this section situate religious traditionalists in various environments, ranging from mid-nineteenth-century Germany and Hungary to twentieth-century colonial north Africa, from Bolshevik Russia to post-Holocaust Israel. Each examines the multiple challenges faced by religious leaders as their traditional communities crumbled around them. Collectively, these essays demonstrate how traditionalists who resisted modern ways nevertheless innovated, even as they claimed to speak for an eternal, unchanging Judaism.

The essays of David Ellenson and Michael Silber introduce two contrasting worlds of Orthodoxy. Ellenson analyzes the emergence of neo-Orthodoxy in Germany as a response of traditionalists to religious reformers. He describes the novel methods employed by neo-Orthodox rabbinic figures, such as their recourse to Kantian categories in defense of the tradition and their secession from established Jewish communities. The latter is especially dramatic in light of the priority placed upon communal unity—a traditional value—by the learned and less acculturated rabbi of Würzburg, whereas neo-Orthodox rabbis risked fragmenting the community in order to insulate their followers from the greater threat posed by reformers. In his effort to understand how such traditionalism worked, Ellenson introduces a motif that will recur throughout this section: namely, that tradionalists seemed oblivious of the radical nature of their strategies, thus displaying a lack of self-consciousness that made it possible for them to clothe themselves in the mantle of tradition.

Ultra-Orthodoxy, another form of traditionalism, first arose in Hungary and in our own time continues to exert a powerful influence due to the dispersal of Orthodox Hungarian Jews after the Holocaust. In light of this group's remarkable impact and resilience, Michael Silber's careful dissection of the crises that gave birth to ultra-Orthodoxy is particularly useful. Interestingly, Rabbi Esriel Hildesheimer appears in both Ellenson's and Silber's essays, but he was regarded very differently by his German and Hungarian colleagues. Whereas Hildesheimer's proposal for a rabbinical seminary provoked a bitter controversy in Hungary, a few years later Hildesheimer successfully established such an institution in Berlin and it became the standard-bearer for neo-Orthodoxy. The disparate assessments of Rabbi Esriel Hildesheimer in Germany and Hungary throw into bold relief the differences between various types of Orthodoxy that emerged in the second half of the nineteenth century. The essays by Ellenson and Silber also highlight the different programs of key religious institutions—synagogues, schools, rabbinic seminaries—established by neo- and ultra-Orthodox Jews.

The essays of David Fishman and Harvey Goldberg examine the responses of traditionalists in two very different environments to massive and rapid social change, in Communist countries and colonial North Africa. Not the least of the virtues of these essays is the attention they lavish on Jews who sought ways to preserve traditional religious and cultural life, a population often overlooked in works that stress the activities of modernizers. Rabbi Joseph Isaac Schneerson, the last Lubavitcher Rebbe to reside in Russia, is the protagonist of Fishman's essay. Sifting through hagiographic literature published by the Habad Hasidic movement and archival documents of Jewish relief agencies, Fishman scrutinizes the efforts of Schneerson to thwart the powerful program to crush Judaism designed by the new Bolshevik regime. Schneerson's efforts ultimately failed and he was forced to flee the Soviet Union. But his clandestine activities to maintain Jewish religious life illustrate a noteworthy reponse by a traditionalist leader to the war of repression waged by Communist regimes against Judaism.

Harvey Goldberg introduces the world of non-Ashkenazic Jewry, principally the Jews of Morocco and Libya. His essay provides entrée into recent historical and anthropological research on the modern history of North African Jewry. Goldberg examines the strategies devised both by elites and the folk to cope with the unprecedented disruption of traditional communal life brought about by colonial governments. He then extends his account to contemporary Israel, where the traditional life of North African Jewry further eroded. Goldberg interprets the public displays surrounding annual days devoted to the veneration of saints as opportunities for even modernized Jews who had abandoned most religious practices to identify for a brief interval with the traditional communities they had left behind. His essay provides a valuable basis for comparing traditionalist responses in Ashkenzazic and Sephardic communities to powerful forces of change.

Both Lawrence Kaplan and Menachem Friedman write about Rabbi Abraham Y. Karelitz, known as the Ḥazon Ish, whose legacy dominates the culture of Ḥaredi Judaism—the ultra-Orthodox, non-Zionist, non-Hasidic Judaism of Ashkenazic Jews in contemporary Israel. Kaplan examines the ideological position and religious rulings of the Ḥazon Ish against the backdrop of east European Judaism in the nineteenth and early twentieth centuries. His essay analyzes the critique leveled by the Ḥazon Ish at two strategies employed by highly traditional rabbis to combat modernity: the method of analytical Talmud study devised by Rabbi Ḥayyim Soleveitchik, and the novel psychological and ethical teachings disseminated by the Musar movement. As Kaplan astutely observes, the Ḥazon Ish criticized proponents of both movements because they "conceded too much to modernity by allowing too great a role for human self-assertion and human autonomy." Kaplan's essay also sheds considerable light on the uses of self-denial and stringency by traditionalists to counter the priority placed by modern culture on expressiveness and relativism.

Menachem Friedman is particularly intrigued by the social implications of the Ḥazon Ish's rulings regarding the proper measure of wine that must be imbibed when Jews sanctify the Sabbath and holidays. With this ruling, the Ḥazon Ish implicitly disqualified the wine goblets passed down through generations in traditional Jewish families. Surely, the *Kiddush* cup handed down from one generation to the next tangibly attests to the transmission of tradition. What was the social function of the Ḥazon Ish's severe decision to rule that earlier generations failed to observe basic rituals properly? And how, asks Friedman, could such a revolution against familial traditions occur? Friedman views the significance of the Ḥazon Ish's ruling within the context of the struggle between yeshivas and other institutions in the traditional communities.

As the former evolved into "total institutions," they replaced the family as the primary vehicle of religious socialization. The rejection of family wine cups signifies the final triumph of the yeshiva over the family: the ways of our family's ancestors were incorrect; only the learned opinion of the rabbis is worthy of emulation. Tradition, as Friedman notes, is no longer in the hands of an organic community but is monopolized by an insulated "total institution." Hence, Ḥaredi Jews today have rejected the PROCESS by which Jewish communities traditionally functioned. The poignant fate of the lost *Kiddush* cup provides a fitting conclusion to this section because it offers powerful evidence that even the traditions of east European Jews prior to the Holocaust have not been spared from radical reinterpretation by present-day traditionalists living in different circumstances.

1

German Jewish Orthodoxy: Tradition in the Context of Culture

DAVID ELLENSON

The study of German Jewish history of the last two hundred years has primarily centered around a description of Jewish religious and cultural reform. Jewish defense organizations and the rise of a small but significant Zionist movement have also garnered considerable academic attention. With the exception of some work on Rabbi Samson Raphael Hirsch, the Orthodox have not been a major focus of these investigations. The reason for this is that Orthodox Judaism has largely been perceived as irrelevant to this tale of how Jewish tradition confronted the challenge of living in a radically changed milieu. As the focus of Jewish academic concerns has been a description and analysis of how Jewish tradition responded to the challenges of a modern world, it has been tacitly assumed that Orthodoxy and tradition succeeded in sealing themselves off hermetically from the effects of a contemporary setting. A study of Orthodoxy would thus have little or no bearing on this tale of oscillation between an undifferentiated medieval past and the excitement and dynamism, the pluralism, of a modern Jewish present.

This, of course, is understandable. After all, the Orthodox, as adherents of Jewish tradition, viewed themselves and their tradition as part of an eternal reality. The German Orthodox Jew, like all religious traditionalists, believed that Jewish tradition endured in an eternal present. Tradition may evoke precedent, but it does not have, for the adherent, a history. Tradition may relate to context, but it nevertheless exists, for the believer, in an enduring moment. This is why, as Peter Berger has observed, tradition requires neither defense nor explanation from its followers. The tradition itself, to its practitioners, provides the internalized contours within which reality is experienced. Life in accord with its beliefs and prescriptions is perceived as the only proper way in which an authentic religious existence can be attained. The "very nature of tradition," writes Berger, is to "be taken for granted."[1] This "taken-for-grantedness" of religious tradition is what allowed Rabbi S. R. Hirsch of Frankfurt to view himself, in contrast to the Reformers, as defender of an eternal, unchanging tradition that measured the contemporary world against the yardstick of an immutable Law. It also permitted Hermann Schwab, the chronicler and apologete of Orthodox Judaism in Germany, to assert, "German-Jewish Orthodoxy was Sinai Judaism."[2]

Recent years have witnessed the emergence of a critical and reflective attitude among academics toward this German Jewish Orthodox self-assessment. There has been a new appreciation that German Orthodoxy, like other Jewish movements and trends in that land, was shaped, in great measure, by the external German environment and that an understanding of its responses to a modern world where no external marks distinguished Orthodox Jews from their non-Orthodox coreligionists is vital if a full portrait of modern Judaism and its struggles with the reformulation of tradition is to be complete. Studies of Samson Raphael Hirsch and his community by Noah Rosenbloom and Robert Liberles, as well as the comprehensive thematic study of German Orthodoxy by Mordecai Breuer, clearly bear witness to this inclusionary trend in modern Jewish historiography.[3]

Undergirding these studies is the proposition that a religious tradition stands in conjunction with, not separate from, the world in which it exists. While adherents of a tradition may constantly proclaim their religion's changelessness, the interpreter of a tradition affirms the axiom, as Heraclitus observed millennia ago, that change, even within the realm of

---

[1] Peter Berger, *The Heretical Imperative* (New York: Anchor Books, 1979), 30.

[2] Hermann Schwab, *The History of Orthodox Jewry in Germany* (London: Mitre, 1950), 11.

[3] Rosenbloom, *Tradition in an Age of Reform* (Philadelphia: Jewish Publication Society, 1976); Liberles, *Religious Conflict in Social Context: The Resurgence of Orthodox Judaism in Frankfurt am Main* (Westport, Conn.: Greenwood, 1985). Breuer's magisterial and comprehensive study of German Orthodoxy is entitled *Jüdische Orthodoxie im Deutschen Reich, 1871–1918* (Frankfurt a.M.: Jüdischer Verlag bei Athenäum, 1986).

tradition, is constant. The task of the student of German Orthodox Judaism is thus to make sense of a particular world of ethnicity and belief. It is to ask about the specific matrix in which German Orthodoxy had its being, and to comprehend the shape and meaning of Orthodox Judaism in Germany by describing the dialectical interplay between Jewish tradition on the one hand and the social and cultural world that was Germany on the other.

Foremost among the concepts social scientists have employed to describe such interplay is the notion of modernization. Modernization is, of course, a multifaceted and complex phenomenon. Yet secularization is among its primary elements. By employing this term, sociologists do not mean that religion or religious tradition disappears when it confronts the process of modernization. Rather, secularization signifies that religion comes to inform and direct fewer activities in the lives of both individuals and communities. Nontraditional, nonreligious warrants and motivations come to fill the vacuum that the disappearance of the religious in various spheres has left. If the attitude of the premodern traditionalist is captured in the words of the Psalmist, "I have placed the Eternal before me always," the paraphrase uttered even by the religious traditionalist in a secularized world is, "I place the Eternal before me, but not all the time." Such a concept provides a fruitful paradigm for comprehending the nature of Jewish Orthodoxy within the context of German culture and for grasping the dynamic that characterized its approach to and reformulation of tradition.

Secularization and the Struggle Over Secession

The German Orthodox, unlike Jewish traditionalists elsewhere, accepted with equanimity the diminution of traditional Jewish influence and guidance in vast areas of life. The dismantling of the political structure of the community, far from being a trauma, constituted a development that the German Orthodox applauded. As Ismar Schorsch has observed, Samson Raphael Hirsch, the leading ideologue of modern German Orthodoxy, "dropped all demands for judicial autonomy and continuance of Jewish civil law."[4] Simply put, the German Orthodox recognized that Jewish tradition now had to confront a political reality where the *Ḥoshen Mishpaṭ* had fallen into desuetude. Acknowledgement

4 Ismar Schorsch, *Jewish Reactions to German Anti-Semitism* (Philadelphia: Jewish Publication Society, 1972), 10.

of this acceptance is seen not only in the position of Hirsch, but in the fact that no course on Jewish civil law was included in the curriculum of the Orthodox Berlin Rabbinical Seminary. The German Orthodox simply surrendered to the facticity of this development and became enthusiastic proponents of Jewish political emancipation. Like their Reform counterparts, they applauded and anxiously embraced the political character of the modern world.

Secularization and its effects, however, were not confined to the political arena. They evidenced themselves in the area of dress, language, education, and religious custom as well. One sees this most clearly if elements of German Orthodoxy are contrasted with the notion of traditional Orthodoxy put forth by their Orthodox peers in Hungary. Rabbi Moses Schreiber, the *Ḥatam Sofer*, leader of Hungarian traditionalism whose legacy continued to inform sectors of Hungarian Orthodoxy throughout the 1800s, discouraged Jewish usage of the vernacular and asked that Jews maintain distinctive garb which would separate them from non-Jews. Schreiber conferred the status of religious obligation upon such items. He, quite clearly, desired to resist those secularizing trends in the modern world that defined such areas in areligious terms. For Schreiber, dress and language were as much matters of religious concern as dietary and marriage laws.[5] It was otherwise for the German Orthodox. Matters of dress and language were seen essentially as items of customs and manners. They were in the strictest sense religiously neutral. Judaism, in their opinion, simply did not demand that Jews distinguish themselves from their gentile neighbors in these ways. Thus, Hirsch, Hildesheimer, and other German Orthodox leaders dressed in contemporary Western garb and mastered and championed the vernacular in their speech and writings, developments that aroused the ire of their traditionalist brethren in Hungary.[6]

This tendency can also be seen in the area of religious customs. The Hungarian Orthodox, gathered in Mihalowitz in 1865, banned entry into

---

[5] See Jacob Katz, "Contributions toward a Biography of the Ḥatam Sofer," (in Hebrew), in *Studies in Mysticism and Religion Presented to Gershom G. Scholem*, ed. E.E. Urbach et al. (Jerusalem: Magnes, 1967), 115–61, for a summary of Schreiber's positions on these matters.

[6] See the translation of Hungarian Rabbi Akiva Y. Schlesinger's polemic, for example, against Esriel Hildesheimer in Alexander Guttmann, *The Struggle Over Reform in Rabbinic Literature* (New York and Jerusalem: World Union for Progressive Judaism, 1977), 289–91. See also the memoir of Hildesheimer's daughter, Esther Calavary, in her "Kindheitserinnerungen," *Bulletin des Leo Baeck Instituts* 8 (1959): 187–92.

synagogues where sermons were preached in the vernacular, where unaccompanied all-male choirs participated in services, where weddings took place within them, where the architecture could be confused with that of a church, and where Jewish religious officiants wore clerical robes like clergymen in non-Jewish religious traditions. The German Orthodox, informed as they were by nineteenth-century standards of German aesthetics and ritual, introduced all these reforms into their synagogue buildings and worship services.[7] Guidelines were often drawn up for German Orthodox synagogues forbidding indecorous or incivil behavior, even on Purim. Clearly, nineteenth-century German standards of behavior, not Jewish tradition, informed the practice of German Orthodox traditionalism on all these matters.[8]

Most significantly, from the perspective of this analysis, the German Orthodox often justified these innovations in the synagogue life of German Judaism on the grounds that such innovations were religiously neutral. That is, the Halakhah, in their view, often took no direct stance on some of these matters. Thus, Esriel Hildesheimer, in responding to these directives issued by the Hungarian Orthodox, said that the architectural style of a synagogue was essentially insignificant to Judaism. Instead what mattered was that a "genuine Jewish spirit" reside in the hearts of those whose worshiped within such a building.[9] Jewish tradition simply was not paramount in informing matters such as ritual dress and synagogue architecture, nor in several of the other items listed above. The impact of secularization—meaning that religion comes to inform fewer spheres of life—can thus be seen even in the liturgical life and practice of the German Orthodox community.

Secularization theory also helps cast light on one of the famous episodes in the history of nineteenth-century German Orthodox history, the struggle over the *Austrittsgesetz* in 1876. As is well known, Samson Raphael Hirsch along with Esriel Hildesheimer led the battle for the passage of a law that ultimately permitted German Orthodox Jews to secede legally, if they so wished, from the *Einheitsgemeinde* in the communities in which they lived. This permitted and fostered the devel-

---

7 These prohibitions are listed in Esriel Hildesheimer, "Ein Beitrag zur Bedeutung von *Chukot Ha Goyim*," in *Rabbiner Dr. I. Hildesheimer, Gesammelte Aufsätze*, ed. M. Hildesheimer (Frankfurt: Kauffmann, 1923), 24–26.

8 See Jakob Petuchowski, *Prayerbook Reform in Europe* (New York: World Union for Progressive Judaism, 1968), 123f., for some representative examples of these Orthodox ordinances.

9 Hildesheimer, "Beitrag" 19.

opment of separatist Orthodox religious congregations in communities such as Berlin and Frankfurt. Of course, such congregations preceded the passage of this law, and many members of these congregations, even after the law was passed by the Prussian Parliament, retained their membership in the larger legal community of Jews in these and other cities—even when such membership was condemned, as it was in Frankfurt, by leaders such as Rabbi Hirsch.[10]

In light of this, it is interesting that Seligman Baer Bamberger, the Würzburger *rav* and greatest talmudist then alive in Germany, much to the dismay of Rabbi Hirsch, opposed passage of this law. The reasons for this are many. Nevertheless, from the perspective of secularization theory, one can assert that for a rabbi like Bamberger, one of the principal reasons for his opposition to passage of the law was his traditionalist commitment to the notion of a unified Jewish community, a commitment that could not be shaken even by the rise and dominance of Reform in most German Jewish communities by the third quarter of the nineteenth century. So long as Orthodox religious interests on matters of kashruth and education were attended to by the larger community, such secession, in Bamberger's opinion, constituted needless splintering of the community.[11]

Hirsch and Hildesheimer, unlike Bamberger, spoke German. They had received educations not only in yeshivas, but in modern German universities. They were undoubtedly more sensitive, on many levels, to the challenges Reform posed for Orthodoxy than was Bamberger. Their stance may well have been more prudential, given the realities of the situation, than Bamberger's. Nevertheless, the same impulse toward Jewish communal unity, an impulse informed by the tradition that had previously led Hirsch and Hildesheimer in the 1840s to fight Reform efforts in several communities to secede from the larger community, continued to inform Bamberger here. However, the reality of a secularized world, and the commitment, knowledge, and observance it brought in its wake, led Hirsch and Hildesheimer to support separatism as a viable Orthodox position in the modern world. Secularization and its consequences caused them to surrender any aspiration for a unified community. It inclined them to formulate the mandate of Jewish tradi-

---

[10] Saemy Japhet, "The Secession From the Frankfurt Jewish Community Under S. R. Hirsch," *Historia Judaica* 10 (1948): 99–122.

[11] For an account of the struggle between Bamberger and Hirsch over secession, see Samson Raphael Hirsch, *Gesammelte Schriften*, 6 vol. (Frankfurt a.M.: Kauffmann, 1908), 4:295–407.

tion on this issue in a way that was distinct from Bamberger's and that departed from the way that tradition had been understood in Germany during the premodern era. The process of secularization indicates that religious tradition could no longer hope to inform all sectors of a modern Jewish community, and a perceptive modern Orthodox leadership understood this. Consolidation of the traditionalist segment of the community, not outreach to the nonobservant, dominated their program for late nineteenth century German Jewish life. The impact of secularization, and Hirsch's and Hildesheimer's awareness of that impact, indicate why this was so. It illuminates this conflict between Bamberger and Hirsch over secession and yields considerable insight into the development of Jewish Orthodoxy's attitude toward the non-Orthodox sectors of the community in the modern period.[12]

This episode also reveals something significant about the nature of tradition itself. Tradition, it is clear, is constantly involved in a process of reformulation. It both contracts and expands in response to a new setting. It does not remain static. The position of Hirsch and Hildesheimer—the champions of Jewish tradition in this German setting—on the matter of secession reveals that tradition neither continues undisturbed nor totally evaporates as it moves on in time and place. Instead, like a river, it flows through set banks and meanders through new channels.

Acculturation and the Defense of Traditional Institutions, Practices, and Beliefs

Cultural integration, as all scholars have observed, was the hallmark of German Jewry. The Orthodox, as much as the liberals, were thoroughly acculturated, and they, like their liberal colleagues, had internalized the Germanic notion of *Bildung* and the educational ideals and sensibilities that were a part of it. Orthodox leaders themselves employed these notions to guide the tradition through the shoals of this new era. One interesting example of such accommodation by tradition to its nineteenth-century German context can be seen in a responsum issued by Esriel Hildesheimer. As rabbi of Congregation Adass Jisroel in Berlin, Hildesheimer had to confront the reality that many of the congregation's

[12] For a fuller account of this episode and the use of sociological theory to illuminate it, see David Ellenson, "Church-Sect Theory, Religious Authority, and Modern Jewish Orthodoxy," in *Approaches to the Study of Modern Judaism* ed., Marc Raphael, (Chico, Calif.: Scholars Press, 1983), 63–83.

children attended *Gymnasium* on the Sabbath and consequently were unable to attend Saturday morning services. Hildesheimer feared that if these children did not hear the traditional Sabbath morning Torah reading, the Torah would be "forgotten in Israel." He therefore issued the unprecedented decree that a Torah reading with the traditional seven Torah readers be held on Saturday afternoon when the students had returned from school. After the Torah reading, the Musaf service was to be chanted, followed by the prescribed Minḥa service. He made no attempt to justify this measure from a Jewish legal point of view other than to label it as an "emergency measure."[13] A generation later, Hildesheimer's successor, David Hoffmann, admitted that this measure was of dubious Jewish legality. However, in defending his own decision to continue this custom into the twentieth century, he quickly cited the verse employed by rabbis throughout the centuries to legitimate extraordinary measures taken in times of stress, "It is time to serve the Lord, make void thy Law" (*Mishnah Berachot 9:5*).[14]

The evolution of tradition as a constant in human history can also been seen in the use German Orthodox leaders made of philosophy in their efforts to conceptualize and defend Jewish tradition in this changed setting. The matters of sacrificial references and prayers for restoration of the temple cult were a point of controversy and great debate in nineteenth century German Jewry. The Reformers, for the most part, labeled such references as atavisms from an ancient past and removed petitions for their return from their liturgy. While a rabbi such as David Hoffmann recognized that no less authoritative a Jewish figure than Maimonides had explained the sacrificial cult in a similar way as a primitive mode of worship, he and other Orthodox leaders realized that Maimonides, whatever his misgivings, retained such passages in his prayer service.[15] As champions and defenders of an eternal tradition, the Orthodox, like Maimonides before them, would not countenance removal of these passages from the liturgy of the synagogue. Sacrifices and the temple cult were simply too integral a part of Jewish tradition and messianic hopes.

Yet for these acculturated leaders of German Orthodoxy, the idea of literally slaughtering animals as a mode of worshiping God appeared

---

13 Esriel Hildesheimer, *The Responsa of Rabbi Esriel, Orah Ḥayyim,* (Tel Aviv: C. Gittler, 1969), 123.

14 Ibid.

15 Hoffmann quotes Maimonides, *Moreh Nevuḥim* 3:32, in David Hoffmann, *Das Buch Leviticus*, 2 vol. (Berlin: Poppelauer, 1905), 1:79.

repugnant. Moreover, for them, no less than for the Reformers, the expiatory function often attributed to sacrificial worship in both the Bible and Christian exegesis not only ran counter to many Jewish interpretations of selected scriptural passages, but, perhaps even more significantly, was opposed to a Kantian notion that a moral act is an autonomous one done at the behest of the individual's own moral will and for which the individual must be prepared to shoulder full ethical responsibility. The contention that an individual's sin could be forgiven through the death of an animal was one which did not appeal to these German bourgeoisie.

The paradigmatic Orthodox response to this dilemma is contained in the writings of Samson Raphael Hirsch. While Hirsch's attention to this subject is voluminous, the key point that emerges from an examination of his interpretations on this matter is that the sacrifices and prayers for their return must be understood on a metaphoric and symbolic, not a literal, level. Symbols, Hirsch wrote, testify to the human ability to "express ideas by physically perceptible signs."[16] They are as natural a means of human communication as the written or spoken word. Symbols, and their contemporary exposition, permit the eternal truth and validity of Jewish laws which might otherwise be branded as outmoded to be affirmed. Indeed, there were those who wished to assert, stated Hirsch, that "if a divine law has only symbolic value," then the act itself "can be discarded like an empty shell."[17]

Such a conclusion, Hirsch felt, was totally unwarranted. Inasmuch as the ideas "which permeate the symbols are eternal," then the symbols possess "a meaning which raises them high above all changes of time and place."[18] Contemporaneous attacks upon the sacrificial cult and prayers for the restoration of temple worship in Jerusalem as literary references to a primitive Jewish past that would better be banished miss the point of their mention. "Must we," asks Hirsch, "see an object or phenomenon simply in terms of its apparently literal meaning or is it possible that the object or phenomenon before us is a symbol?" If the object can be interpreted as such, then removal of the symbol would be tantamount to abrogating the "eternal ideas" which permeate them.[19] This is the mistake the Reformers made in their zeal to either remove such passages from the liturgy or consign them to the past tense.

---

[16] Hirsch, *Gesammelte Schriften,* 3:214.

[17] Ibid., 229.

[18] Ibid.

[19] Ibid., 220.

Hirsch continued his defense of the sacrificial cult, as men such as Naḥmanides and Mendelssohn had done before, by elucidating their symbolic significance. His commentary on Lev. 16:21ff. illustrates the nature of his approach and tells us a great deal about how German Orthodoxy reformulated tradition. These verses, which speak of the he-goat upon whose head the High Priest casts all the sins of the people Israel, are not understood as describing an act of expiation. Instead, the passage is understood allegorically as referring to human rebellion against God's will. "Placed at the threshold of the Sanctuary of His Torah . . .," writes Hirsch, "we fight shy of giving up our selfish living for our own leisure, and, repulsed by and afraid of the demands of God's laws of morality, we hold ourselves stubbornly against Him as a *sa-ir ḥai*, a 'live he-goat.'"[20] However, the Jewish people have the capacity to acknowledge their sins and errors and to vow that these will not be repeated. The goat which is sent out of the camp is "the embodiment of that mistaken way of life which misuses the divine gift of free decision by giving oneself up to be mastered by one's senses, and which turns that which was given to us to devote to moral freedom, to devotion, into moral lack of freedom."[21] The hurtling down of the goat is no offering sent down to appease a demon of the wild, nor is the goat's destruction a substitute "scapegoat" for the sins of the people.[22]

Hirsch, instead, explains in his commentary on Lev. 16:10, "But the he-goat upon which the lot 'Azazel's' fell is to remain standing alive before God, to effect atonement on it, and to let it go as 'Azazel's' into the wilderness," that each of us is the "he-goat" of this passage. Each human being is blessed by God with freedom, and thus with the moral power to resist temptation and do God's will, or else to acquiesce to such temptations and rebel against God and God's "holy Laws of morality." The decision to rebel, to sink "into the power of sensuality in contrast to attachment . . . [to] His laws of morality is here called *l'azazel*. The simplest . . . meaning of this word is *'oz 'azal*, the character of firmness, obstinacy, *'oz*, which *'azal*, which has no future, which disappears, which, in thinking itself *'oz* just thereby digs its own grave."[23] Hirsch, in keeping with rabbinic exegesis of these passages in LEVITICUS, not only avoids interpreting the *sa'ir's* function as an expiatory one. Rather, through his symbolic and metaphoric exegesis he is able to demonstrate that these

[20] Samson Raphael Hirsch, *Leviticus* (Frankfurt a.M.: Kaufmann, 1873), 390.
[21] Ibid., 397.
[22] Ibid., 392.
[23] Ibid., 375.

passages, with their mention of *azazel*, bear no "superstitious" content. Indeed, through his emphasis on the human ability to decide between good and evil, obedience and rebellion, Hirsch supplies a Kantian understanding of these passages in keeping with nineteenth century German moral sensibilities.

Hirsch emphasized that God's Law is a universal law, a "moral law." By allegorizing these passages and interpreting them symbolically, Hirsch was able to transform them into a parable that affirmed humanity's free will and ability to recognize and perform the moral law. Indeed, it is only when humanity turns in sincere contrition to God and earnestly resolves not to sin that God, in a spirit of divine graciousness, will receive humanity's atonement and offer forgiveness of humanity's sins. There is nothing in these passages, as interpreted by Hirsch, that would offend a Kantian notion of ethics. All individuals bear full responsibility for their actions. One's own turning to the good, not the death of an animal, effects reconciliation with God and God's Law of morality. The expiatory function of the animal's death is denied. The supremacy of a modern notion of morality, and the insistence that Judaism possessed an ethic fully in keeping with such a notion, is maintained. Hirsch is thus able to provide, in a world where the tradition was under attack, an Orthodox understanding of atonement and refute those who would literally read such passages in a way that would cast aspersions upon the Tradition and the maturity of its ethic.

Hirsch's exegesis and symbolic approach to the issue of sacrifice indicates that the German Orthodox, like Jews in the world of medieval Islam, employed philosophy as the medium to explain and defend Judaism to Jew and gentile alike. Philosophy, not history, became a weapon to wield on behalf of Orthodoxy in a world hostile to tradition. The role assigned philosophy as a defender of tradition can be seen in all its specificity in the debate Orthodoxy carried on with the Historical School over the issue of divine revelation. Hirsch, anxious to employ dogma as a means of distinguishing Orthodox views of tradition in a time and place where the community's structure had been transformed and where a traditionalistically oriented Positive-Historical trend appeared at the Breslau Seminary, wrote, "The Law, both written and Oral, was closed with Moses at Sinai."[24]

This belief, which denied the possibility that the Law had developed in time, touched off a major controversy between the Orthodox and

---

[24] S.R. Hirsch, *Horeb*, 2 vol. (London: Soncino, 1962), 1:20.

Positive-Historical camps in Germany between 1859 and 1861. Zacharias Frankel, father of Positive-Historical Judaism and head of the Jewish Theological Seminary in Breslau, had maintained in his *Darkhe ha-Mishnah* that elements of the Oral Law had evolved in history. Particularly galling to the Orthodox was Frankel's contention that talmudic laws subsumed under the category, *halakhah le-Moshe mi-Sinai*, were not, as a literal translation would understand it, laws given orally by God to Moses at Sinai. Instead, these laws, he claimed, were of such great antiquity and so firmly established that it was *as if* they had been revealed to Moses. Frankel in effect was asserting that these laws were the enactments of later generations.[25] Frankel had traditional rabbinic warrant for this position.[26] Nevertheless, the need to defend Jewish tradition against the encroachments of this perceived threat to the Law caused Hirsch and others to claim that Frankel had misused this rabbinic precedent.[27] The need to protect the tradition as they understood it led these Orthodox defenders to elevate the dogma of an unchanging law to a position of supreme importance in their struggle to preserve traditional Judaism in the German context. It legitimated their own view that Frankel's position—the position that held that elements of Jewish law had developed in time, in history—posed a grave danger to the normative traditional belief that the Law was eternal and beyond the ravages of time. In a series of articles published by Hirsch in *Jeschurun*, he and Rabbi Gottlieb Fischer accused Frankel of *kefirah*, heresy.[28] Hildesheimer even labeled Frankel as a *meshumad* (an apostate) on account of this book.[29]

Interestingly, Hermann Cohen, who was then a young student at the Theological Seminary, wrote a private letter to Hirsch after these articles appeared describing his teacher Frankel as an observant Jew who conducted himself in all respects in a strict rabbinical manner, "standing in the synagogue with the prayer shawl over his head, singing *zemirot* (hymns) . . . on holiday evenings, and also on occasion in his talmudic lectures zealously commenting; 'A God-fearing person must here be stringent.'" Hirsch printed part of this letter in the pages of *Jeschurun*

---

[25] Z. Frankel, *Darkhe ha-Mishnah* (Leipzig: Hunger, 1859), 20.

[26] Frankel quotes here from the Rosh, *Hilḥot Mikvaot,* to support his nonliteral understanding of the phrase. I am grateful to Professors David Kramer and Eliezer Diamond of the Jewish Theological Seminary of America for bringing this to my attention.

[27] Hirsch, *Gesammelte Schriften,* 6:340.

[28] Ibid., 339–41.

[29] *Responsa, Yoreh Deah,* no. 238.

along with his own reply. Frankel's level of practice, Hirsch charged, was unimportant if it was not accompanied by proper internal beliefs. In fact, affirmation of the divine origins of the Oral Law was as much a sine qua non of an authentic Orthodox Judaism as belief in the Mosaic revelation of the Written Law.[30] A philosophical system which could explain and defend this notion became of paramount importance to the Orthodox in their relationship to contemporary German culture and thought. It was this need which may well hold the key to comprehending how and why the Orthodox leadership of German Judaism at the turn of the century appropriated the teaching of Kant in the way that it did. Kant, because he focused on both the nature of obligation and the ideal of a noumenal, nonphenomenologial realm, was eventually seen, in a way that Hegel was not, as particularly amicable to the doctrines of Jewish Orthodoxy. While this was seen above in Hirsch's interpretation of Leviticus, this entire tendency reaches its zenith in the writings of Hirsch's grandson, Isaac Breuer, in the first half of the twentieth century.

Breuer, one of the leading members and founders of Agudat Yisrael, wrote:

> It is my deep conviction that the God and King of Israel sends enlightened men among the nations from time to time, called and destined to play a part in Jewish 'Meta-History.' . . . And when the hour . . . broke . . . in which Israel . . . had to protect herself against the pressures of the outside world . . . , God caused to rise among the nations the exceptional man Kant, who, on the basis of the Socratic and Cartesian skepticism, brought about that "Copernican Turn", whereby the whole of man's reasoning was set in steel limits within which alone perception is legitimized. Blessed be God, who in His wisdom created Kant! Every real Jew who seriously and honestly studies the "Critique of Pure Reason" is bound to pronounce his "Amen" on it.[31]

Kant, for Breuer, became a weapon to protect Judaism and an Orthodox view of revelation from the presumptions "of the *Kundschafter* (adventurers) of our times."

It did so, as Zvi Kurzweil has explained, in the following way. Breuer employed Kant's well-known distinction between the phenomenal and noumenal worlds to demonstrate that human knowledge was limited to the realm of appearances exclusively. Humans were unable to penetrate

---

[30] *Jeschurun* 7 (1861): 297f.

[31] Quoted in Salomon Ehrmann, "Isaac Breuer," in *Guardians of Our Heritage*, ed. L. Jung (New York: Bloch, 1958), 624f.

into the world of the noumena—the world-in-itself, to use Kant's term. The latter remained unknown to human intelligence and hidden from human perception.[32]

Breuer made use of this distinction to defend the notion that what the Torah records is literally the word of God, as well as to affirm the inerrancy of scripture against attacks launched by biblical critics. In his *Der neue Kusari: Ein Weg zum Judentum,* he criticized both literary and philological attempts to cast doubt upon the accuracy of the Masoretic text of the Bible and maintained the historical veracity of certain biblical narratives. Drawing upon the Kantian distinction between phenomena and noumena, Breuer claimed that Torah was something noumenal, a miraculous appearance of the "metahistorical" in time.[33] Biblical critics and the Higher Criticism fail to grasp this supernal character of the Torah.[34] Academic inquiry into scripture, he concedes, might have validity in the sphere of phenomena. However, it is irrelevant to the noumenal reality of Torah. Scripture, written in Hebrew and endowed with holiness, is both phenomena and noumena, creation and nature. Thus, the contents of scripture, to human understanding, are phenomena. Yet this by no means exhausts the meaning of scripture. The significance of this is articulated by Breuer when he writes, "Philologists, using their methods, view [the Bible] as merely something that has evolved . . . and relate it to a specific language group. Its role as the mouthpiece and the Word of God . . . remains totally concealed from them."[35] In sum, the Torah as *Erscheinung* (appearance) must not be mistaken for the Torah as the *Ding an sich* (thing-in-itself).[36]

Critical methods of inquiry are unable to penetrate the deepest layers and ultimate meaning of the noumenal content of the Bible. Instead, it is only the guiding interpretation of the Oral Law, itself divine in origin, which can rescue us from this dilemma and allow us to unlock the secret, or more precisely, the hidden and true meaning of scripture. As Kurzweil has pointed out, when the Bible narrates human situations, "The Torah speaks in human language." However, when the Torah makes statements of a metaphysical nature, that is, pertaining to acts of

---

[32] See Zvi Kurzweil, *The Modern Impulse of Traditional Judaism* (Hoboken, NJ: Ktav, 1985), 36.

[33] Isaac Breuer, *Der neue Kusari: Ein Weg zum Judentum* (Frankfurt a.M.: Rabbiner-Hirsch-Gesellschaft, 1934), 341f.

[34] Ibid., 326–29.

[35] Ibid., 393.

[36] Ibid., 328.

creation, revelation, and redemption, we can never be sure of grasping their ultimate meaning. As a result, the Oral Law, as well as Kabbalah, must be studied assidiously so as to uncover the noumenal character of Scripture. It was this appropriation of Kant's distinction between the phenomenal and noumenal worlds which provided the epistemological basis for Breuer's immersion, as Gershom Scholem noted over fifty years ago, into the realm of Kabbalah.[37] Kant allowed Breuer to answer the challenges of biblical criticism and the notion of an evolving Jewish law to his own satisfaction.

Breuer was thus able to describe Judaism, as did his grandfather S. R. Hirsch, as a *Gesetzesreligion*. Law was defined by these Orthodox defenders of tradition as constituting the essence of Judaism. However, the law of Torah is not, as Kant characterized it, a heteronomous one. Instead, it is a *Naturrecht*, a "Law of nature," and there is a natural harmony between the law of Torah and the Jewish people. This relationship between God, Torah, and the Jewish people is thus one which points in the direction of autonomy rather than heteronomy. As Breuer phrased it, "The way of Judaism . . . starts out with the heteronomy of God's Law and . . . leads to an autonomy . . . which embodies God's will completely in the will of self."[38] Kant himself correctly perceived, wrote Breuer, "that the world as conceived conforms to law. . . ." Kant's one deficiency, according to Breuer, was that he was unable to identify this law, the content of this law, because he lacked revelation.

> Since he had no share in the revelation of the correct deed, he abandoned the deed as such in despair and only retained freedom—as a motive. From freedom—to Law: he could not tread this path of Judaism since he had not stood before Mount Sinai. So he had to be content with filling up the gap, where the law should have been, with the idea of the law. If they are to be free, men must act as if their action were demanded by a law which is binding upon everyone. Your action is correct if you can wish all men act in the way in which you are now acting. And you possess freedom of action if you act in the way you do solely because you wish that everyone would act in precisely the same way.[39]

---

37 See Kurzweil, *Modern Impulse*, 37. Scholem's essay on Breuer appears in English translation as "The Politics of Mysticism: Isaac Breuer's *New Kuzari*," in *The Messianic Idea in Judaism, ed.* G. Scholem, (New York: Schocken, 1971), 325–34.

38 Quoted in Ehrmann, "Isaac Breuer," 627.

39 Isaac Breuer, *Concepts of Judaism*, ed. Jacob S. Levinger (Jerusalem: Israel Universities Press, 1974), 277.

Breuer can thus be said to outdo Kant in his own application of Kantian principles to an understanding of Judaism and Torah. As an acculturated German, Breuer had internalized Kant and understood his world in light of Kantian teachings. However, he also had a need to defend and explain Judaism in contemporary cultural and philosophical terms. Kant gave him the language to do so. Thus, he was able to write, in words reminiscent of Hermann Cohen, "In Judaism law and ethics are in essence absolutely identical. Our highest goal is to fulfill God's royal law out of love for the Torah. The path leads . . . from man in the multiplicity of his phenomena to man-in-himself; from the Torah of the spoken word to the Torah of the written word—to Torah-in-itself."[40] The words of *Pirke Avot,* 2:4, "Make God's will your own," thus bespeaks the moral task incumbent upon every Jew.

In summary, it is clear that German Orthodox Jewish thinkers were as anxious as their liberal colleagues to articulate a philosophy of Judaism in modern philosophical terms. The manner in which they employed Kant to defend their notion of the place of Law in Judaism is representative of how they did this. Other philosophers, such as Schopenhauer, Hegel, or Schleirmacher, may have played equally critical roles in other areas of their thought. Furthermore, in utilizing these non-Jewish philosophers as the medium to explicate and defend Jewish tradition in a changed world, they were certainly mirroring a path trodden by Jewish philosophers in the Middle Ages. This should not obscure the specificity of their response, however. They were themselves acculturated members of German society who had internalized the values and teachings of *Bildung* and who were addressing their works to a comparably acculturated audience. Because of this background, there was nothing alien or artificial to them about explaining and defending Judaism in contemporary philosophical language. In so doing, the tradition was both defended and reformulated in a novel way.

Epilogue

German Orthodox Judaism, like all historical phenomena, was unique in its individuality. Yet, like other Jews in the modern world, the German Orthodox constructed a meaningful traditional Jewish life and faith in the face of a transformed environment. They did not allow Jewish tradi-

---

[40] Ibid., 280.

tion or Jewish identity to atrophy and die when confronted by modern culture.

An anecdote related by Rabbi Nehemia Anton Nobel, who served as *orthodoxer Gemeinderabbiner* in Frankfurt from 1910 to 1922, illustrates something of German Orthodoxy's synthesis of the contemporary and the traditional, and the distinct way in which German Orthodoxy can be said to have embodied tradition. Recalling his own student days at the *Rabbinerseminar*, Nobel wrote that he was asked to deliver an address at the founding ceremony of *Dibbuq Ḥaverim*, the seminary's student association, in 1894. At the conclusion of his talk, he offered a student toast, a "*Salamander*," in honor of his teacher Rabbi Hildesheimer and the other members of the Orthodox rabbinical school's faculty. According to Alexander Altmann, who remembers similar toasts offered during his student days at the *Rabbinerseminar* in the 1920s, the German, Teutonic student custom of the *Salamander* "consisted in everybody standing up, circling their beer glasses on the table, and draining them to the last dreg."[41]

As graphic testimony to the acculturated nature of German Orthodoxy, this episode bears witness to the symbiotic nature of German Orthodoxy itself and the consciousness of men like Hildesheimer and Nobel who shaped it. Nothing in this scene would have struck Hildesheimer, Hirsch, or any other German Orthodox Jew as dissonant with tradition. After all, these were people who sang Heine to their children along with traditional *zemirot* on Sabbaths and holidays.[42] As such, the episode represents the successful synthesis they had achieved between Jewish tradition and German culture. However, it also suggests that such synthesis succeeds when it is experienced as effective from the inside. That is, Hildesheimer, his colleagues, and his students had so completely internalized the values of the surrounding German-Jewish atmosphere that nothing struck them as discordant about this event.

However, an enigma remains. It seems that the German Orthodox were able to achieve a successful synthesis between Jewish tradition and German culture precisely because they did not too closely examine or reflect on their efforts in this episode or any of the other phenomena described in this paper. This is why Schwab, in all candor, could assert, "German-Jewish Orthodoxy was Sinai Judaism." The German Orthodox, like countless other Jews in the modern world, thus resolved the problem

---

41 Quoted in Alexander Altmann, "The German Rabbi: 1910–1939," *Leo Baeck Institute Yearbook* 19 (1974): 47.

42 See Calavary, "Kindheitserinnerungen," 187–92.

of modernity not through "logic," but through "creation." This study indicates that Orthodox Jews in Germany, like their liberal Jewish peers, adapted the tradition to its German context. They, like other German Jews, possessed a "hyphenated identity." Yet the reformulation of Jewish tradition they provided reveals that a "hyphenated identity" or successful synthesis works not because it is logical. It works because one lives it. The synthesis inheres in the doing. It is this which allowed the German Orthodox, like other Western Jews, to create a modern Orthodox traditionalism that worked. This may be why, in the end, these people hold up a mirror to other modern Jews who are engaged in the same process of constructing and living within a tradition in a modern, pluralistic world. All Jews who affirm their identity and religion in today's world are ultimately engaged in the same task that they were. All Jews who struggle with the Tradition in the modern West employ, as the German Orthodox did, a new language to awaken and defend an ancient faith and tradition.[43]

---

43 On Nobel's tombstone, the epitaph reads, "He awakened an ancient faith through a new language."

2

The Emergence of Ultra-Orthodoxy: The Invention of a Tradition

MICHAEL K. SILBER

Introduction

Of all the branches of modern-day Judaism, ultra-Orthodoxy is undoubtedly the most tradition-oriented.[1] Its rallying cry is "All innovation is prohibited by the Torah!" a clever wordplay on a Talmudic ruling first coined by Rabbi Moses Sofer in the early nineteenth century that captures the essence of its conservative ideology. And yet, like other antimodern conservative movements, ultra-Orthodoxy itself is clearly a recent phenomenon. Belying the conventional wisdom of both its adher-

* I wish to thank Profs. Jacob Katz, James Kugel, Paul Mendes-Flohr and Ḥaym Soloveitchik, as well as the fellows of the research group on "Society and Religion in Contemporary Judaism" at The Institute for Advanced Studies, Hebrew University, for their helpful comments. Research for this paper was funded by the American Council of Learned Societies and the Andrew and Pearl Rosenfeld Project on the History of Hungarian and Habsburg Jewry, Dinur Center, Hebrew University.

[1] Although there is no separate treatment of the emergence of ultra-Orthodoxy as such, there are two important studies on Hungarian Orthodoxy upon which I ground this paper: Mordekhai Eliav, "Rabbi Esriel Hildesheimer and his Influence on Hungarian Jewry" (in Hebrew), *Zion* 27 (1962): 59-86; and Nathanel Katzburg, "The Rabbinical Decision of Michalowce in 1865" (in Hebrew), in *Studies in the History of Jewish Society in the Middle Ages and in the Modern Period Presented to Professor Jacob Katz on his Seventy-Fifth Birthday by his Students and Friends,* ed. Emanuel Etkes and Yosef Salmon (Jerusalem: Magnes, 1980), 273–86.

ents and its opponents, it is in fact not an unchanged and unchanging remnant of pre-modern, traditional Jewish society, but as much a child of modernity and change as any of its "modern" rivals.[2]

Today's ultra-Orthodox have become a familiar presence, clearly identifiable by their peculiar dress and appearance, their religious extremism, their self-segregative way of life, and their all-embracing, communal organization. Within the broader Orthodox community, they constitute a well-defined segment. But this was not always so. The crystallization of ultra-Orthodoxy as a sociologically separate element—as a sect, or better, as a religious order—within Orthodoxy dates back no further than the interwar era, when the Eda ha-Ḥaredit and Neturei Karta were first formed in Jerusalem; and later, after World War II, when their Hasidic counterparts, Satmár, Munkács, and others, established their enclaves in the United States. To a large extent, these groups are an outgrowth of the numerous permutations generated in the Orthodox camp by the rise of modern Jewish nationalism, with the ultra-Orthodox being the most vociferous proponents of a militant anti-Zionism.

Ultra-Orthodoxy, however, has a history which can be traced back to an earlier period, before the rise of Zionism, and it also has a genesis which can be pinpointed to a particular historical juncture. It is no coincidence that Jews from Hungary (or rather, what was once greater Hungary) have predominated among the religious zealots in both Israel and America, for it is in that country that ultra-Orthodoxy first emerged in the previous century. And even if from a sociological perspective ultra-Orthodoxy was then still in its infancy, it was in Hungary of the 1860s that one could discern for the first time, in the strident tones and the militant, uncompromisingly conservative ideology, the familiar contours of the mature phenomenon, and it was in that decade that the initial steps toward institutionalization were taken.

In this paper, I argue that the emergence of ultra-Orthodoxy must be understood within the context of its distinctive Hungarian milieu, and as one of several responses to a severe crisis confronting Orthodox Jewry in the middle of the nineteenth century. The crisis, which is described in the first section, was the result of the convergence of four interrelated challenges which combined significantly to erode Orthodox strength in the

---

[2] For the history of Orthodoxy as a modern phenomenon, see the programmatic statements of Jacob Katz, "Orthodoxy in Historical Perspective," *Studies in Contemporary Jewry* 2 (1986): 3-17; and Moshe S. Samet, "The Beginnings of Orthodoxy," *Modern Judaism* 8 (1988): 249–69 (first published in a different version in Hebrew in 1970).

1860s. These were: the introduction of compulsory secular education by the government; the growing linguistic acculturation of Hungarian Jewry; the increasing pressure to adopt a Magyar national identity; and the steady spread of synagogue reforms. Although it was clear to contemporaries that Orthodoxy was on the decline, the full extent of the damage was revealed only at the end of the decade. By 1870, the Orthodox were confronted with their fifth challenge: the probability that if not yet, then soon enough, they would be reduced to minority status within Hungarian Jewry.

Hungarian Orthodoxy was deeply divided on how to meet these challenges—the subject of the second section. Initially, after the death in 1839 of their world renowned master, Rabbi Moses Sofer,[3] Hungarian Orthodoxy drifted uneasily and without direction. It was during these uncertain years that a confident neo-Orthodoxy on the left made its first appearance in Hungary urging a vacillating center, mainstream Orthodoxy to arrive at greater accommodation with modernity and change. And at first these efforts were crowned with not inconsiderable success. However, the emergence of a group of zealots at the right end of the spectrum in the early 1860s marked a turning point. Invoking the legacy of the Ḥatam Sofer (as Rabbi Moses Sofer came to be called), these ultra-Orthodox crusaders succeeded in checking the influence of left-wing neo-Orthodoxy in Hungary, and by the end of the decade had successfully maneuvered a not entirely convinced mainstream Orthodoxy into a much more uncompromising stance.

The arguments and mode of thinking of the ultra-Orthodox are the focus of the third section. Ultra-Orthodoxy offered its own response to the challenges posed by secular education, linguistic acculturation, national identity, religious reforms, and minority status. They were troubled that tradition, as it was understood by the mainstream, often did not prove up to the task of providing a forceful response. Consequently, the ultra-Orthodox embarked on a course which can best be described as the invention of a new, more potent tradition. Tradition

---

3 Born in 1762 in Frankfurt am Main, he settled in Hungary and served as rabbi of Pressburg from 1806 until his death in 1839. A charismatic figure who left an indelible stamp on the history of Hungarian Jewry, he stood at the head of a yeshiva which was considered the largest in the world at the time. The best introduction to his life and ideology is Jacob Katz, "Toward a Biography of the Ḥatam Sofer," trans. by David Ellenson, in *From East and West: Jews in a Changing Europe, 1750-1870,* ed. Francis Malino and David Sorkin (London: Blackwell, 1990), 223–66 (first published in a slightly different version in Hebrew in 1967).

and the past were interpreted, shaped, filtered, and recast to better serve the cause of traditionalism.

In the course of inventing this tradition, ultra-Orthodoxy innovated in two areas in particular: Halakhah and ideology. In order to preserve tradition uncompromised, these most conservative of men, paradoxically, employed methods in arriving at halakhic decisions which departed from what had been the accepted norm, not only in traditional Judaism, but also in the more recent past, in posttraditional mainstream Orthodoxy. In fact, it is precisely the objections raised by these often scandalized Orthodox authorities that alert the historian to the innovative dimensions of ultra-Orthodoxy. And providing the underlying rationale for these halakhic innovations was a freshly constructed worldview which pulled together often marginal elements of the existent tradition (whether halakhic, aggadic, or kabbalistic) into a consistent "myth" of what authentic Jewishness and Judaism were.[4]

[4] This is perhaps the place to pause for a moment and clarify the terminology used (with some consistency) throughout the paper. In order to avoid semantic confusion, I employ certain conventions when speaking of tradition and Orthodoxy. TRADITIONAL SOCIETY is used here in the Weberian sense to mean a premodern society whose acceptance of tradition as a source of authority is unquestioned. By ORTHODOXY, I mean the adherence to tradition as part of a conscious, self-reflexive, conservative ideology—a traditionalISM if you will—which evolved in response to modernity. Therefore, the shift from a traditional society to an Orthodox one ("Orthodoxization") was part and parcel of modernization, and as such, Orthodoxy must be viewed as a modern phenomenon. This holds true not only of its left-wing, modernist variant, NEO-ORTHODOXY (or as it is sometimes called, "Modern" Orthodoxy), but of all its varieties, including the right-wing, antimodernist ultra-Orthodox. When speaking of Orthodoxy without any modifiers, I usually refer to what I call here the center or mainstream Orthodoxy, a position which is further elucidated below. As for ULTRA-ORTHODOXY, I employ a narrower definition than in current usage. I tend to restrict this term to the sector to the RIGHT of what was traditionally the Eastern European wing of Agudat Yisrael. The Hebrew *Ḥaredim* is a broader classification which encompasses not only the ultra-Orthodox, but also most of what I have labeled here as center or mainstream Orthodox. I would not designate the pre-World War I Lithuanian yeshiva world, nor most of the Russian and Polish Hasidic courts, as ultra-Orthodox. This is not to deny that some of these sectors, especially after World War II, have become increasingly "ultra-Orthodoxized."

The Emergence of Ultra-Orthodoxy (1863–1865)

The Challenge

By the time of the emergence of ultra-Orthodoxy in the 1860s, the *Kulturkampf* between Orthodox and Neologue—as the moderate reform movement in Hungary came to be known—was already several decades old. Although modernization and its concomitant ideologies, the Haskalah (Jewish Enlightenment) and Reform, had begun to make inroads into Hungary even before 1840,[5] that year undoubtedly marked a watershed in the history of the legal status, the national identity, and the cultural and religious profile of Hungarian Jewry. The so-called liberal "Age of Reform" in *Vormärz* Hungary was inaugurated in 1825, but it was only in 1840 that Hungarian public opinion turned seriously to the Jewish question. The dominant stream of Hungarian nationalism in the 1840s was basically liberal and welcomed Jews into the ranks of the Magyar nation. In their approach to Jewish integration, Hungarian nationalists such as Louis Kossuth took their cue from the liberal French model: full acceptance into Hungarian society provided that Jewish identity would be confined and redefined as strictly confessional. During the 1840s, a sizable and influential minority emerged in the Jewish communities of the larger towns and cities, determined to change the face of Hungarian Jewry. They launched a three-pronged attack (though of varying intensity) on traditional society, demanding reforms in education, seeking reforms in the synagogue service, and urging greater identification with the Magyar host nation. Jews began to participate in patriotic clubs, founded societies for the dissemination of the Magyar language, and during the 1848–1849 Revolution, fought in the thousands in the ranks of the Hungarian armies.[6]

---

5 Joseph Ben-David, "The Emergence of a Modern Jewish Society in Hungary in the Beginning of the Nineteenth Century" (in Hebrew), *Zion* 12 (1952): 101–28; Nathanel Katzburg, "Changes in Hungarian Jewry in the First Half of the Nineteenth Century" (in Hebrew), *Bar-Ilan Annual* 2 (1964): 163–77; idem, "The History of Hungarian Jewry" (in Hebrew), in *Pinqas Hakehillot: Hungary* (Jerusalem: Yad Vashem 1976), 14-36; Raphael Mahler, *Divrei yamei yisrael, dorot aharonim mishlehai ha-meah ha-shmonah-esrah ad yameinu* (A History of the Jewish People in Modern Times) (Tel Aviv: Merḥavia 1976), 6:230–70; Michael K. Silber, "The Historical Experience of German Jewry and its Impact on Haskalah and Reform in Hungary," in *Toward Modernity: The European Jewish Model*, ed., Jacob Katz (New Brunswick and Oxford: Transaction, 1987), 107–57.

6 Béla Bernstein, *Az 1848/49-iki magyar szabadságharcz és a zsidók* (The 1848/49 War of Independence in Hungary and the Jews) (Budapest: IMIT, 1898); György Szalai, "The Magyarisation of Hungarian Jewry, until 1849" (in Hungarian), *Világosság* 14

The triumph of the Habsburgs in 1849 introduced the so-called era of neo-absolutism, a decade during which the state intervened forcefully in the internal affairs of Hungary and of Hungarian Jewry. Paradoxically, this conservative state embarked on a series of ambitious economic and educational innovations which ultimately had the effect of greatly strengthening the forces of reform. The most important of these was the introduction of compulsory secular education on a massive, if not yet entirely universal, scale. By the end of the 1850s, there were more than three hundred Jewish schools, perhaps almost ten times as many as there had been in the previous decade.[7]

After a decade of repression and forced inactivity, Hungarian nationalism reemerged in 1860, accompanied by a militant crusade of Magyarization of Hungary's national minorities. The educational system, now firmly in Hungarian hands, served as the key instrument in the campaign. Great strides were also made in the economic development of the country; the urban population swelled as large numbers flocked to the cities.

All these developments greatly altered the cultural profile of Hungarian Jewry on the eve of its emancipation in 1867. The acculturation of Hungarian Jewry, in all but the most backward northeast region, was an accomplished fact. Most of the younger generation were now graduates of the secular educational system, with German having displaced Judeo-German or Yiddish as their primary language. In the heat of the nationalist enthusiasm of the 1860s, a sizable minority of Hungarian Jews switched their linguistic loyalties yet once again, this time from German to Magyar, a process greatly reinforced after 1867, by the introduction of Magyar as the sole language of instruction in the state-supervised Jewish school network.

The balance of power now clearly shifted in favor of the reformers. Perhaps in raw numbers they may still have been short of a majority. However, the trends of the preceding years—economic development, urbanization, and secular schooling—all served to swell their natural

(1974): 216–23; George Barany, "Magyar Jew or Jewish Magyar," *Canadian-American Slavic Studies* 8 (1974): 1-44; Károly Kecskeméti, "Liberalism and Jewish Emancipation" (in Hungarian), *Történelmi Szemle* 25 (1982): 185-209.

7 Bernát Mandl, "The Condition of Jewish Schools of Hungary in the Nineteenth Century and their Important Tasks in the Twentieth Century" (in Hungarian), *IMIT* 1909: 167–99; and Aron Moskovits, *Jewish Education in Hungary (1848-1948)* (New York: Block, 1964); Philip J. Adler, "The Introduction of Public Schooling for the Jews of Hungary (1849-1860)," *Jewish Social Studies* 36 (1974).

constituency and to forecast their eventual triumph. Add to this the sympathy they enjoyed among the newly independent government and Hungarian public opinion, and take into account the disproportionate influence wielded in communal affairs by those advocating reforms—the wealthy and the academically educated—and it all added up to tip the scales decisively in favor of Reform.[8]

The Orthodox Response

Rabbi Moses Sofer, the founding father of Hungarian Orthodoxy, had propounded an ideology which sought to provide new rationale for besieged traditional values and institutions. In a studied antithesis of the Jewish Enlightenment and Reform Judaism, he had argued the merits of the traditional educational curriculum against that of the Haskalah; of exile and alienation against emancipation and integration; of "corrupt" Yiddish against pure German; of the particularist facet of Judaism against its universalist interpretation; of tradition against reason.[9]

Nevertheless, even the teachings of the Ḥatam Sofer were not without ambiguity. Despite his declared opposition to secular education, to German books, to German translations, and to German sermons, and his vehement threat to cut all ties with deviant reformers, in practice one

---

8 The reformers won a clear majority during the nationwide elections for the 1868-1869 Jewish Congress, gaining 57.5% of the 220 seats. See Nathanel Katzburg, "The Jewish Congress in Hungary, 1868-1869," in *Hungarian-Jewish Studies*, ed. Randolph R Braham, 3 vols. (New York: World Federation of Hungarian Jews, 1969), 2:1-33, esp. p. 14.

9 Of the numerous references in the Ḥatam Sofer's works, see Moses Sofer, *Derashot* (Sermons), 2 vols. (Jerusalem: Machon Ḥatam Sofer 1974), 1:140f. (Eulogy of R. Wolf Eger on 8 Tevet 5556), 162f. (Eulogy of R. David Sinzheim on 7 Tevet 5573), 166 (7 Tevet 5574), 187 (8 Tevet 5583), 226 (*Be-shalaḥ* 5571). See also the following: the chapter "Conservatives in a Quandary," in Jacob Katz, *Out of the Ghetto* (Cambridge: Harvard University Press, 1973), 142–60; idem, *The "Shabbes Goy": A Study in Halakhic Flexibility* (Philadelphia: Jewish Publication Society, 1989); idem, "The Orthodox Defense of the Second Day of the Festivals" (in Hebrew), *Tarbiṣ* 57 (1988): 385-434; and a collection of other such case studies to appear in the near future; the path-breaking dissertation (directed by Katz) of Moshe S. Samet, "Halakhah and Reform" (in Hebrew) (Hebrew University, 1967), parts of which have been published in revised form as "The Struggle of the Ḥatam Sofer against the Innovators" (in Hebrew), in *The Jews in Hungary*, ed. M. E. Gonda et al (Tel Aviv: Commission for the Research of the History of Hungarian Jews, 1980), 92-103; "Delayed Burial" (in Hebrew), *Asuppot* 3 (1988/89): 413–65; "Shaving the Beard on the Intermediary Days of the Festivals" (in Hebrew), to appear in a volume on the topic by Meir Benayahu; and "Changes in Synagogue Ritual: The Rabbinic Stance against the Reform 'Innovators'" (in Hebrew), *Asuppot* 5 (1990/91): 345-404.

could find extenuating circumstances in every one of these cases where he adopted contrary positions. In his lifetime and in the following generation, the more extreme statements of the Ḥatam Sofer were still viewed as no more than staking out distant ideals which were meant to serve only as points of reference and orientation. In general, he seems to have been anxious to reassert the validity of hard-line norms, especially in the light of compromises many of his colleagues had been forced to make. Once the principle was established, however, he was quite willing to mitigate theory in practice.[10]

Even had he and his disciples desired to implement some of his more extreme views, such as the expulsion of heretic reformers from the body of Israel, the harsh realities of the preemancipatory era curtailed much of their freedom of action. The state restricted rabbinic authority and compelled the Jewish community to accommodate all Jews who resided in a specific locality. In the light of these constraints, whatever notions the Ḥatam Sofer and other Orthodox rabbis may have entertained of segregating deviants from catholic Israel remained in the realm of theory. A generation had to pass before these state-imposed constraints were removed under greatly altered circumstances, and the Ḥatam Sofer's hard-line theory would be interpreted literally and put into practice.[11]

---

[10] Michael K. Silber, "Roots of the Schism in Hungarian Jewry: Cultural and Social Change from the Reign of Joseph II until the Eve of the 1848 Revolution" (in Hebrew) (Ph. D. diss., Hebrew University, 1985), 42-47, 259; Moshe Samet, "The Ḥatam Sofer–Tradition and Halakhah" (in Hebrew), *Proceedings of the Ninth World Congress of Jewish Studies,* div. B, vol. 2 (Jerusalem: World Union of Jewish Studies, 1986), 17-20; idem "Additional Contributions toward the Biography of the *Ḥatam Sofer*" (in Hebrew), in *Torah im Derekh Ereṣ: The Movement, Personalities, Ideas,* ed. Mordekhai Breuer, (Ramat-Gan: Bar-Ilan University, 1987), 65-73.

[11] See Moses Sofer, *Responsa Ḥatam Sofer* (Jerusalem: Foundation for the Study of Ḥatam Sofer), pt. 6, § 89. This became the classic reference for secessionist Orthodoxy in the following generation. See, e.g., Sigmund Krausz in an article in 1868, cited in his *Wissen und Glauben oder: Der Mensch und der Israelit: Zwei Betrachtungen nebst einer Einleitung als Schlusswort nach beendigtem Kongresskampfe zwischen den Juden orthodoxer und neologer Richtung* (Pest: Bendiner und A. Grünwald, 1871), 60. Urging secession in 1877, Samson Raphael Hirsch too cited the passage and concluded that with the *Austrittsgesetz* of 28 July 1876, governmental permission and authorization was now granted, and "thus this decision, which the Ḥatam Sofer could state only as theoretical, becomes fully valid in practice." See Samson Raphael Hirsch, "Die offene Antwort des Herrn Distr.-Rabbiner S. B. Bamberger," (1877), in his *Gesammelte Schriften,* ed. Naphtali Hirsch, 6 vols. (Frankfurt a.M.: Kauffmann, 1902-1912), 6:400-403. The translation is taken from Leo Levi, "The Relationship of the Orthodox to Heterodox Organizations: From a Halakhic Analysis by Rabbi S. R. Hirsch," *Tradition* 9 (1967): 95-102.

After his death, no one person emerged as the undisputed leader of Hungarian Orthodoxy. Indeed, the next two decades were characterized by a young, indecisive leadership. Most of the Ḥatam Sofer's disciples were men in their twenties and early thirties, and only a few served as rabbis of the more substantial Hungarian communities. The collective impact of the Pressburg school came to be felt only later, in the 1860s, when the mature disciples of the Ḥatam Sofer came to serve in some of the major communities. Hungarian Orthodoxy can be said to have been suspended in a limbo of inactivity, even complacency, in the 1850s. Nothing is as indicative of this vacuum as the ease with which the young rabbi of Eisenstadt, Esriel Hildesheimer (1820–1899), came to seize a virtual monopoly of Orthodox activity during that decade. A recent arrival from Germany, Hildesheimer was a dynamic advocate of neo-Orthodoxy. His crowning achievement was to establish in Eisenstadt the first yeshiva in Europe to incorporate secular Gymnasium studies into its curriculum.[12] Hildesheimer was endowed with exceptional talent and unrelenting energy, which was channeled into a seemingly endless procession of schemes and projects. Had there not been a vacuum of leadership in Hungarian Orthodoxy, however, it is doubtful that a newcomer, no matter how gifted, could have assumed such a central position in its affairs in so short a time.[13]

When the full impact of the crisis hit in the early 1860s, Hildesheimer seemed to be the only one with a clearly formulated response. On the question of linguistic acculturation and secular studies, his was the familiar position of German neo-Orthodoxy. Where the Orthodoxy of the Ḥatam Sofer and his disciples was predicated on the rejection of the

[12] Mordekhai Eliav, "*Torah im Derekh Ereṣ* in Hungary" (in Hebrew), *Sinai* 51 (1962): 127–42; idem, "Rabbi Esriel Hildesheimer and his Influence on Hungarian Jewry" (in Hebrew), *Zion* 27 (1962): 59-86; idem, ed., *Rabbiner Esriel Hildesheimer Briefe* (Jerusalem: Reuven Mass, 1965); Meir Hildesheimer, "Contributions toward a Portrait of Esriel Hildesheimer" (in Hebrew), *Sinai* 54 (1964): 67-94; David Ellenson, "Rabbi Esriel Hildesheimer and the Quest for Religious Authority," *Modern Judaism* 1 (1981): 279–97 idem, "Modern Orthodoxy and the Problem of Religious Pluralism: The Case of Rabbi Esriel Hildesheimer," *Tradition 21* (1979): 73-90.

[13] Hildesheimer's stature can be gauged in several ways. He was approached in the early 1860s to serve as an associate rabbi in Pressburg. His advice was sought early on to recommend candidates for rabbinic positions. He was also the address when both Jewish and government circles wished to resolve one of the numerous communal disputes which racked Hungary in the 1850s and 1860s. Even usually unsympathetic rabbis ended up soliciting his support. See, e.g., Eliav, *Hildesheimer Briefe*, pp. 21, 37-40, 44, 55, 57f, 60f. (Hebrew section); idem, "Hildesheimer and his Influence," 63-65.

Haskalah, German neo-Orthodoxy had internalized much of the Haskalah program already in the first decades of the nineteenth century. Even more, it had adopted most of the synagogue innovations advocated by the early Reform movement, such as those first introduced by the short-lived Westphalian consistory. By the second half of the century, almost every one of the traditional institutions of German Orthodoxy had been transformed: rabbis were increasingly university trained and preached sermons in German; order and decorum reigned in the synagogue; and the educational vision was one of cultural synthesis where Western culture was viewed as a necessary complement to Jewish tradition.[14] As for national identity, while the German-born Hildesheimer may have felt not entirely comfortable with Hungarian nationalism, there is no reason to believe that his position on national identification with the host nation was substantially different from the somewhat reserved but relatively positive attitude of his neo-Orthodox counterparts in Germany.[15]

---

[14] However, it must be noted that order and decorum played a lesser role for Hildesheimer, and he clearly disapproved of several innovations which had been accepted by other German Orthodox rabbis. See Israel Hildesheimer, "Ein Beitrag zur Bedeutung von *ḥuqqot ha-goyim*," in his *Gesammelte Aufsätze*, ed. Meier Hildesheimer (Frankfurt a.M.: Kauffmann, 1923), 20f., 25f. on his opposition to canonicals and moving the *bimah* away from the center of the synagogue. On the innovations of German Orthodoxy, see Isaac Heinemann, "Samson Raphael Hirsch: The Formative Years of the Leader of Modern Orthodoxy, " *Historia Judaica* 13 (1951): 29-54; David Feuchtwang, "Samson Raphael Hirsch als Oberlandesrabbiner von Mähren," in *Samson Raphael Hirsch—Jubiläums-Nummer Israelit*, 25 Siwan, 5668 (Frankfurt: Jisraelit, 1908), 21; Robert Liberles, *Religious Conflict in Social Context: The Resurgence of Orthodox Judaism in Frankfurt am Main, 1838-1877* (Westport, Conn: Greenwood, 1985), 137–64, 227–30. And while most German Orthodox rabbis also objected to moving the bimah, there were surprising exceptions, such as Rabbi Seligmann Baer Bamberger of Würzburg, who made his peace with this innovation. See the testimony of Joseph Carlebach in Naphtali Carlebach, *Joseph Carlebach and his Generation* (New York: Joseph Carlebach Memorial Foundation, 1959), 225f. cited by Liberles, *Religious Conflict*, 277 n. 2, and by Shmuel Grinberg, "Makom ha-bimah be-veit ha-kneset," *Beit ha-Kneset* 14 (1946): 20f.

[15] Ismar Schorsch, *Jewish Reactions to German Anti-Semitism, 1870-1914* (New York: Columbia University Press, 1972), 10. A more ambiguous national identification is argued in Mordechai Breuer, *Jüdische Orthodoxie im Deutschen Reich, 1871-1918: Die Sozialgeschichte einer religiösen Minderheit* (Frankfurt a.M.: Athenäum, 1986), 259–78. In 1866, Samson Raphael Hirsch declared that traditional Hebrew literature is a "Jewish national literature, as the Greek is to the Hellenic people, as the German is to the German nation." Just as it is laudable that German immigrants in the United States promote their German national heritage while declaring their sincere loyalty to their new homeland, so too is it legitimate for Jews in Germany to promote the preserva-

While most of his colleagues of the center did not share his enthusiasm for German and secular studies, they did, nevertheless, recognize the need to adapt to changing conditions. The linguistic shift to German in the northwestern parts of Hungary, the so-called Oberland region, was nearly an accomplished fact, and opposing the state-sponsored school system seemed senseless and foolhardy. In any case, the business careers for which most Jewish youths were destined dictated a solid secular education. In the 1850s, mainstream rabbis could still shut their eyes to the uncomfortable fact that Hildesheimer favored secular culture on principle and delude themselves that his position dovetailed with their own as one of reluctant accommodation.[16]

Differentiation of Hungarian Orthodoxy

In the 1860s, however, this modus vivendi began to come apart. Hungarian Orthodoxy now underwent rapid differentiation, and by mid-decade, three sharply divided positions emerged: a left, a center, and a right. All this took place in the space of two years, 1864 and 1865, stimulated by three separate issues. Each of these issues was seized upon by one of the parties as an opportunity to demarcate its boundaries, and in every instance the overriding concern was to delineate more sharply the border to the left. All three culminated in signed petitions or declarations around which each time a different group of Hungarian rabbis clustered. Even though the signatures are not an entirely reliable indicator of affiliation, the strength of each wing can nevertheless be gauged with a fair degree of accuracy. The 193 Orthodox rabbis in Hungary who signed at least one of the three declarations in 1864–1865, were divided into three camps of almost equal size. Another ninety or so rabbis whose names did not appear among the 1864–1865 signatories, but who signed an anti-Reform petition later in 1872, can be added to the Orthodox

---

tion of their "national literature" ("Einige Andenkungen über den hebräischen Unterricht als allgemeines Bildungselement," in his *Gesammelte Schriften*, vol. 2, esp. pp. 434–36.) Although Hirsch was far from any idea of Jewish nationalism, his American immigrant analogy does seem to point to some notion of ethnic pluralism within the German nation-state. See also Joseph Breuer, "Rabbiner Hirsch und der jüdische Nationalismus," *Naḥlath Ṣewi* 1 (1930/31): 290–97.

[16] There is a revealing correspondence between Hildesheimer and one of the leading mainstream Orthodox rabbis, R. Aszod of Duna Szerdahely, published by Meir Hildesheimer, "Rabbi Judah Aszod and Rabbi Esriel Hildesheimer" (in Hebrew), in *Sefer zikaron le-Rav Yeḥiel Yakov Weinberg* (Memorial Volume for Rabbi Y. Y. Weinberg) (Jerusalem, 1970), 285-302. See also Eliav, "Hildesheimer and his Influence."

roster, almost all of them bolstering the left and the center in equal measures. All in all, of the roughly 280 rabbis who could broadly be identified as Orthodox (there were altogether about 350 rabbis in Hungary at the time), about one quarter formed the right, with the remainder being divided more or less evenly between the left and the center.[17]

Some caveats about the nature of these divisions should nevertheless be kept in mind. First, the strength of the center must not be gauged only by its numbers. The most prominent and influential rabbis adhered to this position, whereas the right and the left had more than their share of relatively obscure and insignificant personalities. Second, while the ideological differences were clear-cut, these failed to harden into firm institutional divisions. Moreover, within each wing a considerable variety of views existed; the center, in particular, had right-of-center and left-of-center factions. And finally, the composition of both the left and the right wings was one with a broad periphery of sympathizers, and only a small core of dedicated true believers who could be designated as neo- and ultra-Orthodox. Consequently, all this suggests that the threefold segmentation of Orthodoxy had not yet institutionalized and was at this time still highly unstable. There was a strong likelihood that these divisions would collapse and revert into a broad, amorphous center (which indeed occurred in the following decades).

The first issue arose over an article published in a Viennese annual by the historian Heinrich Graetz questioning the traditional concept of a personal Messiah.[18] Hildesheimer had long been troubled by the popular

---

[17] I arrive at this number by comparing the signatories of the following: the petition against Kompert; the petition against the rabbinical seminary; the *pesaq din* of Michalowce; and the petition campaign against Viennese reforms led by Rabbi Salomon Spitzer in 1872. See references below in notes 19, 20 and 26, as well as Salomon Spitzer, *Rabbinische Gutachten betreffs vom Vorstande der isr. Cultus-Gemeinde in Wien, am 21. Jänner l. J. gefassten und zur Ausführung gebrachten Reformbeschlüsse* (Wien: Herzfeld und Bauer, 1872), 20-32. I define the left as those who signed ONLY the petition against Kompert (63); the right as those who signed the *pesaq din* (65); and the center as those who signed the antiseminary petition, but did not sign the *pesaq din* (65). I have modified these lists with what I know about the rabbis from other sources. For instance, Salomon Kutna appears on the antiseminary petition but clearly belonged to the left.

[18] In his "Die Verjüngung des jüdisches Stammes," which appeared in *Jahrbuch für Israeliten* in 1863. Graetz stated that Isaiah 2:52f. did not refer to a personal messiah, but rather to the Jewish collective as a whole. The *Kirchenzeitung*, a Catholic newspaper, sued Kompert, the publisher responsible, claiming that not only the Church, but Orthodox Jews, too, viewed these statements as heretical. The preacher Isak Noah Mannheimer and the traditional rabbi of Vienna, Rabbi Eleazar Horowitz, testified on

confusion between neo-Orthodoxy and the historical-positivist school aligned with Zacharias Frankel to which Graetz belonged. All too often the opinion had been expressed that as far as practical observance of the precepts was concerned, there was actually no discernible difference between the two camps.[19] Twenty years earlier, German neo-Orthodox rabbis could still view Zacharias Frankel as a potential ally against Reform. But gradually, first with the establishment of the Breslau seminary in 1854, and later with the publication of Frankel's *Darkhei ha-Mishnah* in 1859, a growing breach opened up between the neo-Orthodox who maintained that the Jewish Law had been revealed at Sinai, and the Breslau school with its historical and evolutionary conception of the Halakhah. The Kompert affair, as the controversy came to be known after the publisher, was a heaven-sent opportunity for Hildesheimer to clarify once and for all that deep-seated IDEOLOGICAL AND DOGMATIC differences did separate the neo-Orthodox from their rivals to their immediate left. In 1864, he orchestrated a petition campaign against Graetz's heretical views, signing up a large number of Orthodox rabbis from Hungary and other parts of central Europe.[20]

But that very year a wedge was driven between Hildesheimer and the Orthodox center over the second issue, that of establishing a rabbinical seminary. The state had been mooting the idea now for several years, and it seemed only a matter of time before it was to be realized.

Kompert's behalf. Hildesheimer attacked Horowitz for obscuring the fundamental differences between the historical-positivist school and Orthodoxy. See Meir Herskovitz, "Rabbi Eleazar ha-Levi Ish Horowitz" (in Hebrew), *Areshet* 5 (1972): 244–46, and idem, "The Historical Background of a Responsum by the Gaon Rabbi Solomon Kluger" (in Hebrew), in *Samuel Belkin Memorial Volume* (New York: Yeshiva University, 1981), 162–80.

[19] See Hildesheimer's letters in 1860 to Rabbi Wolf Feilchenfeld of Düselldorf: the Hebrew translation in Azriel Hildesheimer, "Rabbi Esriel Hildesheimer on Zacharias Frankel and the Jewish Theological Seminary in Breslau (from his Correspondence)" (in Hebrew), *Ha-maʿayan* 1 (1952/53): 66, 68f.; and the original in truncated form in Eliav, *Hildesheimer Briefe*, pp. 24-27. On the controversy unleashed by Frankel's book, see Isaac Barzilay, *Shlomo Yehudah Rapoport [ShIR] (1790-1867) and His Contemporaries* (Ramat-Gan: Masada, 1969), 160–79 and Noah H. Rosenbloom, *Tradition in an Age of Reform: The Religious Philosophy of Samson Raphael Hirsch* (Philadelphia: Jewish Publication Society, 1976), 106-108.

[20] "Die Erklärung von 121 Rabbinen, die bei dem Kompert'schen Pressprozess in Wien vorgekommenen Aeusserungen betreffend," *Israelit* 5 (1864): 95-97, and 145f. for an additional 15 names; "Verzeichniss der 149 Protestanten gegen die Einheit des jüdischen Glaubens," *Neuzeit* 4 (1864): 158f. Altogether 107 Hungarian rabbis signed the petition.

Hildesheimer urged his colleagues to face the inevitable and to preempt the Neologues by suggesting to the government an Orthodox-sponsored seminary. The center resisted this vehemently and submitted a petition with ninety signatures against any form of rabbinical seminary.[21] In the first place, any institution whose primary function was training rabbis was objectionable since it ran counter to the traditional ideal that higher learning was meant for all, regardless of their ultimate professional goals. Such a seminary would echo the earliest educational proposals of the Haskalah (Naphtali Hirṣ Wessely's *Divrei Shalom ve-Emet* [1782]), which had urged that advanced Talmudic studies be pursued exclusively by those who sought to make the rabbinate their career. There was also the traditional ambivalence toward the rabbinate which made the center recoil from explicitly announcing that the purpose of higher learning was meant, a priori, to train professional rabbis. Moreover, it was clear that even an Orthodox institution would flourish at the expense of the traditional yeshivas, especially that of Pressburg, and that in time it would be the seminary that was going to determine the cultural profile of the Hungarian Orthodox rabbinate. "If God forbid the harsh decree of a rabbinical seminary is ordered," Hillel Lichtenstein had declared at a rabbinical assembly, he and his colleagues were prepared "to gather signatures that it should be placed under the auspices of the evil ones [Neologues], not of the Sadducees [neo-Orthodox] . . . who wish to establish it under the guise of holiness!"[22]

As long as Hildesheimer was satisfied to run a yeshiva at Eisenstadt, even one where considerable innovations had been added to the curriculum, only the more extreme figures on the right voiced their opposition. However, when Hildesheimer decided to opt for the more ambitious framework of a rabbinical seminary, this proved too much for the hitherto patient center. If there had been a willingness to overlook the ideological underpinnings of Hildesheimer's combined curriculum, now, as he stubbornly persisted in his campaign for an Orthodox seminary, the ideal of an intentional cultural synthesis came under fire. Rabbi Moses Schick, one of the leading centrist authorities, whose own son had attended the Eisenstadt yeshiva in the previous decade, severely

[21] "Wortlaut der orthodoxen Rabbiner-Petition gegen die Errichtung einer Rabbinerschule," *Ben Chananja* 7 (1864): 907–10. See also Joseph Schweitzer, "The Seminary in the Responsa Literature," in *The Rabbinical Seminary of Budapest, 1877-1977*, ed. Moshe Carmilly-Weinberger (New York: Sepher-Hermon, 1986), 95-105.

[22] *Lev ha-ʿIvri* (Jerusalem: S.M.S. Schlesinger, 1924), vol. 2, fol. 88a, note. Unless stated otherwise, I refer to this edition throughout.

upbraided him. While conceding that the study of secular subjects could perhaps be permitted post factum, after one had mastered the Torah, Schick indignantly denied that a priori one could "make this an obligation for us and for generations to come. . . .One does not say to a man, 'Go and sin!'"[23]

This in general was the basic guideline of the moderate center in formulating their response to the challenges of the 1860s. They were ready to accommodate secular studies and linguistic acculturation, pay lip service to Magyar national identity, and even tolerate some minor changes in the synagogue, but they balked at adopting a neo-Orthodox ideology which clearly overstepped the bounds by making virtue out of necessity and by bestowing legitimacy where only compromise was deemed appropriate.

The Pesaq Din *of Michalowce*

With the third issue the following year, in 1865, it was the turn of the center to be outflanked on its right. An ultra-Orthodoxy emerged which gave a literal interpretation to the conservative and segregative (actually by now the self-segregative) ideology of the Ḥatam Sofer and sought to implement it in practice.

It was led by, or rather, clustered around, an unusually talented troika: the pious Rabbi Hillel Lichtenstein (b. Vágvecse, 1814; d. Kolomea, 1891), a fire-and-brimstone preacher who could rivet crowds for hours on end; Rabbi Ḥaim Sofer (b. Pressburg, 1821; d. Budapest, 1886), an outstanding halakhist, and himself no mean orator (no relation to the Ḥatam Sofer); and Lichtenstein's young son-in-law (and later also his brother-in-law), Akiva Yosef Schlesinger (b. Pressburg, 1837; d. Jerusalem, 1922). Schlesinger, who on principle refused to serve in the rabbinate, quickly earned a reputation as the *enfant terrible* of the Orthodox camp. More than anyone else, he came to embody a new era of religious extremism, what Hildesheimer sarcastically called "the recent Age of Akiva Yosef."[24] And although Schlesinger cannot be said to be typical of ultra-Orthodoxy because of his often maverick views, nevertheless it is he who can best be regarded as the quintessence of the phenomenon. (In this respect, he resembles his neo-Orthodox counter-

---

[23] Moses Schick to Esriel Hildesheimer, 20 Av 1864, cited in Eliav, "Hildesheimer and his Influence," 74.

[24] "Die neueste Akiba-Josef'sche Zeit," in Hildesheimer, "Ein Beitrag zur Bedeutung von *ḥuqqot ha-goyim*," 22. The *Israelit* 7 (1866): 871 refers to "akibajosephischen Doktrinen."

part, Samson Raphael Hirsch.) A firebrand, he became one of the outstanding Jewish publicists in Hungary, making his literary debut in 1863 at the age of twenty-five. In the six years which followed, he wrote half a dozen books aimed at a popular audience and also managed to publish single-handedly a short-lived monthly journal, the first Judaeo-German periodical in Hungary. His most successful work was a running commentary on the testament of the Ḥatam Sofer entitled *Lev ha-ʿIvri* (The Hebrew Heart). The book, which appeared in two parts in 1864 and 1868, became an instant bestseller, quickly running through five editions. And it achieved considerable fame not only in Hungary, but throughout central and eastern Europe. A few years later, the Russian maskil Eliezer Ṣevi Zweifel could write from far-off Zhitomir, "I have never seen any book published in our time which has been greeted by the Jewish public with such great honor and tremendous jubilation as the book *Lev ha-ʿIvri!*"[25] There can be no doubt that Schlesinger was highly influenced by both older men, Lichtenstein in particular, however, since they began to publish their writings only several years later, most of the references in this paper are to Schlesinger's work.

The primary targets of these paladins of ultra-Orthodoxy were not the reformers, who by this time were considered hopelessly beyond the pale. Rather, the most vehement attacks were focused on Hildesheimer and rabbis of his kind. Hildesheimer was viewed by the ultra-Orthodox as a far more dangerous threat than Reform since his very Orthodoxy lent a legitimacy to innovation which had been unhesitatingly denied to the reformers. The exhortations of the ultra-Orthodox were aimed mainly at the mass of vacillating, middle-of-the-road Orthodox who were increasingly tempted to compromise and were on the way to becoming neo-Orthodox fellow travelers.

A broadside issued in 1865 by an anonymous Pressburg scholar in rejoinder to Schlesinger's accusations provides a good illustration of this sector's dilemma. In several publications, Schlesinger had condemned the community for betraying the Ḥatam Sofer's legacy by engaging a preacher to deliver sermons in German. That this man, R. Feish

[25] Eliezer Ṣevi Zweifel, *Shalom al Yisraʾel* (Zhitomir: Shaduv, 1873),4:33. I wish to thank Mr. Motti Zalkin for bringing this source to my attention. This volume of Zweifel's famous work is devoted to mapping out the religious spectrum of his time. He identifies four basic positions: ultra-Orthodoxy (though he does not use this term), as represented by Schlesinger; neo-Orthodoxy, by Hirsch and Hildesheimer; historical positivism, by Frankel and Graetz; and Reform, by Geiger and the Hungarian Leopold Löw.

Fischmann, was not only Orthodox, but even enjoyed a reputation for what many thought was excessive piety, only made matters worse. In reply, the anonymous pamphleteer pointed out that linguistic and cultural conditions in Pressburg were such that in order to safeguard Orthodoxy, it was necessary to compromise and preach in German,

> especially in our time and our town where most of the men and women do not understand Torah and morals in this language [*Jiddisch-Deutsch*] and even if they do, they would not pay attention to it. If [the reformers] will not be opposed by sharp-tongued swords, . . .many who still have their hearts in the right place will succumb.

Unlike the neo-Orthodox, however, the author of the pamphlet stressed the pragmatic factors involved in the latest innovations and stopped short of claiming universal applicability of the Pressburg experience. In an attempt to mollify the ultra-Orthodox militants, he allowed that "in the region where you live [northeastern Hungary], your method is the most useful." Since conditions there were favorable for a culturally segregated life, he saw no need for concessions.[26]

The rabbinic decision, the *pesaq din*, issued at the northeastern town of Michalowce on 28 November 1865 and signed by twenty-five rabbis, was addressed mainly to this hesitant section of the Orthodox population.[27] The nine-point decision, which in time became a sort of manifesto of

---

26 *Ketav Yosher Divrei Emet* (Pressburg: Sieben's Erben 1865), esp. p. [2]. The more dogmatic neo-Orthodox in Hungary such as Hildesheimer no doubt differed on this point. Paradoxically, Samson Raphael Hirsch probably had a more tolerant attitude toward Hungarian ultra-Orthodoxy, but this has yet to be established systematically. Meanwhile see the suggestive article by Hirsch's grandson, Raphael Breuer, "Der Kampf gegen die Assimilation in Ost und West," *Naḥlath Ṣevi* 6 (1935/1936): 143–47.

27 *Pesaq Beit-Din* (Ungvár, 1866). See the fine study by Katzburg, "The Rabbinical Decision." Some of the relevant texts can be found in Jacob Katz, "Sources of Orthodox Trends," in *The Role of Religion in Modern Jewish History* (Cambridge, Mass.: The Association for Jewish Studies, 1976), 31f., 51-58, and in partial English translation in Guttmann, *The Struggle over Reform*, 263–69. For other analyses of the *pesaq din*, see Eliav, "Hildesheimer and his Influence," 75-79; Nathaniel Katzburg, "Assimilation in Hungary during the Nineteenth Century: Orthodox Positions," in *Jewish Assimilation in Modern Times*, ed. Béla Vágo (Boulder, Colo.: Westview, 1981), 49-55; David Ellenson, "Church-Sect Theory, Religious Authority, and Modern Jewish Orthodoxy: A Case Study," in *Approaches to Modern Judaism*, ed. Marc Lee Raphael (Chico, Calif.: Scholars Press, 1983), 73-78, and idem, "The Role of Reform in Selected German-Jewish Orthodox Responsa: A Sociological Analysis," in his *Tradition and Transition: Orthodoxy, Halakhah, and the Boundaries of Modern Jewish Identity* (Lanham, Md.: University Press of America, 1989), 38-46.

ultra-Orthodoxy,[28] proscribed external and internal architectural changes in the synagogue such as moving the bimah away from the center, constructing a tower, and providing inadequate dividers between the men's and women's section. Deviations from the traditional service, such as an accompanying male choir, canonical robes for the cantor, performing the marriage ceremony within the synagogue, and preaching in German were vehemently condemned. Even the slightest innovation in traditional customs was forbidden; a synagogue where such changes were introduced was deemed a house of heresy which one was forbidden to enter.

It would be a mistake, however, to view the *pesaq din* as primarily an attack on Reform. In fact, with perhaps the exception of moving the bimah, nowhere did the *pesaq din* mention the classic synagogue reforms such as changes in the language and text of the prayers or the introduction of the organ.[29] Instead, several of the prohibitions were veiled references to innovations which had only recently been introduced in none other than that bastion of Orthodoxy, Pressburg, the seat of the late Ḥatam Sofer. It was the tactics of accommodation adopted by the moderate center in places like Pressburg which the ultra-Orthodox condemned as tragically misconceived and already having been proved bankrupt in Germany.

In time, altogether seventy-one rabbis signed the Michalowce *pesaq din*. However, as contemporaries were quick to point out, most of the rabbis who had protested the establishment of a rabbinic seminary in the previous year now withheld their signatures, and this held true even of right-of-center allies of the ultra-Orthodox such R. Jeremiah Löw. The *pesaq din* created new divisions within the Orthodox camp.

---

[28] Lipót Kecskeméti, *Egy zsidó vallás van-e, több-e?* (Is There One Religion of More?) (Nagyvárad: Sonnenfeld, 1913), 183, calls the *pesaq din* the "constitution" of Hungarian Orthodoxy.

[29] Which is why I disagree with David Ellenson's interpretation of the *pesaq din*. Ellenson is correct that the *pesaq din* served to provide "clear boundaries for permissible behavior which would aid in the establishment of an Orthodox group identity." However, he is mistaken that at Michalowce "the rabbis prohibited entry into a synagogue which had an organ, even if the organ was not played on the Sabbath" ("The Role of Reform," 39). In fact, the organ is altogether absent from the list of prohibitions issued by the *pesaq din*, because its primary aim was to run the boundaries not between Reform and Orthodoxy, but through the Orthodox camp itself in order to place neo-Orthodoxy beyond the pale.

The Socio-Cultural Basis of Ultra-Orthodoxy

It became increasingly clear that these divisions had distinct regional overtones. Whereas signatures for the antiseminary petition had been solicited from every corner of Hungary, the signatories of the *pesaq din* hailed almost exclusively from the northeast counties, from Unterland.[30] (Although it was so called in contrast to Oberland in the northwest, it was actually a misnomer since the region was even more a mountainous "highland" than Oberland.) Regional differences among the Orthodox came even more to the fore during the 1868–1869 Jewish Congress. The Congress had been summoned by the government in an attempt to create a nationwide Jewish organization. Two hundred and twenty representatives were elected, of whom about eighty can be identified with certainty as Orthodox. A regional breakdown of the Orthodox deputies reveals that Hildesheimer's faction (combining both the neo- and the left-of-center Orthodox) was drawn from Oberland and from the more urbanized areas of the Great Hungarian Plain, regions which had remained largely traditional, but were affected by the educational reforms of the 1850s and 1860s. In contrast, the right-of-center Orthodox and the ultra-Orthodox drew their constituency mainly from the northeast counties.[31]

In every respect the most backward region in the country, Unterland was a corner of eastern European Jewry wedged into Hungary. Though by no means a majority, Hasidim made their presence felt here; there were close family, business, and cultural bonds with Galicia. The density of Jews in the general population was much higher here than throughout the country; a large percentage lived in largely rural areas. The currents of change which had swept over Oberland, transforming it in the previous generation, had largely left this area untouched. Both in schooling and literacy, the Jews of this mountainous region differed markedly from the rest of Hungary. For instance, of the 308 Jewish schools which had been established throughout the country by 1858, only seven were located in the Kassa school district which covered much of Unterland. The contrast with the northwest was striking: while there was one school for every 650 Jews in the largely Orthodox Pressburg school district of

---

[30] "Verzeichniss der Rabbinen, welche die Beschlüsse der Nagy-Mihályer Synode unterzeichnet haben," *Ben Chananja* 9 (1866): 580–82.

[31] My analysis is based on the votes of the 5 and 8 February 1869 sessions of the Congress. See *Az 1868 december 10-ikére összehivott izraelita egyetemes gyülés naplója* (The Diary of the Israelite Assembly Convened on 10 December 1868) (Pest, 1869), session 18, pp. 10, 27f., and session 19, pp. 37f.

Oberland, there was only one per 14,200 in Unterland.[32] The earliest comprehensive statistics on literacy rates (in German and Hungarian) among Hungarian Jews, dating from 1880, confirm that a cultural abyss yawned between these two mainly Orthodox areas. In the Oberland counties of Nyitra, Pozsony, and Trencsén, about two-thirds of the Jewish population was literate; in the neighboring Burgenland—Mosony and Sopron counties—the figure was even higher. To the northeast, however, the literacy rates were substantially lower. The highest percentages was recorded in Zemplén county (42.2%), followed by Ung (36.6%), Bereg (31.0%), Ugocsa (29.5%) and, after a considerable drop, Máramaros (14.9%). Not for another generation would, for instance, Zemplén Jewry even come close to the 1880 rates of Oberland.[33]

Dwelling in the backwater of Unterland enabled one to take a tougher stance, one of resolute rejection rather than weak-kneed compromise. The leader of the right-of-center Orthodox, Jeremiah Löw, rabbi of the Zemplén community of Ujhely, repeatedly urged his Oberland colleagues "not to be afraid or overly cautious" and to follow the more militant lead of Unterland. "Many of the good-hearted in Pressburg lean toward compromise," he confided to a friend, "but I wrote to Oberland that we have no intention of making concessions."[34] In contrast to this combative tone, a spirit of despondency and cultural despair prevailed among many of the Orthodox in the northwest. When summoned to serve in an eastern community, a guilt-ridden R. Moses Schick hesitated over deserting hard-pressed Oberland. An older colleague reassured him. The good fight had been fought, but the situation here was hopeless.

> The rabbis of Oberland nowadays are likened to a commander of a small fort with few men under his command and besieged by the evil inclination. . . . He battles with all his might even if he cannot raise the local children in Torah. He gathers around him cohorts from other places and does what he can. He is comforted by the thought that he has succeeded in at least raising his own children in the way of the Torah and that they

---

[32] K. A. Schmid, ed., *Encyclopädie des gesammten Erziehungs- und Unterrichtswesens* (Gotha, 1866), 5:549; *Statistische Übersichten über die Bevölkerung und den Viehstand von Österreich nach der Zählung vom 31. October 1857* (Wien: Aus der K.K. Hof und Staatsdruckerei, 1859), 392.

[33] *Magyar Statisztikai Közlemények*, n.s. 27 (1909): 160f.

[34] Letter to Ḥaim Sofer, 1864, in *Kan Sofer*, ed. Yakov Ṣevi Sofer (London: Schreiber, 1963), 10; and in the same vein, another letter that year to Moses Schick in *Moriah* 8 6-7 (Kislev 5739 [1978]): 25f.

> have not been entrapped. . . . But if God should summon him to another place and redeem him from prison, . . . should he refuse, saying, "I will continue sitting in prison, I will continue to fight the evil inclination"? . . . I cannot even find a proper *baḥur* for my daughters in order to raise a son-in-law to be like me. . . . Is there at all any doubt or question what you should do?[35]

It is significant that while the mass constituency of ultra-Orthodoxy was clearly located in Unterland, many of its leading figures were born and raised in the non-Hasidic Oberland. Like their revered mentor, the German-born Ḥatam Sofer, they, too, witnessed their native home in crisis and were transformed by the experience. Like him they fled to an uncontaminated, traditional Eden in the east, from where, unfettered by the constraints of a harsh reality, they could hurl their jeremiads against the evils of accommodation.

One of the more revealing episodes of this internecine *Kulturkampf* took place in November 1868. Some two hundred rabbis covering the entire spectrum of Hungarian Orthodoxy had convened in Budapest to discuss strategy for the forthcoming Jewish Congress. As expected, the rabbi of Pressburg, the Ketav Sofer, was elected chairman of the conference; R. Ṣevi Hirsh Friedman of Liszka, the head of the Hasidic camp, and his bitter enemy, R. Jeremiah Löw, were appointed vice-chairmen; and rabbis Esriel Hildesheimer, Salomon Kutna, Pinḥas Stein, and a fourth rabbi were named as secretaries. Each of the major groupings was thus represented in the executive: the secretaries represented Hildesheimer's neo-Orthodox faction; the Ketav Sofer, the left wing of the mainstream; Jeremiah Löw, its right wing; and Ṣevi Hirsh of Liszka, the Hasidim and their allies, the ultra-Orthodox. As a rule, the first two were based in Oberland and western Hungary, the last two in Unterland. During the discussions, the question of secular education arose. A proposal to condemn the establishment of a rabbinic seminary prompted an indignant Hildesheimer and his followers to storm out of the proceedings. After the motion was carried, the Ketav Sofer, suggested a new proposal: "The conference should agree to appoint teachers in the more advanced yeshivas to teach students secular subjects." (This was an unprecedented concession on the part of a traditional yeshiva; we may recall that the great Volozhin yeshiva, Pressburg's Russian counterpart,

[35] Letter of Israel David Margaliot-Jaffe Schlesinger, rabbi of Bazin, 1861, in Moshe Pollak, Introduction to *Derashot Maharam Schick* (Sermons of Rabbi Moses Schick) (Cluj, 1937), fol. 4b-5a.

was shut down toward the end of the century precisely because it refused to countenance such a compromise.) For the rabbi of Liszka, this proved too much. Unable to contain himself any longer, he thundered, "A rabbi in Israel should have nothing to do with *Bildung*, secular subjects, or the sciences! It is enough if he knows how to sign his name in German and Hungarian, and no more!" As on cue, the left wing of the mainstream made a demonstrative exit, only to be followed by Rabbi Löw and his right of center sympathizers who could no longer suffer the Hasidim. "And that is how the conference came to an end!"[36]

The heyday of ultra-Orthodox influence was in the mid 1860s. Although the center, and even the right of center, balked at accepting the extreme formulations of the *pesaq din*, nevertheless the ultra-Orthodox did succeed in inducing a general drift to the right. Even at their zenith, however, they failed to create a sizable, autonomous constituency. While they were capable of generating sympathy among the rabbinic intelligentsia—rabbis, religious functionaries, yeshiva students, and the like—especially in the northeast, they remained dependent upon the good will of the Hasidic leaders in Hungary and Galicia for the backing of the masses. But these *rebbes* had their own agenda and could be unreliable, even treacherous, allies. (After the Congress, most of the Hasidic groups stood aloof from the Orthodox organization. Personal conflicts played no little role in this decision.) Among the economically better-off Orthodox in western Hungary, the dedication of the zealots, their readiness for self-sacrifice, evoked mixed feelings. Many no doubt harbored a sneaking admiration for the principled opposition of the ultra-Orthodox to compromise but were also repelled by their excesses. On the balance, this ambiguous sympathy could not be translated by the ultra-Orthodox into political capital, consequently they made few if any inroads among the middle-class, centrist lay leadership of the Orthodox communities.

Once emancipation was granted in 1867 and the campaign against the Neologues was mounted in earnest, the ultra-Orthodox were brushed aside and it was their archrivals the neo-Orthodox who stepped once again into the limelight. Since 1863, Schlesinger and his colleagues had agitated for the creation of a super-communal Orthodox organization—

---

36 "The Rabbinical Conference in Hungary" (in Hebrew), *Ha-Magid* 12 (1868): 394f. It was probably penned by the poet Simon Bachrach (Bacher). A similar report appeared in *Israelit* 9 (1868), 928. For other descriptions see also *Neuzeit* 8 (1868): 591; "Die jüdischen Hoffnungen in Ungarn," *Jeschurun* 15 (1869): 22f.; the letter of Hildesheimer to S. R. Hirsch, 12 March 1868, in Eliav, *Hildesheimer Briefe*, pp. 61f.; and Hildesheimer, "Die ungarische Rabbiner-Versammlung," *Israelit* 9 (1868): 933–37.

in vain. It took the impending threat of a Neologue-dominated Congress to prod the Orthodox out of their inertia, to set up in April 1868 what was to be the first nationwide, Orthodox organization anywhere, the Shomrei ha-Dat (Guardians of the Faith) Society. The ultra-Orthodox, however, had little to do with the new society.[37] While the rabbinic presidium, headed by the Ketav Sofer, Jeremiah Löw, and Menaḥem Eisenstädter, represented a relatively broad spectrum of the center Orthodox, the lay leaders of Shomrei ha-Dat, who actually set the tone of the society, were either outright left-wing, neo-Orthodox closely identified with Esriel Hildesheimer and Samson Raphael Hirsch, or were their left-of-center sympathizers.[38] Both the statutes of the society and its organ, the *Magyar Zsidó*, were replete with effusive protestations of Hungarian nationalism and enthusiasm for Magyar culture.[39] "Do not call them Guardians of the Faith *(shomrei ha-dat)*!" thundered the ultra-Orthodox, "Call them instead Destroyers of the Faith *(shomdei ha-dat)*!"[40]

The Congress had unexpected results. Dominating the proceedings from the very first, the Neologue by and large ignored the views of the Orthodox minority. However, as a result of intensive lobbying in the wake of the Congress, the Orthodox won over the liberal Hungarian Parliament and in 1871 gained the right to establish an alternative, autonomous association. From this time on, there existed in Hungary

37 As opposed to the commonly held view that they were the moving force behind *Shomrei ha-Dat*. See Benjamin Mintz, "Akiba Joseph Schlesinger," in *Men of Spirit*, ed. Leo Jung (New York: Kymson, 1964), 86f. Contemporary opponents of Orthodoxy also viewed the society as an outgrowth of the *pesaq din* of Michalowce. See *Neuzeit* 8 (1868): 592.

38 The difference between the rabbinic and the lay leadership of the Shomrei ha-Dat society in their relations with Hildesheimer can be seen in Hildesheimer's letter to Sigmund Krausz, July 1868, in Eliav, *Hildesheimer Briefe*, 56-59.

39 See the memorandum of 120 Orthodox communities addressed to Baron József Eötvös, spring 1867, in *A magyar országgyülés mélyen tisztelt képviselőházához intézett emlékirata az izraelita egyetemes gyülés bizottságának az 1868. évi deczember 10-ére meghivott izraelita congressus által hozott határozatok tárgyában* [Memorandum of the Committee of the General Assembly of Israelites Submitted to the Honorable House of Representatives of the Hungarian Parliament Concerning the Decisions of the Israelite Congress Convened on 10 December 1868] (Könyvnyomda-Részvény-Társulat, 1870) (Pest, 1870), no. 66, p. 28 of the appendix, and *A "Hitőr" magyar zsidó egylet alapszabályai. Shomre Hadath. Statuten für den ungarisch-jüdischen Verein "Glaubenswächter"* (in Hebrew, Magyar and German) (Pest: Legrády, 1868), pp. 17 and 19 of the German, and p. 5 of the Magyar version.

40 *Lev ha-ʿIvri*, vol. 2, fol. 117a; and Hillel Lichtenstein, *Maskil el-Dal* (Brooklyn: Rosenberg, 1962), vol. 3, *klal* 8, *prat* 4, fol. 73a-b. The volumes were first published in 1868 and 1869 respectively.

three types of communities, sometimes in the very same town: Neologue or Congress, Orthodox, and the so-called Status quo ante, who refused to join either of the national organizations. (Later, they would set up yet a third national body.) This achievement must undoubtedly be credited to the shrewd campaign led by the lay leadership of Shomrei ha-Dat, who convinced the liberal Parliament that the freedom of religious conscience would be violated if Neologues and Orthodox—"who were further apart than Protestants and Catholics"—were forced to remain under the same organizational roof.[41]

It was ironic that the schism, initiated by the ultra-Orthodox,[42] was ultimately realized by their neo-Orthodox archrivals, who for most of the decade had condemned the zealots precisely because of their schismatic tendencies.[43] But the irony was compounded, because the schism spelled

---

[41] See Jacob Katz, "The Tragic Schism—The Split between the Orthodox and Neologue in Hungarian Jewry: The Origins, Impact, and Consequences of the Schism" (in Hungarian), *Múlt és Jövő* 3 1 (1991): 49-55. That Neologues and Orthodox were further apart than Protestants and Catholics is a recurrent theme. Samson Raphael Hirsch used this argument in Germany already in 1862, and it first appears in the writings of Sigmund Krausz, the leading layman in Shomrei ha-Dat, in the spring of 1868. See Hirsch, "Was hat eine gesetztreue Minorität neologischen Wünschen gegenüber zutun?" (1862), *Gesammelte Schriften*, 2:374; Sigmund Krausz, *Transaction zur Ausgleichung der sich gegenüberstehenden isr. Partheien im ung. Vaterlande: Gesprochen in der Konferenz der Notablenversammlung am 17. Februar 1868* (Pest: M. E. Löwy's Sohn, 1868), 4; "Beleuchtung der die Gemeinden- und Schulen-Organisation betreffenden Vorlagen der ungarisch-israelitischen Konferenzmajorität. Von einem Mitgliede des Schomre-Hadath-Vereines," *Jeschurun* 14 (1868): 229; [Krausz?], "Rückblick auf den ungar.-israelitischen Congress," *Jeschurun* 15 (1869), 151f.; Jacob Ettlinger's opinion in *Rabbinische Gutachten über die Statuten und Beschlüsse des ung.-isr. Kongresses* (Pest: I. Neuer, 1869), 13, 17; . . . c, "Trennung," *Jeschurun* 16 (1870): 35; Sigmund Krausz, *Wissen und Glauben oder: Der Mensch und der Israelit: Zwei Betrachtungen nebst einer Einleitung als Schlusswort nach beendigtem Kongresskampfe zwischen den Juden orthodoxer und neologer Richtung* (Pest: Bendiner und A. Grünwald 1871), p. 60. But cf. n. 43 below.

[42] The bibliographer Ḥaim Lippe, who had taken an active part in the *Kulturkampf* of the 1860s, assigned Schlesinger the central role in causing the schism in Hungarian Jewry: "He was the first, the great hero, to set Jew against Jew, to rend the bonds which held together the holy people into twelve rent pieces!" *Asaf ha-mazkir he-ḥadash: Bibliographisches Lexicon* (in Hebrew) (Wien: D. Löwy, 1881), 325. The history of the schism and the relative importance of the roles played by the ultra- and the neo-Orthodox, awaits its chronicler.

[43] It was only from the spring of 1868 that neo-Orthodox such as Sigmund Krausz, first began to seriously entertain the notion of a schism on a nationwide scale. (See the references in n. 41 above.) But even Krausz changed his mind during the

a Pyrrhic victory for the neo-Orthodox. Once the new national organization came into being, it was the center Orthodox who grasped the reins of power and set the pace for decades to come. In fact, the schism signalled the precipitous decline of both the neo- and the ultra-Orthodox. In time, the two militant wings were re-absorbed into the broad, amorphous mainstream.

No doubt it was more than a coincidence that the two most representative figures of these antagonistic movements, both frustrated by the turn of events, decided to abandon Hungary around the same time. Esriel Hildesheimer accepted the call to serve as the rabbi of a small Orthodox association in Berlin already in 1869, where he finally succeeded in establishing his much-dreamed-of Orthodox rabbinical seminary. And a year later, in 1870, Akiva Yosef Schlesinger made his way up to Jerusalem, where his reveries were to be preoccupied with visions of a different kind.

The Invention of a Tradition

Ultra-Orthodoxy and Halakhic Strategy

What strategy should be adopted on halakhic issues in an age increasingly lax in traditional observance? When the hold of tradition was still strong, leniency or severity was often a matter of the individual authority's personal inclination. Where tradition came to be challenged, however, it often became a matter of policy and general tactics. Should one eschew a stringent approach for fear of further alienating a not entirely committed congregation, or on the contrary, defiantly embrace a hard line, and thus prod a hesitant flock into making a firm commitment?[44]

The Ḥatam Sofer had already established the principle that "it is proper to make a fence around the Torah, to be stringent and not add

Congress and declared that he had abandoned his earlier call for a schism. See his *Worte des Friedens* (Pest: I. Neuer, 1868), 5f.; *Entwurf einer israelitischen Synagogal-Verfassung* (Pest: Légrády, 1869), 6 § 14, which stills calls for one administrative community in each locale; and *Motiven-Bericht zum Entwurf eines organ. Gemeindestatutes* (Pest: I. Neuer, 1869), 8. See also Hildesheimer's letter to Shlomo Ganzfried, 5 April 1869, in Eliav, *Hildesheimer Briefe*, pp. 44f. (Hebrew section). It must be noted, however, that in at least one celebrated case, Székesfehérvár, it was the neo-Orthodox who initiated separate religious institutions albeit on a local, communal level. See on this below.

44 Katz, *The "Shabbes Goy"*; and Mordechai Breuer, "The Method of Judicial Decision of German Rabbis in the Era of Emancipation" (in Hebrew), *Sinai* 100 (1987); 166–86.

lenient rulings,"[45] and Schlesinger assiduously scoured the master's responsa, collecting statements to this effect. This zealous preference for the hard-line became one of the distinctive marks of Hungarian ultra-Orthodoxy. When asked about a possible lenient decision in a matter of kashruth, Ḥaim Sofer made the following revealing remarks to the champion of German neo-Orthodoxy, Samson Raphael Hirsch. "Certainly one could find a permissive ruling," wrote Sofer, " . . . if it were really necessary." The reformers often claimed that the Orthodox adhered to stringent rulings because they were ignorant of the reasons for the customs or lacked the courage to take a lenient stance. Sofer dismissed this as nonsense. Of course the reasons could be known. Even if his generation was sadly deficient in stature compared to previous generations, nevertheless, men of authority were not lacking. "It is not that we do not know [how to rule leniently]. On the contrary. But we do know very clearly that in the present state of decline of our poor generation, faith is endangered on all sides. And everyone must admit that a weak, sick body needs more care and protection than a healthy body." Therefore, instead of seeking ways to lighten the burden, rabbis should find reasons to cling to even the most inconsequential traditions. "In this orphaned generation it is a holy obligation incumbent upon each and everyone to root in his heart from the earliest years to keep and fulfill not only all the commandments, but even the most trifling customs which we received from our ancestors."[46]

Several stratagems were employed. One way which the Ḥatam Sofer sought to arrive at stringent rulings was to collapse the differences between the various levels of precepts. "It is good to elevate a prohibition!" By this he meant to ground a stringent ruling in a new rationale, as well as to "promote" the prohibition to a higher level (e.g., to claim that a rabbinic prohibition was actually a biblical one).[47] Since all elements of the tradition were equally sacred, there was no point in distinguishing between its various strata; that could only lead to its relativization. This was precisely the ploy of the reformers, who eagerly sought to differentiate between the authority of biblical precepts, rabbinical ordinances, and recent customs recorded in the *Shulḥan Arukh*. The Pressburg school

---

45 *Responsa* YD, § 60, cited in *Lev ha-ʿIvri*, vol. 2, fol. 20a.

46 Ḥaim Sofer, *Kan Sofer* (London: Schreiber, 1962/1963), letter § 61, pp. 54-56. The medical analogy of a sick patient who needs severe treatment if he is to be cured crops up often in the literature. See, for example, Israel David Margaliot-Jaffe, *Responsa Har Tabor* (Pressburg: Sieber, 1861), fol. 21b.

47 *Lev ha-ʿIvri*, vol. 2, fol. 21a, citing *Responsa Ḥatam Sofer*, EH I, § 37.

rejected this, collapsing the distinctions. "Every rule in the *Shulḥan Arukh*," stated Schlesinger, "is equal to the Ten Commandments; and every Jewish custom is equal to the Ten Commandments!"[48]

The canonization of the *Shulḥan Arukh* had become the hallmark of Hungarian Orthodoxy already under the influence of the Ḥatam Sofer. This uncritical acceptance of the codes belied an impatience with the give and take of the halakhic process, a quality which set the ultra-Orthodox apart from the general mainstream Orthodox. Unlike the unruly Talmudic deliberations with their cacophony of contending opinions, the codes had the advantage of speaking in a single voice. In an age when tradition was often called into question precisely because of its heterogeneous and at times contradictory nature, the ultra-Orthodox were especially keen on playing down any manifestation of diversity. When the issue of permitting machine-made *matzoth* was raised, Schlesinger complained to Ḥaim Sofer that the open disagreement among the rabbis was creating harmful confusion among the public. "It seems to them as if there are two Torahs. People say just as we are too stringent in this, so are we in everything else."[49] He also leveled critical remarks at an older colleague, the esteemed Solomon Ganzfried, for what he considered errors of judgment in his recently published abridgement of the codes, the *Kiṣur Shulḥan Arukh*. "I am but a young man, immature in wisdom, and had I not known of your humility, most eminent Gaon, I would not have dared say this," he wrote just a month before the *pesaq din* of Michalowce was issued.

> I have noted that in several instances you have ruled not as the *Shulḥan Arukh*, the *RMA*, and the *Magen Avraham*, but relied instead upon the *Ḥayei Adam* like the Gaon Eliahu [of Vilna]. It is my opinion that in this generation, especially when address-

---

[48] "Yad ʿIvri," at the end of *Lev ha-ʿIvri*, vol. 2, (Lemberg: Kugel, Lewin et Comp., 1868), fol. 846, n. 23.

[49] *Kan Sofer*, letter § 15, p. 17. On the issue of machine-made *matzoth*, see Salomon Freehof, *The Responsa Literature* (Philadelphia: Jewish Publication Society, 1955), 181–89. Machine-made *matzoth*, were introduced in Austria in 1857. Rabbi Salomon Kluger of Brody published a prohibition, *Modaʿah le-Veit Yisraʾel* (Breslau, 1859). A year later, Rabbi Joseph Saul Nathanson of Lemberg contested Kluger's ruling in *Biṭul Modaʿah* (Lemberg, 1859). On Kluger's responsum see David Ellenson, "Jewish Legal Interpretation: Literary, Scriptural, Social, and Ethical Perspectives," in his *Tradition in Transition*, 9-32. German rabbis in general sided with the lenient interpretation of Nathanson. See Breuer, "Method of Judicial Decision," 119. Hungarian rabbis, like their Galician counterparts, were divided on the issue.

> ing the masses, it is preferable not to deviate from the customs and the decisions of the *Shulḥan Arukh* even a tiny iota.[50]

But ultimately, even the *Shulḥan Arukh* could not be accepted as the final arbiter. The decisive authority for the ultra-Orthodox resided not in the letter of the law (even as recorded in the *Shulḥan Arukh*), but in its spirit. When an unspecified argument was proposed to Hillel Lichtenstein in 1860 which would have allowed brewing alcoholic beverages on the Sabbath (through the agency of a non-Jew), he vehemently rejected the idea and asked that his response be made public. The Talmud (Yebam. 90b) stated that at times to abrogate the Torah is to preserve it. If this was said in favor of issuing a lenient ruling, argued Lichtenstein, how much more must this hold true regarding a stringent ruling! He recalled the warning of the Ḥatam Sofer, "Take care my children! It is a difficult skill to know the four parts of the *Shulḥan Arukh*, but it can be mastered. But in order to know the fifth *Shulḥan Arukh* [there are only four parts]—to rule and teach in accordance with the state of the generation and the demands of the time and place, to gather and disperse, to rule leniently or stringently—that requires great assistance from heaven!" Therefore, concluded Lichtenstein, "Even if a *bat qol* [celestial voice] were to issue from heaven which would permit brewing based on this lenient ruling, even if Joshua son of Nun would agree to it, I would say this is not in heaven!"[51]

Halakhah and the Pesaq Din of Michalowce (1865)

The preference for the spirit over the letter of the law was best illustrated by the *pesaq din* of Michalowce. Serious problems faced the ultra-Orthodox when they sought to provide the rationale for the nine prohibitions. As its very name suggests, the *pesaq din* was intended to be a halakhically based ruling. Mainstream Orthodox authorities, however, refused to sanction it as such because of its extreme pronouncements. In response to Hillel Lichtenstein's preliminary draft of the *pesaq din*, R.

---

50 *Ha-Ohel* 23 (1976-1977): 2-7.

51 Hillel Lichtenstein to his student, the communal official Yeḥiel, Friday the weekly portion *lekh lekhah*, 5621 in Hillel Lichtenstein, *Responsa Beit Hillel* (Jerusalem: A.Ḥ. Levinson, 1954), § 6, p. 14. The reference was probably to the bill of sale proposed by R. Ḥaim Halberstamm of Sanz in the late 1850s. (It was first published, however, only in 1875.) See Katz, *The "Shabbes Goy"*, 171–75, and on the Hungarian reception of his permissive ruling, pp. 204–15. Katz's remark that "the motif of an 'unruly generation' plays a leading role in their deliberations, sometimes almost preventing serious consideration of the *halakhic* merits of the case" (p. 213) is apposite here.

Moses Schick, who was to become the leading halakhic authority of Hungarian Jewry in the 1870s, wished him success, but balked at endorsing the *pesaq* with its claim to being grounded in halakhah. "When it comes to determining the *din*, love truth and avoid flattery." Were these prohibitions formulated as emergency measures—*migdar milta*—and further if he could be convinced of their efficacy, he would not be averse to lending his support. As it stood, however, the *pesaq din* was misleading, and Lichtenstein could not count upon his signature.[52] And indeed, when the *pesaq din* was issued a few months later, more or less in its original form, Schick, like most mainstream Orthodox rabbis, refrained from signing it. "I saw there things which in my opinion were simply not true," he wrote to Rabbi Menaḥem Eisenstädter of Ungvár, who repeatedly pressured him to sign. If one intends to issue an emergency prohibition, "He is not permitted to claim that it is by force of Halakhah that it is forbidden," and if a court were to do so "as did this *pesaq din*, then according to Maimonides [Book of Judges, Laws of Rebels, chapter 2] it violates the injunction 'Thou shalt not add thereto' [Deut 13:1]."[53]

The rulings of the *pesaq din* can be analytically divided into three elements: the interdictions against the specific synagogue innovations, the prohibition against German preaching, and the status of a synagogue where such changes have been introduced. Not all the points of the *pesaq din* were objectionable; even the neo-Orthodox Hildesheimer was willing to accept some. Although he echoed many of Schick's arguments in dismissing the halakhic authority of the *pesaq din*, he too recognized that if Reform was to be checked, unusual emergency measures were called for. Excepting the interdiction on German preaching, Hildesheimer was sympathetic in varying degrees to the other prohibitions but insisted that in almost every instance custom and not Halakhah was involved. Consequently, while such innovations were undesirable, the Orthodox, if faced with the *fait accompli* of a so-called "choir-synagogue" in their community, should back down and (perhaps with the exception of the *meḥiṣah*) avoid a divisive confrontation.[54] This view could still be shared

---

52 Moses Schick to Hillel Lichtenstein, 2 Av 1865, in *Liquṭei she'elot u-teshuvot Ḥatam Sofer* (Anthology of Questions and Responses of the Ḥatam Sofer) ed. Israel Stern (London, 1965), 73-75.

53 Moses Schick to Menaḥem Eisenstädter, Shevat 1866 in Meir Hildesheimer, "The Responsa of the Maharam Schick: The Book, Its Collection, and Its Editing" (in Hebrew), *Ṣefunot* 1 6 (Tevet 1990); 92f.

54 Hildesheimer, "Ein Beitrag zur Bedeutung von *ḥuqqot ha-goyim*," 1-26. It was originally published in the *Israelit* in 1866 as "Die Beschlüsse der Rabbiner-Versammlung zu Mihalowitz."

by a number of center-Orthodox authorities as late as the summer of 1865, barely months before the assembly at Michalowce.[55] It was to be one of the accomplishments of the right that after the *pesaq din* the center was much less willing to accomodate such *faits accomplis*. And yet, despite this shift to the right, the Maharam Schick and other centrists firmly continued to reject the notion that there was a halakhic basis for condemning such synagogues as "houses of idol worship" (as worded in the draft of the *pesaq din* and emended in the final version to the harsher halakhic category of "houses of heresy") which must be avoided at all cost, even at the risk of life. Such evident exaggerations exasperated even the most sympathetic centrist authorities.

This hyperbolic mode was not entirely the invention of Lichtenstein and Schlesinger; it owed much to an older colleague and disciple of the Ḥatam Sofer, Israel David Margaliot-Jaffe Schlesinger, who had died in 1864, just a year before the Michalowce assembly.[56] Many of the themes which pervade *Lev ha-ʿIvri* and the *pesaq din* appeared previously in a unique polemical volume of "responsa" Margaliot-Jaffe published in 1859 (but which seems to have been written at the beginning of the decade). And indeed *Meḥolat ha-Maḥanaim* is cited by both Lichtenstein and Schlesinger as the chief source for most—but significantly, as we

[55] When queried about the placement of the bimah by the Debrecen community late in the summer of 1865, Nathan Lipschitz, the rabbi of Abauj-Szántó, showed understanding for those "saintly and honest" rabbis who proved helpless to prevent the innovation and had to attend the "choir-synagogues." He probably had his neighbor, Moses Fischmann, the venerable rabbi of Miskolc, in mind. Along with Hildesheimer, Fischmann and his son Feish, the newly elected German preacher in Pressburg, were the prime targets of ultra-Orthodox attacks. See Lajos Blau, "On the History of the Construction of the Debrecen Synagogue," *Magyar Zsidó Szemle* 14 (1894); 25, note.

[56] In his Hebrew books he uses the family name Margaliot-Jaffe; in German, he signed himself David Schlesinger. For biographical details on "David Szered," as he is also called in the rabbinic literature, after his home town, see Mayer Miksa Stein, *Magyar Rabbik* (Hungarian Rabbis) 2 (1905); 157f.; 3 (1906): 41-45, 138f. and 144; Pinḥas Ṣ. Schwartz, *Shem ha-gedolim mi-Ereṣ Hagar* (Brooklyn: Jerusalem, 1959), vol. 1, fol. 53b, no. 10:278; and "Schlesinger, Izráel Dávid," in the *Magyar Zsidó Lexikon* (Budapest: Zsidó Lexikon, 1929), 772f. Born around 1800, he served as rabbi of a small town near Pressburg, Bazin (Pösing). A typographic error in Stein mistakenly lists the date of his death as 24 Nisan 1854 and is taken over by Schwartz and the *Magyar Zsidó Lexikon*. In fact, he appears as a signatory to both the anti-Kompert and the antiseminary petitions. He signed the latter, dated 8 April 1864, just weeks before his death on 1 May 1864. See *Ben Chananja* 7 (1864), 909.

shall see, not all—of the *pesaq*'s interdictions.[57] Individual chapters discussed *ḥuppah* in the synagogue, the placement of the bimah and the canonicals, while the first part of the book was devoted to establishing the general principle that all Jewish customs were invested with supreme importance and absolute halakhic authority. To abandon these customs in favor of imitating the gentiles, argued Margaliot-Jaffe, meant transgressing against no less than eight negative and three positive biblical precepts! By promoting any lowly custom to the level of a biblical precept, and multiplying the number of precepts, he was, of course, following the strategy of his master, the Ḥatam Sofer, "It is good to elevate the prohibition." But the master's "elevations" were relatively selective and pale in comparison to the dazzling extravagance of the disciple.[58] The same unrestrained style characterized Margaliot-Jaffe's attempt to explain the hidden, symbolic meaning of customs such as placing the bimah in the center of the synagogue or performing the wedding ceremony under the open sky. He marshalled no less than seven reasons for the latter, drawing on the authority of the Halakhah, the *Shulḥan Arukh*, the state, the natural sciences, the movement of the stars, astronomy, and finally, philosophy!

This tendency to over-justify clearly betrayed a basic insecurity, an uneasy sense that the halakhic rationale for both the traditional bimah and *ḥuppah* stood on rather shaky ground. And indeed the Orthodox were faced with the embarrassing fact that on both issues the *Shulḥan Arukh* was undeniably open to liberal interpretation.[59] This is why after

---

57 Hillel Lichtenstein to Zusman Sofer, Tuesday the weekly portion of *matot* 1865, in Hillel Lichtenstein, *Maskil el-Dal*, 4 vols. (Brooklyn: Sinai, 1963), vol. 4, at the beginning of the book; and *Lev ha-ʿIvri*, vol. I, fols. 63a-64b, fn.

58 Determining just how many transgressions were involved was an ongoing process of discovery for Margaliot-Jaffe. The number had increased considerably since the summer of 1853 when only *four* negative commandments were mentioned. See his responsum to R. Judah, rabbi of Csongrád, 27 Sivan 5631 in Samuel Margaliot-Jaffe Schlesinger, *Responsa Milei de-Avot* (Bardejov: Horowitz, 1925), part III, addenda, §6, 460–64. His approach to tradition in another context is succinctly summarized by Jacob Katz, "The Orthodox Defense of the Second Day of the Festivals" (in Hebrew), *Tarbiṣ* 57 (1988): 411–13.

59 See R. Moses Isserles's gloss on *Shulḥan Arukh, Even ha-ezer* §61: "SOME SAY the *ḥuppah* should be held under the open heavens" [emphasis added], and the comments of the author of the *Shulḥan Arukh*, R. Joseph Karo, in his commentary *Kesef Mishne* on Maimonides, *Laws of Prayer* 11: 3: "Placement [of the bimah] in the center is not mandatory; everything depends on the time and place. In times when the synagogues were very large, the bimah had to be placed in the center so that all the people would hear. But in our time, when unfortunately our synagogues are small

exhausting specific arguments for adhering to a given custom, Margaliot-Jaffe felt compelled in the final resort to reduce the entire issue to the interdiction against imitating the customs of the gentiles, "Nor shall you follow their laws" (Lev. 18:3). This blanket prohibition (which he claimed, as we have seen, to involve numerous negative and positive Biblical precepts) conveniently sanctified any custom or tradition automatically, regardless of its intrinsic halakhic merit. In fact, he came close to admitting that in their own right these innovations were not prohibited. Referring to the biblical episode of Zimri, the prince who was slain by the zealous Phinehas for having intercourse with a Midianite woman (Num. 25:6-18), he condemned those who like Zimri demanded to know the source of prohibitions.

> In truth this demand is that of Zimri the son of Salu, who insisted that Moses show him the prohibition against having intercourse with a gentile woman. And indeed there is no mention of this prohibition in the Torah prior to the deed of Phinehas, who as we have seen killed Zimri and was praised by God. . . . Thus, too, are those who question and ask for clear-cut answers why it is forbidden to transplant customs of another religion into the vineyard of Israel. This is contemptible! Does it need to be asked or the reason spelled out?! This is exactly the demand of Zimri![60]

By insisting that what was at stake was both SELF-EVIDENT and more FUNDAMENTAL than Halakhah, Margaliot-Jaffe fashioned a potent (almost an omnipotent) weapon for the conservative arsenal. In ultra-Orthodox hands it could preempt any halakhic objection, in effect nipping it in the bud. It is no coincidence that Schlesinger prefaced the passage on the *pesaq din* in his *Lev ha-ᶜIvri* with a warning not to gripe in the spirit of the "demand of Zimri son of Salu".[61]

---

and everyone can hear well, it is more pleasing that it be to one side rather than in the middle." It was in reference to the bimah that the Ḥatam Sofer (Responsa OḤ §28) stated, "All innovation is prohibited by the Torah." There is a large responsa literature on both topics (I counted over thirty on bimah alone), a fraction of which is summarized in Y. Y. Greenwald, "Is it Permissible to Marry in a Synagogue?" (in Hebrew), in his *Oṣar neḥmad* (New York, 1942) 47-54; and Mordekhai ha-Cohen, "On the Issue of Placing the Bimah in the Center of the Synagogue" (in Hebrew), *Noᶜam* 5 (1962): 60-69. For an example of a permissive ruling on bimah, see Moses Feinstein, *Responsa Igrot Moshe*, OḤ, part 2, §§ 41f.

60 Israel David Margaliot-Jaffe, *Responsa Meḥolat ha-Maḥanaim* (Pressburg, 1859), fol. 3b.

61 *Lev ha-ᶜIvri* (1990), 2:61a–b.

It was inevitable that the *pesaq din* would draw the logical consequences of Margaliot-Jaffe's approach. Altering any custom in imitation of the gentiles, it charged, "was more severe, both qualitatively and quantitatively, than eating pork"! Following Margaliot-Jaffe's reasoning, it argued that quantitatively eating pork involved only one negative precept, while by changing a custom in imitation of the gentiles one transgressed against numerous negative and positive precepts. Furthermore, there was a qualitative difference. The reforms involved negative precepts which were *avizrayhu deʿavodah zarah*—acts, which even if in themselves innocent, were prohibited because they were resultant of idolatry—"and it is POSSIBLE that they fall into the category of 'be killed, rather than to transgress'" [emphasis added]. Clearly, as reprehensible as eating pork may have been, it did not obligate martyrdom.[62] Observers could but gape at such logic. Many no doubt shared the assessment of one observer that "there has never been a book which justifies every inconsequential custom, sanctifying it with the holiness of the Torah, of Nature, and of the Sciences, as the book *Meḥolat ha-Maḥanaim!*"[63]

Yet while it is true that *Meḥolat ha-Maḥanaim* proved an inspiration for the ultra-Orthodox, in both substance and style they surpassed Margaliot-Jaffe in several important ways. In fact, nothing illustrates as well the novel elements of ultra-Orthodoxy than the distance separating

[62] *Pesaq Beit-Din* (Ungvár, 1866), paragraph following the nine points. The argument that these innovations were more severe than eating pork was never made by Margaliot-Jaffe. His formulation was also a bit more moderate. Margaliot-Jaffe interpreted the verse *pen tinnaqesh* (Beware of being lured into their ways, [Deut 12:30]) as an additional negative precept which came to teach that even if one were to change a custom without the intention of imitating the gentiles, nevertheless it would also be prohibited because it had the semblance (*marit ʿayin*) of imitation. It falls into the category of *avizrayhu*—an act which stems from a prohibition, but in itself is innocent—which is nevertheless prohibited and obligates martyrdom in the case of idolatry. Yet as soon as he wrote this, Margaliot-Jaffe qualified his statement drastically, to the point of negating that *avizrayhu* or martyrdom was involved. He also consistently used the abbreviation *ʿayin"aleph,* which as he explained nonchalantly in the small print buried away in a footnote on fol. 9b, did not really mean the conventional *ʿavodat elilim,* idol worship. It was rather the abbreviation of *ʿavodah aḥeret,* "another form of worship," because modern gentiles did not fall in the category of idol worshipers. In the body of the text Margaliot-Jaffe continued to use the misleading abbreviation (*Meḥolat ha-Maḥanaim,* fols. 10a-12b). The *pesaq din* understandably overlooked or ignored this fine distinction and used the non-ambiguous abbreviation, *ʿayin zayin, ʿavodah zarah,* idolatry, instead of the creative neologism.

[63] Zweifel, *Shalom al Yisraʾel,* 4:32.

Meḥolat ha-Maḥanaim from *Lev ha-ʿIvri,* published a scant five years later. For one, the passionate, scathing, at times even vulgar and violent polemics of Schlesinger and Lichtenstein were a far cry from the polite, conciliatory tone adopted by Margaliot-Jaffe. And while *Meḥolat ha-Maḥanaim* was addressed to the rebellious "youth" whom Margaliot-Jaffe sought to wean away from Reform, *Lev ha-ʿIvri* viewed any dialogue with Reform as a futile exercise. The analogy Schlesinger used was that of a terminally ill patient with an infectious disease. The patient himself was already beyond cure, it would be pointless to expend energy in seeking a remedy. All that remained for the doctors was to contain the damage by imposing a quarantine.[64]

But the most striking difference between Margaliot-Jaffe and the ultra-Orthodox was to be found in the *pesaq din.* As we have seen, Margaliot-Jaffe's attack on synagogue reforms formed the backbone of the *pesaq din.* However, this constituted only the first (and least controversial) of its three elements. Despite his condemnation of specific reforms and choir-synagogues, Margaliot-Jaffe nowhere quite stated, as did the *pesaq din* that the status of such synagogues was that of a "house of idolatry."[65] Nor did Margaliot-Jaffe suggest (as did many Orthodox authorities in the years to follow) that if a rabbi prove unsuccessful in preventing reforms, he should leave his community.[66] Indeed, he argued that "the prophets did not abandon the remnant of Israel, instead they brought them back gradually. . . . So, too, these rabbis should await salvation from God

---

64 "Third Introduction," *Lev ha-ʿIvri,* vol. 1, no pagination. The analogy is brought in the name of the Ḥatam Sofer.

65 See the seventh point of the *Pesaq Beit-Din.* Moses Schick was of the opinion that the *pesaq din* arrived at this formulation by applying Margaliot-Jaffe's argument that these reforms were *avizrayhu deʿavodah zarah.* Schick rejected Margaliot-Jaffe's argument and added that even if it were acceptable, it would not be applicable here, since God, not idols, is worshiped in the choir-synagogues. *Liquṭei sheʾelot u-teshuvot Ḥatam Sofer,* fol. 73a, end of paragraph 3, s.v. *aval.* And although Margaliot-Jaffe urged that choir-synagogues should be avoided, and that prayer in private even on the high holidays was preferable, nowhere did he equate them with houses of idol worship. Even his harshest statements against Reform synagogues in *Meḥolat ha-Maḥanaim* (fols. 12a-b, 54b) fall considerably short of the *pesaq din.* Schlesinger anticipated these aspects of the *pesaq din* in his *Lev ha-ʿIvri,* vol. 1, fol. 66b, note.

66 As early as the summer of 1866, Moses Schick gave an ambiguous reply to this effect to Leib Klein, a scholar employed by the community of Liptó Szent Miklós. See *Responsa Maharam Schick,* OḤ § 71. Once the schism came into being, it became axiomatic that Orthodox communal employees were obligated to leave Neologue communities.

when his people will repent . . . and the heart of sons will return to their fathers, amen."[67]

More important, despite the recurring leitmotif not to imitate the ways of the gentiles, Margaliot-Jaffe applied this principle only to matters relating to worship, but not to secular studies or to acculturation (linguistic or otherwise).[68] In fact, there was no discussion whatsoever in *Meḥolat ha-Maḥanaim* of German sermons. Of the nine prohibitions in the *pesaq din,* this was the one which most clearly targeted the Orthodox as much as Reform, and it was the issue which set off the ultra-Orthodox from the rest of the Orthodox camp, even those on its right wing such as Jeremiah Löw and Margaliot-Jaffe. While some centrist figures like Moses Schick may have bemoaned the displacement of Yiddish, and even blamed German and secular studies for the decline of traditional Judaism,[69] none insisted as did the ultra-Orthodox that linguistic acculturation and secular education were forbidden according to the Halakhah.

The ultra-Orthodox were hard pressed to substantiate this claim. In his draft of the *pesaq din,* Hillel Lichtenstein listed several sources for the interdiction against German sermons—a passage in the Palestinian Talmud, an early medieval midrash, two responsa of the Ḥatam Sofer—and the unspelled promise of an "et cetera." All were later cited in the introductory and concluding sections of the *pesaq din.*[70]

The first prooftext was based on a talmudic passage in tractate Shabbat on the "eighteen measures" decreed by the Tannaim in the years just before the destruction of the Second Temple. By talmudic times there was an uncertainty what exactly these eighteen were, although it was clear that some of them were interdictions designed to separate Jews from gentiles. The ultra-Orthodox based themselves on the variant account found in the Jerusalem Talmud which (unlike its Babylonian parallel) listed among the prohibitions a decree "on their languages." In his commentary, *Qorban Eda,* the eighteenth century David Frankel

---

67 *Meḥolat ha-Maḥanaim,* fol. 80b.

68 His chapter on preserving Hebrew names only reinforces this impression. It is at best a tepid demand that Jews be called up to the Torah by their Hebrew names and a far cry from Schlesinger's insistence that Jewish names be used in everyday life. *Meḥolat ha-Maḥanaim,* fols. 78a-80b.

69 See for instance his reply to Wolf Sofer, rabbi of Zalaszentgrót, probably in the summer of 1866, in *Responsa Maharam Schick,* OḤ, § 70.

70 The draft is in Lichtenstein, *Maskil el-Dal,* vol. 4, at the beginning of the book.

noted: "'On their languages': One should not accustom himself or his children to speak in the language of idol worshippers."[71]

The second source was drawn from a midrash in *Tanna Devei Eliahu* which, as we shall see below, played a central role in ultra-Orthodox ideology. During their exile in Egypt, the ancient Israelites formed a union and contracted a covenant to observe four things: to practice amongst themselves acts of lovingkindness, to preserve circumcision, not to abandon the language of Jacob, nor to learn the language of the Egyptians because of their idolatry.[72]

The third and last source invoked the authority of the Ḥatam Sofer. In one of his last responsa, he condemned the practice of signing one's name in Latin, even on ordinary documents. "In my opinion the ancients were also well versed in the vernacular but intentionally corrupted the language [German into Yiddish] because of the decree of eighteen measures." He referred to the *Qorban Eda*'s comments in the Jerusalem Talmud, but concluded laconically "because of our sins, I will not elaborate on this."[73] In a second responsum, written a few months earlier, he threatened a straying *shoḥet* with "excommunication" and the loss of his job, if he did not desist reading "external books" *(sefarim ḥiṣonim)*. The community should elect a proper rabbi, "not, God forbid, one of those fraudulent pamphleteers who read external books and employ the vernacular [*loᶜazim belaᶜaz*]. It is forbidden to receive Torah from his lips, it is likened to planting a grove dedicated to idolatry [*asherah*] in the temple."[74]

Again, it is the Maharam Schick, the outstanding representative figure of the mainstream, who is our best guide to the novel methods employed by the ultra-Orthodox. He examined these sources and found them wanting. He reprimanded Lichtenstein for his unequivocal assertion that a halakhic prohibition was involved in preaching or listening to a German sermon. He reminded him that their master, the Ḥatam Sofer was careful to avoid such decisive language in ambiguous situations. Of course it was preferable that Jews speak their own language, indeed the midrash informed us that this was one of the reasons why the Israelites

---

71 *b. Shabb.* 13b, 14b, 17b; *t. Shabb.* 1:4 (Vienna: Schmid, 1820), fol. 6a, and see there the commentary "*Qorban Eda,*" s.v. *ve-ᶜal leshonam*.

72 *Tanna Devei Eliyahu*, 23:2, 4; 24:1.

73 Moses Sofer to Löw Schwab, 11th day of the Omer 1839. *Responsa Ḥatam Sofer*, EH 2, § 12.

74 Moses Sofer to the communal leaders and *dayyanim* of Deutschkreutz (*Ṣehlem*), fourth day of Hanukkah, 1839. *Responsa Ḥatam Sofer*, ḤM, § 197.

merited redemption from Egypt. However, it was not at all certain that a prohibition applied to speaking in foreign tongues. As for the passage in the Jerusalem Talmud which the Ḥatam Sofer also cited, it was contradicted by many statements made by the sages at a later period which did permit Greek or Persian. In any case, Schick concluded, we rule in accordance with the principle that even if something is mentioned in the Jerusalem Talmud, but does not appear in the Babylonian, we are not obligated by the former. Consequently, "it is not clear to us that a prohibition exists here." And while it was true that the Ḥatam Sofer opposed German preachers, this only applied to Reform rabbis, but certainly not those Orthodox rabbis who by force of circumstance resorted to preaching in German, but only in order to shore up the walls of tradition. In fact, he was known to recommend rabbis precisely because of their command of German, just as he gave approbations to German books written by Orthodox authors. It was an unfortunate fact that many in his generation no longer spoke Yiddish; it would be foolhardy to deny them an Orthodox pastor. Therefore, under certain conditions and with a heavy heart, he would permit German preaching by an Orthodox rabbi.[75]

Ultra-Orthodox Ideology

Strict adherence to halakhah is usually viewed as the hallmark of ultra-Orthodoxy. Yet by its very nature the halakhic process, with its meticulous attention to the letter of the law, tended to constrain the impatient zealots. In convincing the Orthodox center to take a rigid, uncompromising stand on secular education, linguistic acculturation, religious reforms, and national identity, the ultra-Orthodox faced the problem that these issues, even most of the religious reforms, fell into gray areas not easily treated within the framework of the Halakhah . The Halakhah was often too flexible or ambiguous, at times silent, or worse yet, embarrassingly lenient, which is the reason why the center, while not above harboring a certain sympathy for ultra-Orthodoxy's utopian ends, could not bring itself to legitimize the latter's often "unorthodox" means.

But if the Halakhah strictly defined did not easily lend itself to the extreme formulations of the ultra-Orthodox, there was no denying that there were traditions in Judaism which did. In the vast storehouse of aphorisms, legends, parables, myths, homilies, scriptural exegesis, moral

75 Moses Schick to Hillel Lichtenstein, 2 Av 1865, in *Liquṭei she᾿elot u-teshuvot Ḥatam Sofer*, 74f. Schlesinger explicitly rejected this watered-down version of the Ḥatam Sofer.

teachings, and the like which made up the aggadic material of the Talmud, the Midrash, and the Kabbalah, there was no lack of such strongly worded statements. These traditions, however, were marked by gross exaggeration and inconsistency. Many seemingly unequivocal pronouncements on this or that subject were contested by just as decisive assertions to the contrary without any attempt to resolve the contradictions. What weight to accord these aggadic or kabbalistic statements in halakhic deliberations was highly problematic.

In general, while mainstream figures did not entirely ignore this extra-legal corpus, they did seek to minimize its impact on the halakhic process. The ultra-Orthodox, on the other hand, adopted a diametrically opposite strategy.[76] While they clearly continued to stick to the notion that Halakhah was the primary source of authority, their tactic was to expand the reservoir of normative traditions which nourished the halakhic process by tapping into the Midrash, Aggadah, Jerusalem Talmud, and Kabbalah. Wherever the body of legal traditions proper proved inadequate, their rule was to mobilize nonlegal traditions to step into the halakhic breach.[77] The methods of casuistic, legal analysis were

---

[76] In 1876, a fascinating exchange took place over the question of the binding force of aggadot between two German rabbis, Samson Raphael Hirsch and Hille Wechsler. Wechsler held that "the authority of the aggadah is equal to that of the orally transmitted halakhah, both originating from Sinai," a position recalling that of the Hungarian ultra-Orthodox. Hirsch left no doubt that this was "a dangerous view to present to our pupils and could even lead to heresy." Hirsch's letters were published by Mordechai Breuer, "R. Samson Raphael Hirsch's Article on Aggadot" (in Hebrew), *Ha-maᶜyan* 162 (1975/1976): 1-16; trans. by Joseph Munk, "Two Letters of Samson Raphael Hirsch: A Translation," *L'Eylah* 27 (April 1989), 30-35. Wechsler's letters appear in a collection of Wechsler's writings, ed. Rivka Horowitz (forthcoming in the *Kuntresim* series of the Dinur Center, Jerusalem, 1992), appendix B. When Wechsler later stumbled upon Schlesinger's writings, he must have immediately sensed a kindred spirit. In time, the two carried on a correspondence on such messianic-related issues as the *tekhelet*, until it was cut short by Wechsler's death in 1891. See Judah Bergmann's letter to Hille Wechsler, 18 May 1878 in Abraham Bartura, *Be-Lev qashuv* (With Open Mind) (Jerusalem: Bartura, 1983), 260f.; and Akiva Yosef Schlesinger, *Brit olam ha-Aḥaron* (Jerusalem: Schlesinger, 1898), 2f.

[77] "Wherever the Talmud does not conflict with the Zohar, the halakhah is like the Zohar" (Schlesinger, "*Yad ᶜIvri*," in *Lev ha-ᶜIvri*, note 24). Actually, this was a comparatively moderate statement. The issue of the complex relations between halakhah and kabbalah has been explored extensively in the collection of articles by Jacob Katz, *Halakhah ve-Kabbalah* (Jerusalem: Magnes, 1984). One of these essays exists in English translation and is especially relevant here: "Post-Zoharic Relations Between Halakhah and Kabbalah," in *Jewish Thought in the Sixteenth Century*, ed. Bernard Dov

indiscriminately applied to this material. By and large, the ultra-Orthodox ignored the mechanism which had guided Jews over the centuries in sifting, weighing, discarding and reconciling the multiplicity of aggadic statements that were often sharply at odds with one another. If in fact there is reason to designate ultra-Orthodox Judaism "fundamentalist," it is precisely because of its tendency to ignore the "tradition" of these traditions in favor of a literal reading. Thus, any one strand of tradition could always be seized upon and cited, no matter how extreme or marginal, because it did after all appear in the written sources.

This was the case of the halakhic status of secular studies. While there existed numerous tough-sounding condemnations of "alien wisdom," "Greek wisdom," "external books," and the like, the study of which could even lead to the loss of one's portion in the world to come, there were countertraditions such as the Maimonidean one which not only permitted Jews to study "wisdom," but even obligated it as a positive precept. Over the centuries, the mainstream avoided both extremes, adopting a sort of filtering mechanism which in theory permitted secular studies under extenuating circumstances for an adult elite first socialized in the traditional curriculum. In practice, this was so broadly interpreted that in fact there was no body of knowledge barred to the adult individual. This modus vivendi was first challenged by the Jewish Enlightenment and later by the modern state's policy of compulsory education, both of which shifted the question of secular studies away from the adult to the child, from the exceptional individual to the entire collective. Although initially there was sharp opposition to what was justly seen as a severe violation of the traditional filter, in time mainstream Orthodoxy learned perforce to live with the state's demands. The basic legitimating device still remained the traditional filtering mechanism, but the social parameters of secular studies had of course greatly changed. What had been essentially a debate over elite culture in medieval Jewish society had shifted in the modern period to a question of popular secular education; a generous ad hoc dispensation had been imperceptibly institutionalized and transformed into a blanket sanction. In effect, the mainstream Orthodox had quietly made far-reaching concessions to the economic and political realities of the time.

Recognizing this, ultra-Orthodoxy sought to do away with the filtering mechanism altogether. In the past a great scholar such as

---

Cooperman, (Cambridge: Harvard University Center for Jewish Studies, 1983), 283-307.

Maimonides may have engaged in secular studies after having "filled his belly" with the Talmud, especially if such studies were necessary for his vocation. However, nowadays who could claim to have mastered the Talmud?[78] Consequently, Schlesinger argued, secular studies are prohibited even—and this was unprecedented—if they are necessary for one's livelihood.[79] It was with good reason that one critic observed, "There has never been in Jewish literature a writer who has issued such a sharp prohibition against any study of secular subjects [*ḥokhmot*] or anything which touches on *derekh ereṣ*, nor books which so denigrate and abuse great, honest, and good men, such as [Schlesinger's] *Naᶜar ᶜIvri, El ha-Adarim, Lev ha-ᶜIvri, Shomer Yisraʾel* [*Amud ha-Yira*], and the *pesaq din* [of Michalowce]."[80]

Division of Labor

The tactic of the ultra-Orthodox in delegitimizing the filtering mechanism was to espouse a strand of tradition which historically was quite marginal, and to pass it off as the only relevant and authoritative one.

---

78 Akiva Yosef Schlesinger, *El ha-Adarim* (Pressburg: Sieber's Erben, 1863), 10. "The halakhah is clear: whoever engages in the study of 'external books' is a sinner and an apostate [*mumar neged kol ha-Torah kulo*], because who is there in our time who has mastered the Talmud and the *poskim* (and even he would be permitted only to study natural sciences [*ḥokhmat ha-ṭevaᶜ*])? Those who read books of passion [*ḥesheq*, meaning novels], and almost all German books are such, not to speak of philosophy and the books of heresy, their fate is clear: R. Akiva states in the Mishnah that they have no share in the world to come" (*Naᶜar ᶜIvri*, fols. 19a-b).

79 See, for instance, *El ha-ᶜAdarim*, 10; and *Lev ha-ᶜIvri*, vol. 1, fols. 25b and 74a, note a. He even condemned reading such works in the toilet—a liminal place and time where by traditional consensus such activity was tolerated. (The paradigm was set by the sage Samuel, who engaged in astrology in the bathhouse, as related in *Deut. Rab.* 8:6.) See *Lev ha-ᶜIvri*, vol. 2, fol. 48a, where he cites approvingly Ṣevi Elimelekh of Dinov's strictures. Nevertheless, the power of the filtering mechanism was such that, later, Schlesinger was to retreat somewhat on his prohibition against secular studies when it came to vocational training. See the following footnote.

80 Zweifel, *Shalom al Yisraʾel*, 4:32. Actually the 1865 *pesaq din* does not condemn secular education. It was only in an 1875 version published by Schlesinger in Jerusalem that he cited parenthetically a tenth point which he claimed had been suppressed in Hungary for fear of contravening state law. "One is forbidden to study, or to educate one's children, in any subject other than the Torah or vocational training. Not in secular studies [*ḥokhmah*], nor in non-Jewish languages or script" (Akiva Yosef Schlesinger, *Beit Yosef Ḥadash* [Jerusalem: Y. M. Salomon-Goscinny et Michel Cohen, 1875], 7). Some later perceptions of the *pesaq din* incorporated this tenth point. See for instance Solomon Schick, *Responsa Rashban* (Munkács: Cohen and Kline, 1900), OḤ, § 140, who wrote toward the end of the century that the *pesaq din* prohibited secular studies and foreign languages.

This was what can be called the idea of DIVISION OF LABOR, and it is in fact with this notion that Schlesinger opens his *Lev ha-ʿIvri*.[81] God created different types of men, each endowed with a different purpose in the scheme of creation. The vocation of non-Jews is to master nature, to explore science, and to invent useful technologies. The vocation of the Jew, on the other hand, is to devote himself solely to the study of Torah. Each to his own, and any attempt to rebel against one's assigned vocation and infringe upon another invited dire consequences.

Here is an opportunity to see how Schlesinger manipulated his sources. He began with a reference to a well-known Talmudic passage: "R. Joḥanan said: A heathen who studies Torah deserves death, for it is written, 'Moses commanded us a law for an inheritance' [Deut 33:4]; it is our inheritance, not theirs" (Sanh. 59a). This type of extreme pronouncement abounds in the Talmud, but it is clearly of a nonlegal, aggadic nature. Later, with the rise of Christianity and Islam, it was interpreted as a warning against teaching gentiles that portion of the Torah which still remained the special preserve of the Jewish people, the Oral Law. Schlesinger may have been justified to pass over in silence the contrary opinion of R. Meir which appears only a few lines down (he held that a gentile who studies the Torah is likened to the High Priest),[82] because R. Joḥanan's opinion was the commonly accepted one. But it is safe to say that it functioned as a general policy guideline and not as a binding legal ruling.[83] More often than not it was observed in the breach, as

81 "First Introduction," in *Lev ha-ʿIvri* I.

82 "An objection is raised: R. Meir used to say, Whence do we know that even a heathen who studies the Torah is as a High Priest? From the verse '[Ye shall therefore keep my statutes, and my judgments:] which, if a man do, he shall live in them.' Priests, Levites, and Israelites are not mentioned, but men: hence thou mayest learn that even a heathen who studies the Torah is as a High Priest!—That refers to their own seven laws" (Sanh. 59a).

83 This point was made by a liberal-minded Orthodox rabbi in Germany. David Deutsch, *Israel und die Völker: Religiöser Vortrag* (Breslau: H. Sulzbach, 1858), Hebrew section, p. 5, note. Parallel to the prohibition on heathens' studying Torah, another passage also prohibited Jews from teaching Torah to the heathen. R. Ami stated: "the teachings of the Torah are not to be transmitted to an idolater" (Ḥag. 13a). A harsh view is also taken by other authorities: The Zohar ("*Aḥarei Mot*," fol. 73a) states that even one letter of the Written Torah may not be taught to a non-Jew, because the Torah is a name of God and the uncircumcised may not enter into its covenant; Salomon Luria, *Yam shel Shelomo: Baba Qama* (Bnei Brak, 1960), ch. 4, para. 9, fols. 27b-28a, emphasizes the original reluctance to write down the Torah and the oral character of its transmission, all measures taken to preclude non-Jewish acquaintance with the Torah; the influential Isaiah Horowitz, *Shnei luḥot ha-brit* (Shanghai, 1947),

demonstrated by the numerous Christian Kabbalists and Hebraists of the Renaissance, many of whom received instruction at the hands of practicing Jews.[84]

Now Schlesinger cannot be entirely faulted for ignoring this "tradition" of slackness and taking the prohibition literally, at its face value. (After all it was one more argument to enlist against German sermons and Mendelssohn's German translation of the Bible—they made the Torah available to the gentiles.)[85] But in the second stage of his argument, he abandons this literal, fundamentalist approach, opting instead for what he clearly understood to be the true SPIRIT of the tradition. Just as a gentile who studies Torah deserves to die, he argued, "so too did the Torah decree conversely" that an Israelite must study only Torah and not the wisdom of the nations. "And if he transgresses," he added, "he deserves death." This clearly followed by analogy, but the fact that nowhere did the sages explicitly state what must have seemed to Schlesinger an obvious, logical inference must have been frustrating indeed. Therefore, Schlesinger could not just leave it at that and felt compelled to resort to one of his typical blanket arguments. In the process, he did not hesitate to compound one aggadic hyperbole with another. The reason for such harsh punishment is that the Talmud taught that "anyone who transgresses against the words of the sages deserves death" (Eruv. 21b, Ber. 4b, etc.) This was the type of exaggerated statement which if taken literally would have had mind-boggling ramifications. It was a variant on the familiar theme of collapsing distinctions between the different layers of tradition; in effect, it would have obviated the need for the fine-tuned gradations of crime and punishment in Halakhah. However, once one embarked on the course of investing aggadic statements with normative power, this followed quite logically.

Schlesinger hastened to add that this did not at all imply a value judgment as to whether Jew or gentile was superior. In a clever analogy

---

on Tractate Shevuot, p. 268, cites Luria and adds the strictures of the Zohar. See also Isaac Lampronti, *Paḥad Yiṣḥak*, ed, B.M. Cohen (Jerusalem, 1977), 4:442f.; Ḥaim Ḥezkiah Medini, *Sedeh Ḥemed (*Brooklyn: Kehot, 1959),8:3119f.

[84] David Kaufmann, "Elia Menaḥem Ḥalfan on Jews Teaching Hebrew to non-Jews," *Jewish Quarterly Review* 9 (1897): 500-508, for a 1545 Italian responsa. On the question of transmitting kabbalah to non-Jews in the Renaissance, see Moshe Idel, "Particularism and Universalism in Kabbalah: 1480-1650" (Paper presented at the Conference on Transformations in Jewish Society in the Sixteenth and Seventeenth Centuries, January, 1986, Van Leer Institute, Jerusalem).

[85] *Naʿar ʿIvri*, 15a–b; *Lev ha-ʿIvri*, vol.1, fols. 25a and 53a.

which he borrowed from Margaliot-Jaffe,[86] he noted that God also set apart the priests from the Israelites, and the High Priest from all the rest. Each of the three classes of Jews was assigned specific rights and obligations, and what was permissible for one was punishable by death for the other. It was clear that if the priestly tithes were prohibited to the Israelites, it was obviously not because there was anything intrinsically revolting about the food. So too it followed by analogy that the customs, the wisdom, and the mode of worship of non-Jews were not forbidden to Jews because there was anything abhorrent about them per se.[87] A benign perception of the gentile world pervaded the writings of the Hungarian ultra-Orthodox. In contrast to the often disparaging attitude of eighteenth century Jews, Schlesinger could not sing praise enough of the spectacular scientific and technological breakthroughs of modern European culture. (Later he will see in the technological explosion of his time a sign of Messianic stirrings).

Not all spheres of life are threatened by the new. True, in religion, tradition ruled and no innovation at all was to be tolerated. "Any change in the custom of our ancestors, even if it is not intended in imitation of the gentiles or even if it is not halakhically interdicted, is nevertheless totally forbidden because it deviates from the tradition of our forefathers."[88] But this did not imply that the pious Jew must be a fanatic opponent of all that is modern. "Someone once asked: why, if we have to be cautious concerning the customs of our forefathers, should we utilize new, useful things which gentile scientists have invented in our times? They answered him: In matters of human affairs, certainly the new is preferred over the old, for all that is new adds benefit; a rule which does not apply in the conduct of religion, whose source is God."[89] The division of labor created a useful mechanism which enabled the Jew to benefit from modern civilization as a consumer, but the ambition to be a cultural producer had to be unambiguously renounced. Not the body of

---

86 *Meḥolat ha-Maḥanaim*, fols. 6b-7a, 14a; *Har Tabor*, fols. 20a-b. He uses another favorite simile in tandem: soldiers from various corps must each wear a different uniform and are forbidden to exchange one for another. Although they all serve the same king, not only does the variety not detract, but rather it enhances his glory. But again, Margaliot-Jaffe employs these analogies only in the sphere of synagogue worship and strictly religious customs, whereas Schlesinger expands the notion to secular studies and acculturation.

87 "First Introduction," *Lev ha-ʿIvri*, vol. 1. See also *Lev ha-ʿIvri*, vol.1, fol. 38b.

88 Ibid., fol. 89b.

89 Ibid., vol. 2, fol. 68a, note a.

knowledge, but the "national" function of knowledge determined what is objectionable and what is permissible.

To be sure, the notion of a division of labor was not an ultra-Orthodox invention. It had its roots in millennia-old midrashim and often cropped up in the anti-Maimonidean polemics of the late Middle Ages. Nevertheless, it was a relatively marginal tradition, more than counterbalanced by contrary ones which expressed a reluctance to abandon "wisdom" to the non-Jews. Ultra-Orthodoxy lent it a centrality and invested it with an intensity it had lacked before. It also diverted the thrust of the cultural confrontation away from Jew versus non-Jew, focusing instead on the internecine conflict between the authentic Jew versus the non-Jewish Jew and on the disastrous consequences which ensued when Jews rebelled against their true vocation.

Sadducees

The principal culprit charged with the breakdown of tradition and the cause of all subsequent evils was the German Haskalah whose ideology of cultural synthesis obscured the once well-defined boundaries between Jewish and gentile cultures. To be sure, the Reform movement was not spared harsh condemnation, but its corrosive effect was seen as largely derivative and epiphenomenal. The original sin had been committed by Moses Mendelssohn, the father of the Jewish Enlightenment. More than anyone, this arch-heretic had beguiled the house of Israel into violating the cultural division of labor and casting aside age-old traditions. Admittedly, Mendelssohn did not explicitly undermine what one would commonly classify as "religious" traditions. What he did damage, perhaps irreparably in Germany, was a layer of tradition more fundamental and comprehensive, what the ultra-Orthodox in their newly evolving vocabulary termed *Jahadus* or "Jewishness." It was primarily his keenly felt shame of this "Jewishness" which induced Mendelssohn to urge acculturation. His translation of the Bible epitomized the notion that to be accepted by the non-Jewish world, gentile wisdom and culture had to be embraced, while the conspicuous—and thus embarrassing—elements of "Jewishness" such as Yiddish, the particular Jewish attire, traditional Jewish names, and numerous irrational customs all had to be discarded.

It was, of course, to be expected that the ultra-Orthodox would condemn Mendelssohn for having fathered the Reform movement. But much worse from their point of view was the fact that throughout his life Mendelssohn had remained—ostensibly—an observant Jew. It was in this role that Mendelssohn posed the greatest threat to tradition. Far preferable were his offspring and disciples who had made a clean break with traditional Judaism by embracing religious reforms or outright conversion. They were enemies who were readily identifiable. The real threat was posed by men like Mendelssohn who did not altogether abandon tradition but rather attempted to graft one tradition unnaturally unto the other, insisting all the while that the integrity of neither would be impaired. It was the observant *maskil* who established the paradigm for the true adversary—neo-Orthodoxy. [90]

The insidious influence of this enemy within—"of you and within you," as Schlesinger called them—was far more dangerous than the open challenge of the Reformers.[91] The ultra-Orthodox were fond of citing the Talmud: "Do not be afraid of the Pharisees, nor of those who are not Pharisees, but only of the hypocrites [*ṣēvuin*] who are similar to the Pharisees; their acts are like that of Zimri, but they ask the reward of Phinehas" (Soṭah 22). By preaching in foreign languages and studying alien wisdom, the neo-Orthodox, like Zimri, brought "the alien woman into the camp of Israel in order to pervert the house of Jacob, all in the name of zealotry."[92] These hypocritical, "righteous" rabbis, smug in their conviction that cultural synthesis was not only traditionally sanctioned, but also the only proper course to save Orthodoxy, were dubbed by Schlesinger SADDUCEES. This was a felicitous choice, pregnant with both the implication that the neo-Orthodox were on the surface "similar to the Pharisees," but actually a sect apart, and the play on the Yiddish

---

[90] Nineteenth-century German Orthodoxy agreed with Schlesinger on this and acclaimed Mendelssohn, if not as the father of neo-Orthodoxy, then at least as a kindred spirit. See Hirsch, "Die Religion im Bunde mit dem Fortschritt: Von einem Schwarzen" (1854), in his *Gesammelte Schriften*, 3:503f., 507f., as well as 2:366. The centennial of Mendelssohn's death produced an outpouring of panegyrics in the neo-Orthodox press, all denying him to Reform and claiming him as one of their own. See the chorus of celebration in [Isaac Hirsch], "Moses Mendelssohn," *Jeschurun* 18 (1885): 833–39; Esriel Hildesheimer, "Moses Mendelssohn," *Jüdische Presse* 17 (1886): 1-3, 13-15; and Marcus Lehmann, "Moses Mendelssohn," *Israelit* 27 (1886): 1-4. Embarrassed by this outpouring of indiscriminate praise, a German neo-Orthodox rabbi presented a more sober and balanced assessment half a century later: Joseph Wohlgemuth, "Moses Mendelssohn und das thoratreue Judentum," *Jeschurun*, n.s. 16 (1929): 321–40. A recent chronicler of German Orthodoxy, after weighing the pros and cons, cautiously comes down in Mendelssohn's favor and rules that "he may be looked upon as one of the forerunners of organized orthodox Jewry in Germany" (Hermann Schwab, *The History of Orthodox Jewry in Germany* [London, n.d.], 14-20).

[91] *Naʿar ʿIvri*, fol. 20a; *Lev ha-ʿIvri*, vol. 1, fol. 51b, note; vol. 2, fol. 68a, note.

[92] Ibid., vol. 1, 4b and 5b, note 4.

pronunciation of *Ṣeduqim* in eastern Hungary—*Ṣʾdikim*—which came close enough to sound like *Ṣaddiqim* ('the righteous'). ("We call their *Ṣadik* a *Ṣeduk*.")[93] Of what use was it if Hildesheimer and his ilk led pious lives, were well learned, and even well intentioned? There were ample precedents in history of such men who like Sabbatai Ṣevi brought only disaster on Israel; after all, even Satan carried on his work "for the sake of Heaven."[94]

These are the Sadducees	They cling to the sake of heaven
Embrace an alien bosom	Advocate alien tongues
Say, "Revive Religion!	Make righteous of sinners!
Join Torah and the Secular!"	And cut short the souls of babes and infants.[95]

These Sadducees pretended to persecute the *apikorsim*—the Reformers, in Schlesinger's vocabulary—but only in order to obscure that they were the "very root of the defilement [*avot ha-ṭumʾah*], murderers of souls." They falsely interpreted *Torah im derekh ereṣ* to mean the synthesis of gentile culture with Jewish religion and considered all but the narrowly defined religious aspect of Judaism dispensable. Neo-Orthodoxy, Schlesinger claimed, had in effect reduced Judaism to a mere confession and thus saw nothing wrong in acculturation. To be a good Orthodox Jew consisted of strictly observing the commandments, but according to the neo-Orthodox, it had nothing to do with speaking the Yiddish language or the preservation of a broadly conceived cultural specifity.

Shalem

Yet precisely these seemingly nonconfessional elements were invested by the ultra-Orthodox with supreme RELIGIOUS valence. "These are the things which our saintly forefathers transmitted to us as the very root of Jewishness [*shorshei ha-yehudut*]," wrote Schlesinger, "name, language,

---

93 Ibid., fol. 38b, note. It is not unlikely that Schlesinger was inspired by that eighteenth century heresy-hunter with whom he had so much in common, Jacob Emden, who consistently referred to the followers of Sabbatai Ṣevi as *Ṣevuin*, pronounced as *Ṣeviyin* in eastern Yiddish dialect.

94 *Lev ha-ʿIvri*, vol. 1, fols. 52a and 55b; vol. 2, fol. 69a, note; fols. 111a-b, invoking *Baba Batra* 16. Hildesheimer is often compared to the seemingly pious Jeroboam ben Navot (*Lev ha-ʿIvri*, vol. 1, fol. 52a). Elsewhere he is referred to as an (unwitting?) agent of Satan: "From his headquarters [in Germany], Satan sent his foolishness to Hungary by his means of his righteous men who perform works of charity only in order to destroy our region as well" (*Lev ha-ʿIvri*, vol. 1, fol. 3b).

95 Ibid., vol. 2, fol. 80b.

and dress." Following the Ḥatam Sofer, these three, *shem, lashon,* and *malbush* in Hebrew, were called by their acronym *shalem,* meaning complete, whole, intact, unimpaired, safe. The acronym alluded to the experience of Jacob who had successfully withstood the cultural temptations at Laban, his father-in-law, and "Jacob arrived intact [*shalem*] in the city of Shekhem" (Gen. 33: 18).

To be sure, the ultra-Orthodox advanced the claim that the preservation of these three items were actual commandments. But here they ran into some complications. In his discussion of the thirtieth negative commandment, not to imitate the ways of the gentiles, Maimonides does indeed mention that "the purpose of all this is that we should avoid the heathen and despise all his customs and his dress." But he is significantly reticent on the issue of language or of names.[96] The *Shulḥan Arukh* in its discussion of the laws of idol worshippers follows Maimonides and warns that Jews must "not wear the dress of idol worshippers." (Typically a filtering mechanism is retained: an exception is made in the case of those who are "near the king.") Again, there is no mention of language or name.[97] Schlesinger blithely ignores this silence and instead invokes the authority of *Sefer Miṣvot ha-Gadol,* which does indeed come close to his formulation: "Israel should be set off from the gentiles [*goyim*] in dress, custom and speech [*dibbur*]." But all this seems to be besides the point, because *shalem* are not ordinary commandments; they are nothing less than the very fundamentals of the Torah [*gufei Torah*].[98] These three things, Schlesinger stated, "were instituted by our ancestors in Egypt, and because of their merit [the Jews] were worthy of being redeemed. On balance, they outweigh all the commandments of the Torah, as it is stated in *Tanna Devei Eliyahu.*"[99]

---

96 Maimonides, *The Commandments,* trans. Charles B. Chavel, 2 vols.(London and New York: Soncino, 1967), vol. 2, *The Negative Commandments,* § 30, pp. 28f.

97 *Shulḥan Arukh,* YD, *hilkhot ḥuqqot ha-ʿovdei kokhavim,* § 178: "not to wear the dress of idol worshippers," subsection 1: Jews should have a special dress; subsection 2: those near the king are permitted to dress like them. (It goes without saying that the issue of whether contemporary Christians can be identified as idol worshippers is obscured by the ultra-Orthodox.)

98 *Lev ha-ʿIvri,* vol. 1, fol. 70b, note, and Moses ben Jacob of Coucy, *Sefer Miṣvot ha-Gadol* (Jerusalem, 1988), Negative Commandments, § 50. It would be quibbling to insist that speech is not necessarily the same as language. Abraham Danzig, *Ḥochmat Adam* 89:1, mentions dress and even names, but remains silent on language. See also his *Beit Avraham* (Vilna, 1821), para. 31.

99 *Lev ha-ʿIvri,* vol. 1, fol. 39b, note.

This collection of midrashim composed relatively late in the gaonic period was a favorite of several Hasidic masters, as well as the Ḥatam Sofer; for Hungarian ultra-Orthodoxy, *Tanna Devei Eliyahu*, especially the following passages dealing with the redemption from Egypt, gained an unprecedented importance.[100]

> King David used to praise those who went out of Egypt. Even the one commandment which they possessed brought much more pleasure to God than several of our commandments. And what was this one commandment they possessed? That they all gathered themselves into one association and drew up a covenant that they will do acts of lovingkindness one with another; that they will preserve circumcision, which is the covenant of Abraham, Isaac, and Jacob; that they will not abandon the language of our patriarch Jacob; and that they will not learn the language of Egypt because of the ways of idol worshippers.[101]

It is interesting that Schlesinger came to favor this variant of an older and better-known midrash. After all, here only the preservation of the language is mentioned, whereas in the older versions both language and names are cited among the four, or at times three, things on account of which Israel was redeemed from Egypt. (Nowhere in the midrash are all three—name, language, and dress—mentioned together.)[102] What was

[100] It should be kept in mind that the zealots considered Elijah the prophet the author of this work (*Lev ha-ʿIvri*, vol. 1, fol. 52a). Schlesinger suggested that at least one page of *Tanna Devei Eliyahu* be studied daily and preferably in public. Schlesinger, *Ḥevrah Maḥzirei Atarah le-Yoshuah im Kolel ha-Ivrim* (Jerusalem, 1955), fol. 33b.

[101] *Tanna Devei Eliyahu* (Jerusalem: Schlesinger, 1906), vol. 1, 23:4, fol. 91b. This edition was published by Schlesinger with his commentary *"Tosefot ben Yeḥiel."*

[102] "R. Huna in the name of Bar Kappara: Israel were redeemed from Egypt on account of four things, viz. because they did not change their names, they did not change their language, they did not go tale-bearing, and none of them was found to have been immoral." *Midrash Rabbah Leviticus*, trans. J. Israelstam and Judah Slotki (London, 1939), *Emor* 33:5, pp. 413f.; *Pesikta de-Rav Kahana*, ed. Salomon Buber (Lyck, 1868), *Vayehi be-shalaḥ*, fol. 83b, esp. n. 66; *Pesikta de-Rav Kahana*, ed. Dov Mandelbaum (New York: Jewish Theological Seminary, 1987), 1:182, esp. n. 8). All these sources are fifth-century midrashim. The *Mekhilta* lists the same four items but attributes the saying to R. Judon in the name of R. Samuel bar Naḥman. See *Mekhilta*, ed. Ḥaim Saul Horowitz (Jerusalem, 1960), 14, *Bo*, § 5; and the *Midrash ha-Gadol Exodus*, ed. Mordekhai Margulies (Jerusalem: Mosad ha-Rav Kook, 1956), *Va-era*, § 14, pp. 101f. *Pirke de Rabbi Eliezer*, trans. and ed. Gerald Friedlander (New York: Hermon, 1965), 387, mentions only three things: "By the merit of three things Israel went forth from Egypt: 1) they did not change their language, 2) they did not change their names, 3) they did not slander one another."

attractive about this particular midrash was its unique depiction of the social or national contract entered into by the ancient Israelites. This pact was designed to set them apart from the other nations; they willed themselves so to speak, into becoming a separate people. The neo-Orthodox erroneously claimed that first came the Torah, and only when it was accepted by the Israelites at Sinai did they become a nation. Just the converse was true. Their becoming a people PRECEDED Sinai, the Torah, and its commandments.[103] In fact, these national characteristics were a necessary precondition and the continuing basis for Jewish religion. "If God forbid you remove these from Israel, then all the commandments are only an empty garment without a body," warned Schlesinger. "For these things are the very body of the Israelite which make him a Jew [*vehu Yehudi*]. Because of them we became a people, as Scriptures state: 'I am a Hebrew, I worship the Lord, the God of Heaven' (Jonah 1:9)." The order of events is intimated in the verse: first came Hebrew nationhood and then followed the worship of the Lord, Judaism.

Here and later, Schlesinger will analytically distinguish between what he called *dat* and *leʾumi*, a religious and an ethnic–national component of Judaism.[104] Significantly, in arguing for the centrality of the latter, he did not rely solely on the authority of tradition. Anticipating a skeptical response, he appealed to common sense. "And even if you should not believe the teachings of our masters, who is so blind as not to see and understand that if you take this away, God forbid, you take away everything? If there are no roots, a wind will come, uproot [religion], and turn it against itself, God forbid. This is what we see before our very own eyes. In whatever country the roots were uprooted, they forgot the Torah

103 "In *Tanna Devei Eliyahu* ch. 14, it is written: It is the way of men to say that the Torah came first . . . but I say Israel came first" (Schlesinger, *Ḥevrah* [Jerusalem, 1955], fol. 33b). Samson Raphael Hirsch had written that the Jews became a nation only as a result of their acceptance of the Torah at Sinai (Samson Raphael Hirsch, *The Nineteen Letters*, trans. Bernard Drachman [New York: Bloch, 1942], Eighth Letter, p. 75).

104 The midrash continued, citing King David: "And who is like Your people Israel, a unique nation on earth, whom God went and redeemed as His people, winning renown for Himself and doing great and marvelous deeds for them [and] for Your land—[driving out] nations and their gods before Your people whom You redeemed for Yourself from Egypt" (2 Sam 7:23). Schlesinger commented on 'nations and their gods': "This wording teaches two things: on the one hand to be a people and nation from '*nations*' [*lihyot le-ʾam goy ve-leʾumi*] . . . and on the other, the unity of his religion from '*their gods*'" (Akiva Yosef Schlesinger, "Tosfot ben Yeḥiel," commentary on *Tanna Devei Eliyahu* [Jerusalem: Schlesinger, 1906], ch. 23:4, fol. 91b, s.v. *goyim ve-elohav*). Throughout his writing career Schlesinger distinguished between what he called *dat ve-lʾeumi*, religion and nation.

and in the end they left Judaism altogether, becoming heretics and Sadducees."[105] The national–ethnic component, *shalem*, is an indispensable guarantee for the survival of religion; Hildesheimer and his camp doomed Orthodoxy from the very start by reducing Judaism to a religious confession. Addressing himself to the Sadducees, Schlesinger asked, "What benefit is there in all the commandments if the body of Israel is missing?"[106]

It is a great paradox that, of all the different groups in Hungary, it was the ultra-Orthodox who came closest to the modern idea of Jewish nationalism and at a time when in all Europe one could count the number of Jewish nationalists on one hand. Elsewhere I expand on this theme, suffice it to say that in my opinion Schlesinger, but perhaps some of his colleagues as well, arrived at a full-blown Jewish nationalism as early as 1863. In fact, this obsession with instantly recognizable national features such as language and costume (as well as the prominent display of sidelocks and *ṣiṣit*, and a full, unshaven beard), is but one more defining characteristic which set off the ultra-Orthodox from the mainstream. Moses Schick had objected in his reply to Lichtenstein to the notion that if a Jew changed his language, he could no longer be called a Jew. "Someone who speaks French or German should NOT be labeled a Frenchman or a German; the noun is defined by the essence, and quintessentially he remains 'a Jewish man, the son of Yair, son of Shimi.' A man like this cannot be called a *lo^cazi*."[107] But this is exactly what the ultra-Orthodox claimed: once *shalem* was removed, one ceased to be not only an Orthodox Jew, but a Jew altogether.[108]

---

105 *Lev ha-ʿIvri*, vol. 1, fol. 39b, note.

106 Ibid., vol. 2, fol. 111a.

107 Moses Schick to Hillel Lichtenstein, 2 Av 1865, *Liquṭei she'elot u-teshuvot Ḥatam Sofer*, p. 74, para. 11, bottom of the second column.

108 The villain of a satire on the Orthodox is none other than a fanatic dubbed Reb Schalem, who declaims:

> "Die Zahl der Frommen vermindert sich immer,
> die Zeiten werden leider stets schlimmer;
> Das machen die Prediger neuer Art,
> die ohne Kutten geh'n und ohne Bart
> Und deutsch herpredigen allerlei Sachen,
> die viele Juden zu Freigeistern machen . . .
> Ha, wie ich mich gräme, wie ich mich kränke,
> wenn ich gar an die Seminäre denke!
> Das sind die echten Schulen den Atheisten,
> das sind die Schulen der Heuchler und Sophisten!

Schism

Ever since the rise of Reform Judaism in the second decade of the nineteenth century, Orthodoxy was plagued by the question of the status of the reformers. The problem had little to do with the actual observance of the halakhic norms. In the past, traditional society had dealt with such sinners with considerable forbearance. As long as it was understood that the spirit was willing, but the flesh was weak, that these men perceived themselves as lapsed sinners, then the authorities were content to prescribe the appropriate punishment and penance, invoking the traditional formula, "An Israelite, even if he has sinned, remains an Israelite." Perhaps because the primordial is such a powerful component in Judaism and, compared to other monotheistic religions, ideology plays a relatively weak role in determining Jewish identity, or perhaps because of a heightened sense of solidarity derived from a long history as a persecuted minority, medieval Jewish society avoided the pattern of Church–sect schisms so prevalent in Christianity. The one exception, of course, was Karaism. The Karaites who repudiated the Oral Law became the archetype of the heretic who was "ruled out of the community of Israel." Yet even in this instance, a significant concession was made by Maimonides in a passage which was to become the classic statement on the subject. Whereas the first Karaites were indeed branded as defiant heretics and condemned accordingly ("he is cast into a pit and is not rescued from it, . . . whoever puts any of them to death fulfills a great precept"), their descendants were considered without rebellious intent, innocents misled in the sinful ways of their fathers. Technically they were "like a child taken captive" by gentiles and raised in another religion who could not be held responsible for his unwitting trespasses.

Die Losung der Orthodoxen sei:
verflucht, verflucht die Fortschritts-Partei!
Verflucht Cultur und Civilisation,
sie sind die Feinde der heiligen Religion!"

(Emil Ludwig Markbreiter, *Die Orthodoxen: Orig. komisches Genrebild* [Pest: Aigner und Rautmann, 1868], 10f).

(The count of the pious keeps getting smaller, The times keep getting tougher; / It's because of the new type of preachers, Who go without cowl and beard, / And preach about everything in German, Who turn many Jews into freethinkers. . . / Oh, how I grieve, how I sicken, When I even think about the seminaries! / They are really the schools of atheists, The schools of the hypocrites and sophists! / The watchword of the Orthodox must be: Cursed, cursed be the Progress Party! / Cursed culture and civilization, They are the enemies of holy religion!)

"Therefore," concluded Maimonides, "efforts should be made to bring them back in repentance."[109]

When the first synagogue reforms were instituted in Hamburg and Berlin, the instinctive reflex of men like the Ḥatam Sofer was to classify the innovators as Karaites, especially since the new reformed prayerbook with its excisions and alterations explicitly challenged such basic dogmas as the Return to Zion.[110] The reform rabbinical conferences in Germany in the mid-1840s evoked the same reaction from R. Moses Schick, who urged the Ketav Sofer to have the reformers "ruled out of the community of Israel" like the Karaites.[111] Significantly, nothing of the sort took place. There may have been some bold talk along these lines, but, surprisingly, much less than one would have anticipated.[112] In fact, by the 1860s a consensus had emerged among German neo-Orthodox authorities: while they continued to condemn Reform as heresy and the few dozen reform rabbis as rebellious heretics, care was taken to distinguish between the rabbis and the mass of lay reformers who were assumed to be nothing more than misguided innocents, "like infants taken captive by gentiles."[113]

---

[109] *The Code of Maimonides: The Book of Judges*, trans. Abraham M. Hershman (New Haven, 1949), "The Laws of Rebels, III:1-3," pp. 143f.

[110] Commenting on the Hamburg reforms, the Ḥatam Sofer had declared in 1819: "If their judgment were in our hands, it would be my opinion to separate them from our domain, not to give our daughters to their sons [or to take their daughters for our sons], so that we should not come to be drawn after them, so that their congregation should be like the congregation of Ṣadok and Beothus, Anan and Saul [the founding fathers of Karaism], they for themselves and we for ourselves. All this appears to me as theory, but not in practice in the absence of permission and authorization of the government—without this [permission], my words should be void and accounted as nonexisting" (*Responsa Ḥatam Sofer*, pt. 6, § 89).

[111] See the undated responsum (probably spring 1845) to Abraham Samuel Benjamin Sofer in his *Responsa Maharam Schick*, OH, §305. Schick passes an uncharacteristically harsh judgment on the reformers: "They are not Jews, but like complete gentiles and even worse, . . . and since they are like complete gentiles, they, their daughters, and their sons are prohibited to us in marriage."

[112] Among those calling to place the reformers beyond the pale of Judaism was the rabbi of Posen, Solomon Eger, who had written a pamphlet to this effect. See his letter to his brother Abraham, undated but on internal evidence written in August or September 1847, in *Igrot Sofrim*, ed. Solomon Sofer (Tel Aviv: Sinai, 1970), pt. I, § 60, p. 84.

[113] One of the earliest to argue thus was Ṣevi Hirsh Ḥayes, "Against the Reformers" (in Hebrew), *Sinai* 6 (1940): 277–85, and "Minḥat Kanaot," in his *Kol Kitvei Maharṣ Ḥayes*, 2 vols. (Jerusalem: Divrei Ḥachamin, 1958), 2:1009–14. Although he does cite the relevant passage in Maimonides, he omits the phrase "like an infant taken captive

Even so, associating with reformers and Sabbath desecrators still posed a problem. Samson Raphael Hirsch's solution had been to draw a distinction between the social and religious sphere. True, technically reformers were not heretics, and therefore he was willing to countenance friendly SOCIAL intercourse with them, however, where RELIGIOUS matters were concerned, he absolutely drew the line: Reform was unquestionably a heresy.[114] Hirsch's solution in Frankfurt, where the Orthodox had been reduced to a small minority by the middle of the century, was to obtain for the Orthodox religious institutions as much independence from the mother community as possible. The degree of independence in the pre-emancipatory period, however, was constrained by the state's insistence that only one Jewish community function in any one locality. This changed only in 1871 in Hungary and in 1877 in Germany when dissenting members were finally allowed to secede and establish their own autonomous community. Until that time, however, a variety of compromises obtained in those communities where there was a willingness to take the Orthodox minority's needs into consideration. The accepted modus vivendi was to allow the Orthodox to establish a separate private society and maintain their own rabbi, school, and synagogue, while continuing to pay taxes to the mother community and sharing the social and welfare institutions.[115] Chafing at this limited autonomy, Hirsch began in the late 1850s and early 1860s to elaborate the notion that a moral imperative obligated the total disengagement of the Orthodox from reform-dominated communities. The demand that the Orthodox pay taxes to the mother community, and thus provide financial support for religious institutions considered by them heretical, amounted to religious coercion. In order not to violate freedom of conscience, the compulsory membership in the community should be eliminated, and all religious associations should become voluntary. The

---

by the gentiles." The landmark decision which does use the phrase and was the most cited in subsequent literature was Jacob Ettlinger, *Responsa Binyan Ṣiyon*, pt. 2 (Vilna, 1878), § 23, dated fall 1860, on the status of Sabbath violators. For a different approach see David Ellenson, "The Orthodox Rabbinate and Apostasy," in his *Tradition in Transition*, 161–84.

114 Samson Raphael Hirsch, "Offener Brief an Sr. Ehrwürden Herrn Distrikts-Rabbiner S. B. Bamberger in Würzburg" (1877), in his *Gesammelte Schriften*, 4:324f.

115 These "structures of accord" are admirably explained by Liberles, *Religious Conflict in Social Context*, 172–74. On Hungary see Katz, "The Tragic Schism" (in Hungarian). I am indebted to Professor Jacob Katz for our numerous conversations on this issue. Prof. Katz is preparing a study of Orthodox secession in Germany and Hungary.

Orthodox should be permitted to set up their own exclusive autonomous communities, whose scope would now include all those services and institutions previously held under the auspices of the mother community. The separation was to be total, not even the cemetery was to be shared. Toward the end of the 1870s Hirsch did succeed in attaining his goal, although many German Orthodox shied away from such total disengagement.

That Hungarian ultra-Orthodoxy arrived at similar ideas was all the more remarkable, since the social conditions of Orthodoxy in Hungary were quite different from its embattled situation in Germany. In the early 1860s, mainstream Hungarian Orthodoxy might have had misgivings about the growing strength of the Neologues, but aside from a few urban communities where the Orthodox were a minority, there was a comforting sense that they were in a position of strength. In confrontations with Reform, coercion rather than freedom of conscience was the rhetoric of the day.

Neither the neo-Orthodox nor the ultra-Orthodox shared this confidence; both keenly sensed that disaster was imminent. Both looked to Germany, or even closer to home, to Bohemia and Moravia, and realized that if the necessary defensive measures were not taken, it would be only a matter of time before traditional Judaism would be swept away in Hungary as well. If the Hungarian neo-Orthodox closely followed events in Germany, the German neo-Orthodox displayed no less interest in Hungarian developments. In fact, a major test of Hirsch's idea of a full-fledged communal schism took place in a Hungarian community several years before the Congress. In the early 1860s, the Orthodox of Székesfehérvár (Stuhlweissenburg), led by a learned layman, Gottlieb Fischer, campaigned for an entirely separate Orthodox community. Although they failed to receive government approval, they did obtain considerable institutional independence. Hirsch, whose son-in-law Dr. Joseph Guggenheim had served as rabbi of the community between 1859 and 1861, wielded considerable influence on the Orthodox party.[116]

The Székesfehérvár incident also had an impact on the ultra-Orthodox. The testament of the Ḥatam Sofer had urged that all contact with the innovators totally cease, and this now became the central theme

[116] Hirsch had been approached by the community for advice as early as 1850. See Jakab Sternherz, "The History of the Jews of Székesfehérvár from their Resettlement until the Present (1840-1892)" (in Hungarian), *MZsSz* 10 (1893), 548–58, 622–27; 11 (1894), 102-106, 177–90, 539–48, 623–37.

of *Lev ha-ᶜIvri.* "Know, my brothers, that the entire purpose of writing these books is to separate the faithful brethren from the evil destroyers, the innovators, the *maskilim,* these *loᶜazim.* It is not my intention in these books to triumph over them and certainly not to conquer them, nor did it enter my mind to reform them."[117] Avoid dialogue, do not try to win them over, for all contact is futile or dangerous. Disengage, live and let live, and strife will cease as each party goes its own way.[118] But whereas the mainstream understood the schism to mean the expulsion of a deviant minority by an Orthodox majority, the ultra-Orthodox already anticipated in the early 1860s that sooner or later the issue was not going to be the segregation of the deviants, but rather the self-segregation of the devout. Cut yourselves off, was Schlesinger's message, even at the price of being relegated to a minority. Resign yourselves to this; after all, what was Jewish history if not the triumph of small numbers against superior odds?[119] A telling choice was the motto Schlesinger picked for his *Lev ha-ᶜIvri*: the verse in Judges where the Lord commands Gideon to dismiss his bloated force of tens of thousands, and instructs him to select an elite unit of three hundred to win victory over the Midianites.

Schlesinger embraced the idea that the Orthodox were a beleaguered minority, he savored being the injured party. "We are the persecuted," he insisted, "not the persecutors!"[120] If the Orthodox in any community are in the minority, "they should immediately seperate themselves entirely for 'It is not because you are the most numerous of peoples [that the Lord set his heart on you and chose you—] indeed, you are the smallest of peoples' [Deut. 7:7]." They should set up a separate synagogue and educational institutions and hire their own ritual slaughterer. "Make an effort to appoint over you a rabbi or a special truly God-fearing lay scholar who follows in the footsteps of our forefathers."[121] If the model Schlesinger proposed in 1864 recalled Hirsch's Israelitische Religionsgesellschaft in Frankfurt, his specific mention of a lay scholar was a transparent reference to Székesfehérvár, where just recently

---

117 *Lev ha-ᶜIvri*, vol. 2, fol. 114a.

118 Ibid., vol. 1, fol. 109a ,and vol. 2, fol. 92b.

119 Ibid., vol. 1, fol. 40a.

120 Ibid., fol. 109a.

121 Ibid., fols. 4b-5a. Further on, Schlesinger appeals to the *ḥevrah qadishah* not to care for the dying reformers or their dead. "Let them expire among the gentiles whom they chose and desired to be with . . . . Eat, drink, and rejoice on the day of their demise, that they are lost to the congregation of Israel" (ibid., fol. 66b). As far as I can tell, this is about as close as Schlesinger comes at this point to demanding separate cemeteries.

Gottlieb Fischer had been appointed as the religious leader of the Orthodox faction. In either case, he adopted what was clearly Hirsch's solution at the time (Hirsch's, but not necessarily Hildesheimer's). And when a few years later under Hirsch's influence Hungarian neo-Orthodoxy moved beyond this to demand autonomous communities, Schlesinger kept pace. On the eve of the Hungarian Congress, as the position of the Orthodox became increasingly grave, he published an appeal in the second part of *Lev ha-ʿIvri* to eliminate religious coercion and compulsory communal membership altogether. Instead he proposed voluntary associations, an organizational framework where everyone could be satisfied. Look to the truly enlightened countries, he suggested.

> In America, everyone can worship as he pleases and no one objects. In New York City there are close to thirty communities called religious societies [*religiöse Gesellschaften*], and they do what they wish without any coercion . . . It may please one to support a society for the upkeep of its synagogue or its rabbi, . . . or he can decide tomorrow that he no longer wants to do so, but would rather go to another society. There is freedom of religion and one does as one pleases. . . . I will write as I wish, they will write as they wish. My friends and I will go to our synagogue, and they will go to their synagogue—what prevents them? Why should they prevent us?[122]

With the growing recognition that they were the weaker party to the conflict, Hungarian ultra-Orthodoxy converged with the neo-Orthodox in their understanding of the politics of separatism and the structure of proper relations between Orthodox and Reform. However, they could not have been further apart in their interpretation of the underlying meaning of the schism, its causes and ultimate solution. For the ultra-Orthodox the religious conflict between the Orthodox and their opponents took on epic, even cosmic proportions: they were convinced that the *Kulturkampf* was none other than the final stage in the eons-long Manichean struggle between good and evil, and what was at stake was nothing less than the Messianic redemption of the end of days.

ʿErev Rav

As the religious conflict gained intensity in Hungary in the 1860s, the focus of the ultra-Orthodox attacks increasingly shifted from the reformers to the neo-Orthodox. If initially they had envisaged a schism between

[122] Ibid., vol. 2, fol. 73a-b.

Reform and Orthodoxy, more and more it became clear that the lines demarcating the two camps had to be redrawn, for the enemy was devious and sought to obscure the difference between friend and foe. The real meaning of the schism had not been immediately apparent; only now did it become clear that its true purpose was to cleave the two camps asunder in a way that would leave no one's loyalties in doubt. And as the confusing fog lifted, the ultra-Orthodox became increasingly certain that this cleavage ran not through the Orthodox–Reform divide, but rather along the lines which separated the authentic Orthodox from the counterfeit ones, the Jews of *shalem* from the neo-Orthodox—the *ʿerev rav*.

The notion of the *ʿerev rav*, the Biblical "mixed multitude" of non-Jews who attached themselves to Israel when they left Egypt (Exod 12: 38), had received new meaning in the Kabbalah. The Zohar and especially Lurianic Kabbalah assigned them a key role in the process of Messianic redemption.[123] The *ʿerev rav* had survived among present-day Jewry, not through biological continuity, but rather through the transmigration of souls. As the souls of virtuous Jews were rooted in the holy *sefirot*, so the souls of the *ʿerev rav* were rooted in the unclean *sitra aḥra*. They were in a metaphysical sense not real Jews. They literally embodied the Lurianic notion of the holy sparks trapped in the unclean shards, of good intermingled with evil. This intolerable unholy mix was to come to an end in the days of the Messiah. The Talmudic statement "The son of David will not come until the world is either wholly sinful or wholly righteous" (Sanh. 98a) was interpreted by Isaac Luria to mean that in the end of

---

123 The classic reference is in *Tikkunei Zohar* in the Zohar I, 25a-b. See Isaiah Tishby, *The Wisdom of the Zohar: An Anthology of Texts*, 3 vols. (Oxford: Oxford University Press, 1989), 3:1470–73. On how the notion of *ʿerev rav* was "politicized" see Gershom Scholem, *Sabbatai Ṣevi: The Mystical Messiah* (Princeton: Princeton University Press, 1973), 71, 228, index; and Yehuda Liebes, "The Ultra-Orthodox Community and the Dead Sea Sect" (in Hebrew), *Jerusalem Studies in Jewish Thought* 3 (1982), 137–52, esp. 143. I owe much that follows to Liebes's analysis of the thought of Asher Selig Margoliot, one of the extreme ideologues of the Jerusalem Neturei Karta from the 1920s on. There are very important differences between Schlesinger and Margoliot, but in general one is struck by the remarkable similarities of their ideas and mentality. There can be no doubt that Margoliot had read Schlesinger, although as far as I can ascertain he cites him only once. The fact that Schlesinger's vision of the Messianic Age came close to that of Religious Zionism probably explains Margoliot's reticence. In any case, both drew upon the writings of the Munkács dynasty. The late Satmar rebbe, Joel Teitelbaum, calls the Zionists the *ʿerev rav*, but this appears only occasionally in scattered remarks. See his *Quntres al ha-geʾula ve-ʿal ha-temurah* (Brooklyn: Jerusalem Publishing, 1967), 64, 107–10.

days vacillation between good and evil will not be tolerated, that it will be necessary to totally separate one from the other. Jews, too, will split in two, those who are totally righteous and those who are totally evil. But as the cosmic process of redeeming the sparks and the separation of good from evil approaches completion, resistance will greatly increase. The *ʿerev rav* will mount a last desperate stand and will enjoy a brief triumph. But this will be their undoing, because then their true natures will be revealed and the final stage of separation will become possible.

The idea of the *ʿerev rav* and its cosmic mission had gained currency in the seventeenth and eighteenth centuries when both sides to the Sabbatian conflict had tarred each other with the label. In the early part of the nineteenth century, such Hasidic masters as Ṣevi Elimelekh of Dinov had applied this notion to the *maskilim*. Those who were drawn to external wisdom, he had taught, "know that they are not of our people, but from the mixed multitude."[124] Nevertheless, it was only in the writings of Schlesinger and Lichtenstein that the *ʿerev rav* became an obsessive litany. Schlesinger even promised to write a separate work on the topic. The *ʿerev rav* were now identified with those who wished to do away with *shalem*. "From the seed of Amalek," wrote Lichtenstein, "from the side of the mixed multitude are those *loʿazim* who strive to make Israel forget its name and tongue."[125] But Amalek, one of the five types of *ʿerev rav* in the Zohar, were not the reformers, but rather the neo-Orthodox. What was the difference between the *ʿerev rav* and the real Jews who left Egypt? Both observed the Torah, but while the *ʿerev rav* discarded the commandment of *shalem*, the seed of Jacob could be easily recognized by one and all as God's chosen people.[126] "The time has come of the Great Purge [*ṣeiruf ha-gadol*] which will take place before the coming of the Redeemer. . . . The time of the *ʿerev rav* has come when evil men will sprout like grass."[127] Proof of the neo-Orthodox deception was that they were engaged in "hybridization" (*harkavah*) at the very moment they should have been striving to separate themselves from evil as much as possible. As was foretold, their perfidy enjoyed at present a

---

[124] See the citation in *Lev ha-ʿIvri*, vol. 2, fol. 47a. For other references, see Ṣevi Elimelekh of Dinov, *Maʿayan Ganim* [commentary on Joseph Yaʿaveṣ, *Or ha-ḥayim*] (Lublin: Herschenhorn, Streisberger und Schneidmesser, 1910), fols. 7a, 15b, 18b and note, 19a, esp. 36b-37a, 40a, etc.

[125] Hillel Lichtenstein, *Maskil el-Dal*, pt. 3 (Brooklyn, 1962) [1st ed. Lemberg, 1869], vol. 3, 8:4, fol. 73a.

[126] *Tanna Devei Eliyahu*, 24:1, "Tosefot ben Yeḥiel," s.v. *ma bein yoṣei Miṣrayim*, fol. 91a.

[127] *Lev ha-ʿIvri*, vol. 1, fol. 86b, and see also 49a-b.

momentary success, for "these new Sadducees and *loʿazim* . . . fulfill what is said in the Zohar, 'In the end of days, the sons of the mixed multitude shall prosper.'"[128] This, however, was only a temporary setback, a time of trial which will soon pass. "I have heard from my mentor," wrote Schlesinger, referring probably to his father-in-law, "that just before a force is destroyed, its power grows. The darkest hour, for instance, is just before the dawn. . . . So, too, in the inception of the Messianic age . . . the *apikorsim* and Sadducees will execute their evil intrigues."[129] The faithful must take heart and counterattack. If the Talmud states, "In the inception of the Messianic age insolence [*ḥuṣpah*] will prevail," then the God-fearing should muster "holy courage" [*omeṣ de-kedushah*] and retaliate in kind, with "holy insolence" [*ʿazzut de-kedushah*].[130]

Such daring was needed if the Gordian knot, intertwining authentic and unauthentic Jew, was to be ruthlessly cut in two. In a declaration which prefaced his second volume of *Lev ha-ʿIvri,* Schlesinger vehemently expressed his disapproval of modern-day converts. Referring to the contradictory aggadic statements on the subject, he argued that converts nowadays, unlike the pious proselytes of the past, had no intention of becoming Jews of *shalem*. In fact, they were exactly like the opportunistic *ʿerev rav* who joined the Jews at their moment of triumph over the Egyptians. The Sadducees joyously welcomed them into the fold, but this was to be expected "for one species of heretic has found another of his kind [*umaṣa min et mino*]." But there was no cause for joy. "If only they would remain in their goyishness [*goyut*]! . . . After all, are not Sadducees and *apikorsim* worse than idol-worshipping gentiles?! . . . We have no wish to increase our numbers. Who would grant us that the gentiles would take some of our own, those thousands and tens of thousands who lust after their ways, their speech and their ideas. Then will Israel truly rejoice! . . . And then will come the Redemption!" Only if the proselyte fully accepted *shalem* and would be distinguished by name, language, dress, by the *ṣiṣit*, sidelocks, and beard; only then was he allowed to convert.[131]

---

128 Ibid., vol. 1, Third Introduction.

129 Ibid., vol. 2, fol. 88a, note.

130 Ibid., vol. 1, fol. 33a-34a, 44a.

131 Ibid., vol. 2, fols. 118b-119b. In this later edition the "Note on the Acceptance of Converts Who Have Increased in Our Time" was placed in back of the volume. Schlesinger dismisses the Lurianic notion that gentiles convert because they recognize that their souls derive from the root of Israel with a casual "we have nothing to do with esoteric teachings, only with the revealed!"

It is difficult to assess just how seriously the ultra-Orthodox took these ideas. It is important to stress that within a few years Schlesinger was to be one of the first to appear in print with the notion that the mass of sinners (not their ideologues) were but "like infants taken captive by gentiles."[132] Nevertheless, for the ultra-Orthodox the idea of secession and schism possessed this added dimension of the *ᶜerev rav,* which as far as I can tell was absent from mainstream Orthodox thinking. They had fewer reservations about making a clean and total break with Reform or even with the neo-Orthodox, because the metaphysical notion of the *ᶜerev rav* freed them of primordial solidarities based on mere biological bonds.

Conclusion

Ultra-Orthodoxy had woven a new tradition, albeit from time-honored, if often neglected, strands. While at times they could disingenuously pretend their teachings were self-understood, often as not, they owned up that in fact these were by no means received traditions. It was therefore necessary to recover that which had been forgotten, marginalized, perhaps even suppressed. In an autobiographical note, Schlesinger recalled his own confusion and equivocation when confronted in his youth by contrary traditions concerning secular studies and acculturation. "At the time I was unacquainted with those statements of the sages which I now know, nor could I offer a sure explanation to many of my God-fearing friends who turned to me for advice."[133] One senses that Schlesinger gloried in his role in having set out and succeeded in recovering lost traditions. He even claimed that the famous testament of the Ḥatam Sofer would have been consigned to oblivion, had he not invested considerable time and effort to retrieve it in a wondrous manner.[134]

---

[132] Ḥaim Sofer, too, when it suited him, could rule just as leniently on the status of Sabbath desecrators as any other halakhic authority. Contrast his vehement attacks in *Shaᶜarei Ḥayim* (Ungvár: Jaeger, 1869) with, for example, his *Responsa Maḥane Ḥayim* (Jerusalem: Divrei Soferim, 1967), p.t 2, OḤ, additions, § 1 on the status of the wine of Sabbath desecrators.

[133] *Naᶜar ᶜIvri* (Stettin [Vienna, 1863]), fol. 9a. In a similar vein, Schlesinger noted that he could readily understand how through ignorance even Orthodox Jews could be easily mislead by modern trends. Now, however, with the recent publication of the Ḥatam Sofer's testament and the relevant volumes of his responsa, there could be no excusing those who persisted in their erring ways. *El Haᶜadarim,* 18, fn.

[134] This is what he reported to his son and son-in-law: see *Naᶜar ᶜIvri* (Jerusalem, 1924), fol. 19b.

In his early publications, Schlesinger gathered scattered and at times inaccessible references, weaving them together into coherent source collections. The most successful of these was the second part of *Lev ha-ʿIvri,* which appeared in 1868, a highly selective compilation of medieval and modern authorities, all expressing hostility to secular studies. He was not the first to do this, and indeed, he made liberal use of the extensive quotes cited by older classics such as the seventeenth-century Isaiah Horowitz's *Shnei luḥot ha-brit* and Ṣevi Elimelekh of Dinov's *Maʿayan Ganim.*[135] However, both in scope and especially in its underlying rationale, Schlesinger's anthology was unprecedented and a model for the future.

In the coming generations, zealot after zealot traveled down the militant trail blazed by Schlesinger, Lichtenstein, and the Hungarian ultra-Orthodox. In style and substance, in their approach to aggadah and halakhah , in their insistence on the qualities of *shalem,* in all this modern day Satmar and Neturei Karta are clearly indebted to their nineteenth century antecedents.[136] And yet their attitude toward these men, Schlesinger in particular, is marked by ambivalence and by a certain reticence or reluctance to acknowledge their paternity. They may have endorsed Schlesinger's prognosis wholeheartedly, but his prescription has been met by puzzlement and deep-seated reservations. For although Schlesinger remained within the ultra-Orthodox fold throughout his life, he proved increasingly critical of an Orthodox establishment content to preserve the status quo. In time, Schlesinger came to propound ideas which his twentieth-century successors found uncomfortably close to

---

135 This last work, itself a commentary on the sixteenth century antirationalist classic by Joseph Yaʿaveṣ, *Or ha-ḥayim,* considerably influenced Schlesinger, as we have seen, and may have been the inspiration for his own commentary on the testament of the Ḥatam Sofer. Published in the mid-1850s, it may also have been the very work which introduced Schlesinger to "those statements of the sages which I now know."

136 This is apparent from reading the following studies: Menaḥem Friedman, "Religious Zealotry in Israeli Society," in *On Ethnic and Religious Diversity in Israel,* ed. Solomon Poll and Ernest Krausz (Ramat-Gan: Bar-Ilan University, 1975), 91-111; Norman Lamm, "The Ideology of the *Neturei Karta* according to the Satmar Version," *Tradition* 13 (1971), 38-53; Allan L. Nadler, "Piety and Politics: The Case of the Satmar Rebbe," *Judaism* 31 (1982): 135–52 and Liebes, "The Ultra-Orthodox Community and the Dead Sea Sect." Of these studies, only Nadler recognizes Schlesinger, Lichtenstein, and Ḥaim Sofer as precursors of Satmar.

that modern arch-heresy, Zionism.[137] The paradoxical logic of an invented tradition led Schlesinger in the years to come to embark upon a new and unexpected path, one that had begun with a conservative ideology but led away to a new, bold, visionary utopia.

---

137 The Satmar rebbe wrote of Schlesinger: "Because he wished to found colonies, even if his intentions were for the sake of heaven, it was a great and terrible mistake" (Joel Teitelbaum, *Va-Yoʾel Mosheh* [Brooklyn: Jerusalem Publishing, 1978], 313).

3

Preserving Tradition In The Land of Revolution: The Religious Leadership of Soviet Jewry, 1917–1930

DAVID E. FISHMAN

Between November 1917 and March 1920, Russian Jewry, one of the most traditional Jewries in the world, came under the control of an ideologically radical, militantly atheistic state. The new Soviet regime was committed to utilizing its full range of coercive powers and its control of public media to combat religious beliefs, practices, and institutions. The primary targets of Soviet power were Russian Orthodoxy and other Christian denominations, but Judaism and Islam were not spared or overlooked.[1]

As the state-sponsored campaign against Judaism was waged, an equally momentous and more positive development occurred: the legal and social emancipation of Russian Jewry. After the Bolshevik revolution, unprecedented opportunities opened up for Russian Jews to participate in Soviet governance, the Communist Party, higher education, economic administration, science, and the arts. For much of the interwar period, Soviet elites were seriously committed to proletarian interna-

[1] R. Marshall Jr., *Aspects of Religion In The Soviet Union* (Chicago: University of Chicago Press, 1967); W. Kolarz, *Religion In The Soviet Union* (New York: St. Martin's, 1961).

tionalism, eschewed anti-Semitism, and proclaimed that "the Jewish bourgeois is our enemy; the Jewish worker is our brother."[2]

The combined forces of emancipation on the one hand, and the state persecution of Judaism on the other, generated a pace of secularization, acculturation, and alienation from the Jewish tradition unparalled in modern Jewish history. In western and central Europe, the emancipation of the Jews had involved an implicit bargain, with European society anticipating that the Jews would shed most or nearly all of their cultural particularism in exchange for their newly granted status. But in the Soviet Union, the emancipation bargain was articulated explicitly by the state, and its terms were extreme and rigid: The new Soviet man of Jewish origin was a full member of society, and could advance to the upper echelons of all its institutions; Judaism, on the other hand, was the reactionary ideology of the Jewish bourgeoisie and clericalists. Its harmful practices would not be tolerated.[3]

The story of the persecution of Judaism by the Soviet authorities, with the active participation of the *Yevsektsiya* (Jewish sections of the Communist Party), has been told in histories of Soviet Jewry and examined in depth in studies by A. A. Gershuni, Zvi Gitelman, and Mordechai Altschuler. The central facts are well known: the forcible confiscation of synagogues, houses of study, and religious schools; the outlawing of the *ḥeder* (religious school) and the widespread prosecution of *melamdim* (religious teachers); public show trials against rabbis, *mohalim* (ritual circumcisers), and *shoḥṭim* (ritual slaughterers of kosher meat); the growing enforcement of the six-day work week, with Saturday as a working day; campaigns of antireligious propaganda and intimidation around the time of Passover and the High Holidays; antireligious instruction in the Soviet Yiddish schools; reprimands and reprisals against party members and state workers who circumcised their children

[2] Two recent surveys of Soviet Jewish history deal with the abovementioned processess: Benjamin Pinkus, *The Jews of the Soviet Union: A History of a National Minority* (Cambridge: Cambridge University Press, 1988); Nora Levin, *The Jews of the Soviet Union Since 1917: The Paradox of Survival,* 2 vols. (New York: New York University Press, 1988).

[3] For much of the interwar period, the Soviet regime tolerated and even supported a third alternative: the development of a secular Soviet-Jewish nationality with its own proletarian Yiddish culture. But the authorities' support for this version of Jewish collective existence was the product of temporary tactical considerations; Leninist and Stalinist ideology remained committed to the rapid disappearance of the Jews as a national group. See Mordechai Altschuler, "The Attitude of the Communist Party of Russia To Jewish National Survival," *YIVO Annual* 14 (1969): 68-86.

or attended synagogue; in the 1930s the banning of the manufacture and importation of matzo, and so on and on.[4]

This paper considers how the religious leadership of Russian Jewry responded to this overwhelming onslaught, how it perceived the challenge it faced, what methods it utilized to preserve Jewish religious life, and how it evaluated its own success or failure. This topic has not been dealt with in the historical literature on Soviet Jewry, in part because primary sources have not been easily available. The Jewish religious leadership had almost no access to printing presses and could not address the Jewish public through mass media. Moreover, it adopted a low public profile early on and kept most of its efforts and activities clandestine. This has made writing its history rather difficult. Scholars have been reluctant to draw any conclusions based on the body of legends and folklore surrounding the Lubavitcher Rebbe, R. Joseph Isaac Schneerson (1880-1950), and other rabbis in the Soviet Union.

The lack of sources on Jewish religious leadership in the early Soviet period has recently begun to be alleviated. In the last ten to fifteen years, a memoir literature has emerged written by rabbis who lived in the Soviet Union in the 1920s and 1930s, and two valuable collections of material have been published by the Lubavitch Hasidic movement: twelve volumes of collected letters by Rabbi Schneerson, who lived in the USSR until mid-1927, and an official history of the Lubavitch movement in the Soviet Union, containing letters, reports, and memoirs by Hasidim, rabbis, and emissaries. These and other materials make it possible to write the history of Judaism in the Soviet Union "from the inside," that is, from the perspective of the rabbinic leadership at the time.[5]

---

4 Jacob Leschinsky, *dos sovetishe yidntum: zayn Fargangenhayt un kegnvart* (Soviet Jewry: Its Past and Present) (New York 1941), 310–22 and passim; Salo W. Baron, *The Russian Jew Under Tsars and Soviets*, 2d rev. ed. (New York: Schocken, 1987), 175–79, 244–47; Zvi Gitelman, *Jewish Nationality and Soviet Politics: the Jewish Sections of the CPSU 1917-1930* (Princeton: Princeton University Press, 1972), 291-318; Mordechai Altschuler, *Ha-Yevseqṣiah be-Vrit ha-Moᶜaṣot* (The Yevsektsiya in the Soviet Union) (Tel Aviv: 1980), 292–303; idem, "The Rabbi of Homel's Trial in 1922," *Michael* 6 (1980): 9-61; A.A. Gershuni, *Yahadut be-Rusiya ha-Sovyetit* (Judaism in Soviet Russia) (Jerusalem: Rav Kook Foundation, 1961) idem, *Yehudim ve-yahadut be-Vrit ha- Moᶜaṣot* (Jews and Judaism in the Soviet Union) (Jerusalem: Feldheim, 1970).

5 R. Joseph Isaac Schneersohn, *Igrot Qodesh Mahariiṣ*, 12 vols. (Brooklyn: Otzar Hasidim, 1982-85; Sholem Duber Levin, *Toldot Ḥabad bi-Rusiya ha-Sovyetit 5678-5710* (History of the Habad in Soviet Russia 1818-1950) (Brooklyn: Otzar Hasidim, 1989); see the list of memoirs cited by Levin, p. 15. The new literature is written almost entirely from a Lubavitch perspective. It is particularly unfortunate that R. Shlomo

The Flight of The Old Elite, The Emergence of the New

In the first years of Soviet rule, the trauma of the antireligious onslaught was so severe that most Russian rabbis emigrated to countries where Judaism could be freely observed. The list of rabbinic emigrés from Soviet territory between 1918 and 1921 is long and impressive. The following are the most noteworthy examples.

1. Rabbi Moshe Soloveitchik, heir to the famous rabbinic dynasty which headed the Volozhin yeshiva, and rabbi of Khislovich, Byelorussia, since 1910, left the Soviet Union for Poland with his family in 1921, taking with him his 18-year-old son Joseph B. Soloveitchik. According to one of his descendants, "it was clear by then that there was no future for them in the Soviet Union."

2. Rabbi Israel Meyer Kagan, popularly known as the Chofetz Chaim, the most revered religious figure of Lithuanian Jewry, lived in Byelorussia and the Ukraine during the years of the World War, the Russian Revolution, and civil war. Only in 1921, that is, after Communist control had been established, did he return with his yeshiva to their home town of Radun, in Poland.

The impetus for Kagan's decision to leave was a drive by the local authorites to force the yeshiva students to work on the Sabbath. Kagan declared that under such circumstances, emigration was an act of *piquaḥ nefesh* (saving a life) and ruled that it was permissible to violate the Sabbath in order to leave Soviet territory.

3. The leaders of the Chernobyl branch of Hasidism—the Rakhmistrivker Rebbe, R. Mordechai (Motele) Twersky; the newly crowned Skverer Rebbe, R. Jacob Joseph Twersky; and the Trisker Rebbe, R. Moshe Mordechai Twersky—all left the Soviet Ukraine during the early years of Soviet rule, taking with them groups of followers.[6]

Yosef Zevin and R. Jacob Klemes, non-Lubavitch rabbis who were active in religious affairs on a national level, never wrote memoirs about their activities in the Soviet Union. Both settled in Palestine in the 1930s. A partial corrective to this bias in the published literature is provided by materials in the archives of the American Jewish Joint Distribution Committee and in the Central Relief Committee collection at the Yeshiva University Archives, utilized in the present study.

6 Professor Ḥayyim Soloveitchik, oral communication, 20 October 1990; Moshe M. Yosher, *Ha-Ḥafeṣ Ḥayim: Ḥayav ve-poʿalo* (The Ḥafetz Ḥaim: His Life and Work) (Tel Aviv: Netzak, 1958), 1:430f., 434–36; Gershuni, *Yahadut*, 134f.; Menashe Unger, *seyfer ha-kdoyshim: rabeyim oyf kidush ha-shem* (New York: Shulsinger, 1967), 5; A. Shrayber, "der skverer rebbe zatsal," *Dos Yiddishe Vort* 15/3 (April-May 1978): 17.

Numerous Lithuanian *rashei yeshivot* who had fled southeast from the invading German armies in 1915, and spent the war years and their aftermath in Russian-controlled territory, streamed back across the border to independent Lithuania and to the Vilna province in independent Poland. Hasidic masters departed for Galicia, Rumania, and Poland. By 1922, Russian Jewry faced a serious crisis of religious leadership. Of the seven-man rabbinic committee which had been chosen to lead orthodox Jewry in the summer of 1917, in preparation for the planned Russian-Jewish Congress, only one member was still alive and residing in the Soviet Union six years later—Rabbi Shmarya Medalia of Vitebsk.[7]

Into this leadership vacuum stepped R. Joseph Isaac Schneerson, the newly crowned Lubavitcher Rebbe, who succeeeded his father R. Sholem Duber in 1920. Young, dynamic, and ambitious, Schneerson began to conceive of himself, in light of this crisis, as the religious leader of all Soviet Jews, and not only of his Habad Hasidim. He acted upon this new self-consciousness and worked aggressively to broaden his influence within the Jewish community. He sought, and eventually achieved, recognition as the uncontested head of Jewish religious life in the USSR.

Schneerson was a masterful organizer and administrator. In December 1917 (prior to his becoming Rebbe), he established Agudat ha-Temimim, an association of former students of the original Tomkhei Temimim yeshiva in Lubavitch (Mogilev *guberniyia*).[8] Upon becoming

7 On the Lithuanian yeshivas' years in Byelorussia and the Ukraine, see *Mosdot Torah Be-Eropah be-binyanam ve-be-Ḥurbanam* (European Torah Institutions: Their Foundation and Destruction), ed. S. K. Mirsky (New York: Ogen, 1956), 99, 151f., 233, 314–16, 329, and passim. The six other members of the 1917 leadership were R. Chaim Ozer Grodzenski (left for Vilna, Poland, in 1918); R. Iser Zalman Meltzer (left for Kletsk, Poland, in 1923); R. Yitskhok Ya'akov Rabinovitch (left for Ponievezh, Lithuania, in 1918); R. Avraham Duber Kahana Shapira (rabbi of Kovna, which belonged to Lithuania as of 1918); The Lubavitcher Rebbe, R. Sholem Duber Schneersohn (died in 1920); and the Bobroisker Rebbe, R. Shmarya Noah Schneersohn of the rival Kapust dynasty (died, and dynasty was dissolved, in 1923). The appeal which they issued in 1917, calling upon all Orthodox Jews to unite in preparation for the Russian Jewish Congress, is reproduced in *Aḥiezer: Qoveṣ igrot* (Ahiezer: Collected Letters), ed. Aaron Surasky (Bnei Brak: Netzale, 1970), 2:643.

8 See the letter on the establishment of Agudat ha-Temimim, and the accompaying by-laws of the association, *Igrot* 1 (1983): 100–10 (an earlier attempt to create such an organization apparently failed; ibid., 41-45). The establishment of such a formal organization structure within Habad Hasidism was influenced by the explosion of Jewish political and cultural organizations in 1917. Agudat ha-Temimim was modeled after the youth movements of the Jewish political parties. Since the Tomkhei

Rebbe, Schneerson transformed the members of Agudat ha-Temimim into the elite avant-garde of Lubavitch Hasidism. He corresponded with them frequently, addressed them individually and collectively, and cultivated their religious fervor, their activism, and their fierce personal loyalty to him as Rebbe. He appointed select *temimim* (members of Agudat ha-Temimim) as the regional leaders of Habad Hasidism in a secret ceremony in 1922:

> I selected eight young *temimim*, people with good brains, hearts, hands, and feet, and I called upon them to assemble in Moscow for a meeting. . . . [There] we took a solemn oath to sacrifice our lives for the sake of the Torah, down to our very last drop of blood. We then proceeded to divide up the work to be done in the country, [with a different region] for each one separately.[9]

Schneerson directed the network of *temimim* and their regional lieutenants from a central bureau (*lishkah*) in his resident city of Rostov. He instructed them to establish *ḥadarim* and branch Tomkhei Temimim *yeshivas* wherever they could, and as a result of their efforts, Lubavitch-run educational institutions began to take the place of the indigenous religious schools which were being abandoned or closed under Communist pressure.

At the same time, Schneerson dispatched individual *temimim* as roving emissaries, to preach in synagogues and encourage communities to maintain religious institutions. Through the emissaries and via correspondence, Schneerson established direct contact with scores of Russian Jewish communities, inquiring about the state of their religious institutions and offering them encouragement and moral support. In doing so, Schneerson broadened his sphere of influence beyond the circles of Lubavitcher Hasidim which had been his father's constituency. Many

---

Temimim yeshiva was founded in 1897, none of its members was above forty at the time of its founding. For a similar development in a non-Hasidic context, see David E. Fishman, "The Musar Movement in Interwar Poland," in *The Jews of Poland Between Two World Wars*, ed. Yisrael Gutman et al. (Hanover, N.H.: University Press of New England, 1989), 247–71.

9 The quotation is from two of R. Joseph Isaac's *sichos*, in 1932 and 1942, cited by Levin, *Toldot Habad*, 55. The special importance Schneerson attributed to the *temimim* was first signalled by his composing a special letter to them (apart from the rest of his Hasidim) upon his father's death; *Igrot*, 1:110–12. See also ibid., 122f., 131–33. On the appointment of regional lieutenants as early as 1921 see *Igrot*, 1:156.

non-Hasidic rabbis and lay leaders who faced the brunt of the Communist onslaught began to look to Schneerson for help and guidance.[10]

Having mobilized his activists and broadened his influence at the grass-roots level, Schneerson turned in 1922 to the task of organizing the Soviet rabbinate. He traveled to Moscow and pressed its rabbinic leaders to convene a clandestine meeting of Soviet rabbis to deal with the crisis facing Jewish religious life. Seniority and etiquette required that the chief rabbi of the capital city, the elderly R. Shmuel Rabinowitz, convene and lead the meeting, but Rabinowitz and his colleagues were opposed to the idea. They feared for the personal safety of the rabbis who would attend, and were concerned that the discovery of an unauthorized rabbinic meeting would lead to an even greater crackdown against Jewish religious life. They quoted the prophet Amos (5:13), "the wise man in this time should be silent".[11]

Schneerson seized the initiative, went over Rabinowitz's head, and convened the meeting himself. The gathering was held in Moscow in the fall of 1922, with rabbis from Moscow, Leningrad, Minsk, Kharkov, Kiev, Vitebsk, Ekaterinovslav, and other cities in attendance. It resulted in the creation of a clandestine Vaʿad Rabane S.S.S.R. (Committee of Rabbis in the USSR) and the selection of a three-member leadership council: Schneerson, Rabinowitz, and R. Eliya Aaron Mileikovsky, chief rabbi of Kharkov in the Ukraine.[12]

The activist and popular Schneerson was the dominant figure on the Committee of Rabbis from its inception. Rabinowitz was a highly regarded Talmudist and *poseq*, but not a distinguished communal leader, having left political and communal affairs to the official "Crown Rabbi" of Moscow, the Zionist leader Jacob Mazeh. Rabinowitz lacked the organizational skills and the political instincts needed to head a body of rabbis and did not have the popular support required to emerge as the leader of religious Jewry. Schneerson, on the other hand, possessed all of

---

[10] *Igrot*, 1:616.

[11] *Igrot*, 1:617

[12] *Igrot*, 1:618; 11, 44f. The criterion for belonging to the leadership council was apparently geographic. It consisted of the chief rabbis of Moscow and Kharkov, the capital cities of the Russian and (in the interim) the Ukrainian republics, and Schneerson, the preeminant rabbinic personality from the Byelorussian territories. Rabbi Shlomo Yosef Zevin of Novozivkov served as Secretary of the Committee throughout most of its existence.

these qualities, and used them skillfully inside the Committee of Rabbis.[13]

By January 1923, Schneerson's rise to preeminence was complete. In a public appeal for financial aid on behalf of religious institutions in the USSR, addressed to Jewish communities throughout the world, he claimed to "speak on behalf of the spirit and soul of the thousands of Jews dwelling in the land of Russia." He was subsequently formally chosen as the Committee of Rabbis' General Director, and later as its chairman.[14]

Consolidation and Organization

From its very inception in 1922, Schneerson conceived of the Committee of Rabbis as more than an occassional forum for consultation. He envisioned it as the executive agency for all of Jewish religious life in the Soviet Union. To his mind, it was imperative that Jewish religious communities be consolidated into a tightly knit, nationwide organization with a centralized leadership. In isolation, the individual synagogue, *ḥeder, melamed,* or rabbi would always be defeated by the more powerful forces of the party and state. A central underground organization could provide the funds to maintain *ḥedarim*, yeshivas, synagogues, and *miqvaot*; it could offer moral support and legal-political advice; it could dispatch religious professionals, books, and supplies (tallith, tefillin, mezuzah, etc.). Schneerson undertook to build such a network of communities under the aegis of the Committee of Rabbis.

The idea was a new one. Jewish religious life had flourished for hundreds of years in eastern Europe on a decentralized basis, with each local community taking care of its own religious affairs. Russian Jewry had never had a "chief rabbi" or a "central consistoire." Schneerson endeavored to apply a distinctly Hasidic model of communal organization—in which the Rebbe supervised the religious affairs of geographi-

---

13 On Rabinowitz and the Moscow rabbinate, see Imanuel Mikhlin, *Ha-Gaḥelet,* (The Glowing Coal) (Jerusalem: Shamir, 1986), 16-24; on Mileikovsky, see Yitskhak Raphael, ed., *Entsiklopedia shel ha-Tsiyonut ha-datit* (Encyclopedia of Religious Zionism), 3 (1965): cols. 415–17,

14 *Igrot,* 1:232–35, 618, 619. Following Rabinowitz's death, his position on the leadership council was assumed by his successor as chief rabbi of Moscow, R. Jacob Klemes (*Igrot,* 1:527). Beginning in 1926, R. Menahem Gluskin, chief rabbi of Minsk, Byelorussia, also appears as a member of the leadership (*Igrot,* 11:73f.).

cally dispersed conventicles of Hasidim—to all of Soviet Jewry, with himself, as chairman of the Committee of Rabbis, at the apex.[15]

In building this structure, Schneerson employed the same organizational techniques he had used with such success to consolidate his own Hasidim and *temimim*. The Committee of Rabbis established an executive office known as the *Merkaz* (Center) to conduct organizational work. Its staff maintained written contact with scores of communities throughout the country, receiving a steady flow of information about the state of religious institutions, as well as requests for financial assistance. The Merkaz kept separate files on each city and town with which it corresponded. In 1925, it sent out a lengthy questionnaire to more than seven hundred communities, with questions on the number of Jews, number of synagogues, synagogue attendance on week-days and Sabbaths, number of young people (under 35) who attend synagogue, the situation of Jewish education, kashruth (kosher meat), *miqvaot* (ritual baths), the names of the local rabbi, and *shoḥeṭ* and so on.[16]

The Merkaz also employed "field representatives," secret emissaries who spent months traveling from one town to another under the guise of wandering preachers. These charismatic personalities, who were handpicked by Schneerson, spoke in dozens of synagogues and homes, energizing and inspiring Jews to form a *ḥeder* for their children or a *shiyur* (religious study group) for adults, and to strengthen religious observance. The emissaries, who did not divulge to anyone that they were sent by an organization, kept detailed records of their travels and served as a discrete back channel of information on the state of religious affairs in the communities. They thus provided confidential assessments of the trust worthiness of the individuals involved in religious affairs and of the financial condition of communities. In 1926, the Merkaz had four different *arumforer* (travelers) in the field, including the legendary R.

---

[15] This centralized approached was viewed by Schneerson's critics as a Lubavitch takeover of Jewish religious life. At the fall 1923 meeting of the Committee of Rabbis, some members protested that "the Lubavitcher [Rebbe] is snatching the Torah into Hasidic hands" (*Igrot*, 1:618).

[16] See the detailed report on the activities of the Merkdaz, written in 1927, in *Igrot*, 1:569–85. A Russian version of the report, entitled "doklad o deyatelnosti Rav inskogo komiteta v S.S.S.R;" and signed by Rabbi Shlomo Yosef Zevin, Secretary of the Committee of Rabbis, is contained in the archives of the American Jewish Joint Distribution Committee (hereafter JDC), USSR file #473. On the questionnaires dispatched by the Merkaz, see Mikhlin, *Ha-Gaḥelet*, p.53. The Merkaz was based at first in Moscow and was transferred to Leningrad in 1924, so as to facilitate its working closely with Scheerson.

Yaakov Moskolik, about whom Schneerson said "if I had twenty Yankelekh I could turn Russia upside down."[17]

As part of Schneerson's effort to consolidate the organization of Jewish religious life, in 1925 the Committee of Rabbis established a central institution for the training of rabbis and *shoḥṭim*, the Bet Midrash le-Rabanim ve-Shoḥṭim (The Seminary for Rabbis and *Shoḥṭim*) in Nevel. This nonsectarian school (for both Hasidic and Mitnaggedic students) broke with the norms of the traditional yeshiva, where Talmud was studied for its own sake, without any particular emphasis on the practical aspects of Halakhah, and geared its curriculum toward the professional training of rabbis and *shoḥṭim*. Connected with the Nevel Bet Midrash was a central placement service which matched communities in need of a rabbi, *shoḥeṭ*, or cantor with young candidates in search of employment. In a time of decreasing human resources in the religious professions (due to emigration, retirements under political pressure, and the passing on of the older generation), it was imperative to train rabbis and religious functionaries and insure that communities desiring or needing a rabbi could find one. Between 1925 and 1928, the Bet Midrash placed 48 graduates as rabbis and *shoḥṭim*.[18]

Funding Mechanisms

Crucial to the Committee of Rabbis' success was its ability to obtain significant funding from abroad. Soviet Jewish communities were in no position to sustain religious institutions on their own. The wars and pogroms had left them in economic shambles. The Jewish middle class, which had traditionally funded such institutions, had been decimated by the policies of War Communism and the nationalization of commerce. The *qehilot* had been liquidated and their assets confiscated. Who was to pay the rabbi, *rosh-yeshivah, melamed,* or *shoḥeṭ*? Who would maintain (or, in the aftermath of wars and pogroms, rebuild and repair) the syna-

---

17 Levin, *Toldot Habad,* 62-65, 154f.; *Igrot,*. 1:578–80 (Zevin's report, 623). Moskolik was a leading figure among the Lubavitch Hasidim in Moscow until his arrest in 1935. He never returned from Siberian exile. See his 1934 letters to Schneerson in *Toldot Habad,* 157f.

18 *Toldot Habad,* 266f.; *Igrot,* 1:578 (Zevin's report); "dokladnaya zapiska pravleniya seminariya 'Bet Yosef,' Nevel", December 1926, JDC archives, USSR file #473. The placement figure is from the "Report on the Accomplishments of the Rabbinical Board in Russia 5688 [1928]," JDC archives, USSR file #476. Unlike the "Tomchei Temimim" yeshivas, the Nevel *Bet Midrash* did not instruct its students in Kabbalah or Hasidism (*Toldot Habad,* 266).

gogue, *miqveh,* or cemetery? With the traditional sources of funding destroyed, a massive infusion of foreign funds was the only hope.

Schneerson's early efforts in this area yielded disappointing results. His appeal to world Jewry in January 1923 was a failure, and even Orthodox organizations in America, such as Agudas Yisroel and Agudas ha-Rabonim, responded to his letters with caution, suspecting that their contributions would fill the coffers of Lubavitch, rather than aid the largely non-Hasidic communities of Russia and the Ukraine.[19]

A breakthrough occurred in 1924, when Schneerson developed ties with the Moscow representative of the American Jewish Joint Distribution Committee (hereafter JDC), Dr. Joseph Rosen. Although the JDC's official mandate for operation in the USSR was limited to economic relief and reconstruction among the Jewish population, including the funding of Jewish agricultural colonies in the Ukraine and Crimea, the organization quietly diverted some of its funds to "cultural work." Schneerson's Committee of Rabbis became the primary recipient of such funds. In the 1925 fiscal year, it recieved $18,000 from the JDC; in 1926, $24,000; and in 1927, over $25,000. Separate annual allocations, of approximately $25,000–$30,000, were granted to the Committee of Rabbis for the distribution of Passover relief.[20]

The connection with the JDC was vital to the activities of the Committee of Rabbis, and Schneerson devoted much effort to cultivating their relationship. He submitted periodic reports and budget requests to the JDC leadership in New York, met with JDC leaders during their visits to Moscow, and corresponded with the chairman of the organization's Cultural Committee, Cyrus Adler. In 1926, he began developing a similar relationship with the Alliance Israélite Universelle.[21]

---

[19] Agudas Yisroel of America responded by requesting a detailed list of the institutions which would be aided through its contributions *Igrot,* 1:263–66. Schneerson complained bitterly about the total lack of response to his appeals in 1923, ibid., 270f., 348. His only sources of support at that time were the small circles of Lubavitch Hasidim in America; see, e.g., ibid., 441.

[20] *Igrot,* 1:619, 624, 630. Only half of the $50,000 budget for religious purposes in 1926 went to the Committee of Rabbis. Regarding Passover relief see ibid., 621.

[21] See Schneerson's letters and reports to the Joint, *Igrot,* 1:472–75, 494–96, 520–28, 11: 72-74, and several unpublished letters in the JDC archives, USSR, files 473–75. Schneerson met twice with the chairman of the Joint, Felix M. Warburg, during the latter's visit to the USSR in 1927. To the second meeting, Schneerson brought a rabbinic delegation consisting of Rabbis Klemes of Moscow, Gluskin of Minsk, Medalia of Vitebsk, Zevin of Novozivkov (Secretary of the Committee of Rabbis), Horinshteyn of Kiev, and Basin of Kharkov (*Igrot,* 1:635). See below n. 59. On his

With the generous support of the JDC in hand, the Committee of Rabbis became the funding agency for most Jewish religious activity in the USSR. The funds disbursed by the Committee were divided into three major categories:

(a) Case-by-case allocations in response to requests from the communities. The Merkaz estimated that it received more than a hundred communal requests for aid per month. "Most of these letters request aid to repair or build a mikveh, to build or repair a synagogue, aid for children in *ḥeder*, for *melamdim*, for religious Jews who are unemployed because of Sabbath observance, etc."[22] There were no firm guidelines for determining the size of such allocations, although grants rarely exceeded 100 rubles.

(b) Regular monthly allocations to institutions of Torah learning. "This includes *yeshiva gedolas* for older students (such as in Minsk, Nevel, Kharkov, etc.), *yeshiva ketanas* for younger students (such as in Kremenchug, Romen, Polotsk, etc.) . . . and, in many cities and towns, the students in *ḥadarim*."[23]

Maintaining yeshivas and *ḥadarim* was the highest funding priority of the Committee of Rabbis. It considered the yeshiva to be the focal point of Jewish spiritual life and the guarantor of the future existence of the synagogue, kashruth, Sabbath, and so on. The yeshivas and *ḥadarim* were also the most seriously threatened religious institutions, since they functioned underground, on an illegal basis, and were frequently hounded by the authorities.[24]

According to a 1928 report, the Committee of Rabbis funded yeshivas in twelve cities, with a total of 620 students, and *ḥadarim* in 22 different communities with a total of 4,200 children. Yeshivas received monthly allocations based on their size, at a rate of 25 rubles per student, plus additional funds for faculty salaries. (The Nevel Bet Midrash le-Rabanim ve-Shoḥṭim was treated as an elite institution for the training of future religious leaders, and was funded at a much higher rate, 50 rubles per

---

relations with Professor Vladimir Haffkin of the Alliance, see *Igrot*, 1:547f., 567–69; *Toldot Habad*, 22, 31 ,41, 75.

22 Zevin's report on the activities of the Committee of Rabbis, *Igrot*, 1:572; for further details see 573-74.

23 Zevin's report, ibid., 577

24 Memo on the state of yeshivas submitted by the Committee of Rabbis, *Toldot Habad*, 292. On the problematic legal status of the yeshiva and *ḥeder*, see below.

month per student.) *Ḥadarim* received monthly allocations according to a rate of 5 rubles per child.[25]

(c) Annual Passover relief funds which were channeled via the Committee of Rabbis to the rabbis of scores of communities.[26]

In addition to these three categories of allocations, the Committee of Rabbis sponsored special projects of its own, such as the publication of a *siddur* (prayerbook) in 1926 (and the abortive attempt to publish a Pentateuch in 1927), and supported Tiferes Bahurim youth leagues in five cities, which furthered religious observance and study among students and young professionals. The remainder of its funds covered administrative expenses and the salaries of staff and emmisaries.[27]

Legal and Political Activity

The Committee of Rabbis also engaged in behind-the-scenes legal and political advocacy for Jewish religious interests in the USSR. Shortly after its establishment, the Committee began lobbying to clarify and improve the status of Jewish religious instruction. Soviet law explicitly prohibited the teaching of religion in schools, and in the early 1920s the *Yevsektsiya*, security police, and Soviet courts waged an aggressive campaign to eliminate the *ḥadarim* and *melamdim*. The Committee of Rabbis responded by making the plight of the *ḥeder* one of its top priorities.

After conferring with legal experts, it was decided that the Committee's Secretary, Rabbi Shlomo Yosef Zevin of Novozivkov, would submit an inquiry to the Central Legal Consultation Office of the Soviet Bar Association, asking whether the private instruction of religion at home, to groups of five or six children, was permissible under Soviet law. The Consultation Office responded that private, home-based teaching of religion was fully protected under Soviet law, and the Merkaz dispatched notarized copies of this opinion to scores of communities across the USSR. The opinion was used by *melamdim* who ran afoul of the local authorities. If they were arrested and prosecuted, it served as the

---

25 The figures are from the above-mentioned report, *Toldot Habad,* 292 and 41, and similarly in the budget submitted by the Committee of Rabbis to the JDC that year, USSR file #475.

26 The Central Relief Collection, Yeshiva University Archives, file 117/21, includes receipts from sixty communities for Passover relief funds (*maʿot ḥiṭṭin*) distributed via Schneerson in 1926.

27 Zevin report, *Igrot,* 1:583; on Tiferes Bahurim see Mikhlin, *Ha-Gaḥelet* 46; Levin, *Toldot Habad,* 51-54.

basis for their legal defense or request for appeal. Five years after its issuance, the Merkaz still processed requests for copies of the ruling.[28]

At about the same time, Schneerson organized a Legal Bureau of three Moscow lawyers (chaired by Y. Oryanson), which worked closely with the Merkaz to provide legal advice to accused *melamdim* and religious functionaries. The Bureau commonly advised defendants to appeal their cases to higher courts, which were considered less subject to overt political presssure from the *Yevsektsiya*. If their case was transferred to a Moscow court, members of the Legal Bureau defended the accused themselves. Schneerson claimed that the Bureau succeeded in overturning several convictions and reducing numerous fines and sentences. Its activity was a source of moral encouragement to *melamdim*, who were the most vulnerable and exposed Jewish religious functionaries.[29]

When, in 1923, the People's Commissariat of Justice proposed amending Article 121 of the Soviet Criminal Statute, so as to outlaw private group instruction of religion to children, the Committee of Rabbis organized efforts to lobby against the amendment. It persuaded the elders of the Moscow synagogue—which unlike the committee was a legally sanctioned body—to submit a memorandum against the amendment to Lev Kamenev, then President of the All-Union Executive Committee (VTsIK). Appended to the memorandum were thirteen petitions collected by the Committee of Rabbis with a total of 4,934 signatures, protesting against the illegal persecution of Jewish religious teachers.[30]

Professor David Shor, one of the elders of the Moscow synagogue, submitted the memorandum and petitions to Kamenev in a personal audience on 22 July 1923. Kamenev expressed his total agreement with its contents and passed it on to N. V. Kirilenko, Deputy General Procurator of the Russian Republic. At the subsequent meeting of the VTsIK, Kirilenko announced that the Commissariat of Justice had decided to withdraw the amendment and stated that "banning group religious instruction for children outside the framework of educational institutions violates the Soviet Constitution, which does not intend to engage in

---

28 *Igrot*, 1:571; Mikhlin, *Ha-Gaḥelet*, 50.

29 *Igrot*, 1:624f.; see the letter of appeal by a convicted melamed from Novozivkov, *Toldot Habad*, 30f.

30 A 1927 memorandum on the legal status of Jewish religious education in the USSR prepared by the Committee of Rabbis includes the text of the memorandum to Kamenev and related materials (*Toldot Habad*, 22-31, esp. 23, 25f.

religious persecution." The session of the VTsIK endorsed Kirilenko's report which included these remarks. The Committee of Rabbis thus succeeded in averting the evil decree against private religious instruction. It proceeded to distribute notarized copies of the minutes of the VTsIK meeting to *melamdim* and communities across the country.[31]

The Committee of Rabbis' Merkaz worked closely with the elders of the Moscow synagogue in those years, relaying to them complaints and petitions from far-flung Jewish communities concerning the confiscation of synagogues and other abuses, assisting them in drafting memoranda to government officials, and helping to arrange private audiences with the latter. Since the Committee of Rabbis was a clandestine organization, the representations themselves were made by the Moscow synagogue.[32]

The Committee of Rabbis' efforts to improve the status of Jewish religious life by working within the Soviet legal and political system were more than just a tactical measure to slow down and confound the process of religious persecution (though they were certainly that as well). Schneerson believed in the integrity of Soviet law and in the reasonableness of Soviet political leaders. He repeatedly told his followers that "the religious Jew is a full citizen of the USSR, and is entirely permitted according to its laws to teach his children Torah and observe all the commandments." He believed that Judaism was being persecuted not by the Soviet state or the Communist party, but by the *Yevsektsiya*, the leaders of the Jewish Communist sections, who were "more pious than the Pope" in their Communist fervor. These fanatical renegades were intent on destroying Jewish religious life in the USSR and abused their power and influence with local Soviet authorities to incite antireligious persecution.[33]

Schneerson's statements regarding the benign attitude of the Soviet government toward Judaism might be taken with a grain of salt, as pro

---

31 *ibid.* The Commissariat of Justice determined, however, that such groups could not exceed three children. The opinion of the Legal Consultation Office, which allowed groups of five or six, therefore remained useful in trials and other situations.

32 *Igrot,* 1:570f.; for other examples, see Gershuni, *Yahadut,* 261. The level of political activity (petitions, audiences, etc.) seems to have declined after 1924, when the Merkaz transferred its headquarters to Leningrad.

33 *Igrot,* 1:627, similarly pp. 263-65, and 486: "It is a lie [to claim] that the government interferes with our observance of the Torah and the commandments. They oppose it, but they do not interfere. On the contrary; in several cases the High Court has acquitted those who have been persecuted, and saved them from their adversaries."

forma expressions of loyalty to the regime, were it not for the fact that he continued to speak in this vein after his departure from the USSR. At a closed meeting of Orthodox leaders held in Riga, Latvia, in November 1927, Schneerson reiterated his position:

> The repressive actions against us do not emanate from the central authorities, but from the *Yevsektsiya*. The latter choose illegal methods to harm our religion. The *melamed* is a legal worker, and the local authorities will not harm him unless the *Yevsektsiya* denounces him with libelous charges as being a counter-revolutionary, a speculator, and so on.[34]

In his first few years after leaving Russia, Schneerson urged that diplomatic channels be used to discredit the *Yevsektsiya* in the eyes of Soviet officials, and to unmask the Yevseks' violations of the law to their superiors. "The Soviet authorities are unhappy with the actions being taken [by the *Yevsektsiya*] against religion, and they certainly aren't happy that as a result, the view has spread that they persecute religion." Eliminating the influence of the *Yevsektsiya* would, he believed, be a major step toward ensuring the treatment of Judaism in accordance with the law.[35]

Economic Program

In his capacity as chairman of the Committee of Rabbis, Schneerson also attempted to address the devastating economic crisis which engulfed Soviet Jews during those years. His efforts in this area were fueled by his self-conception as a Hasidic Rebbe, who considered himself responsible for both the spiritual and material well-being of his followers and of religious Jews at large. In the Soviet context, the spiritual and material realms were inseparable, since it was becoming increasingly

---

34 *Toldot Habad*, 108f.

35 *Ibid.*; letter to Vladimir Haffkin, March 1928, *Igrot*, 2:37f.; similarly, letter to Cyrus Adler, January 28, 1928, JDC Archives file #475. Schneerson had no qualms, however, about defying or ignoring the requirements of Soviet law when it was necessary. The yeshivas funded by the Committee of Rabbis were not registered with the authorities, as required by law, and operated in an illegal, clandestine manner. So long as the Yevseks were engaged in the illegal persecution of Jewish religious life, it would be foolhardy, to try to conduct all activities on a public and legal basis. A combination of open and clandestine, legal and illegal, modes of activity was required.

difficult to find legal employment which would allow for observance of the Sabbath.[36]

In his discussions and correspondence with leaders of the JDC, Schneerson advanced his own economic program for Soviet Jewry: massive retraining of Jews in the handicrafts, so that they could register as *kustari*, self-employed artisans. He repeatedly urged the relief agency to pour its resources into the establishment of craft schools and the shipment of light machinery to the USSR.[37]

Schneerson articulated his position most fully in a memorandum to the JDC in 1928 (i.e., after his departure from the USSR). Soviet Jews, he contended, could enter one of three branches of the Soviet economy: the state bureaucracy, agriculture, or the handicrafts. The third option, the handicrafts, was to his mind the most desirable.

In the state bureaucracy, he argued, work on Saturdays was unavoidable, and Sabbath rest was impossible. Communist party cells waged intense antireligious agitation in the state bureaus, and employees who so much as visited a synagogue risked being dismissed from their jobs. The chances that Jews employed in the bureaucracy would maintain any bonds with Judaism were therefore slim. Indeed, the mingling of young Jews and Gentiles in the workplace led frequently to intermarriage.[38]

---

36 Schneerson received scores of *kvitlekh* from Jews pleading that the Almighty save them from starvation and deprivation. Extracts are cited in *Igrot*, 1:476. One concludes: "O Lord, please save me; do not lead me to a test in which, God forbid, God forbid, I will have to desecrate that which is holy to the people of the God of Abraham."

37 Letters to the JDC leadership, and to the Union of Habad Hasidim in America, June 1925, *Igrot*, 1:472–78; letters to Yekutiel Kremer, New York, and the Agudas ha-Rabonim of America, October 1925, *Igrot*, 1:494–98; letters to M. Warburg, Louis Marshal, James Rosenberg (all leaders of the JDC), May 1926, *Igrot*, 1:520–28; letter by Shlomo Yosef Zevin, secretary of the Committee of Rabbis, to the JDC leadership, May 1926, JDC archives file #475; letter to V. Haffkin of the Alliance, April 1928, *Igrot*, 2:32-36.

38 "About the Handicraft and the Russian Judaism" (in broken English), JDC archives, USSR file #475. On the latter point, Schneerson cited no less an authority than Mikhail Kalinin, the nominal President of the USSR, who stated in his speech to the 1926 convention of the Society for the Settlement of Jewish Toilers on Land (Gezerd): "If I were an old rabbi who is grieved by the disappearance of the Jewish nationality, I would curse all the Jews who go to Moscow to assume Soviet positions, since the latter are lost to the Jewish nationality. In Moscow, these Jews mix their blood with Russian blood, and in the second or at most third generation, they are lost to the Jewish nationality." M. Altshuler, *Ha-Yevseqṣsia*, 201; cited in faulty English in Schneerson's memo, p. 2.

As for the Jewish agricultural colonies, which were then the rave among Soviet-Jewish social engineers (including officials at the JDC), Schneerson viewed the entire enterprise with skepticism and unease. He felt that Jews were generally unsuited for agricultural labor, that few of them would be attracted to the colonies, and that far too many resources were being devoted to an enterprise which was at best only a partial solution to the economic crisis of Soviet Jewry. The agrarianization effort risked aggravating the impoverishment of thousands of Soviet Jews, who would liquidate their possessions in order to resettle in the remote colonies, only to fail in their new callings and be left penniless. Meanwhile, he argued, the agricultural experiment was provoking anti-Semitism among the Russian peasantry, which saw the Jews as "stealing their land."[39]

But most of all, Schneerson was concerned about the consequences of agrarian resettlement for Jewish religious life. Jews were being relocated in colonies under Communist control or influence, where traditional Judaism (e.g., the Sabbath and kashruth) could often not be observed. He warned that the *Yevsektsiya* used the colonies as vehicles for the secularization and communization of Soviet Jews. He demanded that the Joint Distribution Committee ensure the establishment of religious facilities in the colonies, and he committed some of the resources of the Committee of Rabbis to work in the colonies (sending emissaries, placing professionals, allocating funds). But in the final analysis, Schneerson considered the colonization effort harmful to the preservation of Judaism in the Soviet Union. It was difficult enough trying to preserve existing institutions and patterns of life in the heartland of the old Pale of Settlement; transplanting Jewish religious life to new settlements under Communist sponsorship involved even greater hardships.[40]

Handicrafts, Schneerson argued, presented none of these problems or negative consequences. Jews were well adapted to work in the crafts and did not need to relocate anywhere in order to engage in them. The cost of providing training and machinery was much smaller in the crafts than in agriculture, and the return on one's investment was much quicker. The Soviet authorities were committed to restratifying the Jews into productive branches of labor, but they did not have a strong preference between agriculture and the handicrafts. (Only the *Yevsektsiya* pressed the authorities to undertake agricultural resettlement, in order to further its own

---

39 Schneerson, "About the Handicraft," 2. Schneerson noted that the prominence of Jews in the state bureaucracy also generated anti-Semitic resentment. (ibid., 1).

40 Ibid., 4.

goals, according to Schneerson.) And Jewish activity in the handicrafts would not elicit popular resentment and anti-Semitism.

Schneerson's fundamental reason for advocating the handicrafts was its compatibility with preserving the traditional religious way of life. Only as self-employed, home-based *kustari* would religious Jews be able to set their own work schedules and observe the Sabbath, "the axis of the religious Jewish life." The development of cottage industries, in which family members worked together, would strengthen family cohesiveness and intergenerational continuity. "The son and the daughter [will] not want to go to the Comsomol, where they get lost [to] Judaism."[41]

Massive retraining of Jews in the handicrafts would rescue the small-town community of the *shtetl* from economic demise. The *shtetl*, rather than the city or colony, was the milieu in which Jewish religious life could remain intact; where "the *Beys HaMedresh* continues to be the center of the Jewish life, and will dart its beams in[to] the working room."[42]

Based on this socio-economic analysis, Schneerson established a committee for handicraft affairs under the auspices of the Committee of Rabbis. It procured and distributed light machinery to Orthodox Jewish families and helped register *artels* or groups of observant artisans. He actively encouraged Hasidim and religious Jews to learn a craft, so that they and their children could remain Sabbath observers. But due to the fact that the JDC did not fully embrace Schneerson's economic proposals, and considered agrarianization its foremost priority, the scope of the Committee's activity in this area remained relatively modest.[43]

The Committee of Rabbis' spheres of activity were by no means ad hoc improvisations. They represented Schneerson's integrated strategy for the survival of Jewish religious life in the Soviet Union. He was convinced that the combination of tightly knit underground organization and centralized leadership, significant funding from abroad and supervised disbursement, support for legally constituted synagogues and underground illegal yeshivas, political lobbying and legal defense, training in the handicrafts and self-employment as *kustari*, was the formula for the continued viability of traditional Judaism in the USSR. Upon reviewing the Committee of Rabbis' activities shortly after his

---

41 Ibid., 3f. See also the letters to the JDC cited in note 37.

42 Schneerson, "About the Handicraft," 3f.

43 Ibid., 4; and *Igrot*, 1:658; Levin, *Toldot Habad*, 73 reproduces a questionnaire to all *Temimim* asking them whether they would like to be trained in handicrafts.

departure from the USSR, Schneerson concluded that this formula had proven itself successful in the five years of the Committee's existence and that the prospects for Jewish religious life were considerably better in 1927 than they had been in 1922.[44]

Centrifugal Forces

Many of the communities and institutions affiliated with the Committee of Rabbis were headed by Lubavitch *temimim*. The latter served as melamdim, *rashei yeshivot, shoḥṭim*, cantors/*ba'alei koreh, mohalim*, and rabbis in dozens of locales where the indigenous religious leadership had collapsed. The *temimim* were at the vanguard of the struggle to maintain Jewish religious life. Schneerson therefore adamantly opposed their emigration to America or the Land of Israel during the 1920s, when possibilities for leaving still existed. The departure of the *temimim* would leave Soviet Jewish communities bereft of spiritual leadership. He demanded that they make the same existential choice he had made: to stay and fight.

In 1923, Schneerson's regional lieutenant in Georgia, Rabbi Nehemia Sasonkin, reported that there was an opportunity to arrange the emigration of groups of five hundred via the city of Batum, near the Turkish border. He urged the Rebbe to take advantage of the situation and organize the departure en masse of Lubavitch from the country. "I stressed that we would not be able to stay very long in this land in any case," writes Sasonkin. "The day will come when we will have to leave. And who knows if we will be able to do so then. We should exploit this opportunity as long as the border is open." Schneerson firmly rejected the plan: "If the goal is [to build] over there, we already have enough people over there. May they be active and productive. The most important thing is that this place not be abandoned."[45]

The question "to leave or not to leave" aroused turmoil and controversy in the ranks of the *temimim* in the mid-1920s. At a conference of Agudat ha-Temimim in September 1924 (immediately after Rosh Hashanah 5685), a resolution in favor of organized departure from the USSR was passed by majority vote. One member, who subsequently left for the United States, recalls that intense debates continued in the

---

[44] This is the assessment in Schneerson's historical overview of his activities in the Soviet Union, written shortly after his arrival in Riga (*Igrot*, 1:616–37).

[45] Gershuni, *Yehudim ve-yahadut*, 116; Levin, *Toldot Habad*, 339.

ensuing months, even among the group of friends that accompanied him to the train-station:

> "My brother-in-law said to me, 'You're running away. The Rebbe is here, all our Hasidim are here. What are you running for?' But Reb Zalmen Hasdan said to me, 'We're all at the same train-station. We should all leave.'"[46]

In response to the emigration fever which swept through the ranks of the *temimim*, Schneerson vigorously reasserted his position. In the summer of 1925, he issued what became known as his definitive statement on emigration. An anguished Lubavitch emissary had written to him requesting permission to leave for the land of Israel. From the reply, one can reconstruct the emissary's plea: The difficulties in observing Judaism in Russia were overwhelming. His own children were leaving the path of God. Schneerson responded with rebuke and indignation:

> We must understand that we did not come to this land by chance, and not by chance have we encountered the bitterness of exile, darkness and hardship. It is the will of God, blessed be He. He demands of us that we light up the darkness of this land with the light of Torah and worship. . . . The time has come for every one of us to understand this, and not look hither and thither in search of other places. . . . The time has come for us to understand that we have been given a mission in life, the mission of aiding our brethren [here in this land]. . . .
>
> I say to you explicitly: You must stop thinking thoughts about leaving. Instead you should concentrate on the mission with which you are charged—to assist our brethren and strengthen the study of Torah. . . . When I think of those Hasidim who do not pay attention to their mission and obligation, and exaggerate the degree of obstacles and hindrances, my soul becomes stormy and burns like fire. I cry on account of them, and the many losses that they have inflicted on our people by their lack of activity. . . .
>
> The burning question today is, 'What will become of the Torah?' Why then is everyone turning to his own little corner, concerned only with his personal affairs, and thinking day and night about himself—about where it will be better for him, in the Land of Israel or in the United States? . . . Why doesn't he

46 Levin, *Toldot Habad*, 341f.

> consider or take to heart that he, only he, is to blame for the situation from which he is fleeing?[47]

Schneerson reiterated the advice that his great-grandfather had given to a Hasid who had asked to leave for Palestine in the 1850s: "men darf makhn do Eretz Yisroel. Makh do Eretz Yisroel!" (We should make this the Land of Israel. Create a Land of Israel here!)

Most of the *temimim* loyally obeyed their Rebbe's directive. The network of *temimim* remained intact throughout the 1920s and did not suffer significant attrition due to emigration.[48]

Schneerson faced an equally difficult challenge in holding together the members of the Committee of Rabbis. His leadership aroused resentment and suspicion among some of his colleagues, who believed that he was exploiting his position on the Committee to advance the parochial interests of Lubavitch Hasidism. In 1925, these critics lodged complaints with the Moscow and New York offices of the Joint Distribution Committee. In Schneerson's own words:

> I was shocked to hear from Dr. Rosen that due to the many letters he had received . . . claiming that all of my work has been on a partisan basis, for Hasidim—and Habad Hasidim in particular—his promise to provide me with funds for artisans was null and void, and he would also not increase the funds for Torah. . . . At that time I also received information from the bureau in New York that many letters were arriving . . . stating that they were dissatisfied with my activity, which

---

47 *Igrot*, 1:485–89. Schneerson's letter circulated widely among his followers in Russia and was considered his authoritative word (*Toldot Habad*, 344). For a similar (undated) letter, see *Igrot*, 10:418–20.

48 Schneerson's negative attitute toward emigration changed in 1930—three years after his own forced resettlement in Riga, Latvia—when Stalinist terror was unleashed against rabbis and religious functionaries. But by then the difficulties connected with leaving the USSR were formidable and larger scale emigration was impossible. See the materials in Levin, *Toldot Habad*, 345–62. When Rabbi Zevin arrived in Palestine in 1934, he wrote a detailed proposal to Schneerson advocating the use of diplomatic channels to obtain a large number of Soviet exit visas for religious Jews. Knowing Schneerson's earlier opposition to emigration, he approached the topic cautiously and requested Schneerson's assistance "if your holiness agrees to the idea in general, as a matter of principle" (ibid., 359f.). Schneerson agreed and engaged in diplomatic efforts, but without success.

> contradicted decisions adopted at the meeting [of the Committee of Rabbis].[49]

The suspicion and resentment were not totally misplaced. Schneerson did not separate clearly between his roles as Lubavitcher Rebbe and chairman of the Committee of Rabbis. The organizational structures of Lubavitch and the Committee overlapped considerably. The staff of the Merkaz and the roving emissaries in the field were *temimim,* for whom Judaism and Lubavitch Hasidism were difficult to separate. Schneerson's personal control over the disbursement of funds left considerable room for favoritism toward Lubavitch *melamdim,* synagogues, yeshivas, and so on. His position as chairman and his control of the Committee's purse strings strengthened his religious influence and prestige. Mitnaggedic yeshivas came to him (a Hasidic Rebbe!) to request, and sometimes to plead, that they be included in the list of institutions receiving monthly allocations. In some instances, they reportedly felt compelled to profess their admiration of Lubavitch Hasidism, to deprecate the Mitnaggedic traditions of Talmudism and Musar, and even offered to study Hasidism, in order to find favor in his eyes.[50]

The charges of partisanship lodged by Schneerson's critics led to a decision by the JDC in 1925 to disburse half of its annual allocation for Jewish religious activity outside the framework of the Committee of Rabbis. As a result of the division within rabbinic ranks, the Committee of Rabbis failed to become the umbrella agency for all of Jewish religious life in the USSR which Schneerson had envisioned.[51]

---

49 *Igrot,* 1:620. The ellipsis dots within the quotation are found in the published Hebrew version of the letter and indicate passages which have been censored by the editors. The letters of complaint refered to by Schneerson have not been preserved in the archives of the Joint Distribution Committee and its constituent orthodox organization, the Central Relief Committee.

50 See *Igrot,* 2:101–03 concerning the fawning requests of the Minsk and Slutsk yeshivas for aid.

51 *Igrot,* 1:621. A JDC budget for fiscal 1926 indicates that the JDC allocated $43,157.11 for religious purposes in the Soviet Union (JDC archives, USSR file #472). Schneerson reports receiving $24,000 that year (*Igrot,* 1:624).

The identity of Schneerson's critics and opponents who brought this issue to a head can only be surmised, since his published letters have been censored to omit their names. One of them was apparently Rabbi Menahem Gluskin of Minsk. Rabbi Gluskin attempted to establish a separate, direct relationship between his own Union of Congregants of Synagogues and Prayer Houses in Minsk and the JDC. In a letter to the JDC in early 1926, in which he requested $1,000 per month for the religious needs of Minsk Jewry, Gluskin noted that the religious institutions of his community received no funding from sources within the USSR, a not-so-subtle reference to the

Competing Structure

A serious attempt to create a rival leadership structure for Jewish religious life in the USSR was made by the elders of the Leningrad synagogue between 1925 and 1927. They proposed convening a General Assembly of Jewish religious communities in order to discuss the problems facing them, set a common agenda for the future, and elect a leadership. Their proposal was supported by the respected chief rabbi of Leningrad, R. David-Tevl Katzenellenbogen.

The Leningrad elders made preliminary approaches to the local authorities and were confident that they could obtain legal authorization to hold such a conference of communities in their city. The synagogue's chairman, Gurevich, and a number of emissaries toured Jewish communities in the winter of 1925-1926 to propagate the idea of the Religious Assembly, and the proposal was endorsed by the leaders of Odessa and other Ukrainian Jewish communities.[52]

The initiators tried to enlist Schneerson's support early on, but he was adamantly opposed to the idea. He convened a special meeting of the Committee of Rabbis, attended by rabbis from eighteen communities, to discuss the issue and warned them that "the Assembly is impure. . . . Its initiators wish to cause a breach in Israel. . . . Evil lurks in this idea; may God save us from them and their multitudes." When Leningrad

---

Committee of Rabbis. Whether Gluskin refused to join the Committee of Rabbis, seceded from it, or was denied financial support by it remains unclear. The conflict between them was apparently resolved by the late summer of 1926, when Gluskin was appointed to the leadership council of the Committee of Rabbis. See Gluskin's letters to the leaders and rabbis of World Jewry, 24th of Nisan 5686, and to James Rosenberg and Bernard Kahn of the JDC (during their visit to the USSR), 1st of Sivan 5686; Central Relief Committee collection, Yeshiva University Archives, 117/21; Levin, *Toldot Habad,* 18.

The religious community of Leningrad was probably one of the complaintants as well. Leningrad had no representation on the Committee of Rabbis, and its leaders reportedly resented their exclusion from meetings of the Committee, as well as the close ties between Schneerson and the JDC. (*Igrot,* 1:636). On the conflict between Schneerson and the Leningrad community over the leadership of religious life, see below. Schneerson took the attack on his leadership before the JDC seriously enough to organize a letter campaign in his own defense. The rabbis of 28 communities submitted letters to the JDC in early 1926 supporting Schneerson's leadership and the policies he pursued; Central Relief Committee Collection, Yeshiva University Archives, 117/21.

[52] See the report on this entire affair, written from a Lubavitch perspective by R. Elijah Althoyz, in *Toldot Habad,* 78-85. On support for the convention from Odessa and elsewhere, see *Igrot,* 1:610f., 628.

launched its campaign to enlist the support of fellow communities, Schneerson countered with a circular letter in which he denounced the Assembly idea as harmful to the interests of Judaism in the USSR. A rift developed in numerous communities between supporters and opponents of the Assembly.[53]

According to his own testimony and that of his intimates, Schneerson's opposition was immediate and instinctual. The proposed General Assembly conflicted with his fundamental ideas about the conduct of communal affairs, about religious leadership, and Judaism itself—as well as with his personal and organizational interests.

On the simplest level, his opposition was tactical. Schneerson did not believe that public conferences were a desirable forum, given the prevalence of surveillance, infiltration, and informing in Soviet society. Discussions could not be free and candid in a setting where government agents and informers were probably present. Indeed, Schneerson worried that careless statements made from the rostrum could be manipulated and exploited by the *Yevsektsiya* to justify increased persecution of religious institutions. He believed that consultations on religious affairs should be held secretly and behind closed doors (as was the practice of the Committee of Rabbis).[54]

On a more substantive level, Schneerson's opposition revolved around the question of leadership. He realized that a General Assembly of religious communities would be dominated by laymen, and that rabbis would constitute only a minority of the delegates and would not be able to control the decision-making process. The Assembly was, he believed, an assault on the supremacy of rabbinic leadership in communal and religious affairs. He asserted that only the great rabbis of the generation had the authority to convene a General Assembly, "and they alone have the absolute authoritative opinion in matters facing Jewry and Judaism."[55]

---

53 *Toldot Habad*, 78-80, 83f.; *Igrot*, 1:622; see Schneerson's letters of condemnation, ibid., 499-501 (December 1925), 596–98 (May 1927).

54 Althoyz's report, *Toldot Habad*, 79f.; *Igrot*, 1:609, 622, 628. Schneerson therefore initially opposed Rabbi Shmuel Kipnis's plan to hold a public regional conference of rabbis in the Volhynian town of Korosten (*Igrot*, 1:628f.). He subsequently reversed his position on the rabbinic conference and worked to insure that his followers and supporters would be heavily represented among the delegates and guests, and on the presidium and program (*Toldot Habad*, 87-96).

55 *Igrot*, 1:596f. Schneerson could therefore reconcile himself more easily to the rabbinic conference in Korosten, which affirmed the principle of rabbinic leadership.

Schneerson's Committee of Rabbis was based on this model of exclusive rabbinic leadership. Rabbis, and not lay leaders, set its policies and supervised its allocation of funds. The Assembly constituted an organizational threat to the Committee itself. The Joint Distribution Committee followed the developments surrounding the Assembly with interest and may have considered it a positive vehicle for unifying Jewish religious life in the Soviet Union. This must have aroused Schneerson's apprehension, since the Assembly, if convened, would have emerged as a rival funding agency for Jewish religious affairs.[56]

The clash between Schneerson and the sponsors of the Assembly was fueled by ideological differences as well. Most of the elders of the Leningrad choral synagogue were veteran *Maskilim* and Zionists, remnants of the Russian-Jewish intelligentsia which had flourished in St. Petersburg prior to the revolution.[57] Their chairman, Gurevich, had been a member of Ḥevrat Mefiṣe Haskalah (Society for the Dissemination of Enlightenment among the Jews in Russia) and a devoted Zionist. He was joined by Leon Rabinovitch, the former editor of *Ha-Meliṣ* and himself a well-known Zionist publicist. In Schneerson's mind, such men had no right to be leaders in Jewish religious affairs. "The organizers of the 'General Religious Assembly' are a group of people, many of whom have had nothing to do with Torah and *miṣvot* for years. Who is not terrified and alarmed upon hearing this?"[58]

Schneerson viewed the Assembly as a veiled attempt by secularists to take control of Jewish religious life. For him, the struggle against the Assembly was a continuation of the *Kulturkampf* between Orthodoxy and

---

56 The following is an excerpt from the protocol of a meeting of the Committee of Rabbis in May 1927: "Mr. Warburg [chairman of the JDC, then in Moscow] expressed his dissatisfaction that the Orthodox were not united. He meant that they were not united with the intelligentsia and communal activists who were the sponsors of the proposed Leningrad conference. . . . The chairman . . . expressed his absolute opposition to the Assembly of Communities proposed by the Leningrad community, for reasons which he explained."

After Warburg left the meeting, the Committee passed the following resolution: "The Committee expresses its full agreement with the chairman's statement. The members of the Committee reiterate that the Orthodox are united, and that there are no disagreements in the Orthodox camp. There are likewise no disagreements among the members of the Committee of Rabbis, which is the representative of all the different Orthodox parties in our land" ("Protokol Yeshivat Va'ad Ha-Rabanim," 20th of Iyyar 5687, 2).

57 On the latter, see Mikhail Beizer, *The Jews of St. Petersburg: Excursions Through a Noble Past* (Philadelphia: Jewish Publication Society, 1989).

58 *Toldot Habad*, 78-80, 82; *Igrot*, 1:597.

secular Zionists at the turn of the century. He believed that Gurevitch was plotting with his fellow secularists to pack the Assembly with "enlightened" delegates who would ram through all sorts of religious reforms, including a modern rabbinical seminary and changes in the liturgy. "Every good proposal to strengthen religion will be rejected, and every proposal endangering religion will be embraced with enthusiasm."[59]

Some of Schneerson's colleagues on the Committee of Rabbis were initially open to the idea of a democratically elected Assembly of Religious Communities and advocated organizing a vigorous campaign to ensure the election of rabbis and truly pious laymen as delegates. With proper Orthodox and rabbinic representation, the Assembly could be a positive forum for advancing Jewish religious life in the USSR. Schneerson, however, adamantly opposed any arrangement which would legitimize power-sharing between rabbis and moderns. In this respect, he continued the separatist communal politics of his father, who had rejected cooperation with Zionists in any and all affairs.[60]

Despite concerted efforts by its sponsors, the Assembly of Religious Communities was never convened. It remains unclear whether this was due to obstruction by Schneerson, the Soviet authorities, or a combination of both. As a result, the challenge to the Committee of Rabbis' primacy as umbrella agency for Jewish religious life did not come to fruition.[61]

---

59 *Toldot Habad*, 80, 83; *Igrot*, 1:609 (written from Riga).

60 *Igrot*, 1:622; for R. Sholem Duber Schneerson's principled separatism, see *Or layesharim*, ed. Shlomo Zalman Landa and Yosef Rabinovitz (Warsaw: Helter, 1900), 57-61, as well as the remarks cited by R. Joseph Isaac himself in *Igrot*, 1:610f. The members of the Committee of Rabbis subsequently endorsed Schneerson's total rejection of the Assembly; see note 59.

61 There are intimations in Lubavitch literature that the propagators of the Assembly helped bring about Schneerson's arrest in June 1927. Rabbi Katzennelenbogen allegedly warned one of Schneerson's representatives that there were "big *shkotzim*" among the elders of his community, and that Schneerson's activity in opposition to the Assembly put him in grave danger (*Igrot*, 1:636). Schneerson was arrested shortly after issuing his second circular letter against the Assembly. Officials at the JDC also seem to have believed that denunciations from "the Zionists" precipitated Schneerson's arrest; letter from Bernard Kahn to Joseph Hyman, June 22, 1927, JDC archives, USSR file #476.

Decline and Demise

The structures and strategies created by the Committee of Rabbis worked reasonably well until the end of the 1920s. The Committee was able to sustain a network of institutions and communities which, much to the chagrin of the *Yevsektsiya*, could withstand persecution and arrests.

Schneerson himself was arrested by the security police in May 1927 due to his leadership of underground religious activities. He was detained and interrogated in Leningrad's Shpaliarka prison and sentenced to three years' exile in the remote city of Castrama. Thanks to diplomatic interventions from various governments, he was released from Castrama twenty-nine days after his arrest. It soon became evident, however, that the Leningrad security police was intent upon rearresting Schneerson and giving him the punishment he "deserved." He therefore felt compelled to leave the country. After further diplomatic representations, Schneerson was permitted to emigrate, and he left for Riga, Latvia, in October.[62]

Schneerson's departure deprived the Committee of its charismatic and inspirational leader but did not lead to a breakdown of its operations. Schneerson was appointed chairman-in-exile and reestablished the Committee's central office in his new residence in Riga, Latvia. From there he conducted extensive correspondence with Soviet Jewish communities, maintained detailed records on religious life inside the USSR, submitted reports and budgets on behalf of the Committee to the JDC, and raised funds from a variety of sources. He arranged for the illegal transfer of funds to the leadership inside the USSR at an extremely advantageous exchange rate. At first, the JDC even disbursed its funds for the Committee of Rabbis via Schneerson in Riga, but it soon decided to dissociate itself from the latter's illegal financial transactions and issued the funds through its Moscow office.[63]

---

62 There are numerous legends surrounding Schneerson's arrest, interrogation, and brief exile in Castrama. See the account of Avraham Hanokh Glitzenshtein, *Sefer ha-toldot, Rav Yosef Yitshak Schneerson mi-Liubavitch* (New York: Otzar Hahasidim, 1976), 3:103-236.

63 "Protokol shel Yeshivat ha-Va'ad le-Hizuk ha-Torah ve-ha-dat bi-Rusiyah," *Toldot Habad*, 108–11. See the extensive materials kept by Schneerson in Riga on the state of *Ḥadarim, miqvaot*, and antireligious persecution in the USSR, ibid. 36-41, 159–65, 171–86. JDC correspondence on how to administer its Soviet religious account in the aftermath of Schneerson's emigration is contained in the JDC archives, USSR file #475.

The Committee's leadership council inside the Soviet Union consisted of Rabbis Jacob Klemes (of Moscow), Menahem Mendl Gluskin (of Minsk), Eliya Aaron Mileikovsky (of Kharkov), and Shmuel Levitan (listed as representing Kutaisi, Georgia). Shlomo Yosef Zevin continued to serve as secretary. Klemes and Zevin played the central roles; the former maintained contact with the JDC's Rosen in Moscow and controlled most of the Committee's funds, while the latter corresponded with Schneerson in Riga and with communities in the field.[64]

The Committee suffered its first major setbacks in the winter of 1928-1929, when the Bet Midrash le-Rabanim ve-Shoḥṭim in Nevel was discovered and closed down by the authorities, as were two of the largest Lubavitch Tomḥei Temimim yeshivas (in Nevel and Polotsk). R. Shmuel Levitan—the director of the Bet Midrash, a member of the Committee of Rabbis' leadership council, and by many accounts an inspiring religious personality—was arrested, and spent the next three and a half years in prison and Siberian exile.[65]

But the Committee seemed to take these losses in stride. A report on its activities written in early 1929 struck a heroic and confident tone:

> The attacks that are made on the *Yeshivoth*, no matter how hard they are, have not broken the spirit and energy of the *Yeshivoth* students and their deans. Although ten were imprisoned this year as a result of this, the *Yeshivoth* are not destroyed. When the *Yevsrektsia* starts oppressing a *Yeshivah*, the *Yeshiva* moves unto another city, and breaks up into several divisions, and continues studies. With the destruction of the Nevel *Yeshiva*, of which remained only a small number of disciples, the boys have gone to other cities and are studying in groups of fifteen or ten."[66]

---

64 *Toldot Habad*, 111; letter from Committee of Rabbis to JDC, May 1928, JDC archives, USSR file #475; letter from Committee of Rabbis to Agudas ha-Rabonim of America, June 1929, *Toldot Habad*, 125f. Levitan was head of the Bet Midrash le-Rabanim ve-Shoḥṭim in Nevel but was listed as being from Kutaisi, Georgia, where he had spent several years as an emissary; see note 12. Mileikovsky emigrated to Palestine in December 1928; see *Igrot*, 2:164f.

65 *Toldot Habad*, 268–71, 274–76. Rosen, who was not a religious man, considered Levitan the most inspiring religious figure he had met in Russia and noted in a letter to Cyrus Adler that "the Divine light radiates from his face" (JDC archives, USSR file #477).

66 "Report on the Accomplishments of the Rabbinical Board in Russia during 5688," JDC archives, USSR file #476, p. 12.

A letter in May 1929 signed by Klemes, Zevin, and a hundred lesser-known rabbis and "active workers in Orthodox Jewry" still spoke of pursuing the Committee's established agenda and mode of operation:

> In spite of all the hardships lying in the path of the sacred work of spreading the word of the Torah, there exist in many of the Jewish cities and towns *Yeshivoth,* and groups in which Jewish youths are devoting themselves with miraculous self-sacrifice for the study of Torah. . . .
>
> The spreading of Torah requires regular assistance on a large scale; the *Mikvoth* and bath-houses in many communities are in ruins because of the lack of funds for their rebuilding and repair: hundreds of rabbis are starving and a definite aid from without is necessary for them; material aid is also necessary, in one form or another, for all those who want to live by the labor of their hands, so that they might be able to observe the Sabbath and holydays. . . . We are unable to accomplish anything without the assistance of our brethren abroad. . . . Intervene on behalf of our institutions so that the Remnant of Israel in Russia may not perish in spiritual oppression.[67]

The situation deteriorated dramatically in the early months of 1930, when an unprecedented government campaign was lauched against religious functionaries. Numerous communal rabbis, who had previously been recognized as legal workers, were now branded as *lishentsi* —individuals stripped of their civil rights. They were expelled from their apartments, which were confiscated by the state, and could not find legal housing. They were denied ration coupons for food, and medical treatment in public facilities. Their children were not admitted to institutes of higher learning and could not find employment. Finally, rabbis were levied with exorbitant taxes, which forced them to either sell off all their belongings to pay the tax, or face arrest and deportation for tax evasion.[68]

A large number of rabbis resigned from their posts, and announced their resignations publicly, in the local press, in exchange for which they were freed from the exorbitant taxes (but not from the other disabilities). Many more left their communities for distant locales where they would not be recognized and could attempt to evade the legal status of *lishentsi.*

---

67 "An Open Statement," dated Iyyar 5689, JDC archives, USSR file #476.

68 *Toldot Habad*, 200f.; "He'etek ha-mikhtav me-Rusiya she-nitkabel bi-yom shabat kodesh be-shanah 5690," JDC archives, USSR file #477; "Ha'im tamnu ligvo'a?" (anonymous undated declaration), JDC archives, USSR file #477. Some rabbis could only find refuge in the *ezrat nashim* of the synagogue; see for example, R. Moshe Khaskin (of Priluki, Ukraine), *Qalqalat shviʿit*, (Jerusalem: Raphael Hayyim Hakohane Press, 1938), introduction, p. 9.

According to an anonymous letter sent by a group of rabbis to Vilna, the exile and wanderings of rabbis reached startling proportions.

> In the Vitebsk region, not a single rabbi is to be found in his city. They have all left for places where they are not recognized, lest they be destroyed or prosecuted on account of the taxes. Thus, almost all the men of Torah have gone into exile, and their lips rustle with the question, 'Are we doomed to perish?' (Num. 17:28).[69]

The Committee of Rabbis' network of religious communities was in disarray, and its network of educational institutions was crumbling.[70]

A number of prominent rabbis were arrested, including R. Shimon Lazarov, the Hasidic rabbi of Leningrad, who had meticulously avoided any association with the Committee of Rabbis' underground yeshivas and activities. (Lazarov died in Siberian exile.) In Minsk, fourteen rabbis, preachers, and elders of the religious community were arrested, including Chief Rabbi Menahem Gluskin. The local underground yeshiva (the last major Mitnaggedic yeshiva in the USSR), headed by R. David Tsimbalist, was liquidated.[71]

The arrests in Minsk had a chilling effect on the activities of the Committee of Rabbis. The group of fourteen was charged with engaging in counterrevolutionary activity, an offense punishable by death. The charges were based on the discovery by the secret police of "correspondence with Jewish associations abroad . . . a hectograph machine, and other documents proving that the community had engaged in counterrevolutionary activity, by transferring information to those [foreign] associations." Since Gluskin was a member of the Committee of Rabbis' leadership council, these materials must have included Committee documents, including reports and appeals to the JDC. Rosen in Moscow immediately stopped disbursing funds for religious cultural work. He expressed fears that the recipients of such funds would be placed in grave danger, and he must also have worried that continued JDC financing of illegal religious activities would jeopardize the agency's

---

69 "He'etek ha-mikhtav"; on resignations, see "Ha'im tamnu ligvo'a" and Gershuni, *Yahadut*, 71-73.

70 The remaining yeshivas of Kremenchug, Kharkov, and Vitebsk were then discovered by the authorities, or their students scattered to avoid detection in 1930; *Toldot Habad*, 240, 263, 278f.

71 *Toldot Habad*, 88, 166; "He'etek ha-mikhtav;" Meir Hildesheimer, "The affair of the Minsk Rabbis and the Arrest of R. Yehezkel Abramsky" (in Hebrew), *Ha-Ma'ayan* 17/2 (1977) 4-12.

operations in the USSR, especially now that it had been implicated in Minsk.[72] Correspondence from the Committee of Rabbis to the West was discontinued in the aftermath of the Minsk affair, and the organization apparently ceased to exist.[73]

Two other components of Schneerson's strategic plan for the survival of Judaism were swept away by the events of 1930. The first was his trust in Soviet legality and governance, his belief that antireligious persecution was caused by the *Yevsektsiya* and not by the state, and his effort to drive a wedge between the central authorities and the Jewish sections of the CPSU. In 1930, it became painfully evident that antireligious persecution emanated from the state and not from renegade Jewish Communists. The *Yesvektsiya* itself was liquidated in January, as a vestige of nationalist separatism within the Party, and Jewish affairs came under the authority of general party organs. Schneerson had hoped and labored for this very event, believing that it would result in the improved treatment of the Jewish religion. But shortly thereafter came the most brutal campaign against Jewish religious functionaries and institutions in Soviet history, waged by the state secret police, the GPU. The campaign was clearly the product of a policy decision made in the highest quarters and could not be attributed to renegade Communist Jews.[74]

The second strategy to be defeated was Schneerson's plan to preserve Sabbath observance through retraining Jews in the crafts and registering them as self-employed *kustari*. Beginning in 1929, the *kustari* were forced to work in state-managed cooperatives or face being declared *lishentsi*. Self-employment was effectively outlawed. Cooperatives were then forcibly merged with each other and "internationalized," to ensure that Jewish and gentile artisans worked together. Work on Saturdays was

---

72 Hildesheimer, "Affair," 4; correspondence between Rosen, Adler, and Joseph Hyman, JDC archives, USSR file #477. Extensive coverage by the Western press and interventions by American political figures and German diplomats led to the release of the Minsk fourteen after two weeks in detention. They were never tried or sentenced. The rabbis in the group were forced to sign a statement denying the existence of antireligious persecution in the Soviet Union and protesting the anti-Soviet propaganda being spread by Western Jewish organizations.

73 No communications from the Committee of Rabbis or its collective leaders exists after 1930. Zevin continued to funnel some aid from Schneerson to rabbis in the early 1930s; see note 77.

74 On the liquidation of the *Yevsektsiya*, see Gitelman, *Jewish Nationality and Soviet Politics* 472-481.

unavoidable in the internationalized cooperatives, and Sabbath observance became virtually impossible.[75]

Meanwhile, the shocking events of early 1930 caused the linchpin of Schneerson's entire structure—Jewish financial support from the West—to collapse. JDC officials became convinced that the condition of the Jewish religion in the Soviet Union was hopeless. "What was legal is no longer permitted. Rabbis and teachers go around in constant danger of arrest, and have given up most of their religious activity," Adler wrote to Schneerson. The allocation of funds for religious purposes would only endanger the lives of those involved, and could, in fact, have disastrous consequences for Soviet Jewry at large. In the wake of the stock market crash of November 1929 and the deepening Depression, the JDC's income declined, while the demands made on it by Jewish cultural institutions in Europe grew. The JDC could not afford to expend scarce resources on an exercise in futility which would probably cause more harm than good. The agency decided to redirect its Soviet "cultural" funds toward helping extricate rabbis from the Soviet Union, by paying for their exit visas and steamship tickets.[76]

Schneerson's financial support was reduced to the level of providing charity for individuals. The Committee of Rabbis was defunct, and Jewish religious institutions—synagogues, *ḥadarim*, *miqvaot*, and yeshivas—were either closed or rapidly disappearing. Schneerson's focus was on keeping individual rabbis, ex-rabbis, Hasidim, and their families alive; saving them from starvation; sending aid to those held in prison camps, and helping lucky individuals obtain exit visas.[77] The religious network he had built was in shambles. One of the *temimim* wrote to a comrade who had emigrated to America as follows:

---

75 Levin, *Jews of the Soviet Union Since 1917*, 227, 24f.4; *Igrot*, 11:125f.

76 Based on memoranda and correspondence in the JDC archives, USSR file #477. The quote is from a letter dated 28 February 1930. See also the memorandum by Evelyn Morrissey, 12 March 1930, and the letter from Cyrus Adler to Leo Jung, 13 March 1930. Adler, who as chairman of the JDC Cultural Committee had been one of the great supporters of religious aid to the USSR in the 1920s, strongly opposed such aid in the 1930s. Joseph Rosen in Moscow still provided some limited philanthropic assistance for rabbis from his discretionary funds.

77 See Schneerson's memo on aid to rabbis, *Igrot*, 11:125f., and similarly the letter by his son-in-law Samarius Gourary to Leo Jung, 5 June 1931, JDC archives, USSR file #477. Schneerson provided philanthropic aid via Klemes in Moscow, Zevin in Novozivkov, and various other channels. See his letters to Zevin between 1930 and 1934, *Igrot*, 11:205f., 237f., 389f. and more generally *Toldot Habad*, 117–29, 141–53, 202–04.

> The question is always on my mind: How can there be religious Jews here? There is no kosher meat, it is impossible to keep the Sabbath, there are no *miqvaot*, there are no *ḥadarim*. Soon there will be no synagogues, for the festivals, new moons, and Sabbaths have all been abolished. And there are very many uncircumcised ones among us. . . . What can I tell you, my brother? The Lord has poured out his wrath upon us. He is righteous in whatever he brings upon us. Pray for us. Pray that the Lord will hasten our salvation and redeem our souls. May he gather us in, together with the lost in the land of Assyria and the dispersed in the land of Egypt.[78]

By the end of 1930, Jewish religious leadership in the USSR had been crushed. The remaining rabbis were demoralized and isolated, living in fear, poverty and hunger. No one entertained a grand strategy on how Judaism could cope with the situation.

Between 1922 and 1930, the struggle to preserve Jewish tradition in the Soviet Union was waged through the agency of a clandestine, illegal organization, the Committee of Rabbis in the USSR. Many of the tactics of the revolutionary movement under czarism were now appropriated by Orthodox rabbis—tight-knit underground organization, centralized leadership, secret channeling of funds, maintaining close ties with supporters and leaders abroad, and so on. Schneerson's *temimim* were infused with the passionate idealism and heroic spirit of Russian revolutionaries. Tradition assumed the role of a subversive counterculture.

The struggle to preserve tradition in the USSR ultimately failed. But its tenacity, ingenuity, and sophistication do not fail to impress, even at this distance.

---

[78] R. Israel Leyb Lifshitz, letter from January 1930, *Toldot Habad*, 167. Lifshitz emigrated to Palestine in 1937.

4

Religious Responses Among North African Jews in the Nineteenth and Twentieth Centuries

HARVEY E. GOLDBERG

Introduction

The experience of Middle Eastern Jewries with modernization differed in significant ways from that of Jewish societies in Europe. Consequently, the reworking of tradition also took on distinct forms and emphases. Most research on the Jews of the Middle East has underscored their movement from a traditional society toward modernity, as underlined by such titles as *Marche vers l'Occident* or *Évolution du judaïsme marocain*.[1] As a result, many aspects of the religious life of Jews in the Middle East are underexplored, not to say ignored entirely. In the present essay, I examine some of the ways in which North African Jews held on to and reformulated tradition. In the course of this examination I also seek to conceptualize the processes that need be taken into account in order to adequately comprehend the developments in question.

I wish to thank Joëlle Bahloul for helpful comments on an earlier draft of this paper.

[1] A. Chouraqui, *Marche vers l'Occident: Les Juifs d'Afrique du Nord* (Paris: Presses Universitaires de France, 1951); D. Bensimon-Donath, *Évolution du judaïsme marocain sous le protectorat français, 1912-1956* (Paris: Mouton, 1968); A. Rodrigue, *De l'instruction à l'émancipation: Les enseignants de l'Alliance Israélite Universelle et les Juifs d'Orient, 1860-1939* (Paris: Calmann-Levy, 1989).

My discussion draws on examples from all the lands of the Maghrib. Special attention is given to Morocco, however, because much of the available historical material relates to that country. This reflects the fact that the Jews of Morocco were the largest Middle Eastern Jewish population in the mid-twentieth century, and have been the largest country-of-origin group in Israel for the past generation, until the recent mass immigration from the Soviet Union/Russia. A second emphasis results from the author's own work among the Jews of Libya. Because one main purpose of this paper is to contribute to conceptual clarification and to encourage further work, occasional reference is also made to other areas of the Middle East when it is relevant to the question at hand.

There was important variation in the ways that Jewish communities were confronted with modernization even within the countries of North Africa. Most of the Jews of Algeria became French citizens in 1870, experienced virulent European anti-Semitism at the end of the nineteenth century, and left for France in 1963 with Algerian independence. In Morocco, by contrast, there was a significant number of Jews who remained in rural areas, never learned French, and tended to migrate to Israel in the 1950s and 1960s. The dynamics of Jewish identity and the reformulation of religious expression obviously were not the same in these diverse settings.

Among most of the Jews of North Africa, extreme reactions to the challenges of modernization, full-scale assimilation on the one hand and ultraorthodoxy on the other, were not blatant. While many Jews, exposed to French public education in Algeria or to the curriculum of Alliance Israélite Universelle schools elsewhere in North Africa, developed secularizing outlooks and lifestyles, most of the religious responses to the new realities were not far from the middle of the road. This popularly is attributed to a Sephardic "lack of fanaticism" in comparison to European (Ashkenazic) "extremism." Before reaching generalizations, however, based on the inherent characteristics of Sephardic tradition, it is worth attending closely to the CONTEXT within which North African Jews had to come to grips with the dilemmas of modernization and to examine religious trends in the framework of those contexts.

In North Africa, as in Europe, the medieval definition of the Jewish community was undermined and the correlative institutional structures were dismantled. In both instances, the formal power of the rabbinate and the authority of the Jewish community were curtailed, if not entirely eliminated. There were important differences in the two regions, however, in the ways that changes in the wider societies impinged upon

Jewish life. Two major contextual differences were (1) the relation of traditional Jewish society to the surrounding non-Jewish world, and (2) the colonial setting within which modernization took place. Colonial presence not only meant the impact of foreign, European culture, but also entailed the influence of European Jewry upon the Jews of the Maghrib.

In the pages that follow, I explore some of the implications of these processes. My assumption is that there was no single identifiable Sephardic pattern, or school, of response to the changing political and social situation, or at least that it is premature, in terms of research, to identify them. Rather, my method is first to specify the nature of the pressure on Jewish religious identity and behavior that characterized North African settings. After briefly considering some aspects of rabbinic responses to the changing milieu, I then examine several traditionalizing patterns among North African Jews within a situation of diminished rabbinic and communal authority. One pattern, often treated as a residual category, is the selective and pragmatic maintenance of tradition. This form of religious development receives more detailed attention than it usually is given. Another pattern which is cursorily discussed is that of local religious "orthodox" reaction. A third mode concerns the attachment to saints, or *ṣaddiqim,* and the complex of pilgrimage celebrations linked to this system of beliefs and sentiments. My discussion of these various trends highlights the overall perspectives which I deem important in the study of modern religious responses among North African Jews.

External Pressures and Religious Identity in the Maghribi Context

To underline the importance of the relations between Jews and the non-Jewish environment as a contextual factor shaping religious change, it is instructive to consider developments in the Maghrib in the light of a well-known incident that is cited in many discussions of emancipation and modernization among the Jews of Europe. In 1787, the Royal Society of Sciences and Arts of Metz, reflecting social and political developments then under way, offered a prize to the best essay on the question, "Are there means of making the Jews happy and more useful in France?" The winning essays agreed that this was possible, and one argued that "Les Juifs sont hommes comme nous. . . ." According to Katz, "The concession that the Jews were, after all, 'human beings,' indicates that the inclusion of Jews in the family of man was a kind of novelty."[2] This episode may be diagnostic of new ideas which were taking root in European society, but would make little sense in terms of the situation of the Jews in North African lands.

In traditional Muslim society, Jews suffered various political and religious disabilities and were the object of some stereotyping, but they were generally perceived as members both of the "family of man" and of local society. Moreover, their "usefulness" in crafts and commerce was obvious to everyone and did not have to be demonstrated. Paradoxically, their move "out of the ghetto," which was encouraged and abetted by many coreligionists in Europe, did not contribute to their "integration into the surrounding (Muslim) society" but eventually helped sever their ties with the lands that had been their home for centuries.

The labile relationships of the Jews, during the modern period, both with the Muslim population and with local Europeans, had implications for patterns of religious development. A close look at these ties helps explain why patterns of religious reform which emerged in Europe did not find corresponding echoes in North Africa. Maghribi Jews felt no need to modify the style of synagogue worship to make it acceptable to Muslim neighbors. Similarly, there was no issue of rabbis preaching in a language that was not understood by participants in the wider society. Jews and Muslims had lived in proximity so long that there was a similarity in overall religious ambience, even when members of one religious group knew relatively little about the precise details of the behavior and beliefs of the other. More crucially, the Muslims did not constitute the reference group after which Jews sought to model their communal life in the new reality.

It is also worth noting that the organization of Muslim cities in traditional North Africa was predicated on a distinction between the public and private spheres of life.[3] This distinction was NOT identical with the differentiation between the secular national loyalties and individual religious commitments that was the hallmark of European emancipation. It did mean, however, that Jews (and Muslims) could absorb aspects of

---

[2] J. Katz, *Out of the Ghetto: The Social Background of Jewish Emancipation, 1770-1870* (Cambridge: Harvard University Press, 1973), 71f.; S. Schwarzfuchs, *Les Juifs de France* (Paris: Albin Michel, 1975), 199; P. Hyman, *From Dreyfus to Vichy: The Remaking of French Jewry* (New York: Columbia University Press, 1979), 4.

[3] D. Schroeter, "The Jewish Quarter and the Moroccan City" (Paper presented at the Conference on Sephardic Studies, State University of New York, Binghamton, 5-7 April, 1987).

European comportment and points of view in their public activities while retaining many tradition-based beliefs and practices in the "private" realm of religion (which implied family and confessional community as well as "the individual"). It also meant that they could modify and reformulate their religious life along lines that were not necessarily parallel to those which emerged in Europe.

In modern times Muslim religiosity was not a model for emulation, on the part of the Jews, but there was clear and definite movement in the direction of European styles of life. This trend was both advocated by European Jews and followed actively by many North African Jews, particularly the well-to-do. These processes, however, also did not result in far-reaching reformulations of Jewish tradition. There are a number of reasons why this was so. One reason relates to the long-time existence in North Africa of a small, cosmopolitan merchant elite, familiar with European languages, who did not have to change their lifestyle in order to feel comfortable in European society. In a few cases, these wealthy families themselves were objects of imitation on the part of parvenu European settlers establishing themselves in North African towns.

With regard to the mass of Jews in North Africa, they were not presented, on an everyday basis, with a beckoning secularizing or "semineutral society"[4] which pressed them to shed their medieval heritage. Europeans who settled in North Africa, many of whom were immigrants from diverse areas of southern Europe, often viewed the Jews as a competing urban population striving toward middle-class respectability.[5] Reforming Jewish forms of worship was not likely to amelioriate this situation. While the speech, dress, and manners of Europeans were imitated, they did not become a standard for religious comportment.

In French North Africa, the most direct pressure to change both outward behavior and a sense of identity emanated from European Jews. In Algeria, this attitude was coupled to activism on the part of French Jews who advocated that their Algerian brethren be granted citizenship.[6] In other North African countries, the pressure toward westernization received expression in the programs and schools of the Alliance Israélite Universelle, which, from the 1860s on, was an important force in

4 See Katz, *Out of the Ghetto*, 42-56.

5 G. Dermenjian, *Juifs et Européens d'Algérie: L'antisémitisme oranais, 1892-1905* (Jerusalem: Institut Ben-Zvi, 1983).

6 S. Schwarzfuchs, *Les Juifs d'Algérie et la France (1830-1855)* (Jerusalem: Institute Ben-Zvi, 1981).

providing European education and vocational training to Jewish communities in many Middle Eastern countries.[7]

Alliance education focused on the integration of North African Jews into European civic culture rather than on religious matters. It perceived the traditional life of North African Jews, suffused with religious belief and practice, as antithetical to its *mission civilisatrice*. Often, it was perceived as an antireligious force and initially opposed by local rabbis. Eventually, however, the political and educational benefits offered by the Alliance usually were accepted by local lay leaders, who agreed to send their children to the new schools. In most instances, the Alliance worked out a *modus vivendi* with traditional rabbis rather than advocating new forms of religious sensibility. This was another factor which accounts for the coexistence of both modern education and social mobility with varieties of religious traditionalism.[8]

There thus were various reasons why North African Jews did not feel pressured to alter the basic premises of their religious stance, even while

---

7 M. Laskier, *The Alliance Israélite Universelle and the Jewish Communities of Morocco 1862-1962* (Albany: SUNY Press, 1983); Rodrigue, *De l'instruction à l'émancipation*.

8 The concrete policies of the Alliance were adapted to specific situations. At the beginning of the twentieth century, its leaders realized that in some places, such as Algeria, the occidentalization of the Jews had proceeded so far that many Algerian Jews either were strangers to religious life, or experienced it, minimally, in its most traditional forms. It was now the task of the organization to provide an education in the basics of Hebrew, the Bible, and Jewish history. Later in the century, similar problems became acute among some of Tunisia's Jews. This led to a call for the Alliance to provide a new type of rabbinic education. The image of Judaism that informed these plans toward rejudaization was a rational and sanitized European "religion," and the Alliance did not have the teachers to do the job effectively. Traditional North African leadership did not meet this need either. In Morocco, it was only after 1945 that local rabbinic elements began to consider the incorporation of secular studies into schools under their supervision. See Laskier, *The Alliance*, 281; Rodrigue, *De l'instruction à l'émancipation*, 97-110.

The vacuum of a modernizing religious elite is highlighted by another episode. In the late 1920s, the Italian government sponsored a short-lived rabbinic school in Rhodes aimed at providing a modern rabbinic education for Jews from the Middle East. Part of the rationale of this effort was to attract the loyalty of Middle Eastern Jews in ways that the secularizing Alliance, representing French civilization, had not succeeded in doing. This school drew students primarily from Middle Eastern lands, rather than from North Africa, even though Italy ruled one North African country, Libya. See S. della Seta Torrefranca, "The Rabbinical Seminary of Rhodes, 1926-1938" (in Hebrew), *Peʿamim* 37 (1988): 78-112. A recent study of the career of Rabbi Haim Nahoum, active in the Ottoman Empire and in Egypt, also points to developments in those societies which differed somewhat from the North African cases; see E. Benbassa, *Un grand rabbin sepharade en politique 1892-1923* (Paris: CNRS, 1990).

they were acquiring many of the trappings and some of the values of European society. An incident from the history of Tunisian Jewry is suggestive in this regard. In 1879, the Bey of Tunisia ceded a plot to the Jewish community, and, in 1884, after the protectorate had been established, a plan was formulated to build a "Great Synagogue" on the lot, similar in style to European synagogues. The motivation for this plan was that many of the wealthy members of the synagogue had stopped coming to prayers regularly but might be attracted by a building that met modern esthetic standards.[9] Nothing was said about the style of the service or the content of the liturgy. These, apparently, were not seen as a hindrance toward Europeanization.

It therefore also may be that because European civilization was presented by other JEWS, North African Jews were motivated more by considerations of social mobility than by considerations of IDENTITY. They did not have to refigure their fundamental conceptions of group boundaries and belonging to improve their place in society. Moreover, the larger political situation did not press them, in a very direct fashion, to alter their relation to the state. French citizenship was conferred on the Jews of Algeria as a result of lobbying on the part of their metropolitan coreligionists, much before there was a strong demand in this direction on the part of the Algerian Jews themselves.[10] In the other countries of French North Africa, which had the status of protectorates, the issue of citizenship was more remote.[11] In short, the overall context did not require so radical a revision of the Jews' relationship to the surrounding society and polity as was entailed by enlightenment and emancipation in Europe. Correspondingly, North African Jews felt less of a need to reshape their religious life in a fashion that promoted their "acceptance into society."

In some cases, religious changes were imposed from without. Leaders of French Jewry took it upon themselves to modernize Algerian Jewish life and establish the *consistoire* system there. Some synagogue architecture in Algeria came to resemble European patterns, with an elevated

---

9 Y. Abrahami, "A Chapter in the History of the Emanicpation of Tunisian Jewry" (in Hebrew), in *East and Maghreb: A Volume of Researches*, eds. H. Z. Hirschberg and E. Bashan (Ramat Gan: Bar-Ilan University, 1974), 1:259–84.

10 C. Martin, *Les Israélites algériens de 1830 à 1902* (Paris: Herakler, 1936); Schwarzfuchs, *Les Juifs d'Algérie*.

11 On Morocco, see Laskier, *The Alliance*, p. 167–71; on Tunisia, see H. Z. Hirschberg, *A History of the Jews of North Africa*, vol. 2, *From the Ottoman Conquests to the Present Time* (Leiden: Brill, 1981), 133f.

pulpit facing the congregation, and in at least one case an organ was installed in a new synagogue as well. The liturgy underwent no basic change, however, and separate seating for women was taken for granted.[12] Forms of liberal Judaism did not achieve prominence in France[13] and understandably had little impact on North Africa.

In all of these efforts, it was taken for granted by French Jewry that they were to serve as the model for Algerian Jewry to follow, with little thought given as to what might be desirable religious development from the point of view of the indigenous Jews or their leadership. When France conquered Algiers in 1830, the Jews of France, recently having been granted emancipation, had no doubt that their own history of enlightenment and participation in the wider society provided the correct path to follow.[14] A century later, there were those who had second thoughts about the appropriateness of the European road to the evolution of Jewry. This minority response may be illustrated in the case of the Italian Chief Rabbi of Libya, appointed by the fascist government in the 1930s.

Rabbi Gustavo Castelbolognesi of Padua, who was appointed to his post in 1933, was ordered by Governor Italo Balbo of Libya to press the local Bet Din to annul the validity of private *qiddushin* in which an older man married a teenage girl against her parents' wishes. Castelbolognesi refused to do so and was summarily dismissed from his post by the governor, who had assumed that the rabbi would stand by his side in working for the modernization of Libya's Jews. In Balbo's letter to Mussolini explaining his actions, he wrote that the rabbi "was carried away by local religious feelings, . . . He lost the courage to support progress and became almost mesmerized by the Libyan Jews' attachment

[12] In Egypt, by way of contrast, there were innovations in synagogue ritual among some sectors of the modernizing population. These included recognizing a role for young women; See J. Hassoun, "The Traditional Jewry of the Hara," in *The Jews of Egypt: A Mediterranean Society in Modern Times,* ed. S. Shamir (Boulder, Colo.: Westview, 1987), 169–73.

[13] P. C. Albert, *The Modernization of French Jewry: Consistory and Community in the Nineteenth Century* (Waltham, Mass.: Brandeis University Press, 1977).

[14] One case of interaction between a French rabbi and a community in Algiers is analyzed by R. Ayoun, "Un grand rabbin français en Algérie: Mahir Charleville (1864-1877)," in *Les relations intercommunautaires juives en Mediterranée occidentale,* ed. J.-L. Miège (Paris: CNRS, 1984), 162–69. See also R. Ayoun and B. Cohen, *Les Juifs d'Algérie: Deux mille ans d'histoire* (Paris: J.-C. Lattes, 1982), 146–49. A brief interpretation of the traditionality of Algerian Jewry in the face of a modern French rabbinate is found in J.-M. Chouraqui, "Tradition et émancipation," in *Les Juifs d'Algérie: Images et textes,* eds. J. Laloum and J.-L. Allouche (Paris: Editions de Scribe, 1987), 231–38.

to their ancient customs."[15] Interviews with Italian Jews who knew Castelbolognesi[16] indicate that it is not likely that he, in principle, approved of private *qiddushin* or of the isolated cases of bigamy in Tripoli that were carried out in that fashion. Rather, impressed by the unselfconscious religiosity of Tripoli's Jews, and aware of the record of European Jewry's struggles to maintain itself in the context of emancipation, he sought ways of gradually bringing a traditional community into the modern world without splitting it asunder or severing it sharply from its religious heritage. This, however, was an unusual position among European rabbis active in the Maghrib and came late in the day of the history of North African Jewry.

Rabbinic Responses in the New Political Context

Behind the specific forms of contact of North African Jews with European influence were the new political reality of French presence and the basic changes that European rule entailed for traditional Maghrib society. The move against Algeria in 1830 alerted other North African leaders to the possibility of direct European intervention. In certain instances, during early phases of European impact, local North African rulers attempted to maintain power over their Jewish subjects by backing rabbinic authority. In mid-century Tunisia, for example, the bey upheld local rabbinic authority applied to a foreign Jew who was "freer" in his behavior than was generally accepted by local social and religious norms.[17] A similar incident is reported from Tripoli.[18]

Whatever the specific form of rule, however, all North African governments eventually circumscribed the spheres in which rabbinic decisions were binding, limiting their juridical authority to the realm of personal status. This process was complete in Algeria by 1842, and it began under Ottoman rule in Libya in the middle of the nineteenth century (being furthered by the Italian regime in the twentieth).[19] In

---

[15] R. De Felice, *Jews in an Arab Land: Libya, 1835-1970*, trans. Judith Roumani (Austin: University of Texas Press, 1985), 142, 143, 152–60.

[16] In particular, an interview with Clara Levi of Kibbutz Yavneh, 10 April 1986.

[17] Hirschberg, *History of the Jews*, 2:111.

[18] M. Ha-Cohen, *Higgid Mordecaï: Histoire de la Libye et de ses Juifs, lieux d'habitation et coutumes* (in Hebrew), ed. and annotated by H. Goldberg (Jerusalem: Institut Ben-Zvi, 1987), 151, 335f.

[19] Schwarzfuchs, *Les Juifs d'Algérie*, 34; H. Goldberg and C. Segrè. "Holding on to Both Ends: Religious Continuity and Change in the Libyan Jewish Community, 1860-1949," *The Maghreb Review* 14 (1989): p. 161-86. In some instances there arose

Tunisia, too, Bey Mohammad el Sadaq restricted the jurisdiction of the rabbinic courts in 1872, and further steps were taken by the French, while in Morocco, the relevant laws began to be enacted after the establishment of the protectorate.[20]

There are only a few in-depth studies of rabbinic responses in this new situation in Middle Eastern countries. Zvi Zohar has documented a pattern among the rabbis of Egypt, in the late nineteenth and early twentieth centuries, which is indicative of an openness toward some of the trends associated with modernization.[21] His examination of the rabbis of Syria, however, shows a strong assertion of traditional rabbinic norms within communal life.[22]

The case of Libya illustrates other aspects of rabbinic response. It shows that rabbinic influence could be promoted by a Muslim government in the cause of change and provides an example of diverse rabbinic reactions within the same community. Some reforming Ottoman governors in Libya, in seeking to promote social change, enlisted rabbinic support for their program.[23] After having instituted the post of *Ḥakham Bashi* (Chief Rabbi) of the Empire, the Porte appointed, in 1874, a *Ḥakham Bashi* of Tripoli, Rabbi Eliahu Bechor Hazzan,[24] whose outlook fit their efforts toward development and modernization. Hazzan, born in Smyrna, apparently learned both Italian and French, and resided in Tunis from 1872 to 1874 as a rabbinic emissary of the Jerusalem community.[25] He was aware of the effects of emancipation and associated

---

demands, from within, to reform rabbinic legislation and the organization of the courts, but the farthest-reaching changes were those brought about by political fiat from without.

[20] Hirschberg, *History of the Jews*, 2:135; A. Chouraqui, *La condition juridique de l'Israélite marocain* (Paris: Alliance Israélite Universelle, 1950), 121–30.

[21] Z. Zohar, "Patterns of Response to the Challenges of Modernization among Egyptian Rabbis, 1882-1922" (in Hebrew) (M. A. thesis, Hebrew University, 1981); idem, "Halakhic Responses of Syrian and Egyptian Rabbinical Authorities to Social and Technological Change," in *Studies in Contemporary Judaism*, ed. P. Medding (Bloomington: Indiana University Press, 1986), 2:18-51.

[22] Zohar, "Halakhic Responses"; idem, "Halakhic Decision Making in an Era of Change" (in Hebrew) (Ph. D. dissertation, Hebrew University of Jerusalem, 1988).

[23] H. Goldberg, *Jewish Life in Muslim Libya: Rivals and Relatives* (Chicago: University of Chicago Press, 1990), 44.

[24] B. Lewis, *The Jews of Islam* (Princeton: Princeton University Press, 1984), 174f.; Hirschberg, *History of the Jews*, 2:176, 181–83.

[25] See A. Yaʿari, *Shluḥei Eretz Yisrael* (Emissaries of the Land of Israel) (Jerusalem: Mosad ha-Rav Kook, 1951), 748f. and passim; and S. Marcus, "Ḥazzan," *Encyclopaedia Judaica*, 7 (1971): 1541f..

cultural currents among European Jewry, which already were felt in North Africa. His book *Zikhron Yerushalayim* addresses these issues in the form of a debate taking place in Tunis among various representative characters.[26] The goal of the book is to win Jews over to the maintenance of tradition through reasoned debate and persuasion.

Soon after his arrival in Tripoli, Hazzan began to work for educational reform.[27] He sought to establish a central school, rather than have students spread in synagogues around the town, and wanted to limit the number of students to 25 in a class. The most important change he suggested, however, was the teaching of Italian. Hazzan was operating in a complex political situation, in which various European countries were trying to increase their influence in the country. Nevertheless, he had support in this effort from some communal notables, but many local religious leaders opposed it.

Hazzan's opponents claimed that the study of European languages was the means of instilling disbelief in the minds of the young. Even the proviso that the Italian teacher would be Jewish did not placate them. Some of the sermons preached by the Head of the Bet Din on *Shabbat Kallah*, the Sabbath before Shavuoth when it was customary to encourage supporters to contribute to Talmud Torah, appear to criticize Hazzan's effort on the grounds that the study of Torah should not be a source of dissension within the community.[28] Several rabbinic leaders wrote to the Chief Rabbi in Palestine, appointed by the Ottoman authorities (the Sephardi *Rishon le-Ṣion*), trying to enlist his aid in their opposition to Hazzan's school.[29]

Hazzan presented his own views in a long halakhic essay, arguing that there was no religious reason to oppose the study of foreign languages. In addition, he pointed to the needs of the community, particularly the children of the poor. Similarly, he criticized the hypocrisy of his well-to-do opponents who sent their children to obtain an education abroad, out of the context of Jewish communal life, and those who enrolled their children in local Christian schools. Hazzan gained the

---

26 E. Hazzan, *Zikhron Yerushalayim* (Jerusalem Memorial) (Leghorn: Ben-Amozegh, 1874); Hirschberg, *History of the Jews*, 2:181–83.

27 These events are discussed in greater detail in H. Goldberg and C. Segrè, "Mixtures of Diverse Substances: Education and the Hebrew Language among the Jews of Libya, 1875-1951," in *Essays in the Social Scientific Study of Judaism*, eds. S. Fishbane and J. Lightstone (Montreal: Concordia University Press, 1990), 151-201.

28 H. Mimun, *Beʾer Le-ḥai* (Leghorn: Ben-Amozegh, 1888).

29 Hebrew Manuscript Division, Jewish National and University Library, Jerusalem, ARC 40 1512, 20.

written support of rabbinic leaders in Palestine, Smyrna, and Tunis for his stand.[30]

Hazzan's essay also criticizes halakhic approaches which "forbid that which is permitted" and asserts that religious developments in his day are not only a matter of education and of halakhic approach. He insists that failure to follow the Torah stems not from the study of foreign languages but from the fact of political freedom which equates all the religions and prevents rabbinic leaders from punishing the wayward and rebellious. Hazzan clearly understood the challenge of maintaining attachment to tradition in a setting where instituted rabbinic authority was no longer in force.

The available data on rabbinic responses in North Africa indicate that it is premature to generalize about a single orientation among Sephardic rabbis with regard to the developments during the nineteenth and twentieth centuries. Moreover, it is important to recognize that one common rabbinic response was to avoid, insofar as was possible, direct confrontation with the challenges presented by contemporary society. Commenting on the Bet Din in Tripoli, in the period of Hazzan's stay there and the years following, Mordechai Ha-Cohen chides the judges of his generation for their delaying tactics. He attacks their unwillingness to come to clear and quick decisions in cases brought before them, even in matters of personal status which were still explicitly in their jurisdiction. He presents the situation as reflecting the moral fiber of the judges in his day, but these men undoubtedly were reacting to the continuing erosion in the strength of their position. They were reluctant to make unequivocal pronouncements, a stance which most likely further undermined their status and prestige.[31]

If rabbinic judicial caution was one mode of reaction to the new situation, reticence in the realm of written halakhic literature perhaps was its corollary. There is still a great deal of research to be done on the rabbinic writings of Middle Eastern communities in modern times, and one question that should be posed is to what extent rabbis explicitly related to the major questions of the day. A recent study surveys the decisions taken by a committee of Moroccan rabbis with regard to the personal status of women in the years 1947 to 1955 but does not discuss rabbinic reactions during the preceding generations from the time that

---

[30] E. Hazzan, *Taʿalumot Lev*, 1 (Leghorn: Ben-Amozegh, 1879), 14a-18a.
[31] Ha-Cohen, *Higgid Mordecaï*, 255.

European impact began to be felt.[32] Whatever future research may show, the underlying fact is that the rabbis were now functioning in a social and political setting in which the link between them and the community at large was growing more tenuous. In this situation, the religious and traditionalizing responses of "the average Jew" become critical in understanding the development of religious life and institutions.

Responses of the Laymen: Selective Traditionality

While it is possible to debate, as Hazzan did with the local rabbinic leaders in Tripoli, whether religious laxity was due to poor education or the basic changes in the institutional basis of religious life, it is clear that both these factors were operative. In the course of the late nineteenth and the twentieth centuries, many Jews in North Africa, including a growing number of women, became exposed to contemporary secular schooling, an experience that separated them from the background of many rabbinic figures whose education was strictly traditional. In the past, rabbinic leaders had been local scholars who were intertwined by family ties with influential notables, but the new political and economic situation heightened the differentiation between the various forms of leadership.

As stated above, the gap between themselves and their rabbis did not present a problem for most North African Jews. They were able to adapt to new social realities and preserve their identities as Jews without feeling the constraints of rabbinic authority. An attitude of commitment to Jewish tradition, but not necessarily to any specific rabbinic demand, was crucial in maintaining Jewish religious life when the formal power of the rabbis began to weaken.

The fact that the rabbis retained their power in matters of personal status was not challenged. As in the wider Muslim society, internal family life was perceived as a bastion of tradition. In the new situation, ancient biblical and rabbinic rules concerning food and sexual behavior seem to have been invested with additional meanings of preserving Jewish identity. Preparing meals for the Sabbath or Festivals became acts clearly contributing to the continuity of family and community. The valuation of these realms thus accorded a new religious importance to

---

32 M. Amar, "Women's Status in Rabbinical Courts of Morocco in the Twentieth Century" (in Hebrew), *Miqqedem Umiyyam* 3 (1990): 187-202.

the domestic activities of women.[33] That rabbinic authority still held good in the realm of family life was comforting and was not perceived as an impediment toward economic success or social mobility.

In general, patterns of secular life that emerged among the Jews of North Africa did so gradually and selectively. Certain aspects of tradition were abandoned, while others were maintained, but this rarely became a matter of consistent principle or of ideology. The reaction of North African Jews to change was pragmatic. They voluntarily maintained many aspects of religious tradition, even while there was a relaxation of strict compliance with the details of religious law. They did not need ideological justification for their choices.

Jews from Tripoli, for example, beyond the debates over teaching European languages in the 1870s, did not produce any written polemics or debates about religious subjects. They do report instances of textual banter reflecting changing norms of conduct. In the twentieth century, when Italianizing youngsters were faced with the challenge that the *Shulḥan Arukh* enjoins the wearing of a headcovering at all times, a practice they had come to ignore, some of them pointed to a gloss on the passage cited which claims that such behavior was exemplary of piety, but not expected of the common man. For most of them, the question of wearing a headcovering at all times was not a serious issue. Several people explained that they would keep a skullcap in their pocket, in case there was a need for it during the day, but felt no pangs of inconsistency in putting it on their head or in their pocket, according to the situation. North African Jews in general sometimes acted in terms of traditional norms; at other times, as the situation demanded, they behaved in terms of "modern" expectations. Their situational attachment to religious tradition remained a taken-for-granted aspect of life.

Today, it is common to speak of observant Jews from the Middle East as "orthodox," but it may be more appropriate to view their religious

---

33 J. Bahloul, *Le culte de la table dressée: Rites et traditions de la table juive algérienne* (Paris: Métailié, 1983); idem, "Naissance et mariage: Temps forts de la reproduction familiale chez les Juifs nord-africains en France," in *Les Juifs du Maghreb: Diasporas contemporaines*, eds. J.-C. Lasry and C. Tapia (Montreal: l'Harmattan, Presses de l'Université de Montréal, 1989), 239–62; idem, "What You Remember and Whose Son You Are: North African Jewish Families and Their Past," in Fishbane and Lightstone, *Essays*, 217–29; R. Rosen, "Feminine Symbolism, or Women in the Judeo-Moroccan System of Representation in a *moshav* in Israel" (in Hebrew) (M.A. thesis, Department of Sociology and Social Anthropology, Hebrew University of Jerusalem, 1981); E. Friedman, *Colonialism and After: An Algerian Jewish Community* (South Hadley, Mass.: Bergin and Garvey, 1988).

lives not in terms of a systematic reaction to the challenges of modernity, but as the cut-and-paste continuation of traditional patterns. They made little effort toward arriving at explicit philosophies or programs concerned with the place of religion in the contemporary world. Moreover, matters of religion only rarely split communities along ideological lines. The notion of "tradition," therefore, often treated as a residual category, deserves further examination.

The concept of "tradition" has been elaborated in anthropological discourse by Redfield, in his writings on "folk society." He emphasizes the maintenance of tradition in the absence of books, stating that the "ideal" folk society has no legislation, no codification, and no jurisprudence. One implication of this situation is the relative lack of tension, in a folk society, among the various aspects of a world view. People can act on the assumption that "things are the way they ought to be."[34]

The importance of books, however, in setting forth and maintaining tradition has always been central to Judaism. Focusing on Jewish history, Katz has offered a general definition of a traditional society.[35] In such societies, people "assume that all the practical and theoretical knowledge that they require has been inherited by them from their forefathers, and that it is man's duty to act in accordance with the ancient customs." At the same time, Katz recognizes that there may be differences where one seeks ancient wisdom and direction for behavior. On the one hand, the emphasis may be on the "study and absorption of formal knowledge from books and written sources," but there also "were those who claimed that the legitimation of customs lay in the very fact of their practice throughout the generations." He also suggests that recourse to books as a source of tradition may have been characteristic of Jewish society in Europe, while the perception of tradition as being immanent in current social practice may have been dominant in Middle Eastern Jewish communities.

The religious life of the Jews of North Africa reflected an interplay of factors highlighted by these different definitions. Maghribi Jews saw themselves as part of the larger Jewish world and cherished the written

---

34 R. Redfield, *The Little Community and Peasant Society and Culture* (Chicago: University of Chicago Press, 1960), 88; idem, "The Folk Society," in *Human Nature and the Study of Society: The Papers of Robert Redfield*, ed. M. P. Redfield (Chicago: University of Chicago Press, 1962), 1: 231–53.

35 J. Katz, "Traditional Society and Modern Society," in *Jewish Societies in the Middle East*, eds. S. Deshen and W.P. Zenner (Washington, D.C.: University Press of America, 1982), 35-47.

works deemed sacred by Jews everywhere. They placed themselves in the line of religious authority beginning with the Bible and Talmud, but it was the pressure of the existing community which instilled a reverent attitude toward these books among its contemporary members. In addition, they had a keen sense of the legitimacy of their own practices and customary forms. In this regard they were closer to Redfield's "folk society." These two "levels," as diagnosed by an outside observer, were not conceptually distinct in the eyes of North African Jews; they certainly would have resisted any notion that their own praxis diverged from the main norms of Jewish tradition. Rather, the distinction applies to a tendency to keep to familiar ways, reinforced by everyone around, which had been handed down from parent to child within the family and from one generation to another in communal contexts such as the synagogue. This implied that it was not necessary to toe the line with the exactitude expressed in rabbinic texts, as these might be pointed to from time to time, even by a scholar of recognized learning and prestige. This mixture of dependence on communal traditions and the formal "great tradition" played a role in refashioning the religious behavior of North African Jews in the emerging situations of the nineteenth and twentieth centuries.

As the scope of formal rabbinic authority was restricted, the community itself survived as a repository of tradition and control. The main expression of communal existence was the synagogue, and synagogue life continued with vitality. No one challenged the centrality of the synagogue as a religious and social institution. It is possible to speculate that precisely because formal institutions, such as the rabbinic court, no longer commanded attention, voluntary communal worship became more important as a mark of Jewish solidarity.

As emphasized above, identification with the community was not necessarily undermined by adoption of a European style of life. In all major towns of North Africa, economically successful Jews tended to move into the "new city," linking them with the European population, but weekly synagogue attendance was maintained by many of these socially mobile families. Sometimes synagogues were built in the new neighborhoods, while another pattern was that new city residents organized casual synagogues in existing buildings that they owned or rented. It was also common for well-to-do families to pray in the synagogues of the traditional Jewish quarters on festivals, when prayers were longer and more elaborate. From this perspective the festivals reunited members of the community who were growing apart in other ways. On these occasions, families with means gave expression to their social standing by exhibiting their attire, or through their ability to volunteer generous contributions to a synagogue, and thus earn participation in the prestigious portions of the worship or Torah-reading service. It is significant that the poorer Jews of the *mellaḥ* or *ḥara*[36] still constituted a relevant audience in front of whom the rich decided to exhibit their accomplishments. Becoming more French or Italian was a way of getting ahead WITHIN the Jewish community.

As always in Jewish life, the synagogue was used as a base for other activities. Within several synagogues in Tripoli, individuals took it upon themselves to organize children in a "choir," training them in the reading and chanting of psalms and hymns during the late afternoon between the *minḥah* (afternoon) and *ʿarvit* (evening) prayers. At times, children were attracted to this activity by small monetary inducements. These groups had a range of social functions—they served to keep youngsters off the streets but also contributed positively to communal life. These groups (one of which was named *Shirei David*, i.e., Psalms) attended life cycle functions such as circumcisions or funerals and chanted passages and hymns appropriate to these occasions. This brought them both recognition and participation in the festivities (or mourning), including the meals appropriate to each occasion. While this was a traditional form of "youth activity," known elsewhere in North Africa,[37] data from Tripoli suggest ways in which they also reflected new influences. Pictures of two such choirs, from the 1920s, show youths dressed in the equivalent of Italian military uniforms, adding a new element of prestige to this time-honored organization for pious purposes.[38]

New forms of volunteerism, linked to religious values, were also apparent in the lives of women. In Tripoli, in 1896, a group of well-to-do women organized to care for the indigent sick within the Jewish community. They solicited contributions from their husbands and from other women, wrote letters to philanthropists abroad, and tended to ailing individuals. In mid-nineteenth century Mogador (Morocco), Stella Corcos was a leading figure in local philanthropic efforts and established a school for girls. Also in the realm of education, a group of women in

---

36 *Mellaḥ* is the designation of a Jewish quarter or residential concentration in Morocco, while the term *ḥara* was used in Tunisia and Tripolitania.

37 D. Cohen, *Le parler arabe des Juifs de Tunis: Textes et documents linguistiques et ethnographiques* (Paris: Mouton, 1964), 29, 33.

38 F. Zuaretz, A. Guweta, Ts. Shaked, G. Arbib, F. Tayar, eds., *Yahadut Luv* (Jews of Libya) (Tel Aviv: Vaʿad Qehillot Luv Be-yisrael, 1960), 105, 109.

Fez, beginning in 1914, worked along with a Zionist-oriented rabbi from Eastern Europe who established a network of *talmud torah* schools known as *Em ha-Banim*.[39]

Local Religious Reaction

The gradual accommodation of traditional forms to the new realities that I have described does not imply the absence of reactions among religious leaders who opposed the secular developments of the nineteenth century. I have already discussed the resistance to Rabbi Hazzan's attempt at educational innovation in Tripoli. In Morocco, the writings and teachings of Rabbi Yaᶜaqob Abihatsira, of the southern Tafilalt region, stressed piety and moral behavior in a mystical mode. These themes were, in part, a response to European impact on the northern cities of that country and to French influence, which had reached Algeria to the East.[40] Other implications of Rabbi Abihatsira's activities are discussed below.

There is evidence, from mid-nineteenth century Tunisia, of a conservative reaction to internal attempts to reform Jewish education.[41] As already stated, the initial steps of the Alliance Israélite Universelle in establishing modernizing and European oriented schools often evoked a reaction on the part of local rabbinic leaders. For the most part, however, these reactions were not sustained, as the lay leaders of the community and the emerging middle class welcomed the opportunities offered by the new educational system.

Only in Jerba did resistance to the establishment of an Alliance school meet with success over a long period. This resistance sought to preserve the character of Jerban Jewry[42] and was not part of a broader "orthodox" movement. This preservative orientation is reflected in the compendium

---

[39] Ha-Cohen, *Higgid Mordecaï*, 242; D. Schroeter, "Anglo-Jewry and Essaouira (Mogador), 1860-1900: The Social Implications of Philanthropy," *Transactions of the Jewish Historical Society of England* 28 (1984): 60-88; D. Bensimon-Donath, *L'évolution de la femme israélite à Fes* (Aix-en-Provence: Faculté de lettres, Travaux et Mémoires, no. 25, 1962), 43; S. Bar-Asher, "The Jews of Morocco: 1492-1960." *Encyclopaedia Judaica Yearbook: 1983/85* (Jerusalem: Keter, 1985), 179.

[40] D. Manor, *Kabbale et ethique au Maroc: La voie de Rabbi Jacob Abihatsira* (in Hebrew with French summary) (Jerusalem: Institut Ben-Zvi, 1982).

[41] Y. Tsur, "Tunisian Jewry at the End of the Pre-Colonial Period" (in Hebrew), *Miqqedem Umiyyam* 3 (1990): 87.

[42] A. Udovitch and L. Valensi, *The Last Arab Jews: The Communities of Jerba Tunisia* (Chur, Switzerland: Harwood, 1984).

entitled *Brit Kehunah*, which codified hundreds of distinct Jerban customs in the form of a commentary on the *Shulḥan Arukh*.[43] This instance of Jewish reaction may be not unrelated to surrounding cultural influences, for the Jews of Jerba dwelt in the midst of the Ibadi Muslim sect which for centuries had preserved its identity vis-à-vis the wider Muslim environment.[44]

It was more common, as we have stated, for initial rabbinic opposition to retreat in the face of the opportunities created in the new reality. For example, by the first decade of the twentieth century, the opposition to teaching European languages in Tripoli had, for the most part, dissipated. There still were other local and limited responses to the growing presence of European, secular influence in the town. A group of pious individuals led by a rabbi, associated with a synagogue known as Dar Burta, constituted themselves as a "society of reproof." They acted, in the words of one of the former members, as a "secret police," reporting infringements of Jewish law by individuals in the community to their rabbi leader. For example, they might catch a Jew going stealthily into his shop before the Sabbath ended on Saturday evening in order to fetch some item. Such a man would be handed a "summons," demanding that he appear, contritely, at the Dar Burta synagogue. The only sanctions behind such a summons were public opinion and the individual's religious conscience.

There were cruder methods of social control as well. One New City denizen of Tripoli explained that he would not ride a bicycle near the Old City on the Sabbath for fear of being beaten up. Another source cites an incident from 1920 in which young men broke into a wedding ceremony in order to try to disrupt the marriage of a Jewish woman to an Italian officer. These were sporadic incidents, however, reflecting neither systematic ideology nor sustained organization. The overall pattern was to accept traditional norms and practices within the realms of synagogue and family life, but to gradually and pragmatically incorporate European social patterns in a manner which did not invite overt conflict.

---

43 M. Khalfon Hacohen, *Brit Kehunah*, 4 vols. (Jerba, 1941–51).

44 P. Shinar, "Réflexions sur la symbiose judéo-ibadite en Afrique du Nord," in *Communautés juives des marges sahariennes du Maghreb*, ed. M. Abitbol (Jerusalem: Institut Ben-Zvi, 1982), 81-114.

Local Religion

In addition to the synagogue, another important locus of traditional Jewish life[45] in North Africa was the cemetery. The cemetery was not only a place to bury people. Regular visits to the graves of deceased relatives were acts full of religious meaning, complementing deeds of memorialization at home and in the synagogue. Moreover, cemeteries often, if not universally, contained graves of sainted individuals, or *ṣaddiqim,* whom one could supplicate hoping for intercession in the fulfillment of personal petitions, for health, sustenance, successful marriage matches, fertility, and the like. Such visits were very important to women, but the pattern was by no means exclusive to members of that gender.[46]

Within traditional North African religion the devotion to *ṣaddiqim* was also associated with meanings and social configurations far broader than that of the individual and his or her life goals and problems. This was particularly true in Morocco, where the interplay between local Muslim maraboutism and Jewish mystical notions concerning *ṣaddiqim* reached a pinnacle of interpenetration. Prominent here was the celebration of *hillulot,* pilgrimage visits to graves of sainted rabbis.

Pilgrimage festivals constitute the form of saint celebration which is most dramatic in the public eye, but within Maghribi Jewish tradition the devotion to saints also took the form of a *seʿudah,* an elaborate meal in a domestic setting, in honor of a saint on the day of his *hillulah.* During such meals tales were told highlighting the deeds of the particular saint being celebrated, and songs were sung in honor of the better known Moroccan Jewish saints. These celebrations enhanced attachment to particular *ṣaddiqim,* and also reinforced the concept and institution of sainthood in general. The various saints were thus linked metaphorically, in that the lesser local saints stood for the more remote and prominent saints, and ultimately for the archetype of mystical sainthood, Rabbi Shimʿon Bar Yohai, the putative author of the Zohar. They were also

---

45 This section might be called "folk religion," "popular religion," or the like. I follow the terminology chosen by W. Christian, Jr., *Local Religion in Sixteenth-Century Spain* (Princeton: Princeton University Press, 1981), which emphasizes that this is an aspect of religion that relates to local social and cultural realities. Other terms sometimes imply an invidious comparison to "real" religion, but as will be seen, these religious phenomena relate to central life concerns of the participants.

46 H. Goldberg, "The Zohar in Southern Morocco: A Study in the Ethnography of Texts," *History of Religions* 29 (1990): 233–58.

connected metonymically in that all the *ṣaddiqim* become part of a simultaneously revered "pantheon."

Both in Morocco and elsewhere, the complex of beliefs and practices concerning *ṣaddiqim* underwent elaboration and subtle changes of meaning in the modern context.[47] For example, one venerable pilgrimage site, that of "Rabb" at Tlemcen, attracted visitors from both Algeria and eastern Morocco. A description from the first decade of the twentieth century describes how the pilgrims included many French speakers, and how people were dressed both in European fashion and in more traditional garb.[48] At the same period of time, the number of people gathering at the tomb of Rabbi ʿAmran ben Diwan, an important shrine in Ouezzane, Morocco, was in the vicinity of six thousand.[49] This is a large number considering the size of the Jewish population and the means of transportation available at the period. Later in the twentieth century, the introduction of modern transportation served to increase the numbers of visitors to the popular shrines. It also made it easier for women and children to reach the remote shrines, whereas in the past they had been more restricted and mainly visited the sainted graves in their local cemetery. Also, at the larger *hillulot*, the conventional separation of the sexes which pervaded traditional North African life was notably relaxed.

With regard to the organization of pilgrimages, one salient feature which distinguished Jewish hagiolatry in Morocco was that, for the most part, the handling of festive pilgrimage days, including the management of masses of pilgrims and the collection and expenditure of funds, was undertaken by voluntary groups of pious individuals and not by the descendants of a sainted marabout as was common among the Muslims. This may be related to the fact that in Maghribi Muslim settings saints have sometimes been foci for the emergence and consolidation of political power. The relative absence of dynastic conceptions with regard to Jewish saints may be part of the overall configuration of Jewish political weakness and reflect an inverse relationship between supernatural and mundane power. While alive, these North African *ṣaddiqim* were not

47 See I. Ben-Ami, *Ha ʿaraṣat qedoshim be-qerev Yehudei Maroko* (Saint Veneration among the Jews in Morocco), Folklore Research Center Studies 8 (Jerusalem: Magnes, 1984). The section on forms of communal organization, pp. 146–65, discusses some of the developments in the 1930s and 1940s.

48 A. van Gennep, *En Algérie* (Paris: Mercure de France, 1914), 41-58. The site continued to attract pilgrims through the mid-twentieth century.

49 A. Elmaleh, "Aus Marokko," *Ost und West* 10 (1910):779; Anonymous, "Un pèlerinage juif au Maroc," *Univers Israélite* 66, 9, (11 Nov. 1910): 272f.

charismatic characters who attracted masses of followers that might be welded into a social or political force. Tales of Jewish saints performing miraculous acts so that no harm come to their devotees do not refer so much to acts of protection carried out in the lifetime of the saints, as to the continuing guardianship over their adherents after death.

Nevertheless, there are a few instances where a familial or "dynastic" tendency appeared with regard to Jewish sainthood. The most noted instance involved Rabbi Yaʿaqob Abihatsira of Morocco, whose writings were mentioned earlier. R. Abihatsira's prestige became widespread in Morocco and was maintained by rabbi descendants who spread out both in and beyond the Tafilalt. Only a few of his later adherents, however, were familiar with his works or explicit message. The tendency to revere him merged with the more popular and generalized devotion to saintly figures which characterized Moroccan Jewish life and wider Moroccan Muslim culture.

R. Yaʿaqob perished in Damanhur, Egypt, on his way to the Holy Land in 1880. Today, each January, there are pilgrimages to his tomb on the part of Moroccan Jews from Israel and from Europe. Also present are some Hasidim of Eastern European background, who visit from Israel and accord sainthood to this North African rabbi, a phenomenon to be referred to later.

In the Tafilalt itself, many of R. Abihatsira's descendants followed his path of piety and established, throughout the region, yeshivas in which to train a new cadre of religious functionaries and generally to provide spiritual leadership. These institutions were supported by funds collected by members of the family who traveled all over Morocco, even outside the region of the Abihatsira rabbis' immediate influence. With the establishment of an official countrywide Moroccan rabbinate under the French Protectorate, a number of the Abihatsira rabbis were given posts as head rabbis of towns or districts, but this did not eliminate the spontaneous popular support of institutions linked to their name. The tombs of members of the family, which were found throughout the southeastern part of Morocco, continued to be sites of individual and collective visits. When members of the Abihatsira family migrated to Israel, some of them successfully translated traditional sanctity and charisma into political power within the Jewish state, but this topic is beyond the scope of the present paper.

While reverence to *ṣaddiqim* has powerful parallels in local Muslim practice, it also has deep roots in Jewish tradition. It therefore constitutes a symbolic system capable of linking diverse Jewish groups. This has been appreciated keenly by the Habad movement, which began to be active in education in Morocco after World War II and continues to run a school in Casablanca.[50] A picture of the Lubavitcher Rebbe hangs in the homes of many Moroccan Jews today, in various parts of the world, alongside portraits of Moroccan *ṣaddiqim*.

This does not mean that all these North African Jews have adopted Habad's philosophy and lifestyle, even though various observers have commented on the similarity between the veneration of *ṣaddiqim* on the part of North Africans and Hasidim. It does indicate how persuasive symbols can speak successfully to diverse audiences. It still is necessary, however, to understand the phenomenon of attachment to *ṣaddiqim* in terms of its local context.

One clear meaning of the veneration of North African *ṣaddiqim* is the attachment to PLACE, and the Moroccan case shows various ways in which this orientation has been molded to fit new contexts. Although the reasons are unclear, it appears that in the nineteenth century there began a process of proliferation of *ṣaddiqim*, often based on dreams of lay people that such and such a rabbi revealed himself and identified his presence in a given locale.[51] This phenomenon may be connected to the urban-directed migrations that began in the nineteenth century and continued into the twentieth. Several cases from this century indicate that local *ṣaddiqim*, hitherto known only within their small community, achieved prominence and attracted pilgrims from afar AFTER Jews no longer resided in that region. The presence of *ṣaddiqim* in these "emptied-of-Jews" areas may be related to the fact that some Jews still maintained commercial relations there, even while resident elsewhere. More generally, the presence of a *ṣaddiq* in a region represented a claim, understood and partially accepted by Muslims, that the territory was still, in some sense, a place in which Jews had a stake.[52]

The versatility of this religious idiom in adapting to specific historical settings is further underscored by examining other North African examples. In both Tunisia and Libya, the pilgrimage tradition among Jews received prominent expression with regard to sainted synagogues, rather than (or better, in addition to) individual rabbis. This may reflect the fact

---

50 Laskier, *The Alliance*, 248–51.

51 D. Schroeter, "The Politics of Reform in Morocco: The Writings of Yiṣḥaq Ben Ya'ish Halewi in *Hasfirah* (1891)," in *Misgav Yerushalayim Studies in Jewish Literature*, ed. E. Hazan (Jerusalem: Misgav Yerushalayim, 1987), lxxiii–lxxxiv.

52 H. Goldberg, "The Mellahs of Southern Morocco: Report of a Survey," *The Maghreb Review* 8, 3-4 (1983): 61-69.

that tribal organization, stressing the patronage of powerful tribal leaders, was suppressed by the central governments in these regions several generations earlier than it was in Morocco. The symbolic valorization of synagogues, rather than individuals, may point to the heightened importance of the community in the eastern Maghrib.[53] That these synagogues are frequently viewed in anthropomorphic terms, as capable of answering the prayers of individual petitioners for health, marriage of their children, and so forth, highlights the subtlety of transformation that notions of sainthood may undergo.

One such synagogue is the Ghriba on the island of Jerba in southern Tunisia and another, the Bu-Shaif synagogue, is in the town of Zliten to the east of Tripoli, Libya. It may not be coincidental that both shrines are found on sites where older synagogues stood and were rebuilt in the 1860s or 1870s.[54] In the Libyan case, the construction of the synagogue clearly was viewed as a victory for the Jews, for the former structure had been burned down and some local Muslims opposed its reconstruction. In the twentieth century the pilgrimage to Bu-Shaif became firmly associated with Zionist sentiments, including contributions to the Jewish National Fund.[55] While a Zionist orientation did not characterize the community of Jerba, the Ghriba attracted a growing number of pilgrims from outside the region at the end of the last century, resulting in the construction of a hostel to receive them. Such an effort may have been possible only under the conditions of the protectorate.

In the various cases cited, both in Morocco and the eastern Maghrib, there appears a link between sainthood and an overall attachment to Jewish peoplehood. It is possible that the growing popularity of such visits both expressed and reinforced a growing sense of "ethnic" belonging, in addition to the personal and religious motives which brought pilgrims to these shrines. In various ways, then, local practices and beliefs both responded and gave shape to wider forces emerging in the nineteenth and twentieth centuries.

Finally, it should be noted that the celebration of *hillulot* also continues among the small Jewish community of about ten thousand people which remains in Morocco today. Here we find that Jewish sainthood can have

---

53 S. Deshen, *The Mellah Society: Jewish Community Life in Sherifian Morocco* (Chicago: University of Chicago Press, 1989), 23-26.

54 Udovitch and Valensi, *Last Arab Jews*, 123–31.

55 M. Ha-Cohen, *The Book of Mordechai: A Study of the Jews of Libya*, ed. and trans. with an introduction and commentaries by H. E. Goldberg (Philadelphia: Institute for the Study of Human Issues, 1980), 156f.; F. Zuaretz et al., *Yahadut Luv*, 123–25.

implications on the level of international relations, for these celebrations are not only a vestige of a once-thriving cultural complex but have been utilized by the King of Morocco in the context of Middle Eastern politics. For about a decade, the Moroccan government has followed a policy of allowing Israelis of Moroccan origin or descent to visit their native country. Typically the "pretext" for such a trip is a visit to the tomb of a sainted rabbi and participation in the devotional activities there,[56] but such religious tourism carries not-too-hidden political overtones. On the major Jewish pilgrimage festivals, a Moroccan government official may greet the worshipers, and this very fact carries with it ramifications which may impinge upon Israelis, Moroccan Jews in France and Canada, or the leadership of the politically conscious Jews of the United States. Classifying these events as either "politics" or "religion" alone would be missing the point. The creative potential of Moroccan Jewish saints, and their devotees, is yet to be exhausted.

Conclusion

I have traced a number of religious and traditionalizing responses that developed among the Jews of North Africa in modern times, after the dismantling of the medieval Jewish community and the limitation of rabbinic authority. My argument has stressed that the religious developments cited must be examined in their specific historical context.[57] The two forms of response to which I have given special attention are the pragmatic and selective maintenance of tradition and Jewish communal life, and the veneration of hallowed shrines.

Both these forms reflect a heightened sense of the individual and the ability to exercise choice in seeking religious expression. In fact, the two patterns may be complementary. Several authors have suggested that the

---

56 A. Levy, "Ethnic Aspects of the Trips of Moroccan Israelis to Their Country of Birth" (in Hebrew) (M.A. thesis, Department of Sociology and Social Anthropology, Hebrew University of Jerusalem, 1989).

57 In addition to the works cited in our survey, there have been studies of modern Jewish ideologies and movements in the Maghrib, such as Zionism, or the attempt to identify a North African "Haskalah," but these too cannot be simply equated with their European counterparts and must be seen in their local settings. See M. Abitbol, "Research on Zionism and the Aliya of Oriental Jewry—Methodological Aspects" (in Hebrew), *Peʿamim* 39 (1989): 3-14; D. Schroeter, "Politics of Reform"; and J. Chetrit, ed., *Miqqedem Umiyyam*, vol. 3 (Masoret u-moderniyut be-Yahadut Ṣefon Afriqa u-ve-Yahadut ha mizraḥ) (Tradition and Modernity in North African and Oriental Jewry) (Haifa, 1990).

growing popularity of *hillulot* is related to the fact that they allow the expression of piety on the part of people who no longer adhere to all the rabbinic-based strictures of traditional Jewish life.[58] In addition, both of these religious orientations have their social correlates, while also pointing to modes of interrelation between the individual and his or her social setting. The first mode, consisting of pragmatic adherence to tradition, hints at the primacy of current social expectations over ideological commitment in shaping individual behavior. The second points to relations of dependency,[59] and reliance on authority, in seeking an anchor in contemporary society.

[58] S. Deshen, "Political Ethnicity and Cultural Ethnicity in Israel during the 1960's," in *Urban Ethnicity*, ed. A. Cohen, ASA Monograph 12 (London: Tavistock, 1974), 281-309. Much of the developing understanding of the meanings of hagiolatry among Jews in North Africa has grown out of clues based on field studies carried out in Israel.

[59] Y. Bilu, "Dreams and the Wishes of the Saint," in *Judaism Viewed from Within and from Without: Anthropological Perspectives*, ed. H. E. Goldberg (Albany: SUNY Press, 1987), 285-313.

5

The Ḥazon Ish: Ḥaredi Critic of Traditional Orthodoxy

LAWRENCE KAPLAN

I

At the conclusion of Chaim Grade's great novel *The Yeshiva,* the novel's two major protagonists, the fierce, brooding Musarist Tsemakh Atlas and the young tempestuous, passionate ex–*ben-torah* and would-be poet and author Chaikl Vilner, go to the Vilna train station to bid farewell to their mentor, the radiant and serene rabbinic scholar, Rabbi Avraham-Shaye Kosover, who is leaving Vilna for the land of Israel. The novel ends with Tsemakh Atlas and Chaikl Vilner looking thoughtfully at the departing train carrying Rabbi Avraham-Shaye Kosover away from them.

> The platform was now overrun with people waiting for another train. Reb Tsemakh Atlas and Chaikl Vilner still stood beside each other in the crowd; they were like an older brother with a younger one. They stood like two trees at the roadside on the edge of a town, while on the horizon a dense forest sways and rustles. But the two trees are always sad and pensive because the man who lived near them and watched over them has gone off into the wide world and will return no more, return no more. Reb Tsemakh Atlas and Chaikl Vilner realized that many other trials awaited them in life, but both had a feeling that all their struggles would be illuminated by

> the radiance of the man of God - Reb Avraham-Shaye Kosover,
> the author of *The Vision of Avraham.*[1]

Of course, Chaikl Vilner is Chaim Grade himself and Rabbi Avraham-Shaye Kosover, the author of *Maḥazeh Abraham*, (*The Vision of Avraham*), is the famed rabbinic scholar Rabbi Avraham Yeshaya Karelitz of Kossov (1878-1953), better known by the title of the massive series of works of rabbinic scholarship he authored, *Ḥazon Ish*. As Chaikl Vilner was the student of Rabbi Avraham-Shaye Kosover for many years, so Chaim Grade was the student of the Ḥazon Ish. And as Chaikl Vilner at the novel's end senses that all his future struggles will be illuminated by Reb Avraham-Shaye, so, in fact, the image of the Ḥazon Ish accompanied Chaim Grade throughout his long and productive literary career, to the extent that he memorialized him both in this novel and in a number of poems.[2]

But the radiance of the Ḥazon Ish (or his not-so-fictional counterpart Reb Avraham-Shaye) has not only illuminated the paths of the fictional Tsemakh Atlas and Chaikl Vilner and the latter's alter ego, the real Chaim Grade; rather, his writings, his teaching, and above all his persona are a dominant presence and constitute a guiding light for many religious Jews today. In particular, the Ḥazon Ish is seen—and rightfully so—as the spiritual godfather of the present day Ḥaredi (non-Zionist Orthodox) community in Israel and is revered and venerated by its members as the ultimate exemplar of learning and saintliness. The term "charisma" is much used and abused, but with reference to the impact the personality of the Ḥazon Ish made and continues to make on this

---

[1] *The Yeshiva*, trans. Curt Leviant (Indianapolis: Bobbs-Merrill, 1977), 2:393.

[2] See the three poems "Elegye afn Khazoyn-Ish," "Omed ho-Eysh," and "A Keyver in Bney-Brak," in *Af mayn Veg tsu dir* (Tel Aviv: Y. L. Peretz, 1969), 36-55. (This is a bilingual anthology of Grade's poems with the Yiddish originals and Hebrew translations on facing pages.) It is worth noting that Grade wrote these three poems and *The Yeshiva* AFTER the death of the Ḥazon Ish. Indeed, Grade never visited Israel after World War II until after the Ḥazon Ish died. Grade later related, Professor David Fishman informs me, that he felt that had he gone to Israel he would have to meet with the Ḥazon Ish, but such a meeting would have been too difficult an experience. Either the Ḥazon Ish would have been greatly pained by seeing his former student transformed into a secular Jewish writer—the Ḥazon Ish, of course, knew about Grade's break with traditional Judaism and his subsequent literary career, but knowing is not the same as seeing—or Grade would have been impelled, out of respect for and loyalty to his former teacher, to return to traditional Judaism. Neither alternative, Grade concluded, was acceptable to him.

community, it is certainly well deserved.[3] The Ḥazon Ish—except for a brief period during World War I—never held any official position. He was neither a Rav nor a *rosh Yeshivah,* nor a member of any rabbinical or communal organization. Nevertheless, shortly after he arrived in the land of Israel in 1933 and certainly by the end of World War II, he emerged as the unchallenged and unrivalled leader and authority of the Ḥaredi community, an unofficial "position" he occupied until his death. He attained this position solely by virtue of his great personal erudition and scholarship, of his intellectual and spiritual power, of his piety, integrity, and humanity. Unyielding and unbending on what he considered to be matters of principle, a self-declared extremist on matters of religion and faith,[4] the Ḥazon Ish, at the same time, in his personal dealings with individuals displayed great charm, sensitivity, thoughtfulness,

---

3 This, of course, emerges from all the biographies of the Ḥazon Ish and the various studies of the Ḥaredi community. In this connection, I heard recently that it is exceptionally difficult and expensive to obtain a burial plot in the cemetery where the Ḥazon Ish is buried, since so many people wish to have the merit and honor of being buried in ground sanctified, as it were, by his mortal remains.

4 See the Ḥazon Ish's well-known essay in praise of extremism in *Pe᾿er ha-dor*, vol. 1, ed. Shlomo Kohen (Bnei Brak: Neṣaḥ, 1966), 292–94. It is striking that Shimon Finkelman in his biography, *The Chazon Ish* (New York: Mesorah, 1989), 218-219, translates *kiṣoniyyut*, "extremism," as "absolute commitment." Moreover, while he does translate *kiṣoniyyim* as "extremists," he revealingly puts quotation marks not to be found in the original text around the word. Obviously, Finkelman either personally feels uncomfortable with the notion of extremism or is concerned about the possible negative impact this very sharp and forthright praise of extremism on the part of the Ḥazon Ish might have upon the reader. It is, of course, very clear what the Ḥazon Ish would have to say about Finkelman's unacknowledged watering down of his views.

It should be noted, however, that on many important issues the Ḥazon Ish adopted what might be considered a "moderate" stance and opposed positions that he evidently considered to be "overly" extremist. For example, he pours withering scorn on the view that it is a halakhic obligation to secede from "Kenesset Israel," the autonomous Jewish community in the land of Israel during the Mandatory period. See *Qoveṣ iggerot Ḥazon Ish* (Collected Letters of the Ḥazon Ish) ed. Rabbi Shmuel Greineman, vol. 3 (Bnei Brak: Greineman, 1990), 129–34 (letters 111 and 112). (For historical background regarding this issue, see Menaḥem Friedman, *Ḥevrah ve-dat* [Society and Religion] [Jerusalem: Yad Yiṣḥak Ben-Zvi, 1978], 185–213.) Cf. as well the famous and oft-quoted statement of the Ḥazon Ish (*Yoreh de῾ah, siman* 13) that in the absence nowadays of visible and miraculous divine providence, nonbelievers do not fall into the halakhic category of heretics, indeed, that that category lacks any contemporary practical relevance. Rather, the Ḥazon Ish concludes, "It is incumbent upon us to draw them [the nonbelievers] to us with bonds of love, so that the light of truth will illuminate their ways to whatever degree possible."

and modesty. Perhaps it is this special blend of humility and forcefulness that accounts for the fascination the personality of the Ḥazon Ish exerted on all who knew him, whether they identified with him ideologically or not.

Recently two individuals who as young people knew the Ḥazon Ish personally related to me their own memories of him. A well-known Israeli bookseller rather pointedly contrasted the breadth and vision of the Ḥazon Ish with the narrowness and conventionality of his rabbinic successors in the Ḥaredi community, however great their traditional talmudic scholarship may be.[5] Sarah Meyers of Chicago, the daughter of the well-known philanthropist Mr. Bernard Meyers, who provided the Ḥazon Ish with a home in Bnei Brak—for which the Ḥazon Ish insisted on paying taxes and upkeep[6]—recollected the Ḥazon Ish's warmth, saintliness, integrity, and unremitting devotion to study. "My father helped support a number of prominent rabbinic scholars," Ms. Meyers related. "The other rabbinic scholars would, at times, utilize some of the funds he provided them to take—with his understanding, of course—a vacation in Switzerland or to spend a weekend at the beach in Netanya. And why not? But never the Ḥazon Ish."

We are fortunate in having much material to draw on in delineating both the ideology and personality of the Ḥazon Ish. In addition to his massive, strictly halakhic writings, which, however, at times contain some striking general theological or ideological observations,[7] his collected letters[8] and his brief but concentrated work *Emunah u-biṭaḥon*[9] provide us with a vivid picture of his religious world-view and, perhaps even more important, allow us to hear his distinctive and highly individual voice. There are several collections of his teachings by his

---

5 Since the bookseller has both personal and economic connections with the Ḥaredi community, he wishes, understandably, to remain anonymous.

6 See Finkelman, *The Chazon Ish*, 63f.

7 See the many theological and ideological statements culled from his halakhic writings to be found in the anthologies cited in note 10. Cf. R. Yiṣḥak Hutner, *Iggerot u-mikhtavim* (Jerusalem, 1981), 71-74, for an analysis of the link between the halakhic and theological elements in the Ḥazon Ish's famous ruling concerning milking on the Sabbath.

8 *Qoveṣ iggerot* (many reprints). While much of the material found in vol. 3 has already appeared in the anthologies cited in note 10 and the biographies cited in note 11, the volume does contain, as far as I have been able to determine, a good deal of highly interesting, hitherto unpublished material as well.

9 (Faith and Trust) (Bnei Brak, 1954), and reprinted many times.

disciples and followers, generally organized topically.[10] While these collections draw primarily on the letters and *Emunah u-biṭaḥon,* they also contain a fair amount of uncollected and unpublished material. There are also a number of extensive biographies of the Ḥazon Ish, in both Hebrew and English.[11] These biographies are hagiographical and consequently undiscriminating in nature, but they do contain a good deal of otherwise unavailable primary material, provide helpful historical context, and, if used with critical care and caution, can often prove illuminating. Finally, as mentioned earlier, we have the marvelous portrait of the Ḥazon Ish in Grade's *The Yeshiva.* Grade's portrait dovetails beautifully with what we know of the Ḥazon Ish from both his own writings and the more conventional biographies, and it serves to bring the Ḥazon Ish to life in a way the more conventional and uncritical biographies cannot hope to equal.[12] Moreover, it provides us with much personal data that those worshipful biographies omit, no doubt deliberately, the Ḥazon Ish's unhappy married life, for example.[13]

II

The Ḥazon Ish grew up in the milieu of east European Orthodoxy as that Orthodoxy had crystallized in the late nineteenth and early

---

[10] *Hitʿorrerut* (Awakening) (Bnei Brak: Greineman, 1989); *Liqquṭ dinim ve-hanhagot mi-Maran he-Ḥazon Ish,* (Anthology of Rulings and Practices of Our Teacher the Ḥazon Ish) vol. 1, compiled by Rabbi Meir Greineman (Bnei Brak: Greineman, 1988); *Orḥot Ish* (Jerusalem: Greineman, 1989).

[11] Kohen, *Peʾer ha-dor;* Aharon Sorasky, *He-Ḥazon Ish be-dorotav* (The Ḥazon Ish in His Times) (Bnei Brak: Yad He-Hazon Ish, 1984); Finkelman, *The Chazon Ish.* As Finkelman indicates (p.8), his biography draws heavily upon the two Hebrew biographies, and, indeed, as he does not indicate, is, in many places, little more than an abridged English paraphrase of these works. I have, nevertheless, refered to Finkelman's biography wherever possible because of its ready availibility.

[12] A full comparison of the portrait of the Ḥazon Ish painted by Grade both with his spiritual profile as reconstructed from his own writings and with the various hagiographical portraits found in the standard biographies would make a fascinating study. Meanwhile, compare *The Yeshiva,* 2:143, 190, and 190f. with *Emunah u-biṭaḥon,* . 40-43, 16f., and 5f., respectively.

[13] The recently published personal recollection of the Ḥazon Ish by Ḥayyim Kolitz, *He-Ḥozeh mi-Liṭa: Perakim be-Ḥayyei he-Ḥazon Ish* (The Visionary from Lithuania: Chapters in the Life of the Ḥazon Ish) (Jerusalem: Rubin Mass, 1990), though it also tends to hagiography, does, unlike the standard biographies, speak openly about the Ḥazon Ish's troubled marriage. While most of Kolitz's discussion of this matter (pp. 41-46) seems to be based on Grade, he reveals new important information, not found in Grade, concerning the more intimate side of the Ḥazon Ish's marriage (see p. 61).

twentieth centuries. More specifically, he grew up in the spiritual climate of Lithuanian Mitnaggedism. His father was a prominent Lithuanian Rav, and many of his ancestors from both his paternal and maternal sides were leading members of the Lithuanian rabbinic elite.[14]

Scholars have examined how traditional east European Jewish society in the nineteenth century under the multiple challenges of modernization—Haskalah, secularism, nationalism, and so on—transformed itself and emerged as a self-conscious Orthodox movement.[15] The rise and efflorescence of the great central Lithuanian yeshivas, first Volozhin and later Ponovezh, Slobodka, Telz, Mir, and many others; the development of new methods of analytic talmudic scholarship in those yeshivas, pioneered by R. Ḥayyim Soloveitchik and others; the spread of the Musar movement under the guidance of R. Yisrael Salanter and his followers, a movement which at first sought to direct itself to the community as a whole, but later turned its attention to the yeshivas; the publication of such rabbinic journals as *Ha-Tevunah* and orthodox newspapers as *Ha-Levanon*; and the founding of a wide variety of rabbinic and communal organizations culminating in Agudat Yisrael—all these developments are well known and have been extensively studied. It was this Orthodoxy, more specifically, the Lithuanian Mitnaggedic branch of that Orthodoxy, that formed and shaped the personality and thought of the Ḥazon Ish. And yet, as the title of my essay indicates, the Ḥazon Ish, in my view, developed and maintained a dialectical relationship with that Orthodoxy, in particular with Lithuanian Mitnaggedism. While in many respects he deepened and intensified the already existing and ongoing trends and tendencies in east European Orthodoxy, in other respects he developed a rather subtle, oftentimes more implicit than explicit, but nevertheless powerful and far-reaching critique of that Orthodoxy. What emerges from an examination of the Ḥazon Ish's writings is that the Ḥazon Ish felt—though he never put it that way—that east European Orthodoxy—and again, more specifically, late nineteenth- and early twentieth-century Lithuanian Mitnaggedism—in the laudable battle it waged against the forces of modernity had, perhaps unwittingly, absorbed many of modernity's values, in particular the value of self-affirmation and the many different guises it assumes: self-expression, autonomy, personal creativity, and so on.

---

14 On the family background of the Ḥazon Ish, see *Pe'er ha-dor*, 27-65.

15 See the many studies of Jacob Katz, Gershon Bacon, Immanuel Etkes, Ehud Luz, Joseph Salmon, Eli Schweid, Shaul Stampfer, and others on this subject.

Let us, however, before we present the more fundamental critique, begin with some externals. The Ḥazon Ish once noted that the Gerer Rebbe, R. Abraham Mordecai Alter, criticized the students of Lithuanian yeshivas for three things: 1) they wore short jackets, following the modern fashion; 2) they were clean-shaven until they got married; and 3) they married at a late age. And the Ḥazon Ish commented that no valid response can be made to these three criticisms; rather, all the explanations and rationalizations offered for justifying such behavior are forced and lack any basis.[16] Of course, that the Gerer Rebbe, the leader of Polish Ḥasidism, would level such criticisms against Lithuanian yeshiva students is not surprising. But that the Ḥazon Ish, who after all, as we have seen, emerged from the midst of the Lithuanian Mitnaggedic tradition and was one of its outstanding rabbinic representatives, would endorse them is significant. Nor was this endorsement just a casual comment on the part of the Ḥazon Ish. Rather, throughout his writings he emphasizes the importance of wearing traditional rabbinic garments,[17] forcefully sets forth his opposition to using shavers and depilatories,[18] and stresses the need for marriage at an early age, preferable between the ages of 18 and 20 as mandated by the Sages.[19] We are, of course, dealing here with externals, and yet, as all historians, sociologists, and anthropologists know, externals ought never be underestimated, particularly in connection with the phenomenon of acculturation. Nor, in endorsing the Gerer Rebbe's criticisms, was the Ḥazon Ish just finding fault with the behavior of Lithuanian yeshiva students. Rather he was also, if only by implication, criticizing the great *rashei yeshivah* of such outstanding Lithuanian yeshivas as Mir, Slobodka, and Kletzk who, at least tacitly, lent their approval to their students' behavior. As we shall see immediately, his criticisms of the leadership and philosophy of the Lithuanian yeshivas went much deeper than questions of clothing, beards, and the average age of marriage, as important as such matters might be.

Let us turn to the issue of Torah study. In the late nineteenth century, R. Ḥayyim Soloveitchik developed a new, innovative method of Talmudic study, variously known as *havanah, ḥaqirah,* or *hegyon,* which

16 *Pe'er ha-dor,* 250 n. 31.

17 *Dinim ve-hanhagot,* 34; *Qoveṣ iggerot,* 1:178 (letter 196).

18 See Rabbi Moshe Werner, *Hadras Ponim Zokon,* 2nd ed. (New York: Moshe Wiener, 1978), 16, 17, 19, 34f., 40, 56, 304-307, 349–51; *Qoveṣ iggerot,* 1:179 (letters 197f.).

19 *Qoveṣ iggerot,* 2:123f. (letter 135).

was highly abstract, conceptual, and analytic in character.[20] This method became the rage in all the yeshivas and swept all before it.[21] It has been shown that although the Ḥazon Ish in his early halakhic works oftentimes engaged in this mode of abstract analysis and classification à la Rav Ḥayyim, he gradually moved away from it and adopted a much more text-centered and *peshaṭ*-oriented approach.[22] Why? and of what significance was such a move? In order to arrive at a possible and, I trust, plausible answer to these questions, let us first place the analytic approach in its proper historic context and seek to determine the source of its appeal.

My teacher, the noted contemporary rabbinic scholar and theologian R. Joseph B. Soloveitchik, in describing the great intellectual power of his grandfather, Rav Ḥayyim, has written, "Were it not for him, Torah would have been forgotten from Israel"[23] Of course, this statement is no doubt partially—and perhaps more than partially—motivated by pardonable family pride. And yet, Rabbi Soloveitchik is, at the same time, making, if in a rather exaggerated and hyperbolic manner, a serious historical point.

Rabbi Soloveitchik has had the occasion to explain orally that many talented east European and more specifically Lithuanian yeshiva students were drawn to the new, expansive, and highly attractive external and secular intellectual horizons that opened up before them in the modern world. Was there anything in traditional Jewish learning, in traditional talmudic scholarship that could compete, could hold its own, with the excitement, the intellectual challenges of the humanities, the sciences, philosophy, and all? The analytic approach, Rabbi Soloveitchik

---

[20] On the analytic method of the school of R. Ḥayyim Soloveitchik, see R. Shlomo Yosef Zevin, *Ishim ve-shiṭot* (Men and Methods) (Tel Aviv: A. Tsiuni, 1966); the various studies of N. Solomon, "*Ḥilluq* and *Ḥaqirah*: A Study in the Method of the Lithuanian Talmudists," *Dine Israel* 4 (1973); lxix–cvi; "Definition and Classification in the Works of the Lithuanian Halakhists," *Dine Israel*, 6 (1975), LXIII-CIII: "Concepts of *Zeh Neheneh* . . . in the Analytic School," *The Jewish Law Annual* 3 (1980), 49-62; R. Joseph B. Soloveitchik, "Mah dodekh mi-dod," in *Be-Sod ha-yaḥid ve-ha-yaḥad* (Jerusalem: Orot, 1970), 212–35; and Yiṣḥak Adler, *Iyyun be-lomduṭ* (New York: Composition by Beit Shʿar Press, 1989).

[21] See Rabbi Henoch Eigis, Introduction to *Marḥeshet*, cited by R. Zevin, *Ishim ve-Shitot*, 195f.; Rabbi Prof. Samuel Bialoblocki, "R. Iṣele mi-Ponevezh," in *Eym le-masoret* (Ramat Gan: Bar Ilan University, 1971), 259. See note 35 below.

[22] See Zevin, "Ḥazon Ish," *Ishim ve-shiṭot*, 316. The biography of the Ḥazon Ish, *Peʾer ha-dor*, 273f., lifts the entire analysis of Rabbi Zevin, almost word for word, attributing it to anonymous "knowledgable observers" ("*yodʿei davar*")!

[23] "Mah dodekh mi-dod," 213.

argues, answered this need. It provided the yeshiva students with a new, exciting method of talmudic study that encouraged conceptual creativity and innovation, that allowed a student's intellectual powers full range of expression, and that was as demanding, as rigorous as any discipline the secular world had to offer. Only a method of talmudic study like that of R. Ḥayyim, a method that was the intellectual equal of secular disciplines, stood a chance of keeping the most intellectually talented of east European Jewish youth within the confines of the *bet midrash*. Indeed, then, were it not for Rav Ḥayyim, Torah would surely have been forgotten from Israel!

Of course, the fact that Rabbi Soloveitchik is one of the towering rabbinic scholars of our age does not necessarily mean that we have to accept his historical judgments. However, this particular historical claim of Rabbi Soloveitchik is supported by such other knowledgeable rabbinic observers as Rabbi Isser Unterman[24] as well as by such outstanding contemporary historians of the Lithuanian yeshiva world as Professor Mordecai Breuer[25] and would seem to be well founded.

It should be noted that Rabbi Soloveitchik himself is, of course, a modern halakhic thinker, perhaps the outstanding modern halakhic thinker of our time. And for him the greatness of his grandfather's method is precisely the scope it allows for *yeṣirah* and *ḥiddush,* for conceptual creativity and innovation. Moreover, for Rabbi Soloveitchik, this method of Talmudic study ultimately turns out to be one of the major means whereby one reconciles the rational religious consciousness, with its emphasis on self-expression and intellectual autonomy, and the revealed religious consciousness, with its emphasis on self-abnegation and submission to external authority.[26]

---

24 R. Isser Yehudah Unterman, "Torah Maḥzeret el Akhsanya Shelah," in *Sefer ha-Yovel le-Rav Shimon Shkop* (Jubilee Volume for Rav S. Shkop) (Vilna, 1937), 12-20. Rabbi Unterman recollects, "The students felt the wonderful delight of creative activity, and this was as vital for them as air for breathing . . . . Some thought that this method [of R. Ḥayyim] served as protection against the attractive power of secular Haskalah."

25 Mordecai Breuer, "Tradition and Change in European Yeshivot: Seventeenth–Nineteenth Centuries" (paper presented at the conference "Tradition and Crisis Revisited: Jewish Society and Thought on the Threshhold of Modernity," Center for Jewish Studies of Harvard University, October 1988).

26 See his essays "Ish ha-halakhah," (Man of the Law), in *Ish ha-halakhah: Galui ve-Nistar* (Halakhic Man: Revealed and Concealed) (Jerusalem: Alpha, 1979), 11-113 (repr. from *Talpiyyot* 1/3-4 [1944]: 651-735) (=*Halakhic Man,* trans. Lawrence Kaplan [Philadelphia: Jewish Publictation Society, 1983]); "Mah dodekh mi-dod;" "U-bikashtem mi-sham," *Ha-Darom* 47 (1978): 1-83. Cf. my essay, "Rabbi Joseph B. Soloveitchik's Philosophy of Halakhah," *Jewish Law Annual* 7 (1987): 139–97. I discuss

It is precisely at this point that we are ready to return to the Ḥazon Ish. For if R. Soloveitchik is one of the great MODERN halakhic thinkers of our time, the Ḥazon Ish was one of the century's great ANTIMODERN halakhic thinkers. Therefore, so I would argue, if it is precisely the innovative, creative, and expressive aspect of Rav Ḥayyim's approach that made this approach so popular to begin with and so attractive to his grandson, it is this very same aspect that made this approach so suspect to the Ḥazon Ish. For the Ḥazon Ish, this approach was too innovative, too creative, too expressive. The Ḥazon was very wary of *ḥiddush*. As he oftentimes had the occasion to state, "*Ḥiddush* is alien to my nature."[27] Or, as he wrote on another occasion, "One should not innovate (*le-ḥaddesh ha-devarim*) but search out (*le-vakkesh ha-devarim*)."[28] Of course, the Ḥazon Ish could not dismiss the time-honored role of *ḥiddush* in Talmudic studies. However, *ḥiddush*, for him, does not mean conceptual creativity or innovation, but rather the clarification that derives from diligent study.[29]

In this connection it is worthwhile to examine the critical glosses of the Ḥazon Ish on R. Ḥayyim Soloveitchik's *Ḥiddushim al ha-Rambam* (Novellae on Maimonides), the work which is generally viewed as the quintessential embodiment of the analytic method.[30] A full comparison of the varying approaches of Rav Ḥayyim and Ḥazon Ish is beyond the scope of this paper. We may, however, note the following. The Ḥazon Ish in his glosses never resorts to the type of conceptual terminology that typifies the analytic approach. He opposes a number of Rav Ḥayyim's conceptual distinctions as being overly subtle and unfounded.[31] Above all, he consistently and firmly opposes what he views as attempts on the

---

these matters further in two as yet unpublished essays, "Rabbi Joseph Soloveitchik as a Modern Halakhic Thinker" and "From Freedom to Necessity and Back Again: Man's Religious Odyssey in the Thought of Rabbi Joseph Soloveitchik."

27 *Ḥazon Ish, Shevi*ʿ*it, siman* 7.

28 *Ḥazon Ish, Likkutei Sanhedrin, siman* 22.

29 *Qoveṣ iggerot* 1:28f. (letter 4). In offering this definition, the Ḥazon Ish bases himself on a statement of R. Ḥayyim of Volozhin. For an analysis of the educational philosophy of R. Ḥayyim Volozhin, see Norman Lamm, *Torah Lishmah: Torah for Torah's Sake in the Thought of Rav Ḥayyim Volozhin and His Contemporaries* (New York: Yeshivah University Press, 1989), 28-31. See note 58.

30 In most of the recent reprints of *Hiddushei Rabbeynu Ḥayyim ha-Levi*, the *Gilyonot he-Ḥazon Ish* (Marginalia of the Ḥazon Ish) may be found appended at the back.

31 See, for example, *Gilyonot*, 11, on *Hilkhot Tefillin* 1:1, s.v. *ve-nireh de-be-sefer torah*.

part of Rav Ḥayyim to read certain concepts and ideas into the Rambam or the gemara which are not stated clearly therein.[32]

One may argue, of course, that in his opposition to the analytic method and his espousal of a more rigorously impersonal, text-centered, *peshaṭ* approach, the Ḥazon Ish was just adhering to good scientific methodology.[33] But, as I have sought to indicate, there is a more fundamental ideological point being made here, if only by implication.[34] For the Ḥazon Ish, the analytic approach allows too much room for self-expression, for the play of the individual's own intellectual powers unconstrained by the discipline of the text. In this respect, though the analytic approach may be an admirable attempt at making talmudic study more attractive and exciting to the student, it concedes too much to the modern temper, to the modern emphasis on the self and its intellectual autonomy, even if it is a self engaged in exercising its intellectual autonomy in the realm of traditional talmudic scholarship.[35] It is striking

---

32 See, for example, ibid., 1, on *Hilkhot Tefillin* 1:11, s.v. *ve-nireh de-mi-shum hakhi*; ibid. 8, on *Hilkhot Maʾakhalot Assurot* 4:3, s.v. *ve-ha-nireh lomar, de-be-emet*; ibid. 12, on *Hilkhot Maʾaseh ha-Korbanot* 10:12, s.v. *ve-hinneh be-sof perek bet*; and ibid. 14, on *Hilkhot ʿAvodat Yom ha-Kippurim* 5:31, s.v. *ve-nireh be-daʿat ha-Rambam*.

33 An acquaintance of mine who has made a careful study of the *Gilyonot* wittily remarked that the Ḥazon Ish judged Rabbi Ḥayyim's interpretations of the Rambam by the wrong criterion; he wanted to determine if they were true!

We may add that in his exceptionally comprehensive, text-centered, *peshaṭ* approach, as well as in his avoidance of analytic "*lomdut*," the Ḥazon Ish may justly be compared to his relative, the great rabbinic scholar of our generation, the late Professor Saul Lieberman. (This, of course, is not to deny the many important differences between their approaches.) It is interesting that the methods of study of both were often compared to that of the Vilna Gaon. For the Ḥazon Ish, see R. Yeḥiel Yaakov Weinberg, *Seridei esh*, vol. 3 (Jerusalem, 1966), 249. With reference to Professor Lieberman, Professor David Halivni informs me that when Lieberman published his *Tosefet Rishonim*, the venerable Hungarian rabbinic scholar Immanuel Löw, wrote Lieberman a letter in which he said that he could see from *Tosefet Rishonim* that Lieberman possessed a spark of the Gaon. For the Ḥazon Ish's favorable evaluation of the scholarship of Professor Lieberman, see S. Abramson, "R. Saul Lieberman's Method of Investigating Talmudic Literature" (in Hebrew), in *Le-Zikhron shel Shaul Lieberman* (In Memory of S. Lieberman) (Jerusalem: Israel National Science Academy, 1984), 29.

34 As to why the Ḥazon Ish is not more explicit in his criticism of the analytic approach, see note 57 below. It would seem, however, that when discussing matters with his close acquaintances the Ḥazon Ish was more open in his criticism. See note 39 below.

35 I would suggest in light of this point, that the Ḥazon Ish's largely tacit critique of the analytic method differs from the highly explicit critique of this method by such contemporaries as the Ridbaz (R. Jacob David Willowsky) and R. Aryeh Karlin,

that while the key terms that Rabbi Soloveitchik, the great modern halakhic thinker, uses in describing talmudic study are *yeṣirah* and *ḥiddush,* conceptual creativity and innovation,[36] the key terms used by the Ḥazon Ish, the great antimodern halakhic thinker, are *sheqeidah, yegiaᶜ,* and *ᶜameilut,* diligent unremitting study, effort, and toil.[37] Indeed, in one letter the Ḥazon Ish writes:

> What is required is to study and review the text several times, even without any *ḥiddush,* and to carefully examine matters in which the intellect, to being with, takes no pleasure, matters which, on the contrary, it finds burdensome. But such toil [*ᶜamel*] is the toil of Torah, and all the special qualities [conferred by] the study of the Torah are acquired precisely through this toil. However, after this toil, a new gate of light is opened and the intellect will take endless delight in it.[38]

In a word, what the Ḥazon Ish feels is called for in the area of traditional Jewish learning is not intellectual self-assertion but intellectual submission, submission to the authority of the text. And only such intellectual submission will bring in its wake true intellectual delight.

We would further argue that, for the Ḥazon Ish, this ethic of submission must express itself not only in the area of traditional Torah learning, *talmud torah,* but also, and perhaps primarily, in the area of observance of the commandments, *shemirat ha-miṣvot.* In this respect, the Ḥazon Ish's largely implicit critique of the analytic method of Talmudic scholarship,[39]

---

insofar as the critique of the Ḥazon Ish is, paradoxically, more fundamental than those of his contemporaries, for, as we shall see, it derives from a comprehensive world-view. For the critiques of Rabbis Willowsky and Karlin, see the relevant excerpts cited in Louis Jacobs, *A Tree of Life* (New York: Oxford University Press, 1984), 59f. Interestingly enough, the critiques of both testify, from a hostile standpoint, to the exceptional popularity of the analytic method. See note 21 above.

36 See the essays referred to in note 26.

37 A convenient collection of relevant passages may be found in *Orḥot Ish,* 63-72. Note as well the frequency of these terms in the writings of R. Ḥayyim Volozhin. See Lamm, *Torah Lishmah,* 31, 117. See note 29 above, and note 58 below.

38 *Qoveṣ iggerot,* 1:26 (letter 2).

39 After this article was completed and submitted, there appeared a very interesting, albeit rather hagiographical, new portrait of the Ḥazon Ish, *Be-Meḥiṣat he-Ḥazon Ish,*(n.p., 1991), by Raphael Halperin. Halperin as a young man was very close to the Ḥazon Ish and many letters in the volumes of *Qoveṣ iggerot* are addressed to him. Halperin, on the basis of what appears to be personal knowledge, categorically states, "The Ḥazon Ish did not at all approve of the method of logical analysis [of the Talmud] developed in the Lithuanian Yeshivot" (p. 241).

pioneered by R. Ḥayyim Soloveitchik, dovetails neatly and is of a piece with his more explicit critique of the Lithuanian Musar movement.

Unlike previous Musar ideologies which sought, in the main, to set forth and delineate the religious and pietistic ideals to which a Jew ought to aspire, Lithuanian Musar took for granted the traditional values of study of the Torah and observance of the commandments as those values were understood in the world of east European Orthodoxy. The problem with which Lithuanian Musar was concerned was the gap between theory and practice.[40] It is not that the average Jew did not known what he ought to do—it is that he oftentimes did not do it! Of course, while Lithuanian Musar focused on the internal, psychological obstacles to proper observance, it was clearly formulated against the backdrop and partially in reaction to the general breakdown of tradition in nineteenth-century eastern Europe. In this respect, the Musar movement, as we have already noted, was one of the major means whereby the new, emerging east European Orthodoxy sought to defend itself against the challenges to tradition posed by modernization and secularization. What the Musar movement did, as Emmanuel Etkes has noted, was to develop what is in effect a religious and pietistic psychotherapy based on an astute and penetrating psychology.[41] Without entering here into the details of either

---

[40] It should be noted that previous Musar ideologies, for example that of R. Jonah Gerondi, were also concerned with this psychological problem, though, unlike the Lithuanian Musar movement, they did not place it at the center of their interest. See the important observation of Yisrael Ta-Shema in, "Ḥasidut Ashkenaz bi-Sefarad: Rabbenu Yonah Gerondi - Ha-Ish u-Poᶜalo," *Galut aḥar Golah: Meḥkarim Mugashim li-Professor Ḥayyim Beinart* (Ashkenasi Hasidism in Spain: R. Jonah Gerondi—The Man and His Work, in *Exile and Diaspora: Studies in the History of the Jewish People Presented to Professor Ḥaim Beinart*), edited by Aharon Mirsky, Avraham Grossman, and Yoseph Kaplan (Jerusalem: Ben-Zvi Institute, 1988), p.182, note 42.

[41] See Emmanuel Etkes, *R. Yisrael Salanter ve-reishitah shel tenuᶜat ha-Musar* (R. Y. Salanter and the Beginning of the Musar Movement) (Jerusalem: Magnes, 1982). My general characterization of the Musar movement here is based on my own reading of the works of R. Salanter and on the recent studies of Etkes, Silman, Goldberg, and Pachter. See the aforementioned work of Etkes, certainly the best and most rounded study of R. Salanter; Yoḥanan Silman, "The Psychological Doctrine of R. Yisrael Salanter" (in Hebrew), *Bar-Ilan Annual* 11 (1978): 288-304; Hillel Goldberg, *R. Israel Salanter: Text, Structure, Idea* (New York: Ktav, 1982); and Mordecai Pachter's important Introduction to his edition of *Kitvei R. Yisrael Salanter* (Writings of R. Y. Salanter) (Jerusalem:Bialik Institute, 1972), as well as his major review essay of both Etkes and Goldberg, "R. Yisrael Salanter in a New Light" (in Hebrew), *Tarbiṣ* 53/1 (1984): 621–50. It should be noted that all these works focus on R. Yisrael Salanter and the Musar movement during his lifetime. For recent scholarly studies of the thought of R. Salanter's successors, see Tamar Ross, "Ha-Maḥashvah ha-ᶜiyyunit be-kitvei

the psychology or the psychotherapy, we may just briefly enumerate the methods that Rabbi Yisrael Salanter, the founder of the Musar movement, and his followers devised in order to help the individual overcome the gap between theory and practice: intense study of those areas of Jewish law which were generally neglected by the multitude; study of Musar texts with enthusiasm, with "lips aflame"—the content of the Musar texts was secondary; the cultivation of worldly wisdom in combating the evil instinct; unsparing introspection; and, finally, *protim* or *peᶜules,* the deliberate undergoing of trials "designed to cultivate certain positive character traits or eradicate negative ones."[42] This last method, associated particularly with the radical Novaredok school of Musar, was perhaps the best known of these means, certainly the one which best caught the popular imagination. The anecdote about the Novaredok yeshiva student going into an apothecary to ask for some nails is almost legendary. The point of this self-imposed trial, of course, is to endow the Musarist with the inner strength necessary to withstand and ignore the ridicule of the ignorant and scornful rabble, to give him the opportunity to display his contempt for the opinion of the multitude.

The Ḥazon Ish was critical of all these Musar techniques, with the, to be expected, exception of the technique of studying those areas of Torah which are generally neglected.[43] He was critical for two reasons. First, he felt that these techniques, unless strictly limited, would take away valu-

---

mamshikhav shel R. Yisrael salanter bi-Tenuᶜat ha-Musar" (The Speculative Teachings of the Successors of R. Y. Salanter) (Ph. D. diss., Hebrew University, 1986); idem, "The Musar Movement and the Hermeneutic Problem in Torah Study" (in Hebrew), *Tarbiṣ* 59/1-2 (1989-1990): 191-214.

42 David Fishman, "The Musar Movement in Inter-War Poland," in *The Jews of Poland between the Two World Wars,* ed. Yisrael Gutman et al. (Hanover, N.H.: University Presses of New England, 1988), 250. My brief characterization of Novaredok immediately following is based largely on Fishman's essay.

43 See *Emunah u-biṭaḥon,* 25f. (3:9), 27f. (3:12), citing R. Salanter's famous *Iggeret Musar.* In his use of R. Salanter's writings, or rather, certain very carefully selected excerpts therefrom, to criticize the Musar ideologies of the twentieth century, the Ḥazon Ish follows in the path of an already long line of opponents of Musar who sought to distinguish betwen R. Salanter himself and his successors. See Dov Katz, *Pulmus ha-Musar* (The Musar Controversy) (Jerusalem: Weiss, 1977). (In the same way, critics of Maimonideanism often attempted to distinguish betwen the views of the Great Eagle himself and those of his "unworthy" disciples who, so the critics claimed, inadvertantly or deliberately distorted the teaching of the Master.) It is ironic that R. Salanter's emphasis on the ethical and pietistic significance of intensive Torah study in the *Iggeret Musar,* given the use the Ḥazon Ish makes of it, may have been designed, at least in part, as a concession to traditional sensibilities. See Silman, "The Psychological Doctrine," 293-95.

able time from the study of Torah.[44] The second reason, however, is more fundamental.

The Ḥazon Ish was of the opinion that the fundamental Musar approach of working on oneself, of turning inward, in order to develop one's spiritual personality and overcome the obstacles standing in the way of proper observance was fundamentally misguided. Again, we may suggest that the Ḥazon Ish was suspicious of the focus on, the concern for, the self, even if that focusing, that concern, was for religious purposes. Rather, the Ḥazon Ish developed what we may term a counter-Musar, based on his own psychology, his own analysis of the human personality.[45] This counter-Musar is the subject of chapter 4 of *Emunah u-biṭaḥon.* At the beginning of the chapter the Ḥazon Ish states, "At the root [of man's manifold evil traits] there is only . . . one evil trait. This evil trait is allowing one's natural life to flow along its natural course."[46] On the other hand, "The [sole] positive trait is [man's] absolute commitment to give preference to the ethical sensibility over the natural sensibility."[47] Moreover, for the Ḥazon Ish, man's manifold evil traits—laziness, pride, and so on—and in particular, his fundamental evil trait of "allowing one's natural life to flow along its natural course," stand in the way of his fulfilling not only the commandments between man and man but also the commandments between man and God.[48]

How then can man overcome his fundamental negative trait and cultivate his fundamental positive trait? The Ḥazon Ish answers:

> After we have established that the rectification of one's [evil] traits is necessary for observing both the statutes [between man and God] and the judgments [between man and man], it follows that the method for rectifying those traits is through observing the Halakhah. For though the practical commandments on a superficial level . . . appear easy to perform, those who know the strict requirements of the law [*ḥomer ha-din*] and who have fixed in their heart the love of Halakhah find them exceptionally difficult to observe. . . . For a person who seeks to observe a commandment in all its fine particulars will find himself confronting many awesome trials . . . and he will have to combat his [evil] traits, at times the trait of laziness . . . and,

44 This is one of the major points made throughout chapter 3 of *Emunah u-biṭaḥon.* See, for example, 27f. (3:11f.), 30–32 (3:17f.), 37-40 (3:25-27).

45 See Etkes, *Salanter ve-reishitah,* 346, n. 21. Etkes, however, refers in this note to chapter 3 of *Emunah u-biṭaḥon,* when, in fact, he should refer to BOTH chapters 3 and 4.

46 *Emunah u-biṭaḥon,* 44 (4:1). Cf. *Qoveṣ iggerot,* 3:186f. (letter 184).

47 *Emunah u-biṭaḥon,* 44 (4:1).

48 Ibid., 47 (4:5).

> at times, [he will suffer] the scorn of others and a thousand such like.[49]

Even more important:

> The constant adhesion to the precise requirements of the law [*dikduk ha-din*], [which involves struggling] against one's inborn inclinations, accustoms a person to give over the staff of rulership into the possession of understanding and the bridle into the hand of intellect. It strengthens his heart to be constantly aware that he must submit himself to his inner [moral] sensibility and his noble conscience.[50]

Thus for the Ḥazon Ish it is precisely the DIFFICULTY in observing the commandments, the countless trials involved in their precise performance, the ongoing struggle against one's natural inclinations that their fulfilment calls for, that serve as the means whereby one overcomes negative character traits and develops positive ones.

The Ḥazon Ish, then, is in agreement with the Novaredok school of Musar that the only means of character improvement is undergoing trials; however, for the Ḥazon Ish, these trials need not and should not be self-imposed, like Novaredok *peʿules*, but must be trials that flow from the unremitting struggle to observe the precise, extensive, and exceptionally difficult requirements of the Halakhah. As the Ḥazon Ish argues—and here it is clear that he has Novaredok in mind though he does not say so explicitly—

> One could almost say the precise fulfillment of the law is the only way to rectify one's [evil] traits. For in other respects it is a commandment to keep far away from trials. And a person should not seek out trials in order to train himself in the rectification of his [character] traits; on the contrary, it is an ethical obligation to avoid a situation in which one might be subject to a trial. . . . However, the person who observes the commandments and all their precise details constantly finds himself confronted with trials . . . and he is able to train himself well to incite his good *yeṣer* against his evil *yeṣer*; and precisely because he encounters trials at every moment, his [spiritual] ascent is certain and his improvement is assured.[51]

What we have here, then, is an ethos of stringency, of *ḥumrah*. Scholars have discussed to what extent the Ḥazon Ish was a *maḥmir* or a *meiqil*,

49 Ibid., 48 (4:7).
50 Ibid., 48f. (4:8).
51 Ibid., 49f. (4:9).

was stringent or lenient, in his halakhic rulings.[52] People oftentimes point to his famous ruling concerning *shiʿurim,* concerning the proper determination of halakhic measurements, such as the precise size of a cubit (an *amah*) or a *kezayit,* as an example of the Ḥazon Ish's halakhic stringency. This ruling requires, for example, that the quantity of wine consumed for *Kiddush* or the amount of matzah consumed on Passover be considerably greater than was previously assumed to be the case.[53] However, the Ḥazon Ish himself says that this ruling cuts both ways and that he would rely on his view concerning measurements to issue a decision permitting a woman to remarry in a case of doubt (*le-hatir eyshet ish*).[54] But what is important is not whether the Ḥazon Ish was a *maḥmir* or *meiqil* in this or that halakhic ruling, or even whether in terms of the totality of his halakhic rulings he could be described as a *maḥmir* or a *meiqil.* What is important is that his fundamental world-view involves an ethos of *ḥumrah.* According to this view, one should not seek out *qulot,* leniencies, for it is precisely the DIFFICULTY involved in fulfilling the precise requirements of the Halakhah that enables one to break one's evil character traits.[55] At the same time, we must add, the Ḥazon Ish would

---

52 See Finkelman, *The Chazon Ish,* 104; Shila Raphael, "On the Image of the Gaon R. Shlomo Yosef Zevin," (in Hebrew), *Sinai* 82/1-2 (1977): 4. It should be noted, however, that the well-known *qulot* of the Ḥazon Ish with reference to the issues of the Sabbatical year (*Qoveṣ iggerot* 3:108–10 [letter 84]), milking on the Sabbath (ibid., 111f. [letter 86]), and Yom Kippur in Japan (Ibid., 2:114 [letter 167]) are all examples of particular, limited, lenient rulings that only slightly offset his fundamentally stringent rulings on these issues.

53 See Menachem Friedman, "Life Tradition and Book Tradition in the Development of Ultra-Orthodox Judaism," in *Judaism Viewed from Within and from Without,* ed. Harvey Goldberg (Albany: SUNY Press, 1987), 237f., 251f. Idem, "The Lost *Kiddush* Cup" (this volume).

54 *Qoveṣ iggerot* 1:175 (Letter 194). My contention, however, needs to be qualified. While the ruling of the Ḥazon Ish on the issue of *shiʿurim* involves both halakhic leniency as well as stringency, certainly the ACCEPTANCE of his ruling "by almost all of the Ḥaredi community in a relatively short time," as that ruling affects the consumption of wine for *Kiddush* or the consumption of matzah on Passover, is, as Friedman, "Life Tradition," 235–38, correctly argues, an example of that community's movement in the direction of greater stringency. It is also an instance, as Friedman notes, of the triumph of the "book tradition" over the "life tradition" in ultra-Orthodox Judaism. On this last point, see section IV below.

55 A convenient collection of passages from the Ḥazon Ish on the importance and vital necessity of *dikduk ha-din* may be found in *Orḥot Ish,* 105–13. (For examples of the Ḥazon Ish's own personal, exceptionally stringent behavior in halakhic matters, see Finkelman, *The Chazon Ish,* 166–72, though, of course, one should not confuse the PRIVATE adoption of personal stringencies with stringency in one's PUBLIC function as

be opposed to seeking out artificial or unnecessary *ḥumrot*.[56] For him, simply observing in a proper fashion the multitude of commandments set forth by the Halakhah in all their fine details and particulars is difficult enough.

In this respect, it is instructive to contrast the view of the Ḥazon Ish with that of the leading rabbinic decisor (*poseq*) of our generation, the late R. Moshe Feinstein. Rav Moshe was often wont to say that the trouble with Judaism started with the popular saying, "*Siz shver tsu zayn a yid*" (It is difficult to be a Jew). Rather, people ought to say, "It is wonderful to be a Jew." For the Ḥazon Ish, however, the whole point of the Halakhah is that it is "*shver tsu zayn a yid*," it is difficult to be a Jew; and precisely because it is difficult to be a Jew, it is also wonderful to be a Jew.

In sum, we are arguing that the Ḥazon Ish's critiques of both the analytic method of Talmudic scholarship and the Musar ideology stem from the same source. For him, to reiterate, the proponents of both the analytic method and the Musar ideology in their praiseworthy efforts to bolster tradition and combat the attractions of modernity tacitly conceded too much to modernity by allowing too great a role for human self-assertion and human autonomy, even within a strictly traditional framework, and by not sufficiently insisting on the absolute submission of the individual to the authority of the tradition in the realm of both study and practice.[57]

---

a *poseq*.) It would be worthwhile to establish a typology of the different ethoi of *ḥumrah* found in the Jewish tradition. To limit ourselves to more recent times, we have the kabbalistic ethos of the Shelah, the pietistic ethos of the Ramḥal, the psychological ethos of the Ḥazon Ish, and the more purely halakhic ethos of the contemporary rabbinic scholar, Rabbi Moshe Sternbuch. For some very preliminary but nonetheless suggestive remarks on this matter, see David Horowitz, "R. Moshe Sternbuch's Halakhic Novellae," *Tradition* 20/3 (1982): 265–72.

[56] See, for example, *Qoveṣ iggerot*, 2:130 (letter 149), 3:161 (letter 149), 3:169 (letter 155); and Finkelman, *The Chazon Ish*, 171.

[57] One may ask why the Ḥazon Ish was not more explicit in his criticisms of the analytic method of *lomdut* and the Musar ideology and his ideological basis for those criticisms, and why we have had to tease these views of his from his writings. I would suggest that the Ḥazon Ish felt very strongly that the Lithuanian yeshivas of his day were the last bulwarks of a tradition under siege, and that the analytic method and Musar ideology were the foundation stones of these yeshivas. One would have to be very careful and circumspect, then, in leveling any critique, lest by overly sharp and explicit remarks about the analytic method or about Musar one would somehow inadvertently weaken these yeshivas and thereby the tradition as a whole. It is striking that when an acquaintance of the Ḥazon Ish publicly retailed certain criticisms that the Ḥazon Ish had leveled in private against the Musar movement, the Ḥazon Ish wrote him a strong letter of rebuke (see *Qoveṣ iggerot*, 1:152f. [letter 154]). In this letter, written in 1939, the Ḥazon Ish does not deny that he made

His own method of talmudic study and his own counter-Musar were designed to provide and ensure that requisite degree of submission. In this respect, the ideology of the Ḥazon Ish must be seen as the Lithuanian Mitnaggedic counterpart of similar ideologies of religious submission and heteronomy that were flourishing at that time in the Hasidic world of east European Orthodoxy.[58]

---

the critical remarks ascribed to him, but argues that his comments would, in the course of being spread about in public, be distorted, blown out of proportion, and thereby give rise to dissension and discord. In the letter he also refers to a period in his life during World War I when he spent much time with both R. Nosson Ṣevi Finkel, the *Alter* of Slobodka, and R. Yeruḥam Levovitz, the *Alter* of Mir, and their disciples, as well as with leading representatives of the Novaredok school of Musar. He states: "A boundless love always existed between us, and they were completely devoted to me. Never would I refrain from [leveling] a sharp critique [of the various Musar ideologies]. And they delighted in this (for true scholars delight more in attempted refutations of their views than they do in support being adduced in favor of their positions) and I would delight in them." An oft-told story about the Ḥazon Ish relates that he once attended a Musar discourse of the *Alter* of Slobodka. At the discourse's conclusion, the *Alter* approached the Ḥazon Ish and queried, "What is my friend doing here? I thought he was opposed to the Musar doctrine?" The Ḥazon Ish replied, "True, but I am even more opposed to your opponents!"

Perhaps it was this felt need on the part of the Ḥazon Ish for a circumspect critique of the analytic method and the Musar ideology that was responsible for his not publishing his critical glosses on *Ḥiddushei Rabbenu Ḥayyim* and his work of counter-Musar, *Emunah u-biṭaḥon*, during his lifetime. For the former work makes quite clear his profound disagreement with the analytic method, while the latter is quite openly and forcefully critical about the Musar ideology. The Ḥazon Ish thus may have felt ambivalent about "going public" with such relatively unambiguous criticisms and therefore allowed these works to remain in manuscript. I have been told that when *Emunah u-biṭaḥon* appeared posthumously, the well-known Musar exponent R. Yeḥezkel Lewenstein delivered a very forceful address taking sharp issue with the views of the Ḥazon Ish as expressed therein and defending Musar against his criticisms. Certainly, then, the Musar exponents grasped full well the thrust of the book's argument and against whom it was directed.

58 See Mendel Piekarz's important monograph, *Ḥasidut Polin: Megammot Raʿayoniyot beyn Shtai ha-Milḥamot u-bi-Gezerot 1940-1945 ("Ha-Shoah")* (Ideological Trends of Hasidism in Poland During the Interwar Period and the Holocaust) (Jerusalem: Bialik Institute, 1990), chapters 3 and 4. We would suggest that the Ḥazon Ish himself, however, saw both his method of Talmud study and his view of the proper relationship between Torah study and Musar as a return to the approaches taken by the Gaon of Vilna and his disciple, R. Ḥayyim Volozhin; i.e., he saw himself as an upholder of the TRUE Lithuanian Mitnaggedic tradition. I have already indicated in note 33 that the similarity between the Ḥazon Ish's method of Talmud study and that of the Gaon has often been remarked upon. Moreover, the Ḥazon Ish bases his view of *ḥiddush* on a statement of R. Ḥayyim Volozhin (see note 29 above). That there may be similarities between the Ḥazon Ish's views concerning the proper

III

The above completes our presentation of the Ḥazon Ish as a critic of traditional Orthodoxy, particularly Lithuanian Mitnaggedism of the late nineteenth and early twentieth centuries, in the name of his own ethos of submission. In this section, I show how this ethos of submission is a fundamental and central element of the religious world-view of the Ḥazon Ish, how it keeps reappearing in his writings and determines his stance on a wide variety of issues. I limit myself to the Ḥazon Ish's views regarding two basic issues, but could easily multiply examples.[59]

First, the Ḥazon Ish sharply opposed the enactment of any new *taqqanot* (rabbinic ordinances) by the rabbinic authorities of his day. In 1943, the Chief Rabbinate of Israel, as part of a series of *taqqanot* on matters of family law, proposed to issue a *taqqanah* modifying the existing Jewish law of inheritance by allowing daughters to inherit along with

---

relationship of Musar and Torah study and those of the Gaon and R. Ḥayyim of Volozhin has not to my knowledge ever been suggested, but a very preliminary and tentative study does point in that direction. The matter requires and deserves further investigation. In any event, it is ironic and revealing that the great upholder of the Mitnaggedic tradition found himself, in the last years of his life, playing, perhaps against his will, the role of a Mitnaggedic Rebbe!

59 Other issues which ought to be discussed in this connection are the Ḥazon Ish's attitude toward the Rishonim; his prohibition of the zebu, an animal which appears to have the distinguishing characteristics of kosher animals but which lacks a tradition testifying to its kosher status; his views regarding textual criticism and the use of manuscripts; and his stance on *Daʿat Torah*. On the issue of the Ḥazon Ish's attitude toward *Rishonim*, see the sources collected in *Orḥot Ish*, 212–17. But see *Qoveṣ iggerot*, 3:50f. (letter 22). Cf., as well, Zevin, *Ishim ve-Shiṭot*, 318f. On his prohibition of the Zebu, see *Qoveṣ iggerot*, 1:115f. (letter 99), 2:87f. (letter 83), and 3:134–37 (letter 113) [= Rabbi Isaac Herzog, *Pesakim u-Ketavim*, Vol. 4 (Jerusalem: Mossad ha-Rav Kook, 1990), 68f.]. For different halakhic perspectives, see R. Isaac Herzog, 59–66; and Rabbi Moses Tendler, *Chavrusa* (March 1985), 3. For a discussion of the Ḥazon Ish's views on textual criticism and the use of manuscripts, see Ẓvi Yehuda, "The Ḥazon Ish on Textual Criticism and Halakhah," *Tradition*, 18/2 (1980): 172–80; Shnayer Z. Leiman, "The Ḥazon Ish on Textual Criticism and Halakhah: A Rejoinder," *Tradition*, 19/4 (1981): 301–10; and Daniel Sperber, "On the Legitimacy, or Indeed Necessity, of Scientific Disciplines for True 'Learning' of Talmud," paper delivered at the Fourth Conference of the Orthodox Forum of Yeshiva University, November, 1991. Finally, for an analysis of the Ḥazon Ish's stance on *Daʿat Torah*, see my article "Daas Torah: A Modern Conception of Rabbinic Authority," which will appear in a volume of essays on rabbinic authority, edited by Moshe Sokol, to be published by Yeshiva University.

sons.[60] When the Ḥazon Ish heard of this proposal, he wrote a very strong letter to R. Iser Zalman Melṣer condemning the idea. He viewed this proposal as a sign of weakness of faith—more significantly, as a craven type of apologetic stemming from the deep inferiority feelings of the middling believer in the presence of the unbeliever.

> And those in our generation who are weak [of faith] capitulate to the heretics and take pleasure in the heretic's approval [of him] by displaying weakness of faith [so that the heretic will think] that he is not a fanatic and is not an unworldly idler, but knows that it is necessary to forgo prohibitions in vital matters and to find permissive rulings [*heterim*] when called for by contemporary life. But the heretic rejoices in his victory and in his heart has but contempt for this counterfeit believer. . . . To our consternation, hearts have been stopped up and instead of displaying strength and fortitude of spirit by firmly maintaining the certain belief that the judgment belongs to God and that we have received [the Halakhah] thus from God, the Master of all, Lord of the earth, there are those of base thought who seek devices to prostrate themselves before heresy and to keep the law in the *Ḥoshen Mishpaṭ* [on the books], but in practice to conduct themselves like the nations of the world, [to the effect] that the daughter will inherit like the son. They thereby give praise to our enemies [by, in effect, conceding] that indeed the law of inheritance in the Torah does not accord [with the status] of an enlightened people, and this constitutes complete agreement with the abomination of heresy. Woe unto the ears which hear thus![61]

Of course, the Ḥazon Ish was criticizing here a controversial *taqqanah,* one which certainly modified the already existing Halakhah in a significant way. But in this letter he goes further and denies the power of the rabbis of his day to issue any type of *taqqanah* at all.

> And have we not heard from our masters that we are an orphaned generation and are not worthy of enacting any ordinances at all? For [the power to enact ordinances] requires greatness in Torah to an extraordinary degree. We, however, have descended wondrously, and are like laypersons [*hedyoṭim*]. How then can we be so brazen [*naʿiz paneynu*] and obstinate as to claim that we are sages and have the power to declare money ownerless and enact permanent ordinances?[62]

60 On these *taqqanot* of the Chief Rabbinate, see Menaḥem Elon, *Ha-Mishpaṭ ha-Ivri,* (Hebrew law) (Jerusalem: Magnes, 1973), 2:661–75.

61 *Qoveṣ iggerot,* 1:111f. (letter 96).

62 Ibid., 112.

It is this sense of the unworthiness of his generation and of its rabbinic leaders and of their consequent lack of ability to legislate in any way at all that was behind the Ḥazon Ish's famed opposition to a proposed rabbinic *taqqanah* establishing a fast day in memory of the victims of the Holocaust.[63] When this proposal was put forward, the Ḥazon Ish set forth his objections to it in a letter that clearly calls to mind his just-cited letter to Rav Isser Zalman.

> Establishing a fast for all generations is in the category of a rabbinic commandment—all existing fasts are from the times of the prophets. Dare we, a generation that had best be silent, be so brazen [*naᶜiz paneynu] as* to even think of establishing matters for generations? This proposal bears witness to a denial on our part of all our sins and our lowly state, at a time when we are mired in our transgressions and iniquities, impoverished and bereft of Torah and *miṣvot*. Let us not seek that which is too great for us. Let us examine our paths and repent. This is our obligation, as it is said, "Is this not the fast I desire?" (Isa 58:6).[64]

In response to an argument that the great seventeenth-century rabbinic scholar and decisor the Taz had established the 20th of Sivan as a fast day in commemoration of the Chmielnicki massacres of 1648–1649, the Ḥazon Ish is reported to have offered two replies: first, this was not a permanent ordinance, and it was, for that reason, not recorded in the Taz's commentary on the *Shulḥan Arukh*; and second, the spiritual level of the present generation and its leaders is not as great as that of the Taz and his generation. The Ḥazon Ish added, "For all we know, succeeding generations may be superior to our own—who are we to establish new ordinances for them?"[65]

Here we arrive at the heart of the Ḥazon Ish's position. Scholars have noted that the doctrine of "the decline of the generations" (*nitqaṭnu ha-dorot*) has served in traditional Jewish circles as a barrier against halakhic

---

[63] For a discussion of the Ḥazon Ish's view as well as the views of others on this question, see Joel Wolowelsky, "Observing Yom Ha-Shoaᶜ," *Tradition* 24/4 (1988): 46-58; Nathanel Helfgot, Letter to the Editor, together with Wolowelsky's comment, *Tradition* 25/2 (1990): 109f.

[64] *Qoveṣ iggerot*, 1:113f. (letter 97).

[65] Finkelman, *The Chazon Ish*, 174. See, however, Taz, *Oraḥ Ḥayyim* 516:3. (I am indebted for this reference to Rabbi J. J. Schacter who is currently preparing a major study on the fast of the twentieth of Sivan.) That the Ḥazon Ish seemed to be unaware of this comment of the Taz is surprising, but as he himself stated once, "it is humanly impossible for anyone nowadays to master completely *(la-daᶜat al buryan)* all four parts of the *Shulḥan ᶜArukh.*" See *Qoveṣ iggerot*, 3:76 (letter 53).

change.[66] But such a doctrine serves only as a barrier against the type of halakhic change which modifies already existing Jewish law, such as the *taqqanah* concerning the inheritance of daughters. For who are we to modify, even through halakhic means, the practices of previous generations that were greater than ours? At the same time, however, this doctrine WOULD allow for such halakhic change as instituting new *taqqanot* which ordain practices arising out of and responding to entirely new situations, such as ordaining a fast in commemoration of the victims of the Holocaust. For the doctrine of the decline of generations implies that if the present generation is inferior to all previous generations, it is superior to all future generations! Therefore, as long as the present generation would not be enacting a *taqqanah* modifying the practice of previous generations, it COULD legislate for all future generations. For the Ḥazon Ish, however, the course of Jewish history is like a V and the present generation is at the bottommost point, inferior to BOTH past and future generations. It can, therefore, neither modify past practice nor determine future practice. The sole task of the present generation, thus, in his view, is to receive the tradition in its totality from the previous generation, to study it and obey it, to submit to its authority, and to hand on that tradition, unchanged, intact, to the next generation.

This leads us to the second issue. I just stated that for the Ḥazon Ish the task of the present generation is to submit to the authority of the tradition IN ITS TOTALITY. But for him that totality includes not only the realm of Halakhah but that of aggadah as well. Thus, in a famous letter replying to a correspondent who was apparently critical of certain aggadic statements of the sages, the Ḥazon Ish begins by saying that it is our obligation to keep far away from speculation [*meḥqar*], goes on to say that he just wishes to be a "simple Jew" who is concerned with the "what," not the "why" of Judaism, and climaxes his letter with the remarkable statement: "We recoil upon hearing the casting of doubt on any statement of Ḥazal, whether Halakhah or aggadah, and view [such critical remarks] as constituting blasphemy, heaven forbid."[67]

---

66 For a discussion of some of the sources regarding *nitqaṭnu ha-dorot*, as well as sources expressing contrary tendencies in the Jewish tradition (e.g., "on the shoulders of giants," *halakhah ke-batrai*, etc.), see Norman Lamm, *Torah u-maddah* (Torah u-Maddah: The Encounter of Religious Learning and Worldly Knowledge in the Jewish Tradition), (New York: Jason Aronson, Inc., 1990), 48, 73, 86-103, 106-109. See, particularly, notes 15, 39, 41, and 47 (106-108) for bibliographic references and documentation.

67 *Qoveṣ iggerot*, 1:42f. (letter 15). Cf. 3:43 (letter 14), where the Ḥazon Ish's insistence that all *aggadot* in the Talmud are authoritative results in a rather forced inter-

This insistence on submitting to the authority of the sages in all realms also accounts for the thrust of the fifth—and last complete—chapter of *Emunah u-biṭaḥon*.[68] This chapter bears the title "Imagination and Intellect." But its true subject is the greatness of previous generations in the realm of theoretical scientific knowledge, indeed, their superiority in that realm to the present generation, though the present generation may surpass previous generations in the sphere of technology. Of course, the point of this chapter is to defend the truth and accuracy of scientific statements of Ḥazal and the Rishonim. The present generation must not delude itself into imagining that by virtue of its great technological achievements, it surpasses the wisdom of previous generations. Rather, once again, its task is both to acknowledge and to submit to the wisdom and authority of the tradition as handed down to us by previous generations, in the realm of science as well as in all other realms.[69]

In his insistence, then, on the acceptance and submission to the authority of the tradition in its totality, the Ḥazon Ish makes no concession to modernity at all. Perhaps here we arrive at the critical dividing point between the fundamental stance of the Ḥazon Ish and that of the previous east European traditional rabbinic scholars whose views he crit-

---

pretation on his part of a statement of the Rashba. Contrast this view of the Ḥazon Ish with the views on aggadah of R. David Ṣevi Hoffman in his Introduction to his commentary on *Va-Yiqra* and R. Samson Raphael Hirsch in his two Hebrew letters to R. Hille Wechsler, published by Mordecai Breuer in *Ha-Maʿayan* (Tevet 5736) and translated into English by Joseph Munk in *L'Eylah* no. 27 (Pesach 5749): 30-35. The attempt on the part of R. Yosef Avraham Wolf, the well-known head of the Beth Jacob movement in *Ereṣ Yisra'el* and confidant of the Ḥazon Ish, to reconcile the view of the Ḥazon Ish with that of R. Hoffman—R. Wolf was unaware of the two then unpublished letters of R. Hirsch—in his essay, "Shiluv Emunat Torah she-be-ʿal peh be-Hora'ah" in *Ha- Tekufah u-Baʿayotehah* (Bnei Brak: Y. A. Wolf, 1981), 125f., is exceptionally strained and singularly unconvincing, as, indeed, is R. Wolf's entire valiant but quixotic and ultimately misguided attempt to harmonize the Haredi ideology of the Ḥazon Ish with the *Torah im derekh ereṣ* ideology of Rabbis Hirsch, Hoffman, and Yehiel Yaʿakov Weinberg. There really are limits as to how far one can go in attempting to square the circle!

68 pp. 60-67.

69 In this connection, see as well *Qoveṣ iggerot*, 2:37f. (letter 24). For a full discussion of this letter and its background, see, *Orḥot Ish*, 186f., n. 2. Contrast Norman Lamm, *Torah u-maddah*, 93f. For a very strong statement of the Ḥazon Ish forbidding the questioning of the historical accuracy of the rabbinic tradition regarding Second Temple chronology, see *Qoveṣ iggerot*, 1:182 (letter 206). It must in all candor be said that the argument set forth in this letter does not really come to grips with the seriousness of the issue and appears to be an intellectual dodge that is difficult to take seriously.

icized. These scholars, though they resisted the temptations of modernity, though they were acutely aware of its dangers, nevertheless felt its pull, sensed its attractions. They may, therefore, have believed that precisely in order to better combat modernity it was necessary to incorporate some of its external forms or internal values within the framework of tradition. For the Ḥazon Ish, however, the modern world HELD NO ATTRACTION AT ALL.

In the fall of 1952, a famous meeting took place between Ben-Gurion and the Ḥazon Ish, at the latter's modest house in Bnei Brak, regarding the issue of *sheirut le'ummi*, compulsory national service for women. Ben-Gurion asked the Ḥazon Ish how, in his view, religious and secular Jews could live together in harmony. The Ḥazon Ish replied:

> The Talmud states:[70] Two ships are traveling down a river; one is laden, the other is empty, and they meet—if they attempt to pass one another both will sink: the empty ship must back up and allow the laden ship to pass. The ship of the religious Jews, of *Yisra'el Sabba*, which is laden with thousands of years of sanctification of the divine Name, of devotion for the sake of Torah, has encountered in the narrow straits of our era the empty ship of the secularists. There can be no compromise. There can be no harmony. The collision between the ships is inevitable. Therefore, whose ship ought to back up before whose? Should it not be your empty ship before our laden one?[71]

Ben-Gurion, of course, heatedly protested that the ship of the secularists was by no means empty. Be that as it may, the Ḥazon Ish's exceptionally sharp and uncompromising comment during this very charged and highly symbolic encounter perfectly encapsulates his perception of the modern world as a whole: an empty ship.

IV

The tradition, the authority of which the Ḥazon Ish, as we have seen, accepted in its entirety was not so much the living tradition of east European Jewry, but the tradition as found in the classic texts of halakhic Judaism, in the teachings and rulings of its great scholars and decisors. It

---

[70] *Sanh.* 32b.

[71] The story of this meeting between Ben-Gurion and the Ḥazon Ish has often been retold. My own reconstruction of their conversation is based on Finkelman, *The Chazon Ish*, 238f. and the novel of Haim Be'er, *'Et ha-Zamir* (The Time of Trimming) (Tel Aviv: Am oved, 1987), 44-46.

was not so much the tradition of the community as it was the tradition as reconstructed by the Ḥazon Ish himself by virtue of his prodigious intellectual powers, of his complete mastery of the totality of rabbinic learning. It follows that though the Ḥazon Ish was opposed to formal halakhic innovation, he was one of the great halakhic innovators of our century; if not through legislation, then through interpretation, or, to be more precise, through a willingness to draw the appropriate halakhic conclusions from his theoretical study and to put these conclusions into practice. In this respect as well, the approach of the Ḥazon Ish, as Professor Menaḥem Friedman has correctly argued, constitutes a break with that of the traditional world of east European Orthodoxy where the role of the living tradition was so central.[72]

It should be noted that the Ḥazon Ish functioned neither within the framework of that traditional world nor, for that matter, within the framework of the traditional world of the land of Israel of his day. As we indicated earlier, he never served as either a Rav or rosh yeshivah, nor was he ever a member of any rabbinic or communal organization. While he was still in Europe he remained a completely private individual. He spent all his time immersed in study and writing. Although he was a confidant of Rav Ḥayyim Ozer Grodzinski, the great Rav of Vilna, and advised him about a number of matters, the Ḥazon Ish himself never spoke out publicly or took a stand on communal matters or halakhic issues of general concern. People heard about this mysterious figure, a great rabbinic scholar who spent day and night absorbed in learning, but he had no public profile or persona.[73]

---

72 This is the thrust of Friedman "Life Tradition." For a contemporary example of a halakhic figure who openly proclaims the superiority of the "book tradition" over the "life tradition" in Judaism, see the multivolume, *Moʿadim u-Zemanim ha-Shalem* of Rabbi Moshe Sternbuch (Jerusalem: n.p., 1968), in particular the preface to volume 3. In this preface, Rabbi Sternbuch suggests that while the "life tradition" may suffice for the common folk, certainly Torah scholars and *benei torah* ought to conduct themselves solely according to the "book tradition." (Rabbi Sternbuch, of course, does not use those terms.) For a preliminary analysis of the ideology and methodology underlying Rabbi Sternbuch's work, see Horowitz, "Sternbuch's Halakhic Novellae."

73 See Beruriah David's memoir of her father, R. Yiẓḥak Hutner, in *Sefer ha-zikkaron le-Maran Baʿal ha-Pahad Yiẓḥak* (Memorial Volume for R. Yiẓḥak Hutner), (Jerusalem: Gur Aryeh, 1984), 36. Professor Isadore Twersky once commented to me that Chaim Grade's portrait of the Ḥazon Ish in *The Yeshiva* is extraordinarily accurate in all respects except one: Grade, Professor Twersky claimed, exaggerated the prominence of the Ḥazon Ish while still in Europe.

In 1933, the Ḥazon Ish left Vilna for the land of Israel. When he arrived there he did not settle, as might have been expected, in Jerusalem, but rather in the newly formed religious community of Bnei Brak. Why the Ḥazon Ish did not settle in Jerusalem remains something of a mystery. But perhaps one reason for his decision was precisely a desire on his part to function outside an already existing communal framework, a wish to help fashion and shape a new framework.

Soon after the Ḥazon Ish arrived in the land of Israel, he began to speak out forcefully and issue definitive rulings concerning the burning halakhic issues of the day: the proper mode of observance of the Jewish agriculture laws in general (*miṣvot ha-teluyot ba-ʾareṣ*) and the Sabbatical year in particular; the problem of milking on the Sabbath; the determination of the international date line; and, later on, the general question of what ought to be the Ḥaredi attitude to the newly established state of Israel and such related matters as *ḥinukh ʿaṣmaʾi, sheirut leʾummi,* and others. As I pointed out earlier, the Ḥazon Ish became accepted by the Ḥaredi community solely by virtue of his personal standing, his charisma, his *daʿat Torah*. It was a community that he was fashioning and shaping through his rulings, through his teachings, through his unofficial but very real leadership; and despite—perhaps because of—his lack of any official standing, the community looked to him for guidance and direction. His word, then, for that community, was binding and final.

With the end of the Second World War and the destruction of the great Jewish communities of eastern Europe and the living tradition they embodied, the authoritative position of the Ḥazon Ish and the reconstructed halakhic tradition he embodied became even more dominant and even more central within the world of traditional Orthodoxy. A striking symbol of this entire historical process may be found in the passing of the mantle of leadership of the traditional Orthodox Jewish community from Rav Ḥayyim Ozer before the war to the Ḥazon Ish after the war. Rav Ḥayyim Ozer, of course, was a great Talmudic scholar, but, even more, he was preeminently the communal Rav of the great city of Vilna. His standing thus reflected the traditional role of the communal Rav as leader of the Jewish community. To put the matter another way, it was Rav Ḥayyim Ozer's personal charisma and learning, FILTERED THROUGH and MEDIATED BY his position of communal Rav, that was the source of his great authority. The Ḥazon Ish neither needed nor desired such a filter. His own authority was purely personal, was entirely individual.

In this respect, it is instructive to contrast the Ḥazon Ish not only with his predecessor, Rav Ḥayyim Ozer, but also with a great luminary of an earlier generation to whom he has often been compared—and with much justice—the Gaon of Vilna. Both the Ḥazon Ish and the Gaon of Vilna were private individuals. Neither served as Rav or rosh yeshiva. Both derived their immense authority from their unparalleled Torah learning and—in both cases—unique charisma. But in the time of the Gaon of Vilna, the traditional communal structures were still in place. Therefore, when the challenge of Hasidism arose, the Gaon, working in tandem with the community's lay leaders, lent his immense prestige to the COMMUNAL ban issued against the Hasidim by those lay leaders, acting in their capacity as representatives of the community of Vilna.[74] By contrast, when the Ḥazon Ish spoke out on the issue of *sheirut le᾽ummi,* he expressed his opposition purely on the basis of his own authority, presenting his view as *da῾at Torah.*[75] He was the community.

And yet, and here we come to the final twist of the argument, despite the Ḥazon Ish's immense role in forming and shaping the ethos of the Ḥaredi community,[76] in a certain respect he was a failure. Certainly the full dimensions and implications of the Ḥazon Ish's critique of the traditional world of Lithuanian Mitnaggedism were never really absorbed, much less acted on, by the Ḥaredi community. Despite his criticisms of the analytic method of talmudic scholarship, it is that method which is prevalent in the Ḥaredi yeshivas today, and which was and continues to be espoused by his closest disciples, the late R. Yaakov Kanievsky and the venerable Rabbinic sage R. Eliezer Schach. And despite his criticisms of Lithuanian Musar, the Musar approach, in a rather attenuated form to be sure, is still a force in those yeshivas. Moreover, no individual has

---

74 See S. Dubnow, *Toledot he-Ḥasidut* (History of Hasidism) (Tel-Aviv: Debir, 1967), 114–17. One ban was signed by the Gaon himself, by the Rav of Vilna, Rav Samuel, and by the *dayyanim;* another ban was signed by Rav Samuel, the *dayyanim,* and the *parnasim.* An examination of the various bans and proclamations against the Hasidim will easily reveal the preeminent role played in the entire episode by the lay leaders of the various communities.

75 *Qoveṣ iggerot,* 1:122-126 (letters 111–13); cf. the public announcement of the *da῾at Torah* of the Ḥazon Ish on *sheirut le᾽ummi* in Finkelman, *The Chazon Ish,* 252.

76 As a striking example of the Ḥazon Ish's deep influence on the Ḥaredi community, we may note that it was he who was the first to enunciate the view which "singles out Zionism explicity as bearing direct responsibility for the Holocaust," a view which has since acquired the status of almost official dogma in the Ḥaredi community. See Menachem Friedman, "The Ḥaredim and The Holocaust," *Jerusalem Quarterly,* 53 (Winter 1990): 107.

succeeded in achieving the halakhic position and authority of the Ḥazon Ish by virtue of a purely personal charisma. The notion of *daʿat Torah* has become almost entirely institutionalized.

Perhaps the vision of the Ḥazon Ish was too austere, his demands too uncompromising. He was calling for a type of self-renunciation of which, paradoxically, only he, with his great intellectual powers and deep piety, with his unyielding extremism, complete commitment and—yes—genuine saintliness, was capable. The ethos of submission is still alive and well and flourishing within the world of traditional Orthodoxy. But, at the same time, the need for self-assertion and some measure of personal autonomy has proved too strong. We cannot all be saints. Most of us, even the great rabbinic scholars among us, occasionally need a weekend at the beach.

6

The Lost Kiddush *Cup: Changes in Ashkenazic Ḥaredi Culture—A Tradition in Crisis*

MENACHEM FRIEDMAN

A Rift in Tradition

A binding attachment to tradition is perhaps the hallmark of Ḥaredi Judaism within the framework of postwar Jewish society. This phenomenon is reflected above all in the affinity for and attitude toward primary symbols of personal and collective identity: dress, appearance (beards, sidelocks), and language. Obviously, I do not contend that all Ḥaredi Jews wear the traditional Eastern European garb, grow beards, and speak Yiddish, but more of them than ever before have adopted all or some of these identity symbols. I do claim that such symbols are perceived as an a priori expression of wholeness, whereas deviation from them is at most tolerated a posteriori.

However, affinity for these external symbols of identity is no more than a manifestation of the Ḥaredi historiographic conception, which undoubtedly exists even if no systematic written evidence thereof is available. Moreover, I believe that this conception constitutes the basis of the perceived confrontation with other Jewish identities common to all varieties of Ḥaredi society. From a point of view that is simplistic—although adequate for our purposes—we may note that Ḥaredi society divides Jewish history into two main periods, of which the first arguably commences with the Patriarchs, receipt of the Torah, or perhaps the mishnaic and talmudic eras and concludes with the inception of the

Haskalah. According to Ḥaredi historiography, there was only one kind of Jewish identity during this period, one whose sole legitimate expression was unconditional commitment to Halakhah, as interpreted by approved scholars, generation after generation. The saying attributed to Rabbi Saadiya Gaon, "Our nation is only a nation by virtue of its Torah (both the Written and Oral Law)," is quoted frequently by Ḥaredi leaders to express the complete and legitimate Jewish identity. Contrasting with this age of fulfillment and wholeness is the modern period, which began, as indicated, with the Haskalah. This period was marked by a substantial and fundamental rift, as great masses of Jews abandoned the traditional Jewish identity and unconditional commitment to Halakhah yet considered themselves legitimate Jews nonetheless. Today, a decisive majority of Jews do not consider themselves bound by Halakhah in any way. Ḥaredi society perceives this historical development as a process accompanied by a cruel and painful social and cultural struggle of good versus evil, of the weak versus the strong, and the many versus the hapless few. The contemporary mythology of Ḥaredi society may well be based primarily on this interpretation of historical realities during the age of schism. The rift was so vast and so dramatic that even those who remained loyal to the values and customs of the previous age, to that consummate world of Jewish fulfillment, were somehow affected by it, whether consciously or not. Ḥaredi society hardly perceives its own situation as an ideal one, but rather as a distorted reflection of the prerift world. Awareness of flaws, of incompleteness relative to the previous era, is a central component in Ḥaredi society's self-perception. The traditional society which preceded the Haskalah, especially that of eastern Europe, is therefore considered a frame of reference (in the sociological sense), a way of life which Ḥaredim aspire to maintain .

Awareness of the rift, and the perceived incompleteness of both individual and collective Jewish life, introduce tension and dynamics in the structure of Ḥaredi society. Paradoxically, however, this conception also enabled Ḥaredi society to adjust to modern realities while relating to tradition differentially. The perception of the contemporary situation as one of catastrophic crisis, with inevitable consequences, engenders a tolerant attitude toward deviance from tradition, on condition that one recognizes the situation of crisis and realizes that such deviation represents a compromise, a manifestation of post factum behavior. In other words, using Ḥaredi terminology, deviation should not become *shiṭah* (literally 'method'), that is, it must not be accorded full a priori ideological justification within the overall traditional *Weltanschauung*.

This analysis elucidates the extensive variety of customs and lifestyles in Ḥaredi society, based on differential acculturation to modern Western culture and society and on the Ḥaredim's self-awareness of their social uniqueness qua Ḥaredim facing the surrounding Jewish world. Perhaps the best example of this characteristic mechanism of adjustment and acculturation to modern realities may be seen in Ḥaredi attitudes toward the German neo-Orthodoxy established by Rabbi Samson Raphael Hirsch. Without discussing this complex issue in detail, I note that Ḥaredi society did perceive Hirsch's community as an integral part of the history and mythology of the struggle between the giants of religious-traditional Judaism and the Haskalah. The facts, however, are ignored and Hirsch's efforts are perceived as an a posteriori act.

The rupture in German Jewish society was so vast and so comprehensive that it was impossible to turn back the clock. Therefore, it was necessary to salvage whatever one could, to compromise and adjust to the modern reality. It was thus possible to perceive neo-Orthodoxy as a legitimate part of the Ḥaredi traditional heritage and at the same time to dissociate oneself virtually absolutely from the application of its norms and values in prewar eastern European religious-traditional society and in present-day Ḥaredi communities alike. A similarly tolerant attitude prevails today in Israel regarding practices of American Ḥaredim which deviate from accepted eastern European Ḥaredi tradition, especially in the spheres of general education and modesty for women, which are justified by the formula: "It's permissible for THEM."

As indicated, this adjustment mechanism originated in the tensions which developed between an awareness of the rift and a perception of prerift traditional society as the epitome of complete Judaism. From this same point of departure, the postwar Ḥaredi society developing in the West began to manifest tendencies toward stringency and extremism in both the ritual and social spheres, reflecting a kind of dialectic attitude toward tradition. Here, I emphasize the fact that traditional society considers stringency, especially in the halakhic-ritual sphere, to be no less dangerous than laxity, as attested to by numerous cases in halakhic literature. The best example may be found in the polemics against Hasidism In an early record of the dispute between Hasidim and Mitnaggedim, a letter sent by Rabbi Avraham Katzenellenbogen to Rabbi Levi Yitzhak of Berditchev, he decries the changes (i.e., restrictions) in Ashkenazic tradition which were introduced by the Hasidim, such as adoption of a variant prayer liturgy (that of the Ari, known as *Nusaḥ Sefarad*) and differences in methods of ritual slaughter. Rabbi Katzenellenbogen asks, "How can you find fault with [the practices of] our forefathers?"[1] His argument is only significant and valid within the framework of traditional society. One who seeks to change time-honored customs in favor of a more stringent halakhic perspective is effectively declaring that the religious practices of our holy ancestors (in traditional society, all ancestors are holy) were inferior to our own. This strikes a severe blow at the very foundations of traditional society. Or, as Rabbi Katzenellenbogen wrote, it necessarily "finds fault with our forefathers."

> All who challenge [a practice as contrary to Torah law or as lenient where it should be stringent] should realize that our ancient forefathers and sages, whose esteem is immeasurably greater than our own, were not unapprised of the reasons for their customs. It would be better to ascribe the challenge to a deficiency in one's own knowledge than to a shortcoming in our ancestors and sages, whose wisdom was as vast as the earth and as deep as the sea.[2]

The vast social phenomenon under consideration here is called "religious extremism," as expressed in the dynamics of stringency in the Halakhic-ritual sphere, combined with occasional intentional deviation from the traditions of one's ancestors within the framework of a society which demands commitment to tradition. I now seek to determine how such deviation was rendered possible from a structural point of view. I address this question through analysis of a story concerning a *Kiddush* cup which was lost, found, and then lost again for eternity.

The Lost *Kiddush* Cup

The story is told by Dov Genachowski, a well-known journalist, talmudic scholar, economist, and amateur researcher of the history of Jerusalem. Dov is the scion of a Lithuanian family of rabbis and scholars. His father, Rabbi Eliyahu Moshe Genachowski, was a member of Knesset on the ha-Poel ha-Mizraḥi list. The Genachowski family lived in Bnei Brak, in the Givat Rokaḥ neighborhood, near the home of Rabbi Avraham Yeshayahu Karelitz, better known as the Ḥazon Ish.[3] The Genachowski family was friendly with the Ḥazon Ish, and Dov, as a

---

[1] Simon Dubnov, *Toldot ha-ḥassidut* (A History of Hasidism) (Tel Aviv: Debir, 1967), 251–351.

[2] Menahem ben Solomon Meiri, *Magen avot*, I. M. Last (ed), London, 1909, p. 10.

[3] For a sketch of the life and career of the Ḥazon Ish, see the preceding essay by Lawrence Kaplan.—ED.

young man, would often spend time at his home. The families already knew each other in Lithuania: Dov's mother's grandfather, Rabbi Shneur Zalman Hirschowitz (an outstanding student of Rabbi Israel Salanter), was once the *ḥavrutah* (study partner) of the Ḥazon Ish's father, Rabbi Shmaryahu Karelitz, the Rabbi of Kossovo.

During the early 1950s, a new Halakhic concept began to spread throughout Ḥaredi society: the *shiur* (measuring standard) of the Ḥazon Ish. Within a very short time, the concept became so entrenched that in halakhic applications, the *shiurei Ḥazon Ish* have become an accepted norm among nearly all sectors of Ḥaredi society. The concept of *shiur* and its halakhic implications are as follows: A *shiur* is a measure of volume, area, length, or width which is critical to the performance of major precepts.

The first Mishnah of tractate *Beiṣa,* for example, recalls a dispute between the house of Shammai and the house of Hillel concerning the *shiurim* relating to observance of Passover: "The house of Shammai says: a *kezayit* (olive's measure) of sourdough or a *kekotevet,* (dried date's measure) of a leavened product [violate the prohibition against possessing leavened products on Passover]; the house of Hillel says, a *kezayit* of either." Because sourdough is unfit for consumption and is only used as leavening, one does not violate the prohibition against possession of leavened products on Passover unless one possesses AT LEAST a *kezayit.* In contrast, according to the house of Shammai, the prohibition on eating leavened products is only violated if one has eaten at least a *kekotevet.* The House of Hillel is more stringent and claims that in both cases, the minimum size is a *kezayit.* Similarly, one must eat a *kezayit* of matzo at the Seder to fulfill the commandment to eat matzo on Passover (a positive injunction from the Torah).

Another such measure is the *kebeiṣah* (egg's measure), the minimum quantity of food mandating Grace After Meals, or the *reviʿit,* (a measure of volume, one quarter of a *log.*) Referring to Sabbath eve *Kiddush,* the *Shulḥan Arukh* declares that "One must drink . . . most of a *reviʿit* [-sized glass of wine]" (Laws of the Sabbath, 271:13). These three measures, the *kezayit,* the *kebeiṣah,* and the *reviʿit,* are related in a fixed ratio: a *kebeiṣah,* is equal to two *kezayit*s and a *reviʿit* is equal to one and a half *kebeiṣah*s.

The *kezayit* and *kebeiṣah* are based on products of nature. However, the Sages also defined the ratio between them and even offered several alternative means of measurement. Hence one would not have anticipated the differences of opinion regarding their relative size that subsequently emerged. Comparison of the results of experimental measurements yielded a marked incompatibility. The first to notice the incongruity was Rabbi Yehezkel Landau (the Nodah be-Yehudah) of Prague, in the eighteenth century.[4] Others who repeated his experiments likewise noted discrepancies. To solve the problem, the Nodah be-Yehudah raised the possibility that today's eggs are only half as large as the average egg was in talmudic times, invoking a phrase first coined by the tosafists in an entirely different context: "Nature has changed." Rabbi Israel Meir Hacohen (the Ḥafetz Ḥayim), author of the *Mishnah Berurah,* cites the dispute on this matter and declares that "some people who are very strict about *shiurim* have proved that the eggs of our time are half as large." The Ḥazon Ish had no doubt, declaring axiomatically that "today's eggs are smaller." The Ḥazon Ish's views were first formulated in the "Booklet of *Shiurim* "which concludes his book *Ḥazon Ish* (Laws of the Sabbath). At first glance, they seem to be part of an ordinary difference of opinion, as is common throughout halakhic literature. Moreover, the Ḥazon Ish appears not to have stated anything particularly innovative, as the Nodah be-Yehudah and other halakhic experts had also suggested that "Nature has changed" and that our eggs are smaller than the average eggs of the talmudic era. Nevertheless, a substantive change has indeed taken place.

Previously, such disputes were essentially theoretical alone, argued purely for the sake of Torah study. In contrast, the Ḥazon Ish's stipulation was also of practical significance, as it created a new halakhic norm, the *shiur Ḥazon Ish,* which is accepted today by almost all Ḥaredi society and even by some non-Ḥaredi religious Jews. In most if not all Ḥaredi homes, the volume of *Kiddush* cups (at least a *reviᶜit*), the *kezayit* of matzo eaten on Seder night, and even the dimensions of the *tallit qatan* worn by men all conform with the *shiur Ḥazon Ish.*

Returning to Dov Genachowski's story: Rabbi Eliyahu Moshe Genachowski had two *Kiddush* cups which were brought from "home" in Lithuania. The first was given to him on his wedding day by Rabbi. Meir Simha Hacohen (the Or Sameaḥ), Rabbi of Dvinsk (Duenaburg), Latvia, a relative of the bride. The second cup kept by the Genachowski family belonged to Dov's grandfather, Rabbi Shneur Zalman Hirschowitz, who was, as indicated, an outstanding student of Rabbi Israel Salanter and the *ḥavrutah* of the father of the Ḥazon Ish. Neither of these cups held a *reviᶜit* according to the Ḥazon Ish's calculations.

---

4 Ṣalaḥ (Ṣiyun le-Nefesh Ḥayah, ad *Pesaḥ*. Prague, 1783), 109a.

When the concept of *shiur Ḥazon Ish* began gathering momentum in yeshiva circles, Dov Genachowski was a typically audacious young Sabra. He took the *Kiddush* cups out of the closet and presented them to the Ḥazon Ish at the latter's home. The Ḥazon Ish refused to react, but would not relent, either. Numerous anecdotes circulate in the religious community concerning the Ḥazon Ish's "revolution." For example, Rabbi Yitzhak L. Rabinowitz remembered the daughter of the Ḥafetz Ḥayim complaining that her sons would not use their grandfather's cup for *Kiddush* because "it doesn't hold a *shiur Ḥazon Ish*." The Ḥafetz Ḥayim, it should be recalled, was the author of the *Mishnah Berurah*.

I proceed to analyze the social significance of institutionalizing the *shiur Ḥazon Ish* in Ḥaredi communities in the context of the following question: How did a religious change of such significance, one which concerns key Jewish religious ceremonies, gain acceptance and popularity so simply and rapidly within a society for which awareness of continuity of eastern European traditions is a central component of its self-identity?

The *Kiddush* cup is not only a ritual object. More than any other artifact, it symbolizes tradition, the affinity between past generations and the present one. The *Kiddush* cup is passed down as a legacy: "Grandfather's cup." Consider an extended family in a traditional community, gathering to celebrate the Passover Seder. The table is set and the elder of the family, the grandfather, sits at the head of the table, with a *Kiddush* cup before him. The cup would usually be one passed down from a previous generation or generations. It symbolizes the family's common roots and expresses its solidarity with generations gone by. The cup thus embodied not only religious significance, but also social significance of the highest level. It was generally given to the eldest or favorite son on the father's demise, as a sign of his assuming the role of head of the family or as a token of some special relationship. The *Kiddush* cup is thus bequeathed as a legacy, reflecting attachment to former generations and consequently also mutual affinity for one another. There are indeed other sacred artifacts of similar significance, but the *Kiddush* cup is outstanding among them because of its function in important ceremonies which express family solidarity and attachment to ancestral tradition: the Sabbath Eve meal and the Passover Seder. The Genachowski family's cups were stored in the closet, together with the Passover dishes, and were indeed present before the family on Seder night. The fact that most Ḥaredi families now have relatively new *Kiddush* cups hints at a dramatic change in history and in the structure of Ḥaredi society.

One explanation of the "lost cup" situation concerns the structure of Ḥaredi society, which, like all Ashkenazi Jewry, is a society of immigrant-survivors. Until the Second World War, Jews emigrating from eastern Europe were relatively young people who left their extended families behind them, as well as their *Kiddush* cups, which, as indicated, were of great symbolic value. Furthermore, Holocaust survivors were usually unable to salvage *Kiddush* cups and similarly symbolic artifacts from destruction. Consequently, a considerable part of Ḥaredi society did not experience a direct confrontation with tradition (represented by their families' *Kiddush* cups from their destroyed ancestral homes) when a personality of high halakhic standing, such as the Ḥazon Ish, enjoined them to use cups holding at least a *reviʿit* based on his calculations.

According to an alternative explanation, the Holocaust destroyed the extended family which had gathered at the Seder table. Those who remained and migrated to the West most often did so as individuals. Thus, the large family, which was a significant and perhaps primary means of transmitting tradition from generation to generation, no longer existed. However correct this explanation may be it is insufficient and perhaps not the essential response, as it does not address the social changes which introduced the new cup into the Jewish home. The harbingers of change were members of the new Ḥaredi generation, raised at the great postwar yeshivas of Israel and the United States.

I contend that from the outset, the higher yeshivas, as they developed in Lithuania from the second half of the nineteenth century, laid the foundation for Ḥaredi society as we know it today. These yeshivas represented a long-standing tradition of Torah study and simultaneously reflected processes of comprehensive social change. Eventually, they succeeded in implementing many of their ideals in postwar Western society, establishing the basis for the Ḥaredi "society of scholars." I will not examine this development in detail at present, but rather attempt to explain the background for the dialectic of tradition which enabled institutionalization of the *shiur Ḥazon Ish* as it accelerated other processes of religious extremism and the continual institution of new strictures.

Higher yeshivas of the Volozhin type developed in Lithuania against the background of a religious, social, and political crisis. The processes of modernization and secularization which engendered this crisis shattered the traditional Jewish community, which was an integral unit identified with the religious way of life, one which considered Halakhah and tradition, as formulated throughout the generations, as an entity which binds the individual and the collectivity alike. One reaction to these processes was the establishment of a new type of educational institution: the higher yeshiva exemplified by Volozhin. One may consider this institution as an integrative religious community, a kind of "total institution," that is, a closed social system whose members remain under its aegis all day long for several years. As indicated, the archetype of this formula was the Etz Ḥayim Higher Yeshiva, established in Volozhin at the beginning of the nineteenth century. For purposes of discussion, however, I concentrate on the higher yeshiva format which prevailed at the turn of the century, under the influence of the Musar Movement. The Volozhin-type yeshiva differs from the traditional one because it transcends community boundaries, attracting students from the broad periphery. It is not a part of the community, but rather a parallel and largely isolated institution. By its very definition, it comprises a community of young people, a kind of youth society, which intentionally develops the consciousness of a religious elite, facing the crumbling external society (the rank and file or *baalei batim* according to standard yeshiva terminology). The yeshiva society is characterized by a social and economic moratorium; it is isolated from everyday affairs and maintains a direct and unmitigated affinity for religious culture, as expressed not in living tradition but in the literature of Halakhah and Musar. This closed society, which develops an intensive religious culture and considers itself an elite group, necessarily engenders a rather uniform halakhic culture which binds all students, a kind of yeshiva tradition, which is less committed to living tradition as practiced by Jewish communities than it is to the written stipulations of halakhic decisions. This tradition obligates yeshiva students with variant customs to dissociate themselves from the particularist traditions of their families and communities. In the yeshiva social system, the literature of halakhic decision-making can "defeat" family and/or community traditions. The book has become a virtually exclusive source of authority, tolerating no substantive conflict with family or community mores.

Before the Holocaust, the relatively few yeshivas were on the periphery. Most young people from traditional families did not apply to them. The economic crises compelled the young people to learn a trade and join the labor force pursuing *takhlit* (practical ends) to help support their families. The political crises, in turn, led many young people to question their future in eastern European countries. The yeshivas themselves became more and more dependent on American assistance (the Joint Distribution Committee) and found it difficult to function. Many students left in favor of socialism and Zionism. After the Holocaust, however, a new economic and social situation emerged.

The financial situation of the Volozhin-type higher yeshivas, reestablished in Israel and the United States, was far better than it had been in eastern Europe. Among the primary factors contributing to this improvement were guilt feelings about Holocaust victims and the attendant obligation to preserve the memory of a tragically and cruelly destroyed traditional world, as well as the economic prosperity characterizing Western countries and the development of the modern welfare state. The yeshivas began to accept increasing numbers of Israeli and American-born students, who considered them as an idealistic counterpoint to the materialism and permissiveness of Western society. Moreover, because of the material prosperity and social security of the welfare state, Ḥaredi parents could now afford to send their children to yeshiva, which they believed was the only way of keeping them from free and unmediated contact with the modern secular world and guaranteeing the continuity of traditional Jewish culture. The yeshiva thus represented the dominant educational pattern for boys within Ḥaredi society. Concomitantly, the Lithuanian-style yeshiva, as a total institution, enabled its religious leadership to mold the spiritual image of virtually all Ḥaredi youth as it saw fit. Ḥaredi parents who sent their children to yeshivas effectively forfeited their role in the socialization of their children. I refer specifically to Lithuanian-type yeshivas, although these observations are also essentially valid regarding Hasidic Ḥaredi circles, who in attempting to rehabilitate their status in the Western world, have adopted the Lithuanian yeshiva pattern to mold the spiritual and social image of the next generation under the conditions prevailing in the modern, open city.

This was not the end of the "revolution," however. The cultural change in Ḥaredi society, as reflected in its transformation into a "society of scholars," was realized when the influx of students to yeshivas gave rise to the *kollelim*, institutes of advanced yeshiva studies for married students (*avrekhim*). Nearly every yeshiva student gets married while still studying and continues his education at yeshiva for at least another seven or eight years. A considerable number continue for many more years, sometimes for their entire lives. This development necessarily led to a cultural and social upheaval.

As I indicated, Ḥaredi parents who sent their boys to yeshivas had relatively little influence on their religious socialization, because these boys were kept within the framework of a total institution, subject to constant indoctrination and supervision. Another social development of equal significance is a rapidly developing sense of superiority among yeshiva students, who feel that they have surpassed their parents in learning, access to halakhic literature, and conformity with the norms stipulated in Musar literature. Yeshiva students in Lithuania may have felt the same, but they faced a multigenerational extended family of grandparents, uncles, and aunts. In Israel and the United States, however, the confrontation involved only a single set of parents versus a scholarly, self-confident son, backed by yeshiva custom and literature. Parents were somewhat confounded by their children, who were adopting new religious norms and challenging their accepted traditions. The children often succeeded in convincing their parents to change their customs, which they, in turn, had learned from their own parents.

The Ḥazon Ish did not appeal to the parents' generation. For them he was a Jew, a sage, but no more. Instead, he addressed the younger generation directly, those who studied his books, admired his scholarly acumen, and were influenced by his ascetic, authoritative personality. The young yeshiva students of the 1950s and 1960s represented a kind of "first generation of redemption," whereas their parents were the "wilderness generation." The Ḥazon Ish enjoined these children to fulfill the ideal of total devotion to Torah study, although many of their fathers had never studied at a yeshiva at all. It is therefore hardly surprising that they felt free to mold their religious lives without considering family traditions, particularly when the new customs were perceived as more stringent, more complete. When the Ḥazon Ish demanded that they eat approximately three fourths of a matzo on Seder night, which was his estimate of the requisite *kezayit* for fulfillment of the commandment, they did not view this stricture as an injustice to their sacred ancestors. Rather, they considered it a better and more complete fulfillment of the commandment, as prescribed in the literature which they accepted as a total expression of Halakhah and tradition alike. This attitude paved the way for new stringencies within a society which purports to maintain authentic tradition.

The New Rift

The *Kiddush* cups used by our forefathers in the Exile of Europe were lost in the Holocaust, along with their owners, our grandparents, aunts, and uncles. Dov Genachowski thought that he had found them and hastened to bring them to the Ḥazon Ish. He did not understand that they had already been lost forever, because vessels, artifacts, and the like do not constitute tradition. Tradition constitutes uninterrupted affinity for past generations, as manifested by a living community, down through the ages, where everyone knows everyone else, young and old alike. Tradition means an extended family, in which the individual is only a part and never an independent whole, a family in which a young man inherits his father's place at the synagogue, as his grandfather lies buried in the adjacent cemetery. Tradition means a sacred community, comprising simple, ignorant Jews, ordinary *baalei batim,* and a handful of scholars who live together in harmony and share a sense of mutual responsibility. When the entire nation is composed of scholars, the power of tradition weakens and becomes the custom of *baalei batim,* of the masses. Upon the disappearance of the traditional community, the *Kiddush* cup, too, loses its power, only to be forgotten and lost for eternity.

PART II

The Retrieval of Tradition in Modern Jewish Culture

Our focus now shifts from the responses of traditionalists who fought modernization to the efforts of modern Jews to retrieve aspects of traditional Jewish religion and culture. Paula E. Hyman's essay serves as a bridge because she pays due attention to the persistence of Jewish life in rural areas, thereby countering exaggerated portraits of the rapid disintegration of traditional Jewish societies, and also reflects on the emergence of a new Jewish culture in urban centers. For much of the nineteenth century, Jewish life in small-town and rural areas of eastern France, southern Germany, and parts of the Austro-Hungarian empire retained vitality and changed only gradually. This village experience has been overshadowed by the rapid mobility and rise to prominence of urban Jews. Hyman brings to life the folk customs of small-town Jews. She notes the important role played by individuals born into this culture in the development of Jewish urban society later in the nineteenth century.

Hyman also analyzes the social role of Jewish ghetto tales, a new genre of Jewish literature which grew in popularity in nineteenth century cities. Through their evocation of the village life abandoned by Jews who now resided in the cities, these accounts served both as sources of nostalgia, as well as tools for coming to terms with a traditional society left behind by urban Jews. In an era of change, as Hyman notes, the ghetto tales helped Jews reflect on their relationship to tradition and modernity.

The modern practice of collecting and displaying Jewish art, served a parallel purpose. By analyzing which objects were collected, where they were displayed in public, and how exhibits were mounted, Richard I. Cohen reveals much about the changing agenda of nineteenth-century Jewry. The public display of Jewish art forced exhibitors to clarify which aspects of the past they sought to retrieve, which aspects had continuing meaning. Significantly, Cohen, like Hyman, situates the new nostalgia for the past within the broader cultural movements of nineteenth-century Europe and links it to the dislocating effects of rapid transformation.

The ethnographic expedition organized by S. Ansky in the two years prior to World War I served as yet another movement of retrieval. Ansky sought to reclaim "the oral Torah" of the Jewish masses in eastern Europe by collecting folktales and songs, as well as physical artifacts of Jewish life, just as traditional *shtetl* culture disintegrated. This act of retrieval was the culmination of a personal odyssey carefully reconstructed by David G. Roskies. For Ansky, Roskies argues, is paradigmatic of the modern Jewish cultural figure who retrieves aspects of the tradition for a distinctly modern purpose. Ansky's act of return to his people, language, and traditions was inspired by the modern culture he had imbibed and was informed by its values, no less than by the values of the Jewish culture to which he returned. Roskies' subtle reading of Ansky's "return" lays bare the complexities of selective retrieval.

In contrast to the concern with literary and artistic developments evinced by the first three essays in this section, the three concluding essays focus more sharply on religious questions. Jay M. Harris examines the manner in which modern critical scholarship challenged Jewish researchers to rethink the origin and purpose of traditional rabbinic exegesis. Inspired by Spinoza's critique of Jewish learning, French and German enlightenment writers mercilessly ridiculed the methods of *midrash halakhah*, the foundation of rabbinic legal exegesis. Practitioners of the new Jewish learning known as *Wissenschaft des Judentums* (the science of Judaism) were forced to confront this criticism. Harris shrewdly notes the irony of reformers supporting the traditional understanding of the role of *midrash halakhah*, whereas more religiously traditional scholars "reshaped tradition in order to rescue it." In defending the exegesis of rabbinic law against modern criticism, traditional scholars retrieved traditions of historical understanding that had fallen into disuse.

Paul Mendes-Flohr analyzes how two of the most influential Jewish thinkers of the early twentieth century—Martin Buber and Franz Rosenzweig—understood the process by which modern Jews might return to tradition. How do Jews who have lost their "innocence" and who fully participate in modern liberal societies find their way back to tradition? How can they do justice to the modern world-view they have absorbed and simultaneously recover a "second innocence" when they approach the sources of their tradition? Mendes-Flohr skillfully contrasts the solutions offered by Buber and Rosenzweig. In the process, he touches on fundamental issues confronted by all modern Jews who wish to remain modern but also seek Jewish renewal through a retrieval of tradition.

The remarkably popular retrieval of one specific tradition—the holiday of Hanukkah—is the subject of the concluding essay in this section. Long treated by rabbinic culture as a minor holiday, Hanukkah has enjoyed an unprecedented revival in the United States. The reasons for Hanukkah's new-found importance are not difficult to fathom given the inordinate attention America's consumer society lavishes on the December holiday season. But there is much to be learned about American Jewish folk religion and culture from an examination of how holiday practices have evolved and how Hanukkah's promoters have continuously revised their rationales for the holiday's observance. These are the themes of Jenna Weissman Joselit's careful reconstruction of Hanukkah's history in the United States since the mid-nineteenth century. Examining this family-oriented holiday within the context of the Jewish home and Jewish consumer culture, Joselit offers a dramatic instance of how modern Jewish folk culture has reappropriated and thoroughly transformed a traditional observance.

7

Traditionalism and Village Jews in 19th-Century Western and Central Europe: Local Persistence and Urban Nostalgia

PAULA E. HYMAN

At the beginning of the nineteenth century, the majority of the Jews of western and central Europe lived in villages and small towns among the rural populace of their lands.[1] Although contemporary observers and later historians alike paid particular attention to the disruption of European Jewish culture promoted by the combination of Enlightenment ideas, revolution, and war that characterized the end of the eighteenth century and the first decades of the nineteenth, in the villages traditional Jewish culture proved more resilient than contemporary critics would have predicted. As the village economy declined in the latter part of the century and young Jewish men and women, village-born and bred, sought their fortunes in the burgeoning cities, they brought with them a familiarity with popular Jewish culture along with a sentimental attachment to their home town and their memories of childhood. Even as they abandoned many of the customs rooted in the Jewish milieu of the village, they related to the village, now depicted nostalgically in the

---

[1] Jacob Toury, "Der Eintritt der Juden ins deutsche Bürgertum," in *Das Judentum in der deutschen Umwelt,* ed. Hans Liebeschütz and Arnold Paucker (Tübingen: Mohr, 1977), 139f.; Steven Lowenstein, "The Rural Community and the Urbanization of German Jewry," *Central European History* 13/3 (September 1980): 220, 230f.

growing literature of "ghetto tales," as a source of a particularist Jewish identity within the modern city.

It is no surprise to discover that traditional Jewish culture survived longer in the countryside than in the cities; the stereotype of rural stagnation and backwardness as opposed to urban vitality and innovation is deeply rooted and based, at least partially, on observable cultural differences. Yet it is not sufficient simply to point to the rural–urban distinction as an explanation for the persistence of traditional practices in Jewish village society and their erosion within the urban environment. It is important to understand the factors which enabled village Jews to both preserve and adapt their traditional culture in response to the changing conditions of the nineteenth century. It is equally important to explore the ways in which city Jews selectively retained links to aspects of Jewish tradition that prevailed among village Jews even as they routinely deemed most of those practices inappropriate to the demands of an urban society.

The prevalence of the village in the experience of European Jews in the years when the idea of emancipation was gaining currency among the Jewish elites of western and central Europe is striking. According to an estimate by the sociologist Werner Cahnman, "At the beginning of the nineteenth century about ninety percent of the Jews living in the German-speaking countries of Central Europe resided in villages and tiny country towns."[2] Of the Jews of France, the German states, Bohemia, and Moravia, only those who lived in Prussia, and especially East Prussia, were found in any considerable numbers in urban areas. Although the rural percentage declined in the course of the century as Jews throughout these lands embraced the opportunities offered by vibrant urban economies, most of that decline occurred in the second half of the century. Even as late as 1900 there remained residual village and small town Jewish populations in such regions as Alsace, the southwestern German states, and Bohemia and Moravia.[3] Because of the predomi-

---

2 Werner Cahnman, "Village and Small-Town Jews in Germany—A Typological Study," *Leo Baeck Institute Yearbook*, 19 (1974): 107.

3 Vicki Caron, *Between France and Germany: The Jews of Alsace-Lorraine, 1871-1918* (Stanford: Stanford University Press, 1988), 162f.; Marsha Rozenblit, *The Jews of Vienna 1867-1914: Assimilation and Identity* (Albany: SUNY Press, 1983), 38; Utz Jeggle, *Judendörfer in Württemberg* (Tübingen: Tübingen Vereinigung für Volkskunde, 1969), 198. On the socioeconomic evolution of rural Jewry in Germany, see Monika Richarz, "Emancipation and Continuity—German Jews in the Rural Economy," in *Revolution and Evolution: 1848 in German-Jewish History*, ed. Werner E. Mosse, Arnold Paucker, and Reinhard Rürup (Tübingen: Mohr, 1981), 95-115.

nance of the village in the demography of western and central European Jews at the turn of the nineteenth century, most Jewish communal leaders between the French Revolution and World War I, while based in cities, were born in village communities and had personal experience of the traditional patterns of Jewish life that prevailed there.

The attitudes of these socially aspiring members of the nineteenth-century urban Jewish elites to the society they had left were complex and ambivalent. Only too happy to break out of the narrow confines of the village, many were avid critics of what they saw as the superstitiousness of village Jewish customs. Like Gentile critics during the preemancipation public debates on the "Jewish question," they focused on the need to "improve" or "regenerate" the Jews of the countryside. Yet they also acknowledged the strength of Jewish solidarity and religious observance that characterized village Jewry at its peak, even as they criticized its excesses.[4] This ambivalence enabled the Jews who had migrated from village to city, once they were acculturated to the mores of urban life, to use the village—either in actual visits home or, as we shall see, in literary excursions—as a measure of how far they had traveled, but also as a resource for reflection upon the status of the Jew in their contemporary world.

Several factors contributed to sustaining traditional patterns of Jewish behavior in European villages. Village Jewish communities were small, generally numbering from a few score to a few hundred persons. Their members were bound together by socioeconomic as well as religious differentiation from their neighbors, for they played a distinct economic role as middlemen between the urban and rural economy. Unlike the local Christians, they were neither peasants nor—at least in the case of Alsace-Lorraine and the southwest German states—artisans. The clustering of Jews in distinct sectors of the economy, and the survival throughout the nineteenth century of a village Jewish economy in which self-employment was the dominant pattern, created a climate supportive of traditional religious observance. Village Jewish society was also reinforced by external factors. Although they were often deeply rooted in the local environment and had adapted some local customs for Jewish use, Jews living in the countryside were objects of popular antipathy and occasionally victims of popular violence. Thus the bonds forged by

---

4 See, for example, the articles in *La Régénération*, published in Strasbourg in 1836-1837. On the efforts of French Jewish leaders to "regenerate" their fellow Jews, see Jay Berkovitz, *The Shaping of Jewish Identity in Nineteenth-Century France* (Detroit: Wayne State University Press, 1989).

kinship, shared communal institutions and economic networks, and external pressure created powerful social constraints that hampered deviance.

Although Jews living in villages and small towns, because of their commercial pursuits and contact with the urban economy, were often the first to introduce elements of urban fashion and manners into their milieu, their patterns of popular Judaism were reinforced by the surrounding rural culture. Thus, for example, the village Jewish custom of the communal procession during funerals, widely criticized as undignified by urban Jewish elites and persisting into the second half of the century, mirrored Christian festival processions. The village *shulklopfer*, who went from house to house to summon Jewish men to prayer, depended upon a compact, geographically restricted, and mutually dependent population for the success of his endeavors. Village Jews who visited wonder-working rabbis like the Baʿal Shem of Michelstadt seeking protective talismans and hung his portrait on their walls or who consulted Jewish faith healers when they were ill scarcely differed from their peasant neighbors who would turn to Christian faith healers. Similarly, there was no local incentive to suppress the Jewish folk practices that surrounded childbirth—including the use of amulets, the drawing of circles to ward off evil spirits, and the custom of the *hollekreisch* (the ceremony of lifting the newborn's cradle and conferring a secular name upon the infant on the sabbath the mother first returned to the synagogue). These practices paralleled popular Christian custom and were a mark of the cultural integration of village Jews into their milieu. Memoir and ethnographic literature indicate that the *hollekreisch*, in particular, survived into the twentieth century.[5]

The paucity, or even absence, of secular or nonsectarian social institutions in villages and small towns also fostered the survival of traditional Jewish institutions that were transformed or disappeared in the urban

---

5 On popular Jewish custom in Alsace see Freddy Raphael,"Rites de naissance et médecine populaire dans le judaisme rural d'Alsace," *Ethnologie française*, 1/3-4 (1971): 83-94; and Freddy Raphael and Robert Weyl, *Regards nouveaux sur les Juifs d'Alsace* (Strasbourg: Istra/Editions des Dernieres Nouvelles, 1980), 239–44; S. Debré, *L'humeur judéo-alsacien* (Paris: Rieder, 1933); and my "Emancipation and Cultural Conservatism: Alsatian Jewry in the 19th Century" [in Hebrew], *Uma veToeldoteha*, 2 (Jerusalem: Merkaz Zalman Shazar, 1984), 39-48 and *The Emancipation of the Jews of Alsace: Acculturation and Tradition in the Nineteenth Century* (New Haven: Yale University Press, 1991); for references to customs in a Jewish village in Baden, see Jacob Picard, "Childhood in the Village: Fragment of an Autobiography," *Leo Baeck Institute Yearbook* 4 (1959), 280f., 283-86.

environment. The village Jew seeking leisure-time activity had no recourse but to Jewish institutions. Often traditional philanthropic associations, whose mandate was strengthened by common knowledge of communal welfare needs, survived not only because of the acceptance of the obligation of *ṣedaka* (charity) but also because of the social role the association played. The traditional *ḥevra* (confraternity) for the study of rabbinic texts, as another example, persisted in some village Jewish communities in Alsace at least until mid-century. A reading of the minute books of these *ḥevras*, and particularly of their records of fines levied upon members for infractions, indicates the importance of sociability, in addition to the ostensible religious goals of the group, in the functioning of the *ḥevra*.[6]

Village Jews, of course, were not untouched by the political, economic, and cultural developments of the nineteenth century. But their rootedness in a relatively stable economic environment seems to have fostered the persistence of traditional patterns of life. Even as the youth acquired facility with the national language, village Jews continued to speak their own local Yiddish dialect among themselves. Memoir literature, journalistic accounts, and studies by gentile observers all note that the Jewish calendar continued to determine the regular routine as well as special occasions for festivity among Jews in the countryside into the twentieth century. The linkage of that calendar with family life was a powerful incentive for the perpetuation of traditional religious practice for Jews whose communal and domestic frames of reference were interwoven.[7] In Alsace, the region that I have studied most intensively, nineteenth-century village Jews also continued to feed wandering beggars from across the Rhine, even when the local and national consistorial leadership banned such philanthropy, and they compiled *memorbikher* (memorial books) of martyrs and prominent local rabbis and pious laymen (and laywomen) throughout the nineteenth century to provide

---

6 See, for example, Takonos shel Hachevro d'Shocharei Hatov, Riedseltz, 5697 [in Yiddish], ms. HM 5521, and Pinkas Cheshbonos shel Chevras Shocharei Hatov b'Riedseltz (1837-1849) [in Yiddish], ms. HM 5528, Central Archives for the History of the Jewish People, Jerusalem.

7 See *Jüdisches Leben in Deutschland: Selbstzeugnisse Zur Sozialgeschicte*, ed. Monika Richarz, 3 vols. (Stuttgart: Deutsche Verlags-Anstalt, 1976-1982), passim; Marion Kaplan, "Priestess and Hausfrau: Women and Tradition in the German Jewish Family," in *The Jewish Family: Myths and Reality*, ed. Steven M. Cohen and Paula E. Hyman (New York: Holmes and Meier,1986), 62-81; Edouard Coypel, *Le judaïsme: Esquisse des moeurs juives* (Mulhouse, France: Imprimerie Brustlein, 1876).

an ongoing link with the Jewish past.[8] The preservation of these traditions suggests the survival of a sense of Jewish solidarity that transcended both geographical and chronological boundaries.

This stable environment also promoted the synthesis of the new with the old, rather than wholesale abandonment of past custom. Thus village Jews in Alsace combined contemporary regional and even national motifs with traditional Jewish religious (and semireligious) artifacts. A recent exhibition at the Jewish Museum on the Jewish folk art of Alsace included the use of the popular Alsatian folk art of cut paper flowers to create a Torah crown, a typical Alsatian painted large floral display on a *mizraḥ* (plaque to mark the eastern wall), the inclusion in a *shiviti* wall plaque of a military conscription number, and the incorporation of the tricolor French flag on Seder show towels and Torah binders.[9] The latter two examples, in particular, provide a visual articulation of the compatibility of the new status of the Jew as citizen with traditional Jewish practice and suggest that historians would do well to pay attention to material culture in their attempts to understand the acculturation of Jews in the modern world.

Since those Jews with the highest aspirations and a measure of accumulated capital as well as the least attachment to religious tradition were the first to leave the villages for more promising economic environments—as several scholars have demonstrated, at least for France and Germany—the smaller village Jewish communities that survived into the twentieth century became increasingly orthodox in their orientation.[10] More prosperous and culturally urbanized than their village forebears of the prior century, they were nonetheless a living reminder of the Jewish past.

By the middle of the nineteenth century, village Jews existed in two forms: as flesh-and-blood representatives of a declining type of Jewish society, and, increasingly, as characters in a new genre of literature, often referred to generically and misleadingly as "ghetto tales." These literary recreations of village Jewish life were the product of Jewish writers who had left behind the villages of their childhood for integration into the high culture of the larger society in which they lived. At least three of

---

[8] Debré, *L'humeur*, 273-76; Moïse Ginsburger, "Les Mémoriaux alsaciens," *Revue des études juives* 40 (1900): 231-47; 41 (1900): 118-43.

[9] "Memories of Alsace: Folk Art and Jewish Tradition," The Jewish Museum, New York, 18 May–14 August 1989.

[10] Lowenstein, "Rural Community," 234f.; Hermann Schwab, *Jewish Rural Communities in Germany* (London: Cooper, 1956).

them—Berthold Auerbach (1812-1882) of Württemberg, Leopold Kompert (1822-1886) of Bohemia, and Alexandre Weill (1811-1899) of Alsace—abandoned traditional rabbinical study, the career of choice for the intellectually gifted male Jewish youth of the preemancipation village, for the world of the university and literary pursuits.[11] Yet they chose to integrate their childhood experiences with their adult personae by focusing upon Jewish village society as the scene for much of their fiction.

Along with a fourth writer, Daniel Stauben (1822-1875), who, like Weill, depicted the traditional village Jews of Alsace, all three of these pioneers in tales of Jewish village life were political liberals. However, their fictional representation of Jewish life depended on the romantic currents then prevailing in European literature and the rediscovery of the peasant folk in general. They were early examples of a phenomenon that was to become common at the end of the nineteenth century. The French historian Eugen Weber, for example, has commented that the development of the study of folklore after 1870 in France was a sign of "the wholesale destruction of traditional ways;"[12] and the British historian Eric Hobsbawm has pointed out that certain official political and unofficial social traditions both in Great Britain and on the Continent were invented in the same *fin-de-siècle* period in order to maintain social cohesion in the wake of transformations wrought by industrialization and mass politics.[13] In a similar vein, the somewhat earlier literary efforts of Jewish writers of village origin reflect their perception that the traditional culture of their youth, though still visible, was doomed to disappear as urbanization, secularization, and acculturation to bourgeois cultural patterns took their inevitable toll. In the introduction to his *Scènes de la vie*

---

[11] For a broad assessment of nostalgia among nineteenth-century European Jewry, see Richard I. Cohen, "Nostalgia and 'return to the ghetto': a cultural phenomenon in Western and Central Europe," in eds., J. Frankel and S. J. Zipperstein, *Assimilation and Community: The Jews in Nineteenth-Century Europe* (Cambridge: Cambridge University Press, 1991), 130–55. On Auerbach, see *Encyclopedia Judaica* 3 (1971): 845f., and David Sorkin, *The Transformation of German Jewry, 1780–1840* (New York: Oxford University Press, 1987), 140–55; on Kompert, ibid., 10 (1971): 1177f.; on Weill, see his autobiography, *Ma jeunesse*, 2 vols. (Paris: E. Denty, 1870), and Joë Friedemann, *Alexandre Weill: Ecrivain contestaire et historien engagé (1811-1899)* Société Savante d'Alsace et des régions de l'est, 29 (Strasbourg: Libraire Istra, 1980).

[12] Eugen Weber, *Peasants into Frenchmen: The Modernization of Rural France, 1870-1914* (Stanford: Standford University Press, 1976), 471.

[13] Eric Hobsbawm, "Mass-Producing Traditions: Europe, 1870-1914," in *The Invention of Tradition*, ed. Eric Hobsbawm and Terence Ranger (Cambridge: Cambridge University Press, 1984), 263-307.

juive en Alsace, published in Paris in 1860, Daniel Stauben, the pen name of the professor Auguste Widal, displayed this perception, commenting that after reading about rustic life in one region of France,

> there were aroused in me a flock of reminiscences connected to a world at once analogous and different; analogous in the simplicity of its customs, the antiquity of its practices, and the originality of some of its personages; different in its religion. . . . Le Berry, I . . . said to myself, is not the only region of France where there live populations of distinct character, . . . of picturesque idiom. One could oppose to the peasants of the Indre . . . the Jews of our hamlets of Alsace. . . . I asked myself why, . . . with my qualification as an Alsatian and a Jew, born and raised in the village, I should not attempt to initiate the secular reader in this [way of] life so little known and so worthy of [being known]. . . . We have sought to depict as well as we can this sort of contemporary Judaic antiquity, alas ready to disappear; for at the pace in which our century is going—progress and railroads assisting—within several years there will remain no vestige of these primitive customs.[14]

Stauben was part of a generation of Jewish authors of village origin who began to write about village Jewry in a nostalgic tone in the 1840s. His own volume on Alsace depended heavily upon a series of lengthy "Letters on Alsatian Customs," derived from his visits home to Alsace, that were published (under the name Auguste W) from 1849 to 1853 in the *Archives israélites*, a self-styled progressive journal of Jewish opinion.[15] Berthold Auerbach had taken the lead with his *Schwarzwalder Dorfgeschichten*, tales of the Black Forest region in which he grew up, that appeared from 1843 to 1854. Leopold Kompert (whose work Stauben would translate into French) published his first tale of Jewish life, "Die Schnorrer," in 1846, followed by several other collections of stories that appeared from 1848 to 1865. Finally, Alexandre Weill published his first stories of village life in Alsace in German in 1847 and in French in 1850. The work of Auerbach, Kompert, and Weill was exceedingly popular in their own time and went through many editions; Auerbach and Kompert were also translated into several foreign languages.

A second, and somewhat less illustrious, generation of writers who wrote about traditional Jews living in western Europe emerged in the

---

[14] Daniel Stauben, *Scènes de la vie juive en Alsace* (Paris: Michel Lévy Frères, 1860), ii–v.

[15] "Lettres sur les moeurs alsaciennes," *Archives israélites* 10 (1849): 643-56; 11 (1850): 72-87, 246-51, 425-32, 465-69; 12 (1851): 65-71, 95-99, 204-209, 461-68; 14 (1853): 374-83.

1880s. Foremost among them was Léon Cahun, born in Haguenau in 1841 and the grandson of the rabbi of Rosheim, whose *La vie juive*, published in 1886, celebrated and romanticized the traditional life of the Jews of Alsace, now threatened not only by progress but also by the German conquest that had wrested the province from the benevolent protection of France.[16] (Also active in the 1880s was a Christian writer, one Sacher-Masoch, whose ghetto stories were published in French literary reviews and favorably cited in the French Jewish Press).[17]

These tales of village Jewish life seem to have found their primary audience among urban Jews seeking a tie with what they saw as the authentic Judaism of their childhood or, for some, of their forebears. Preliminary research indicates that Jewish publishing houses brought at least some of these books to the reading public.[18] But the presentation of these stories first in prestigious general literary journals, such as the *Revue des Deux-Mondes* and the *Revue bleue* in France, was especially important in legitimating these works for a bourgeois Jewish public. In 1852, for example, the *Archives israélites* found two elements of Leopold Kompert's work worthy of note—his "remarkable output" on the society he wanted to make known, on the one hand, and, on the other, "the reflections that these pictures *[tableaux]* and the society that furnished them have inspired in a man of letters, Christian and French."[19]

On the whole, the Jewish press appears to have greeted this new literary genre warmly. Articles in the *Archives israélites*, the *Univers israélite*, and the *Allgemeine Zeitung des Judenthums* reflect a complex appreciation of the significance of these tales for the Jews of their own time. In 1852 the *Archives israélites* found the center of the Jewishness of Leopold Kompert's work, recently translated into French, in "the inspiration of a race long oppressed and always courageous [that] makes itself felt

---

16 Léon Cahun, *La vie juive* (Paris: E. Monnie de Brunhoff, 1886), illustrated with lithographs by Alphonse Lévy. On Cahun, see Elisabeth Christine Muelsch, *Zwischen Assimilation und jüdischen Selbstverständnis: David Leon Cahun (1841-1900)* (Bonn: Romantischer Verlag, 1987).

17 I. C., "Contes Juifs, par Sacher Masoch," *Archives israélites* 49 (1888): 418f; another novel, "La petite colporteuse," is cited by the *Univers israélite* 43 (1887–88): 80–82. Leopold von Sacher-Masoch was an Austrian novelist who lent his name to the phenomenon of Masochism, which he described in his works.

18 For example, in Paris the Quantin publishing house, Archives israélites 49 (1988): 419 and Michel Lévy frères, which published Stauben and Kompert.

19 *Archives israélites* 13 (1852): 225f. Stauben's *Scènes de la vie juive en Alsace*, for example, appeared in the *Revue des Deux-Mondes* before its publication in book form.

there."[20] Referring to yet another of Kompert's books on a rural Jewish family in Bohemia, the *Archives israélites* noted in 1855 that "these publications . . . bring so much pleasure to every Jew and even to every man of heart and intelligence."[21] Four years later it spelled out the roles this literature played: it served to dispel lingering prejudice and to mark progress. In the words of the reviewer,

> In casting a glance backward, one measures the distance traveled and one derives from it hope for the future. . . . Let us therefore . . . protect our Jewish writers! For they are our avant-garde, and they are the ones who have delivered the first blows to the old fanaticism and the ancient intolerance."[22]

The *Allgemeine Zeitung des Judenthums* saw village tales as a natural human response to change and as evidence that Jewish sources could serve as an inspiration for literary creativity. In 1850 an article on Jewish folk life commented that "the life of the Jewish masses has in the past fifty years been almost entirely transformed . . .; Jewish folk life has in part come to an end in modern general life," and then referred to the expressed desire of the author of a recent volume of village tales to write down his stories "to fix the forms of an earlier time."[23] Five years later the paper reflected on Kompert's work:

> The readers of earlier volumes of this newspaper will remember how we crowned the young Kompert with a . . . laurel wreath when his *Aus dem Ghetto* appeared. Kompert has remained true to himself. He has not considered Jewishness [*Judenheit*] as a stick with which he is only learning to walk; rather he strides unswerving further along the road that he has chosen. Therefore, honor to him. This is the way we must yet come so that writers and artists not believe that Jewish material is merely like children's shoes that they wish to outgrow but so that they may also invest the strength of an adult in it to raise up and create greatness from Jewish soil.[24]

Jewish reviewers of this literary genre used such nostalgic terms as "picturesque" and "age-old" to describe popular Jewish custom to which they no longer adhered because it was inappropriate to their circumstances as modern, acculturated urban Jews; they praised the courage, fidelity, and fortitude of the heroes of these tales while dismissing their

[20] Ibid., 226.
[21] Ibid., 16(1855), 293.
[22] Ibid. 20 (1859): 661.
[23] *Allgemeine Zeitung des Judenthums*, 14 (1850): 497f.
[24] Ibid. 19 (1855): 307.

superstitiousness and religious fanaticism as the fruit of persecution and segregation happily transcended. Thus, they (and presumably other Jewish readers as well) sought both to appropriate the village experience, as depicted in literature, as a connection to the past and a source of pride insofar as the general values of village Jews were admirable; and to distance themselves from the specific characteristics of the Jewish culture of the village by denying their contemporary relevance. In this balancing act they were assisted by the authors of these tales themselves. In recreating the village milieu and its Jewish characters, they wrote with affection and respect, dwelling not on poverty, the petty squabbles that could disrupt small communities, or the tensions with Christian neighbors, but on social harmony and the simplicity of a rural life. Their very idealization of the village distanced it psychologically for their readers.

The Jewish readers of Jewish village tales could use these works not only as a source of entertainment but also as a way to locate themselves on a historical continuum in a period of perceived rapid change. They were from the village—and proud of that fact—but no longer of it; their roots went deep but their urban transplantation was successful and pointed to the future. Village tales could also stimulate reflection on the problematics of tradition and change. As one French reviewer of Kompert put it,

> How can we reconcile attachment to the centuries-old religion of our fathers with the obligations that emancipation imposes upon us, how combine together prescriptions that had as their goal the prevention of any mixing of the races with the sentiments of fraternity necessary vis-à-vis fellow countrymen and non-Jewish friends?[25]

The stories of Jewish life in the village thus posed for some of their readers the central question of the nature of Jewish particularity within modern European society.

---

[25] *Archives israélites* 13 (1852): 228.

8

Self-Image Through Objects: Toward a Social History of Jewish Art Collecting and Jewish Museums

RICHARD I. COHEN

When the noted Russian art critic Vladimir Stasov recorded his impressions of the first public exhibition of Jewish ceremonial art at the World Exposition in Paris in 1878—the collection of Isaac Strauss—he surmised how Jews walking through the exhibition would respond to its content. He wondered whether they would be able to recognize its importance or dismiss it as "a new and curious game which flatters more or less their national sentiment, but basically has only mediocre importance." He presumed that they preferred the wealth of European art over "the minuscule objects, rings . . . and chandeliers . . . (for) here there was nothing monumental . . . a minuscule collection." For Stasov, who actively encouraged various Jewish artists to assert their national identity, this anticipated rejection was obviously annoying, since it "denies their own interest. Is it not from 'trifles'" (figure 1), he asked, "that emerge all the important collections of national objects? One must begin by first loving that which is small and modest, . . . that which does not attract because of its majesty and colossal forms . . . but where are hidden the characteristic traits of the nation, hidden by the futile modes of despotism, ignorance, and persecution."[1] Stasov's astute premonition of

[1] Vladimir Stasov, "Art israélitea l'Exposition Universelle," *Archives Israélites* 41/5

the "Jewish response" to the Strauss collection of Jewish ceremonial art[2] touches on some of the inherent issues that an inquiry into Jewish art collecting raises; foremost among them is the way in which the collection of art and its appreciation are at the point of intersection of some of the major social and cultural strains and currents of Jewish life in *fin-de-siècle* Europe. Indeed, Stasov perceived an essential element that a century later historians and anthropologists of museums turned into an axiomatic framework of their thinking—the public display of objects and their acceptance by the public involve a wide range of interactions, be they political, social, cultural, historical, or economic.

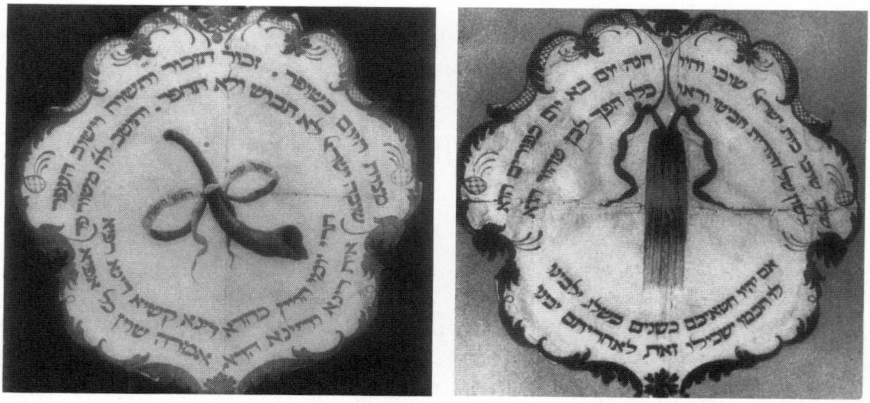

FIGURE 1: An example of the "trifles" referred to by Stasov: Cloths for Rosh Hashanah and Yom Kippur, Italy, 18th century. Silk taffeta, silk, and gold. Strauss Collection, Musée de Cluny 12338a–b.

(1878): 14f.; also 21, 30, 37, 46. On Stasov's role in bringing Jewish artists to repossess their national culture, see *Tradition and Revolution: The Jewish Renaissance in Russian Avant-Garde Art in 1912-1928,* ed. Ruth Apter-Gabriel (Jerusalem: Israel Museum, 1987), passim. See also Mark Antokolsky, *Zikhronot uzeror Mikhtavim* (Memoirs and Letters) (Jerusalem: Bialik Institute, 1952), 160-62; D. Maggid, *Antokolsky* (in Hebrew) (Warsaw, 1897), 206-209. Compare Stasov's review of the exhibition with that of the noted Jewish scholar David Kaufmann, "Aus der Pariser Weltausstellung," *Israelitische Wochenschrift* 9 (1878): 301, 309, 312, 325, 333, 341, 349. Kaufmann discussed in depth certain objects while appealing to German Jewry to emulate Strauss's effort and establish a similar collection.

[2] On Strauss and his collection see Victor Klagsbald, *Catalogue raisonné de la collection juive du musée de Cluny* (Paris: Éditions de la Réunion des musées nationaux, 1981); Moïse Schwab, "Les médailles de la collection Strauss," *Revue des Études Juives* 23 (1891): 136-38; idem, "La collection Strauss au Musée de Cluny," *Gazette des Beaux-Art* 5 (1891): 237-45; idem, "Manuscrits hébreux du Musée de Cluny," *Revue des Études Juives* 50 (1905): 136-39.

Various scholars of visual culture have reflected on the social significance of removing cultural artifacts from the private sphere to the public domain. Common to their thinking is that with the change of context the object takes on a wholly new dimension. On the one hand, its accessibility to the public entails recognition and acceptance of a community's right to view and react critically, with no guarantee of a uniform response—though the display is often designed to instil a particular interpretation and experience. Instruments of knowledge and historical identification, exhibited to arouse spiritual uplift and enjoyment, objects have also been likened "to a book in print or a play on the stage"[3] that necessarily engender response and criticism. However, the dialogue between the public and object is far more extensive. As the objects in a public collection or a museum continue a cultural tradition, they are conceived as links between the spectators and the inhabitants of previous worlds and experiences, as connections between the tangible and intangible or visible and invisible worlds. On the other hand, the new open space in which they are exhibited, an expression of the democratization of art, allowed for the interaction of diverse elements of society that were not likely to encounter each other. This new meeting ground often necessitated the establishment of a particular set of regulations and codes of behavior that were to guarantee a proper atmosphere for the display. But here too, museums and public collections projecting a particular self-image offered diverse alternatives for that desired milieu.[4] Exhibitions of Jewish art and the creation of Jewish museums, in one form or another,

---

3 Thomas E. Crow, *Painters and Public Life in Eighteenth-Century Paris* (New Haven: Yale University Press, 1985), 14.

4 This perspective draws on diverse approaches to the study of public collections and museums, and some of their conceptual orientations underlie the thrust of this article. Though further works are mentioned later, the following studies proved particularly valuable and insightful: Crow, *Painters and Public Life*; Krzysztof Pomian, *Collectionneurs, amateurs et curieux: Paris, Venise:XVIe–XVIIIe siècle* (Paris: Editions Gallimard, 1987). Also available in English translation in Krzysztof Pomain, *Collectors and Curiosities* (Cambridge, England: Polity Press, 1991); Daniel Sherman, *Worthy Monuments: Art Museums and the Politics of Culture in Nineteenth-Century France* (Cambridge: Harvard University Press, 1989); Mary Douglas, *How Institutions Think* (Syracuse: Syracuse University Press, 1986); *The Origins of Museums. The Cabinet of Curiosities in Sixteenth- and Seventeenth -Century Europe*, ed. Oliver Impey and Arthur Macgregor (Oxford: Clarendon, 1985); Bernard Deneke and Rainer Kahsnitz, *Das Germanische National-museum. Nürnberg 1852-1977, Beiträge zu seiner Geschichte* (Munich: Deutscher Kunstverlag, 1978); Édouard Pommier, "Naissance des musées de province," *La Nation, vol. 2, Les lieux de mémoire*, ed. Pierre Nora (Paris: Gallimard, 1986), 451-95.

emerged consciously and unconsciously from these working hypotheses and provide ample evidence of the multidimensional aspect that is embedded in such enterprises. It is the intention of this article to inquire into some of the impulses involved in collecting and displaying Jewish art—ceremonial objects, painting and sculpture, medals and memorabilia—and show how they are related to cultural processes in European and Jewish society and figured prominently in the initiatives toward establishing Jewish art museums and societies from the late nineteenth century until World War II. Underlying the analysis is the premise that a certain self-image shapes attitudes to the visual material, and that self-image offers a further perspective for analyzing Jewish cultural integration in the postemancipation period.

The act of collecting objects of one sort or another, of both a refined and a mundane character, dates back to the beginning of culture. As such, attitudes and traditions associated with economic interests, religious beliefs, and even medical needs were part and parcel of the collection and preservation of material objects in various cultures. Take the example of Tutankhamun, the thirteenth century B.C.E. king of Egypt, who believed that when he died he could take his possessions with him and so had his collection of walking sticks and staves placed in his coffin. By so doing he gained a form of immortality. The king's motive was not economic but bent on perpetuating his particular setting, enabling him to view his prized objects as he was accustomed to during his lifetime. Yet collections of valuables also provided economic leverage. Homer in the *Iliad* relates how Priam, the King of Troy, gathered a "splendid treasure" to redeem the body of his beloved son Hector from Achilles and the Greeks. In classical Greece, where artists and artisans were not regarded on a particularly high level, works of art were essentially public property and shown in various public spaces, especially in the temples, where they served as a kind of bank or royal treasury. Though the word museum is derived from the Greek *mouseion*, the Greek museum was of a different nature—a place where the Muses were glorified.

In the history of art collecting, Christianity offers still another model. For almost a millennium, individual artists were of little concern. Art was created through communal effort and enjoyed as such. The Church, the fountain of knowledge and intellectual ferment, was also the source of artistic appreciation and aesthetic taste. And as art was conceived as a means of edifying the Church's power and glory, educating the public and convincing it of Christ's dominion over the world, individual collection of former artistic achievements was inconsequential, having no place in the hierarchy of ideas. The Church thus became the major repository of treasures of art, scrupulously determining what need be shown to the public for its education, providing complete accessibility only to a select few, except on special occasions and festivals when its wares were publicly exhibited. However, art remained by and large invisible for most of European society even when the almost monolithic hold of the Church on collections of art dwindled in early modern Europe. Royalty and wealthy individuals who built vast collections during this period were concerned neither with disseminating their knowledge nor with revealing their possessions to the public at large.[5] Thus it was not until the eighteenth century, with the spread of Enlightenment ideas and the eclipse of the aristocratic monopoly over art, that Europe sees the creation of public museums that were, in the words of Alma Wittlin, "a confirmation of the [masses'] claim to participation in life's offerings."[6]

Jewish tradition, from biblical times, placed a major symbolic importance on objects that were designed to serve God and service the Temple, but it is only at a later time and setting, Jerusalem and Egypt of the 11th and 12th centuries, that we have evidence of the storing of ritual objects in synagogues with specific descriptions of these objects.[7] Thus the collecting of Jewish ritual objects was traditionally a function of the synagogue. Jewish religious objects were housed in the sacred space of the synagogue (*heikhal*) and community registers (*pinqasim*) of certain communities (*qehillot*) attest to regulations commonly instituted to determine how the objects should be kept and preserved, on what occasion they should be used, and who was allowed to remove them from the *heikhal*. Accessibility was limited. Jewish religious objects of a communal nature were visible when they served a particular function, but they remained basically out of sight for most of the community, as was common with ritual objects in other cultures. The objects, collected over generations in a particular *qehillah*, not only served a religious function but were also charged with a social meaning for both the original patron and the *qehillah*. Products of patronage, ceremonial objects of the

---

5 Antoine Schnapper, "The King of France as Collector in the Seventeenth Century," *Journal of Interdisciplinary History* 17/1 (1986): 185-202.

6 Alma S. Wittlin, *Museums in Search of a Usable Future* (Cambridge: MIT Press, 1970), 81; cf. Dillon Ripley, *The Sacred Grove. Essays on Museums* (New York: Simon and Schuster, 1969); Crow, *Painters and Public Life*, passim; Jean Cassou, "Art Museums and Social Life," *Museum* 2/3 (1949): 155-58.

7 S. D. Goitein, "The Synagogue Building and its Furnishings according to the Records of the Cairo Genizah" (in Hebrew) *Eretz-Israel* 7 (1964): 81-97.

community allowed for the invocation of past figures and deeds while enabling the contemporary patron to assert his place in society and for posterity. To fulfill these social functions, artistic techniques were harnessed to the making of the objects (figure 2).[8]

FIGURE 2: Torah shield, Frankfurt, Germany, late 18th century. Silver, repoussé, and engraved diamonds and semiprecious stones. Master: Johann Jakob Leschhorn. Courtesy of The Israel Museum, Jerusalem. Note the way in which the inscription with the name of the donor is integrated stylistically into the object.

[8] I am hinting here at the ways in which inscriptions with special dedications gradually became an integral part of the ritual object, eventually contributing to its shape and form.

Private homes also maintained Jewish ceremonial objects for performing certain rituals, but, as far as we know, it was not until the middle of the eighteenth century that we encounter an individual, Alexander David (1687-1765), whose religious artifacts not only served his private synagogue but constituted a veritable collection of Judaica.[9] Prior to David and among his contemporary Court Jews, collections of non-Jewish objects existed, and of course Jews actively established vast libraries of printed books and manuscripts,[10] yet it was not until the second half of the nineteenth century that a tendency to assemble Jewish ceremonial objects begins to emerge. And only at the end of that century do we witness the first strides toward the establishment of Jewish museums in various European cities, where Judaica was to be exhibited publicly. Indeed, this phenomenon remained rather limited prior to 1945, after which its scope extended considerably. In the interim Judaica had established itself as an area of interest and study that had previously been almost completely neglected by Jews and gentiles. The turning point, then, in the collection and exhibition of Judaica was that juncture in the history of European Jewry when the process of leaving the "ghetto" was fully matured and the bulk of western and central European Jewish society had achieved emancipation. It is that nexus which offers an insight into a predisposition on the part of elements in Jewish society to openness, to an internal recognition that Jews need not fear exposing their religious and cultural tradition, and to the assumption that an exhibition or a museum may serve as a public meeting ground for Jews and gentiles alike in the spirit of culture and in appreciation of Jewish culture.

At this point let us recall Stasov's concern that Jews would by and large prefer to disassociate themselves from the Strauss exhibition. It would appear that he was well aware of the evolution of bourgeois Jewish taste in the nineteenth century and convinced that the possible Jewish patrons of the arts would turn their heads in another direction, looking for more monumental art. He had evidence to back him up. Bourgeois Jews in western and central Europe were becoming an increas-

---

[9] G. Rulf, "Das Museum der israelitischen Gemeinde Braunschweig," *Mitteilungen zur jüdischen Volkskunde* 19 (1906): 89-94; Vivian Mann, "Forging Judaica: The Case of the Italian Majolica Seder Plates," *Art and Its Uses: The Visual Image and Modern Jewish Society,* ed. Ezra Mendelsohn (*Studies in Contemporary Jewry* 6), (New York: Oxford University Press, 1990), 218f.; 223f.

[10] Azriel Shohet, *Im Hilufer Tekufot* (Beginnings of the Haskalah among German Jewry) (Jerusalem: Bialik Institute, 1960), 29-35.

ingly important market for *objets d'art* of almost every variety—ranging from the decorative arts to the finest of European paintings. As part of their accommodation to the upper middle class and emulation of the aristocracy, they built magnificent homes and furnished them with precious possessions.[11] Some prominent Jewish collectors also emerged during the *fin-de-siècle* as leading patrons of the arts, rising at times to a dominant position in certain branches of art—as was the case with the Secessionist movement and to a certain extent with the Impressionists[12] —a fact that did not escape the attention and antagonism of the surrounding society. In a lighter vein, Evelyn Waugh gave vent to the mythic nature of the Jewish capability to capitalize on art in a humorous passage in *Work Suspended*. Jews were blamed for fostering worthless Impressionist paintings (such as those of Cézanne) "just to get something for nothing. . . . They've made thousands out of it."[13]

One example of this class of Jewish collectors/patrons will suffice. Isaac de Camondo, a descendant of the Turkish banking philanthropist Abraham Camondo, was a voracious collector. In an extraordinary hotel

---

[11] This cultural dimension of Jewish integration into European society has not received adequate treatment and lies beyond the scope of this essay. Distinguished collectors could be found in the major cities of Europe, and their homes often became the hub of artistic interaction. In some cases, as that of C. Sedelmeyer in France, their collection was considered of unusual quality and value and deemed of pivotal importance. A sample of the literature in which some of these legendary collectors are discussed: Colin Eisler, "Kunstgeschichte American Style: A Study in Migration," in *The Intellectual Migration: Europe and America 1930-1960*, ed. Donald Fleming and Bernard Bailyn (Cambridge, Mass.: Belknap, 1969), 554; Ernest Samuels, *Bernard Berenson: The Making of a Legend* (Cambridge, Mass.: Belknap, 1987), passim; Carl E. Schorske, *Fin-de-Siècle Vienna: Politics and Culture* (New York: Knopf, 1981), passim; Steven Beller, *Vienna and the Jews 1867-1939: A Cultural History* (Cambridge: Cambridge University Press, 1989), 26-29; *Les Arts* (Paris, 1903-1908) surveys significant collectors in France, many of whom were Jewish. When the Sedelmeyer collection was publicly sold in 1907, it netted one of the highest sums in auctioning history.

[12] Study of the role of Jews as patrons of the arts in *fin-de-siècle* Europe, a flip side of their collecting passion and economic achievements, remains a historical desideratum. Several examples of initial forays will suffice: Abraham Gilam, "Erich Goeritz and Jewish Art Patronage in Berlin during the 1920s," *Journal of Jewish Art* 11(1985): 60-72; James Shedel, *Art and Society: the New Art Movement in Vienna 1897-1914* (Palo Alto: Sposs, 1981), 60-62; Margarete Merkel Guldan, *Die Tagebücher von Ludwig Pollak. Kennerschaft und Kunsthandel in Rom 1893-1934* (Vienna: Österreichische Akademie der Wissenschaften, 1988), 213-67. My thanks to Michael Silber for this reference.

[13] Evelyn Waugh, *Work Suspended and Other Stories including Basil Seal Rides Again* (London: Chapman and Hall, 1967), 114. My thanks to Ezra Mendelsohn for bringing this reference to my attention.

he had built in Paris by the famous French architect Charles Garnier, he housed a diverse collection that Camondo himself likened to the composition of an opera. It consisted in part of Japanese art and eighteenth-century French furniture and was distinguished by its breadth of modern art, in particular avant-garde Impressionists—the now classic paintings of Manet, Degas, Cézanne, and others—that were eventually donated to the Louvre in 1911. The case of Camondo is instructive. A very wealthy Jew, Camondo based his collection on what was part of the new French experience and did not seek out either the French historical paintings then in vogue or the Old Masters, the goal of the native aristocracy. He excelled in the innovative field of French art and then donated his collection to the French nation—the Louvre—well expressing his sense of appreciation for France, as did other members of the family when they willed the family mansion and collections to the state a generation later.[14] Art patronage—particularly in the form of donations to public museums—was clearly a manner in which the elite Jewish upper class hoped to legitimate their standing in society and to display their patriotic attachment to their country. Not so secure in their status as for example, the English aristocracy, who during this same period sold major paintings to wealthy collectors in the United States,[15] Jewish collectors by and large preferred to donate their collections rather than have them sold. Examples of their patronage abound, and it was not limited to the national museums of their native country but included emerging provincial museums as well.[16] This drive, to reach the plateau

---

14 *Musée Nissim de Camondo* (Paris: Union Centrale des Arts Decoratifs, 1973); Arsène Alexandre, "Collection de M. le Comte Isaac de Camondo," *Les Arts* (November 1908): 1-32; Eugen Weber, *France, Fin de Siècle* (Cambridge, Mass.: Belknap, 1986), 157f. On the Camondo family see Aron Rodrique, "Abraham de Camondo of Istanbul: the Transformation of Jewish Philanthropy," in *From East and West: Jews in a Changing Europe, 1750-1870*, ed. Frances Malino and David Sorkin (Oxford: Oxford University Press, 1990), 46-56. As an aside it is interesting to note that Gustavo Sforni, a Jewish collector and patron of the arts, was "possibly the first in Italy to buy works by Vincent van Gogh and Paul Cézanne" (Emily Braun, "From the Risorgimento to the Resistance :One Hundred Years of Jewish Artists in Italy," in *Gardens and Ghettos: The Art of Jewish Life in Italy*, ed. Vivian B. Mann [Berkeley and Los Angeles: University of California Press, 1989], 158).

15 David Cannadine, *The Decline and Fall of the British Aristocracy* (New Haven: Yale University Press, 1990).

16 Sherman, *Worthy Monuments*, 207, discusses the gifts of Baron Alphonse de Rothschild to French provincial museums. Jewish newspapers at the end of the nineteenth century followed closely this form of Jewish involvement in European society and reported on various donations of paintings to public institutions and museums.

of art patronage and social legitimacy, as was the case of Jewish integration into other areas of the arts, certainly worked against an attentiveness to a particularistic "Jewish art," though now and again one comes across leading Jewish collectors who had some Judaica in their possession.[17] Stasov's reading of this element of Jewish society was thus astute and perceptive.

But the Strauss collection revealed an aspect of postemancipation bourgeois and urban Jewry which Stasov may not have been privy to. With Strauss too we have a case of a well established Jew, one who became publicly acknowledged as director of the court balls and composer of its music in Vichy during the reign of Louis Napoleon. Isaac Strauss (1806-1888), a minor collector of *objets d'art*, began in his later years to collect Jewish artifacts—sabbath lamps, *Kiddush* goblets, spice boxes, Hanukkah lamps, and the like. By the time he died, his collection had grown to 149 objects (only 82 were exhibited in 1878) of diverse Judaica.[18] Can we assume that for this scion of a rabbinic family in Strasbourg, who had gone the route of many French Jews in the nineteenth century by migrating from Alsace to Paris (1827), collecting Judaica had an element of returning to his childhood and was a subconscious means of reviving memories thereof without actually returning to that experience? Could his urge to collect not be seen as an effort to obliterate time's passing? Strauss was apparently motivated by what I have called elsewhere a nostalgic yearning for a vanishing Jewish world.[19] Strauss made

---

The *Jewish Standard* (19 September 1888, p.4) glowingly reported that the Rothschild family in Paris had begun making plans to establish a Rothschild museum. "The happy thought to immortalise thereby the memory of the head of this famous family finds unconcealed sympathy even in those circles which are not favorably disposed toward Jews." The project was seemingly discarded. I have yet to uncover the reasons for the change in heart.

[17] These include some members of the de Camondo family; Rodolphe Kann, who was the owner of Rembrandt's "Aristotle Contemplating the Bust of Homer" and works by Ruisdael, Metsu, Mals, and others; Léopold Goldschmidt, Hart-Derembourg, and Ludwig Pollak. Pollak had seemingly little Judaica in his possession but after purchasing a mediaeval manuscript of the *Haggadah*, he carried it with him on several of his European trips almost as an amulet, eager to display it to established collectors and friends (Guldan, *Tagebücher*, 263-66).

[18] Klagsbald, *Catalogue raisonné*; idem, *Jewish Treasures from Paris: From the Collections of the Cluny Museum and the Consistoire* (Jerusalem: Israel Museum, 1982); and the following note.

[19] Richard I. Cohen, "Nostalgia and 'Return to the Ghetto': A Cultural Phenomenon in Western and Central Europe," in *Assimilation and Community in European Jewry, 1815-1881*, ed. Jonathan Frankel and Steve Zipperstein (Cambridge:

Judaica the core of his collection and asserted therein his identification with his Jewish past—*mutatis mutandis* with the paths of individuals involved in *Wissenschaft des Judentums* (science of Judaism) in earlier periods. Strauss's personal motives hint at a later social phenomenon—the juncture at which bourgeois Jews, well integrated into European society, utilizing their means to accumulate *objets d'art,* choose to focus on "Jewish" objects. That is, they adopted the bourgeois behavior of collecting and legitimated their status in society, yet opted for a particularistic realm of objects undeniably related to their private lives, past or present. Their orientation coincided with and supported the emergence of Jewish artists (e.g., Moritz Oppenheim, Maurycy Gottlieb, and Isidor Kaufmann) who drew on Jewish religious experience and life and found in these collectors a sympathetic market (figure 3).[20] In this sense, and possibly in their socioeconomic status, these bourgeois Jewish collectors embodied a less "assimilated" and less "successful" model of the Jewish bourgeoisie than the one Camondo provides.

Moreover, the public exhibition of the Strauss collection necessarily expressed a certain desire to merge Jewish cultural artifacts within the wider framework of European art and diverse cultures. Here too a definite sociocultural statement was being made. Jewish religious artifacts could now be perceived objectively as art, in a neutral territory, and divested somewhat of their purely religious implications. The Palais de Trocadéro, where the exhibition took place, had become the home of various ethnographic shows inspired by the French geographer Siebold, and it thus lent itself to viewing this "curious collection" in the context of little known cultures. Here we can see that in the study of collections and exhibitions several factors need to be considered simultaneously—the motives of the collector, the impression, impact, reception, and experience of the viewers, and the nature of the public/private space where the exhibition is held.

Cambridge University Press, 1992), 130-55.

20 On Oppenheim, see *Moritz Oppenheim: The First Jewish Painter* (Jerusalem: Israel Museum, 1983), esp. Ismar Schorsch, "Art as Social History: Oppenheim and the German Jewish Vision of Emancipation," 31-61; on Kaufmann, see Norman L. Kleeblatt and Vivian B. Mann, *Treasures of the Jewish Museum* (New York: Universe Books, 1986), 168f.

FIGURE 3: Isidor Kaufmann (1853–1921), *Friday Evening,* ca. 1920. Oil on canvas. Courtesy of The Jewish Museum, New York.

Siebold's perception of ethnology as a supplement indispensable to the historian, the student of natural science, and the philosopher became a central orientation for Jewish figures in the west and east in their collecting and exhibiting of Judaica. The Anglo-Jewish Exhibition at the Royal Albert Hall in 1887 and its coordinators, Joseph Jacobs and Lucien Wolf, exemplify this trend. The conception of this second Jewish exhibition was more encompassing than the first. Alongside the Strauss and private English collections, the organizers assembled archeological relics, documents from Anglo-Jewish history, manuscripts, portraits of prominent Anglo-Jewish figures, and a model of Solomon's Temple (figures 4 and 5), all told almost three thousand items. What was behind this extravagant effort? It appears that a definite connection exists between the successful attempts of figures in the community to prevent the demolition of a historic Jewish landmark in London—the Bevis Marks synagogue—and the original proposal of the exhibition. It was hoped that interest in Anglo-Jewish history could be generated on the basis of popular antidemolition sentiment. In turning to a public exhibition as the medium to further an interest in Anglo-Jewish history, these Jewish individuals proved loyal children of the age. Not only did they respond to the "destruction" of the past by turning to it, as was common throughout *fin-de-siècle* Europe, but they also focused on one of the nineteenth century's "favorite vehicles to convey . . . messages to posterity" (to use Schorske's felicitous description of museums)[21]—as a form of preserving and developing Jewish historical and group consciousness. And once the idea surfaced, the coordinators read into and built on it their conceptions of Judaism. For Jacobs, a prominent ethnographer of his day, the exhibition was a confirmation of his view that Jews "were men, not merely theologians," and it emphasized their "human aspect," in the manner of their jargons, names, and customs;[22] for Wolf, who was engaged in historical research, the possibility that the exhibition would promote a Jewish historical society was a paramount concern.[23]

In displaying Judaica, in the widest meaning of the term, in a public setting, members of the Anglo-Jewish community were intent on using objects to convey a message.[24] In so doing they revealed an apologetic strain in Jewish museology that has continued well into the twentieth century. For in celebrating their own history and its distinguished figures in honor of Queen Victoria's Jubilee within a purely English context—as opposed to a community setting—the organizers were confident that the public would see in the exhibition a vindication of the Jewish presence in England. Representative spokesmen of the community made this clear at various occasions.

---

21 Schorske, *Fin-de-Siècle Vienna*, 104.

22 Report of a lecture given by Jacobs on the Jewish diffusion of folklore in which he took Solomon Schechter to task for being concerned only with theology and seeing "nothing worthy of attention except Jewish theology . . . . He thought lightly of the history of the Jewish race in its social aspects . . . . One of the objects of the late Historical Exhibition . . . was to emphasize this purely human aspect" (*Jewish Standard* [11 May 1888]: 4); *Jewish Chronicle* [11 May 1888]; on Jacobs and his ethnographic work, Haim Schwarzbaum, "Anglo-Jewish Contributions to Folklore Research" (in Hebrew), in *Studies in the Cultural Life of the The Jews in England* , vol. 5, ed. Dov Noy and Issachar Ben-Ami (Jerusalem: Folklore Research Center Studies, 1975), 97-102.

23 *Jewish Chronicle* (London, 1886-1888); Lucien Wolf, "Origin of the Jewish Historical Society of England," *Transactions of Jewish Historical Society of England* , 7 (1911-1914): 212–14. Isidore Spielman originally proposed the idea of the exhibition and saw its ramifications for creating a historical society.

24 *Jewish Chronicle* (21 May 1886).

FIGURE 4: An example of how ceremonial objects were displayed at the Anglo-Jewish exhibition, 1887.

The *Jewish Chronicle* devoted much attention to the Jewish image that the exhibition evoked, emphasizing especially the themes of Jewish–Gentile relations and interest in Jewish history. Reporting on the gala opening, the *Chronicle* in an editorial remarked on the presence of many Jewish notables:

> But there was a goodly number of Gentile celebrities who showed their friendliness to all that interests Jews by their sympathetic presence. . . . From all sides were to be heard expressions of admiration at the successful display of objects. . . . The exhibition is of an educational character. It is calculated to remove something of the mystery which somehow seems in the mind of the outside world to environ all that is Jewish.[25]

As for the anti-Semitica exhibited, the *Chronicle* noted:

> A phase of English opinion of the past . . . but survivals of which still linger on in popular talk. The Gentile visitor will be ashamed of these misrepresentations, and his shame will be to his credit. . . . England has to be proud of her treatment of Jews and Jews have to be grateful to a great country that has held up the beacon of tolerance thru so many years of misrepresentation and ill-will. From this point of view the Exhibition is

[25] Ibid. (8 April 1887): 9f.

truly Anglo-Jewish, and in the best sense of the word, national.[26]

FIGURE 5: A sculpture commemorating Moses Montefiore's intervention on behalf of the Jews of Damascus in 1840. Montefiore memorabilia were lavishly displayed at the Anglo-Jewish exhibition.

As the exhibition placed Judaism in the limelight, it confronted Jews with questions about their self-image and their image in the eyes of English society. Effort was made to display and promote a Judaism that was cultured, respectable, and elegant: concerts with Jewish music were performed during the exhibition, lectures by distinguished scholars were offered, and an exclusive, numbered catalogue was produced.[27] The

---

26 Ibid.

27 Joseph Jacobs and Lucien Wolf, *Catalogue of the Anglo-Jewish Historical Exhibition* (London: Office of the *Jewish Chronicle*, 1888). Two editions of the catalogue were published (1887, 1888), the latter in a limited edition of 250 copies. William L. Gross,

Delegate Chief Rabbi of England, Dr. Hermann Adler, recognized the novelty in this form of Jewish self-representation and admitted that individuals in the community had voiced their displeasure, questioning the wisdom of placing Judaism in the public view. They claimed that Judaism's strength and wisdom lie in its dignified reserve, "in the absence of all ostentation." Adler responded that the intention of the exhibition was wholly educational—*inter alia* "to remove something of the mysteriousness which, in the mind of the outer world, seems to encompass everything relating to our observances," to acquaint society "with the history of our race in the British Empire," and to stimulate interest in Anglo-Jewish history.[28] Knowledge of the past was deemed a universal value, and if it could mediate between peoples, then it validated turning Judaism into an open, accessible culture. On that level, Adler's perspective was almost prophetic. An outcome of the exhibition was the establishment in 1893 of the Jewish Historical Society of England, almost forty years before the creation of a Jewish museum in London, an indication that the material objects were primarily intended to inspire historical consciousness.

In a sense, the attitude that characterized British Jewry was typical of an earlier period in Victorian England when art was associated with moral teachings, social amelioration, and didactic purposes. Everything but art for art's sake.[29] Whether Queen Victoria would grace the exhibition with her presence was of more concern to leading figures in the community than what was actually being shown. Few were taken with the nature of the artifacts in the way that David Kaufmann, a collector in his own right, had been nine years earlier when he saw the Strauss objects: "[They] contain such an abundance of magnificent silverwork that its description and reproduction would justify a special undertak-

"Catalogue of Catalogues: Bibliographical Survey of a Century of Temporary Exhibitions of Jewish Art," *Journal of Jewish Art* 6 (1979): 134f.

[28] *Jewish Chronicle* (22 April 1887): 8. Similar motivations lay behind the initiative to open a Jewish museum in Manchester almost a hundred years later, after scores of Jewish museums had been opened across the globe: among its proclaimed purposes, it planned "to counterbalance the external prejudice and misunderstanding with which the Jewish community is perenially faced" (quoted in Tony Kushner, "Looking Back with Nostalgia? The Jewish Museums of England," *Immigrants and Minorities* 6[1987]: 206); for a portrait of the Adler family, Eugene C. Black, "The Anglicization of Orthodoxy: The Adlers, Father and Son," in *From East and West*, 295-325.

[29] Cf. Dianne Sacko Macleod, "Art Collecting and Victorian Middle-Class Taste," *Art History* 10 (1987): 328-51.

ing."[30] For English Jewry, as the historian Heinrich Graetz rightly put it, this was a great achievement which could not, he assumed, be carried out on the Continent. Graetz read the exhibition as a statement of Anglo-Jewry's sense of continuity with Israel's history and its deep and fervent attachment to England. For Graetz, as well, the meaning of the enterprise and the sentiment it provoked were the crucial aspects—for the objects themselves could by no means compare to those of other nations:

> You desired rather to give evidence of your true Jewish convictions. You wished to display the inner connection of your Past and your Present. You wished to show that while you, as English patriots, are attached to this happy isle with every beat of your hearts, you wished to preserve your connection and continuity with the long series of generations of Israel. And without exactly wishing it, you have thereby raised a practical protest on the one side against thoughtless indifference, and on the other against unprincipled apostasy, two hateful types within the ranks of Judaism, which—to your honour it be said—are rarer here than on the Continent.[31]

The ethnographic premise of Joseph Jacobs was thus expanded by the viewers, for if Judaism was more than simply theology it impinged on all elements of its relationship with the outside world and its past.

The Anglo-Jewish exhibition was a landmark in the history of Jewish collecting and Jewish museums. Almost an official community enterprise, it had brought together several dimensions—private Jewish art collections, archival documents from various authorities, and objects from English museums and English collectors. Its public nature and comprehensive illustrated catalogue were unprecedented, and created a new awareness of forgotten aspects of Jewish culture. This in itself was insufficient to elicit philanthropic support for the establishment of a Jewish museum. Such a project required an appreciation for the intrinsic value of Jewish art and an understanding that masterpieces were not the only standard for a museum. It also was predicated on the implicit recognition of a Jewish ethnic identification. As Daniel Sherman has argued, "The transcendence of the art object is not a self-evident concept; only an influential constituency, for whom it serves particular ideological

[30] Quoted in Avram Kampf, "The Jewish Museum: An Institution Adrift," *Judaism* 17 (1968): 282f.

[31] Quoted in *Jewish Chronicle* (24 June 1887): 18. Graetz came to London specially to address the exhibition.

needs, has the means to construct an institution to embody it."[32] British Jewry failed on this account.

Some twenty years later, it again reveled in a vast exhibition of Jewish art and antiquities, held at the Whitechapel art gallery in the West End of London, where tens of thousands of Jewish immigrants from eastern Europe lived. Initiated by Canon Barnett, the exhibition included this time contemporary Jewish artists from various countries and was designed to encourage participation by the local immigrant community. Once again, prominent Jewish figures, among them Chief Rabbi Adler and Rabbi Moses Gaster, dismissed criticism of the exhibition and lauded its distinct educational contribution to society: it would improve relations between immigrant and native Jews, and between Jews and gentiles; and it would dispel "reserve and mysteriousness about our religious observancy in the past," the source of "foul aspersions."[33] The inclusion of contemporary Jewish artists in the exhibition added an extra dimension of communal self-pride, as it rejected the notion that the "Jewish race" had no talent for graphic arts. However, it raised the question whether "Jewish art" exists as a special category, and the delicate issue of which sources influence Jewish creativity. Should Jewish artists be viewed within the context of their particular country, or did they constitute a particular "national" association that bound their work together? The exhibition, which was transplanted a year later to Berlin in reduced form, thus provided individuals within the Anglo-Jewish community the opportunity to temporarily "transcend" (in Sherman's terminology) the art objects and view them within their particular community agenda. But it failed to recruit enthusiastic supporters who saw Jewish art as an independent entity worthy of its own institution. A gap still existed between the readiness to exhibit Judaism temporarily and lavishly, and a commitment to institutionalize it as an independent cultural vehicle.

---

[32] Sherman, *Worthy Monuments*, 106.

[33] *Jewish Chronicle* (9 November 1906): 8; also ibid., special supplement with many illustrations of the modern paintings; also descriptions in contemporary German-Jewish newspapers. German Jews also believed that a Jewish museum would serve an important purpose in removing the common ignorance of Judaism—the major source of anti-Semitism. This idea was strongly upheld by the important Berlin-Jewish art collector Salli Kirschstein. S. Kirschstein in *Jüdisches Jahrbuch für Gros-Berlin* [1928]: 88-95; Hermann Simon, *Das Berliner jüdische Museum in der Oranienburger Strasse. Geschichte einer zerstörten Kulturstätte* (Berlin: Berlin Museum, 1983), 15. See below fn.35.

The fate of British Jewry's brief public exposure was to have parallels among other Jewish communities. It was only in 1932 that a Jewish museum was established in London. The museum's location reveals a recurring internal social process: the museum's opening coincided with and was conditional upon the establishment of a Jewish community center at Woburn House (where it resides to this day on one of its floors as a kind of "auxiliary" to communal affairs).[34] Here came to an end a social process that began in 1887. The first exhibitions aroused much praise and interpretation, more for the mere act of presentation and perceived hidden messages than for the objects themselves. Turning a temporary show into a permanent independent entity required a different self-image, both on the part of communal figures and entrepreneurial, wealthy members of the community. That self-image was missing. Thus, even though important collectors of Judaica emerged on the English horizon, they found no social legitimation in making their collection accessible to the public on a permanent basis through donations to a Jewish museum.

The drive during the *fin-de-siècle* to preserve and develop historic consciousness through museums found a clear resonance within Central European Jewry. Several factors combined with those already discussed to encourage this tendency in some Jewish communities. At the outset one cannot dismiss as merely coincidental their setting—modern, urban centers in the midst of massive renewal which included the construction of new districts; specialized museums were promoted by local elites who envisioned monuments appropriate to their city. Vienna, Prague, and Budapest—three cities with important Jewish concentrations—experienced the act of renewal and demolition of older buildings and quarters, which engendered a craving for past glory. This dialectical tendency was buttressed by the contemporary interplay between ethnographic interest and historical memory, exemplified by the establishment of ethnographic museums or ethnographic departments in prominent museums, often specializing in native peoples.[35] These currents, along with particular efforts of individual collectors of Judaica, helped place the idea of

34 The Ben Uri Art Society, established in London in 1915, went through a similar process. See *Jewish Artists. The Ben Uri Collection,* ed. W. M. Schwab (London: Ben Uri Art Society, 1987).

35 *Museums in Budapest* (Budapest: Corvina Kiado, 1985). Salli Kirschstein has left an interesting memoir on how the encounter with the Ethnology Museum in Berlin inspired him to begin collecting Judaica. See Joseph Gutmann, "The Kirschstein Museum of Berlin," *Jewish Art* 16/17 (1990/91): 172-176.

creating Jewish museums on the agenda in various cities—Vienna (where the first Jewish museum was founded in the 1890s),[36] Prague, Danzig, and Budapest, to name but a few. In each of these communities, individuals began to explore the material culture of their region and to assemble Jewish art as a means both of promoting historical consciousness and of preserving local Jewish history. Driven by a similar impulse as that which inspired Zunz and his coworkers at the beginning of the century—a sense of responsibility for the image of the Jewish past and implicitly the Jewish present—these figures were concerned with the rapid disappearance and decay of Jewish ritual objects and dwindling interest in Jewish material culture.[37] Also in the charged spirit of early *Wissenschaft des Judentums,* some of the supporters of the Jewish museums attached definite social and cultural relevance to their undertaking. These individuals were not necessarily part of the wealthy Jewish bourgeoisie and might lack the means to develop their own private collection, but often they brought a more academic approach to the collection of Judaica. However, in certain cities, as we will see, their work received the backing of private Jewish collectors and established representatives of the Jewish bourgeoisie who hoped to enhance the image of their Jewish community.

Several of the Jewish museums whose foundations were laid prior to World War I emphasized their attachments to their native city or country. The Prague collection provides an instructive paradigm. Prague underwent a major facelift in the last decade of the nineteenth and the first decade of the twentieth century that included the historic Jewish ghetto and several of its celebrated synagogues. Prague Jewry now confronted a dilemma similar to that encountered by Anglo-Jewry when the Bevis Marks synagogue faced demolition. How to preserve, if not the buildings themselves, the synagogues' contents? Where could these

---

[36] In Vienna, as in other cities, the "founding" date of the "museum" depends upon one's definitions of the terms involved. This is the source of discrepancies in the relevant literature.

[37] For example, this was the prevailing animus of the founders of the Budapest Jewish museum (Ilona Benoschofsky and Alexander Scheiber, *The Jewish Museum of Budapest*, tr. Joseph W. Wiesenberg [Budapest: Corvina Kiado, 1987), 7-16). Jewish folkloristics also emerged in this period, motivated by similar tendencies. Mutual bifurcation is apparent in the evolution of these fields, especially in Vienna and Hamburg, where Max Grunwald was active (Dan Ben-Amos, "Jewish Studies and Jewish Folklore," *Proceedings of the Tenth World Congress of Jewish Studies*, division D, part 2 [Jerusalem: World Union of Jewish Studies, 1990): 1-20; Barbara Kirshenblatt-Gimblett, "Problems in the Early History of Jewish Folkloristics," ibid., 21-31).

objects be housed? From a different perspective, the community faced a common phenomenon in the history of culture: due to the changing function of a traditional institution, at times due to destruction or relocation, its treasures previously held in private or ecclesiastical possession undergo a complete transformation. They become part of the public sphere.[38] As a new home was needed in these situations to house the dislocated objects, public museums were often created. Prague's Jewish museum began under such circumstances.

FIGURE 6: Circumcision bench from Údlice, Bohemia, ca. 1805. Carved, stained, and painted wood; silk damask. Courtesy of State Jewish Museum, Prague. Formerly in Old Jewish Museum, Prague.

Salomon Hugo Lieben was the guiding force behind Prague's new venture. Typical of the vast majority of Czech Jews, he received a thorough German education yet viewed favorably the gradual transformation of Bohemian Jewry into "Czechs."[39] Eventually to emerge as a

---

38 Pomian, *Collectionneurs, amateurs et curieux*, 47-50.

39 Hillel J. Kieval, *The Making of Czech Jewry: National Conflict and Jewish Society in Bohemia, 1870-1918* (New York: Oxford University Press, 1988), 48-63; Vladimír Sadek, "Salomon Hugo Lieben—Founder of the Prague Jewish Museum," *Judaica*

significant scholar of the history of the Jews in Bohemia and Moravia, Lieben played an instrumental role in formulating the Czech orientation of the Verein zur Grundung und Erhaltung eines jüdisches Museums in Prag during 1906, several months after the demolition of two Prague synagogues (the Zigeuner and Great Court Synagogue).[40] Undaunted by the severe criticism directed in those years at the Czech–Jewish alliance from certain Jewish quarters, Lieben aligned himself with individuals like August Stein,[41] Markus Brückner, and Adolf Hahn, who were forthrightly involved in promoting Czech–Jewish relations. The Verein's statutes reiterated this premise: the collection and preservation of Jewish artifacts that originated in either Prague or Bohemia were seen as the ultimate goal of the society.[42] Lieben actively pursued this nationalist orientation, combing Prague and the local surroundings in search of objects that would represent each Jewish holy day and ritual ceremony. His findings were impressive and sometimes of a unique quality, like the circumcision bench from Údlice, Bohemia (figure 6), an authentic expression of the Jewish link to the Bohemian countryside.[43] He took great pride in the imprint of the native land on the autochthonous and homogeneous nature of the collection. Clearly, Lieben saw the evolution of the museum as a link in the historical development of Czech Jewry for which his generation was responsible. On several occasions Lieben reflected on that matrix, expressing the impact of the historic moment and the pull to commemorate the past. Describing the destruction of the Prague synagogues and the background to the museum, Lieben remarked:

> A disquieting question was posed—what should be done with all the valuables and treasures that our fathers and forefathers through centuries, under great self-renunciation, offered as consecrated donations to the sanctuary? Should the history of the nineteenth century repeat itself, that each supposed urgent modernization of a synagogue and Jewish properties simply

---

Bohemiae 22/1 (1986): 3-8; Hana Volavková, *A Story of the Jewish Museum in Prague* (Prague: Artia, 1968), 72f.

[40] Arno Pařík, *The Prague Synagogues in Paintings, Engravings and Old Photographs* (Prague: Státní Zidovské Muzeum, 1986).

[41] Kieval, *The Making of Czech Jewry*, 31-34.

[42] Arno Pařík, "Das Jüdische Museum in Prag (1906-1942)," *Judaica Bohemiae* 24/1 (1988): 8-10; S.H. Lieben, *Das jüdische Museum in Prague* (Prague, 1924), 1-5.

[43] For a catalogue description of this object see *The Precious Legacy: Judaic Treasures from the Czechoslovak State Collections*, ed. David Altshuler (Washington: Smithsonian Institution Traveling Exhibition Service, 1983), 198, 259f.

> let valuable objects of great art-historical, familial history, and historical value disappear and cause irreplaceable damage forever? To avoid this I, with several supporters, founded then in the community our Jewish museum.[44]

Lieben's enterprise was wholly identified with the community, and it immediately attracted the support and following of hundreds of Prague Jews.[45] Within three years the Verein held its inaugural exhibition in a community building and in 1912 moved into a more permanent location in the recently reconstructed home of the Prague burial society. Adjacent to the old, impressive Jewish cemetery, the museum thus assumed a venerable place within the cultural nexus of the community, its exhibitions evoking the spiritual and cultural world of the community and the diverse levels of Jewish involvement and association with Prague and Bohemian society. Within a decade Lieben had succeeded in juxtaposing religious and secular artifacts in a significant manner such that their display celebrated the community's confidence in the Czech–Jewish alliance and its commitment to the historical past and future.[46]

The local and national aspirations that the Verein placed high on its agenda were not wholly unique. Other Jewish museums of the period and at later stages were similarly motivated. The museum was thus at times meant to be a showcase, bearing witness to the deep-seated connection of Jews to their particular place of settlement and their historic presence in the respective country. Lesser Gieldzinski's collection in Danzig is a case in point. A Polish-born Jew, Gieldzinski moved to Danzig in 1860 at the age of thirty, where he thrived as a grain merchant and achieved local prominence. A photograph taken late in his life (figure 7) shows Gieldzinski in formal attire wearing the decorations he received from Kaiser Wilhelm II. It conveys the image of a successful individual at the peak of his life.

---

44 S. H. Lieben, "Das jüdische Museum in Prag," *Gemeindeblatt der jüdischen Gemeinde zu Berlin* 21 (1931): 33; also quoted in Pařík, 6f. Cf. Lieben, *Das jüdische Museum*, 2f.

45 Pařík, *jüdische Museum* 10; for its impact on a personal level see Guldan, *Tagebücher*, 270f.

46 Lieben's guide to the museum, *Das jüdische Museum*, 5-10, is an excellent primer for our thesis. He shies away from loading his descriptions with national or moral comments; it is a dry, descriptive narrative, unlike the language of Anglo-Jewry's leaders, allowing the objects to carry the ideological message. His slim 1924 exposition remained the basis for later texts even though the war period dramatically changed the dimensions of the collection. *The State Jewish Museum in Prague*, ed. Vilém Benda (Prague: Olympia, 1967); cf. Sherman, *Worthy Monuments*, 246.

FIGURE 7: Lesser Gieldzinski (1830–1910). Courtesy of The Jewish Museum, New York.

Gieldzinski exemplifies that bourgeois Jew whose collection of decorative arts, paintings, and Judaica reflects an affirmation of his citizenship and religious affiliation. Secular objects associated with Danzig and its history became the hallmark of his private collection, which he labored to convert into a public landmark. To the acclaim of local dignitaries, distinguished visitors to the city, including Kaiser Wilhelm II, were directed to his expansive home where his collection was exhibited. Gieldzinski also earned consistent public recognition for donations of Danzigiana to major civic buildings.[47] His attachment to the city perme-

[47] This comes out very clearly from the local newspapers that followed closely Gieldzinski's development as a citizen of Danzig and recognized his "treue Anhänglichkeit an unsere Stadt." See also the lavish descriptions in the Danzig papers of his funeral. My thanks are extended to Dr. Vivian Mann, Curator of Judaica, The Jewish Museum, New York who kindly put at my disposal a collection of Danzig newspaper clippings relating to Gieldzinski.

ated no less his Judaica collection. Here too Gieldzinski sought to merge worlds, and he succeeded in assembling many a unique Danzig object that could honorably stand beside his general Danzig acquisitions. By exhibiting a miniature Torah ark (figure 8), apparently modeled after the seventeenth-century Brigittenkirche tower in Danzig, or the miniature reader's desk and furnishings, or the Biedermeier wedding sofa (figure 9), Gieldzinski was able to show how minuscule objects of Jewish culture could express both integration and particularism. Different from Isaac Strauss, Gieldzinski made his present status as a Danzig citizen the guiding feature of his collecting zeal. Yet this patron of arts proceeded to distinguish his Judaica from the general collection, donating the former to the community and its synagogue in honor of his 75th birthday in 1904.[48] In so doing, Gieldzinski thus returned the religious objects to the community and its synagogue; they had, so to speak, traveled from the religious sphere to the secular, and then were reunited by the collector and returned to the religious domain. This route became a common one in various Jewish communities in Germany and elsewhere. Gieldzinski asserted thereby that these artifacts could not possess an independent existence outside the community framework, nor was it appropriate for them to mingle with the rest of his Danzig collection.[49] The dislocation sharply limited the number of potential viewers and changed the interrelationship between viewer and object. German dignitaries rarely made a special visit to the Gieldzinski Judaica collection housed from 1904 in the local synagogue. The attraction the objects may have once evoked among visitors to Gieldzinski's house, as part of the larger collection, now receded. Though still affirming respect for the Jewish past and local patriotism, they now reassumed part of their original function as objects of sacred observance, viewed primarily by members of a small Jewish community.[50] Gieldzinski, through his personality and his multi-

[48] Upon his death in 1910 it was assumed that the collection would be left to the city of Danzig, but it was sold by his heirs at an auction in 1912. We have not determined the reason for this turn of events (*Die Woche* [Berlin, 11 June 1910]).

[49] This discussion is based on *Danzig 1939: Treasures of a Destroyed Community* (Detroit: Wayne State University Press, 1980); *Sammlung jüdischer Kunstsgegenstände der Synagogen-Gemeinde zu Danzig* (Danzig: Bäcker, n.d. [1933]); and the newspaper clippings cited in note 47.

[50] Danzig Jewry remained a community of less than three thousand prior to World War I (Elijahu Stern, "The History of the Jews of Danzig from the Emancipation until their Deportation in the Nazi Era" [in Hebrew] [Ph.D. diss., The Hebrew University, 1978]; Samuel Echt, *Die Geschichte der Juden in Danzig* [Leer and Ostfriesland: Rautenberg, 1972]).

dimensional Danzig collection, had granted this community an added representative presence in the city, one that the Jewish museum could not sustain.

FIGURE 8: Miniature Torah ark, Danzig, 19th century, Brass and copper: cast and chased; wood. Courtesy of The Jewish Museum, New York.

The ethnographic interest that surfaced in European society at the turn of the century was marked by an openness to the Jewish cultural world. In some cases, Christians played a determining factor in the initiative to collect Jewish art and in the formation of Jewish museums. Stasov's persistent efforts to encourage Jewish artists to discover their national expression in art went hand in hand with his proposals to safeguard their cultural and religious artifacts. His vision and involvement were instrumental in convincing secular Jewish intelligentsia and wealthy Jews to retrieve Jewish art through ethnographic and anthropological work. The St. Petersburg Jewish Historical and Ethnographic Society (1908), infused with Stasov's perspectives, pursued this goal and supported Ansky's celebrated Jewish ethnographic expedition of 1911-1914, upon which the future Jewish museum in Petrograd was formed

(1916).[51] In Hungary, organizers of the millennary celebrations of the Hungarian conquest (1896) encouraged Jewish participation at a national exhibition that proved to be a catalyst to promoting the preservation of Jewish valuables—visual and textual.[52]

FIGURE 9: Wedding sofa, probably Danzig, 1838. Birch veneer over pine: lindenwood; painted and gilded; upholstery. Biedermeier sofa. Courtesy of The Jewish Museum, New York.

Frankfurt's Jewish museum owed its initial strides to the interest of the director of the Düsseldorf Kunstgewerbemuseums, Heinrich Frauberger. In 1895, Frauberger was consulted about a design for a railing around a Jewish grave. Not knowing how to respond, he consulted various individuals and combed the museum's vast collection, but his inquiries were to no avail. While pursuing this question, Frauberger was struck by the scarcity of photographs or drawings of Jewish relics of the past as opposed to the rich collection relating to other religions, whose adherents, unlike the Jews, did not even inhabit the area. Driven by a cultural and museological instinct "to rescue and collect" remnants from the past before technological development would

51 Seth L. Wolitz, "The Jewish National Art Renaissance in Russia," in *Tradition and Revolution*, 24-27; John E. Bowlt, "From the Pale of Settlement to the Reconstruction of the World," ibid., 43-47; Avram Kampf, *Jewish Experience in the Art of the Twentieth Century* (South Hadley, Mass.: Bergin and Garvey, 1984), 15-23.

52 Benoschofsky and Scheiber, *The Jewish Museum of Budapest*, 7.

erase all memory of various cultures,[53] Frauberger began to lay the groundwork for a society that would collect and study the cultural remains of the Jewish past and contemporary Jewish cultural creativity. His concern and systematic efforts to preserve Jewish culture need to be seen within the context of a pluralistic, museological ethos prevalent in Europe at the time, and not within the nationalist agenda that informed Stasov's approach. An interest in and fascination with foreign cultures had evolved in western and central Europe and found institutionalization in "world exhibitions," museums of religions, and ethnographic societies and museums. Within this framework, several German museums already collected Jewish artifacts and one, the renowned Hamburg Museum für Kunst und Gewerbe, showed a particular interest in developing its collection of Jewish religious artifacts; the Alsatian museum of Strasbourg also devoted a special wing to Jewish artifacts from Alsace–Lorraine.[54] But Frauberger's perspective was more encompassing. He endeavored to cover all visual aspects of Jewish life and creativity, past and present, with no limitations on the geographic origin of the objects. Ultimately, when the collection was assembled, the role of Jews in the formation of culture would be determinable. Frauberger thus brought to the collection of Judaica an objective position, groomed by the advanced German museological school of the nineteenth century. Judaism was to have a rightful place among the cultures of mankind through collection, study, and exhibition.

With this inclination, Frauberger proposed to members of the Frankfurt Jewish community the establishment of a society that would further the basic goals of an interdisciplinary approach to Jewish visual material. Frankfurt's Gesellschaft zur Erforschung jüdischer Kunstdenkmäler, established in 1901, brought together a cross section of the successful bourgeois integration into Frankfurt society. Bankers, lawyers, city officials, merchants, dealers in books and art, and two university trained rabbis constituted the Jewish core of the society, to which were added the local directors of the Frankfurt library and historical

---

53 Heinrich Frauberger, "Zweck und Ziel der Gesellschaft zur Erforschung jüdischer Kunstdenkmäler zu Frankfurt A.M.," *Mitteilungen der Gesellschaft zur Erforschung jüdischer Kunstdenkmäler* 1 (1900): 3-7, 37-39; *Israelit* 39 (1898).

54 Justus Brinckmann, "Die Sammlung jüdischer Kultgeräte im Hamburgischen Museum für Kunst und Gewerbe," *Mitteilungen der Gesellschaft für jüdische Volkskunde* 2 (1898): 86-89; the Alsatian museum responded to the request of the Gesellschaft für die Geschichte der Israeliten in Elsass–Lothringen in 1907 and opened a permanent Jewish exhibition a year later. M. Ginsburger, "Juedische Altertuemer in Elsass–Lothringen," *Ost und West* 12 (1912): 1095-1108.

museum.[55] Guided by Frauberger's approach and leadership, the society laid out an ambitious program, that aside from collecting Judaica, included support for contemporary Jewish art and the publication of scientific research. It also began the publication of the *Notizblatt der Gesellschaft zur Erforschung jüdischer Kunstdenkmäler* that appeared intermittently until 1937. But it was Frauberger who remained the pivotal factor in the society's growth. The author of the first six issues of the society's bulletin, covering a wide range of topics on Jewish visual material, Frauberger also curated the first public exhibition in Germany devoted to Jewish ritual objects. Frauberger and the society brought together in 1908 an impressive collection of objects and reproductions, for which he prepared a comprehensive descriptive catalogue.[56] Frauberger's decision, supported by the society, to concentrate the objects in the Düsseldorf museum and to hold the exhibition on its premises was exemplary of their pristine museological approach. Objects of Jewish ritual belonged in the cultural sphere and neither he nor members of the society had any intention of turning the collection into an arm of the synagogue. Frauberger thus collapsed into one period a process—collecting, description, and analysis—that in the evolution of museums often took several generations.[57]

Yet the determination to establish an institution devoted to Jewish ritual objects was always a more complicated matter, even with strong financial backing: only after World War I, in 1922, was the society successful in establishing a home for the collection—it was granted a floor in a historic home donated by the Rothschild family to the Jewish community in 1912. In this new setting several exhibitions were held that placed a strong emphasis on Frankfurt Jewry and bore the imprint of a new generation of German Jews dedicated to making the study of Jewish

---

55 For the list of names see *Was Übrig Blieb: Das Museum jüdischer Altertümer in Frankfurt 1922-1938,* ed. Felicitas Heimann-Jellinek (Frankfurt: Jüdisches Museum Frankfurt, 1988), 15; a similar professional distribution is found in other societies for Jewish museums. For Budapest, see Benoschofsky and Scheiber, *The Jewish Museum,* 8f.; for Vienna, S. Weissenberg, "Jüdische Museen und Jüdisches in Museen: Reiseeindrücke," *Mitteilungen zur jüdischen Volkskunde* 23 (1907): 86; for Berlin, Simon, *Das Berliner jüdische Museum,* 30-38.

56 *Ausstellung von jüdischen Bauten und Kultus-Gegenständen für Synagoge und Haus* (Düsseldorf: Kunstgewerbe-Museum, 1908); Weissenberg, "Jüdische Museen": 79-81; Guldan, *Tagebücher,* 264; *Allgemeine Zeitung des Judentums* 72 (1908).

57 Cf. Thomas J. Schlereth, "History Museums and Material Culture," in *History Museums in the United States: A Critical Assessment,* ed. Warren Leon and Roy Rosenzweig (Urbana: University of Illinois Press, 1989), 296f.

material objects a scientific discipline and an integral part of Jewish culture.[58] Here the objects had moved from a source of nostalgia and proof of Jewish creative ability to an integral element in Jewish historical development. This was in no small measure part of the heritage that Frauberger's wide-ranging museological approach bestowed on his talented successors. Freed from the various self-perceptions that enveloped Jewish society, Frauberger, Stasov, and other gentiles regarded Jewish objects in the light of their intrinsic cultural value. They point to a type of interaction that challenges blanket appraisals of Jewish–gentile relations in the highly charged atmosphere of this period.

How did the institutionalization of Jewish art take place? Two models seem to have prevailed. In one, the "museum" is formed almost simultaneously with the emergence of the collection. A sudden development—as in Prague or St. Petersburg—created a collection that needed to find a repository. A second model, as in the case of Frankfurt, Budapest, and London, suggests that a certain incubation period was necessary. A generation often elapsed from the original interest in various aspects of Jewish visual creativity at the turn of the century until the collection found an abode within a community facility. In Berlin, for example, collectors and students of Jewish art appeared from the turn of the century and brought Jewish art consciousness to the Berlin public, yet the local Jüdische Museumsverein was founded only in 1929, four years before the opening of the museum.[59] In the interim local obstacles often surfaced necessitating makeshift solutions. In both models the original design of an independent institution gives way to the recognition that for the museum to be sustained it had to be incorporated into the community's structure. This had several social implications. First, to form a permanent monument to Jewish visual culture, the collecting and exhibiting process had to go beyond the intrinsic and implicit value of the objects. Art itself was not sufficient. Its ramifications for illuminating Jewish life/creativity/history in one form or another were thus necessarily entwined in the museological message. Second, Jewish art—in particular Jewish ceremonial art—had to return almost invariably to the community's parameters, having no independent existence. Granting art a role in

---

[58] This was especially true of Erich Toeplitz, who was a curator of the museum in the 1920s.

[59] Bezalel Narkiss, "Rachel Wischnitzer, Doyenne of Historians of Jewish Art," Rachel Wischnitzer, *From Dura to Rembrandt. Studies in the History of Art* (Milwaukee, Vienna, and Jerusalem: Aldrich Center for Jewish Art, 1990), 17-20, 177–80; Simon, *Das Berliner jüdische Museum*, passim.

Jewish expression, beyond the sphere of religion and text, was an innovation for the community. Promoters of Jewish visual material widened the forms of attachment for the Jewish public, opening themselves up to the criticism that they were embarking on a new definition of Jews[60]—as an ethnic group, a people or even a nation—but by returning the objects to the communal context they in essence reconsecrated that art as a visual form of the religious experience.

In identifying motivations that inspired Jewish art collecting and museums at the turn of the century, the drive to promote a Jewish national consciousness must be regarded as a most significant one.[61] Art was to assume a new priority in the hierarchy of Jewish values—no longer a problematic area of creativity due to the biblical restriction on representation nor a mere external trapping but, as in Martin Buber's formulation, an essential element for refashioning the national soul. Art was conceived as a basic attribute of a modern people; and by uncovering its past form, through creating and collecting, its renaissance was guaranteed. Already in 1888 Boris Schatz, the future founder of Bezalel, lauded art's spiritual qualities and its capacity to lift the human spirit and unearth higher values. Citing the impact of Courbet's paintings on French society, he lamented that Jews failed to collect and display in their homes art that was either inspired by their own national spirit or that treated themes and individuals from their past.[62] It was also with this intention in mind that Stasov and Gunzburg published *L'Ornement hébreu* in 1905, through the Calvary publishing house, bringing together examples of Jewish ornamentation from what they affectionately called "remnants from another age and relics of a vanished civilization which continue to live under the accumulated ruins of centuries of ignorance

[60] For criticism of Jewish museums, ibid. Simon, *Das Berliner jüdische Museum;* similarly when Max Grunwald established in Hamburg in 1897-1898 the Gesellschaft fur jüdische Volkskunde with plans for a Jewish ethnographic museum, members of the community expressed severe reservations; Kirschstein maintained adamantly his independence from the burgeoning, political identification and stated: "To reveal the culture which through the centuries has held together a people, is a tie so strong, that when it is visually presented as it can be through Jewish museums, it would more strongly emphasize the inner unity of the community and cause it to carry on more than any other endeavor." Gutmann, "The Kirschstein Museum," 173.

[61] Michael Berkowitz, "Art in Zionist Popular Culture and Jewish National Self-consciousness," in *Art and Its Uses,* 9-42; N. Shilo-Cohen, *Bezalel* (Israel Museum Catalog, Jerusalem, 1983), (in Hebrew) (Jerusalem: Israel Museum, 1983), 319–338.

[62] Boris Schatz, "Melechet Machshevet," (A Work of Art), *Haṣefirah,* 216–217 (1888); Yigal Zalmona, "Schatz as a Thinker," in Shilo-Cohen, *Bezalel,* 137-40.

and destruction."[63] This impulse, to penetrate to the inner characteristics of a people through art and to stimulate national pride and dignity, took on many forms and expressions.

Rather than luxuriate in self-satisfaction that Jewish artists were being exhibited in a particular exposition or salon and note each Jewish artistic success with ravenous delight—a common trait of Jewish newspapers across the Continent at the turn of the century—the nationalist trend inspired joint exhibitions of Jewish artists. These became more common from their first collective showing at the Fifth Zionist Congress in 1901, when, for example, paintings on a biblical theme by the convert Eduard Bendemann were exhibited alongside the works of Ephraim Moses Lilien (figure 10), Josef Israels, Jehuda Epstein, and other *fin-de-siècle* Jewish artists. The emphasis on contemporary Jewish artists was not by chance. Jews possessed a history, but Jewish artists could illuminate through their unique background different facets of the modern experience, ranging from humanity's existential predicament to its links with the past. Moreover, their joint appearance confirmed the Jews' acceptance of modernization and their ability to succeed in artistic disciplines.[64] But it had another internal goal. Combined displays were designed to arouse a sense of national pride in Jewish achievement, to engage the beholders in the rare constellation of Jewish national feeling, and to reconnect the Jew with his lost sense of aesthetics. The Ausstellung jüdischer Künstler that opened in Berlin in 1907 afforded such an opportunity. Modern painting and sculpture were exhibited alongside ceremonial art and other Jewish artifacts, but this time the former were at the center of attention. Certainly this is what Alfred Nossig, then a Zionist, wanted to achieve in organizing the exhibition of Jewish artists from all of Europe. He wanted to stir the hearts and arouse the minds into thinking about the nature of Jewish creativity and what constituted the "racial uniqueness of Jews in art." Furthermore, in his search for a social interpretation of art, Nossig claimed that the exhibition illuminated how Jewish artists subjectively evoked the impact of Jewish homelessness. Public response to the exhibition bore out Nossig's intentions. Critics and reporters focused on these

63 David Gunzburg, "Avant-Propos," in Vladimir Stasov and David Gunzburg, *L'Ornement hébreu* (Berlin: Calvary, 1905), 5; Wolitz, "Jewish National Art Renaissance," 24.

64 Lilien's letter to the editor, *Ost und West* (1902): 110-12, offers a fascinating critique of the overemphasis in Jewish museums on the past; Berkowitz, "Art in Zionist Popular Culture," 19.

issues, questioning or affirming their premisses.[65] The exhibition was an actualization of Buber's vision of unity between present and past, between the individual and the group, the Jew and the complete person, and between feeling and aesthetics and the intellect.

FIGURE 10: E. M. Lilien (1874–1925), illustration for Morris Rosenfeld's "The Jewish May," in *Lieder des Ghetto,* 1902. Entrapped in thorns, the pious Jew lifts his hands toward the sun, symbolizing Zion.

The Zionists were not, however, the first to make this connection between the arts and the national ethos. Stasov had spoken of the need to unite Jewish artists and art since the 1870s—so as, in the words of the Kultur Lige in Kiev that pursued his lead in 1920, to "place a sovereign national stamp upon their art" and "to bring to fruition the distinctive-

65 *Ausstellung jüdischer Künstler* (Berlin, 1907). Nossig's introduction to the catalogue was reproduced in *Ost und West* 7 (1907): 743–52. The exhibition was held in the Galerie für alte und neue Kunst; G. Kutna, "Zur Ausstellung jüdischer Kuenstler," *Ost und West* 8 (1908): 18-26; idem, "Urteile der Presse ueber die Ausstellung jüdischer Kuenstler," ibid., 25-28; idem, "Berliner Ausstellung," ibid., 495–98; K.S. [Karl Schwarz], "Die Ausstellung jüdischer Künstler zu Berlin," *Allgemeine Zeitung des Judentums* 71 (22 November 1907): 573. Schwarz, future curator of the Berlin Jewish museum, had encouraged bringing the exhibition from England to Berlin; ibid., 49 (1906).

ness of Jewish . . . expression."[66] It was not only historical consciousness that was now being sought, but a drive to assert unique Jewish creativity, as other nations and cities had done in their museums.

FIGURE 11: Boris Schatz (1866–1932), *Self-Portrait*, ca. 1930. Oil and resin on panel. Harry Friedman Collection. Courtesy of The Jewish Museum, New York. Above the self-portrait the inscription reads, "I am for my people and my people are for me" (a paraphrase of Song of Songs 6:3).

The national orientation in collection found its embodiment in the Bezalel museum founded by Boris Schatz in Jerusalem in 1906 alongside a school for arts and crafts (figure 11). Yet Bezalel presents a certain anomaly. In many aspects its beginnings resembled more the development of museums in Europe in the nineteenth century than that of the Jewish museums in the early twentieth, as it shows a greater reconciliation with diasporic history and religious culture than the

---

[66] Quoted in Introduction to the Catalog of the "Jewish Exhibition of Scupture, Graphics and Drawings" (February–March, 1920), Apter-Gabriel, *Tradition and Revolution*, 230.

accepted image of early Zionist history. Bezalel as a museum faced the same dilemma which countries that underwent revolutions encountered—how to deal with art that represented ideas and images that the revolution rejected. Should one collect and display that art as part of the cultural past of the country, leave it to deteriorate, or even destroy it?[67] Bezalel, an outgrowth of the Zionist revolution, opted for the former alternative, seeing the museum as a national inheritance and Jewish religious artifacts as an integral part of it. Related to a nationalist longing for a central Jewish museum that would assemble "everything" associated with the Jewish past and present,[68] Bezalel in Schatz's vision was intended to be both a source of inspiration for artistic creativity—to offer craftsmen in the school of arts and crafts fine ceremonial art as objects of study—and a monument to Jewish history (figure 12).

FIGURE 12: An exhibition hall in the early years of Bezalel. Schatz views his display. In the center, above a chest with bottles of liquids containing various minerals, is a photograph of Herzl. Various archeological remains and reliefs of Jewish figures are also exhibited. Courtesy of The Israel Museum, Jerusalem.

[67] This predicament appears in fascinating ways during the French Revolution and in European revolutions ever since. Pommier, "Naissance des musées," 451-78.

[68] S. Weissenberg, "Jüdische Museen," 88. Cf. *Bezalel Exhibition: Palestine Arts and Crafts 1926* (New York: Select Printing Company, 1926), 54; for another possible influence on Schatz's thinking see Mirjam Rajner, "The Awakening of Jewish National Art in Russia," *Jewish Art* 16/17 (1990/91): 116-21.

Bezalel's initial strides showed a close affinity to the development of local museums in Europe in the nineteenth century. From the outset, the Bezalel complex was an independent entity, unrelated to any communal or synagogal structure, enabling it to pursue its own course and strive for influence in the formation of the new society. Situated in the center of the new Jerusalem, making it easily accessible to Jews, Christians, and Muslims, Bezalel endeavored to be recognized as Palestine's national museum. Conceived as an integral unit with an intimate link between museum and art school, an occurrence unprecedented among Jewish museums, Bezalel followed a common procedure in the evolution of certain nineteenth century museums. There, as with Bezalel, priority was allocated to the art school: on the one hand, the museum's collection was to serve as an educational paradigm for students' work, and on the other hand the museum was to open its walls to their art. Typically, Schatz was responsible for both "institutions," constantly stressing their interrelationship but giving preference and greater attention to the art school, the avant-garde of the nationalist renaissance.[69] Yet since the museum was designed to be a place of memory, an expression of a local heritage, and a cultural tradition, it held its own in attracting public interest and support. Indeed, "as the property of the Jewish nation," a conception taken from national museums in Europe, Bezalel was meant to be an institution that the entire Jewish people could identify with proudly and feel responsible for maintaining.

But in the establishment of the Bezalel museum a tendency appeared that proved a factor in the first exhibitions of Judaica and in the foundation of earlier Jewish museums: collecting was a means of retrieving disappearing worlds. In Schatz's flowery, romantic declaration:

> We are collecting in one place all that the genius of the Jewish people created and preserving it from destruction. Now, in the hour of emergency, when so many communities have been destroyed and synagogues silenced, and the only corners where the soul of Israel remains is in the synagogue decorations and ceremonial art, it is incumbent upon us to collect them all and send them to our national treasure in Jerusalem, where they will be eternally preserved and regenerated by the Hebrew cultural creativity that Bezalel regenerates in Eretz-Israel.[70]

---

[69] Cf. Sherman, *Worthy Monuments*, 97-121; Pommier, "Naissance des musées," 478-90; Stephen Bann, "Historical Text and Historical Object: The Poetics of the Musée de Cluny," *History and Theory* 17 (1978): 251-66.

[70] *Bezalel Exhibition*, 54; Richard I. Cohen, "Collecting and Preserving the Jewish

Collection to avoid extinction was not, however, sufficient for Schatz. Almost foreshadowing Gershom Scholem's nationalist critique of the early stages of *Wissenschaft des Judentums*, Schatz presented a three-stage perspective that can be encapsulated in the following way: history is to be collected from all corners of the Diaspora, stored in its historic and religious center, and rejuvenated by the national craftsmen of Bezalel. This orientation, together with the other national tendencies, produced a collection that in its embryonic stage juxtaposed natural and artificial objects, reminiscent of the encyclopedic collections in seventeenth- and eighteenth-century Europe that were to be mirrors of the entire world.[71] Bezalel's earliest collection consisted of botanical and zoological objects indigenous to Palestine—live animals, stuffed birds, butterflies, and flowers. Schatz imagined that these objects from the Holy Land were to inspire local artists to create artifacts (rugs, tapestries, pottery,etc.) with native Palestinian ornamentation and enable Bezalel to be "as original as other nations."[72] A special room was allocated to the natural history collection (figure 13), reminiscent of the early *Wunderkammer*; later the collection was to be removed from Bezalel in order to constitute a separate zoological museum. Alongside the zoological material Schatz assembled archeological remnants—clay lamps, glass work, ceramics, and so on—and paintings by Jewish artists. In each collection a different aspect of the national thrust and Schatz's vision are apparent. The connection with the historic past in Palestine is emphasized along with a didactic and apologetic element—bringing together paintings by Jewish artists that "would prove to the world that there is such a thing as Jewish art and that it may lay an example for Jewish artists, and prompt them to create in the Jewish spirit."[73] In the following years, before Bezalel opened its doors officially to the public in 1925, Schatz actively solicited paintings, sculptures, and medals of famous contemporary Jews and self-portraits of prominent Jewish artists—including the likes of Albert Einstein and Max Liebermann—to establish a Jewish Pantheon, as a source of hope and direction. Schatz's interpretation of the museum as a national monument recognized the importance of historical memory, and he also allocated a special exhibit to the sufferings of the past. Objects

---

Past:Judaica in The Israel Museum," *The Israel Museum Journal* 9 (1990): 53.

71 Cf. Impey and Macgregor, *The Origins of Museums*, passim.

72 Israel Aharoni, *Zikhronot Zoolog Ivri* (Memoirs of a Hebrew Zoologist) (Tel Aviv: Am Oved, 1943), 194.

73 Letter, Schatz to Harry Friedenwald, 15 September 1930, Central Zionist Archives, Jerusalem, L42/6.

were still being employed to represent the self-perception.

The museum, which Schatz spoke of in terms of a "temple" (a concept used at times to depict certain French museums in the nineteenth century),[74] was greater than its parts. Already containing fourteen exhibition rooms in the early 1920s, it asserted within Jerusalem, the bastion of the "Old *Yishuv*," a different form of continuity with Jewish tradition. Heralding the return home to Palestine, as in Hirschenberg's huge "Wandering Jew" canvas (figure 14), and celebrating Jewish creativity through the products of Bezalel's craftsmen, the museum established a moral interrelationship between the viewer's history and future. Bezalel displayed art that affirmed the nationalist ideology of Zionism and extended its modernizing vision but could hardly live up to its self-appointed title as the museum of the Jewish people. Unsuccessful in attracting the assistance and patronage of the Jewish haute bourgeoisie in Europe,[75] Bezalel grew from the grass roots of Jewish society, for whom in essence it was originally designed.

FIGURE 13: Photograph from ca. 1909 in which the zoologist Aharoni is seen studying an object while Schatz looks on. Courtesy of The Israel Museum, Jerusalem.

74 Sherman, *Worthy Monuments*, 184f.

75 Boris Schatz, *Bezalel: Its History, Nature and Future* (Jerusalem: Smunith, 1910), 21; letter, Schatz to Felix Salten, 1923 (?), Israel Museum Archive.

FIGURE 14: Samuel Hirschenberg (1865–1908), "The Wandering Jew," 1899. Oil on canvas. Courtesy of The Israel Museum, Jerusalem. This dramatic and anguished portrayal of *galut* often served as a background for photographs taken in Bezalel of visiting dignitaries.

With the emergence of a Jewish national perspective in the east and west, a further significant dimension was added to the collecting impulse. Though ideologically at odds with the premise of bourgeois Jewish society, the Jewish national idea complemented and solidified a new vista of Jewish involvement that emerged from the embourgeoisement of central European Jewry and penetration of bourgeois values in the *fin-de-siècle*. Jewish society had wrestled throughout the nineteenth and into the twentieth century with the vacuum that was created by leaving the ghetto and with the challenges of modernity. Previously, Judaism had been an all-encompassing phenomenon for the bulk of Jews, but as its hold weakened and the distance from the ghetto experience widened, individuals turned to a myriad of different occupations and callings. Within this process of integration, there emerged diverse attempts to reclaim parts of that past experience, in some cases through denying modernity and in others through merging modernity with aspects of that past.[76] In the postemancipation era, different elements of Jewish society found contrasting ways to reappropriate the past without succumbing completely to its previous tenets. Collecting and exhibiting "Jewish art" was part of that process. Jews of opposing ideologies from across Europe and abroad were engaged by this cultural domain and found in it a viable expression of their association with the Jewish past. For various reasons—apologetics, nostalgia, patriotism, historical consciousness, and nationalism—they turned to display Jewish art and promote their particular self-image. They had come to appreciate the ability of art to convey traditions and evoke memories of the past, while asserting a particular view of the Jewish present and future.

[76] Cf. Michael A. Meyer, *Jewish Identity in the Modern World* (Seattle: University of Washington Press, 1990), 4-7.

9

S. Ansky and the Paradigm of Return

DAVID G. ROSKIES

The archetypal modern Jewish plot is a plot of return. This would not have been evident in 1920, when millions of Jews throughout the world were still casting about for new identities; and this would not have been evident when all their escape routes were blocked in 1940, but in the wake of the Holocaust and after Jewish political sovereignty was achieved in Israel, the return to one's people and one's past has emerged as a mass phenomenon.

So powerful and normative has this path of return become in our view of the modern Jewish experience, that the complexity of individual lives is systematically reduced to a simple, uncomplicated plot. While to his contemporaries Theodor Herzl stood for a brave new kind of international diplomacy, and upon his death, his unrealized dream was captured in that famous photo of him standing on a bridge and gazing off into the distance like Moses on Mount Nebo, today, in the light of everything that has transpired, the essence of the man has become his legend. I refer to Herzl's rude awakening in Paris while covering the Dreyfus Affair for Vienna's *Neue Freie Presse*. His reaction to the frenzied Parisian mobs prefigures that of countless assimilated Jews the fact of whose Jewishness was brought home to them under far more brutal conditions. Herzl—the man, not the politician—stands for all the Jews who came in from the cold under duress.

There are other lives that fairly cry out for an epiphany, that make no sense without a scene of dramatic self-confrontation. Franz Rosenzweig's turn from Catholicism to the total embrace of Halakhah and history is one such celebrated example. To a generation of Jews for whom politics was a religion, the rallying cry of return was uttered by Jacob Glatstein in April 1938 when he slammed shut the gate on the "big stinking world" of Western democracy and east European Marxism.[1]

Even in the heyday of Jewish rebellion and apostasy, then, there were prodigal sons who performed acts of public penance. In the annals of Jewish nationalism, Moshe Leib Lilienblum's *Derekh teshuvah* (The Path of Return, 1899) established the pattern for writers who doubled as public figures. They were especially prone to confess their sins out in the open. Perhaps the most dramatic such occasion was the celebration honoring S. Ansky's twenty-fifth anniversary as a writer.

The august group of Jewish intellectuals and cultural activists who gathered in St. Petersburg on 27 December 1909 to honor him had every reason to celebrate. If they belonged in the nationalist camp, they could point to Ansky, né Shloyme-Zanvl Rappoport, as the prodigal son par excellence. For here was a man who had left home at the age of seventeen to spread enlightenment among the benighted *shtetl* masses but soon took up the cause of the Russian masses instead, changed his name to Semyon Akimovich so as to share the miserable fate of Russian miners in the Donets Basin, spent a heady year in St. Petersburg as a trusted member of the Russian Populist elite, and then followed the lead of other radicals by emigrating to Paris where he worked for the cause in the cradle of the Revolution. But by the time the political amnesty of 1905 brought him back to Russia, this "Old Narodnik" was ready to assume a leadership role in the Jewish cultural and political arena. He began an extensive lecture tour through the provinces under the auspices of the Jewish Literary Society that hosted this very gathering. He was literary editor of the newly founded Russian-Jewish monthly *Evreiski Mir*. He was active in the Jewish Education Society and Jewish Historic-Ethnographic Society, both based in St. Petersburg.

Jewish socialists, in turn, applauded the author of their new Bundist anthem and sang more muted praises of his recent novel *In shtrom* (With the Stream) that documented the rise of their movement. Yiddishists of every stripe took pride in the ever-growing corpus of Ansky's original poetry and prose written since 1901 in the *mame-loshn* (mother tongue). Finally and most unusually for this period of rising anti-Semitism and

[1] For a recent translation of Glatstein's most famous poem, "A gute nakht, velt," see *American Yiddish Poetry: A Bilingual Anthology*, ed. Benjamin and Barbara Harshav (Berkeley: University of California Press, 1986), 304-307.

political reaction, Russian liberals and revolutionaries also joined in the festivities. Ansky had sterling credentials as the protégé of Gleb Uspensky and later in Paris as private secretary to Populist theoretician Pyotr Lavrov. Attesting to Ansky's lasting commitment to the Socialist-Revolutionary Party was his recent arrest and exoneration for the possession of subversive documents. Here, indeed, was a man for all seasons.[2]

But at a more intimate gathering held in his honor two weeks later at Mikhalevitsh's restaurant, Ansky used the occasion to do penance for his sins. "Bearing within me an eternal yearning toward Jewry," he confessed to his audience in Russian, "I nevertheless turned in all directions and went to labor on behalf of another people. My life was broken,

[2] These, in chronological order, are the major biographical sources on Ansky: (1) the special Ansky Issue (7/8) of Moyshe Shalit's *Lebn* (Vilna, 1920), containing memoirs by Zemach Szabad, Khaykl Lunski, S. L. Citron, J. Wygodsky, and M. Shalit and a valuable biographical essay by Zalmen Reisen. This issue appeared on 8 December 1920, at the conclusion of the thirty-day mourning period, but was later republished with the full text of Ansky's will (68-70). (2) Hillel Zeitlin, "Der lebnsveg fun Sh. Anski," *Almanakh tsum 10-yerikn yubileum fun "Moment"* (Warsaw, 1921), 49-72, which reacts critically to the published memoirs in *Lebn* and then offers its own reading of Ansky's career. (3) P. Shargorodskaya, "On An-sky's Legacy" (in Russian), *Evreiskaya Starina* 11 (1924): 306-11, an inventory of the Ansky Archive that found its way to Leningrad and may still be there (summarized by Nachman Meisel in *Literarishe bleter* no. 20 [1924]: 5). (4) Reisen's biography in the *Leksikon fun der yidisher literatur*, 3rd rev. ed. (Vilna: Kletskin, 1928) with an extensive bibliography. (5) Moyshe Shalit, "Der An-ski arkhiv: zayn inhalt un vert," *Literarishe bleter* no. 259 (1929): 313f. (6) The Ansky Issue of *Literarishe bleter* no. 340 (1930) with essays by Meisel, Shalit, and E. J. Goldshmidt. (7) Chaim Zhitlovsky, *Zikhroynes fun mayn lebn* 1 (New York: Yubilee Komitet, 1935): 9-114 and passim, which are extremely self-serving but offer the only independent version of Ansky's adolescence. (8) Extensive and important selections from Ansky's Archive in Moyshe Shalit's *Fun noentn over* 1 (Warsaw, 1937-1938). (9) R. Lichtsztein, "An-skis ershter aroysfor," *YIVO-bleter* 12 (1937): 443-53. (10) Viktor Chernov, *Yidishe tuer in der partey sotsyalistn revolutsyonern* (Jewish Activists in the Socialist Revolutionary Party: Biographical Essays), trans. from the Russian by Viktor Shulman (New York: Workmen's Circle Branch 247, 1948), 52-90, which offers a perspective on Ansky completely different from that of any of the Jewish sources. (11) The Ansky Issue of *He'avar* 11 (1964): 53-105, with memoirs by A. Kaufman, Rosa Monoszon-Etinger, Shraga Entobil, and David Vardi and Ansky's correspondence with Bialik and Monoszon (the letters to Monoszon written in Russian between 1915-1917 reveal Ansky at his most personal and metaphysical). (12) *An-sky, Jewish Folklorist: Memorial Exhibition on the 50th Anniversary of his Death* (Tel Aviv: Ginza Section for Jewish Folk Art, 1970). (13) *S. Ansky (1863-1920): His Life and Works* (also available in Yiddish) catalogue of an exhibition compiled by Eleanor Mlotek (New York: YIVO, 1980).

On Ansky's trial for the possession of subversive documents, see Shalit, *Fun noentn over*, 226-28.

severed, ruptured. Many years of my life passed on this frontier, on the border between both worlds. Therefore, I beg you, on this twenty-fifth year of summing up my literary work, to eliminate sixteen years."[3] Ansky's profession of undivided loyalty to the Jewish masses reads with especial poignancy if one knows what was to come—that from 1912-1914 he would lead the Jewish Ethnographic Expedition to rescue the artifacts and the "Oral Torah" produced by the Jews of Eastern Europe; would risk life and limb to aid the Jews of war-torn Galicia; would author *The Dybbuk,* that most perfect distillation of Jewish folklore and mysticism; and finally would be buried alongside I. L. Peretz and Yankev Dinezon in the Warsaw Jewish cemetery.

Thus it appears from this biographical sketch—inspired by his anniversary celebration—that Ansky's life follows the second of the two variants I outlined above. If the Herzl legend and the Glatstein poem represent the political act of return, performed under historical duress, then Rosenzweig and Ansky represent the spiritual variant. The latter is more a conversion experience than a rude awakening, an internal upheaval rather than a strategic reassessment. What the political and the spiritual odysseys of return have in common is that both are neatly divided between Before and After, between innocence and knowledge, skepticism and faith. Once any life is so grossly simplified, it can serve as a mnemonic of the Jewish collective experience.

But there exists a third possibility of return which is dialectical in nature. Here the plot combines both rebellion and return; indeed, in this model there can be no return without a prior rebellion. That is where the UNTOLD story of Ansky's life comes in, which in turn suggests a new understanding of his work. Because Ansky made his life the sum and substance of his work, he invites just this kind of analysis. Because he ultimately lays bare what others have hidden, the dialectical pattern he reveals may help clarify the complex nature of return in the modern age.

Found in his archive was the outline of an unwritten autobiography. This one told of a more graduated and aboveground path of return.

---

[3] As quoted by Lucy S. Dawidowicz, *The Golden Tradition: Jewish Life and Thought in Eastern Europe* (Boston: Beacon Press, 1968), 305. For the full text of his remarks, translated into Yiddish, see Shalit, *Fun noentn over,* 231. In an unpublished paper, my student Michael Krutikov argued persuasively that the death of Lavrov in 1900 marked the critical turning point for Ansky. Thus, working backwards, we arrive at 1884 as the date of Ansky's "defection."

> A young man, born and raised in the thick of Jewish life, underwent a very paradoxical evolution; works in the Hebrew language forcefully and violently tore me away from ancient Judaism and its traditions and awakened within me a hatred and contempt for its traditions, thrusting me [instead] toward Russian letters, so that later, in the Russian language, I would discover the beauty of the poetry that lies buried in the old historical foundations and traditions.[4]

The "young man" of this passage is anonymous because so many like him made a total break with the Jewish past after reading heretical works in Hebrew. Taking the next logical step, the hero embraced the majority culture to which the Hebrew Haskalah (Enlightenment) was merely a bridge. Russian became his measure of progress, of excellence, of true belonging. But somehow—and this is the crucial gap in the narrative that I shall be laboring to fill in—his total immersion in Russian culture led to the discovery of what he had repudiated in his past. And so the hero "returned" to reclaim his lost patrimony. Note, however, that he did so in borrowed terms. While he spoke obsessively of "tradition," a catch-all that revealed his estrangement and angst, what he rescued was primarily of aesthetic value—"the beauty of the poetry that lies buried in the old historical foundations and traditions."[5] The hero was an archeologist dusting off the accumulated debris of the past in order to salvage the old, the classical foundations. Far from being a pious act of self-negation, Ansky's was a Western sensibility engaged in a highly self-conscious act of retrieval.

As a typical product of an ultra-Orthodox home, Ansky Rappoport arrived at Russian via works of the Hebrew Haskalah. But because he came of age in the 1870s, when the Haskalah itself had arrived at a self-critical stage, he could avail himself of Moshe Leib Lilienblum's *Ḥaṭṭot neʿurim* (Sins of Youth, 1876), the first work of Hebrew literature to turn one person's life into an indictment of a whole civilization.[6] Lilienblum's

---

4 An undated autobiographical fragment quoted by Shargorodskaya, "On Ansky's Legacy," 307, trans. in Moyshe Shalit, "Naye protim vegn Sh. Anski," *Literarishe bleter* no. 340 (1930): 839. My guess is that he wrote this sometime between 1909, when he began writing autobiographical essays in earnest, and September 1918, when he fled the Soviet Union leaving most of his archive behind.

5 On "tradition" as a modern concept, see David Lowenthal, *The Past Is a Foreign Country* (Cambridge: Cambridge University Press, 1985) ch. 7.

6 See Alan Mintz, *"Banished from Their Father's Table": Loss of Faith and Hebrew Autobiography* (Bloomington: Indiana University Press, 1989), 29-48; Ben-Ami Feingold, "Autobiography as Literature: a study of M. L. Lilienblum's *Ḥaṭṭot neʿurim*" (in Hebrew), *Jerusalem Studies in Hebrew Literature* 4 (1983): 86-111.

excruciating confession of personal failure was Rappoport's blueprint for rebellion, his nihilist scripture. Lilienblum's sobering exhortations to Jewish "sons" inspired Rappoport to take up a manual trade while still living "in the thick of Jewish life." Lilienblum's condemnation of the "fathers" added historical weight to Rappoport's own adolescent rebellion. *Ḥaṭṭot neʿurim* was, however, only the first in a series of heretical texts in the self-education of a young Russian Jew. If we have reason to believe that in his later autobiographical fiction Ansky greatly exaggerated the influence of this one Maskilic classic, it is because his hometown of Vitebsk was no provincial backwater.[7] It was as good a school for radicalism as any in the Czarist empire.

Too poor to attend the local gymnasium, young Shloyme-Zanvl learned Russian on his own and was tutored on the side by those of his friends who came from the better part of town. Together they read the radical works of Pisarev and Chernichevsky and learned to loathe everything that the bourgeois establishment stood for. Even though they still didn't know a single Russian gentile, what they knew of Jewish life was bad enough: the stifling and sadistic *ḥeder*, the immorality of the marketplace, the conflict between rich and poor. Rappoport's first literary endeavors (in Yiddish) were a melodrama on the evils of *ḥeder* education and a novel about the economic and moral collapse of a Jewish family.[8]

Once a young Jew went on the offensive, the utopian fervor of Russian radicalism would hardly have kept him at home. It is enough to recall the fate of Rappoport's *landsman* and exact contemporary Abraham Cahan, who left to establish an agrarian commune in America after a chance meeting with a leader of the Am Olam movement in 1882.[9] The formative influence in Rappoport's life was Russian Populism, the *Narod-*

---

7 Why Lilienblum loomed so large in Ansky's reconstruction of his youth is something I discuss in "The Maskil as Folk Hero," *Prooftexts* 10 (1990): 219-35.

8 Zhitlovsky is our only source of information on the melodrama; see *Zikhroynes fun mayn lebn,* 15, 25. Unable to find a Yiddish publisher for his novel, Ansky published it as "Istoria semeistvo" (The Story of a Family) in *Voskhod,* nos. 9-12 (1884). A pirated retranslation by A. Litvak was published under the title *Di milkhome far'n lebn: eyne ertseylung fun dem yidishn folks-lebn in tsvey teyl* (Vilna: Shriftgiser, 1895). Once Ansky rejoined the ranks of Yiddish literature, he cut the novel in half and published a revised version, "A toyter lebn," in *Di tsukunft* (1905). This version later appeared as "Shtifkinder" in the *Gezamlte shriftn,* 15 vols. (Vilna–Warsaw–New York: Farlag Ansky, 1920-1925), 7: 105-64; and as "Pasinki" in *Sobranie sochinenii S. A. An-skovo* (Collected Works of S. An-sky), 5 vols. (St. Petersburg: Samoobrazovanie, 1915), 1: 175-240.

9 Jonathan Frankel, *Prophecy and Politics: Socialism, Nationalism, and the Russian Jews, 1862-1917* (Cambridge: Cambridge University Press, 1981), 93.

nichestvo, to which he may have been exposed while still living in Vitebsk but whose messianic force became dominant only after he left for Dvinsk.

At that time, in the early 1880s, the focus of Russian Populist thought was the peasantry. Did the *obshchina*, the Russian peasant commune, already embody the essence of the just and equal society (as Zlatovratsky maintained), or did the peasants lack independence and originality (as Uspensky believed)? Did one take up Kropotkin's challenge that Socialists adopt the life of peasants and workmen and merge with them, or did one become part of the village in order to enlighten it, to bring social and political reform?[10] Whichever side was right, reforming the rigidly hierarchical, exploitative, and parasitic Jewish community was a moot point. Lilienblum's plea to learn a useful trade was useless so long as one remained "in the thick of Jewish life." The legacy of guilt between *shtetl* fathers and their sons was dwarfed by the unpaid debt that weighed on the conscience of the privileged groups toward the millions of Russian workers of this generation and those of the past.[11] Fired by Lavrov's panhistorical sense of duty, steeled by Chernichevsky's personal model of total dedication to the cause, and armed with a specific eschatology, any idealistic young Jew would leave the stifling fold in order to redeem Mother Russia.

For several years Solomon Rappoport earned his meager living teaching Russian to Jewish boys and girls in various *shtetlakh* and villages. It was a lonely life, living "on the border between two worlds," far from the camaraderie of his fellow heretics back home and never fully partaking of the radical chic flaunted by children of the Russian well-to-do.[12] But by 1888 he had chosen the Donets Basin and Yekaterinoslav as his base of operations. "I feel good here," he wrote to his lifelong friend Chaim Zhitlovsky. "I like the simple working life of the *narod*, its naiveté,

---

[10] For a summary of positions, see Franco Venturi, *Roots of Revolution: A History of the Populist and Socialist Movements in Nineteenth-Century Russia*, trans. from the Italian by Francis Haskell (Chicago: University of Chicago Press, 1983), ch. 18; and Zhitlovsky, *Zikhroynes fun mayn lebn*, 43-45.

[11] Venturi, *Roots of Revolution*, 450.

[12] "Der hungeriker" (The Hungry One, 1892) in *Gezamlte shriftn*, vol. 14, *Noveln*, 71-100, is a superb fictionalization of this period in his life. The story was originally written in Russian as "Twenty Years Old." The oldest document in the Zhitlovsky file (YIVO Archives) is a postcard of 16 December 1883 written in a very Russified Yiddish to Shmuel Gurevitsh. "There is no society of heretics here [in the shtetl of Osvey]," Ansky complains, "no antagonism toward me, nothing to remind me of the [heady] phrases self-sacrifices. All they care about is fleecing the goyim."

poverty, truth, its lack of malice. Here I shall find a cause for myself."[13] Because the villages were swarming with spies and police agents, Ansky could not adopt the "natural" habitat of the folk. He found his niche among the coal miners instead; every kind of misfit came to work in the mines. Backbreaking and debilitating, this hard labor was the great leveler of society. In the *shtetl*, everyone had been spying on the Russian tutor who was undermining the morals of the young, while here one could even go around without an internal passport.[14] The miners, who found the name Solomon Aranovitsh unassimilable, Russified Rappoport's name to Semyon Akimovich and thus it remained to his dying day.[15]

By accepting their name for him, Rappoport signified that he had also adopted their lifestyle, their "poverty, truth, and lack of malice" as his own. Everyone who met him, whether in Paris, Bern, St. Petersburg, Moscow, Vilna, or Warsaw, attested to his spartan surroundings, his modest dress, his practice of self-denial. His personal affinity for those who inhabited the lowest depths of Russian society then carried over to Ansky's scholarly and artistic concerns as well. While living and working among the miners he began to study their folklore, their political views, and their reading habits.[16] In the tactical debate on effective agitation among the masses, Semyon Akimovich found proof that the campaign to enlighten them from above had failed. By the time he left—finally flushed out by the ever-vigilant Czarist police in 1891—he had discovered the reason why.

The *narod* (the folk, the masses), Ansky argued in his detailed analysis of their reading habits, were culturally and psychologically distinct.[17] By "folk" he meant the peasants who were still tied to the land. As distinct from the more well-to-do kulaks, the petty clerks, or the urban working class, the landed peasantry had made little progress since the liberation of the serfs. Their formal schooling primitive and short-lived, the peasant folk read *lubok* (didactic and sensational) literature if they read anything

---

[13] Quoted by Frankel, *Prophecy and Politics*, 268.

[14] Chernov, *Yidishe tuer*, 66f. Zhitlovsky gives a diametrically opposite account of Ansky's life in the mines; see *Zikhroynes fun mayn lebn*, 51.

[15] Zhitlovsky, ibid., 55.

[16] As historian Jacob Shatzky reminds us, "The Russian Populists of that period were not all folklorists, but most of the folklorists were Populists." See "Sh. Anski, der meshulekh fun folklor," *Jewish Book Annual* 9 (1950-1951): 113.

[17] S. An-ski, *Ocherki narodnoy literaturi* (Essays on Folk Literature) (St. Petersburg: B. M. Wolf, 1894). First serialized in the leading Populist journal *Russkoe Bogatstvo* in 1892.

at all; the pamphlets, books, and journals of the radical or reform-minded intelligentsia simply could not reach them. Nor could the classic works of Lermontov, Pushkin, and Gogol, no matter how they were packaged and even if read to them aloud.[18]

To write for the folk, Ansky concluded, one had to be of them. The great Leo Tolstoy had briefly succeeded in penetrating their ranks with his ethical tales in the folk vein, and his Posrednik Publishing House found effective means of distribution in the villages, but the brief lifespan of this venture proved that intellectuals could not merely stoop to conquer.[19] The peasant-folk had their own ethos, their own sense of beauty. They were a distinct "social-psychological type." The folk saw all truths that derived from a single individual (like Tolstoy) as illusory and transitory; they bowed only before the truth of the collective. Therefore, Ansky maintained, the intellectual, armed with his individual truths alone, must merge with the folk in order to achieve a new and higher synthesis.[20]

The search for that synthesis ultimately led Ansky in new directions: to a heady year spent in a charmed circle of Populist intellectuals in St. Petersburg; to the life of a Russian émigré in Paris complete with love affairs with *shiksas*, heated ideological debates, a bohemian lifestyle.[21] Finally, on the eve of his return to Russia, he found his man in Father Gapon, the legendary hero of the January Revolution of 1905 and a survivor of its bloodbath. They met in Geneva, where Gapon was in hiding and where he joined the ranks of the Socialist Revolutionary Party. What most impressed Ansky, recalling their brief collaboration some years later, was Gapon's pamphlet written in solidarity with the Jewish pogrom victims in Russia. Here was more than agitprop under

---

18 Ansky returned to this subject many years later in his public lectures. See Moyshe Shalit, "Sh. An-skis referatn," *Fun noentn over* 1 (1937-1938): 314f.

19 Ansky, *Ocherki*, ch. 7. For a more positive assessment, see "*Posrednik*," in *Handbook of Russian Literature* ed. Victor Terras (New Haven: Yale University Press, 1985), 351f. For Tolstoy's stories in the folk vein, see *Twenty-Three Tales*, trans. Louise and Aylmer Maude (London: Oxford University Press, 1906).

20 S. An-ski, *Narod i kniga* (People and Book) (Moscow, 1914), 1-41. My thanks to Michael Krutikov for summarizing the contents of this book, the only locatable copy of which is in the Lenin Library, Moscow. For a critical discussion of Ansky's theory, see Chaim Zhitlovsky, "Shloyme-Zanvl Rapoport An-ski un der sotsyal-politisher folklor," intro. to Ansky's *Gezamlte shriftn*, vol. 15, *Folklor un etnografye* (1925), 43-51.

21 For this "inside story" of Ansky's life as a radical, see Chernov *Yidishe tuer*; Zhitlovsky, *Zikhroynes fun mayn lebn*, 52-66; and Ansky's "Hinter a shtumer vant" (1909) in *Gezamlte shriftn*, vol. 11, *Zikhroynes*, pt. 2:5-20.

cover of piety. As a man of the people, Father Gapon could appeal to their conscience in the name of Christian values and in the style of an Eastern Orthodox sermon.[22]

If this fusion of radical thought and folk religion was the desired goal of the intelligentsia, then someone like Ansky was ideally positioned to do the same for the Jews. All he had to do was redirect his populism back to where it belonged. With hindsight, some have described the turn in Ansky's life as simply as that. Historian Jacob Shatzky saw Ansky's sojourn among the Russian *narod* as merely an apprenticeship for his true calling as the *meshulekh*, the inspired messenger of Jewish folklore.[23] This reading of Ansky's career as a seamless ideological progression from the Russian to the Jewish sphere was not, however, shared by his contemporaries, who labored long and hard to find some dramatic explanation.

Was it the hand of history that seized Ansky from his slumber? Sobered by the pogroms in Russia in 1905-1906, the native son returned to lead his abandoned flock.[24] Or was it the hand of God that dispelled Ansky's love of the Russian *narod*—nothing but an aberration anyway, a youthful escapade that ended in a last fling of revolutionary politics in exile? This third map, charted by Zionist biographer S. L. Citron, drew Ansky's itinerary within the Jewish world alone. It began in Vitebsk and ended, melodramatically, with Ansky undergoing a conversion experience in a small Vilna synagogue between afternoon and evening prayers.[25]

To be sure, there is some truth in each of these readings. Shatzky is right to maintain that what Ansky discovered in Jewish folklore is what he had already found among the Russian *narod*. Ansky himself admitted as much in the autobiographical sketch cited earlier. The hand-of-history

---

[22] "Gapon" (1920), *Gezamlte shriftn*, vol. 11, *Zikhroynes (fun der rusisher revolutsyonerer bavegung)*, 43-47.

[23] Shatzky, "Anski, der meshulekh," 114. This view is echoed by Y. Zerubavel, "Sh. An-ski (shtrikhn tsu zayn kharakteristik)," *Di goldene keyt* 48 (1964): 7.

[24] Among the memoirists who credited the pogroms were Sh. Rosenfeld and Zalmen Reisen. For a convenient survey of theories on Ansky's "conversion," see Zeitlin, "Der lebnsveg fun Sh. An-ski," 56-59. Ansky's response to anti-Semitism, pogroms and blood libels was in fact extremely complex, often alienating him from Jewish nationalist sentiments. See, for instance, Zhitlovsky, *Zikhroynes fun mayn lebn*, 102f. (on the Dreyfus Affair); Frankel, *Prophecy and Politics*, 143 (comparing the 1880 pogroms to the Kishinev pogrom); and especially Ansky's angry letter to Bialik of 1913 (*Di goldene keyt* 48 [1964]: 205). See also his "Pogrom Impressions" of the Bialystok pogrom (1906) in *Sobranie sochinenii*, 4:221-45.

[25] Sh. L. Citron, "Eyner fun dray (vegn Sh. An-ski)," *Lebn* 7-8 (December 1920): 35-37. For a trenchant critique, see Zeitlin, "Der lebnsveg," 58f.

theory is true insofar as Ansky had to experience the fatal predictability of his people's history before he could decode the symbolic language of their folklore. And Citron is right that a return of such intensity points to some kind of spiritual upheaval. But the model I am positing, for Ansky's life as well as for his work, is a dialectical one in which the move from *narodnik* to *meshulekh* is neither a lazy progression nor a leap of faith.

Whether we credit Ansky's lifelong commitment to Russian Populism or whether we require a melodramatic scenario to explain how his Jewish loyalties could suddenly reassert themselves, there can be no doubt that the turning point of his life came between 1900, when Lavrov's death robbed him of his source of livelihood, and the political amnesty in October 1905 which enabled émigré radicals to return home. With dramatic coincidence, this was when the new Jewish politics in Russia, Europe, America, and Palestine had entered into a period of "nationalization." During these years of Storm and Stress, as Jonathan Frankel has shown in his magisterial work *Prophecy and Politics*, even the most hardened cosmopolitans from across the radical spectrum were asking themselves whether the Jews as a nation did not require their own strategy, platform, solution.[26] Victor Chernov, a Russian non-Jew who personally sought out Ansky's help in establishing the Agraro-Socialist League, also tried to persuade his Jewish comrade-in-arms to take a more positive attitude to the Jewish national revival.[27] "How come you people don't fight for your own kind?" he might have asked. Ansky's populism, for all that it inspired his studies of Russian and, later, French folklore, was strictly universalist. It would take a great deal of persuasion to convince Ansky that the Jews were also—let alone exclusively—worthy of his efforts.

The major catalyst of Ansky's return was I. L. Peretz. In his moving eulogy to Peretz written in 1915, Ansky recalled the revelatory impact that reading Peretz's *Collected Writings* had had upon him in 1901. For the first time, he discovered a modern European sensibility expressing itself in the Yiddish language. When he finally had occasion to meet the great writer in St. Petersburg in 1908, what most impressed him was that Peretz did not look at all like a Jew. "In his whole demeanor—no hint

---

26 Frankel, *Prophecy and Politics*, part 2, "The Party Ideologies until 1907."

27 Chernov, *Yidishe tuer*, 79-86; Frankel, *Prophecy and Politics*, 274.

whatsoever of *goles* (diaspora)! Such liberation from exile I had never seen in the expression of any of the assimilated Jews of St. Petersburg."[28]

As an immediate result of reading Peretz, Ansky went back to writing in Yiddish, after a nineteen- or twenty-year hiatus.[29] His best early effort was a sequel to Peretz's mock-epic poem *Monish* (1888). Where Peretz had focused on the seduction of the young hero by an agent of Lilith, Ansky farcically put the temptress herself on trial. Now it was Lilith standing trial in Hell for having been swayed by the "Linen Rebbe" to repent of her evil ways. Lilith was caught "between two worlds." Otherwise the poem was a cheap imitation of the master, from its pseudo-folk narrator, its super-Hebraized style, and its anti-Hasidic jibes, to its overuse of talmudic "folklore" and common superstition.[30] More impressive was Ansky's subsequent attempt to folklorize his own lived experience with the Haskalah movement of the 1870s. Written in Russian, this fictionalized "chronicle" exposed the roots of Jewish political radicalism: its collective strengths as well as its individual muta-

---

[28] "Yitskhok Leybush Perets," *Gezamlte shriftn*, vol. 10, *Zikhroynes*, pt. 1: 155. There is general agreement on the Peretz connection among recent biographers. See Frankel, *Prophecy and Politics*, 274; and Dov Noy, "The Place of Sh. An-ski in Jewish Folkloristics" (in Hebrew), *Jerusalem Studies in Hebrew Folklore* 2 (1982): 98. Noy, however, vitiates his own argument by claiming that Ansky never lost touch with Yiddish literature, citing Ansky's visit with Sholem Aleichem in 1890 as proof. As I read it, the visit proves the very opposite: that even Sholem Aleichem, at the height of his wealth and in the heat of his reformist activities, could not bring Ansky back to the fold.

In his private correspondence, unlike his public pronouncements, Ansky criticized Peretz for his egomania. "A khokhem mekhukem, an emeser kinstler," he described Peretz during his recent visit to St. Petersburg, "nor a fardreyter moyakh. Tsulozn fun di varshever yinglekh. Halt zikh far a got un trogt a groysn varshever khlyumper. Vi Ash un andere" (The wisest of wise men, a true artist, but of a confused mind. Spoiled rotten by the Warsaw youngsters. Thinks he's a god and walks around in a big Warsaw-style cape. Like [Sholem] Asch and the others) (Letter of 11/24 [Old Style/New Style] April 1911 on *Evreiski Mir* stationery, Zhitlovsky file, YIVO Archive).

[29] The only thing Ansky published in Yiddish by his own hand prior to 1901 was a sketch titled *Di ksovim* (The Writings). Apparently translated from the Russian, by L. Reynish, it appeared in Peretz's *Yontef-bletlekh, Oyneg-shabes* (1896). Ansky included the sketch (dated 1882) in vol. 1 of *Sobranie sochinenii* but never reprinted it in Yiddish. His inauspicious Yiddish debut appears to have come with the poem "Dos elnt" (Loneliness) in the Zionist newspaper *Der yid*, 3/46 (1901): 12.

[30] *Ashmeday (a poeme)*, serialized in *Der fraynd* (1904); rpt. in *Gezamlte shriftn, Humoreskn un lider*, 8:5-80. The "between two worlds" motif appears on 76.

tions.[31] Closer to Peretz the crusader and satirist than to Peretz the neoromantic, Ansky may have had the will but he still lacked the way to reclaim the language and spirituality of the Jewish folk.

If Peretz embodied the longed-for synthesis of modernity and tradition, politics and culture, what Ansky found upon his return to St. Petersburg was a more rarified atmosphere than that of Polish-Hasidic Warsaw where Peretz made his home. For one thing, the circle of Jewish activists in St. Petersburg was entirely Russian-speaking, and its approach to matters of the Jewish spirit was somewhat academic. Here, in 1908, the groundwork was laid for a network of Jewish cultural institutions designed to preserve the facts and artifacts of Jewish folk culture and to disseminate a highbrow version thereof in the Russian language. That same year the Jewish Historic-Ethnographic Society and Society for Jewish Folk Music received their formal charters; the Jewish Literary Society was founded in June; the Jewish Education Society (OPE) expanded its activities, and the Russian-Jewish monthly *Evreiski Mir* was established with Ansky as its literary editor.[32] Under their auspices, Ansky began the lecture circuit throughout the Pale of Settlement, spreading the word about Jewish folklore and language, Yiddish literature and theater, about war, the folk, and the revolution.[33] In the inaugural issue of *Perezhitoe*, the official organ of the Jewish Historic-Ethnographic Society, Ansky published his epoch-making essay on Jewish ethnopoetics.[34]

Everything now seemed to be in place for Ansky to "discover the beauty of the poetry that lies buried in the old historical foundations and traditions." The universalist tendencies of Russian Populism had been overcome through a decisive shift to romantic nationalism; Jewish folklore and the east European Jewish past were now deemed respectable subjects of study; specialized journals and institutions had been established to oversee the means of cultural reproduction. In practical terms this meant that a person like Ansky, who habitually lived from hand to mouth, could now make a living as a JEWISH writer, journalist, lecturer.

---

31 *Pioneri* (Pioneers), serialized in *Voskhod*, nos. 1-9 (1904). Its sequel, *Pervaya bryoshch* (The First Breach), was written in 1905. For a discussion, see my "The Maskil as Folk Hero."

32 On the Society for Jewish Folk Music, see Albert Weisser, *The Modern Renaissance of Jewish Music* (New York: Da Capo, 1983), ch. 3.

33 Shalit, "Sh. An-skis referatn," 311-14.

34 "Di yidishe folks-shafung," trans. from the Russian by Zalmen Reisen in *Gezamlte shriftn*, vol. 15, *Folklor un etnografye*, 27-95. For a different version, see "Der grund-motif fun dem yidishn folks-shafn," *Dos naye lebn* 1 (1909): 224-40.

And so the archeology of the past could proceed unencumbered. Yet for a man whose life had for so long been "broken, severed, ruptured," who had spent so many years "on the border between two worlds," the price of achieving wholeness was total self-transformation. The event that would turn theory into creative practice and archeologist into inspired messenger was actual contact with the Yiddish-speaking folk, Ansky's physical return to his own *narod*.

Now forty-eight years old and ailing (he never physically recovered from his life as a miner), Ansky barely understood the Jewish folk imagination, but he was moving in the right direction. Though all he had to go on was the Ginzburg–Marek anthology of Yiddish folksongs (1901) and Ignatz Bernstein's collection of proverbs and sayings (1908), the paucity of authentic data did not stop him from building a theoretical edifice whose central pillar was the absolute spirituality of the folk. The idea of biblical monotheism (*akhdus haboyre*), he wrote in his synthetic essay on Jewish ethnopoetics, "is inimical to any form of struggle and places spiritual integrity above the material, and certainly above the physical." Whereas the Bible still retained some traces of vengeance and bellicosity, in Jewish folklore all forms of struggle were spiritualized. Who were the Hasidic *rebbes* and wonder workers, he asked, if not the Jewish equivalents of knights in shining armor? Hasidic folklore in particular (which Ansky thus far knew only from chapbooks and sacred histories) transformed the errant knights into tsaddikim traveling the globe to redeem Jewish captives; turned chivalrous men rescuing damsels in distress into tsaddikim restoring purity of soul to penitent sinners; made tournaments into theological debates.[35] The spiritual greatness of the Torah was finally realized only by the folk.

Moving beyond the glowing description of Jewish folklore to its recreation, Ansky began to write pseudo-Hasidic tales (in both Russian and Yiddish) that tested this spiritual fortitude in the bloody arena of east European Jewish history. The heroes, whether leaders or footsoldiers, male or female, rich or poor, were everywhere ready to sacrifice themselves for the sake of the Jewish collective. Wondrously, their *mesires-nefesh farn klal-yisroel* always prevailed, whether against Czar Nicholas I or the King of Romania.[36] And how could they not succeed,

---

35 *Gezamlte shriftn,* vol. 15, *Folklor un etnografye,* 34, 74-80.

36 Virtually all the tales and narrative poems collected in sections 2-4 of *Fun eybikn kval,* vol. 1 of the *Gezamlte shriftn,* exemplify this heroic pattern. Add to that "A din-

seeing as powerless Jews had always faced off against all-powerful rulers and lived to see the vindication of God's justice? *A din-toyre* (A Rabbinical Lawsuit, 1909) began with the storyteller invoking the memory of the Temple's Destruction. *Mesires-nefesh* (Self-Sacrifice, 1906), Ansky's first neo-Hasidic tale, ended with an extended comparison between this folktale rescue and the story of Purim.[37] Through folklore, Ansky discovered the oneness of God. Through his folklorized reading of the modern Jewish experience he discovered the symbolic language of historical archetypes. Through his encounter with the living folk he would discover how to make that language his own.

Why venture forth into the field at all if so much could be accomplished at home? Ansky himself counseled that the Jewish classics be mined for their folkloric material.[38] Leo Wiener and Y. L. Cahan had already begun to record Yiddish folksongs among the Jewish immigrant masses in America. Neither books nor studying "culture at a distance" would satisfy the old *narodnik*, however. "No," Ansky wrote emphatically to Zhitlovsky in America, "Yiddish tales, legends, and the like must be collected among old folks who carry the past with them in unadulterated form."[39] Just as the Russian peasant was a species apart so long as he remained ON THE LAND, so too were the Jewish "old folks" who never left the *shtetl* or village for either the big city or America. It was only in the thick of Jewish life, the scene of his own rebellion, that the lost treasures were to be found.

The Jewish Ethnographic Expedition bearing the name of Baron Naftali Horace Günzburg (father of its largest donor), was launched on 1 July 1912. Ansky was still short the 30,000 rubles he needed to see the project through to the end, but he already had the support of a stellar group of scholars and a staff of energetic young fieldworkers.[40] By the end of the first year of fieldwork, the expedition had grown in Ansky's eyes into "a survey of Jewish life on a national scale, if not larger." Waxing more eloquent still, he compared himself to a mountain climber

---

toyre" (A Rabbinical Lawsuit; subtitled "A Hasidic Tale"), published concurrently in *Der fraynd* no. 62 (1909) and *Dos naye lebn* 1 (1909): 142-46 but never anthologized.

37 *Gezamlte verk*, vol. 1, *Fun eybikn kval*, 213-17. Ansky later reworked this into an article on the Revolt in Mastislav, *Perezhitoe* 2 (1910): 248-59.

38 See his letter to Bialik of Erev Pesach 1912, *Di goldene keyt* 48 (1968): 200.

39 Yiddish letter to Zhitlovsky on *Evreiski Mir* stationery, 11/24 April 1911. Zhitlovsky File, YIVO Archives.

40 For the most extensive account of the expedition, and Isaiah Trunk, "Ḥomer bilti-yaduʿa shel 'mishlaḥat Anski' bashanim 1912-1926" [New material on the "Anski Expedition" (1912-1926)], *Gal-Ed* 6 (1982):229-45.

who, from his elevated vantage point, could finally see "with eyes of flesh and blood the people, the nation."[41] After estimating the huge number of folktales, folksongs, photographs, and other valuable artifacts they had already amassed, Ansky expressed his indescribable joy at digging out with his own hands a broken tombstone riddled with holes from the time of the Chmielnicki massacres of 1648-1649.

The expedition was the sacred mission of his life. In discovering that the Jews were a people with vast cultural treasures, in literally unearthing the stigmata of their collective suffering, and by exploring their holy sites—the tomb of the Baal Shem Tov, the synagogue in Ostro—Ansky had gone beyond Peretz and beyond anything the young *narodnik* Semyon Akimovich himself had ever done. The image of the mountain was no mere conceit. For in the introduction to the published questionnaire used during the expedition, Ansky identified Jewish folklore with the Oral Torah itself, created by the folk through centuries of trial and tribulation.[42] If this was the Torah, Ansky was its prophet: not Moses on Mount Nebo staring out at the Promised Land, but Moses on Sinai receiving the Tablets.

If it had been the fate of his generation to be torn between body and soul, between gentile and Jew, between tradition and modernity, then folklore held out the promise of reconciliation. In folklore one found no such thing as outright assimilation or national self-effacement. Here the Slavs and Jews were engaged in "mutual cultural influences," with the folktales and folk beliefs of one being transmuted into the idiom of the other.[43] In Hasidic folklore, the boundaries between this world and the next broke down as well. The tsaddik negotiated freely between the two realms and could effect change in the cosmos by directing human activity down below. According to Jewish folk belief, the living remained in dialogue with the dead. Just as the Written Torah was the source of all prior Jewish creativity, so the Oral Torah, this language of symbol and memory, was to become the wellspring for Jewish creative artists of the future.[44]

---

[41] Yiddish letter of 26 August/8 September 1913 on stationery of the Ethnographic Expedition, Zhitlovsky file, YIVO Archives. Misquoted and misdated in the YIVO exhibition catalogue, no. 60.

[42] See Ansky's "Forrede" to *Dos yidishe etnografishe program*, ed. L. I. Shternberg (Petrograd, 1914), 9-12.

[43] See "Gegnzaytike kulturele aynflusn" (1920), in *Gezamlte shriftn*, vol. 15, *Folklor un etnografye*, 257-68.

[44] As indeed it did. See John E. Bowlt, "From the Pale of Settlement to the Reconstruction of the World," in *Tradition and Revolution: The Jewish Renaissance in Russian*

Yet never in his life was Ansky more true to his revolutionary past and more consistently Russian than now, in his great homecoming. When he appealed to the conscience of his fellow intellectuals to rescue and preserve Jewish folklore in the name of the people's suffering, he was following in the path of his beloved teacher Pyotr Lavrov. Both the pathos of his appeal and its historical consciousness bespoke Ansky's Russian persona: "Our past," he wrote, "over which so much blood and tears of holy martyrs have been shed, that has been sanctified with so much self-sacrifice, is being lost or forgotten."[45]

We imagine today, after the destruction of east European Jewry, that people of Ansky's generation had easier access to the folk traditions than we do: that no matter how far they strayed, they just had to stretch out their hands and reap the rewards. Not so. Their act of reclaiming the past was ever so painstaking and self-conscious. Nothing less than a full-scale expedition seemed to be required, complete with questionnaires, trained fieldworkers, and elaborate disguises. In some towns, the only way Ansky could win the trust of the local inhabitants was to pose as an orthodox Jew and to appear in *shul* wearing tallith and tefillin.[46] Ansky and his fieldworkers did not come there to pray. They came to sanctify the relics.

The guns of August ended the expedition abruptly. In the midst of the Great War that followed, Ansky returned to the heartland of Yiddish, to the quaint *shtetlakh* where old-timers still preserved the past in its unadulterated form. What he found was ubiquitous ruin. As a talisman and memento, he would carry with him to his dying day the shards of the Ten Commandments from the desecrated synagogue of Dembits with only the words *tirṣaḥ, tinʿaf* (thou shalt . . . kill . . . commit adultery") still intact.[47] Yet even in the midst of this apocalyptic landscape, he insisted that one not return to the Jews as to a suffering nation. Rather, one should return to a people secure in its own identity; to the creative joy and cultural self-confidence of the Jews; to the song that resounded through every fiber of their being. Whosoever returned to such a people

---

Avant-Garde Art 1912-1928, ed. Ruth Apter-Gabriel (Jerusalem: The Israel Museum, 1987), 43-60.

45 Ansky, "Forrede," 11.

46 Khaykl Lunsky, "A halb yor zikhroynes vegn An-ski," *Lebn* 7-8 (1920): 22.

47 See Moyshe Shalit, "Der An-ski-arkhiv—zayn inhalt un vert," *Literarishe bleter* no. 259 (1929): 313; and my *Against the Apocalypse* (Cambridge: Harvard University Press, 1984), 54. For a folklorized version of the same episode, see Rechtman, *Yidishe etnografye*, 16.

was not sacrificing anything at all but was tapping the wellspring of eternal happiness.[48]

Ansky's career lays bare the dialectical movement of modernism and return in Jewish life. Because Ansky's debt to Russian culture was so great and because Russian Populism provided so clear a blueprint for rediscovering the folk, we can see how the selective retrieval of the Jewish past could never have come about without his prior immersion in the culture at large. Peretz, Sholem Aleichem, Berdyczewski (among writers of his own generation); Der Nister, Manger, and Isaac Bashevis Singer (among writers of the next) all went a similar route, only they mostly managed to cover their tracks. Because Ansky's act of *teshuvah,* of penitent return, was so dramatic, because he launched one rescue operation after another, he became a prophet in his own time. The prophetic call that transformed and redeemed its recipient was to reimagine himself as a member of the folk.

Instead of a bifurcated life, half of which was lived in error, the other half in a state of grace, Ansky's career was a four-act drama. First came the break with Jews and Judaism, accompanied by the total embrace of Russian radical culture. Then came a series of jolts—political, cultural, and, if the tale of conversion has any validity at all, spiritual—that awakened in him a longing for what he had left behind. Seeking a renewed affiliation, Ansky did public penance and turned his attention to the study of Jewish folklore. Thus far, the standard homiletical reading of his life as a typical tale of rebellion–loss–and penitent return. But the very culture that seduced him away provided him with the rationale for and the means of retrieval. It was as a Russian Populist that Ansky took the critical next step toward a creative, dynamic appropriation of the east European Jewish past. He did not renounce his modernism or his radical faith in order to become a good Jew; he acted upon that faith and reinvented Jewish culture accordingly. He turned the disparate remains of Jewish folklore and folk life into an all-embracing Oral Torah.

His return, in all its complexity, was the paradigm for the Jewish cultural renaissance as a whole. The hero of the modern age was a born-again Jew in a Judaism of his own remaking.

---

48 Letter of 18 February 1916 to Rosa Monoszon-Ettinger, trans. from the Russian (by I. Latzky-Betholdi?) in *He'avar* 11 (1964): 97. According to a footnote on the same page, a German translation of this segment was published in *Jüdische Rundschau* in the late 1930s to bring solace to the Jews living under Nazi rule.

10

Modern Students of Midrash Halakhah: *Between Tradition And* Wissenschaft

JAY M. HARRIS

In the rabbinic literature of the first five Christian centuries, there is perhaps no feature whose presence is as pronounced as the legal exegesis of the Torah, or *midrash halakhah*. In the nineteenth century, the history, significance, and quality of this exegesis was to become one of the central scholarly points of contention between religious traditionalists of various kinds and religious liberals of various kinds. Studying the different models emerging from this area of contention yields some surprising results regarding traditional assumptions and their continuity in the modern period. However, before dealing with this in detail, it is necessary that we first examine the premodern *status quaestionis* if we are to make any sense of the modern debates.[1]

In classical rabbinic literature, most *midrash halakhah* revolves around the tannaim, the earliest rabbinic sages. They are either understood as the authors of much of it—both specific texts such as the Mekhilta, Sifra, and Sifre, or the many *beraitot* contained in the talmuds—or else the midrash

1 The discussion of the premodern state of the question represents a summary of the results of my research; these results will be presented in full in a later book-length study. Similarly, the discussion of modern authors represents a brief overview, in accordance with the theme of this volume, of the issues dealt with by nineteenth-century *Wissenschaft* scholars. A fuller treatment must await the completion of the aforementioned book.

is presented as the source of their particular legal opinions. In the second case, while the tanna in question is not necessarily seen as the author of the exegesis, the midrash represents his thinking as reconstructed by later hands. In either case, the midrash was seen as an authentic representation of the thinking of the tanna to whom it is attributed.[2]

In the tannaitic texts, we often find significant diversity regarding the meaning of a particular biblical verse or phrase, perhaps traceable to different systems of exegesis in general, perhaps to other, more local concerns. This diversity, as well as the question of what is and is not acceptable exegesis to the ancient sages, gave rise to considerable reflection, starting with the two talmuds and proceeding up to our own day.[3]

When we examine the way the two talmuds make use of the midrashic materials that were bequeathed to them, it is easy to discern that each takes a distinct approach. The Bavli's approach is to treat the diversity of techniques and results as, in essence, a virtue, leaving it free to deal with the material as it sees fit. To take some concrete examples, in the tannaitic materials we often find sages deriving a law from a scriptural repetition. Sometimes other sages oppose the law, and therefore, it is presumed, the exegesis. Sometimes they may agree with the law, but yet reject the proffered exegesis, preferring some other to establish the point. At some moment in time, opposing the exegesis of repeated phrases was justified by the position that the Torah speaks in human language, and therefore the repetition is devoid of significance; it is merely a concession to human style. In the Bavli, as was noted by a number of medieval commentators, the position that the Torah speaks in human language is attributed to perhaps a dozen different tannaim, ranging over a number of generations. Further, the same tanna who in one place supposedly refrains from interpreting repeated phrases is often cited in other contexts as interpreting them. It appears, then, that to the redactors of the Bavli, everyone agrees that in general the Torah does not speak in human language; everyone also agrees that sometimes the Torah does. Thus, most repetitions are to be interpreted, but some are

---

[2] For the purposes of this paper it makes little difference how we date this material. My own view is that the Mekhilta, Sifra, and Sifre are products of the first half of the third century. In any event, I take for granted that, whenever these specific texts emerged, much of the material contained therein was known to the redactors of the talmuds and was considered by them to be legitimately tannaitic.

[3] This diversity of opinion may result in an exegetical dispute in which the principals agree regarding the law but disagree regarding its biblical "source," or it may result in an actual legal dispute in which the principals disagree regarding the legal contours of the verse(s) in question.

not.[4] Similarly, with the technique of *doresh vavim* (deriving meaning from the presence of the conjunctive 'and'); while strongly associated with R. Akiva,[5] the Talmud assumes that numerous rabbis might use this technique, and having used it in one place will yet refrain from using it in another.[6]

It seems, then, that the redactors of the Bavli took from the earlier materials the stance that there are among the tannaim no systems of exegesis exclusive to an individual or a school. All techniques are available; they therefore felt free to attribute to any tanna any exegetical position consistent with the legal position adopted by that sage.[7]

When we turn to the Yerushalmi, we see that the situation is quite different. While scarcely maintaining consistency throughout all the tractates, the Yerushalmi often divides the earlier tannaitic materials into two schools, that of R. Akiva and that of R. Ishmael. Numerous times, after reconstructing the putative exegetical stance of a particular tanna, or amora, the Talmud will state that thus far the law is grounded according to the system of R. Akiva; it will then ask, whence do we know the law according to R. Ishmael's system? The answer to this question will always be another *derashah*. In many of these cases, it is to be noted, the midrash that is ostensibly according to the system of R. Ishmael is attributed to an amora, who gives no indication that he is interpreting according to anyone's system. However, because the midrash uses techniques of which R. Ishmael allegedly approves rather than those he rejects, the redactors of these passages issue the judgment that this midrash belongs to his system.[8] Thus the redactors of the Yerushalmi

---

4 See the comments of the tosafists at *b. Soṭa* 24a, s.v. "*ve-Rabbi Yoḥanan,*" etc. and at *b. Menaḥot* 17b, s.v. "*Mai heʾakhel yeʾakhel*" etc. See also Samson of Qinon's *Sefer ha-Keritut*, pt. 5, 1:30.

5 See *b. Yebamot* 68b and the parallels noted there.

6 See the Tosafot at *b. Menaḥot* 51b, s.v. "*vav lo darish,*" and the parallels noted there. See also *b. Yebamot* 72b, where the anonymous voice of the *gemara* (the "stam") states that even those who do not interpret "*vavin*" interpret "*vav ve-he*", again indicating how the redactors are prepared to attribute techniques to tannaim to suit their own needs.

7 The one exception concerns the use of the techniques of *ribui u-miʿuṭ* and *kelal u-feraṭ*. Already the Tosefta (*t. Shebu.* 1:7) associates the former with R. Akiva and the latter with R. Ishmael, and this position is echoed by the talmuds. See the discussion in Michael Chernick's *Hermeneutical Studies in Talmudic and Midrashic Literature* (Lod: Haberman Institute, 1984). Even here, as Chernick makes clear, the distinction is often blurred.

8 One example is the passage at *y. Shabb.* 19:2. Here the Talmud asks whence we know that both *periʿah* and *milah* are required for an acceptable circumcision. It cites a

react to the chaotic nature of the earlier materials by imposing system on it, arguing that there are two different approaches to scripture that dominated the tannaitic world, one expanding the range of acceptable techniques, one resisting that expansion.

When we examine the subsequent history of the question, we find that the position of the Bavli prevailed. Later commentators show little or no awareness of any consistent exegetical distinctions between Rabbis Akiva and Ishmael. To be sure, they are everywhere recognized as rabbis who often disagree with one another in legal and exegetical matters. However, neither students of rabbinic midrashic exegesis, such as Samson of Chinon in his *Sefer Keritut*, nor the many chroniclers of rabbinic tradition recognize these two figures as founders of exegetical schools nor as people whose exegetical approaches are systematically opposed to one another's. Indeed, even one of the major eighteenth-century commentators on the Yerushalmi will interpret certain passages in that talmud in accord with the Bavli's judgment that any rabbi might be willing to interpret repetitive phrases.[9] While these commentators are sometimes perplexed by the Bavli's unsystematic approach, they nevertheless accept it, ignoring the Yerushalmi's position entirely.

Furthermore, to anticipate an issue that will become relevant later on, no premodern scholar recognized any systematic distinctions among the tannaitic *midreshei halakhah*, the Mekhilta, Sifra, and Sifre. Virtually all chroniclers since Maimonides follow that master's claim that Rav, a third-century Babylonian transitional figure, authored these texts (at

---

scriptural repetition (*himmol yimmol*, Gen 17:13) and comments that this *derashah* is in accord with the system of R. Akiva, who interprets such repetitions. Whence, the Talmud goes on to ask, do we know the law according to the system of R. Ishmael? It then cites the *derashah* of R. Yudah b. Pazi, an amora, who interprets the plural word *lamulot* as signifying the requirement in question. Now, the first, allegedly Akivan, *derashah* is found in *Gen. Rabb.* (46:13, Theodor-Albeck, vol. 1, p. 468) without any mention of R. Akiva. As to the second *derashah*, nowhere does R. Yudah indicate that his interpretation is in accord with the system of R. Ishmael; nor does he indicate that he is opposed, in principle, to the allegedly Akivan *derashah*. This is also the case in the parallel passage found in *Deut. Rabb.* (very beginning of *parshah* 6, p. 111d in the Vilna edition), in which both *derashot* are presented but there is no mention of Rabbis Akiva and Ishmael at all. Finally, it is to be noted that same *derashah* is presented at *y. Ned.* 3:9 anonymously, again with no mention of its place in R. Ishmael's system. It is the redactors of this passage who link R. Ishmael to this *derashah*, on the assumption that he would oppose the "Akivan" *derashah*, but still agree with the legal requirement of *periʿah* and *milah*.

9 See the comments of R. David Frankel in his *Qorban ha-ʿEdah* and *Sheʿarei Qorban* to *y. Ḥag.* 2:1.

least the last two), without any sense that there are distinctions to be drawn among them. Even the most recent and most critical works produced by the traditional world—such as the *Seder ha-Dorot* of Yehiel Heilprin, the *Shem ha-Gedolim* of Hayim Yosef David Azulai (Hida),[10] or the *Rav Peʿalim* of R. Avraham b. Eliahu, the son of the Gaon of Vilna[11]—attribute authorship of these works to Rav. In addition, they follow the tradition of the Bavli (Sanh. 86a) that the anonymous content of these works represent the views of R. Akiva's students, all, including the Sifre to Numbers, in accord with the views of their teacher. Nowhere in premodern historiography do we find any systematic differentiation among the existing *midreshei halakhah.*

When we turn from this set of concerns to the question of the legal function and status of the midrashic material, we turn to an issue that is fraught with theological concerns, and surrounding which an extensive literature has grown. Since the thirteenth century, the primary focus of the discussion has been a famous dispute between Maimonides[12] and Naḥmanides. Maimonides, in the second of the fourteen principles that preface his enumeration of the commandments, argued that any law derived by the standard exegetical principles is to be considered rabbinic in origin and function, unless otherwise specified by the rabbinic sages. What this means is that Maimonides denies that rabbinic legal midrash can actually create laws having scriptural authority. That is, legal midrash does not make manifest what is latent in the divine text; it is the creation of the sages, and other sages may disagree. When the rabbis specify that the derivation actually has the status of Torah, it is, claims Maimonides, because they have an unbroken tradition that the law in question was part of the oral communication by God to Moses. The verse is not halakhically creative at all, but is simply an *asmakhta,* a support, perhaps for mnemonic purposes.

While Maimonides had many predecessors here, his particular formulation is quite stark, and his legal conclusions are more venturesome and far-reaching than are those of his predecessors. Thus, from his time

---

[10] See his entry for Sifra and Sifre in the "*Maʿarekhet Sefarim*" of the *Shem ha-Gedolim*.

[11] See *Rav Peʿalim* (Warsaw, 1894),. 12f.

[12] To be sure, Maimonides had predecessors in his devaluation of the central role of *midrash halakhah*. Most important among them were Saʿadia Gaon (882-942) and Abraham Ibn Ezra 1089/1092-1164/1167). Yet Maimonides' position was more radical than theirs, and it was his work that became the lightning rod for subsequent discussion.

forward the debate took a new turn. The most prominent rabbinic scholar of the thirteenth century, Naḥmanides (1194-1270), felt compelled to sharply disagree with Maimonides' position. He argues that the results of legal exegesis are the very essence of Torah; to midrashically interpret scripture is itself part of the divine mandate communicated at Sinai. The results of such an exegesis are always *de-ʾoraita*, of scriptural status, unless otherwise specified. Only in such cases is the verse an *asmakhta*.

Without venturing further into the technical details, we may summarize the debate as follows. For Maimonides, knowledge of the divine mandate vouchsafed to Israel is not dependent on legal exegesis of the Torah. Midrash is an important intellectual exercise designed to support this divine mandate, or to supplement it with rabbinic enactments. For Naḥmanides, on the other hand, *midrash halakhah* is indeed the foundation stone on which stands the divine message to Israel. The exegesis of the rabbis is an extremely serious business; it may not be reduced to a supportive or supplementary role in the emergence of the Halakhah.

Subsequent to this debate, almost all traditional commentators agreed with Naḥmanides. Even those who defend Maimonides' position do so on the grounds that he actually agrees with Naḥmanides regarding the place of midrash in the development of the Halakhah. They reduce the debate to one of nomenclature relevant only to how one enumerates the 613 commandments, but which does not trample on the sacred status of the results of *midrash halakhah*. Defending Maimonides by saying he actually agrees with his opponent is itself, of course, to affirm the position of Naḥmanides.[13]

Thus, as we enter the modern period, it is clear that Jewish traditional historiography recognized no systematic distinctions among the various midrashic texts, nor among the various midrashic techniques. Further, most Jewish thinkers affirmed the position of Naḥmanides that rabbinic legal midrash was indeed the genuinely creative foundation of the halakhic system, although here occasional reservations were voiced.

---

[13] A full review of this literature may be found in Jacob Neubauer, *Ha-Rambam al Divre Soferim* (Maimonides on the Sayings of the Sages) (Jerusalem: Mosad Harav Kook, 1954), passim. Neubauer's discussion is limited to those who explicitly refer to the dispute between Maimonides and Naḥmanides. A study of other rabbinic literature from the Middle Ages would also show the marked preference of talmudists for Naḥmanides' point of view. One representative example from the very end of the Jewish Middle Ages is R. Yehezkel Landau of Prague (d. 1793); see his *Ṣiyyun le-Nefesh Ḥayyah* (*Ḥiddushe ha-Ṣelaḥ*) *Berakhot, petiḥah*.

Jewish traditionalists dealing with *midrash halakhah* in the nineteenth century had to contend with yet another "tradition" that had enormous impact on the development of modern Judaism. For when we turn to the treatment of midrash in modern times, we find that for nearly two centuries, starting with Spinoza in the middle of the seventeenth, rabbinic legal exegesis came under relentless attack. Virtually all scholarly attempts to take account of Judaism noted its reliance on unusual exegetical methods and judged Judaism as primitive and corrupt. For Spinoza, any exegesis of the Bible not based on the literal and historically appropriate understanding of the language was illegitimate. Further, claiming possession of an exegetical tradition to justify such an exegesis was equally illegitimate. Thus rabbinic legal exegesis, which certainly violated Spinoza's interpretive standards, in no way reflected the actual or latent meaning of the text. It was simply the result of flawed presuppositions or primitive thought patterns. How else could the rabbis have come to believe that the text says what it clearly does not? From this it follows that the only practices genuinely demanded by the scriptural text are limited to those explicitly stated therein. As is well known, for Spinoza, even they are valid only during periods of Jewish political sovereignty.

Similarly, many other scholars reflecting on halakhic midrash noted its obfuscation of the biblical text. Richard Simon, the seventeenth-century pioneer of biblical criticism, excoriated the rabbis for their reading of scripture, for their inability or unwillingness to maintain a reasonable understanding of the text.[14] Jacques Basnage, the Huguenot historian of the Jews, noted that rabbinic midrash, which entailed the abandonment of the literal meaning of scripture, was directly responsible for the multiplication of Jewish practices. The result, he insisted, was a religion that enslaved rather than saved.[15]

Denis Diderot, a leading figure of the French Enlightenment, noted that rabbinic midrash could be very helpful in recovering the meaning of the ancient scriptural text, particularly so since Jews remain obligated to perform "certain ceremonies of the law." However, this is mitigated by the fact that "often, instead of seeking the literal sense of scripture, they seek the mystical sense, which causes the obfuscation of the intent of the

---

14 See his *Histoire critique du Vieux Testament* (Rotterdam, 1685), 130ff. Elsewhere he points to Abraham ibn Ezra and Isaac Abravanel as individuals who were partly able to break away from this aspect of rabbinic culture; ibid., 28f., 45, 599.

15 See his *L'histoire et la religion des Juifs depuis Jesus Christ jusqu'à présent* (1709), tome neuvième, première partie, p. 257.

writer, itself sufficiently obscure."[16] While Diderot's comments are directed primarily against aggadic interpretation, halakhic midrash is also included in the indictment.

Even figures otherwise sympathetic to Jews could muster little tolerance for *midrash halakhah* or for the rabbinic culture that proceeded from it. Gotthold Ephraim Lessing, perhaps the most significant figure in the German Enlightenment, and certainly a friend of the Jews, explains the providentially ordained shift from the Old Testament, the first stage in human education, to the New Testament, a higher stage of human education, as follows:

> Every primer is only for a certain age. To delay the child, who has outgrown it . . . is harmful. For to be able to do this in a way that is at all profitable, you must insert into it more than there is really in it, and extract from it more than it can contain. . . . This gives the child a petty, crooked, hairsplitting understanding: it makes him full of mysteries, superstitious, full of contempt for all that is comprehensible and easy. The very way in which the Rabbis handled *their* sacred books. The very character which they thereby imparted to the spirit of their people! A better instructor must come and tear the exhausted primer from the child's hands. Christ came.[17]

The Jews in refusing to advance beyond first grade, as it were, had no choice but to find all kinds of new meanings in their Dick and Jane stories. Accomplishing this required adopting a ridiculous hairsplitting method that read into the text far more than it could reasonably bear.

Johann Gottfried Herder, another figure often sympathetic to Jews, noted that upon the return of the Jews from the Babylonian exile, "Their religion was pharisaism; their learning a minute nibbling at syllables, and this confined to a single book."[18] It is probably safe to say that Herder too was not overly impressed with rabbinic midrash.

The attack on midrash was not limited to historians and scholars. Missionaries of various sorts, posing as scholars, or perhaps the other way around, also got into the act. Luigi Chiarini, an Italian abbot, a professor of Oriental languages at the University of Warsaw in Poland, was hired by the Russian government to translate the Talmud into

---

[16] Denis Diderot, *Oeuvres completes*, ed. J. Assezat, vol. 15 (Paris: Garnier frères, 1876), 372f.

[17] G.E. Lessing, "The Education of the Human Race," in *Lessing's Theological Writings*, ed. and trans. Henry Chadwick (Stanford: Stanford University Press, 1956), 91.

[18] J.G. Herder, *Ideen zur Philosophie der Geschichte der Menschheit*, in *Sämmtliche Werke*, ed. Suphan, vol. 14 (Berlin: Weidmann, 1877), 62.

French, on the assumption that once Jews had unmediated access to this document they would of course recognize how ridiculous it was and how far it stood from the message of Moses' Torah. He prefaced his translation with a two volume work called *Théorie du Judaïsme,* in which he notes among many other things the distorting nature of rabbinic legal interpretation. Similarly the British missionary Alexander McCaul, whose *Old Paths* created quite a sensation in the middle of the nineteenth century. First published as a book in English in 1837, it was almost immediately translated into Hebrew and German, subsequently appearing in French as well. The primary target of McCaul's pen was the superstition and immorality of the aggadic section of the Talmud that found expression in the liturgy. By focusing on the liturgy, McCaul cleverly insulated himself against the counterclaim that the aggadic passages in question were not meant to be taken seriously. If, after all, they found expression in the Piyyutim of the synagogue service, they must have been taken literally and seriously. In any event, although very much a secondary target, *midrash halakhah* also does not fare well in McCaul's treatment. Many *halakhot* derived from scripture are derided by McCaul as obviously false readings, the result of rabbinic lack of charity and inability to read the scriptures correctly.

One could go on and on with this, although it would serve little purpose. It is clear that in the non-Jewish world *midrash halakhah* was regarded with contempt, as a result of which the question of *midrash halakhah* took on a particular urgency for Jews.

My treatment of *midrash halakhah* in *jüdische Wissenschaft* cannot hope to be exhaustive in this paper. I can, however, examine the major figures in the debates, in particular those who developed a new historical picture of the emergence of this genre.

From all that has been said to this point, it is should come as no surprise that those who were hostile to rabbinic halakhah took a very negative view of *midrash halakhah*. Even someone such as Michael Creizenach, for example, while noting the indispensibility of rabbinic interpretations for many biblical passages, nevertheless insists that much rabbinic exegesis distorts the Halakhah and makes it unnecessarily severe. For him, the desired reform of Judaism entails an undoing of this rabbinic midrash and the reestablishment of the less severe premidrashic interpretation.[19]

---

19 See his *Schulchan Aruch,* 4 vols. (1833-1841).

Certainly the most hostile voice against rabbinic midrash in the Reform community was that of Abraham Geiger. While later in his career, from the publication of his *Urschrift* (1857) forward, Geiger was to display a sympathetic attitude to rabbinic exegesis,[20] through the 1840s he emerged as its implacable foe. As he wrote in a notorious essay published in 1841,[21] rabbinic exegesis manifested a "turbid," indeed, a defective, exegetical sense. Everywhere *midrash halakhah* was infected with a ridiculous *Buchstäblichkeit*, here meaning an excessive concern with words, half-words, even letters, ripped from their context and natural meaning.[22]

What is of particular interest in Geiger's essay is that his criticism of *midrash halakhah* explicitly affirms the traditional historical framework in which midrash had generally been seen. On the question of how seriously the midrash was intended as exegesis, Geiger affirms throughout the essay that rabbinic midrash seriously represented what the rabbis thought the verses of scripture actually meant. Later, in response to a critical reaction to his essay—one that argued for Maimonides' position—Geiger explicitly affirms the position taken by Naḥmanides, considering it beyond dispute. For him, there can be no doubt that *midrash halakhah* represented the backbone of the halakhic system, and this fact served to indicate that halakhic practice was devoid of intellectual foundations.[23]

Not only does Geiger affirm the generally accepted position of Naḥmanides, but his writings prior to the *Urschrift* indicate that he accepted the traditionally accepted consensus in favor of the Bavli's approach. Thus Geiger explicitly denies that there is any rabbinic

[20] It seems that Geiger in his later work felt that an attachment to a reformed Judaism could not bypass rabbinic culture, whereas earlier in his career, he focused on those elements of Jewish culture that were at odds with "mainstream" rabbinic thinking as Geiger would have reconstructed it.

[21] That Geiger's essay actually appeared in late 1841 or early 1842 is evident from the material cited by Neubauer, *Ha-Rambam*, 165; and Ismar Schorsch, "Emancipation and the Crisis of Religious Authority: The Emergence of the Modern Rabbinate," in *Revolution and Evolution: 1848 in German-Jewish History*, ed. Werner Mosse et al. (Tübingen: Mohr, 1981), 224 n. 60. This despite the fact that the date given for the publication of the complete volume 5 of the *Wissenschaftliche Zeitschrift* is 1844. See next note.

[22] See his "Das Verhältniss des natürlichen Schriftsinnes zur thalmudischen Schriftdeutung," *Wissenschaftliche Zeitschrift für jüdische Theologie* 5 (1844): 53-81, 234-259. See also his *Lehr- und Lesebuch zur Sprache der Mischnah*, vol. 2, *Lesestücke aus der Mischnah, mit Anmerkungen und einem Glossare versehn* (Breslau, 1845), 7-11.

[23] See his *Nachgelassene Schriften* (New York: Arno Press, 1980), 1:102-105.

exegetical system that is less inclined toward *Buchstäblichkeit*. The various midrashic principles that harness the tendency toward it are considered by Geiger specific exceptions directed *ad locum*. Thus the principle that the Torah speaks in human language is not understood as a general rejection of midrashic excess on the part of an identifiable rabbinic school. It is understood, precisely as in the Bavli, as the refusal of a particular rabbi to apply an otherwise acceptable technique to a specific situation, and no more.[24]

Geiger's acceptance of the traditional understanding of midrashic literature should not surprise us. The attack on midrash buttressed the more general attack on Halakhah. Yet this attack could only be effective if midrash was understood as playing a genuinely creative role in the development of the Halakhah, and if the exegetical defectiveness it displayed applied to the entire rabbinic estate. That is, combining the positions of the Bavli and Naḥmanides provided for the greatest vulnerability, given the distance between halakhic midrash and modern, that is, nineteenth-century, exegetical assumptions. To put this more bluntly, debunking halakhic midrash only made sense if all the significant rabbis really believed that nonsense.

Another interesting example of a reformer who insists on traditional historical assumptions is Samuel Holdheim. He too insists that Naḥmanides (and Rashi as well) understood far better than Maimonides (and Ibn Ezra as well) the nature of rabbinic midrash. The latter made the single Torah into two, placing their faith in *peshaṭ*, while guiding their actions by *derash*. The reality is that such assertions had no place; the rabbis did not recognize the distinction between *peshaṭ* and *derash*, but took their *derashot* very seriously. Of course, as a result, Holdheim can insist that rabbinic exegesis is far inferior to that of the Karaites, and the rabbinic practice is therefore not based on truth.[25]

We may add, not only Geiger and Holdheim, but virtually all modern critics of midrash accepted the traditional position that all rabbis shared the same basic exegetical assumptions, and that midrash was for them the source of Halakhah, and thus the true meaning of scripture.

Of course, one could scarcely expect that traditionally committed voices would remain silent in the face of this onslaught, and indeed they were not. There were two major responses to this barrage of criticism.

---

24 See "Das Verhältniss," 78-80.

25 Samuel Holdheim, *Ma'amar Ishut al Tekhunat ha-Rabbanim veha-Karaim* (Berlin, 5621),. 155–60, esp. n. 1, beginning on p. 156.

The first is to be found in the traditional Bible commentary of the nineteenth century. The century saw a plethora of commentaries emerging from the yeshiva world, all devoted to harmonizing the written and oral laws, thereby placing midrash on sounder footing. I do not wish to deal with this at any length here, except to note that many of these commentators, particularly Naftali Ṣevi Yehudah Berlin (NṢIV) and Yaʿakov Ṣevi Mecklenburg, endorsed a modified version of the position of Maimonides in his debate with Naḥmanides. In effect, they insisted that the *halakhot de-ʾoraita* antedated the development of midrash. Thus midrash is not to be understood as halakhically creative per se. It does, however, create a strong connection between oral and written laws, since, for NṢIV, midrash helped to unlock many of the secrets encoded within the poetic structure of the biblical text. This preference for the Maimonidean position is understandable in light of what we have seen, and we will encounter it among traditionalists yet again.

The second response to the attacks against midrash came from traditionally oriented *Wissenschaft* scholars,[26] and it is here that we first find an entirely new historical conception of the emergence of midrash—one, by the way, that remains the consensus among many scholars to this day.

Heinrich Graetz took the lead in developing this new conception. In the fourth volume of his *Geschichte der Juden*, published in 1853, Graetz revived the Yerushalmi's conception of midrash by insisting that Rabbis

---

[26] My use of the term "traditionally oriented" to refer to Graetz, Fränkel, and Weiss requires some comment. Certainly, the Orthodox would not have recognized them as "traditional." The issue of course is one of perspective; for the purposes of this paper I call TRADITIONALIST anyone who understood their own efforts as being directed toward preserving the tradition in the face of Reform. That they may not have accepted every aspect of Jewish tradition (who did?), and did not claim to, is beside the point. In any event, we must recognize the extent to which the boundaries of tradition are fluid. For example, the rabbinic defenses *Beit Yehudah* and *Zerubabbel* written by Isaac Ber Levinsohn were excoriated by the radical Maskil Yehoshua Heshel Schorr; he viewed them as totally devoid of the critical spirit. As the same time, the erstwhile yeshiva student Moshe Leib Lilienblum describes his reading of *Zerubabbel* as an important stop on his path toward his self-described heresy, for it acknowledged that the Halakhah had a history. From Schorr's perspective these were traditional works masquerading as scholarship, while to Lilienblum they were scholarly works undermining tradition. To add further complexity to the matter, it is reported that R. David Luria of Bikhov in Lithuania, a traditional rabbi of the old school, actually considered Levinsohn's *Zerubabbel* an important work, worthy of being read. Thus the boundaries are hard to draw. Again, for the purposes of this paper, scholars who rejected Reform and sought to defend the tradition, or some major aspects of it, are considered "traditionally oriented."

Akiva and Ishmael represented entirely different approaches to scripture. More than this, Graetz makes explicit what to the redactors of the Yerushalmi was, at best, implicit. He found in R. Ishmael an approach to scripture that was logical and natural. He writes, "[R. Ishmael] represented the natural meaning and, so to speak, healthy human understanding in the interpretation and exegesis of the scriptural laws." Unlike R. Akiva, he understood that the Torah speaks in human language, and therefore contains many concessions to style. Repetitions are mirrors of colloquial usage, as are many other biblical expressions. "His views regarding the relationship of the oral law to scripture are characterized by a judicious, unartificial attitude that seems to be directed particularly against R. Akiva's artificial system of learning." Finally, in one of his notes, Graetz argues that R. Ishmael represents the logical approach to scripture, R. Akiva the allegorical.[27]

In claiming that R. Ishmael's system represents a natural and healthy exegesis, he is locating within the classical rabbinic literature precisely those qualities Geiger insisted it lacked. Indeed, he uses the exact same language as Geiger (e.g., *gesunden Menschenverstand*). Further, despite expressing admiration for many of his accomplishments, Graetz leaves no doubt that he considers R. Akiva's approach to scripture to be, at times, beyond the limits of good judgment. Finally, Graetz makes it clear that the exegesis of scripture adds details to and supplements the existing laws, but the main body of Halakhah originates not in midrash but in the older traditions. Thus where Geiger insisted on combining the positions of the Bavli and Naḥmanides in order to challenge the foundations of Halakhah and rabbinic learning, Graetz affirmed the positions of the Yerushalmi and Maimonides (sufficiently historicized) in order to defend Halakhah and the reputation of rabbinic learning. The Halakhah was the product of a historical process grounded in the life of the people, not in exegesis. Further, when the rabbis sought to understand scripture in light of these traditions, they were not all engaging in excess; some were able to read scripture with a healthy human understanding and still affirm the validity of the traditional Halakhah.

The next to pick up this line of argument was Zechariah Fränkel in his *Darkhei ha-Mishnah*. Relying almost exclusively on the Yerushalmi, Fränkel too put forth the argument that R. Ishmael followed an independent exegetical path opposed to that of R. Akiva. While acknowledging that sometimes R. Akiva's position appears more committed to *peshaṭ*, in

27 See Heinrich Graetz, *Geschichte der Juden*, 4th ed. (Leipzig, 1897), 4:57-59, 394–97.

general, according to Fränkel, R. Ishmael was devoted to *peshaṭ* while R. Akiva often pursued far-fetched interpretations. It was R. Ishmael who insisted that the Torah speaks in human language, and who therefore refrained from fanciful exegeses. It should be noted that both Graetz and Fränkel extend the purview of the principle "the Torah speaks in human language" far beyond the limits of its usage in the Talmud. There it refers strictly to refusal to interpret repetitions; for these two scholars, it symbolizes a general commitment to natural, healthy exegesis.[28]

For Fränkel, too, the position taken by Naḥmanides must be rejected. Fränkel cannot endorse Maimonides' position entirely, for, like Graetz, he cannot affirm that the Halakhah extends back to Sinai. He insists, however, that it is the product of a long, organic process of growth rooted in the life of the Jews, extending back into antiquity. The *midrash halakhah* was designed to find support for this body of Halakhah in scripture, not to actually derive it from scripture. Thus once again the two main features of the earlier consensus, shared by the modern critics of midrash, is rejected.

Next to fall in line was another traditionally oriented scholar, Isaac Hirsh Weiss. Weiss adds little to the discussions of Graetz and Fränkel, except his insistence that R. Ishmael's commitment to the principle that the Torah speaks in human language extends to a rejection of anthropomorphism. The adoption of this principle to explain anthropomorphic usages in the Bible became a staple of medieval Jewish thought; however, such an adoption is unattested before the tenth century.[29] Weiss, however, reads it into R. Ishmael's alleged system, thereby portraying him as deeply committed to rational theology, advancing his stock that much further. In Weiss, far more than in Graetz and Fränkel, we find genuine anger at R. Akiva for developing his far-fetched exegetical system; this anger, it seems to me, is eloquent testimony of Weiss's embarrassment at midrashic excess. Locating rejection of such excess in the rabbinic system rescues it from the judgment that it is based on unsupportable exegesis.[30]

---

28 See *Darkhei ha-Mishnah* (Tel Aviv: Sinai Publishing, 1859), 113.

29 See *inter alia* Wilhelm Bacher, *Die Bibelexegese der jüdischen Religionsphilosophen des Mittelalters vor Maimûni* (Budapest: Országos rabbiképzö intézet, 1892 [repr. Farnborough, England: Gregg International, 1972]), 72 n. 1; idem, *Die Bibelexegese Moses Maimûni's* (Budapest: Országos rabbiképzö intézet, 1896 [repr. Farnborough: Gregg International, 1972), 19-22.

30 Isaac Hirsh Weiss, *Dor Dor ve-Dorshav* (Berlin: Platt and Minkus), 2:101–18. See esp. p. 106.

To be sure, in this "traditionalism" there is substantial deviation from traditional historical conceptions. Not only is the medieval consensus challenged, but the belief in an oral law extending back to Sinai is as well. Thus, some more "traditional" traditionalists were uncomfortable with this shift in historical understanding. Samson Raphael Hirsch, who was particularly sensitive to historiographical motivation, recognized immediately that there was a subtext behind this historical conception. It seems to me, though, that Hirsch missed the point. For to him, what these historians, specifically Graetz, were trying to accomplish was to justify easing the halakhic burden by showing that (way back when) there was a moderate voice within the rabbinic movement, a voice opposed to the Akivan system that prevailed, a voice that can be revived today. He misses the extent to which these scholars limit their discussion to *midrash halakhah*, not halakhic practice, from which midrash is distanced in their presentations. Thus he fails to see that they are defending halakhic observance—by describing midrash as potentially rational, and, in any event, historically secondary—in the face of the attacks outlined earlier. For R. Akiva and R. Ishmael agreed on most religious practices; if R. Akiva justified them *post factum* with far-fetched exegeses, R. Ishmael justified the self-same practices through a more "natural and healthy" exegesis. Thus, both *midrash halakhah* and halakhic practice—if not traditional historical conceptions—are buttressed by this new historiographical model.[31]

If Hirsch's rigid dogmatism blinded him to the possibility that traditional life could be well served by historiographical innovation, a younger German Orthodox rabbi saw this quite clearly. In 1886, David Zvi Hoffmann published his *Zur Einleitung in halakischen Midrasch*, in which he completed the revolution begun by Graetz. Here Hoffmann was not content to simply argue for a systematic exegetical distinction between Rabbis Akiva and Ishmael. He went on to insist that all rabbinic midrash be seen as deriving from one of these two schools. Thus while no previous historian had ever insisted on the connection between the Mekhilta and Sifre Numbers, Hoffmann argued, based almost entirely on the Yerushalmi's conception, now applied to the presumably tannaitic documents, that they each are the product of R. Ishmael's *beit midrash*. Similarly, the Sifra and Sifre Deuteronomy were the product of R.

---

31 See *Collected Writings of Rabbi Samson Raphael Hirsch*, vol. 5 (New York: Feldheim, 1988), 161–71.

Akiva's *beit midrash*.[32] This was a revolutionary historical conception, one that has become the consensus among scholars of midrash, despite a judicious, and in my view correct, critique by Hanokh Albeck.[33] For Hoffmann's work has a strong appeal to those sympathetic to halakhic midrash. Here R. Ishmael's position—the one modern traditionalists like—is not a dissenting voice in a literature dominated by R. Akiva's less appealing midrash but is, rather, an equally dominant voice. Further, he like the others insisted that R. Ishmael was, for the most part, committed to *peshaṭ* and simpler midrashic techniques, and that the midrashic texts attributed to him—fully half of the major bodies of halakhic midrash—displayed this characteristic.[34]

Further, as we might expect, Hoffmann enunciated a categorical endorsement of Maimonides' position, *en passant* in the *Einleitung*, but forcefully in his introduction to his commentary on Leviticus.[35] Thus, in Hoffmann's view, *midrash halakhah* played a primarily supplementary role in the development of Jewish practice. Both Rabbis Akiva and Ishmael were attempting to support this practice by connecting it to

---

[32] David Zvi Hoffmann, *Zur Einleitung in die halakischen Midraschim* (Berlin: Driesner, 1886), passim, esp. pp. 5-12.

[33] See his *Untersuchungen über die halakischen Midraschim* (Berlin: Akademie-Verlag, 1927), passim, esp. pp. 126–39.

[34] He wrote, "Oft gewinnt R. Akiba eine Lehre vermittels tiefer Deutungsregeln aus dem Schrifttexte, während R. Ismael dieselbe Lehre durch einen einfachen logischen Schluss folgert oder aus deutlichen Schriftwort ableitet" (*Zur Einleitung*, 6). At times Hoffmann's claim that R. Ishmael was committed to *peshaṭ* itself involves a "midrashic" reading of his teaching. For example, at *y Shabb.* 9d, Hoffmann sees R. Ishmael's reliance on the word *niddah* as affirming the simple meaning of this word. Actually, R. Ishmael is learning a *gezerah shavah* (inference by analogy), since, viewed philologically, the word *niddah* does not connote temporary disqualification. Only by virtue of its application to a menstruant does it achieve that legal significance.

[35] He wrote, "Wie wir schon vorher bemerkt haben, sind uns sehr viele Bestimmungen der göttlichen Gesetze nicht durch die Schrift, sondern nur durch mündliche Überlieferung mitgetheilt worden. Nun aber haben sich unsere Weisen bemüht, für diese traditionellen Bestimmungen Anhaltspunkte in der Schrift zu finden. Dies gelang ihnen durch ein tieferes Eindringen in den Sinn der Schriftworte oder durch ein tieferes Forschen in der Schrift . . . . Diese Ansicht über den midrasch, welche auch Rambam und viele Andere ausgesprochen haben, wollen wir unsere Schrifterklärung zu Grunde legen. Nach dieser sind die halakhot, die im midrasch aus der Schrift hergeleitet werden nicht erst in Folge dieser derash entstanden, sondern sie sind traditionelle Lehren, für die man nur durch diese derashah einen Anhaltspunkt suchte, entweder um sie besser zu begründen, oder um sie vor Vergessenheit zu bewahren" (*Das Buch Leviticus, übersetzt und erklärt von Dr. D. Hoffmann* erster Halbband [Berlin: Verlag M. Poppelauer, 1905], 3f.).

scripture. In this activity, R. Ishmael was guided by exegetical assumptions quite hospitable to the modern mind. The Halakhah, then, is not the product of twisted exegetical minds, as many of its opponents would insist. It is the product of revealed traditions, supported by two distinct exegetical systems, one of which was devoted to simple, logical deductions from the biblical text.

What emerges from this brief overview of *midrash halakhah* in modern historical treatment is that with the shift in values accompanying the advent of the modern age, traditional historical assumptions are often held by opponents of tradition. On the other hand, those committed to the continuity of traditional values and practices who eschew seeking refuge from modern historical scholarship are compelled to develop new historical models, or, more accurately, to revive old ones that had ceased to address the needs of earlier traditionalists, to successfully orient themselves in their chosen world. In other words, the traditional segment of the world of *jüdische Wissenschaft* had to reshape tradition in order to rescue it.

11

The Retrieval of Innocence and Tradition: Jewish Spiritual Renewal in an Age of Liberal Individualism

PAUL MENDES-FLOHR

A Second Naiveté

It is told that on a stroll in a Berlin park Franz Kafka met a little girl weeping over the loss of her doll. Kafka sought to comfort her, explaining that the doll merely went for a trip, and in fact he had just seen and spoken to her. And Kafka added that the doll had promised with all her heart that she would send her, the little girl, a letter from time to time. "Come to the park again tomorrow and I will bring you a letter from her." And so he did, and every morning for weeks on end he would bring the little girl a letter from her wandering doll. The correspondence ceased only when increasingly grave tuberculosis obliged Kafka to return to Prague and then to enter a sanatorium, where he died several months later. Before leaving Berlin, he sent the girl a new doll, but (heaven forbid) not as a replacement, because she could have no replacement. Although the new doll was obviously different, Kafka insisted she was actually the same. He explained this paradox to the girl in the letter accompanying the doll. Due to the influence of her adventures in distant and strange lands, the doll's appearance had changed, but she was in essence, nonetheless, the same.[1]

This tale is related by the late Israeli philosopher Ernst Akiva Simon (1899-1988) to illustrate what he celebrates as a "second naiveté," that innocence which is necessary to regain faith after having experienced the purgatory of secularization.[2] But the tale of Kafka's efforts to comfort the child over the loss of her doll may also be understood as a parable of the desired "second naiveté" itself. The doll—the original innocence—is lost; and what eventually comes in its place is not really a replacement but merely bears the marks of its travels to distant and alien lands. The doll redivivus—the second innocence—has a different countenance because she cannot, and perhaps does not wish to, rid herself of the memories and all she has learned during her journeys. Such, indeed, is the "second naiveté" of which Simon, following the Catholic philosopher Peter Wust (1884–1940), speaks.[3] The attitude that allows the children of the Enlightenment to affirm religious faith bears within its bosom the doubts, uncertainties, and skepticism attendant to the secular experience. Faith is achieved not by denying or rejecting the insights and sensibilities of modern, secular culture; rather they are honored and, as a Hegelian would say, *aufgehoben*, sublated and integrated into a new cognitive posture. While remaining alert to the critical concern of the secular order, a "second naiveté" allows one to encounter the Presence of God, to be open to the transcendent claims of tradition, and to humble oneself in prayer.

The difficulty of achieving this second innocence is perhaps no more poignantly depicted than by Kafka. He desperately sought such an innocence in love and in faith, and both eluded him. His encounter with the

---

[1] This tale was first related to Max Brod by Kafka's companion, Dora Dymant. Brod published it in the New York German Jewish journal *Der Aufbau* (19 August 1963) and later included it in his *Brod über Kafka* (Frankfurt a.M.: Insel, 1966), 339. When I told this charming anecdote to a colleague, Yaron Ezrahi, he commented that Kafka's delightful playfulness was presumably prompted by an eagerness to preserve for the child a coherent world, a world that supported her "naive" expectation of a just order to things. Knowing that in the "adult" world this expectation will surely be disappointed, Yaron further remarked, Kafka's intent effort to protect the child may have been "as much an act of self-pity as it was compassion."

[2] E. Simon, "ʾaz ʾitam. ʿal ha-tmimut ha-sheniah," [On the Second Naiveté], in idem, *Haʾim ʿod yehudim ʾanahnu. Masot* (*Are We Still Jews? Essays*) (in Hebrew) (Tel Aviv: Sifriat Poʿalim, 1982), 164.

[3] Peter Wust, *Naivität und Pietät* (1925), in him *Gesammelte Schriften* (Münster: Regensberg, 1964), vol. 2.

little girl, which took place shortly before his death two weeks shy of his forty-first birthday, was but a game, a fantasy he shared with the girl, a brief interlude in his tortured life buffeted by ambivalence, fear, and distrust. His fanciful play with the child was no more than an indication of what he longed for but knew that the adult world which he perforce inhabited denied him.

Kafka understood his existence, and that of each of us, to be under the curse of the expulsion from Paradise.[4] Having eaten of the Tree of Knowledge, we are no longer able to behold the divine Presence in spontaneous innocence. Eager to taste the fruit of the Tree of Knowledge, we deprived ourselves of the nurture of the Tree of Life. To be sure, Kafka acknowledged, with the revelation of His Torah God graced us with another opportunity to gain access to the Tree of Life. He well realized that the revealed Torah—the divine Law which frees life of its ever-confounding ambiguities and provides existence with a coherent, just structure—is, as the rabbis proclaim, the Tree of Life. But for Kafka, a denizen of the modern world, the Law is no longer intelligible, and although he so profoundly wished to comprehend it, he could not.

Upon reading Kafka's *The Castle*, the religious philosopher Franz Rosenzweig (1886–1929) wrote that he "never read a book that reminded me so much of the Bible as [this] novel [. . .], and that is why reading it certainly cannot be called a pleasure."[5] Commenting on Rosenzweig's observation that Kafka's novel presents a genuinely biblical problem, Nahum Glatzer explains:

> With the expulsion from Paradise man lost his name (Kafka's heroes go mainly by initials), lost his language (there is no real communication), lost his love (only sex remains); time which could be man's is now confused, distorted, paralyzed eternity. Man (K), World (village), and God (Castle) exist, but their existence is not correlated.[6]

Glatzer adds, "Rosenzweig meets man exactly where Kafka left him."[7] Rosenzweig would indicate how the divide which separates human

---

4 See Nahum N. Glatzer, "Franz Kafka and the Tree of Knowledge," in *Arguments and Doctrines: A Reader of Jewish Thinking in the Aftermath of the Holocaust*, ed. Arthur A. Cohen (Philadelphia: Jewish Publication Society, 1970), 86-97.

5 Rosenzweig to Gertrud Oppenheim, 25 May 1927, *Briefe*, ed. Edith Rosenzweig and Ernst Simon (Berlin: Schocken, 1935), 596.

6 Glatzer, Introduction to Rosenzweig, *Understanding the Sick and the Healthy: A View of World, Man and God* (New York: Noonday, 1954), 19f.

7 Ibid., 20.

beings from one another and ultimately from God may be overcome. His friend Martin Buber (1878-1965) assumed the same task, although his strategy would be different. Both sought to guide their fellow Jews in attaining what their common disciple Ernst Simon called a "second naiveté."

Kafka's Predicament

Despite his passionate yearning for such an innocence, Kafka's skepticism and distrust were probably too unbending to yield to the theological discourse of Buber and Rosenzweig. Although he seems not to have known Rosenzweig, whose major writings were not yet widely circulated before Kafka passed away, he did know Buber personally and was inspired by several of Buber's Hasidic stories, which, transmuted, found their way into his writings.[8] But he was also frightened by the implicit appeal to folk solidarity borne by Buber's Hasidic tales.[9] Not that Kafka lacked such sentiments, but Jewish responsibility based solely on such sentiments he found oppressive and unacceptable. He would require something more, and whatever that power might be, he feared he would never have the resolve to accept it.

His incorrigible ambivalence pinioned his ability to affirm anything with certainty, with unbridled conviction. All relations and commitments could at most be engaged in with a wary tentativeness, and thus would invariably falter. He passionately yearned for relationships and commitment, and yet he could not fully allow himself either. As a Jew he longed for the innocence of faith and an unambiguous bond to his people and its traditions, but his recurrent efforts to achieve a creative relationship to Judaism and the Jewish people all led to an emotional cul-de-sac.

Kafka has been regarded as an emblem of the modern Jew, for he seems to give expression to the predicament of the modern Jewish experience, albeit in an extreme and hyperbolic fashion. He himself thought

---

[8] On Kafka's relation to Buber and his indebtedness to him, see my "Fin-de-siècle Orientalism and the Aesthetics of Jewish Self-Affirmation," in my *Divided Passions. Jewish Intellectuals and the Experience of Modernity* (Detroit: Wayne State University Press, 1991), ch. 3: 80, 83, 100.

[9] Ronald Hayman, *Kafka: A Biography* (New York: Oxford University Press, 1982), 299. Cf. "What have I in common with Jews? I have hardly anything in common with myself and should stand very quietly in a corner, content that I could breathe." Kafka, *Diaries, 1914–1923*, ed. Max Brod, trans. M. Greenberg and H. Arendt (New York: Schocken, 1949). Entry dated January 8, 1924.

of himself as "the most typical west European Jew." As he wrote to a lady friend:

> This means, expressed with exaggeration, that not one calm second is granted me, nothing is granted me, everything has to be earned, not only the present and the future, but the past too—something after all which perhaps every human being has inherited, this too must be earned, it is perhaps the hardest work. When the Earth turns to the right—I'm not sure that it does—I would have to turn to the left to make up for the past. But as it is I haven't the least particle of strength for these obligations, I can't carry the world on my shoulders, can barely stand my winter coat on them.[10]

Kafka's predicament was, *mutatis mutandis*, indeed shared by his fellow Western Jews: How to retrieve the Jewish past and an innocent faith without forfeiting knowledge; how to affirm traditional wisdom without undergoing a mental lobotomy excising Western culture and secular sensibilities? How to eat of the Tree of Knowledge and partake in the sweetness of the Tree of Life?

Religious Faith and Liberal Individualism

Sociologically, Kafka's—and the modern Jew's—predicament may also be understood as that of one trapped by the ethic of liberal individualism. The Western, or liberal, ideal of liberty held that one is first and foremost a human being, an individual. Unencumbered by feudal restrictions, an individual's fortunes were now to be determined solely by one's talents, enterprise, and merit. Graced by liberty, one was also accorded the right to define oneself independent of one's inherited culture and its expectations; under the banner of liberty, one need not acknowledge any primordial loyalties. One was free to develop one's own personality, interests, and talents in utter disregard of the dictates and precepts of one's parents' tradition. But the ethic of a free individualism[11] has also often meant isolation, and a loss of genuine community.

---

[10] *Letters to Melina*, ed. Willi Haas, trans. Tania and James Stern (New York: Schocken, 1953), 219.

[11] "Free individualism" is a term used in German discourse; it is virtually equivalent to what in a recent sociological study of the American ethos has been called "expressive individualism": a view "that each person has a unique core of feeling and intuition that should unfold or be expressed if individuality is to be realized." Robert N. Bellah, Richard Madsen, et al., *Habits of the Heart. Individualism and*

As former residents of the Ghetto, Jews were naturally drawn to the ideal of liberty and in ever-increasing numbers embraced the ethic of a free individualism. With the emancipation the Jewish individual was liberated; her or his talent and enterprise were duly rewarded. The annals of the modern world amply record the many splendid achievements of talented and enterprising Jews.[12] To be sure, in pursuit of their personal dignity and well-being not all Jewish votaries of the liberal ethos felt obliged to break with Jewish tradition, but surely to varying degrees many did.[13]

Perhaps they were beguiled by the vision of the German writer Johann Gottfried Herder (1744–1803) that in the new liberal order "no one will any longer ask who is a Jew and who is a Christian."[14] One assumed that despite all the nasty resistance to the new order, and especially to the Jew's putative role in it, one's background was ultimately irrelevant. The liberal era was said to pave the way to a Neutral Society in which the accidents of one's birth would be "neutralized" and rendered insignificant.[15] But the liberal order, as the historian Jacob Katz has observed, was not quite—and perhaps could never be—as neutral as envisioned by its more febrile prophets, for it was hardly bereft of particular historical memories and ethnic and religious sentiments.[16]

Even in the most insistently liberal countries a "civil religion" arose to occupy the space supposedly reserved for the "neutral" society.[17] A

Commitment in American Life (New York: Harper & Row, 1985), 333f. For a differentiation of various types of individualism, see Ibid., 332–36.

[12] Jews, of course, still faced many obstacles placed in their way by anti-Semitism and general prejudice against minorities.

[13] Viewing Jewish secularization from the perspective of the ethic of free individualism may add needed nuance to an understanding of Jewish acculturation and assimilation, which, in my opinion, is inadequately characterized as a process of self--abnegating accommodation to non-Jewish culture and society.

[14] J.G. Herder, *Reflections on the Philosophy of the History of Mankind,* trans. T. O. Churchill, abridged and ed. by Frank E. Manuel (Chicago: University of Chicago Press, 1968), 15.

[15] Jacob Katz, *Tradition and Crisis: Jewish Society at the End of the Middle Ages* (New York: Free Press of Glencoe, 1961), p245–59.

[16] Accordingly, Katz argues that at best one must speak of a "semi-neutral society": *Out of the Ghetto: The Social Background of Jewish Emancipation, 1770-1870* (Cambridge: Harvard University Press, 1973), pp.42-56.

[17] Coined by Rousseau (*The Social Contract*, bk. 4, ch. 8) but largely forgotten, the term "civil religion" was reintroduced and given a sociological definition by Robert Bellah, "Civil Religion in America," *Daedalus* (Winter 1967), reprinted in idem, *Beyond Belief. Essays on Religion in a Post-Traditional World* (New York: Harper and Row, 1970), 168–86. Bellah underscores that although it draws from the historical religions,

public culture emerged embroidered with an eclectic skein of symbols, myths, and rites drawn from the historical experience of the nation and often from the dominant religion. Hence, in virtually all liberal societies in the West, public culture was in effect colored by what may be best characterized as a laicized Christianity. In the employ of the "laity" and shared social and cultural values, the Christian motifs of the civil religion, it may be claimed, were so theologically diluted as to be rendered innocuous. The laicized Christianity of the civil religion became offensive only when enjoined by true believers (i.e., those who insisted on the pristine theological contents of that which was borrowed from Christianity), or when harnessed to an ethnic nationalism. As such, civil religion manifestly conflicted with the liberal ethos.[18]

By projecting shared values and purpose, civil religion may be viewed as the modern state's attempt to provide a sense of community and thereby compensate for the loss or at least attenuation, of traditional religious and communal bonds.[19] From this perspective, nationalism may be viewed as an intensification of civil religion and the attendant sense of community.[20] The more passionate the nationalism, the greater the sense of community and *a fortiori* the more it threatens the liberal ethic of a free individualism. Needless to say, Jewish liberals in particular would be

---

civil religion has its own integrity with its own distinctive set of sacred persons, events, beliefs, rituals, and symbols. As a result of Bellah's article, much scholarly attention has been given to the concept. See, for example, the superb collection, *American Civil Religion,* ed. Russell E. Richey and Donald G. Jones (New York: Harper and Row, 1974).

18 Civil religion and nationalism need not be antagonistic to liberalism. American civil religion, for instance, is said to support "a synergistic religious cosmopolitanism" and "republican beliefs" that unite and transcend the multiple ethnic and religious groups that make up the United States; see Sidney E. Mead, "The Nation with the Soul of a Church," in *American Civil Religion,* 45-75. Challenging the charge of the inherent illiberality of nationalism, the British historian John Plamenatz reminds us that nationalism often has a democratic and liberal impulse: "Two Types of Nationalism," in *Nationalism: The Nature and Evolution of an Idea,* ed. Eugene Kamenka (London: Edward Arnold, 1976), 22-36. On the relation of nationalism and religion, see J.H. Carlton Hayes's classic study on the subject, *Essays on Nationalism* (New York: Macmillan, 1926), ch. 4.

19 See Mead, "Nation with the Soul of a Church," 65-71. We have, of course, examples, such as the effort of the Jacobins in revolutionary France, deliberately to design a civil religion to displace the historical religions in a given society. See Robert Nisbet, "Civil Religion." *The Encyclopedia of Religion,* ed. Mircea Eliade (New York: Macmillan, 1987), 3:525.

20 See George L. Mosse, "Mass Politics and the Political Liturgy of Nationalism," in Kamenka, *Nationalism,* 38-54.

threatened by a civil religion bearing the exclusive inflections of Christianity and ethnic nationalism.

Here, the experience of German Jewry is most instructive. Due to the peculiar circumstances of their emancipation, German Jewry identified the liberal order with *Bildung,* the humanistic culture of learning and aesthetic refinement.[21] *Bildung,* as George Mosse has recently pointed out in his masterful monograph, *German Jews beyond Judaism,* became the civil religion of German Jewry.[22] The tragedy was that in time the culture of *Bildung* became nigh-exclusively the civil religion of German Jews and theirs alone (although they continued to the very end, across the threshold of Auschwitz, to view it—and themselves—as quintessentially German). The isolation they felt was thus twofold. First, they were estranged from German nationalism, the civil religion of the majority of Germans;[23] and second, they experienced an existential isolation—the anguished lost community—of a consequential liberal. In addressing this situation, Buber and Rosenzweig, who together became the focus of a veritable spiritual renaissance of German Jewry, demonstrated an acute sensitivity to the predicament of their fellow Jews.

Buber and Jewish Renewal

Both Buber and Rosenzweig realized that the challenge posed by the liberal predicament was not simply to provide German Jews with their own civil religion and ethnic nationalism. Both appreciated that, though disaffected by the ethic of a free individualism, German Jewry was for the most part not ready to compromise other liberal values. The paroch-

[21] On the formation of the distinctive German-Jewish identity, see David Sorkin, *The Transformation of German Jewry 1780-1840* (New York: Oxford University Press, 1987).

[22] "The centrality of *Bildung* in German-Jewish consciousness must be understood from the very beginning—it was basic to Jewish engagement with liberalism and socialism, fundamental to the search for a new Jewish identity after emancipation. The concept of *Bildung* became for many Jews synonymous with Jewishness. . . . [The concept of *Bildung*] easily provided a new identity for many articulate and intellectual German Jews, for despite its emphasis on the individual and the critical mind, it could be lifted into immutability and become a secular religion" (G. Mosse, *German Jews beyond Judaism* [Bloomington: Indiana University Press; Cincinnati: Hebrew Union College, 1985], 4, 18).

[23] A given society may have a variety of competing, contradictory, and overlapping civil religions, which in turn may be understood differently by each of its members. See Martin E. Marty, "Two Kinds of Two Kinds of Civil Religion," in *American Civil Religion,* 139–57.

ialism of ethnic nationalism could hardly appeal to one who still adhered to the universal vision of liberal humanism; and the external, seemingly contrived, trappings of a civil religion could hardly satisfy the spiritual yearnings of many of their generation. Accordingly, Buber and Rosenzweig taught that the renewal of Jewish community must be grounded in the renewal of Judaism as a spiritual reality of transcendent and thus universal significance.

Buber made his debut as a Jewish teacher when in 1909 he accepted an invitation to address the Bar Kochba Association of Jewish university students of Prague. These students, who included the likes of Shmuel Hugo Bergmann, Max Brod, Franz Kafka, Hans Kohn, and Felix and Robert Weltsch, turned to Buber, whom they had known previously as a writer on Zionist cultural affairs and the author of two volumes on Hasidism,[24] to instruct them as to how they as assimilated urban youth "could convert what remains of Jewish existence into their own."[25] In appealing to the then thirty-two-year-old Buber to make the journey from Berlin to Prague, they noted that "we have nobody in the West, or anywhere else for that matter, who can interpret Jewish being as sensitively as you."[26] What they meant was that Buber presented a view of Jewish spirituality that was beholden to neither the Orthodox nor the Liberal conception of Judaism—both of which they found jejune and objectionable.[27]

Buber developed a special relationship with the Bar Kochba Association and would return annually to Prague to deliver an address and hold workshops. His first three addresses, published together in one slim volume, *Drei Reden über das Judentum (1909–1911)*[28] became the vade mecum of several generations of young German-speaking Jews in search

---

[24] Buber, *Die Geschichten des Rabbi Nachman* (Frankfurt a.M.: Rutten & Loening, 1906); *Die Legende des Baal Schem* (Frankfurt a.M.: Rutten & Loening, 1907).

[25] Leo Herrmann to Martin Buber, 14 November 1908, *Martin Buber: Briefwechsel aus sieben Jahrzehnten*, ed. Grete Schaeder (Heidelberg: Lambert Schneider, 1972), 1:269.

[26] Ibid.

[27] On Buber and the Bar Kochba Association, see Leo Hermann, "Erinnerungen an Bubers 'Drei Reden' in Prag," *Mitteilungsblatt der Hitachdut Olej Germania* (Tel Aviv) no. 48 (26 November 1971):4f.; Hans Kohn, *Martin Buber: Sein Werk und seine Zeit. Ein Beitrag zur Geistesgeschichte Mitteleuropas 1880-1930*, 2nd rev. ed. (Cologne: Joseph Melzer, 1961), 90f., 314f.

[28] *Drei Reden über das Judentum* (Frankfurt a.M.: Rutten & Loening, 1911), 102. These addresses, together with other speeches he gave to the Bar Kochba Association of Prague, have been translated in Buber, *On Judaism*, ed. Nahum N. Glatzer (New York: Schocken, 1967).

of Jewish community, guiding them in their initial steps back to a spiritually meaningful Judaism.[29]

Buber spoke as a Zionist. In contrast to political and cultural Zionists, however, he spoke of the "personal Jewish question."[30] He spoke to the INDIVIDUAL Jew, acknowledging "the great ambivalence, the boundless despair ... and pathetic inner chaos of many of today's Jews."[31] He told Jewish youth disaffected with their parents' assimilation and with bourgeois ideals that human personality could never achieve fulfillment in isolation. Human personality, he averred, only truly flowers in community and in the acceptance of a call to super-personal tasks.

What these tasks might be was no longer clear, however. They cannot be determined, Buber emphasized, by a mere return to Jewish tradition, by a return to "inherited custom" primed by a sense of fidelity, a desire for continuity, or a conviction that tradition per se is the fount of Jewish authenticity. An affirmation of tradition out of motives extraneous to faith cannot but deaden true religious sensibility, for while "tradition constitutes the noblest freedom for a generation that lives it meaningfully, . . . it is the most miserable slavery for the habitual inheritors who merely accept it, tenaciously and complacently."[32] Pride and defiance, even when clothed in the garments of tradition, cannot be the basis of a spiritually truthful Jewish existence. Judaism must once again become an "autonomous reality"[33]—a spiritual power that is neither contrived nor feigned, but existentially genuine, and thus compelling. That Judaism could be such a power was Buber's most fundamental and abiding conviction.

It was also Buber's conviction that the renewal of Judaism as a spiritual power could not be effected by the mere adoption of a set of creeds and ritual practices. Even the affirmation of a Jewish national identity,

---

[29] "[Buber's *Drei Reden*] exuded a considerable magic in their time. I would be unable to mention any other book about Judaism of these years, which even came close to having such an effect . . . among a youth that here heard the summons to a new departure" (G. Scholem, "Martin Buber's Conception of Judaism," in idem, *On Jews and Judaism in Crisis: Selected Essays*, ed. and trans. W. J. Dannhauser [New York: Schocken, 1976], 138). See also Chaim Schatzker, "Martin Buber's Influence on the Jewish Youth Movement in Germany," *Leo Baeck Institute Year Book* 23 (1978): 151–71.

[30] "Judaism and the Jews," in *On Judaism*, 19. "Judaism and the Jews" was Buber's first Prague address.

[31] "Renewal of Judaism," in *On Judaism*, 39. "Renewal of Judaism" was Buber's third Prague address.

[32] "Judaism and the Jews," 11.

[33] Ibid., 13.

although necessary, is insufficient.[34] Indeed, Jewish renewal is not a question of renewing this or that aspect, doctrine, or practice.[35]

For Judaism is a multifarious, ongoing "spiritual process" (*geistiger Prozess*)[36] which one only distorts when one seeks to grasp it creedally and ritually. Orthodox and Liberal attempts to define the "essence" of Judaism, in fact, have done a grave disservice to Judaism as a creative spiritual process—a process, moreover, that unfolds in the life of Jewish individuals and not in creedal catechisms or ritual manuals.[37] Accordingly, Buber also rejected an "elitist" conception of Jewish renewal and warned that the flourishing of Jewish literature and scholarship may be misleading:

> This is the danger threatening the Jewish people: that it may lose the life of the spirit. We cannot comfort ourselves that the danger has passed by pointing to the flourishing of a new literature or to any other values we are accustomed to calling "Jewish Renaissance," an expression of hope rather than reality.[38]

Genuine renewal "must originate in deeper regions of the people's spirit,"[39] that is, Judaism must be renewed as a spiritual process engaging the life—the existence, the imagination, the soul—of the Jewish individual. "Only such a life can create not merely an aggressive or defensive but a positive consciousness of peoplehood."[40]

Only when the individual Jew feels him or herself to be part of a spiritual process shared with fellow Jews can one properly speak of a renewal

---

34 Rather than "nationality," Buber preferred to speak of *Volkstümlichkeit* and *Volkstum,* terms derived, of course, from the German term *Volk* 'folk, people'. Relying on meanings German Romanticism attached to these terms, Buber regarded *Volk* as preeminently a spiritual and moral entity, and "nationality" as a political phenomenon. See my detailed discussion in "The Politics of Covenantal Responsibility: Martin Buber's Hebrew Humanism," in *Divided Passions,* ch. 8: 194-206.

35 "Nor is it enough for only single ideas to be renewed, whether it be one or another, or even the one and the other" (Buber, "Renewal of Judaism," 54).

36 Ibid., 39; "Erneuerung des Judentums," in *Drei Reden,* 71.

37 In consonance with this position, Buber made a distinction between "religion," or the formal and institutional organization of faith, and "religiosity," or the spontaneous, expressive manifestation of faith. In light of this distinction, he asserted that the "renewal of Judaism means in reality renewal of Jewish religiosity. . . . I say and mean: religiosity. I do not say and do not mean: religion" ("Jewish Religiosity," in *On Judaism,* 79f).

38 "Renewal of Judaism," 53.

39 Ibid.

40 Ibid.

of Judaism. As such, each Jew must feel a personal responsibility for Jewish existence:

> Once, [the individual Jew] arrived at a sense of belonging [to the Jewish people] out of external experience; now, out of an internal one. On the first level, his people represented the world to him; now they represent his soul. The people are now for him a community of [human beings] who were, are, and will be—a community of the dead, the living, and the yet unborn—who, together, constitute a unity. It is this unity that, to him, is the ground of his I, this I which is fitted as a link into the great chain. [. . .] Whatever all the [individuals] in this great chain have created and will create he conceives to be the work of his own unique being; whatever they have experienced and will experience he conceives to be his own destiny. The past of his people is his personal memory, the future of his people his personal task.[41]

This sense of responsibility, Buber tirelessly reiterated, flows out of participation in the spiritual process of Judaism and, accordingly, cannot be simply evoked by an act of affirmation and sacred pledges, or even charitable or communal deeds. These are external acts, and although they may engender welcome feelings of solidarity, they do not touch the "deeper reality" of Judaism as an inner, spiritual process, which Buber deemed to be the ultimate ground of Judaism as an enduring and existentially meaningful community of faith.

And since the "deeper reality" of Judaism as a spiritual process cannot be defined in abstract terms, and allegiance to a particular conception of Jewish deed and practice is beside the point, access to the spiritual process, in Buber's judgment, can only be attained through the study of the sacred texts of Judaism—the Bible, Midrash, Kabbalah and Hasidica,[42] "the scroll of words and deeds whose letters tell the chronicle of [the Jewish] people's relation to its God"[43] and record the recurrent struggle of Israel, from the Patriarchs to the Baal Shem Tov—to find symbols and a language to express this relation. Re-connecting with this corpus of symbols and language allows the individual Jew to find a way to articu-

---

[41] "Judaism and the Jews," 15f.

[42] It has often been pointed out that Buber was rather selective in the sacred texts of Jewish tradition he considered worthy of attention, neglecting those sources that did not conform to his conception of Jewish spirituality, for instance, halakhic writings. See Scholem, "Buber's Conception of Judaism," 130–41.

[43] "Herut: On Youth and Religion," in *On Judaism*, 154f.

late his or her own personal struggle to comprehend the encounter with the Divine:

> How could an adequate response develop in individual man, how could he even conceive of an appropriate symbol, were he not part of the continuity of mankind's spiritual process? Response and symbol, however, are given to individual man directly only in the absolute, that is, the religiously creative, life of his people. Here mankind's wordless dialogue with God is condensed for him into the language of the soul, which he is not merely able to understand, but to which he himself can add new expressions, as yet unspoken. Without this language, he could do no more than stammer and falter. . . . Without a bond to his people, man remains amorphous and adrift when God calls him; it is only from this bond that he derives contour and substance, so that he can dare to confront his Caller.[44]

Jewish education is, then, not a question of Jewish erudition, a mastery of Jewish texts and knowledge. On the other hand, familiarity with—if not mastery of—the sacred texts of Jewish tradition is indispensable. Hence, Buber declared that Jewish youth bent on a renewal of Judaism

> must no longer permit itself the illusion that it can establish a decisive link to its people merely by reading Bialik's poems or by singing Yiddish folksongs; nor by the addition of a few quasi-religious sentiments and lyricisms. It must realize that something bigger is at stake: that one must join, earnestly and ready for much struggle and work, in Judaism's intense creative process, with all its conflicts and subsequent reconciliations; that one must recreate this process from within, with reverence of soul and awareness of mind. . . . The idea of renewal must not . . . degenerate into a comfortable slogan that would exempt us from the effort of struggling, studying, and building, a slogan in which the emotions may luxuriate and the mind go slack.[45]

For Buber, the renewal of Judaism as a spiritual process—as is suggested by the German term *Geist*, which means both spirit and mind—had a decisive intellectual dimension. Jewish renewal thus requires a resolve to participate anew in the ever-unfolding process of Jewish learning and "spiritual creativity":

> We must therefore reject commitment to a claim that Jewish teaching is something finished and unequivocal. For us, it is neither. It is, rather, a gigantic process, still uncompleted, of

---

[44] Ibid., 155f.

[45] Ibid., 159f.

> spiritual creativity and creative response to the unconditional. It is in this process that we want to participate with our conscious, active life, in the hope that we, too, may not be denied a creative spark. But to achieve this participation, we must fully discern this process—discern not merely some of its isolated aspects or effects, not only maxims or theses, but, in earnest awareness, its whole development up to the present, recreating it in its entirety from within.[46]

Buber explored various hermeneutical strategies for revitalizing this process, which was threatened in the modern period with utter ossification, finally focusing on what he called the dialogical principle. But it would, of course, be mistaken to understand dialogue as merely a principle for reading sacred texts and retrieving their meaning. For Buber, reading these texts dialogically bore directly upon the overarching and urgent goal of living a Jewish life of personal fulfillment and responsibility.

Buber attached to the study of sacred texts not only hermeneutical and existential significance, however. The study of these texts also had an intrinsic theological import. Representing a realm of "unconditionality," the "absolute"—or what Buber's friend, Paul Tillich the Protestant theologian called "ultimate concern"—sacred literature and its study serve to detach one from the immediate environment (*Umwelt*) of mundane cares and objectives. "Unbinding our soul from the utilitarian bustle [of everyday life]," the study of sacred texts directs one toward "unconditional" truths and tasks.[47]

Sacred detachment from the mundane, of course, is but a dialectical pause: spiritually requickened by the study of sacred texts, one returns to the here and now. For

> renewal must also mean . . . that the spirit enters life. Only when Judaism once again reaches out, like a hand, grasping each Jew by the hair of his head and carrying him, in the tempest raging between heaven and earth, toward Jerusalem, as the hand of the Lord once grasped and carried Ezekiel, the priest, in the land of the Chaldeans—only then will the Jewish people be ready to build a new destiny for itself where the old one once broke into fragments. The bricks may be, indeed must be, assembled now; but the house can be built only when the people have once more become builders.[48]

---

[46] Ibid., 164.
[47] "Renewal of Judaism," 55.
[48] Ibid., 54.

By reintegrating his or her life into the spiritual fabric of the Jewish community, Buber taught, the individual Jew acquires not only a language and symbolic universe allowing for personal fulfillment, namely, the ability for a cogent and sustained spiritual expression. *Pari passu,* he or she also becomes a "builder" in the reconstruction of Judaism battered by the confusions attendant to the entry of Jewry into the liberal order initiated by the French Emancipation.

Rosenzweig and Jewish Renewal

"Builders" is an image borrowed from a famous midrash: And all thy children shall be taught of the Lord, and great shall be the peace of thy children! (Isaiah, 54:13). Do not read *'banayikh'*, thy children, but *'bonayikh'*, thy builders.[49] Referring to the same midrash, Rosenzweig questioned Buber's summary rejection of the *miṣvot,* the traditional ritual precepts set by tradition, as the proper context of Jewish spirituality and divine service.[50] Since these precepts have been codified as laws strictly regulating the spiritual life of the Jew, Buber concurred with those who dismissed the *miṣvot* as a heteronomous distortion of biblical teachings, and insisted that "God is not a lawgiver, and therefore the Law has no universal validity for me."[51]

Rosenzweig criticized Buber for yielding to Western bias regarding traditional Jewish ritual practice, which has been ironically supported by the defensive posture of modern Orthodoxy and its efforts to shield the tradition with the protective mantle of a Law demanding unswerving obedience. Had Buber sought to consider the *miṣvot* phenomenologically, Rosenzweig commented, he would have readily acknowledged that as experienced—as lived—by the pious Jew the *miṣvot* are hardly laws but are a rhapsodic occasion to behold God's Presence. On the basis of this observation, Rosenzweig formulated a theological principle for Jewish renewal: Regarded as a personal address, the *miṣvot* may, in fact, be the occasion for renewing the individual Jew's dialogue with God.

Buber failed to see this possibility, Rosenzweig implied, for he misunderstood the dialectical nature of tradition. Reenactment of the rituals and rites, the *miṣvot,* performed by one's ancestors is not to be construed as an atavistic exercise depriving one of the freedom of an autonomous

49 Midrash Seder Eliyahu, ch. 17; cf. *b. Berachot,* end.

50 "The Builders: Concerning the Law," in F. Rosenzweig, *On Jewish Learning,* ed. N.N. Glatzer (New York: Schocken, 1965), 72-92.

51 Buber to Franz Rosenzweig, 13 July 1924, cited in *On Jewish Learning,* 115.

expression of devotion. Jewish tradition, Rosenzweig argued, is rather informed by a unique dialectic whereby one is by virtue of the very same ritual act both the child of his or her ancestors and one's grandchildren's ancestor. Through renewing the *miṣvot*—to be sure, renewed with passion and existential integrity—one's becomes a vital link in an ever-renewing eternity, an eternity that allows Jewry to attain the sacred detachment that Buber was prepared to find only in the study of sacred texts:

> For what may be a hard task for the other nations, that is to turn back in [i.e., resist] the onrushing stream of life—because they consider themselves united by time and space [i.e., secular history and territory] and only on festive days and in hours of destiny do they feel as members in a chain of generations—this is just the very basis of our communal and individual life: the feeling of being our fathers' children, our grandchildren's ancestors. Therefore we might rightly expect to find ourselves again, at some time, somehow, in our fathers' every word and deed; and also that our own words and deeds will have some meaning for our grandchildren. For we are, as Scripture puts it, "children"; we are, as tradition reads it, "Builders."[52]

The venerable vessel of Jewish tradition, Rosenzweig reminded Buber, comprises not only sacred texts but also sacred deeds, and in remaining true to the tradition, the Jew paradoxically conserves and renews.[53]

Rosenzweig also differed with Buber's Zionism. As an "eternal people," he held, the Jews must remain above history and the mundane struggles of the nations. Exiled from their ancestral home with the destruction of the Second Temple, he explained, the Jews perforce withdrew from history, and reconstituted themselves principally as a community of prayer, a "Synagogue," their life and imagination no longer nurtured by worldly affairs. Sequestered in the Synagogue and governed solely by the eternal rhythms of liturgical time, Rosenzweig observed, the Jews of the Diaspora prefigure Messianic existence, thereby serving to inspire the Christian nations still locked in history.[54] Hence, the Jews

---

52 Rosenzweig, "The Builders," 91.

53 The debate between Buber and Rosenzweig regarding the *miṣvot* is discussed in detail in my "Law and Sacrament: Religious Observance in Twentieth Century Jewish Thought," in *Jewish Spirituality*, ed. Arthur Green (New York: Crossroad, 1987), 2:327–35.

54 See Alexander Altmann, "Rosenzweig on History," in *The Philosophy of Franz Rosenzweig*, ed. Mendes-Flohr (Hanover: University Presses of New England, 1988), 124–37.

would betray their vocation should they not resist the Zionist call to return to history.[55]

Yet Rosenzweig shared many of Buber's more basic theological presuppositions and similarly placed supreme emphasis on education as the bedrock of Jewish renewal. Indeed, he made his own debut as a Jewish thinker as the author of several tracts on Jewish education[56] and regarded his crowning achievement to be not his works in philosophy and theology but the *Freies Jüdisches Lehrhaus*, the school of adult Jewish education he founded in Frankfurt am Main in 1920.

At the heart of Rosenzweig's conception of Jewish education as the fulcrum of Jewish renewal was the study of Hebrew, the language of Jewish prayer and sacred literature. His affirmation of the centrality of Hebrew to Jewish education and renewal was born of both sociological and theological considerations. True to the Hegelian underpinnings of his thought, both these aspects, the sociological and theological (or metaphysical), are interlaced and dialectically interrelated, conflating into a protest against all attempts to reduce Judaism to the civil religion of the Jews. "Civil religion," of course, is a contemporary term unknown to Rosenzweig; he spoke of the danger of an "atheistic theology"—the tendency (shared with many Christians in the modern world) to remove God in all but name from one's religious consciousness, projecting onto the exalted altar formerly occupied by the Almighty the community's values, self-image, and even interests.[57] To fend off this danger, Rosenzweig advocated, *inter alia*, the re-introduction of Hebrew—QUA Holy Tongue, it should be emphasized—as the language of Jewish imagination and passion.[58]

---

[55] On Rosenzweig's attitude toward Zionism, see Stephane Moses, "Politik und Religion: Zur Aktualität Franz Rosenzweigs," in *Der Philosoph Franz Rosenzweig: Internationaler Kongress Kassel 1986*, ed. W. Schmied-Kowarzik (Munich: Karl Alber Freiburg, 1988), 2:855–75.

[56] These essays are translated in Rosenzweig, *On Jewish Learning*, pp.27-71.

[57] "Atheistische Theologie," in *Franz Rosenzweig: Der Mensch und sein Werk, Gesammelte Schriften*, vol. 3, *Zweistromland*, ed. Reinhold and Annemarie Mayer (Dordrecht: Nijhoff, 1984), 687–98.

[58] As a Holy Tongue, as the language of Jewish prayer, Rosenzweig contended, Hebrew should be taught according to the Ashkenazi system of pronunciation, in contradistinction to the Sephardic system advocated by the Zionists. For a comprehensive discussion of Rosenzweig's attitude toward Hebrew, see my "Hebrew as a Holy Tongue: Rosenzweig on Hebrew," in *Hebrew in Ashkenaz*, ed. Lewis Glinert (New York: Oxford University Press, 1992).

The sociological considerations informing this position were most forcefully articulated in Rosenzweig's analysis of the state of Jewish religious education in Germany. It was mistaken, he held, to regard the problem of Jewish education as identical to that of religious education in general. For Christians the problem of religious education is to provide "an emotional center"[59] for the society in which the pupil lives, to lend emotional support to the values and ideas to which one is introduced through other subjects taught at school. Christian religious instruction thus serves to strengthen one's emotional bond to the society and culture in which one lives; in a word, religious instruction is in effect an educational adjunct to the prevailing civil religion. This cannot, Rosenzweig protests, be the role of Jewish education.

Jewish education, Rosenzweig argued, must seek to introduce the Jewish pupil and student into a "Jewish sphere," a reality which, by definition, is not Christian and is thus APART from, indeed, often opposed to, the surrounding society, its values and self-image. Yet, of course, since the emancipation the Jew is intimately part of the surrounding society; it would be foolish to deny this fact or to seek to sever the bond the Jew has with, in this case, German culture and society. How is the Jew, then, to lay claim to the contrasting Jewish world without rejecting his or her attachment to the surrounding non-Jewish reality?

Clearly, Rosenzweig argued, the whole strategy of Jewish education must be different from that of a Christian education. In devising this strategy it must also be noted that in fostering the Jew's integration into non-Jewish society the emancipation often led to the attenuation of the Jew's tie to a specifically Jewish world. All that is left for most modern Jews is some vague affiliation with the synagogue:

> Those Jews with whom we are dealing have abandoned the Jewish character of the home [i.e, the Jewish social reality outside school] some time during the past three generations, and therefore for them that "Jewish sphere" exists only in the synagogue. Consequently, the task of Jewish religious instruction is to re-create that emotional tie between the institutions of public worship and the individual, that is, the very tie which he has lost.[60]

---

[59] "It is Time," in *On Jewish Learning*, 28.
[60] Ibid.

The re-creation of this tie requires, in the first instance, that the Jew recognize the "Jewish sphere" as being utterly apart from the world of his or her everyday, "non-Jewish" cultural and social reality.

Accordingly, Rosenzweig observed, one does not enter the Jewish world simply by acquiring Jewish knowledge and by adding to one's library a shelf of Judaica aside the works of Goethe, Kant, and Hölderlin. For, "to possess a world does not mean to possess it within another world which includes its possessor"[61]—one does not simply make room in one's existing world for Judaism. It is not a question of extending one's *Kultur* to include Jewish knowledge.

Hence, Rosenzweig warned, it would be amiss for Jewish educators and all those intent on promoting Jewish renewal to seek to smuggle Judaism into the heart and mind of the Jew through the ideal of *Bildung*—an ideal, as we have already noted, that so enchanted emancipated Jewry—which encourages in the name of intellectual and spiritual cultivation a cosmopolitan—or rather a syncretistic—pluralism:

> The [cultivated] German may possess another civilization—ancient or modern—because insofar as it also belongs to the spiritual world that includes him; therefore he can acquire it without leaving his own world, maybe even without understanding its language; because in any event he will understand it only as translated into the "language" of his world; and experience has always shown that knowledge of the words of a language does not necessarily imply possession of its civilization.[62]

As a world unto itself, Rosenzweig taught, Judaism has a soul of its own, "a language of its own."[63] Herein is the significance of Hebrew—but surely not in the mere technical sense. Hebrew is more than a linguistic instrument by which a given people communicate with one another: it is the vessel bearing the Jewish soul.

At this juncture, Rosenzweig's sociological argument merges with his theological considerations for asserting the centrality of Hebrew. As the bearer of Israel's "soul," he averred, Hebrew is intimately and indissolubly linked to the sacred literature of the Jews: this literature is the numinous ground that nurtures Hebrew and gives it life, but a life that is distinct from that of all other languages. Hebrew is a Holy Tongue animated by the breath of eternity. And it is through Hebrew as a holy

61 Ibid., 29.
62 Ibid., 29f.
63 Ibid., 30.

language that the Jewish people gains its life as a Holy People, as an eternal people. "The language of the eternal people," Rosenzweig says somewhat cryptically in *The Star of Redemption*, "drives it back to its own life which is beyond external life, [and] which courses through the veins of its living body and is, therefore, eternal."[64]

Messianic Time, Faith and the Recovery of Innocence

For Rosenzweig the experience of eternity, of an existence beyond external life, as previously noted, is achieved by assuming a meta-historical posture. By sequestering itself in the synagogue and the sacred rhythms of the ancient Hebrew liturgy, Israel gains an intimation of Messianic time. Anticipating redeemed existence, Israel stands above not only the invidious wiles of history but also the divisive cadences of secular time.

Observing that the Jew does not pray when it moves him or her, but at a given time and in the community of fellow Jews, who have gathered in accordance with a fixed schedule, Rosenzweig discerns in synagogal prayer a cultic quality. With a ceremonial exactness reminiscent of the Temple cult, the prayer service follows an agenda that might seem to the outsider to be gratuitously rigid and even legalistic. The Sabbath begins this week in Jerusalem on Friday evening at 5:43 and not at 5:30 or 5:46, and all of the House of Israel recite the same prayers, celebrate and commemorate with the same words and at the same time. The "cultic prayer" of the synagogue, according to Rosenzweig, thus has the unique power to quicken the experience of eternity, of redeemed time which witnesses the primal unity of humanity:

> But does [synagogal] prayer really have the power to force eternity to accept [its] invitation? Is the cult really more than just the preparation of food and drink, the setting of the table, the dispatch of messengers to bid the guests? Admittedly we realize that eternity can become time in the cult, but how are we to understand that it *must* become time, constrained with the power of magic? The cult too appears merely to build the house in which God may take up residence, but can it really force the exalted guest to move in? Yes it can. For the time which the cult prepares for the visit of eternity is not the time of an individual; it is not mine, nor thine, nor his secret time. It is the time of All. Day, week, and year are the common prop-

---

[64] *The Star of Redemption*, trans. William W. Hallo (New York: Holt, Rinehart and Winston, 1970), 292f.

> erty of all. They are based on the cosmic orbit of an earth which patiently bears them all, and in the law of the earthly work which is common to all. The bell tolls the hour for every ear. The times which the cult prepares are owned by none to the exclusion of all others. The prayer of the believer takes place in the midst of the believing congregation. "In assemblages" he praises the Lord. The enlightenment [*Erleuchterung*] which befalls the individual can here be none other than that which can befall all others too. And in this enlightenment, since it is supposed to be common to all, the same thing should be enlightened for all. It is common to all, beyond all individual points of view and beyond differences of perspective conditioned by the differences of these points of view, and so it can be but one thing: the end of all things, the ultimate things. Whatever lies along the way would appear differently to each person according to the place where he was standing; every day has a different content for each person according to the day that he is living. Only the end of days is common to all. The searchlight of prayer illuminates for each only that which it illuminates for all, only the farthest: the kingdom.[65]

Borne by the proleptic power of synagogal prayer, the congregation of Jewish worshipers gains a glimpse of redemptive eternity, overcoming for a glorious moment the existential isolation that characterizes human existence in ordinary, unredeemed time—an isolation that Rosenzweig well appreciated was radically deepened with the ascendancy of liberal individualism and the concomitant weakening of community.

Rosenzweig also acknowledged that with the conclusion of the prayer service, the Jew exits the synagogue and returns to the mundane order. But the experience of eternity, he insisted, is not confined to the synagogue and the occasion of cultic worship. The experience in the synagogue—and other sacred acts (viz., *miṣvot* and *talmud torah*) in which the Jew participates[66]—casts what Walter Benjamin would call "chips of Messianic time"[67] into the world of quotidian struggle and ambition.

The synagogue is thus for Rosenzweig not simply a Messianic refuge protecting the Jew from the fury and torments of history.[68] Facilitating

---

[65] Ibid., 292f.

[66] In *The Star of Redemption*, Rosenzweig confines his view of Jewish spirituality to the synagogue proper and its liturgical calendar; in his subsequent writings and practice, he expands his purview to include the *miṣvot* and *talmud torah*.

[67] *Illuminations*, ed. Hannah Arendt, trans. Harry Zohn (New York: Schocken, 1969), 265.

[68] It is a misreading of Rosenzweig to regard his teaching of the metahistorical posture of the synagogue as indicating an indifference to history. See my

the experience of eternity, the synagogue is a beacon illuminating the eschatological horizon, humbly reminding secular humanity (which includes both Jews and Christians in their everyday lives) of the Last Things and prompting it to push forward and not to despair.[69] In a world increasingly bereft of community and hope, the synagogue as a prefiguration of the Messianic future becomes especially urgent and that much more compelling.

Conclusion

The proleptic power ascribed by Rosenzweig to the synagogue to anticipate the redeemed future and render it a palpable and thus inspiring "pocket" of a superior reality in the present is but a particularly intense instance of a characteristic of faith in general. The poet Ludwig Strauss (1892-1953), accordingly, referred to faith as projecting one onto "islands of Messianic time" where one periodically sojourns to behold a future and blessed reality—a reality that for Strauss personally was disclosed by a faith expressed not in ritual and formal religious rites but in the imaginative deed of writing poetry.[70] For Buber, dialogue also had a proleptic quality: dialogue is an act of faith, a reaching out in trust to the other, and anticipating a world which, in bold contrast to ordinary experience, is amenable to the dialogical gesture.[71] Dialogue is guided by a trust that in turning and thus opening oneself to another—a Thou—with attentive care one will not be rebuffed, misunderstood, and hurt. Faith, therefore, reaches beyond the precincts of secular experience and assumes or anticipates an alternative, "Messianic" reality. So conceived, faith may also be the path to the longed-for "second naiveté." For from

---

"Rosenzweig and the Crisis of Historicism," in *The Philosophy of Franz Rosenzweig*, 138–61.

69 To be sure, Rosenzweig holds that the synagogue inspires "secular" Jewry and Christianity in decisively different ways. For Christianity the synagogue, as a metahistorical configuration anticipating the promise of redemption, serves as a "mute admonisher" reminding it that the affairs of the world are at best a necessary byway to the *eschaton*. For Jews, the Synagogue as the experience of eternity is a constant reminder that their ultimate place is not in history and its conceits.

70 "Wintersaat: Ein Buch aus Sätzen," in Strauss, *Dichtungen und Schriften*, ed. W. Kraft (Munich: Koesel, 1963), 753; cited in Simon, "Die zweite Naivität," 275.

71 In this respect, Buber's understanding of the noumenal reality posited by dialogue displays an affinity to Kant's concept of the *summum bonum*. On Buber's relationship to Kant, see my "Buber's Conception of God," in *Divided Passions*, ch. 10: 237–82.

the shores of the Messianic islands (to return to Strauss's image) whither faith brings us, we do not, indeed cannot, forget the raging waters of unredeemed time but view them with what Ernst Simon calls an "optimistic skepticism"—a skepticism emboldened by hope—and, alternatively, a "critical Messianism"—a critical evaluation of the present informed by a vision of the future.[72]

Both Buber and Rosenzweig presented their respective conceptions of Judaic faith as a path to this renewed and sober innocence, and also as an alternative to the *ersatz* community and solidarity proffered by nationalism and what we now call civil religion. Rather than the solidarity of shared pride and sentiment—emotions that are notoriously mercurial and are often defined over and against the other who is not a member of one's group—they raised the vision of bonds, forged in faith, of love and mutual trust.

---

[72] Simon, "Die zweite Naivität," in Simon, *Brücken. Gesammelte Aufsätze* (Heidelberg: Lambert Schneider, 1965), 275.

12

"Merry Chanuka": The Changing Holiday Practices of American Jews, 1880-1950

JENNA WEISSMAN JOSELIT

> "Let us now celebrate the national feast of dedication, merry Chanuka, about which cluster so many sweet and fragrant reminiscences . . . "
> — "The Call of Chanuka," *Jewish Messenger*, December 20, 1878

"In our town," noted suburban parent Grace Goldin in 1950, "Chanukah is no longer a Jewish holiday; it's a major competitive winter sport." [1] Recast as the functional equivalent of Christmas, the Maccabean festival enjoyed a decided measure of revival during the post–World War II era. At a time when the number of American Jews who observed kashruth and the traditional Sabbath fell off markedly, Hanukkah was one of the few Jewish ritual practices actually to grow in popularity. "It is the good fortune of Hanukah," explained the author of a 1951 article entitled "More About Hanukah in the Home," to become the first [Jewish holiday] to revive in an American setting," an observation confirmed several years later by Marshall Sklare in his pioneering study of the

---

[1] Grace Goldin, "Christmas-Chanukah: December Is the Cruelest Month," *Commentary* (November 1950), 417.

In the New World, the festival of Hanukkah lent itself to multiple orthographic as well as behavioral expressions: spellings vary from "Chanukah" and "Chanuka" to "Hanukah" and "Hanukkah." When not otherwise quoting from historical materials, the text uses "Hanukkah" as its standard spelling.

postwar suburban experience.[2] "Chanukah," he wrote in the mid-1950s, "is the only single religious practice that registers any gain."[3]

Several factors help to explain Hanukkah's latter-day appeal. An example of Jewish cultural adaptation at the grass roots, it brought together in one formidably effective entity the shared concerns and interests of the postwar "baby boom" generation: the renascence of Jewish cultural identity engendered by the rise of the state of Israel in 1948 on the one hand and the intense child-centeredness of postwar suburban society on the other. Then again, the growing ecumenism of postwar society, captured vividly in Will Herberg's analysis of America as a tripartite culture, gave parity to Hanukkah, making room for that holiday within America's civic religion.

Though it reached its apogee in the 1950s, the revival of Hanukkah capped a long process of reinterpretation and reevaluation, a process whose origins date back some eighty years earlier, to the 1880s, and whose development owes much to the American celebration of Christmas. At that time, significant numbers of American Jews, many of them German in origin, marked the advent of the winter season by celebrating some form of Christmas. "Have you never . . . entered a Jewish home to be confronted by the Christmas tree instead of Chanukah lights," asked Sarah Kussy in the pages of the *American Jewess*, intimating that many of her readers had shared her experience.[4] Indeed, if editorials and feature articles in the Anglo-Jewish press of the late nineteenth century are to believed, the number of American Jews "who hanker[ed] after Gentile customs" by celebrating Christmas far outnumbered those who celebrated Hanukkah.[5]

Admittedly, the extent of Christmas observance differed from Jewish home to Jewish home and ranged from those who actually placed Christmas trees or "illuminations in their parlors" to those who merely exchanged gifts.[6] Whatever its variations, the desacralized, commercialized American Christmas of the late nineteenth century, itself in the process of expansion, attracted a significant number of Jewish followers.

---

[2] Mrs. David Goldstein, "More about Hanukkah in the Home," *Outlook* 22/2, (December 1951): 16.

[3] Marshall Sklare and Joseph Greenbaum, *Jewish Identity on the Suburban Frontier*, 2nd ed. (Chicago: University of Chicago Press, 1979), 53.

[4] Sarah Kussy, "Judaism and Its Ceremonies," *American Jewess* (November 1896): 79.

[5] "Hanukkah Lights," *Jewish Messenger* (3 December 1880): 4.

[6] Quoted in Stanley Chyet, "Hanukkah and Christmas: 1866," *Jewish Frontier* 30 (December 1963): 30.

In the years following the Civil War, the American Christmas began to change from a restrained, religious occasion into a veritable "festival of consumption" by lending itself to the "quickening and fertilizing influence" of commercialization.[7] During the 1870s and 1880s, a period when the exchange of Christmas greeting cards and the custom of decorating one's home with a Christmas tree became normative and widespread, department stores like Macy's pioneered the display of "Christmas windows" while Woolworth's, the national chain of five and dime stores, first introduced consumers to its mass-produced selection of Christmas tree decorations. By the early years of the twentieth century, Christmas became, in the words of historian Daniel Boorstin, "overwhelmingly a season of shopping."[8] Given these developments, it was no wonder that American Jews were beguiled by the holiday. As one American Jew of that era explained, "no one who has an eye for beauty and sweetness can withstand the marvelous charm exercised over young and old by the advent of [Christmas] night."[9]

It was not just the inherent attractiveness of the American Christmas that drew American Jews to the holiday; it was also the perceived absence of such qualities, the "lack of romance" in the Jewish festival.[10] When compared to the charms of Christmas, those of Hanukkah paled in comparison. "How humble and insignificant does the one appear by the side of the other," remarked Dr. Kaufmann Kohler, a leading Reform rabbi, at once capturing and promoting the image of Hanukkah as pallid, enervated, and even meek.[11] With its exuberance and profound family spirit, Santa Claus, and Christmas tree, Christmas "give[s] a zest to life that all the Chanukah hymns in the world, backed by all the Sunday-school teaching and half hearted ministerial chiding, must forever fail to give," related Esther Jane Ruskay, the author of the widely read *Hearth*

7 Daniel Boorstin, *The Americans: The Democratic Experience* (New York: Random House, 1973), 158; Kaufmann Kohler, "Chanuka and Christmas," *The Menorah* 9/6 (December 1890): 306.

8 Boorstin, *The Americans*, 159. See also James H. Barnett, *The American Christmas: A Study in National Culture* (New York: Macmillan, 1954), and William R. Leach, "Transformations in a Culture of Consumption: Women and Department Stores, 1890-1925," *Journal of American History* 71 (September 1984): 319–42.

9 Kohler, "Chanuka and Christmas," 306.

10 Rabbi Louis Grossman, *The Hanukkah Festival: Outline of Lessons for Teachers* (Cincinnati: Teachers' Institute of Hebrew Union College, 1914), 9.

11 Kohler, "Chanuka and Christmas," 305.

and Home Essays and an astute Jewish observer.[12] The Yiddish press, in turn, admitted that "modest" Hanukkah stood little chance in its confrontation with Christmas.[13]

No wonder, then, that Hanukkah appears to have languished, a victim of growing neglect. As early as 1884, Dr. Gustav Gottheil remarked on the apparent drift away from Hanukkah practice. "The customary candles disappear more and more from Jewish homes," he observed while Louis Marshall, writing approximately a decade later, ruefully confirmed the continuation of that trend.[14] "The children of the present day," the Jewish civic leader explained, "are kept in ignorance of the ancient holiday whose name they scarcely can pronounce and to whose meaning they are growing deaf . . . "[15] Though statistics on the diminishing number of Hanukkah celebrants in the years prior to World War I are hard to come by, the frequency of exhortations to light the menorah, which surfaced annually during the holiday season in both the contemporary Anglo-Jewish and Yiddish press, suggest the extent to which that practice had fallen off. "Kindle the Chanukah lights anew, modern Israelite! Make the festival more than ever before radiant with the brightness and beauty of love and charity," urged Dr. Kohler, while the *Jewish Messenger* suggested "try[ing] the effect of the Hanukkah lights. If just for the experiment, try it."[16] The *Tageblatt*, in turn, called dramatically on the "spirit of the Hasmoneans to vanquish the Christmas tree and to enable the Hanukkah lights to speak to our hearts."[17]

By the 1890s, several key members of the Reform community, alarmed by the diffusion of Christmas practices within their own circles and the concomitant abandonment of Hanukkah, sounded a collective alarm of dismay. "Is it right to discard the Chanukah in order to celebrate the Christmas?" they asked rhetorically; "Would it not be wise to restore the Jewish Chanuka and to discard the pagan Christmas?"[18] Theology, as well as a kind of religious patriotism, fueled their concern. Sensitive to the larger "theological implications" that suffused Christmas, these

[12] Esther Jane Ruskay, *Hearth and Home Essays* (Philadelphia: Jewish Publication Society, 1902), 37.

[13] See, for example, *Yidishes Tageblatt* (19 December 1900): 4; (21 December 1903): 8.

[14] Rev. Dr. Gustav Gottheil, "What Christians Owe the Maccabees," *Jewish Messenger* (4 January 1884): 6.

[15] Louis Marshall, "When I Was a Boy: Part Two—Chanuka," *Helpful Thoughts* 3/8 (December 1898): 131.

[16] Kohler, "Chanuka and Christmas," 313; "Hanukkah Lights," 4.

[17] *Tageblatt*, (19 December 1900): 4.

[18] *Helpful Thoughts* 3/8 (December 1898): 132; Marshall "When I Was a Boy," 131.

moral custodians, especially the rabbis among them, viewed the holiday in classic terms: as a religious event that marked the birth of the Christian deity and not as a harmless social occasion for shopping and "festive mirth." However liberal the Reform rabbis might have been in other matters, they drew the line at the notion of Christmas trees in Jewish homes and construed the practice as a supreme act of disloyalty to the tenets of Judaism.[19] "How can the Jew, without losing self-respect, partake in the joy and festive mirth of Christmas? Can he without self-surrender, without entailing insult and disgrace upon his faith and race, plant the Christmas tree in his household?" Dr. Kohler asked rhetorically, resorting to uncharacteristically fierce language.[20] Those with similar views picked up on Kohler's rhetoric by lambasting the Jewish celebrants of Christmas as traitors to the Jewish people, as a "mark of opprobrium to their own race," while deriding their affinity for Christmas as an act of social cowardice, a "weak, coldly and sickly imitation" of a "borrowed custom," not their own.[21] One of the most perceptive critiques even brought etiquette, then a matter of pressing concern, into the discussion. Jews who observed Christmas, Esther Jane Ruskay stated categorically, are most guilty of a lapse in good taste; such Jews, she declared, are characterized by an "ignorance of racial properties, and ill breeding so rank, so utterly un-American, not to say un-Jewish as must always place them beyond the pale of civilized notice."[22]

In making a case for Hanukkah, Jewish apologists insisted that Jewish traditions, when properly channeled, could be as heartwarming, convivial, and engaging as those found elsewhere. The American Jew, insisted Emil G. Hirsch, pleading the merits of Hanukkah in the pages of the *Ladies Home Journal*, has little "excuse" for substituting Christmas for Hanukkah, "since his synagogal calendar provides at the identical season of the year an occasion for as intense a manifestation of joy."[23] Chiding his coreligionists for forgetting that Christmas was riddled with theological considerations, Hirsch suggested that Jews look inward, a suggestion echoed repeatedly by his colleagues. Hanukkah possesses all the right qualities, stated educator and rabbi Louis Grossman, subtly implying

---

19 Maurice Harris, "Why Should Jewish Children Not Have Christmas Trees," *Helpful Thoughts* 6/4 (December 1900): 140f.

20 Kohler, "Chanuka and Christmas," 307f.

21 Ruskay, *Hearth and Home Essays*, 40.

22 Ibid.

23 Emil G. Hirsch, "How the Jew Regards Christmas," *Ladies Home Journal*, 24/1 (December 1906): 10.

that these qualities, which he catalogued as "a vigorous story, dramatic incidents, strong personalities, fine home-scenes, abundance of imagery, plenty of traditional customs, home-cheer," resembled those of Christmas. [24]

FIGURE 1: With its emphasis on the familial and domestic qualities of Hanukkah, Moritz Oppenheim's painting enjoyed widespread popularity in both the Old World and the New. Courtesy The Israel Museum.

Even as they ringingly extolled Hanukkah's virtues, its advocates altered the holiday's raison d'etre. Conscious of the appeal of Christmas's "sweet virtues," concerned rabbis and educators alike transformed Hanukkah from an avowedly nationalistic and profoundly spiritual

---

24 Grossman, *The Hanukkah Festival*, 28.

occasion into a vaguely Judaized version of the prevailing late-nineteenth century Christmas. These champions of Hanukkah downplayed its distinctive theological message, preferring to domesticate and sentimentalize the Jewish holiday in familiar secular terms. "Family gatherings, merry making, presents, feasting the poor and giving the little ones a good time are things in which the Jew takes as much pleasure as his Gentile neighbor. With these habits he falls in, regardless of name and event," insisted Gottheil as he played up Hanukkah's seeming kinship with the heavily secularized and popular Christmas.[25] "It is gratifying to note," added the *Jewish Messenger*, "how more and more Hanukah has become a children's day and an occasion for kindliness," while *Helpful Thoughts*, a Jewish children's magazine of the era edited by Julia Richman, described the Maccabean festival as one of "joy, a season for giving gifts and making our companions happy."[26]

In its late nineteenth and early twentieth century incarnation, then, Hanukkah became the domestic Jewish holiday or "Home Festival" par excellence.[27] The modernized Hanukkah, newly reconstituted as a "whole week of games, of music and song, of gathering together of the various family clans," evoked feelings of warmth, good cheer, and camaraderie even as it symbolized the ordered world, bourgeois probity and family centered values of the American middle class.[28] Ruskay's *Hearth and Home Essays*, published in 1902, is characteristic of the evocatively bourgeois approach to Hanukkah. Writing in the effusive style of her era, Ruskay captured and doubtless helped to promote the notion of Hanukkah as a domestic festival, stressing repeatedly the themes of family togetherness, holiday cheer, and well-being. Following the candle-lighting ceremony, the Jewish family, she wrote in one characteristic sentence, "entered upon an evening of such unrestricted enjoyment and pleasant family intercourse as is rarely witnessed in these busy and too enlightened days."[29]

Thanks to formulations like these, Judaism was reshaped: it became more of a state of mind or a cluster of warm and resonant associations having to do with childhood and family than a matter of specific behavior—of lighting the menorah, say—or of theological imperatives. Much

---

25 Gottheil, "What Christians Owe," 6.

26 *Jewish Messenger* (19 December 1890): 4; *Helpful Thoughts* 3/8, (December 1898): 132.

27 Grossman, *The Hanukkah Festival*, 29.

28 Ruskay, *Hearth and Home Essays*, 45.

29 Ibid., 46.

like Moritz Oppenheim, whose enormously popular images emphasized the familial, domestic qualities of the modern German Jewish experience (figure 1), Ruskay and other American advocates of Hanukkah turned to words to make a similar point. "Pleasant memories of childhood are awakened by the approach of the Festival of Chanukah," Louis Marshall related. "Bright, flashing eyes, merry laughter, deep and enthusiastic emotions are conjured from the past."[30]

Despite efforts at reinvigorating the holiday, Hanukkah remained a "quaint" affair and, for the growing number of immigrant residents of the Lower East Side in the years prior to World War I, a minor, "unassuming" event on the Jewish calendar.[31]"Chanukah! To the Yiddish-speaking the word smells of reeking buckwheat cakes and resounds with the buzz of spinning `Chanukah tops,'" explained an overexuberant Abe Cahan to the non-Jewish readers of the *Commercial Advertiser*.[32] But in most homes, the holiday was marked (more quietly) by lighting the menorah, eating latkes, playing card games, an "imported custom," and spinning a dreidel.[33] For many Lower East Siders, the relative insignificance of Hanukkah was a carry-over from the Old World where that festival, unlike Passover or Purim, was "never a festival of revelry."[34] A modest occasion at best, Hanukkah traditionally entailed consuming latkes, distributing a modicum of "Hanukkah gelt," and playing cards, a "sanctioned" holiday activity.[35]

The Yiddish press, for its part, also tended not to make much of the holiday. With the exception of occasional advertisements for a "Hanukkah Sale" (*lekavod Hanukkah*) or announcements of a "grand celebration" at a local synagogue, the holiday went virtually unmarked. "I was losing track even of the calendar," explained a recently arrived

---

[30] Marshall, "When I Was a Boy," 130.

[31] Abraham Cahan, "Feast of Chanukah" (20 December 1897), in *Grandma Never Lived in America: The New Journalism of Abraham Cahan*, ed. Moses Rischin (Bloomington: Indiana University Press, 1985), 79, 80.

[32] Ibid., 80.

[33] Ibid., 82.

[34] Hayyim Schauss, *The Jewish Festivals: From Their Beginnings to Our Own Day* (Cincinnati: Union of American Hebrew Congregations, 1938), 235.

[35] Cahan, *Grandma Never Lived in America*, 82. For a more extended discussion of eastern European Hanukkah practices, see Schauss, *Jewish Festivals*, 231–36. Originally published in 1933 as *Dos Yom Tov Buch*, Schauss's work drew on both literary and autobiographical sources to reconstruct the nature of Jewish holiday practices.

immigrant, homesick for the Old World. "Did I know that last week was the Feast of the Maccabees? How could anyone know it in America?"[36]

Ironically enough, New York's Yiddish speaking population seemed to be more acutely aware of Christmas than of Hanukkah. They encountered the Yuletide season in the marketplace and on the street where the sight of Jewish peddlers stocking their pushcarts with Christmas decorations, "gaudy whirligigs, candy crucifixes and shrines of Madonna" was not uncommon.[37] Downtown, on the Lower East Side, the public school and the settlement house were particularly active in the diffusion of the Christmas spirit. Staging Christmas pageants and cantatas, settlement houses on the Lower East Side were often lavishly decorated with illustrations drawn from the New Testament and with other "conventional paraphernalia" of the holiday, including Christmas trees.[38] New York City public schools, in turn, routinely displayed Christmas trees along with decorations of holly and mistletoe and convened assemblies in which "distinctly Christian" hymns and recitations were performed and "little Jewish boys" dressed up as Santa Claus until a series of public protests by Jewish immigrant parents curbed the practice.[39]

The Yiddish press, with its keen sociological imagination, greatly contributed to disseminating an awareness of Christmas. In an attempt to allay and dispel commonly held notions—and experiences—of Christmas, Yiddish newspapers like the *Forverts* took great pains to familiarize readers with the particular nuances of American Christmas traditions, especially those that related to gift-giving and the excesses of shopping. Where Christmas in the Old World had been a time of pogroms and anti-Jewish sentiment, dramatizing the Jew's marginal status, in the New World, the *Forverts* carefully explained, the holiday

---

36 Marcus Ravage, *An American in the Making* (New York: Harper, 1917), 118.

37 Archibald Hill, "The Pushcart Peddlers of New York," *The Independent* 61 (1906): 921.

38 "Christmas Celebrations," *Jewish Daily News* (24 December 1903): 8.

39 On Christmas celebrations in the public school, see Leonard Bloom, "A Successful Jewish Boycott of the New York City Public Schools—Christmas, 1906," *American Jewish History*, 70/2 (December 1980): 180–88; *American Hebrew* (28 December 1906): 189, 203; "Christmas Celebrations," *Tageblatt* (24 December 1903): 8. Questions over the permissibility of this practice continued unabated well into the post–World War II era. In 1954, no less a ritual authority than the Committee on Law and Standards of the Rabbinical Assembly deliberated on the matter. It recommended that Jewish children refrain from participating in public school programs where the holiday plays and hymns contained "distinctly recognizable" Christian themes. *Proceedings, The Rabbinical Assembly* 18 (1954): 52.

was an occasion for merriment, gift-giving, and feasting. In editorials and feature articles—such as "Christmas Presents," a discussion of holiday shopping practices; "How Christmas Became A Christian Holiday," an analysis of the historical Jesus; or "Christmas and Yom Kippur: Fantasy and Reality," a comparative look at the philosophies behind the two holidays—Yiddish newspapers made sure their readers understood the nature of Christmas in America, seeking to minimize their fears of alien, non-Jewish practices.[40]

Some readers, in fact, may have understood the Christmas spirit all too well. According to the *Forverts*, many greenhorns took quickly to the *minhag* (custom) of buying Christmas presents as proof of their new status as Americans. "Who says we haven't Americanized?" the paper inquired rhetorically, pointing to the large numbers of Jewish shoppers among those thronging the department stores. "The purchase of Christmas gifts is one of the first things that proves one is no longer a greenhorn," it noted, pointing out that the exchange of gifts among Jewish tenement dwellers was as widespread and popular as "*shalokh manos, lehavdil.*"[41] Like the *Forverts*, the *Tageblatt* was also highly alert to the existence of these practices, but where the Socialist paper mocked them, the more religious daily fiercely condemned them. "The same voice that blesses the Chanukah lights cannot sing the praises of the Yule-tide and be reckoned as an honest voice," the paper stated categorically, adding that "the same hand that lights the long yellow tapers in the Menorah cannot light the gaudy candles on the Christmas tree and be reckoned an honest hand."[42]

To be sure, it is hard to know whether or not the *Forverts'* observation or, for that matter, the critique of the *Tageblatt* was merely a rhetorical gambit or a bona fide sociological observation. What is clear, though, is that well into the post–World War I era, Christmas had a larger hold on the public imagination than did Hanukkah. By the 1920s, though, Hanukkah began to come into its own as both a major Jewish domestic occasion and an exercise in consumption. Though initially lagging far behind Christmas, Hanukkah celebrations of the 1920s showed clear signs of having been thoroughly Americanized, modernized, and com-

---

40 Respectively, *Forverts* (24 December 1910): 6, (25 December 1910): 5, and (26 December 1910): 4.

41 "Pious They May Be but They Still Observe Christmas," *Forverts* (25 December 1904): 4.

42 *Tageblatt* (21 December, 1903): 8; see also "Christmas and Hanukkah," *Tageblatt* (14 December 1909): 4.

modifed. No longer a quaint and unassuming little holiday, the Maccabean festival by the interwar years shared much in common with its Christian "competitor," and in its own way reflected the growing affluence of postwar New York Jewry.

The Yiddish press vividly documents this transformation. In contrast to the prewar era, when Hanukkah-related promotions were in short supply, the Yiddish press of the interwar era was replete with dozens of tempting advertisements for Hanukkah gifts. "A Hanukkah Present for the Entire Family—The Greatest Bargain [*meṣiʾah*] in the World," trumpeted an advertisement for a Hudson motor car in the December 1925 issue of *Der Tog,* while the *Morgen Zhurnal* carried a series of ads from the Colgate Company extolling such "Hanukkah Pleasures" as Colgate perfumes, shaving equipment, and dental creme.[43] Brunswick Phonographs and Records followed suit by promoting recordings of the legendary cantor Zvulun Kwartin in connection with the holiday (figure 2). The format of this advertisement, which combined images of the top-hatted cantor, a shining menorah, a modern phonograph, and a contented nuclear family listening attentively to Kwartin's vocalizing effectively summed up the ethos of the postwar Hanukkah.[44] Readers were also encouraged to use a wide range of food products *"lekavod Ḥanukkah"* from Canada Dry ginger ale and Goodman's noodles to Aunt Jemima pancake flour, "the best flour for latkes," and Crisco shortening, which allied "Hanukkah latkes and Modern Science."[45]

Editorials in the Yiddish press also reflected these changes. Some, like the impassioned "Hanukkah and Our Children," emphasized taking a more spiritual, educational approach to the *yontef,* suggesting the extent to which a commercialized Hanukkah had taken hold among the Yiddish-speaking. "Jewish Mothers! It is up to you to celebrate Hanukkah! Keep in mind your children! See to it that the days of Hanukkah are experienced differently than those of the other days of the year. . . . Tell you children why in their veins courses the blood of those ancient Jewish heroes—the Hasmoneans."[46] More typical, perhaps, was

---

43 *Der Tog* (12 December 1925): 7; *Morgen Zhurnal* (8 December 1920): 10, (5 December 1925): 3. Banks like the East River Savings Institution urged Jewish consumers to "Save for Hanukkah" by opening up a "Christmas plan." *Der Tog* (14 December 1925): 6.

44 *Morgen Zhurnal* (6 December 1923): 3.

45 See, for example, *Der Tog* (16 December 1919): 10, (19 December 1919): 10, (9 December 1925): 6, (15 December 1925): 6; *Morgen Zhurnal* (10 December 1925): 3.

46 "Hanukkah and Our Children," *Froyen Velt* 1/8 (December 1913): 1.

an editorial in the *Morgen Zhurnal* entitled "Hanukkah Must Become a True Children's *Yontef.*" Recounting the heroic exploits of the Maccabees is not enough, counseled the daily, for in order to counter the lure of Christmas, Hanukkah must become an occasion for storytelling, gift-giving, and general festivity. The paper then went on to advise its readers to add the exchange of presents to the roster of "Hanukkah *minhagim.*"[47]

The pressures of consumerism were not the only forces making for Hanukkah's revitalization at this time. The publication during the interwar years of guidebooks to Hanukkah observance further encouraged and sustained the spirit of improvisation and cultural adaptation. Emily Solis-Cohen's *Hanukkah: The Feast of Lights* was one of the most popular of such texts. With detailed suggestions for "A Hanukkah Party" and descriptions of costumes, props, puppet shows, and dances for such characters as "The Top," "The Pancakes," and "The Spirit of Giving," this volume promoted the notion of Hanukkah as a lively, fun-filled, child-centered occasion.[48] Much the same can be said of *The Jewish Home Beautiful*, yet another immensely popular publication of the interwar era. Joining together floral design, coordinated table settings, and recipes, this guidebook to Jewish ritual practice touted the merits of a home "bright with candle lights and gay with parties and the exchange of gifts."[49] Hanukkah is a "period for mirth and for spreading of goodwill," noted the text, advising would-be celebrants to use orange as a color scheme, to create place cards in the shape of hammers, and to prepare latkes and Menorah vegetable salad, a composition of cottage cheese and fruit that, when molded, resembled a menorah. The Maccabean sandwich, generally tuna fish or egg salad shaped in the form of bite-sized Maccabees, was another highly popular culinary suggestion.[50] The preparation and consumption of such holiday-related fare was deemed critical to the holiday's success. Manifestly appealing to children, Menorah salads and Maccabean sandwiches popularized the holiday

---

47 *Morgen Zhurnal* (14 December 1925): 5.

48 Emily Solis-Cohen, *Hanukkah: The Feast of Lights* (Philadelphia: Jewish Publication Society, 1937).

49 Althea O. Silverman and Betty Greenberg, *The Jewish Home Beautiful* (New York: Women's League of the United Synagogue, 1941), 24. On this text, see Jenna Weissman Joselit, "'A Set Table': Jewish Domestic Culture in the New World" in Susan Braunstein and Jenna Weissman Joselit, *Getting Comfortable in New York: The American Jewish Home* (New York: Jewish Museum, 1990), 51-53.

50 *Jewish Home Beautiful*, 52, 69f., 100-102.

FIGURE 2: An example of the commodification of Hanukkah, this advertisement in the *Morgen Zhurnal* of the 1920s promoted the recordings of the legendary cantor Zvulun Kwartin as an appropriate holiday gift. The New York Public Library, Astor, Lenox and Tilden Foundations.

even as they contributed to the ceremonializing of Jewish identity through its association with food. As Betty Greenberg, one of the authors of *The Jewish Home Beautiful*, advised, "nor should we overlook the value of latkes in the building of Jewish memories."[51]

---

[51] Betty Greenberg, "Chanukah Ramblings and Reflections," *Outlook* 7/2 (December 1936): 3.

Still other texts, like "A Hanukkah Manual," a pamphlet published by the Women's League of Conservative Judaism, reflected an unabashedly playful approach to the holiday by adding games to the traditional repertoire of recipes and decorations.[52] A Hanukkah peanut hunt, a Jewish version of Scrabble®, and Hanukkah bowling in which the pins represented Antiochus and his warriors further enlivened the holiday. So too did the manual's fanciful suggestions for holiday decor. These ranged from cardboard menorahs and tinfoil Stars of David to Hanukkah mobiles made of pipe cleaners and dreidel-shaped candy containers of colored crepe paper. Encouraged by the "Hanukkah Manual" and related materials, Hanukkah party-goers indulged in a flurry of inventiveness: "mount[ing] cardboard Jews and Syrians in Maccabean creches, or past[ing] together paper chains of cream-colored menorahs, orange stars of David, pink dredels, purple elephants."[53]

Suggestions like these were directed explicitly toward the mother of the house. While the ritual responsibility for actually lighting the menorah fell to the father, that of creating an appropriately festive atmosphere was a maternal matter. The Maccabean festival, observed one contemporary writer in 1951, "offers a challenge to the creative powers of Jewish mothers," enlisting her feminine qualities and seemingly innate artistry.[54] At the same time, Hanukkah also demonstrated, and heightened, the increasingly popular notion that Jewish women served as agents of Jewish cultural identity, transmitters of Jewish ritual, and that the Jewish home served as the primary source of Jewish moral authority and of socialization. The Hanukkah lights have a special message for women, noted the Jewish Home Series, affirming the woman's role as the standard-bearer of Judaism. "If but something of the Maccabean spirit could fortify us against these invidious onslaughts [of assimilation]!" the text exhorted its all-female readership. "If we could be roused from the chronic indifference that is petrifying our souls! Let us hope that these little Chanukah lights may kindle in our hearts anew the zeal to defend our Judaism even as did the Maccabees twenty-one centuries ago."[55]

---

[52] Jewish Family Living, "A Hanukkah Manual," 5th ed. (New York: Women's League of Conservative Judaism, 1972).

[53] Goldin, "Christmas–Chanukah," 417.

[54] Goldstein, "More About Hanukkah in the Home," 16.

[55] Hadassah Levine, "The Minor Festivals," *The Jewish Home Series,* ed. Leo Jung (New York: Women's Branch of the Union of Orthodox Jewish Congregations of America, 1926), 10.

Ironically enough, the notion that the role of the Jewish mother embraced, and presumed, the conscious transmission of Jewish identity was itself a reflection of acculturation; modernity conferred on the Jewish woman manifold responsibilities for the maintenance of Jewish culture and continuity. As the "priestess of the home," it was up to the Jewish woman to uphold and sustain the "reign of religion" and, as Paula Hyman has written, to fulfill the role of domestic educator. "Bourgeois ideology," she explains, "conferred on wives and mothers responsibility for the moral and religious tone of the home."[56] "Upon the Jewish woman of today rests a greater responsibility than ever before," wrote one such woman, Sarah Berman, in the pages of *Outlook,* the national publication of the Women's League for Conservative Judaism. "In her keeping lies the shaping of minds of the coming generation. . . . It is she who decides whether the Chanukah lights be required as a shrine for the eternal spirit of freedom and justice or as an outworn symbol. . . . Will she give them the place of honor in her home?"[57] Conversely, it fell to the Jewish mother to see to it that Christmas trees did not intrude on the Jewish home. Every Jewish woman, exhorted *Outlook,* should use her influence to dissuade Jewish mothers from bringing Christmas trees into their homes. "Let them beware that by bringing the light of Christianity to their homes they might dim the light of Judaism. Let the tree of lights from the Menorah serve to strengthen our Jewish pride."[58]

Whether motivated by Jewish pride or outside pressures, including what one parent called the "need to compensate Jewish children for the glory and glamour of the Christmas season," the theologically neutral Hanukkah of "merry-making and gifts" caught on quickly within the American Jewish community; by the eve of World War II, this kind of Hanukkah had not only evolved its own aesthetic, social dynamic, and set of unique domestic rituals but had also emerged as the most popular form of the holiday and, even more to the point, as an occasion for "Jewish gift-giving."[59] At once symptom and cause, toy manufacturers and Judaica importers throughout the late 1930s, 1940s, and 1950s were quick to capitalize on the growing importance of Hanukkah by developing an inventive array of holiday novelty items, games, records, books,

---

56 "Save the Sabbath," *American Jewess* 7/2 (May 1898): 97; Paula E. Hyman, "The Modern Jewish Family: Image and Reality," in David Kraemer, ed., *The Jewish Family: Metaphor and Memory* (New York, 1989): 188–90, esp. 188.

57 Sarah Berman, "The Spirit of Chanukah," *Outlook* 5/2 (December 1934): 3.

58 "Chanukah Trees and Christmas Candles," *Outlook* 2/2 (December 1931): 4.

59 Goldstein, "More about Hanukkah in the Home," 16.

and papier-mâché decorations. "Chanukah is Gift Time at M. Wolozin, 28 Eldridge Street, The House of a Thousand Traditional Hebrew Gifts," this Judaica distributor related, while Bloch Publishers as early as 1931 enthusiastically promoted its latest product, a cutout Menorah with candles and a headband. This "charming new design," the advertisement explained, "afford[s] amusement and instruction for young children."[60] So too did the emergence at this time of a nascent American Jewish children's literature (figure 3). *The Adventures of K'tonton,* the "Jewish Tom Thumb," one of the earliest examples of that genre, first appeared in serialized form in 1935 and was immediately hailed as a way to "bring the holidays and festivals to your children in an attractive way."[61]

Through their production of a wide array of menorahs, manufacturers of American Judaica participated in the cultural diffusion of the holiday. Where once American menorahs had been limited in style, shape, design, and material, those of the late 1940s and early 1950s were distinguished by their variety. "Many new and beautiful Hanukah lamps of modern design are available," observed one determined Jewish homemaker. "Every home should own at least one."[62] The success of a musical menorah fashioned from chromium is a vivid illustration. The invention of Ziontalis, a leading American manufacturer of Judaica, this newfangled menorah was not only available in forty-seven different styles but "always gleams, needs no polish and will not tarnish" as it played selections from Hatikvah or the Rock of Ages.[63]

The ingenuity of Judaica and toy manufacturers seemed to peak during the 1950s with the invention of an oversized, electrified revolving dreidel known as the "Maccabee." Made of laminated plastic and standing four feet tall, the "Maccabee," touted its creators, the Dra-Dell Corporation of North Bergen, New Jersey, "expresses a true holiday spirit in the home where modern children may share the wonder of Chanukah. It becomes a center for gift-giving. It decorates and illuminates the season of proud traditions [and] joy tastefully, meaningfully for the child and

60 *Jewish Life* 20/2 (November–December 1952): 68f.; "New Chanukah Cut-out," *Outlook* 2/2 (December 1931): 11.

61 *Outlook* 5/4 (May 1935): 12.

62 Goldstein, "More about Hanukkah in the Home," 16.

63 "The House of Zion for the Ideal Chanukah Gift," *New York Post* (2 December 1942).

for the family. The Maccabee," the manufacturers concluded, "is a fine addition to the Chanukah atmosphere."[64]

FIGURE 3: Brightly illustrated children's books like Jane Bearman's 1943 *Happy Chanuko* contributed to Hanukkah's appeal as a child-centered holiday. Courtesy The Union of American Hebrew Congregations.

Thanks to the successful transformation of Hanukkah into what the editor of the *World Over*, a Jewish children's pictorial magazine, called "one of our jolliest festivals for fun and games,"[65] the holiday came to assume a prominence it did not traditionally have. "Chanukah occupies

64 Press release of the Dra-Dell Corporation, United States Territorial Collection #415, YIVO Archives; for an illustration of "The Maccabee," see Joselit, "A Set Table," 63.

65 *The World Over* 3/4 (12 December 1941): 2.

a unique place in the lives of American Jews," observed Rabbi Albert Gordon, attesting to its hold on his suburban congregants, an assessment shared by other observers of contemporary American Jewish society.[66] "Hanukkah is only one of our festivals, and a minor one at that; but we exalt it above all our holidays," a writer in *The Reconstructionist* critically related in 1948, adding, "we magnify it beyond all reason, and establish it as a major holiday day in our children's minds."[67] Sociologist Marshall Sklare, studying Jewish communal life on the "suburban frontier," confirmed these trends: "Hanukkah, in short, becomes for some the Jewish Christmas," he stated unequivocally.[68]

Admittedly, many American Jews continued to celebrate some form of Christmas, sharing in what one observer called the "loveliness of the day."[69] And yet, the confluence of market and social forces ensured that Hanukkah could indeed serve as a powerful "antidote" to Christmas.[70] "A Yuletide spirit," observed one student of postwar contemporary Jewish life, has "infused into [sic] the Hanukkah greeting cards, the home decorations, the Hanukkah napkins, the giant candelabra, and the exchange of gifts in Hanukkah wrapping, complete with colorfully decorated Hanukkah ribbons."[71] Thanks to these developments, the modern American Jew, it seemed, no longer had cause to dread the "cruel month" of December: Hanukkah with its range of "better facilities," from Jewish storybooks to decorative napkins, could now serve as a fulfilling and viable cultural substitute.[72]

Interestingly enough, the outside world in the years following World War II came increasingly to share that assessment, not only freighting

---

66 Albert Gordon, *Jews in Suburbia* (Boston: Beacon, 1959), 140.

67 Abraham Segal, "Christmas in the Public School—The Problem," *The Reconstructionist* 14/16 (10 December 1948): 22.

68 Sklare, *Jewish Identity*, 58.

69 Louis Witt, "The Jew Celebrates Christmas," *The Christian Century* 56 (6 December 1939): 1499. See also Milton Matz, "The Meaning of the Christmas Tree to the American Jew," *Jewish Journal of Sociology* 3/1 (June 1961): 129–37. This late 1950s study of the attitude of 53 middle-class Chicago Jews toward Christmas pointed to growing acceptance of the Christmas tree as a secular symbol of American unity. Where 14.2% of second-generation American Jews in Matz's sample had Christmas trees in their home, a substantial 39.9% of third generation Jews resorted to that practice.

70 Goldin, "Christmas–Chanukah," 417.

71 Irving Canter, "Uncle Sam, the Hanukkah Man: Assimilation or Contra-Culturation," *The Reconstructionist* 27/15 (1 December 1961): 5-13.

72 Goldin, "Christmas–Chanukah," 416; Sarah L. Kopelman, "President's Page," *Outlook* 20/2 (December 1949): 3.

Hanukkah with the same cultural and social significance as Christmas but yoking the two together in demonstration of America's "cultural oneness."[73] Joint Christmas–Hanukkah observances in the public schools were the most apparent, and far-reaching, examples of the growing parity between the two holidays, and, as Will Herberg explained in 1955, an unmistakable indication that "the very notion of a tripartite arrangement is something that increasingly commends itself to the American mind as instrinsically right and proper."[74] As a case in point, public school educators developed the strategy of convening a "holiday" assembly on a "compromise date" in December that not only featured both a Christmas tree and a "Menorah candle" but also the singing of Hanukkah hymns and Christmas carols.[75] The same prevailing spirit of postwar ecumenism and neighborliness even affected the new medium of television: special holiday broadcasts, including those produced by the Jewish Chautauqua Society in conjunction with the Central Conference of American Rabbis, reiterated these themes by having Christian and Jewish neighbors exchange visits and gifts with one another during the week of Hanukkah.[76]

To be sure, Hanukkah's "transfiguration" into a "Jewish Christmas" was not without its detractors, who viewed both the process and the end product as a pallid and inappropriate imitation of non-Jewish practices or, more harshly still, as a "back-door means to participation in a Christian festival."[77] While those more traditional in outlook tended to be the most vociferous in their criticism, a more liberal element within the American Jewish community shared that concern, insisting that "Hanukkah CAN NOT compete with Christmas, or leaven it or weaken its

73 Thomas A. Clemente, "Double or Nothing," *Commonweal* 53/11 (22 December 1950): 274.

74 Will Herberg, *Protestant–Catholic–Jew: An Essay in American Religious Sociology* (Garden City, N.Y.: Doubleday, 1955), 259f.

75 Clemente, "Double or Nothing," 273f. An adumbration of this spirit of ecumenism can be seen in the practice, common at the Henry Street Settlement, of hosting a "Midwinter Festival" in which such "common symbols" as a Yule log, a lit Christmas tree, a Chinese lantern, and a Hanukkah lamp were collectively displayed. See, for example, *Twentieth Anniversary Pamphlet, The Henry Street Settlement, 1893-1913* (New York: Holt, 1913), 29. For a critique of ecumenical public school celebrations, see Segal, "Christmas in the Public School," 17-22; "Hanukkah, Christmas and the Public Schools," *The Reconstructionist* 23/17 (27 December 1957): 3f.; Sylvia Rothschild, "Christmas in Suburbia," *Hadassah Magazine* 46/4 (December 1964): 11, 16.

76 See, for example, "A Time of Valor," a 1950s production of the Jewish Chautauqua Society, National Jewish Archive of Broadcasting, The Jewish Museum.

77 "Chanukah," *Jewish Life* 20/2 (November–December 1952): 5f.

influence."[78] "True Young Judeans will abstain from Xmas [sic], programs and celebrations and will urge their friends to do likewise," advised the leadership of that secular American Jewish youth movement. "It should be made clear to members that Xmas [sic], unlike Thanksgiving and Lincoln Day, is not a National American holiday. It is rather a purely Christian religious festival. It may also be necessary to explain that Chanukah is not the Jewish Xmas [sic]," they added. "There is not the slightest similarity between the two."[79] Meanwhile, publications like *Jewish Life*, the house organ of the Union of Orthodox Jewish Congregations of America, contended that the menorah "has become an apologetic cloak for a non-Jewish content" and urged celebrants to infuse the holiday with overtly Jewish content. Chanukah "needs no apology and will sustain no borrowings," this magazine insisted.[80] Reflecting an increasingly common position at the grass roots level of American Jewish life, parents, too, gave voice to a sense of frustration as they found themselves in competition with Christmas. As one highly articulate Jewish mother explained, "The character of the holiday has been transfigured by an accident of timing: what used to be a festival of freedom "becomes a festival of refuge."[81]

Despite the pressures of conformity, American Jews in search of a more authentically Jewish rationale for and expression of Hanukkah did not have to look too far afield: they could draw on Zionism to legitimate the Hanukkah experience and to provide a more positive, less compensatory, role for that holiday. Although the overwhelming majority of American Jews seemed to relate their celebration of Hanukkah to that of Christmas, Zionism had the potential to supply an appropriately Jewish idiom and context for the display of Hanukkah spirit and, at the same time, to lessen the reliance on external "borrowings." "Recently, the observance of Chanukah has gained added vitality," the editors of *Outlook* observed in 1935, pointing to the promise of "Modern Zionism." "Color is given to Jewish life by the development of a new art, drama, music and literature in Palestine."[82] In fact, the association between

---

[78] Segal, "Christmas in the Public School," 22.

[79] "Leader's Manual of Programs and Projects for 1931-32/5692," Prepared by Ben M. Edidin for Young Judea, p. 23, Hadassah National Archives, Young Judea Collection.

[80] "Chanukah," *Jewish Life*, 5f.

[81] Goldin, "Christmas–Chanukah," 417.

[82] Emma Bienenfeld, "Days of Dedication—Days of Light," *Outlook* 6/2 (December 1935): 3.

Zionism and Hanukkah preceded that statement by several decades. During the pre–World War I era, editorials in the religiously oriented Yiddish press, for example, frequently stressed the connection between the donation of *sheqalim* to the Zionist cause and the Maccabean festival, thus underscoring the particularly philanthropic cast of the holiday.[83] In subsequent years, the flowering of cultural Zionism and then later still the establishment of the state of Israel in 1948 heightened the cultural importance and relevance of the Hanukkah story, leading American Jews to identify the soldiers and citizenry of Israel, those "modern brave warriors," with the ancient Maccabees and to reinterpret their ancient triumph as a "vehicle for secular nationalist sentiment."[84] "Hanukah 5703 Finds the Maccabean Spirit Alive Again in Palestine," triumphantly reported the *Hadassah Newsletter* in 1942, thus helping to concretize the reality of the Maccabees and their struggle for religious and national freedom while the Zionist Organization of America produced a "portfolio" of Hanukkah materials, replete with readings, recitations, songs, and games, designed to emphasize the organic ties between that holiday and Zionism.[85] "The festival of Chanukah makes December a most important month in the life of a Young Judea club," noted the leaders of this national Zionist movement. "Chanukah more perhaps than any other Jewish holiday, recalls the heroism of the Jewish people. . . . The festival, therefore, lends itself readily to dramatic presentations, and to many other interesting club activities."[86]

The relationship between the embryonic state and the increasingly popular celebration of Hanukkah was not only spiritual and cultural but also graphic and material. Throughout this period, the wholesale introduction into the American Jewish mass market of mass-produced Palestinian and then Israeli menorahs made of the characteristic patinated bronze ("greenware"), or bearing the iconic symbols of the new state, underscored the association between the two. In fact, the popularity of Israeli-made menorahs and of Israeli products in general fueled and in a real sense legitimated the transformation of Hanukkah into a gift-giving

83 See, for example, "The Shekel and Hanukkah," *Tageblatt* (10 December 1909): 4; "Hanukkah and the Jewish National Fund," *Morgen Zhurnal* (11 December 1925): 10; "Hanukkah," *Der Tog* (12 December 1925): 4.

84 *Outlook* 20/2 (December 1949): 2; "Chanukah," *Jewish Life* 20/2 (November-December 1952): 5.

85 *Hadassah Newsletter* (December 1942–January 1943): 2; "Hanukkah Program," *American Hebrew* (13 December 1940): 22.

86 "Leader's Manual," 22.

occasion (figure 4). "Make it a real happy Chanukah with Jewish gifts for Jewish children," Jewish newspapers advised, pointing to the proliferation of Jewish children's books, records, menorahs, toys, and Israeli souvenir items.[87] Kosher chocolate manufacturers also indulged the American Jewish public's fascination with Israel by producing a line of overtly nationalistic games to accompany their Hanukkah candies. Lofts Chocolates, for example, introduced a spinwheel game entitled "Valor against Oppression" which featured contemporary Israeli heroes like Moshe Dayan and Yigael Yadin. Barton's, in turn, introduced the "Barton's Race Dredel," an Israelified version of Monopoly® whose board featured a map of Israel, miniature Israeli flags, menorahs, and the following text: "Every Jewish boy and girl thrills to the heroic story of the Maccabees. . . . We light the candles every night, . . . recite the blessings, sing the songs, play chess, go to parties and dance the hora."[88]

However it was celebrated or understood, the American commemoration of Hanukkah provides a fascinating case study of how American Jews invigorated a languishing tradition, transforming what had once been a relatively minor moment on the Jewish calendar into a momentous occasion. As one observer presciently put it in the 1930s: "In reality, the American celebration of the Hanukkah festival is a step in the evolution of what the future Jewish historian will refer to as American Judaism."[89] Pressures from within and without, from the marketplace and the suburban neighborhood, combined to make the ancient Maccabean victory increasingly relevant to modern urban Jewish life even as they inspired a variety of institutional, commercial, and homegrown attempts to render Hanukkah an attractive and compelling alternative to Christmas. Illuminating the process of ritual change and adaptation, the reappropriation and reinterpretation of Hanukkah suggests the continuing vitality of Jewish tradition in twentieth century America, the plasticity of Jewish ritual, and the cultural ingenuity of American Jews. As one suburban rabbi related, noting the attention his congregants lavished on Hanukkah: "It all goes to show that if you work away at it, you CAN REVIVE a holiday."[90]

---

[87] "Chanukah Presents," *Outlook* 8/2 (December 1937): 4. See also Joselit, "A Set Table," 61-65.

[88] Quoted in Morris Freedman, "Sweets for Heterodox New York: The Story of Barton's," *Commentary* (May 1952): 478.

[89] "Hanukkah in American Judaism," *American Hebrew* (20 December 1935): 1.

[90] Albert Gordon, *Jews in Transition* (Minneapolis: University of Minnesota Press, 1949), 117 (emphasis added).

FIGURE 4: In this display of American Jewish cultural ingenuity, a Cincinnati Jewish family, ca. 1960s, poses in front of an arrangement of Hanukkah gifts. A homemade Judah Maccabee doll, suspended overhead, attests to the children's belief that Judah Maccabee himself brought them presents. Courtesy Dr. Jonathan Brumberg-Krauss and the Krauss Family.

PART III

The Reappropriation of Tradition in Contemporary Judaism

The essays in this section examine ways in which contemporary Jews appropriate aspects of the Jewish tradition for radically new purposes: Shulamit Magnus surveys the range of new ceremonies and liturgies created by Jewish women who seek reconciliation between their religion and contemporary feminist perceptions; Stuart Schoenfeld carefully reconstructs the educational experience of women preparing to celebrate an adult bat mitzvah, a rite of passage which is doubly new—because it serves as an unprecedented analogue for the male bar mitzvah and because it provides a new opportunity for adults who had missed out on celebrating their coming of age as Jews at the age of puberty; Barry Holtz evaluates the uses of midrash by literary critics and teachers in settings where the midrashic mode is often quite alien to the thinking of contemporary audiences; Joseph Reimer writes as both a participant and observer of *ḥavurot*, communities based on models of Jewish fellowship first created by rabbis some two thousand years ago, yet informed by uniquely American sensibilities of the 1960s; Charles S. Liebman analyzes the dynamic impact of life in a newly founded Jewish state on the way Israelis understand the essence of Jewish tradition; and Arnold M. Eisen writes of the varying efforts of modern Jewish thinkers to define the nature and limits of Jewish tradition. Collectively, these essays attest to the receptivity of contemporary Jews to traditional ways and simultaneously illustrate the complexity and challenges inherent in the reclamation of tradition.

New programs designed to accommodate the changing role of women in Jewish life serve as a prime case in point. With the onset of the feminist revolution in the mid-1960s, Jewish women have assumed a more active role in synagogue life and other religious institutions. The adult bat mitzvah has provided some women with a belated education that enables them to participate more knowledgably in Jewish life. Stuart Schoenfeld's ethnographic study well illustrates the complex interplay of new and old ways in the adult bat mitzvah: both the content of study and the setting within the synagogue link students with the Jewish past; but the entire enterprise of adult women preparing for full participation in Jewish religious life represents a radical departure from traditional patterns. The rite of passage is hallowed by tradition, but the role transition and the participants in the rite are distinctly modern.

The interplay between tradition and change is even more complex within feminist Judaism. As Shulamit Magnus notes, some ceremonies and liturgies reclaim traditional women's observances—such as New Moon celebrations, welcoming a newborn girl, and so on. But feminist Judaism also challenges the conventional wisdom about the nature of Jewish tradition when it poses the provocative question, WHOSE tradition? So much of the tradition recorded in Jewish texts reflects the perceptions and needs of Jewish elites—which, with rare exceptions, consisted of males. Only limited information has survived on the traditional life of Jewish women. Accordingly, contemporary Jewish women have struggled to retrieve a usable past. Magnus is sensitive to the quest for authenticity that drives feminist Jews back to traditional forms, but she is also aware of the radical discontinuity inherent in their quest.

Whereas feminist Jews struggle to retrieve a USABLE tradition, contemporary Jewish educators seek an ACCESSIBLE tradition. One of the greatest impediments to the reclamation of tradition by Jews today is the alien quality of that tradition. The essays of Stuart Schoenfeld, Barry Holtz, and Joseph Reimer reflect on the educational challenges that arise when Jews seek to return to the sources of their tradition after having internalized the assumptions of modern Western culture. Schoenfeld's description of the liminality experienced by women in the adult bat mitzvah group suggests that such women suffer a degree of social isolation when they immerse themselves in intensive Jewish study.

Barry Holtz, by contrast, is concerned with the foreign world-view and interpretive mode of rabbinic texts which pose an obstacle to adult

Jews studying the sources of their tradition. Noting the recent infatuation of some contemporary literary critics with the midrashic mode of exegesis, Holtz questions the accessibility of midrash to the modern worldview. He is particularly concerned with the obstacles modern Jews encounter when they confront the values and perceptions of the sages recorded in the classical texts of midrash. (Holtz's prime example also reflects the dissonance between the outlook of those texts and contemporary feminist values.) Reimer addresses yet a third aspect of the confrontation with traditional study, namely the process of interactions during adult education. On the basis of his personal participation in two pioneering *ḥavurot*, he examines how an environment can be created which will permit adults to feel secure enough to become receptive to education.

Few events have forced modern Jews to reconsider their relationship with tradition as much as the establishment of a Jewish state in 1948. In truth, Zionist thinkers since the end of the nineteenth century hoped for a thoroughgoing reassessment of this relationship, believing it necessary for the remaking of the Jewish people's collective psyche. Charles Liebman analyzes the way in which the experience of living in the Jewish state has propelled Jews to reassess the essential components of Jewish tradition. Suddenly, the land of Israel and Jewish sovereignty have assumed a central role after many centuries of peripheral existence in Jewish consciousness and traditional texts. Liebman is especially interested in the new recognition accorded in Israel to rabbis as the custodians of tradition and the ways in which religious traditions have become nationalized through the widespread acceptance within religious circles of the ideology of Rabbi Kook. Through his sophisticated analysis of how Israelis understand and relate to the tradition, Liebman implicitly suggests that the selective retrieval of tradition by one segment of the Jewish people can also isolate them from other segments: there is little congruence between the construction of Jewish tradition by Israeli and American Jews.

Arnold Eisen's essay provides a fitting conclusion to this section because he directly confronts the problematic issues that arise when modern Jews appropriate from the tradition in a selective fashion. Eisen is primarily concerned with the efforts of contemporary Jewish thinkers to define their relationship with Jewish tradition and to characterize the authority of that tradition. Does the tradition have an essence? Is it binding? How selective can one be and still remain true to the tradition? Is it even appropriate to speak of "the tradition?" Ranging widely over the course of modern Jewish history, Eisen elaborates on themes adumbrated in earlier essays in the book. His trenchant analysis raises psychological questions about the ties that bind contemporary Jews to tradition. And he concludes by asking contemporary Jews to consider limiting their autonomy in order to preserve the tradition, a question that reflects the temper of our times and the self-conscious struggle with tradition in some sectors of contemporary Jewish society.

13

Re-inventing Miriam's Well: Feminist Jewish Ceremonials

SHULAMIT S. MAGNUS

Rabbinic legend tells of a miraculous well, created according to one account on the second day of creation, according to another on the twilight of the sixth; a well which accompanied the Israelites during forty years of desert wandering, sustaining their lives. According to yet another account, the waters of the well would spring up, when bidden, with such plenitude that they created rivers between the different tribes, obliging the women to use ships when visiting one another. The waters nourished a plain where all manner of plant and fruit-bearing tree flourished, and they brought fragrant herbs to the women, who then had no need of perfumes. The well was given to Israel because of the merit of Miriam for having watched over her infant brother Moses in the reeds, saving his life, and it was called after her "Miriam's Well." When she died, it departed, leaving the Israelites to fend for themselves, although according to many medieval authors, Miriam's Well moves from river to river and well to well at the conclusion of every Sabbath.[1]

My thanks to Penina Adelman, Rebecca Alpert, and Paula Hyman for comments on my original paper.

[1] See the many Miriam legends collected in Louis Ginzberg, *Legends of the Jews*, 7 vols. (Philadelphia: Jewish Publication Society, 1909-1938, 1946). Those I cite appear in 1:265, 3:52f., 6:22, n. 135.

"Miriam's Well" is a fitting metaphor for the contemporary phenomenon of Jewish feminist creativity, not only because Miriam, a prophet leading liberated women in song and dance, is the most popular figure in feminist midrash and ritual—something I learned only after I chose the title for this paper and researched it—but because the well symbol so perfectly conveys the spirit of the Jewish feminist endeavor.[2] The notion of abundant creative resources lying dormant but accessible if women but bid them to the surface underlies the entire feminist enterprise. Equally basic is the conviction, conveyed in the myth of the waters nourishing an entire people, that the resources of women can sustain not just themselves but Judaism as a whole.

The flourishing of the Jewish feminist endeavor is one of the greater surprises of our times. The general feminist critique of all established religions as inherently and irredeemably patriarchal would seem to make feminism and Judaism irreconcilable antipodes. Traditionalists have made this argument; so have radical feminists of Jewish birth, such as Starhawk, who have joined Goddess cults. In the latter cases, not the

---

[2] The popularity of Miriam as a figure and symbol of women's creativity is illustrated in the very title of Penina V. Adelman's compendium of Jewish women's rituals, *Miriam's Well* (Fresh Meadows, N.Y.: Biblio, 1986), as well as several rituals cited there. Notable is the Sukkoth ritual (11-13) in which Miriam and her well were literally called up to inspire women gathered for a "women's night in the *sukkah*." Responding to the theme of hospitality which marks the Sukkoth festival, as well as to the absence of women from the traditional *ushpizin* (the "guests"—seven patriarchs—"invited" to the *sukkah*), the women invited Miriam to join them and instruct them in the art of celebration: "Now close your eyes and imagine Miriam with her bells and tambourine [proposed the hostess]. The bells chimed, the tambourine jangled and when we opened our eyes again, Miriam seemed to be sitting with us . . . . 'I have brought you a gift, my women friends, since you have invited me to celebrate . . . with you . . . . Do you know how long it has been since anyone thought to invite me into the *sukkah*? My brothers, Moses and Aaron, are always being asked, but not I. In gratitude for such long-awaited hospitality, I give you these . . . . 'Miriam carefully placed the letters on the table before us . . . they formed the words—*Be*ʾ*er Miriam*, the Well of Miriam."

Ms. Adelman informs me that a new ritual, entitled "Kos Miriam," has recently been conceived by a Boston women's Rosh Hodesh group. Created for use at the Passover seder ("We begin our seder with *Kos Miryam*, Miriam's cup, which we symbolically fill with *mayim ḥayyim*, living waters from Miriam's Well . . . we symbolically invoke this sustenance"), the ritual has also been used on the Sabbath, Yom Hashoah, and at bat mitzvahs (correspondence and conversation, 15 May 1990). Miriam often figures as a symbol of feminist assertiveness as well, as in Rita J. Burns, *Has the Lord Indeed Spoken Only Through Moses? A Study of the Biblical Portrait of Miriam* (Atlanta: Scholars Press, 1987).

treatment of women alone but the very structure of Judaism, and particularly its relation to the natural world, are found fundamentally offensive and intolerable. Indeed, Judaism's stance toward women is seen as a natural and necessary expression, even the basis, of a whole system of violation of the cosmos. As such, Judaism is irremediable.[3]

The feminist challenge can be a secular one; that is, it may undermine loyalty to religion per se. But the feminist challenge can also be religious, posing an alternate and sometimes antithetical system of values to those of Judaism. Yet it is already clear that this challenge is, for the most part, proving not to be a death-blow to Judaism or to the affiliation of feminists, but rather an immense spur to creative adaptation. It is the latter phenomenon, expressed in the creation of feminist Jewish ritual, that I examine here.

Two notes about terminology. First: specialists in religion and culture make theoretical distinctions between "ceremony" and "ritual," but I employ both terms generically to connote conscious and voluntary stylized expressions.[4] More poetically, I would say with Joseph Campbell that "Ritual is mythology made alive"—noting, however, that in the feminist case (as in Hasidism and Zionism, to cite but two possible examples), the mythology is also actively being elaborated and in some instances, created outright.[5]

Second: I choose the term "feminist Judaism" rather than the more common "Jewish feminism" for the same reason that we call ourselves "American Jews" rather than "Jewish Americans." Just as the primary identity is defined by the noun and then modified by the adjective, so too, in this case. More profoundly, however, it is because the amalgam of feminism and Judaism is reshaping Judaism as a whole. It is not a movement "out there"; it is in the blood and marrow of Judaism, including Orthodoxy. The demand that we pass beyond equality, beyond the "first stage" of feminism, which sought to achieve the right of women to

---

3 Starhawk, *The Spiral Dancę: A Rebirth of the Ancient Religion of the Great Godess* (San Fransisco: Harper and Row, 1979); idem, *Dreaming the Dark: Magic, Sex and Politics* (Boston: Beacon, 1982).

4 On the theoretical distinction, see Evan M. Zuesse, "Ritual," and Bobby C. Alexander, "Ceremony," *The Encyclopedia of Religion* (New York: Macmillan, 1987); I have borrowed from Zuesse in constructing my definition.

5 Joseph Campbell, *The Masks of God: Primitive Mythology* (New York: Penguin, 1970), 118. I will not begin to cite here the literature on the "invention of tradition" in these and other modern Jewish movements (or earlier ones, for that matter); on the historical phenomenon of creating mythology, see *The Invention of Tradition,* ed. Eric Hobsbawm and Terence Ranger (Cambridge: Cambridge University Press, 1983).

assume traditionally male roles, to the "second stage," where women redefine and create new roles reflective of women's experience and sensibilies, is being met.[6] There is a veritable explosion of creativity underway, the vast majority of it not in established, institutionalized settings. Aviva Cantor has aptly characterized the creation of new rituals, nonsexist liturgy, and feminist midrash—and, I would add, feminist music—as a "cottage industry."[7] Some of what is being produced is woefully ignorant Jewishly, for example, a *simḥat bat* celebration in whose liturgy the word *simḥah* was spelled with a *samekh*. Some of it, on the other hand, is quite informed Jewishly, as for example Linda Hirschhorn's brilliant song "Miriam's Slow Snake Dance," in which the opening English words and one Hebrew biblical phrase are set to the distinctive *trop* of *shirat ha-yam*.[8]

All this is a welling up of popular religion; this is its significance and its unavoidability. Despite the fact that much of it takes place outside established Judaism, the sheer breadth of "second-stage" feminist Judaism is making it a central rather than a peripheral phenomenon. The conscious, articulated sensibilities of women are being read back into Judaism and are transforming it, feminizing it.

The distance we have traveled in just a few years is conveyed precisely by this distinction in title, reflected in the different names, for example, a mere six years apart, of Susannah Heschel's book *On Being A Jewish Feminist* and the conference of the Jewish Women's Resource Center in December 1989 entitled "Feminist Judaism."[9] The substantive significance of this semantic distinction is evident in the difference

---

[6] For a succinct statement of the second-stage demand, see Paula Hyman, quoted in Charles Silberman, *A Certain People* (New York: Summit Books, 1985), 267. For an incisive criticism of the Jewish feminist movement for focusing "on getting women a piece of the Jewish pie [rather than on baking] a new one," see Judith Plaskow, "God and Feminism," *Menorah*, 3/2 (February 1982): 1. See, too, idem, *Standing Again at Sinai: Judaism from a Feminist Perspective* (San Francisco: Harper and Row, 1990), which came out after I had completed the work for this project.

[7] Aviva Cantor, *The Jewish Woman, 1900-1985: A Bibliography* (Fresh Meadows, N.Y.: Biblio, 1987), iii f.

[8] Miriam Hirschhorn, "Miriam's Slow Snake Dance," on Hirschhorn's cassette, *Gather Round: Songs of Celebration and Renewal*, (Berkeley: Oyster Albums, Kehilla Publications).

[9] ed. Susannah Heschel, *On Being A Jewish Feminist: A Reader* (New York: Schocken, 1983); "Feminist Judaism: A Jewish Women's Resource Center Conference," 3 December 1989. Plaskow *Standing Again at Sinai*, routinely and deliberately speaks of "a feminist Judaism," the creation of which is one of the author's central goals.

between Heschel's pervasively negative, even hopeless tone and the Resource Center's proclamation of the conference as its "bat mitzvah" celebration, the first item of whose agenda is "to share nachas." As one of the chief archival repositories of feminist Jewish ritual, a burgeoning collection, the Resource Center knows whereof it celebrates. The feminist current is feeding into the ocean of Judaism and reshaping what Judaism is, not just for women but for all Jews. We have only begun to experience the changes which will take place, and I daresay the changes are unstoppable.

Feminist Judaism is much more in the nature of radical innovation than continuity; to suggest anything else is disingenuous. Nevertheless, when feminist Jews scour the tradition for a "usable past," they certainly find it. They claim, with justice, that there was a distinct and powerful women's culture within male Judaism, Ashkenazi and Sephardi. They point to *zeved ha-bat* birth ceremonies for girls in Sephardi tradition, a normative ritual whose text appeared, and still appears, in standard Sephardi prayer books.[10] They point to women's *tekhines*, petitionary prayers and guides to ritual sanctification of every conceivable aspect of women's daily lives, life cycles, and holiday observances.[11] They cite the existence of semiofficial women religious functionaries in traditional Ashkenazi communities: *sogerkes* (also called "vorsorgerinnen"), who led other women in synagogue prayer; *gabetes*, who undertook pious works for the sick, the dead, the poor—but also for wealthy women, serving, for instance, as confessor-priestesses (as I would term them), to other

[10] For a rich treatment of Sephardic women's lives as depicted in Cairo Genizah sources, see S. D. Goitein, *A Mediterranean Society;* vol. 3, *The Family* (Berkeley and Los Angeles: University of California Press, 1978).

[11] The research of Chava Weissler into women's *tekhines* is spurred both by a scholarly desire to uncover Jewish women's spiritual universe and a personal commitment to encouraging its contemporary expression. Weissler's scholarly works are: "The Traditional Piety of Ashkenazic Women," in *Jewish Spirituality From the Sixteenth Century Revival to the Present*, ed. Arthur Green (New York: Crossroad, 1987), 2:245–75; "The Living and the Dead: Ashkenazic Family Relations in the Light of Hebrew and Yiddish Cemetery Prayers," (Paper presented at the Annual Conference of the Association for Jewish Studies, December 1986); "The Religion of Traditional Ashkenazic Women: Some Methodological Issues," *Association for Jewish Studies Review*, 12/1 (Spring 1987): 73-94; "Women in Paradise," *Tikkun*, 2/2 (April-May 1987): 43-47, 117–20; "Traditional Yiddish Literature: A Source for the Study of Women's Religious Lives" (The Jacob Pat Memorial Lecture, Harvard College Library, 1987); "Images of the Matriarchs in Yiddish Supplicatory Prayers," *Bulletin of the Center for the Study of World Religions* 14/1 (1988): 45-51.

women on *ʿerev* Yom Kippur.[12] They cite the ubiquitous presence of Jewish midwives and healers, whose activities were suffused with religious sensibility, and who also functioned as priestesses.

The nineteenth-century memoirs of Pauline Wengeroff, a full treatment of which I am now writing, amply attest to the existence of a rich women's culture in the Jewish Pale, and other memoirs by both women and men do likewise.[13] Feminists may thus claim with justice that Jewish women as well as men inhabited an "enchanted" universe, to borrow from a recent title by Jacob Neusner, and that there is a vast tradition with which we have lost touch in modernity (whose existence, indeed, was ruthlessly stamped out in modernity), but which is there for the reclaiming.[14]

One of the chief observances which has been reclaimed, and which has been a tremendous spur to the reclaiming or outright creation of other rituals, is the Rosh Hodesh celebration. This is one of the best examples of creative adaptation of tradition, since, as participants always point out, traditionally Rosh Hodesh was a women's holiday.[15] While the specific rituals feminists now practice at Rosh Hodesh celebrations are clearly innovations, the fact of Jewish women sharing a sacred moment is certainly not new, and this is its charm: the sense, even while innovating, of being part of a generational chain. This feeling is given stark expression in the words of two feminist writers, who, in best midrashic tradi-

---

[12] The activities of such functionaries are richly detailed in Pauline Wengeroff's *Memoiren einer Grossmutter* (Berlin: Poppelauer, 1908). Another, more famous memoirist, Gluckel of Hameln, frequently and unselfconsciously (the most telling testimony) mentions women's piety and regular synagogue-going, saying offhandedly of herself, "I had risen for morning prayers and gone to the synagogue"; and of her daughter, Esther, "she never missed a synagogue service" (*The Memoirs of Gluckel of Hameln,* trans. Marvin Lowenthal [New York: Schocken, 1977], 130, 240).

[13] Wengeroff, *Memoiren;* Bella Chagall, *Burning Lights* (New York: Schocken, 1946); Israel Joshua Singer, *Of a World That is No More* (New York: Vanguard, 1970); Chaim Grade, *My Mother's Sabbath Days* (New York: Knopf, 1987). Glimpses of traditional women's culture which existed in parts of eastern Europe until World War II are also to be found in *From A Ruined Garden: The Memorial Books of Polish Jewry,* ed. Jack Kugelmass and Jonathan Boyarin (New York: Schocken, 1983).

[14] Neusner, *The Enchantments of Judaism* (New York: Basic Books, 1987). Wengeroff's is an eloquent, aggrieved voice recording the eradication by modernity of traditional Jewish culture in general, and traditional Jewish women's culture in particular.

[15] Arlene Agus, "This Month Is For You: Observing Rosh Hodesh as A Woman's Holiday," in *The Jewish Woman: New Perspectives,* ed. Elizabeth Koltun (New York: Schocken, 1976), 84-93; Adelman, *Miriam's Well,* 6f.

tion, utterly collapse time when describing Rosh Hodesh celebration. "During Biblical times," they say, "sacrifices were offered. . . . [It] was a day of rest for women when WE refrained from traditional distaff tasks . . ." (emphasis added).[16]

Rosh Hodesh rituals may be anything from a scholarly (or hagiographic) presentation on some aspect of Jewish women's history, to artistic renderings—verbal, musical, or plastic—of women's experience, to cooking of symbolic foods, to guided imaging and myth-writing. In all instances, the rituals articulate with received tradition while consciously inventing new ones.

Perhaps the best example of this is the creation of midrash around women's themes in the weekly Torah reading, or from a theme in an upcoming holiday, a particularly popular activity of Rosh Hodesh groups. Midrash writing allows participants to "enter" a story, a term I would use for a process very different from fixed retelling, in that the story is filled out or even radically rewritten in ways that are felt to be more affirming to women than the originals. An example of both processes is midrash-writing about Dinah, whose yearning for female companionship is both elaborated beyond the sparse biblical verse and given a positive valuation, as opposed to that ascribed to it in traditional midrash.[17] In "entering" Dinah's story, contemporary feminists explore their own yearning for female friendship and solidarity. Needless to say, the rape of Dinah, about which the biblical text says nothing in Dinah's own words, becomes the occasion for both the elaboration of Dinah's experience and the expression of contemporary feelings of societal violation.[18] If Miriam is the mythic figure of feminist liberation and self-expression, Dinah is the archetype of the silenced, atomized woman.[19]

---

[16] Judith Chalmer and Fran Stolin, *Lilith* no. 21 (Fall 1988): 17.

[17] For rabbinic midrashim on Dinah, see Ginzberg, *Legends*, esp. 1:66, 395, 396, 397, 399, 412; 2:10, 38; 4:259; 5:299, 313, 314.

[18] The fact that Dinah, an offspring of Leah and Jacob no less than the six sons who later become tribes in Israel, is not made the progenitor of a tribe has led to a pointed "correction," expressed in the title of an anthology of feminist Jewish writings, *The Tribe of Dinah: A Jewish Woman's Anthology*, ed. Melanie Kaye/Kantrowitz and Irena Klepfisz (Montpelier: Sinister Wisdom, 1986).

[19] "Dina . . . went out of her father's house seeking other women. What did she want? What did she want to give? . . . No words, no hints. Only what the men felt and thought . . . . Did Dina ever speak to the women? Did they gather secretly? Comfort each other? . . . Did they want something for themselves?" (*The Tribe of Dinah*).

Another favored story to "enter" and elaborate is that of the midwives who defied Pharaoh's order to drown male Israelite infants. Although the biblical text clearly signals approval for this act, very little is made of it in traditional (i.e., male) Jewish lore.[20] Far less slighted (because they center around Moses and the royal palace), yet still relatively uncelebrated, are the tenacity and inventiveness of Miriam standing guard over her brother and the altruism and heroism of Pharaoh's daughter, who saved and raised an infant she knew to be Hebrew. Feminists write midrash around these themes for three purposes: to assert that Jewish women have a mythic past; to fill in the blanks of women's sacred history; and then to fill out Jewish sacred history generally—in these instances, to balance the prominence of Moses and Aaron with a new conspicuousnesss for Shifra, Puah, Miriam, and Bithya/Bathya, as Pharaoh's daughter is named in rabbinic midrash.

Most importantly, feminists write midrash about these women in a very different vein from prior, rabbinic midrash. Feminists assert that these women, qua women, defied patriarchal tyranny, and they then use their stories to explore the nature and social implications of women's solidarity. Indeed, there is something of a women's "liberation theology" emerging from discussion of the midwives' defiance in particular, which is seen as the paradigm for resistance to patriarchal oppression generally.[21]

---

[20] For rabbinic midrashim on the midwives, see Ginzberg, *Legends,* 2:251, 257; 5:393; among the many references to Pharaoh's daughter, see 2:271, 275, 278, 369; 5:33, 96, 165, 258, 398, 401, 435; 6:186, 297, 412.

[21] For a fascinating comparison of the treatment of Pharaoh's daughter, and women generally, in the Zohar and in the *Sheloshah sheʿarim,* a classic compendium of *tkhinus* of the eighteenth and nineteenth centuries, see Weissler, "Women in Paradise." For the midwives as a paradigm of resistance to patriarchal oppression, see Geela Rayzl Raphael's song, "Shifra and Puah," in "Shira Hadashah," unpub. pamphlet submitted to the Melton Center for Jewish Education in the Diaspora, Senior Educator's Program, Hebrew University of Jerusalem, 1989; and Irv Ackelsberg, Shoshana Bricklin, Jan Cooper, et al., "Midwives of Justice: A Hagaddah Honoring the Struggle for Human Rights in Latin America" (unpub. pamphlet [Philadelphia: New Jewish Agenda, 1987]). "The midwives' disobedience was the first stirring of resistance among the Jewish slaves . . . . It was the forerunner of later resistance . . . . For this reason . . . we say that Shifra and Pu'ah were not only midwives to the children . . . but also to the entire Jewish people . . . . Our sages affirmed this when they said: 'The Jews were liberated from Egypt because of the righteousness of the women.' (Talmud, Sota, 11b)." An early expression of this theme is in Arthur Waskow, *Seasons of Our Joy: A Celebration of Modern Jewish Renewal* (New York: Bantam, 1982), 156. My thanks to Dr. Waskow for bringing this to my attention.

Feminist midrash writing in the Rosh Hodesh context, and in general, is such an important agent of syncretizing feminist and Jewish consciousness that one writer has formulated it as a feminist Jewish *miṣvah.* In terms reminiscent of the Haggadah's injunction to retell the exodus in every generation, Irene Fine exhorts, "Therefore, it is incumbent on contemporary women to study the text and to write modern stories that maintain a relationship with the text, incorporating their own experiences and consciousness into Judaism."[22]

The creation of ceremonials to mark passages in the lives of women is one of the most central, ongoing activities of feminist Judaism. In this, the movement has passed beyond its early criticism of received tradition for what has not been provided, to creative remedy. It is inconceivable that the workings of the bladder and intestines, but not those of the uterus, would have been sanctified had women had anything to do with the creation or codification of blessings, early feminists said. Now women have this involvement, and such blessings and full-blown rituals to accompany them, abound.

If birth rituals for girls have some precedent in Jewish tradition, completely new are ceremonials to mark menstruation and menarche, first menstruation. Such rituals stand traditional attitudes on the head by consecrating a natural function which, in traditional understanding, plunges women into *ṭum'ah,* a state of ritual impurity. Such ceremonials can in no way be considered a continuity or reworking of prior tradition, though some familiar observances may be worked into them. Thus the inventors of one menarche ritual, which they have called *bagrut* or "coming of age," have slated its observance for a Rosh Hodesh, in order to mark the consonance of women's cyclical biology with lunar cyclicality. This, of course, would also achieve the ultimate goal of any successful ritual: the appearance of its being "natural," organic, rather than contrived.[23]

Other women have suggested reclaiming *miqvah* for menarche ceremonies, appropriating a symbol traditionally related to menstruation but infusing it with a completely new signification which embodies, in fact, fundamental criticism of the old one. The classic feminist critique is that men go to the *miqvah* to prepare themselves for God, while women go to the *miqvah* to prepare themselves for men. Now, it is suggested, a Jewish girl should go to *miqvah* for the first time to mark the maturation of her

---

22 Introduction to *Taking the Fruit: Modern Women's Tales of the Bible* (San Diego: Women's Institute for Continuing Jewish Education, 1989), 6.

23 See Adelman, *Miriam's Well,* 73f.

own body, with no reference to men. "The point" of going to *miqvah* for the first time at menarche, according to one writer—who, it should be stressed, herself observes the traditional laws of family purity—was "not to emphasize the reproductive or sexual aspects of woman's life but to bring [these] fully into a whole Jewish life . . . "[24]

Numerous versions of blessings for menstruation now circulate; a particularly ingenious one is to be found in "Siddur Nashim," by Naomi Janowitz and Maggie Wenig.[25] My point here is not the specifics, but the revolutionary inclusion of a core feminist value, namely, positive images and valuation of the female body, into Judaism.

At the other end of the female life cycle, ceremonials to mark menopause are also being created, though, perhaps because of the demographics of the Jewish feminist movement, they are not so widespread as menstruation ceremonials; one would expect this to change with the aging of the current feminist population.[26] Adult bat mitṣvah ceremonies, on the other hand, for women "from their 20s to their 80s,"[27] have become common and are one feminist rite most likely to be celebrated within established synagogues. Indeed, synagogues welcome and encourage them as a means to introduce fresh, eager

---

24 Whether this or other feminist Jewish rituals will also be "felicitous," as Lawrence Hoffman puts it, remains to be determined over time ("Criteria for Evaluating Liturgy," *Sh'ma* 14/264 (23 December 1983, p. 30–32); On the use of *miqvah* for menarche rituals, see Evelyn Hutty Dodd, *Lilith* 2 (Winter 1976-1977). See, too, Shulamit Magnus, "More Light on Menarche," in *New Menorah*, 2nd series, 1 (Winter 1985): 10, a response to Phyllis Berman, "Enter: A Woman," *Menorah* 6/1–2 (November–December 1984).

25 "Siddur Nashim: A Sabbath Prayer Book for Women," trans. and supplemented by Naomi Janowitz and Maggie Wenig (unpub. pamphlet), 96.

26 Penina Adelman informs me that this is already happening. See *Miriam's Well*, 67f. See, too, one ceremony on "Becoming A Crone: Ceremony at 60," by Marcia Cohn, *Lilith* 21 (Fall 1988), 18f.

27 Ruth Mason, "Adult Bat Mitzvah: Changing Women, Changing Synagogues," *Lilith* 14/4 (Fall 1989): 21. Rabbi Avis Miller of Adas Israel Congregation in Washington, D.C., leads what may be the largest adult bat mitzvah program in the United States; Helen Belitsky, "Adult Bat Mitzvah Enriches Jewish Life for Women of All Ages," *Women's World* (B'nai Brith Women) (April/May/June, 1987). Some 180 women have completed the course since the program began in 1978; a group ceremony is celebrated in the synagogue on a Sabbath morning, in which the women conduct the entire service (Conversation with Rabbi Miller, 23 May 1990). Mason, "Adult Bat Mitzvah," 21, estimates that thousands of women have undergone adult bat mitzvahs in the last ten years.

talent—service leaders, Torah chanters.[28] For participants, the ceremonies are not so much a rite of passage in their personal as in their Jewish lives, a "commitment to community . . . a middle-aged realization that the time had come for me to address community. I wanted to say 'we' instead of 'I,'" in the words of one.[29]

By far the most popular ceremonial innovation for the life cycle is birth ceremonies for girls. The extent of the perceived need for such ceremonials is indicated by their ubiquity in all branches of Judaism, including Orthodoxy, less than three decades after they first appeared. The specifics may differ immensely in different denominational settings, but the point again is not only WHAT is done, but that SOMETHING is done. In all cases, ritual is innovated because of a perceived imbalance in the value assigned to the birth of male and female Jews; and in accepting that view, all the ceremonies, however cautious, are responding to an internalized feminist critique.

Some of the most interesting theoretical arguments about ritual within feminist circles have centered around birth ceremonies for girls. To what extent should such rituals be based on the circumcision ceremony for boys? The most radical argument for complementarity has resulted in the proposal of hymenotomy, a ritual rupturing of the hymen to consecrate the regenerative organ for girls, just as the penis is consecrated for boys in circumcision. Strict complementarity would also dictate holding this or any other ritual on the eighth day after birth. But taking the ritual for the boy as the determining reference for rituals for the girl seems to some feminists a fundamentally flawed procedure, and the arena is then opened wide for an outpouring of creative alternatives. Some of the better known are ritual footwashing, recalling the welcoming custom in the Bible; immersion of the infant in a real or simulated *miqvah,* to symbolize covenanting through the female image of water; a verbal covenanting ceremony held specifically on the Sabbath, since this day is called a "covenant" between God and Israel; or the use of the *Havdalah* ceremony to mark the distinction between prenatal and postnatal life, for the infant and her family.[30]

---

28 Rabbi Melvin Glazer of the Jewish Center of Princeton, New Jersey, said of one adult *bat miṣvah,* "When she came, she knew nothing. Now she's an ace Torah reader. She's one of the major players around here" (quoted in Mason, "Adult Bat Mitzvah," 22).

29 Quoted in Mason, "Adult Bat Mitzvah," 22.

30 See Daniel I. Leifer and Myra Leifer, "On the Birth of a Daughter," in *The Jewish Woman,* ed. Koltun, 21-30; "Blessing The Birth of a Daughter: Jewish Naming Cere-

These and other life cycle rituals for women have come under generic attack on both Jewish and feminist grounds for accentuating biology as the foundation of identity, personal and religious. Cynthia Ozick has denounced such ceremonials as a betrayal of the basic feminist and, she says, Jewish fight against the assertion that "anatomy is destiny."[31] Penina Adelman addresses this dilemma in the introduction to her compendium of women's rituals by stating,

> We have no desire to return to the oppressive conditions of our female ancestors whose lives revolved around key points in the lifecycle . . . to the exclusion of other aspects of their development . . . Our challenge is to become aware of our bodies without idolizing them; to discern transcendant meanings in our physicality without bypassing its blood, sweat and tears.[32]

But perhaps the best response comes from anthropologist Barbara Myerhoff who, paraphrasing Claude Lévi-Strauss, writes, "We belong both to Nature and Culture."[33] This dual identity and the tensions it produces are part of the human condition and underlie all cultures and religious systems. Feminist Jews will have to address its paradoxes along with everyone else.

The strength of Jewish feminist ceremonials is their individuality and the creative involvement of their authors, who have the greatest emotional investment in them. Thus one of the prime problems of established ritual in any culture—staidness, or to use Jewish idiom, *keva*, lack of *kvona* (focused intentionality), is absent here. This same strength is also the rituals' weakness, since they lack a shared symbolism and the

---

monies for Girls," ed. Toby Fishbein Reifman with Ezrat Nashm (unpub. pamphlet); "Birth Ceremonies—Brit Banot: Covenant of Our Daughters" (unpub. pamphlet, Jewish Women's Resource Center, 1985) and the copious collection of rituals in the Center's New York collection; Mary Gendler, "Sarah's Seed: A New Ritual for Women," *Response* 24 (Winter 1974-1975): 65-75; Sharon and Michael Strassfeld, "An Appropriate Ceremony for Daughters," *Sh'ma* 14/264 (December 1983): 27f; Rebecca Trachtenberg Alpert, Nancy Fuchs-Kreimer, Linda Holtzman, et al., "The Covenant of Washing," *Menorah* 4/3-4 (April–May 1983): 5f.; Susan Weidman Schneider, *Jewish and Female: Choices and Changes in Our Lives Today* (New York: Simon and Schuster, 1985), 121f., and the literature cited there.

[31] Ozick, "Torah as the Matrix for Feminism," *Lilith* 12–13 (Winter–Spring 1985): 47f.

[32] *Miriam's Well*, 9.

[33] Myerhoff, "Rites of Passage: Process and Paradox," in *Celebration: Studies in Festivity*, ed. Victor Turner (Washington, D.C.: Smithsonian Institution Press, 1982), 109.

immense power of rites so ancient and pervasive as to be anonymous. Yet, to borrow from Myerhoff once again,

> The absence of unifying, axiomatic common symbols does not alter the possibility of our use of rites to provide and state meanings of life on a smaller scale . . . [although] we do so alone, often in ignorance and always in uncertainty. . . . [It] is heroic to assemble meaning, find symbolic expressions for them, gather a small society of one's choice, then enact the story in a ritual. . . . Instead of having rites performed on us, we do them to and for ourselves and immediately we are involved in a form of self-creation that is potentially community-building, providing . . . regeneration by revitalizing old symbols from the perspective of the present.[34]

I stated earlier that Jewish feminist ceremonials are more radical innovation than continuity; this is so for two reasons. First, while there was a distinct women's culture in traditional Jewish society, the creation of the ceremonials described here derives inspiration from outside Jewish tradition, from contemporary feminism, and is not in a direct line with anything that preceded it. This much is apparent from the clearly datable launching of the phenomenon in the 1960s and 1970s. For many, though by no means all, of the women who actively create women's rituals, the activity is the bridge between a highly developed, prior, feminist consciousness and a far newer and less grounded Jewish connection. For these women, a feminist Judaism is the only affirmable Jewish identity. Not having been raised on *tekhines*, never having heard of *sogerkes* (ignorance they share with most postwar Orthodox women), they are not so much building on a past as discovering one—with immense relief, for its existence means that both feminism and Judaism can be affirmed. But even for women with extensive traditional backgrounds, feminism, not the women's court, is the catalyst for current feminist Jewish creativity; that provenance, and often a severe clash of values between tradition and feminism, are felt only too sharply.[35]

---

34 "Rites of Passage," 129–31.

35 The best-known expression of this conflict is Blu Greenberg, *On Women and Judaism: A View From Tradition* (Philadelphia: Jewish Publication Society, 1981), but see too Sara Reguer, "Kaddish From the Wrong Side of the Mehitzah," in *On Being a Jewish Feminist*, 177–81, and more recently and most poignantly, Norma Baumel Joseph, (Paper presented at the American Jewish Congress Conference on "The Empowerment of Jewish Women," Session on Rites and Rights: Women in Religious Life," Philadelphia, 17 September 1989).

Second, for all their use of tradition, contemporary feminist ceremonials are an innovation because the women's culture of the past existed alongside male Judaism as a separate sphere which women inhabited at male behest and, whatever women may have made of it, for male convenience. The current feminist thrust, by contrast, is for a transformation and feminization of Judaism as a whole. While feminists indeed create separate "women's space" (more on which below), it is by their choice and for very different reasons than was the creation of the traditional women's domain. Replication of a women's domain within patriarchy is not, of course, what contemporary feminists wish to accomplish.

However, while I would argue that the lineage here is undeniably alien, the PROCESS of creating new traditions by grappling with the old ones, discerning their meanings, and applying them in new guises when possible, is quintessentially Jewish. Don Saliers has said that through ritual it is possible "to actualize the tradition."[36] Actualizing Jewish tradition for women is what feminist Jewish ceremonials are about. In an age when Jewish survival is threatened by mass apathy on the one hand and principled rejection of tradition on the other, that is very good news for the Jews.

I would like to close with some reflections not on feminist ceremonials but on the feminists who create them, as a group phenomenon.

Cultural anthropologists, following the work of Arnold van Gennep, distinguish three stages of rites of passage, rituals which mark transition from one culturally recognized state to another. The first stage is SEPARATION, in which the individual or group of potential initiates is marked apart from the rest of the group. The second is MARGINALIZING, or pushing the separated individuals utterly to the margin of society and culture, to a position on the threshold (*limen*, in Latin), a state called "liminality." The third stage is AGGREGATION, or rejoining the group after changed status has been conferred.

For our purposes, it is the theory of liminality, elaborated by the noted anthropologist Victor Turner, which is of primary interest. In his landmark study *The Ritual Process,* Turner says that "if liminality is regarded as a time and place of withdrawal from normal modes of social action, it can be seen as potentially a period of scrutinization of the central values and axioms of the culture in which it occurs." He says further that "liminality, marginality and structural inferiority are conditions in which

---

[36] Quoted in Theodore Weinberger, "Re-Examining Ritual: The Passover Seder," *Response,* 16/3 (Winter 1989): 17.

are frequently generated myths, symbols, rituals, philosophical systems and works of art."[37]

What marks feminist Jewish consiousness is precisely a sense of liminality within Jewish tradition, a radical perception by women of marginality of self in Judaism. What Turner notes about liminal entities, such as neophytes in initiation or puberty rites, applies to these feminists: the scrutiny of received Jewish tradition and established culture from an outsider's stance; and a subsequent explosion of creativity on the part of those who choose to continue articulating with that culture in some way.

The feminist case differs fundamentally from those which Turner studies in that not the larger culture, but the women induce liminality: the women initiate self-separation, thrusting liminality upon themselves. Sometimes the self-separation takes physical expression, in feminist retreats, prayer groups (including Orthodox women's "*tefillah* groups"), and Rosh Hodesh groups, but underlying all these behaviors is a liminal MENTALITY: the radical awareness of being apart in a way that is liberating rather than oppressive.[38] The feminist case is different, too, from tribal instances Turner studies, in that the physical states of liminality, rather than being one-time affairs followed by permanent absorption into the larger group, are passed into and out of regularly.[39] The liminal MENTALITY of feminism, moreover, is permanent, more reminiscent of the liminal social types (poets, court jesters, monks), movements (millennarian cults), and social concepts (matrilineality in patrilineal systems) which Turner also cites.[40]

There is a further element of Turner's theory which I believe also has bearing on our case, the social state Turner terms "communitas." "Communitas," as distinct from "community," which envelops disparate individuals, is a state of identity-melding between those who share a liminal state. Typically, in the cases Turner studies in preindustrial

---

37 Victor Turner, *The Ritual Process: Structure and Anti-Structure* (Ithaca: Cornell University Press, 1977), 128, 167.

38 This in contrast to marginalization in its conventional sense, with its denigration and effacement of women; imposed from without, often internalized by women, this is one of the core sins of patriarchy, Jewish and otherwise.

39 My thanks to Dr. Rebecca Alpert for bringing the need to make this distinction to my attention.

40 See Barbara G. Myerhoff, Linda A. Camino, and Edith Turner, "Rites of Passage," *Encyclopedia of Religion* 12 (1987), 382. Jews, of course, can be seen as a liminal group, with attendant consequences for cultural creativity. See John Murray Cuddihy, *The Ordeal of Civility: Freud, Marx, Lévi-Strauss and the Jewish Struggle with Modernity* (New York: Basic Books, 1974).

African tribes, such a state is induced in initiands in puberty rites, who are removed physically from their families and separated off with each other, often for weeks, while undergoing the initiation process. All previous aspects of individual or family identity are made irrelevant—wealth, property, or status in the tribe: the chief's son and those of lowly tribal families have the same status in this liminal stage. "Communitas," or radical bonding, often results and, for all the harsh rigor of the process which produced it, is often remembered with intense fondness by those who experienced it.

I believe that gender bonding is one of the most important yet overlooked aspects of Jewish society in modern times. Experience of male bonding—in the *kloyz*, the yeshiva, the *kolel*, the rebbe's *tish*—is, I believe, one of the radical innovations of ultra-Orthodoxy; the amount of time involved, often years, and the intensity of contact made these contexts qualitatively different from simple participation in the premodern, all-male *minyan*. Given the overall numbers of men involved in the Hasidic and Musar movements, it was an innovation with necessary and extreme consequences for women, something which thus far has not systematically been explored.[41]

Female bonding in contemporary feminism is the more "obvious" to us, the word "obvious" highlighted, because what we see is what we choose to see or are prepared by cultural conditioning to see. (The examples of male bonding just cited are no less obvious, yet are less culturally "visible," hence ignored. Men, the norm in social groupings, are not perceived in terms of gender; women, being "other," are.) And female bonding is an essential aspect of the feminist phenomenon.

I believe that some form of communitas is achieved in Rosh Hodesh groups, particularly those with stable membership, and in feminist

[41] A passing reference to the lowering of the "the status of women" in Hasidism is in Jacob Katz, *Tradition and Crisis: Jewish Society at the End of the Middle Ages* (New York: Free Press of Glencoe, 1971), 243. Cf. Ada Rapoport-Albert, "On Women and Hasidism: S. A. Horodecky and the Maid of Ludmir Tradition," in *Jewish History: Essays in Honor of Chimen Abramsky*, ed. Ada Rapoport-Albert and Steven J. Zipperstein (London: Halban, 1988), 495-525. Although he does not make it a primary focus, Emmanuel Etkes is alert to the implications for women in the Musar movement's innovation of prolonged advanced Torah study for large numbers of male adolescents and young adults; see his excellent "Family and The Study of Torah among Lithuanian Talmudist Circles in the Nineteenth Century" (in Hebrew), *Zion* 51/1 (1986): 87-106. Of interest, too, is Shaul Stampfer, "Shelosha Yeshivot Lita'iot be-Me'ah ha-19" (Three Lithuanian Yeshivas in the Nineteenth Century) (Ph.D. dissertation, Hebrew University, 1981).

retreats, and is one of the prime underpinnings of the feminist Jewish movement. Feminists have repeatedly described the ecstasy of entering such groups where individual aspects of prior identity—marital staus, sexual oritentation, profession, class—become irrelevant and all that is left is shared femaleness.[42] I believe that something of this nature has taken place in a group in which I have been active, the "Women of the Wall," which comprises women from every conceivable strand of Jewish life, radical feminists to Orthodox and everything in between, who have bonded around a shared experience of affirmation: women's group prayer, with Torah reading, at the Western Wall. Although this was not the original intent, the very experience of bonding across ideological and denominational lines has become one of the most precious aspects of the group's existence to its members, emboldening them to take on no less than the Israeli religious establishment in the cause both of women's spiritual expression and pandenominational *ahavat yisraʾel*.

The experience of "communitas" and the creative fruits of feminist liminality are the most significant characteristics and contributions of feminist Judaism. They are the functional equivalents of the gushing waters of Miriam's Well.

---

[42] See Adelman, *Miriam's Well*, 7: "In the Rosh Hodesh group, the boundaries between women which operate in society are no longer so sharply felt, because we no longer act in reaction to society but in freedom from it."

14

Ritual and Role Transition: Adult Bat Mitzvah as a Successful Rite of Passage

STUART SCHOENFELD

> I was sitting in my seat, my knees shaking. As I was walking up, I heard F's voice behind me, 'It's between you and God. You'll be all right.' When I got up there I was calm.
>
> — a member of the adult bat mitzvah class describing her ascent to the bimah.

In the spring of 1988, over the course of the morning services on the first and second days of Passover, eighteen women ascended the bimah of a large Reform temple, received their first aliyot, read or chanted from the Torah, and delivered brief commentaries on their Torah portions. This ceremony was the culminating event of the group bat mitzvah class in which they had participated for a year and a half.

The group bat mitzvah of adult women is a contemporary adaptation of well-established, although not ancient, Jewish rituals of early adolescence. Puberty appears in Jewish law in an age-of-majority context in the Mishnah, the second-century code of Jewish law. Marking a boy's thirteenth birthday with a synagogue ritual followed by a reception appears to have become common in the late Middle Ages.[1] A corre-

[1] Isaac Rivkind, *Le-ot u-le-zikaron toledot "bar miṣvah" ve-ha-tiftakoto be-hay ha-am ve-ha-raboto be-ṣaruf bibliografia im ha-arot.* (Hebrew) . . . (Bar Mitzvah: A Study in Jewish Cultural History, with an Annotated Bibliography) (New York: Bloch, 1942);

sponding bat mitzvah ritual was introduced in 1922 when Rabbi Mordecai Kaplan called his eldest daughter, Judith, to the Torah.[2]

The elaboration of bar/bat mitzvah into a ritual for adults is a contemporary adaptation of a traditional form. This elaboration was not done at the initiative of the leadership of any branch of Judaism. Rather, it began as a local practice which spread because of its popularity. It is possible to characterize adult bar/bat mitzvah as a "folk" innovation that has been incorporated into "elite" Judaism.[3]

Initially the idea of a belated bar mitzvah was expressed by men who felt that their Jewish identity was incomplete without having one. A television drama in the 1950s used this as a plot device, as did an episode of "The Dick Van Dyke Show." This feeling has no basis in Jewish tradition, as a youth becomes *bar miṣvah* at age thirteen with or without a ceremony. However, rabbis welcomed men who came in search of a ritual confirmation of their Jewish identity, creating opportunities for study and applying the name "bar mitzvah" metaphorically to the adult ritual. In those settings where the movement for gender equality in Judaism had been successful, women were welcomed as well. By the 1970s, descriptions of adult bar/bat mitzvah ceremonies were in print.[4]

Abraham Millgram, *Jewish Worship* (Philadelphia: Jewish Publication Society, 1971), 466.

[2] Paula Hyman, "The Introduction of Bat Mitzvah in Conservative Judaism in Postwar America," *YIVO Annual* 19 (1990): 133.

[3] On the distinction between "folk" and "elite" Judaism see Charles Liebman, *The Ambivalent American Jew* (Philadelphia: Jewish Publication Society, 1973); idem, "The Religious Life of American Jewry," in *Understanding American Jewry,* ed. Marshall Sklare (New Brunswick, N.J.: Transaction Books, 1981), 96-124: on the applicability of the distinction to the role of bar/bat mitzvah in contemporary Judaism see Stuart Schoenfeld, "Folk Religion, Elite Religion and the Role of Bar Mitzvah in the Development of the Synagogue and Jewish School in America," *Contemporary Jewry* 9 (1988): 67-85; for other applications of the concept of "folk religion" to Judaism see Joshua Trachtenberg, *Jewish Magic and Superstition: A Study in Folk Religion* (New York: Athenaeum, 1987 [1939], and Mordecai Kaplan, *Judaism as a Civilization: Towards A Reconstruction of America-Jewish Life* (New York: Schocken, 1967 [1934]). As noted by Liebman, "Religious Life," the folk-elite distinction, while widely cited, requires further theoretical elaboration.

[4] Richard Siegel, "Adult Bar Mitzvah," *Moment* (October 1975): 66f.; Albert Axelrad, "Belated Bar/Bat Mitzvahs," in *The Second Jewish Catalog* (Philadelphia: Jewish Publication Society, 1971), 78-81. Axelrad was at the center of the innovation and diffusion of this new ritual practice. For a description of a 1989 adult bar mitzvah see Bob Greene, "Herman Gollub's Bar Mitzvah." *Esquire* 112/1 (July 1989): 33f.

Formal programs leading to group adult bar/bat mitzvah have been in place for over a decade.[5]

The movement for increased involvement of women in Judaism has had many consequences: the entry of women into rabbinic and cantorial positions in the Reform, Conservative, and Reconstructionist movements;[6] the assumption of gender equality in the schools and other settings for the youth of these movements; and greater opportunities for female study and worship in some Orthodox settings. It has also brought many women into contact with the Torah for the first time.[7] As bat mitzvah has become almost as common as bar mitzvah only within the past generation,[8] many more women than men have not had contact with the Torah as adolescents. By the late 1980s, the enthusiastic response of Jewish women to the opportunity to have a bat mitzvah as an adult was noted as a major new development.[9]

---

5 Stuart Schoenfeld, "Ritual Performance, Curriculum Design and Jewish Identity: Towards a Perspective on Contemporary Innovations in Bar/Bat Mitzvah Education," *Bikkurim* 6/2 (Winter-Spring 1989): 19-22.

6 While most congregations still have male rabbis and cantors, female enrollment in the seminaries of the Reform, Conservative, and Reconstructionist movements is quite high, indicating a likely gradual but substantial change over the next generation.

7 Arleen Stern, "Learning to Chant the Torah: A First Step," in *On Being a Jewish Feminist,* ed. Susannah Heschel (New York: Schocken, 1981), 182-85.

8 The historical research on bat mitzvah is remarkably sparse; for the only work so far and a discussion of issues for future research, see Hyman, "The Introduction of Bat Mitzvah."

9 Ruth Mason, "Adult Bat Mitzvah: A Revolution for Women and Synagogues," *Lillith* 14/4 (Fall 1989): 21-24. A previous study of an individual adult bat mitzvah explored the motivations of one woman and the meaning she ascribed to her role as a Jewish woman; see Stuart Schoenfeld, "Integration in the Group and Sacred Uniqueness: An Analysis of Adult Bat Mitzvah," in *Persistence and Flexibility: Anthropological Perspectives on the American Jewish Experience,* ed. Walter Zenner (Albany: SUNY Press), 117-35. The group which is described here shares in much of what was reported there about the individual, but there are important differences. The individual bat mitzvah was not unique but it was institutionally exceptional. It was not part of a program sponsored by the congregation at which it occurred, and the *bat miṣvah* made almost all of her own arrangements. The group bat mitzvah reported here was institutionally structured. To some extent it followed the precedents of previous ones at the congregations. It was largely structured by the rabbis who led it; other congregational staff were also involved. It was, in many ways, institutionally routinized, in form like the adult bat mitzvah classes which are conducted elsewhere, and consequently a more typical structure for adult bat mitzvah than the individual case reported previously. Another important difference was the group experience. The individual who had a bat mitzvah was not Jewishly isolated. She participated in a

The women who went through the process described in this paper experienced the process as a successful rite of passage. The framework of the rite of passage, as initially stated by Arnold van Gennep and elaborated by Victor Turner into a general model of the ritual process, divides the process into three stages: separation, liminality, and reaggregation.[10] In this process, the individual is separated from his or her social role; goes through dramatic, sometimes bizarre, always emotional adventures; and returns to society a different person. The liminal phase of this process "is a no man's land betwixt-and-between the structural past and the structural future."[11] Turner calls the structured relationships based on status and role "societas." Those who go through the liminal phase together experience possibilities and potentialities. Uncertainty and spontaneity are heightened because they have broken away from clear status and role expectations. Instead, the social relationships of those who go through the liminal stage together are based on intuition, insight, shared feelings. Turner applies the term "communitas" to these types of relationships.[12]

In the process of becoming *bat miṣvah* as adults, the women were, in a subjectively important way, transformed. It is important to note, however, that the transformation was one of role, not of status. They did not go from child to adult as in a life-cycle rite of passage, but from one way of playing the role of Jewish woman to another.[13]

Jewish women's group and in other settings. Nevertheless, the process reported in this paper was one of joint preparation. The women felt that one of its important consequences was the way in which the relationships to each other developed through the process.

[10] Arnold van Gennep, *The Rites of Passage,* trans. Monika B. Vizedom and Gabrielle L. Caffee (Chicago: University of Chicago Press, 1960 [1909]); Victor Turner, *Dramas, Fields and Metaphors: Symbolic Action in Human Society* (Ithaca: Cornell University Press, 1972); idem, "Variations on a Theme of Liminality," in *Secular Ritual,* ed. Sally F. Moore and Barbara G. Meyerhoff (Amsterdam: Van Gorcum, 1977), 36-52; idem, "Are There Universals of Performance in Myth, Ritual, and Drama?" in idem, *On the Edge of the Bush: Anthropology as Experience,* ed. Edith Turner (Tucson: University of Arizona Press, 1985), 291-301.

[11] Turner, "Are There Universals," 295.

[12] Turner, *Dramas, Fields and Metaphors.*

[13] The rite of passage framework was used to organize and interpret their experience on the basis of a lengthy tape-recorded interview with nine of the eighteen women. Subsequent conversations and questionnaires received from the women not present at the interviews were consistent with the interpretation.

It may be objected that the researcher's familiarity with the rite of passage process influenced the topics raised in the interviews, the specific wording of questions asked, and the general direction of the discussion at the interviews. In other

Separation

The congregation had previously had adult bat mitzvah classes leading to a ceremony, which two or three women at a time had completed. In the summer of 1986, several women attending the annual retreat organized by the congregation's department of family programming approached the rabbi in charge of continuing education with the request

---

words, what about the dreaded "interviewer effect"—the tendency of those being interviewed to tell the interviewer what it is they think the interviewer wants to hear? Several aspects of the data should lay this objection to rest, while at the same time contributing to the understanding of the group.

The interview was easily and quickly arranged. The researcher was almost invited. The women felt that they had gone through something important. Some were more private about it, but some saw the research as an opportunity to tell more people about it. These responses to the interview indicate that the feeling of having gone through a rite of passage was present in the group and not subtly insinuated by the researcher. At the interview, women spoke in great detail about their experiences and with considerable emotion—behavior not consistent with the tendency to politely try to fit responses into the interviewer's preconceived theory. The women being interviewed also out-numbered the interviewer nine to one. This numerical imbalance made it harder for the researcher to impose his "authority" than in a one-to-one setting. Finally, much of the conversation consisted of the women talking to each other. Near the end of the interview, when the group was thanked for participating, the researcher was thanked for giving the group the chance to get together and relive the experience.

The applicability of a rite of passage framework to this group experience is itself interesting, as the framework does not really fit conventional bar/bat mitzvahs. Conventional bar/bat mitzvahs are more rituals of identification than they are of initiation. They are rarely associated with the intense personal change that has led Mircea Eliade to see death and rebirth as the central metaphors of rituals of initiation. (*Rites and Symbols of Initiation* [New York: Harper and Row, 1975], Previously entitled *Birth and Rebirth,* 1958). In conventional bar/bat mitzvahs, parents and children usually come out of the process much the way they went it—more or less committed or ambivalent about the tradition and community with which they are ritually identifying. This does not deny that many, perhaps most, families experience bar/bat mitzvah as meaningful and happy occasions. Other research on bat/bat mitzvah indicates that they do: Stuart Schoenfeld, "Some Aspects of the Social Significance of Bar and Bat Mitzvah Celebrations," in *Essays in the Social Scientific Study of Judaism and Jewish Life,* ed. Simcha Fishbane and Jack Lightstone (Montreal: Concordia University, 1990), 277-304; idem and Leo Davids, "Practical and Symbolic Social Cohesion in the Bar Mitzvah Practices of an Orthodox congregation" (ms., 1987): Judith Davis, "Mazel Tov: The Bar Mitzvah as a Multigenerational Ritual of Change and Continuity," in *Rituals in Families and Family Therapies,* ed. E. Imber-Black, J. Roberts, and R. A. Whiting (New York: Norton, 1988), 177-208. But they are not experienced as rituals initiating the bar/bat mitzvah into an emotionally richer experience of Jewish life. This is exactly what happened to these women.

to have an adult bar/bat mitzvah class. He told them that he anticipated a drop-out rate of 50%; they could have the class if they signed up a minimum of seven participants. When they returned with twelve or fourteen names, the class was approved and announced in the temple bulletin. The announcement brought in more women and one man, but he did not remain in the group past the first few sessions.

Since the group was voluntary, the separation from previous unsatisfactory role-playing came out of processes that were already under way in the women's lives. The things that were happening in their lives that brought them into the class were quite varied. For example:

> I think I've always had a religious nature but I've been sitting on it all my life. . . . During the High Holidays I made a New Year's resolution. . . . The first service I attended all on my own was Simhat Torah. Coming to that first service . . . was a turning point for me. . . . I was sitting at home . . . around the Christmas holidays . . . just ripe for this, waiting and hoping that I might see some kind of announcement for adult bat mitzvah. And I opened my bulletin.

A few women mentioned wanting to participate in the services, knowing what was going on, as their motivation. Although socially identified as Jews, they felt that was not enough:

> I didn't have the opportunity to study Hebrew or get a Jewish education. I've always felt a lack.

> I had no Jewish education. We had joined [the temple] and over the course of years I became active. . . . I was most embarrassed and frustrated when High Holidays would come around. My husband would say, "Turn the page." I was holding the book and [my husband] with his other hand was turning the page.

> I am taking the Jewish Studies program at X University. In many of my courses, there were very young people who were very comfortable with reading Hebrew, particularly in the Bible. I realized that was a building block in what I wanted to learn. It seemed to me that an adult bat mitzvah made it possible to do that. . . . I was very frustrated, just like D, because I didn't know enough to follow properly.

> I went to [the temple school] from nursery to confirmation. Unfortunately I had no interest in Jewish education or in Hebrew. So I learned next to nothing. It was like I wasn't even Jewish. . . . I married someone from an Orthodox background. I felt ignorant in a lot of things and I wanted to learn more. . . . Every high holidays we'd go to different [synagogues]. . . . We

> joined [the temple] after we had two children, with the intention of sending them to kindergarten there, which we didn't do. . . . We both became active. . . . When H told me there was going to be an adult bat mitzvah class, I'd never heard of that. When she mentioned it I was really excited about the ideas because I was at the stage of my life where I wanted to know about Judaism and I really wanted to know Hebrew. My husband and I had decided that we would send our children to [a Hebrew day school]. I wanted to know what they were learning.

The desire expressed in the last comment to study in order to be more fully involved in the Jewish lives of children was shared by several others. Mothers with young children wanted to be informed about what their children were learning. Others were anticipating the bar or bat mitzvah of their own children and wanted to be able to participate without embarrassment. Two of the members of the class were a mother and daughter. When the married daughter decided to join, her mother also decided to make up for the deficiencies in her Jewish education.

Two women in the group were converts, but they came into the group in different ways. A single woman had recently converted.

> By the end of the Jewish Information Class I was feeling terrific about being Jewish but feeling sad that I didn't have any Jewish friends or family in [the city]. . . . I wanted to meet some people and thought, what better way . . .

A married woman who had converted was in a very different situation. She has a Jewish home and has been active in the congregation for years.

> It has become the main focus of my life in many ways. . . . I've been involved with many things at the temple. I've carried the Torah on Simhat Torah as an honor for being chairperson of different committees, but I've always wanted to read from the Torah. I felt it was time to take steps in that direction.

The desire to make a personal feminist statement about the legitimacy of women's participation in ritual was expressed, but not often, and only as one of several reasons. The specifically female dimension of their bat mitzvah was important, as quotations below indicate, but they saw the bat mitzvah as a consequence of the change in women's status in society, not as a setting in which that change was being promoted as a major innovation.

The decision to enter the class was not always supported by family members. The woman who joined the class after making her New Year's resolution' to attend services was coming by herself; her family, longtime members of the congregation, resisted her desire to become more religious. Another woman described her grown children as "antireligious." In most cases, though, the women in the class reported that members of their families were supportive.

The Liminal Phase

Like other processes of initiation, this process involved taking the initiates out of society and subjecting them to experiences which gave them the esoteric knowledge needed to confirm the new identities for which they were being prepared.[14] However, as Turner's writings on liminality stress, the emotional work of rites of passage is at least as important as the cognitive work. As the process moved toward completion, the emotional side became more intense.

Since these women had families, jobs, university courses, and other obligations, they only left society partially, attending class together for two hours a week. The special relationship that they built up in class, however, remained when they would see each other at services, study groups, or committee meetings. In addition, the sense of being in transition was sustained by the individual studying each would do to prepare for class.

The classes began in January 1987, stopped for the summer, resumed after the high holidays, and continued until after Pesach 1988. The first hour followed the chapter headings in Louis Jacobs, *The Book of Jewish Belief*.[15] Other topics were added and additional shorter readings were used. The topics covered included approaches to understanding God, study of the structure and language of Jewish worship, the evolution of the Reform movement's principles, an introduction to basic traditional religious texts and their usage by Reform Jews, and contemporary issues in Jewish life—such as the relationships between the various branches of Judaism, living after the Holocaust, and contemporary anti-Semitism. Since the women came into the class at different levels, they had different reactions to the text by Jacobs, ranging from "fascinating" to "boring." The readings, however, were used as a takeoff point for discussions, which were consistently remembered as enthusiastic.

---

[14] J. S. La Fontaine, *Initiation: Ritual Drama and Secret Knowledge around the World* (Harmondsworth: Penguin, 1985): Eliade, *Rites and Symbols.*

[15] Louis Jacobs, *The Book of Jewish Belief* (New York: Behrman House, 1984).

> You opened up during the study sessions. This was not a group of thirteen-year-olds who had to get through it. . . . What came together in the actual study sessions was a lot more than just "these are the basics of Judaism."

During the second hour, the class was divided into three groups according to their level of Hebrew, with three Hebrew teachers as instructors. Some, at the most elementary level, began with the letters and vowels of the Hebrew alphabet.

> M handed us the sheet [of the Hebrew alphabet] and I can still remember asking [one of the advanced readers], "What am I supposed to do with this?" My heart was going. . . . I didn't even know what to do with it.

There are other settings at the temple for learning elementary Hebrew. An annual introductory course called "Hebrew without Tears" is taught. Nevertheless, those who began as complete beginners in Hebrew were reassured by the group and the instructors. "It didn't take long—one or two sessions—to realize, 'Everyone is friendly. It's okay to admit that you know nothing.'" Supportive family members also helped.

> To prepare I'd make my husband sit beside me and we'd read over and over and over again. Then I realized that that's where the tears came in, having your husband beside you because he really didn't have the patience and didn't want to be there. Then F made us a tape and I could use my walkman and relieve my husband of the burden.

The combination of discussion in the first hour and Hebrew study in the second seems to have given a particular balance to the process. While the first-hour session had content issues, it was conducted as a discussion group. The issues were serious and were typically open-ended. In the discussion, the members of the group were encouraged to express their opinions and allowed to draw different conclusions. In the second hour, the group's energies were focused on acquiring esoteric skills. Learning Hebrew was in itself an esoteric activity to the absolute beginners. For others, the esoteric skill was learning to read or chant Hebrew from the *tiqqun* (a volume presenting the vocalized and unvocalized text on facing pages) in order to read or chant from the Torah scroll.

In addition to the technical esoteric skills the women were learning in order to read from the Torah, several of the women spoke about their feeling of awe for it.

> Being up there with the Torah was very emotional. . . . We had a woman rabbi a few years ago who had a short study session

> for women. . . . She made all of us go up and hold the Torah. It was an incredible experience.

> The feeling one gets when they actually go up to read from the Torah is so intense. . . . It has to do with time. It has to do with connection from generation to generation. This is the book. This is the document that has been like the silver thread throughout the ages of Judaism. It's such a personal honor to stand before it and read a part.

One woman, who had been active in the congregation and was used to carrying the Torah was unable to breathe at the rehearsal a few days before the ceremony. She commented, "Only during the rehearsal. I got very nervous. I got intimidated by the scroll, not by the people, by the scroll."

Several women associated the feeling of intensity with the recent access of women to the Torah. One woman said,

> [For me] it's not a sacred object, but performing the ritual and having my family there, having the freedom to perform the ritual was very intense.

Another woman corrected a reference to the tradition that "all Jews" read the Torah to "all male Jews" and continued, "Because we're women and so connected with time, and so connected with generations, emotionally I think it was even much more meaningful."

During the winter–spring 1987 session, the atmosphere was more of a class than of preparation for a ritual. Several members had joined the class with the intent of learning Hebrew and how to read Torah but without the intention of participating in the bat mitzvah ceremony. As long as the class dealt with Torah study in a general way and not with learning the particular verses to be chanted or read in the ceremony, the question was moot.

When the group began to meet again in the autumn of 1987, the rabbi who had been conducting the class had left and it was taken over by the temple's senior rabbi. He simply announced that there were so-many weeks left, and that in January each person would get her individual portion. The women vividly recalled their reactions.

One woman remembered that when the rabbi announced that they'd be getting their portions, "We all looked at each other and we all went, uhh!" Another continued,

> I don't know about you, but that's when I started having an anxiety attack [group laughter] because that was the first time he said we were going to get our portions. [interjection: "So

> this was really coming down."] I remember when he actually handed out the portions, you and I and I think B, the ultimate beginners, we had this anxiety attack. [laughter. interjection: "Oh my God, I can't do it, so what, what am I going to do!"] I realized, . . . calm down, [everything's] going to be fine. C kept saying everything is going to be OK, everything is going to be OK. C was wonderful, she was very supportive.
>
> What was happening was that the class was coming together as a real cohesive group through all this. We were becoming very supportive of each other. We were getting to know each other better. We were getting close.

They were well into the liminal phase. Those who had begun committed to a public ceremony in which they could be reintegrated with the knowledge, spiritual growth, and legitimate participation that they had previously lacked were developing confidence in the skills they needed to successfully make the transition. Those who had not intended to participate in the ritual were carried along by the emergent solidarity of the group.

> I wanted to learn Hebrew, that's what I basically came for, and I sort of got sucked into this bat mitzvah business. I got in so deep that I couldn't get out. [comment: "And now she's glad, though."] There was only one way out and that was to go through with it. I'm really grateful.'
>
> You were given the option but there was a certain group pressure, it was an unspoken group pressure [at this point two women commented: "come on" and "encouragement"].
>
> You just got caught up in the motion. You were on this merry-go-round and there was just no getting off it. Besides, you didn't want to get off. These were your peers. It was this whole thing with this group . . . coming together. . . . It became a strong commitment.

As the ceremony came closer, each woman worked on her "drash"[16]—a brief commentary on her verses, which was delivered before reading

---

[16] "Drash" is informal for *derashah.* A *derashah* is, formally, a learned commentary on a point of Jewish law, using the Talmud and other, more recent legal writings. A *derashah,* delivered by the *bar miṣvah,* a relative, or a rabbi, became part of the celebration of bar mitzvah in early modern times. The term, and its more informal form "drash," are loosely used to refer to any commentary on the Torah. The Hebrew plural of *derashah* is *derashot.* It is common, however, for Jews who know some Hebrew to use English grammatical forms when using these words in English conversation, and the word "drashes" is often used, as in this setting, instead of *derashot.*

from the Torah and which were all printed in an attractive volume. Preparing the drash combined the ideas raised in the discussion part of the class with the technical skills of reading the Hebrew from the Torah learned in the second part.

Each drash was also the opportunity to make a personal statement to the congregation. The women used this opportunity in different ways. Some wrote explications of the text using secondary sources. Others wrote personal commentaries on the meaning of the text to them. Preparing the drashes contributed to the bonding that was taking place. They discussed them with each other, with the rabbis, and with the Hebrew teachers.

As the women recalled going through the class, they explored several of the things—the openness about feelings (in which the rabbi also participated), the practical assistance given by the more advanced to the beginners, the rabbi's growing rapport with the group—which they felt accounted for the enthusiasm that built in the group.

> There were a lot of personal interconnections and experiences that came out that brought you closer to the group, that made you more aware of being religious within that. . . . Everybody who was scared—all the others said, "we can do it," and C said, "I'll privately coach if you have troubles." F helped those who couldn't. Mechanisms sprang into place for those who were less assured of themselves about the actual ceremony.

> I think it was amazing just to see the turnout every week [15 or 16 out of 18]. That continued to amaze me and I'm sure it amazed the rabbi.

> T had a baby and was right back in the class a week later.

> I saw a side to [the rabbi] that I'd never seen. . . . When he was talking to us about kosher, he just opened up his heart to us. He told us all kinds of things. There were no secrets in this group. That's the way it was. He would open his heart to us and we would open up. . . . For me, that's why I kept coming back.

During this part of the interview, the "communitas" that Turner describes as characteristic of liminal situations was much in evidence: spontaneity, trust in each other, commitment to the group. As the selections from the transcript indicate, they felt comfortable interrupting each other, completing each other's thoughts, taking up the topic where another had left it. One of the women recalled the joke they told each other when they got their portions: "Now your mother has to book the hall."

The feeling of mutual interdependence and valuing each one's special contribution to the group was strongly expressed in the following statement: "Everybody had a strength or skill that they brought to the group in some way. I don't know what it was, but everybody contributed something at some point or another and gave something special."

Reaggregation

The reaggregation phase of the process consisted of the bat mitzvah ceremony and the associated social activities. At the ceremony, the women were returned to the congregation in their new roles. They publicly demonstrated that they were able to act as members of the congregation in a way in which they could not when the process began. The reactions to the ceremony recognized and approved the changes.

Because of the size of the class, the ceremony was scheduled for two days, the first and second days of Passover, 1988. As the date of the ceremony came closer, business meetings were added to the schedule.

> Something would come up—we had to get gifts for all the people that had helped us, we had to contact the temple, put a notice in, collect money, etc. . . . Even the logistics of the ceremony were something that we had to do a lot of business meetings over. Whether we should all be up on the bimah or whether we shouldn't be on the bimah. Whether we should wear the choir type of uniform or not.[17] These were things we felt we really should discuss.

What they accurately referred to as the choreography of the ceremony was a particular concern of the rabbi. The rabbi suggested that the group to participate each day should sit on the bimah through the Torah reading. The group considered the opinions of various people involved with them and decided instead that each day's group would sit in the front row and go up one by one. They wanted each person reading the Torah to have her moment to be on the bimah alone. They also wanted to be able to see and to hear and appreciate each other's reading, and especially their drashes.

The group also decided to follow the common practice of twinning their bat mitzvahs with families of refuseniks in the USSR. Individual bar and bat mitzvahs are twinned with children. The adult bat mitzvah group contacted the temple's Soviet Jewry Committee and were told about a group of refusenik women, with whom they decided to twin.

---

17 They decided against uniform dress.

In these concerns about gifts, dealing with temple staff, presenting themselves before the congregation, and making a symbolic gesture of solidarity, the group was now preparing for reaggregation. The liminal phase had been one of community-building, creating bonds, and going through emotionally important experiences together. Although that phase was not over, they were now also orienting themselves to "society"—the network of formal statuses and clear role expectations—that they were going to rejoin.

Inviting guests to the ceremony was part of the preparation for reaggregation. Most invited about twenty people, family and friends.

> Some of us felt that this was just going to be a celebration that we were going to have on our own and we didn't want to call anyone up and make them feel obligated to come. I certainly felt that way. Then towards the end, I started thinking. . . . I did invite twenty people.

A few invited more; the number forty was jokingly used, seeming to mean in context, "twice as many as the rest of us." One woman, for whom the event had a primarily private meaning, invited only her husband, children, mother, and brother.

The date was publicized through an article written for the temple bulletin by the senior rabbi. The local Jewish newspaper was invited to send a reporter.

All the women attended on both days. On each day, the group that was taking part in the service sat together in the first row, with those participating on the other day sitting immediately behind them. During the Torah reading, each woman was called up individually. She would deliver the drash on her verses, recite the blessings, read from the Torah, and recite the closing blessings.

> I can still remember, as each person went up, we were all excited and we followed. But at the end, the rabbi and the cantor had called the first group up [each had returned to her seat as the next came up] and they did the sheheḥiyanu. Everybody—tears were just—we were just crying. Then they came down—and I'll never forget this (and my husband said the same thing after the second day)—they came down and it was over and the rabbi invited everybody down for *Kiddush*—it was like we were in a football huddle. We were just hugging each other and kissing each other and wishing each other mazel tov. There was a feeling there, I can see it like it was yesterday.

This spontaneous outpouring of emotion at the end of the service may be seen as the point marking the emotional awareness of the transition from "communitas" back to "societas." All along they had been intending to return to society. Their relationship with each other was a part-time one and did not require relinquishing their involvement in the other relationships in their lives. Nevertheless, the relationship had become special. They had helped each other prepare for a collective ordeal. With the conclusion of the services, the task on which they had focused their collective energy had been accomplished.

Reaggregation with a change in role was a personal event and a social one. The successful conclusion of the ceremony was followed by the acknowledgment of their accomplishments by family and friends, other members of the congregation, and members of the Jewish community outside the congregation.

The articles in the local Jewish newspaper and the temple bulletin made it an event known to many who were not there.

> It was interesting to see the number of people who came up, who had seen your name in the bulletin. A few weeks afterwards, they would wish you mazel tov.

> People, women particularly, who were raised in a traditional way were absolutely knocked out. [interjection: "yeah"] They were jealous. [researcher: "what did they say?"] "Could you arrange it so that we could do it too."

> I took my kids swimming. . . . Women came up to me saying, "I saw your picture. It was wonderful. Tell me how you did it." [interjection: "The picture was terrible, but you were wonderful."] A woman came up to me and said, "How can I get bat mitzvahed at [the temple]?" I said, "They're starting another class." It turns out that she was a member at [an Orthodox synagogue]. She said, There is no way they are ever going to do this for us. I admire you women for what you have done. I would give my eye teeth." I said,"You'll have to join [the temple]; that's the only way you can do it." A lot of Conservative women, more towards Orthodox really, that were swimming there were really excited about it, really moved by it, in terms of "How do I get it going? What happens?" I was in [a Jewish book store], picking out a book, and somebody said, "Mazel tov." Someone else asked me what happened and I told them I'd had a bat mitzvah at [the temple]. Out of the clear blue, behind the stacks, somebody said, "Only at [the temple] would you find anything like this happening!" This young man, with a yarmulke on, came up to me and said, "It's wonderful," and he really gave it to that

> man. He said, "I belong to an Orthodox synagogue. We have a lot of very young Jewish women studying and learning and going on." He says, "Mark my words, in the next fifteen, twenty, thirty years you're going to see a big change in the Orthodox women because they want this. They want to learn. The feminist movement is taking hold on our Orthodox Jewish women." I hope he's right.

In addition to the congratulations after services, the lunches at home the women had for their invited guests, and the unexpected public reactions, the process of reaggregation continued at a small party the group held the following week for those who had helped them. They each received a book, *A Feast of History,* from the brotherhood (the brotherhood gives a book to each *bar* or *bat miṣvah*), and cards and donations in their honor from people who had helped the class prepare. However, the transition to the social role of people who were able and willing to give back was also continuing. As successful initiates, they were no longer on the receiving end of the process, but were in a position to confer praise on others and to give gifts as well as receive them. For example, they thanked the cantor by presenting him a taped thank-you message sung in trup and a T-shirt with his name in Hebrew letters.

Consequences: Institutional, Familial, Personal

There was no change in formal status as a consequence of the experience. The women began the process as members of the congregation. Some were already very much involved in congregational life; others were not. After the bat mitzvah some who were not previously involved took on or were asked to assume positions of responsibility. The bat mitzvah process had prepared them for this, but the process was not a formal prerequisite. They moved into these positions not as a change in status but as a change in role.

The women in the group expected the close personal ties to each other to continue after the bat mitzvah, even as they were involved in other ways with other people in the congregation.

> A lot of us meet during the 5:45 services and we talk. There is a sisterhood, if you will. . . . When we get together.a certain feeling stays with us.'

One of the women simply stated, "I've made lifelong friends." This sentiment was more pronounced for those women who had been feeling spiritually and socially isolated before the class, but it was shared by others as well. Many of the women in the adult bat mitzvah class have attended the various study groups at the temple and continue to do so. Nevertheless, they were planning to continue to study together with the senior rabbi in the coming year. An artistically talented woman, who had designed the cover for the booklet of drashes, was beginning work on a series of silk scarves inscribed in calligraphic script with verses from each woman's portion.

The senior rabbi was also beginning to use the individual skills and talents of members of the group to fill congregational needs. At the interview, the feeling was expressed that the group as a whole was now a resource on which the congregation would draw. Two examples were given. One woman who attends regularly on Saturday morning was acting as gabbai—in this congregation, with many people coming on and off the bimah during the Torah reading, this role is one of "directing traffic" and helping things go smoothly. Another woman, a professional singer, had begun to lead the early Friday night services and was asked to be cantor at one of the auxiliary services on the High Holy Days.

Most of the women who went through this rite of passage had husbands, and children of various ages. In a few cases, discussed above in the section on "separation," the immediate family was not supportive. In other families, husbands encouraged participation. Children's reactions varied.

The successful ceremony of their mothers made it difficult for children approaching bar/bat mitzvah to engage in the common complaint about how hard it is to learn the required Hebrew chant. Mothers of younger children told stories of their toddlers imitating mother studying and inviting their classmates to their far-off bar/bat mitzvahs. One mother quoted her nine-year-old, "Oh, four years to my bar mitzvah, mom, isn't that wonderful!"

The significance of the bat mitzvah for family life was a issue in many relationships. One woman reported that her husband asked apprehensively whether a kosher home was the next step. Another reported and analyzed some dialogue:

> My husband pats me on the head and says, "My *yeshiva bocher*." But I feel, like he's saying, "This is enough already."

On the other hand, in one of the families that was not supportive, the ceremony was thought to make some positive difference:

> I think on that day they were proud. At this point, they are taking me a little more seriously. . . . I have to be careful,

> because otherwise they'll feel threatened. I have to let them know that they're important to me, not just Judaism. I have to keep reminding them. But things did get better.

Two of the women had written drashes in which they spoke of spiritual travel and finding God as they went through the class. The one who was present at the interview explained:

> I always believed in God but I didn't much think about it. The difference between me then and me now is that I'm actively thinking about it. I guess to put it very simply I'm developing—and it's an ongoing process—my own personal, private relationship with God.

Those participating in the interview placed themselves at different stages along this spiritual route. At a basic level, a few commented on the relief of having spiritual needs recognized. One said, "What's nice is to be able to talk about God without having people look at you like you're crazy." Another woman described herself as someone who "always had very strong spiritual feelings" and has a "simple-minded approach to God. . . . I just talk to Him—Her [laughter]."[18] She contrasted the bat mitzvah class with the attitudes of other Jewish friends who said, "We liked you better before you were so frummy."[19]

Other women spoke of coming into the process with uncertain beliefs and leaving with uncertain beliefs, but with their commitment to Jewish life strengthened.

> I'm still not certain about my beliefs. I don't worry about it that much. . . . As long as one ponders God, I don't think you absolutely have to believe in Him. [The bat mitzvah] reminded me that it is important to act and to continue acting.

Another woman spoke about how she talks about belief with her children.

> There's a lot of myth built into what we are reading and studying. I deal with [the question], "Is God real" or "Is this story true" [by asking,] "What is the moral to take from this?" I guess the only way I'll really know if there really truly is a God is when I die that maybe one day She will be there to

---

18 This ambiguity about God's gender introduced the following tangential exchange: "God has to be female. There's not enough compassion in God to be male . . . ." "I wish he were female, but I somehow don't think He is. I wish I could get myself around that thought."

19 "Frummy" is colloquial, a degenerate form of the Yiddish *frum* 'observant of Jewish ritual'.

> welcome me to the heavens. Until then, my feeling when I'm dealing with my children is, "What is the lesson that we are to be learning from this, what is the moral?" It seems to be working.

A third continued,

> I don't think I've changed my beliefs, but I'm a firm believer in rituals as guides in our everyday life. I think that what you remember are rituals of your childhood. The rituals, maybe more for women anyway than for men, are life-affirming and comforting in many ways. Maybe I just sort of, with the rituals, feel that way about myself. Maybe I'll give God a second chance. I can't say that I'm too crazy about God. So I feel that, with this, I've given, truly I've given God a chance to make up for all the terrible things that had to happen in the world throughout the centuries. You know, everybody has their own theological concept of God. I've sort of given Him the opportunity—It the opportunity—to work in positive ways, without direct connection. So it's a bit harrowing to me.

A Successful Rite of Passage: Role Transition, Personal Pilgrimage, And The Spiritual Quest

The experience of the bat mitzvah class could be interpreted from a number of distinct perspectives. The comments which follow use the bat mitzvah class to probe the meaning of a positive religious experience in contemporary society. This is a complex topic; the interpretation is intended to be suggestive rather than definitive.

The rite of passage process has structural similarities to the experience of a pilgrimage. Eliade, for example, interprets the ritual process of separation, transition, and return as a metaphor of death and rebirth, just as the pilgrimage has been used as a metaphor of the human journey. The human journey, when understood as a pilgrimage, is more than birth, life, and death. The end of the pilgrimage, like the end stage of the ritual process in general, is not death, but rebirth.[20] Turner, who elaborated the rite of passage model into a general model of ritual process, also wrote about the pilgrimage as a special type of ritual process, showing how it follows the three stages of separation, liminality, and reaggregation.[21]

The theme of spiritual growth through a process of exile and return, of death and rebirth, has implications for understanding the transitions

---

[20] Eliade, *Rites and Symbols.*

[21] Turner, *Dramas, Fields and Metaphors.*

of the women in the group. It is clear that they were doing something very different from going through the form of ritual without commitment. Like pilgrims, they had voluntarily stepped out of their normal roles in the human journey to let the sacred work on them, in order to be able to return the same, but not the same. What they said about their experience may be linked to the metaphor of the pilgrimage. This linkage clarifies what it can mean to modern people to become engaged with religious institutions.

The image of pilgrimage is an old one, and it remains powerful in modern culture. There is a difference, though, between the older conception of pilgrimage and the modern one. Traditional pilgrimages brought people in groups to sacred shrines. The biblical pilgrimage festivals, for example, were intensely communal, as are the Muslim pilgrimages to Mecca to this day. The traditional pilgrim traveled in company, like Chaucer's group on its way to Canterbury, to communally accepted sites of spiritual revelation. The modern pilgrim is, in contrast, a spiritual descendent of Bunyan's Pilgrim, Goethe's Werther, and the poor, wayfaring stranger of the American folk song—an individual on an interior journey seeking "salvation" or enlightenment, without a reassuringly fixed destination. The modern pilgrim, rejecting the passive acceptance of inherited wisdom, is on a journey of self-discovery, seeking personal truth to live by.

The modern image of the pilgrim may be related to what has been written about the contemporary transformation of religion. For most sociologists, the important data about modern religion have been the clear declines in participation in organized religion and in adherence to formal theologies.[22] A relatively small group of social scientists who work in the specialized area of the sociology of religion have tried to account for those data which indicate that religion is somehow persisting. In various ways, they seem to have come to what may be termed an "existential" view of religious persistence.[23] Even though more and more

---

[22] Social scientists have discussed the declining significance of organized religion and formal theologies for the way of life of modern society in great detail. Some have followed Durkheim's analysis of the shift from social cohesion symbolized through ritual to social cohesion based on functional interdependence. Others have developed Weber's concept of "disenchantment"—the replacement of ways of acting justified as directives of a sacred tradition with skepticism about inherited wisdom and new ways of acting based on technical rationality. Still others continue the Marxist tradition of critiquing religion as false consciousness.

[23] I would put the following works in the group that accounts for the persistence of religion on existential grounds: Ernest Becker, *The Denial of Death* (New York: Free

people turn away from the imposed discipline of organized religion and from the acceptance of authoritatively defined dogma, they continue to require ideas which interpret their life experience as meaningful.

Religions have, of course, historically presented themselves as meeting the human need to find the "Truth." In the Western tradition, collective acceptance of revealed "Truth" has been followed by institutionalization: an organized authority structure and formal dogma. While in the modern West, institutionalized meaning systems have weakened, the search for meaning continues. As a continuing feature of modern society, religion seems more and more to specialize in what the popular culture calls "spirituality" or, to return to the image of the pilgrim, "the spiritual quest."

This quest is a personal one, but it does not have to be undertaken in isolation. The individualistic pilgrim often needs other people and some degree of organizational support. The web of group affiliations through which the individual is connected to others needs to show sufficient flexibility to accommodate an individual's change. The process of change receives powerful support from others going through similar processes and from organizations which justify the change and give access in a structured way to the resources needed to change. Consequently the personal spiritual quest expresses itself through the continuation of relatively large scale, formal religious organizations which facilitate the coming together of individuals into small groups that support each other in the process of personal change.[24]

Press, 1973); Daniel Bell, "The Return of the Sacred? The Argument on the Future of Religion," the *The Winding Passage* (Cambridge, Mass." ABT Books, 1980 [1970]); Victor Turner, *Dramas, Fields and Metaphors;* Thomas Luckmann, *The Invisible Religion* (New York: Macmillan, 1967); Colin Campbell, "The Secret Religion of the Educated Classes," *Sociological Analysis* 39/2 (1978): 146-56; and Robert N. Bellah et al., *Habits of the Heart: Individualism and Commitment in American Life* (New York: Harper and Row, 1985). Each makes particular contributions to this view of modern religiosity; these contributions have not yet been synthesized. Those named in this list, of course, do not exhaust it. For a sample of the debate on the persistence of religion, see the essays by Dupre, Berger, Douglas, Schluchter, and Marty in *Religion and America: Spiritual Life in a Secular Age,* ed. Mary Douglas and Steven Tipton (Boston: Beacon, 1983).

24 Even those small-scale groups that do not have change as part of their overt agenda many be seen as part of this pattern. Groups of regular worshipers or attendees at study classes move through the life cycle together; the personal ties established through these patterns and the common language that they share through these ongoing experiences are important resources for coping with normal life cycle changes. Here we touch on a phenomenon to be incorporated into the as yet undone theoretical elaboration of the concept of folk religion.

The individualistic spiritual quest as a feature of modern society may be understood sociologically. Various sociologists have pointed out the complexity and multiplicity of statuses and roles which individuals have in the modern division of labor. Moreover, people are constantly going through changes in statuses and roles. As a consequence of having continually changing social relationships of many different types with many different people, individuals may experience a problem of "role integration." Subjectively, the problem of role integration is experienced as identity confusion (or crisis), as role conflict, or as role fragmentation. The search for some transcendent principle of identity integration is one response to this experience.[25]

As a process, the search may follow a scenario like the following: Events in a person's life make the person conscious of a problem of role integration. The work of reconciling apparently conflicting roles leads the individual to try to identify elements of identity—values and commitments—that cut across the various roles. This work, whatever rhetorical label the individual uses to describe it, is a spiritual quest of "getting in touch with yourself" and getting in touch with the world (as experienced through various role expectations). It is cognitive work, but it is emotionally driven, and, when successful, emotionally satisfying. The goal of the quest is a sense of wholeness, of having a center of gravity which keeps the constantly changing configuration of personal roles together. This private search for meaning is characteristic of modern religiosity[26] even when individuals do not think of what they are doing as conventional "religious" behavior.[27]

Some people may never go through such a spiritual quest. They may acquire a sense of who they are and a plan for how to live that identity early in life. If events simply allow them to live out the plan, there is no crisis to confront. Others may go through a spiritual quest in adolescence or young adulthood, the socially structured periods of identity uncertainty in our society. If the goal is achieved, the spiritual quest is remembered as the central activity in the drama of one's early life. The practical pressures of role obligations keep others busily fragmented. Yet others may drift and experiment rather than engage in a cumulative process of self-discovery.

---

[25] For a discussion of the work of identity integration among the elderly, see Barbara Myerhoff, *Number Our Days* (New York: Simon and Schuster, 1977), 222 and passim.

[26] Campbell, "Secret Religion."

[27] Luckmann, *Invisible Religion.*

The spiritual search may also be put aside—perhaps with a tentative resolution—under the pressure of role obligations, only to reappear later in life. Events later in life may challenge a previously acquired strategy of role integration. Or the private search for meaningful role integration may not be understood as an "existential" search for ultimate truth, but simply as a pragmatic activity of working on and reconciling particular problems of role conflict and fragmentation.

These considerations about modern religiosity help to explain why the women experienced their bat mitzvah as a meaningful rite of passage. The women in the bat mitzvah class had chosen to participate in organized religion, to engage in reading and discussion about the meaning of Judaism, to develop the skills needed for participation, and to present themselves in a congregational ritual. For some the process was—or became—an element of a self-conscious spiritual quest. Those who found God or rediscovered God or who saw the class as a follow-up to conversion were finding the center of gravity, the personal point from which to place the many statuses and roles of their lives into a coherent, meaningful framework.

In many ways, though—and this was true of those for whom the bat mitzvah was especially intense as well as for the others—the bat mitzvah class served the practical spiritual need of working on quite particular problems of role integration.

To begin with, the women in the bat mitzvah class had made a commitment to Judaism as a central focus of their identities, but they had not had the experience of gender equality in religious participation. Being called to an aliyah and reading from the Torah was for them symbolic that they had moved toward a resolution of this discrepancy.

There were also practical issues of role integration that the bat mitzvah addressed for particular women. Their private quests for meaningful role integration had brought them into the temple, but there were aspects of their lives which were inconsistent with that commitment. Some felt they could not meet the obligations of a Jewish family and a Jewish household without improving their understanding and skills. Others needed social contacts and support for their Jewish commitments. Others, already involved in congregational life, were bothered by gaps in their understanding and skills. The bat mitzvah class provided a structure to transform their roles along these lines. The ceremony dramatically reincorporated them into their families and the congregation with their role transition acknowledged.

Broader Issues: The Female Experience of Judaism and "The Return of The Sacred"

This chapter is introduced with a quotation in which one of the women described what it was like to ascend to the bimah for her aliyah. This woman, and the others in the group, experienced the bat mitzvah as a successful rite of passage. They had separated themselves from previously unsatisfactory role integration, gone through a process of transformation and returned to their social networks through a ritual which expressed their role transitions. They went through a process of initiation, but in a modern spirit, as an element of the individual spiritual quest for meaningful role integration. Going through the process as a group, they revived something of the ancient experience of a pilgrimage.

The primary task of this chapter has been to use a framework of ritual analysis which organizes and interprets the experience of this group of women from their own perspective. Beyond this task, the experience recounted here raises two questions. What is the relationship of the ritual experience of this group of women to the feminist movement within Judaism? What does the positive experience of this group indicate about the potential place of Judaism in the lives of contemporary Jews? Each question is discussed in turn.

The general feminist critique of "patriarchal religion" has led to three ideological options: (1) the withdrawal of women from religious activities and organizations, (2) the development of female religiosity which aims at the rehabilitation of female images of divinity and the valuation of such (allegedly) female virtues as nurturance in opposition to the (allegedly) male worship of power, and (3) the movement toward gender equality within Christian and Jewish thought and practice. The third option has had a major impact on Judaism, and is in fact now normative in its liberal branches.

A significant debate within Jewish feminism turns on the relationship between the last two responses. Is the goal of feminism within Judaism equal participation, or participation in the transformation of Judaism to incorporate female as well as male sensibility?[28]

---

[28] See the contrasting positions of Ozick and Plaskow, as well as other articles, in *On Being a Jewish Feminist*, ed. Susannah Heschel (New York: Schocken, 1983); also Judith Plaskow, *Standing Again at Sinai: Judaism from a Feminist Perspective* (San Francisco: Harper and Row, 1990); and *Womanspirit Rising: A Feminist Reader in Religion*, ed. idem and Carol P. Christ (San Francisco: Harper and Row, 1979). For a detailed ethnographic analysis of how the tension between formal equality for women and the more ambitious agenda of transforming Judaism became a major

The adult bat mitzvah class clearly falls into the strategy of equal participation. The women were enlarging their skills and becoming more comfortable as participants in congregational life as members of the congregation, not as women. The classes were led by male rabbis, as was the service in which they participated. The texts they studied addressed Jewish issues, not Jewish women's issues. The women spoke about the bat mitzvah as a consequence of feminism, a reconciliation of their Jewish and female identities, not as a route to feminism. They did not think of themselves as making a feminist statement through their ritual, but of making a Jewish statement that was made possible by feminism. Their disinclination to view their bat mitzvah as a feminist ritual would probably be shared by many feminists.[29]

Nevertheless, there was a specifically female dimension to the process, even thought it was only intermittently articulated. A female rabbi who had been at the congregation for several years before moving to a more senior position elsewhere[30] had created the first opportunity for some members of the group to hold the Torah. The invitation to be part of the group was extended to all members of the congregation, but the man who responded soon dropped out. The group's style of relating to each other included characteristics that are often presented as conventionally female: a concern with the aesthetic and emotional, the creation of social bonds by sharing personal stories, an emphasis on bringing the whole group along instead of giving priority to an outstanding individual performance. It is possible to debate whether these traits are "feminine" or "feminist."[31] In either case, they implicitly accentuated the female dimension of the process through which the women were going.

Some women in the group were identified as more "feminist" than others. This meant having greater sympathy for a more thorough redefinition of women's role and using more female symbolism. As well, the women's conversation showed familiarity with the more far-reaching feminist agenda of transformation. There were references to the gender

---

issue in a *ḥavurah,* see Riv-Ellen Prell, *Prayer and Community: The Havurah in American Judaism* (Detroit: Wayne State University Press, 1989), ch. 7.

29 A bat mitzvah class led by a female rabbi or with a leader of either sex specifically concentrating on feminist issues would be different from the one described in this chapter and could also conceivably occur within a large congregation.

30 A typical career pattern in the Reform rabbinate consists of an initial, short-term appointment at a large congregation followed by one or more moves.

31 That is, traits which are socially acquired as the result of the inferior power position of women or traits, whether biological or social in origin, which would be desirable in a more humane society.

of God and to female as well as male understandings of the Torah. The specifically female meaning of the experience was left unresolved or implicit, but it was present. The *benot miṣvah,* by agreeing on the immediate task of equal participation and agreeing to disagree about how "feminist" they ought to be, left open the long-range implications of what they were doing.

The relationship of the bat mitzvah to the general question of the religious experience of contemporary Jews was also left unresolved. In this the *benot miṣvah* have plenty of company. Certainly the literature on trends in twentieth-century Jewish life emphasizes declines in general religiosity, balanced only partially by the revival of Orthodoxy and the continuation of *ḥavurah*-like groups which developed from the Jewish counterculture.

The social scientists referred to above have raised the questions of the extent of religious persistence and the reasons for it. Their work is often tentative and controversial, and much of the argument depends on exactly what is meant by "religion." In general, they argue that religious groups have traditionally met basic human needs—needs for a way of understanding the world, for shared standards of proper conduct, and for membership in a community that cares and shares.

Our research on contemporary religion tells us little about how people now use religious groups to meet these needs. People seem to be particularly conscious of these needs at transition points in the life cycle (birth, puberty, marriage, death), at those times in the annual cycle when attention is focused on values and symbols of values, and at those idiosyncratic times of profound personal reexamination. If we want to do research on religion in contemporary society, it might be appropriate to focus on how people go through these experiences.

Put another way, an exploration of the religion of American Jews means investigating its folk aspects in the same detail in which its elite aspects have been studied. This exploration would involve more than asking how often Jews attend synagogue on the Sabbath, whether they light candles, keep any degree of kashruth, and so on. Rather than asking whether they attend synagogue on Rosh Hashanah or fast on Yom Kippur, it would ask how they spend these days, why they have made the choices that they have, and how they feel about what they do. Rather than questioning whether they light Hanukkah candles and attend Seders, it would question how they interpret the symbolism of these holidays, how this interpretation is shared with others, and how they feel about it. Instead of asking whether Jews have *berit milah* and naming ceremonies, bar/bat mitzvahs, Jewish weddings and burials (which most surveys on Jewish religious behavior do not include), this exploration would inquire into the experience of these rituals, the feelings they evoke, the decisions that have to be made around them, the relationships that they acknowledge, the way in which those participating are able to use them in their personal lives.[32] Some of this research will be on the folk Judaism of the home and community.[33] This study of adult bat mitzvah indicates that some of the research will be on the relationship of folk Judaism to congregational life.

Other areas of vitality in congregational life will also show, as is the case with adult bar and bat mitzvah, the intersection of personal agendas and institutional opportunities. The women entered the class with a variety of personal goals: resolving the discrepancy between formal equality and their lack of technical skills, searching for a more meaningful Judaism, enriching their family lives and their relationships with their children, making social contacts, offering and receiving emotional support for their Jewish commitments. Their individual goals were somewhat different, but they were congruent. As a group they were able to meet their individual goals better than they could have on their own.

One might ask to what extent their enthusiasm and feeling of having made successful transitions was a consequence of an intense group experience and to what extent it was the consequence of having a "religious experience." Just as there is a debate about what "religion" is, the answer to this question depends on what is meant by "religious experience."

In Judaism we have ample precedent for the mingling of the social and the religious. The adult bat mitzvah had personal, social, institutional, and communal dimensions. These multiple dimensions are consistent with the traditional Jewish view that spiritual life can only fully take place in a community; the individual's ongoing encounter with the

---

[32] See the articles cited at the end of note 13 for an application of this perspective to the study of bat/bat mitzvah; also Stuart Schoenfeld, "Theoretical Approaches to the Study of Bar and Bat Mitzvah," *Proceedings of the Ninth World Congress of Jewish Studies,* div. D. pt. 2 (1986): 119-28. This proposal to study the "folk" rather than the "elite" aspect of religion, of course, has analogies to the movement among historians to write history from the "bottom up" rather than from the "top down."

[33] Jonathan Woocher, *Sacred Survival: The Civil Religion of American Jews* (Bloomington: Indiana University Press, 1986), documents a particular kind of folk Judaism: the Judaism that has emerged out of the need of communal leaders to explain to themselves in terms which reflect their life experiences the reasons for their organizational commitment.

sacred is sustained by the community and, in turn, sustains the community.[34]

Adult bar and bat mitzvah groups, especially bat mitzvah groups, may be found in many congregations, and they are generally considered successful rituals. They are an example of another route of "return" within Judaism[35] indicating that even in large, conventional congregations it is possible to find spiritual pilgrims and the opportunities for ritual creativity which allow these Jews to use their tradition as they travel together.

---

34 Fully working out the relationship of the social and the religious dimensions of Jewish experience would require detailed consideration of at least several topics: whether Judaism, as it has been historically interpreted, is distorted by fitting it into the modern category of "religion"; the relationship between the halakhic understanding of the scrupulous observation of *miṣvot* as a "religious experience" to the mystical interest in the emotional side of the "religious experience"; whether the conventional understanding of "religious experience" shows a bias, most clearly expressed in Protestant Christianity, toward using the direct, personal encounter with God as the paradigm of the "religious experience."

35 For a discussion of the possibility of Jewish renewal under modern conditions, see Jacob Neusner, *Death and Birth of Judaism* (New York: Basic Books, 1987).

15

Midrash and Modernity: Can Midrash Serve a Contemporary Religious Discourse?

BARRY W. HOLTZ

The reappropriation of religious tradition for contemporary life is an endeavor that can take many different forms. One might, for example, investigate the ways that classical ritual practices or theological ideas or norms of behavior are adapted, reconceptualized, embraced, or rejected in the light of the values and attitudes of the culture of modernity. My particular concern in this paper, however, is to look at one traditional Jewish LITERARY genre, midrash, and to examine in brief the ways that it has been adopted by the academic intellectual community, and then to explore at greater length the educational challenge that midrash presents.

I would suggest that the "reappropriation of tradition" is at heart a problem for education; indeed it is one of the essential tasks of education in general: How does one mediate the past for the world of the present? What I want to examine here are the pedagogical impediments to any such enterprise and the difficulties occasioned in attempting to solve them. Such an exploration will, I hope, give a clearer sense of what precisely the nature of the educational task may be and where the road-blocks to "reappropriation" might lie.

Midrash and the Literary Critic

In recent years we have witnessed a virtual explosion of interest in the study of midrash. Particularly in the world of academia, midrash has become the focus of considerable scholarly enterprise. This scholarship has both taken conventional lines—such as scientific editions of texts or new translations into English[1]—while at the same time it has moved in interesting ways into new areas, using methodologies not conventionally employed in Jewish studies, such as literary theory and interpretation.[2] Similarly, scholars such as David Weiss Halivni and Jacob Neusner, whose work has generally focused on talmudic studies in the past, have now turned their attention, at least in part, to midrash.[3]

Midrash, then, flourishes in the world of higher learning. Why this is so may be due to a number of factors, but in the case of the second kind of midrash scholarship mentioned above—literary theory—it is clear that some of the interest emanates from the concern with the general issue of interpretative methodology that has gripped the university in the past two decades. Whether it be feminist scholarship or Jacques Derrida and deconstructionism or Clifford Geertz and the *Interpretation of Cultures* or Thomas Kuhn and nature of scientific discovery, scholars have sought to examine the ways in which we interpret ANYTHING and to look carefully at the underlying assumptions we bring to such acts of interpretation.

Midrash offers a fresh perspective on the issue of interpretation because its assumptions about the limitations and logic of the interpreted text seem so different from the history of Western literary criticism. Midrash, as many have pointed out, when looked at as a whole does not seek to find THE interpretation of a scriptural passage, it does not assume that there is one right reading exclusive of all others, rather it seems to delight in the very multiplicity of explications that can be generated.[4]

---

1 For example, Avigdor Shinan's editon of *Shemot Rabbah* (Jerusalem: Dvir, 1984), or Reuven Hammer's translation of *Sifre Deuteronomy,* Yale Judaica Series 24 (New Haven: Yale University Press, 1986).

2 For example, see Geoffrey H. Hartman and Sanford Budick, *Midrash and Literature* (New Haven: Yale University Press, 1986). See also the journal *Prooftexts,* which for some time has been an important locus for literary approaches to midrash.

3 For example: David Weiss Halivni, *Midrash, Mishnah and Gemara* (Cambridge: Harvard University Press, 1986); Jacob Neusner, *Midrash in Context* (Atlanta: Scholars Press, 1988), or idem, *Midrash as Literature* (Lanham, Md.: University Press of America, 1987).

4 Of course, individual pericopes in any given midrashic text may assert a particular reading of the scriptual lemma at hand, but the effect of the edited text as a whole, the "literary midrash," as it were, is to show a multiplicity of interpretation.

"Turn it and turn it again," as the oft-quoted phrase from *Avot* (5:22) puts it—the Torah text is limitless. No interpretation can exhaust it.

Midrash, however, offers another attraction for the contemporary literary critic. For midrash is not only a body of work which INTERPRETS SOMETHING ELSE (namely, the Bible), a second-order writing, in other words; rather, midrash itself becomes a first-order body of work, A LITERATURE—indeed a sacred text—in its own right. As Robert Alter has put it, "Through exegesis, midrash develops literary coherences of its own, both narrative and rhetorical that are sometimes quite compelling."[5] Of course, in the traditional Jewish hierarchy the level of holiness inherent in rabbinic texts is significantly lower than that in the Revealed Word of God, but midrash is, nonetheless, *torah she-be-al peh*, Oral Torah, with the emphasis here on the word Torah.

Thus in the milieu of contemporary culture, particularly in the world of the academy, midrash offers a comforting, in fact inspiring, model for the importance and weight of the enterprise of criticism. It becomes the model for the way that a contemporary literary theorist might see his or her own work. No longer mere explication, no longer second-order, criticism in the midrashic mode becomes the EQUAL of literature; it too is part of the "canon," taking that word with its full religious implications.

Such a position can be seen quite clearly, for example, in a recent article about the role of criticism by Geoffrey Hartman, a leading literary theorist who has taken a considerable interest in midrash. Hartman argues that we have for a long time too narrowly defined the arena of art and creativity. We have been subject, he asserts, to "a hierarchical prejudice that holds that creativeness can be achieved only in certain genres, to which other genres are subordinate."[6]

Criticism, in other words, has been seen as handmaiden to the work of art, rather than as its coequal. But, Hartman goes on to say, "a critical essay, a legal opinion, an interpretation of scripture or a biography can be as inspiring and nuturing as a poem, story or painting."[7] The list here is not accidental. By placing "interpretation of scripture" between "legal opinion" and "biography," Hartman manages both to prepare us for an analogy to midrash which is about to come and to secularize the act of

---

5 Robert Alter, "Old Rabbis, New Critics," *The New Republic* 196/1–2 (5–12 January 1987): 27.

6 Geoffrey Hartman, "Criticism and Restitution," *Tikkun* 4/1 (January–February 1989): 30.

7 Ibid.

biblical interpretation by placing it squarely in the midst of other contemporary "critical" activities.

Midrash becomes Hartman's key analogue for the act of criticism. "Criticism has its own strength," he writes;

> even commentary. . . does not disappear into the code or scripture it interprets, but must itself be interpreted. A salient example of this is the Jewish Oral Law, the Talmud and adjacent compilations called midrash. They cannot be reduced to a purely exegetical function. They extend or reenvision the original, the "primary" text.[8]

In this light there no longer is a primary text and a secondary commentary. Rather, all is primary. Thus Hartman adds:

> My plea is not for midrash as such, but for an enrichment or even a reconstitution of the literary-critical field. . . . Midrash is more important for literary criticism than the latter is for midrash. By including midrash, criticism would exercise its power to revalue an alienated practice, and it would enlarge itself at the same time.[9]

This vision of the exalted role of criticism in contemporary culture is not one that is universally embraced, of course. In a recent book, for example, George Steiner has presented a sharp attack on precisely the kind of vision that Hartman offers. In Steiner's view, we are witnessing "the dominance of the secondary and the parasitic" over the primary experience of art and of religion. We today, says Steiner, are subject to a "radical misconception of the functions of interpretation and of hermeneutics."[10]

Steiner, in his own way, explores the model of midrash. But for him viewing midrash and "criticism" as coterminous is a dangerous misunderstanding. For one thing, according to Steiner, modern critical writing "takes over from scriptural and theological exegesis its essential methodological and practical instruments. At the same time, the modern explicator-critic reverts to the elucidation and assessment of secular, mundane texts."[11] In Steiner's view such a mingling of sacred methodology with secular literature is highly problematic. But more than that, he reminds us that the ultimate goal of midrash was not "pure" explication, but something else:

---

8 Ibid.

9 Ibid., 31.

10 George Steiner, *Real Presences* (Chicago: University of Chicago Press, 1989): 7.

11 Ibid., 31.

> The rabbinic answer to the dilemma of the unending commentary is one of moral action and enlightened conduct. The hermeneutic exposition is not an end in itself. It aims to translate into normative instruction meanings indwelling in the manifold previsions of the sacred message.... Via ever-renewed interpretations, this very same biblical verse, this very same parable, shall, in times and places of need as yet unknown, deploy illuminations and practical, existential applications as yet unperceived.[12]

Midrash, in other words, is ultimately about people's lives. It is "normative" in the sense that midrash intends to influence the way people act and make sense of their experience.

Midrash and the Layperson

Other issues can be raised about the current romance of criticism and midrash. Robert Alter for one has pointed out some of the essential differences between the underlying assumptions of midrash and those of contemporary literary theory.[13] However, I have raised the examples of Hartman and Steiner not to enter that particular debate itself, but rather to show the way that midrash, both in practice and as theoretical construct, has come to play an important role in the intellectual agenda of the academic world. But outside the world of the academy, in the lives of Jews who know very little about this literature, midrash is a strange animal. There is in these texts a whole dimension of difficulty, impediments to learning midrash, that it is essential to explore if we wish to talk about the "reappropriation" of tradition.

These difficulties in the pedagogy of midrash emanate from a number of different factors. To name just two, we cannot, first of all, ignore the simple fact that those of us who already have some connection to this material—Jewish educators, rabbis, professors—often just do not see what makes it hard. And second, teaching midrash has become difficult because it has become so unfamiliar for the vast majority of Jews today. At least until the last century, midrash had always been alive in the world of ordinary Jews, not just the elites. Indeed, in rabbinic times the *derashah*, as scholarship has shown, was a sermon that served as a kind of

---

12 Ibid., 30-40.

13 Alter, "Old Rabbis," a review of Hartman and Budick, *Midrash and Literature*. See also the exchange between David Stern and Susan Handelman concerning her book *The Slayers of Moses* (Albany: SUNY Press, 1982) which appeared in *Prooftexts* 4/2 (May, 1984): 193-204 and 5/1 (January 1985): 75-95, 96-103.

public entertainment for the general Jewish community, the group we today would call "laypeople."[14] But today, quite obviously, that is no longer true.

For the person who is not a scholar, the impediments to understanding midrash are not to be underestimated. There are difficulties of language, historical distance, and complexity of thought. We can try to consider the ways that we might create a bridge between midrash and the lives of people seeking religious meaning, by looking at one midrashic text here which may help us uncover the various pedagogical obstacles of such a mission.

> Afterwards (*ve-aḥar*) she [Leah] bore him a daughter and named her Dinah. Now God remembered Rachel. God heeded her and opened her womb (*raḥmah*). She conceived and bore him a son . . . and she called his name Joseph, saying May the Lord add (*yosef*) to me another (*aḥer*) son."
>
> (Gen. 30:21-24)

> After Leah had given birth to six sons, she saw by way of prophecy that there would be twelve tribes in the future emerging out of Jacob. She had already given birth to six sons and was pregnant with her seventh. The two maid servants [Bilhah and Zilpah] had given birth to two sons each, hence a total of ten. Leah arose and called out to the Holy One, blessed be He: "Master of the World, twelve tribes in the future will emerge out of Jacob; I already have six sons and am pregnant with my seventh and the maid servants have two each. If my next child is a male, my sister Rachel will be even less than the maid servants. Immediately, the Holy one, blessed be He, listened to her prayer and transformed the fetus within her into a female, thus it says: Afterwards, she bore him a daughter and named her Dinah. *Aḥar* not *aḥeret* [the feminine form of *aḥar*] is the word used. And why was she called Dinah? Because Leah the righteous stood before God with a judgment (*din*) and God said to her, "you are *raḥmanit* [kind person, merciful person] and so I will be merciful to her," hence: "Now, God remembered Rachel." (Gen. 30:22).
>
> —*Mid. Tanḥuma, parshat Vayeṣe*, 7

This, to my mind, is a very compelling and beautiful text which accomplishes a number of different religious (and rhetorical) things at

[14] The classic scholarly article on the issue is Joseph Heinemann, "The Proem in Aggadic Midrashim," *Studies in Aggadah and Folk Literature*, Scripta Hierosolymitana 22 (Jerusalem: Magnes, 1971): 100-22. For a discusssion of the pedagogic role of the public sermon, see the essay by Marc Bregman, "The Darshan: Preacher and Teacher of Talmudic Times," *Melton Journal* no. 14 (Spring 1982), 3f.

the same time. To begin with, it is about the rehabilitation of Leah, or at any rate it is about the rehabilitation of her relationship with Rachel, as it is portrayed in Genesis 29–30. There, we recall, the text vibrates with the hostility that exists between the two sisters, a hostility which emanates out of their individual unhappiness.

Each is unhappy about different things; each has what the other wants: Rachel is barren, but she is loved by Jacob, while Leah though unloved gives birth to many children. It is almost as if the narrative is trying to create a balance in the relationship between the two women. But it is an economy of deprivation—being only partially fulfilled, it is as if each has nothing. The glass is not half full. It is felt to be completely empty.

The tension between the two is expressed in a kind of childbearing contest that ensues in these two chapters. As Leah continues to have children and Rachel is unsuccessful, we hear in the biblical etymologies of the sons' names the very nature of the conflict between the sisters (as in, "She conceived again and bore a son, and declared, `This is because the Lord heard that I was unloved and has given me this one also'; so she named him Simeon" (Gen. 29:33). But no love comes to Leah and no child to Rachel.

Taking that biblical situation, the midrash here depicts a different relationship between the two women. In our midrash above, the values represented are the sisterly love and sacrifice that Leah shows for Rachel. Leah sacrifices her own happiness and prays for Rachel so that her sister will not be humiliated by having fewer sons than the maidservants. There is no revenge here, as we might expect; there is only compassion.

A second thing that this midrash does is to answer a literary difficulty within the biblical text. The Torah says, "Now God remembered Rachel," but it does not tell us why. Or, to be more precise, why "now," why at this moment? Looking at the whole flow of Genesis 29 and 30, the rabbis noted a sudden narrative break: What leads God to "remember" Rachel, especially since we have no apparent cause that would lead to God's action? In the Exodus narrative, by contrast, we are told that God "remembers" the Israelites when he hears their cries and moaning (Exod. 2:23f.). What occasions the change with regard to Rachel? The midrash invents a scenario: it is Leah's prayer which influences God.

And finally the midrash accomplishes another task: it gives us an etymology for Dinah's name. It fills in a gap in the biblical text. In the Genesis narrative, all the sons of Jacob receive both names and etymologies for those names, but Dinah receives only a name. But with this text from *Midrash Tanḥuma,* a legendary origin for her name is supplied. (And of course in conclusion we receive another meaning or context for the conventional etymology of Joseph's name.)

For all these reasons, it is not difficult to find this midrashic text impressive, even charming. But consider all the difficulties that one would have to surmount in teaching the text to an "inexperienced" reader.

To begin with, the whole premise of our midrash is based on the rabbinic vision of biblical language. To the rabbis every word, indeed every letter, of the Torah was a potential midrash waiting to happen. Nothing was superfluous, and through their hyper-intensive reading of the Torah, every element of the Bible could be examined under the rabbinic microscope and used as an occasion for midrash. In our midrash, to take just one example, the rabbis pick up on the slight oddity in biblical language of *ve-aḥar* (afterward) to ask, as it were, After what? The answer: After the prayer that Leah offers. We might call this approach "non-contextual reading," and it is the heart and soul of midrash, but to explain the process to the unfamiliar reader is no mean feat.

We should remember that this is not the kind of approach to literature that most people have learned. In fact, in many ways it is precisely the opposite of the careful contextual examination that we wish students to engage in when reading a literary text. For example, we do not expect readers to examine each word of a play by Shakespeare while disregarding the context of the sentence in which the word appears. No one would consider legitimate an interpretation of Hamlet's "To be or not to be" speech which took the word "be" as related to the bee of the insect world, and yet in midrash we find "readings" that are equally outrageous.[15] This "atomistic" view of the biblical text, in James Kugel's apt term,[16] is yet another significant issue in looking at the relationship between midrash and literary criticism.

Moreover, this text, like many others in midrash, centers around wordplay. Here we have a number of examples. One is the association of Leah's *raḥmanit* (kind) qualities with the opening of Rachel's *reḥem*

---

[15] To choose just one well-known example, take the connection made between *nisah* "to test" as used in the beginning of the binding of Isaac story, Gen 22:1, and *nes,* flag or banner, as interpreted in *Gen. Rab.* 55:1. See the discussion in Joseph Heinemann, *Derashot be-ṣibbur be-tkufat ha-talmud* (Public Sermons in the Talmudic Age) (Jerusalem: Mosad Bialik, 1970): 39f.

[16] James Kugel, "Two Introductions to Midrash," *Prooftexts* 3/2 (May 1983): 147.

(womb); another is a much more obscure play on the words *aḥar* meaning after, *aḥer* meaning another in the masculine form, and *aḥeret* meaning another in the feminine form. The midrash seems to suggest that the use of the masculine rather than the feminine is a hint that the child originally was going to be a male and then was miraculously transformed into a female. The midrash does not seem to be terribly concerned with the fact that its proposed usage of the feminine would make for a syntactically strange Hebrew phrase. For midrash, the precision of the wordplay is of little importance. What matters more is the sense that the Torah is a kind of codebook waiting to be unraveled. But it is precisely this quality of midrash, this central premise, that helps make the pedagogy of midrash so difficult.

As academics, we are able to look at the rabbinic approach to Torah from outside. We can say, "Yes, that is the way the rabbis read." But what about the reader we might be teaching, the Jew who says, "I want this text to live in my own life, but I don't believe the rabbinic assumptions about the nature of scripture"? How do we enable that inexperienced reader to connect with the experience of reading midrash?

Even more than issues of rabbinic methodology, we are faced with the pedagogic challenge of the MESSAGE of midrash. Midrash raises questions of perspective and values and how those values speak to the contemporary reader. For example, I have often seen this text from *Tanḥuma* as a kind of proto-feminist midrash, and for me that is part of its appeal. After all, this is quite literally a text about sisterhood, and the picture of Leah's self-sacrifice for Rachel is noble and moving. Here we have a woman who is so sensitive to her sister's needs that she will intercede with God, indeed even change God's mind.

But, of course, it is by no means a feminist text. At its heart this is a text about the way that childbearing defines a woman's identity and, truth be told, it is about the importance of having SONS. Now for me and for most experienced readers of such texts, seeing this in midrash is not an insurmountable problem. I am willing to accept that the rabbis' values, like their approach to Torah itself, are different from my own. I am pleased that the text goes as far as it does—it promotes sisterhood; it redeems Dinah from bearing a name without an etymology. But the new reader of midrash may not be so generous. It is not difficult to imagine that the disparity between a reader's own contemporary values and the values of the rabbinic text can lead to a dismissal or rejection of the latter.

Midrash and the Student

How, then, should we approach the pedagogy of midrash for this type of student? To me it seems that the primary goal of such teaching should be, first and foremost, something that we might call "fostering openness" to these traditional texts. But how precisely such openness might be created is a complicated matter.

One possible direction is to look at the teaching of Jewish texts as something similar to transmitting any cultural artifact distant in time, consciousness, or values from a contemporary student. Hence it could be argued that teaching midrash is no different from teaching Shakespeare or Mark Twain or Giotto or Mozart. Each of these figures speaks with a language or artistic style whose conventions are different from our own, and each works out of a set of cultural assumptions which we may not share. Thus to learn Shakespeare means to confront Elizabethan English, iambic pentameter, and the notion of the great chain of being.[17] To understand a painting by Giotto means one must have familiarity with the language of medieval Christian iconography, and so forth. Obviously, teachers dealing with such figures have confronted the disparities between students today and the world of the past and such difficulties can surely be bridged.

There is something appealing in such a point of view, and there is some truth in it as well. But "fostering openness" to Shakespeare or Mozart is significantly different from a similar task in teaching the Jewish classics. We can see the differences by looking at one educational stance that is often suggested as a possible pedagogic strategy to overcome some of the difficulties mentioned above. I want to consider how such a strategy may be useful, but I also want to look at it as a way of pointing out that the matter of finding such approaches may be considerably more complex that it first appears.

I have pointed out that one of the key difficulties in teaching midrash to adult students is the distance between contemporary values and the values and consciousness of the rabbinic world. This sense of distance, for the previously uncommitted student, often creates a tension that leads to discouragement or to rejection of the classical text.

One familiar strategy—employed in teaching Shakespeare and Mark Twain as well—used for dealing with this problem is to ask the students to temporarily put their difficulties on hold and to attempt to approach

[17] See, for example, E. M. W. Tillyard, *The Elizabethan World Picture* (New York: Macmillan, 1943).

the text "on its own terms." Usually this pedagogic strategy chooses between two different routes. The first suggests that the text is to be understood as a document from the past that can be viewed "historically." In other words, the task is to learn what the rabbis' "value concepts," as Max Kadushin put it, were in their own context.[18] This approach might be termed the pedagogy of *Wissenschaft*, using the term associated with the historically oriented scientific study of Judaism (*Wissenschaft des Judentums*).

Nonetheless, such a strategy does not entirely eliminate the difficulty of the content problems raised by older texts (such as the gap between their ethical values and ours) for present-day readers, especially if we also have educational objectives that go beyond the historical perspective alone, if we want to find ways to reappropriate the text for the contemporary reader. Thus if the attitude of *Huckleberry Finn* toward blacks or of *Oliver Twist* toward Jews makes us feel uncomfortable, it is not so simple to say, "Well, back then they had a different way of thinking about things." We may not want to judge history by the standards of today, but are we willing to stand calmly and at a distance in listening to ideas we may find repugnant? And, indeed, do we not argue that the roots of CONTEMPORARY anti-Semitism or racism or sexism are to be found in precisely those iconic texts of the past?[19]

In the second version of this strategy, the students are asked to "willingly suspend their disbelief" about the text before them. I will come back to this phrase in a moment, but for the time being let us simply say that this approach does not—like the *Wissenschaft* approach—wish to focus on the historical dimension per se, but rather asks the students, one might say, to tolerate strangeness. That is, the reader is asked to ignore those archaic or strange aspects of the text which may be distracting to its appreciation. Thus we ask students to read *Hamlet* despite the fact that we do not require them to believe in ghosts or to value violent revenge. One might call this approach "anthropological pedagogy," in the sense that when studying an exotic culture, we do not expect to mimic, say, the Balinese in order to appreciate the significance or richness of Balinese culture.

---

[18] Max Kadushin, *Organic Thinking: A Study in Rabbinic Thought* (New York: Jewish Theological Seminary, 1938), and *The Rabbinic Mind* (New York: Jewish Theological Seminary, 1952).

[19] For an interesting discussion of this issue, see Wayne C. Booth, *The Company We Keep: An Ethics of Fiction* (Berkeley and Los Angeles: University of California Press, 1988).

Both of these strategies are appealing, and both are widely used, but we should clearly understand that both of them are problematic as well, particularly for the type of student that has been my focus here. The difficulty with the *Wissenschaft* pedagogy is that it misunderstands the primary underlying motivation behind most adult religious education. For, in fact, the goal of this kind of student is not so much acquiring knowledge as it is searching for personal meaning.

Although it is true that adults do seek to expand their repertoire of "facts" about Judaism (and here I use the term "fact" in its broadest sense), both research and personal observation seem to suggest that the dimension of personal meaning is far more significant.[20] This meaning may include the practical skills needed for ritual observance (and this seems to have an important dimension in experiments in Jewish family education,[21]) but it is even more prevalent in what Theodore Roszak has termed "the contemporary hunger for wonders,"[22] and to my mind it is an important motivating factor in adult religious education. To view the rabbinic world as a matter of historical interest may work for graduate students (or even for undergraduates, given the pedagogic style of most undergraduate education), but it will not fulfill expectations in the realm of meaning which are sought by adult students.

Nor does the second approach produce a simple solution. Less purely "intellectual" than *Wissenschaft* pedagogy, anthropological pedagogy also has the primary disadvantage of distancing students from their encounter with the text. We might consider in this regard the commonly used phrase to describe what teachers ask of their students in the course of anthropological pedagogy, "the willing suspension of disbelief."

---

[20] See, for example, *Religion and America,* ed. Mary Douglas and Steven M. Tipton (Boston: Beacon, 1983); Charles Y. Glock and Robert N. Bellah, *The New Religious Consciousness* (Berkeley and Los Angeles: University of California Press, 1976); and Robert N. Bellah et al., *Habits of the Heart* (New York: Harper and Row, 1985). For a discussion of this whole question in contemporary Jewish education, see Barry W. Holtz and Eduardo Rauch, "Education for Change: Toward a Model of Jewish Teacher Education," in *Studies in Jewish Education,* vol. 3, ed. Janet Aviad (Jerusalem: Magnes, 1988), 62-91.

[21] See, for example, the various programs described in *Learning Together: A Sourcebook on Jewish Family Education,* ed. Janice P. Alper (Denver: Alternatives in Religious Education Press, 1987), and the discussion in Vicky Kelman, "Of Scaffolds and Life-supports: Toward a Theory of Jewish Family Education" (Paper presented at the annual Research Conference at Oconomoc, Wisconsin on Jewish Education, 1989).

[22] Theodore Roszak, "On the Contemporary Hunger for Wonders," in *The Pushcart Prize,* vol. 6, *Best of the Small Presses, 1980-81,* ed. Bill Henderson (New York: Avon, 1981), 108–12.

In its original context the phrase has nothing to do with education but is rather the invention of the English poet Samuel Taylor Coleridge in one of the most influential works of literary criticism ever published, the *Biographia Literaria* written by Coleridge in 1817 as a kind of poetic manifesto for the age of Romanticism. In chapter 14 of the *Biographia Literaria,* Coleridge describes the circumstances which led him and Wordsworth to write the joint book of poems, the *Lyrical Ballads,* published in 1798, which essentially began the Romantic movement in English poetry.

According to the plan, Wordsworth was to write poems about ordinary experience which would "give the charm of novelty to things of every day and would excite a feeling analogous to the supernatural." Coleridge, on the other hand, would write poems dealing with feelings of a "supernatural, or at least romantic" sort and try to show "the dramatic truth of such emotions." The latter type of poem was meant to convey the "reality" of this supernatural, romantic dimension of experience. The goal, in Coleridge's famous phrase, was "to transfer from our inward nature a human interest and a semblance of truth sufficient to procure for these shadows of imagination that willing suspension of disbelief for the moment, which constitutes poetic faith."[23] It is clear from the statements here and from other writings of Coleridge that he is referring to reading poems which include images that are supernatural or dreamlike in quality. Indeed, one need only look at his poem "Kubla Khan" to see what he means. Readers must suspend their disbelief in the reality of such images to allow themselves to penetrate to the poem's inner truth.

To be sure, there ARE times when we use the phrase in a manner similar to Coleridge's usage. We might say to a class studying Exodus, "Suspend your disbelief about the reality of these plagues that the Bible describes and let us see what the underlying message of the text is." Like Coleridge, we want the reader to get at the dramatic truth beneath the tale, although it appears that Coleridge is talking more about personal experience than about the sort of communal events described in Exodus.

But generally speaking, this is not what we mean when we use the phrase in the classroom. We do not mean suspend your DISbelief, but rather suspend your BELIEF, as in, "Suspend the intellectual belief you hold about the issue that the midrash is addressing." This is far different

---

23 The quotations are from Samuel Taylor Coleridge, *Biographia Literaria,* ed. James Engell and W. Jackson Bate (London: Routledge and Kegan Paul, 1983), Bollingen Series 75 (Princeton: Princeton University Press) 2:5-7.

from Coleridge's desire to let the emotional magic of the "romantic" image work on the reader's imagination.

And here, of course, the difference between teaching midrash and teaching Shakespeare becomes quite apparent. Students have the option of distancing themselves from Shakespeare or Mark Twain or even Giotto because none of these artists demands religious commitment from those who wish to study them. I can love Shakespeare and take from Shakespeare that which speaks to me without having to apologize for Shakespeare's "shortcomings" from the point of view of contemporary values. But midrash, like other Jewish classics, is premised upon religious seriousness. Midrash demands an active, living connection from the Jew. True, as Maimonides pointed out, one need not accept the literal truth of events described by aggadah:

> The words of the sages contain both an obvious and a hidden meaning. Thus, whenever the sages spoke of things that seem impossible, they were employing the style of riddle and parable which is the method of truly great thinkers
> (commentary on Sanhedrin, ch. 10,)[24]

But one must think hard about these texts, "trying anxiously to grasp its logic and its expression, so that you may find its genuine intellectual intention and lay hold of a direct faith."[25] Such commitment of "faith" is not required of the reader of Shakespeare.

Now, it may be that there is one aspect of the study of midrash which comes closer to the Coleridge position, namely, suspending one's disbelief about the METHOD of midrash, the use of puns and word associations, disparate verses from the Bible, and texts broken down into their tiniest elements. For here we are asking the reader to enter the illusive quality of midrash, the magical side of the text which looks at Torah the way one might see a monumental code.

The skepticism we might have about such "tricks" of interpretation may give way to an appreciation for the poetic truth which lies beneath. The student may even come to value the charm and elegance of a good midrashic reading. But this is only one aspect of teaching the classics. A deeper challenge lies in the message—or messages, to be more accurate—of these marvelous texts. In a world little given to accepting the authority of tradition, no easy pedagogic solutions are to be found for

---

[24] See the translation in *A Maimonides Reader,* ed. Isadore Twersky (New York: Behrman House, 1972), 409.

[25] Ibid., 410.

such an endeavor. This is not to say that the texts cannot be or should not be taught. It is only to recognize the educational challenge that they present.

For such students I often say Jewish texts are something like long-lost family: we may not always recognize the resemblance, but at least we want to give the new acquaintances the benefit of the doubt. But for many people—those who do not come to the tradition with an already built-in level of commitment—this may not be an argument that is going to work. The greatest impediment to pedagogy lies in the wide gulf between text and life in the world of most Jews today.

16

The Ḥavurah *as a Context for Adult Jewish Education*

JOSEPH REIMER

The field of adult Jewish education is yet in its infancy. While the American Jewish community has struggled for most of this century to establish schools and informal educational settings for the young, Jewish education for adults has remained episodic. A few institutions have devoted effort to developing thoughtful approaches to educating adults, but the standard fare has been familiar lectures of Jewish interest. In that format, the lecturer may have a name recognizable to the audience, but is essentially a stranger who will leave after taking a few questions. No ongoing teacher–student relationship will develop; no continuous pursuit of a subject matter will follow; no community of learning will emerge.

One need not have read the growing literature on general adult education to realize that, by any serious criteria, the typical lecture series does not merit the designation of "adult education."[1] But what is less well known is that a reenvisioning of this field has begun. In recent years

---

[1] Of the growing literature on adult education, some of the best known works are: Stephen B. Brookfield, *Understanding and Facilitating Adult Learning* (San Francisco: Jossey-Bass, 1986); Patricia K. Cross, *Adults as Learners* (San Francisco: Jossey-Bass, 1982); Malcolm S. Knowles, *The Modern Practice of Education: From Pedagogy to Andragogy* (New York: Adult Education Comapany, 1980); Alan B. Knox, *Adult Development and Learning* (San Francisco: Jossey-Bass, 1978).

a number of new projects, informed by contemporary theories of adult education, have emerged that go well beyond the lecture format in meeting the needs of adult learners. These programs generally are targeted to more specific audiences, involve commitment to continuous learning, utilize different forms of cooperative learning and call upon adults to be active in setting goals for Jewish learning and achieving them at their own pace and according to their own learning style.[2]

What is encouraging about these developments is that they come from many different corners of the Jewish community. Heilman has offered a careful exposition of *lernen* as it is practised in contemporary Orthodox circles. Schoenfeld has shown the power of the adult bat mitzvah ceremony to motivate the Jewish learning of mature women. Zachary has written suggestively of the role of adult Jewish learning in leadership development for federation circles.[3]

The focus of this paper is on the *ḥavurah* as a context for adult Jewish education. Much has been written on the contemporary North American grouping known as the *ḥavurah,* but not much attention has been focused on its functioning as an environment in which adult Jews, with relatively little or no previous Jewish educational background, have learned to become practicing members of an ongoing worship and study group.[4]

Two Ḥavurot

The data for this paper derive from my own longstanding involvement as a member in two *ḥavurah* groups, Havurat Shalom from 1968 to 1972, and the Harvard–Radcliffe Hillel Worship and Study Congregation from 1980 to the present. Each is a freestanding group not part of a larger congregation; each was founded by a rabbi who continued as a leader in the group; each is located in the same broad university community and

---

[2] *The Pedagogic Reporter* 40 (January 1990). The entire issue is devoted to new developments in adult Jewish education.

[3] Samuel C. Heilman, *The People of the Book* (Chicago: University of Chicago Press, 1983); Stuart Schoenfeld, this volume; Lois J. Zachary, "Lay Leadership Development," *The Pedagogic Reporter* 40 (January 1990): 29f.

[4] Of the many pieces on the *ḥavurah,* I have found these to be most helpful: *Contemporary Judaic Fellowship in Theory and in Practice,* ed. Jacob Neusner (New York: Ktav, 1972); Riv-Ellen Prell, *Prayer and Community: The Havurah in American Judaism* (Detroit: Wayne State University Press, 1989); Bernard Reisman, *The Chavurah: A Contemporary Jewish Experience* (New York: Union of American Hebrew Congregations, 1977); Lenore Weissler, "Making Judaism Meaningful: Ambivalence and Tradition in a Havurah Community: (Ph.D. diss., University of Pennsylvania, 1982).

attracts members from that community; each has as its main point of gathering a *Shabbat* morning service that combines *davening* and communal study; and each is constituted by members of varied Jewish backgrounds, some of whom came as virtual novices to Jewish living and learning, and others of whom came with a variety of more extensive Jewish backgrounds.

There are as many salient differences as similarities between these two groups, which is often the rule among contemporary *ḥavurot*. I have cited similarities which are of particular relevance to the focus on adult Jewish learning, and now enumerate several of the relevant differences.

1. Havurat Shalom began in 1968 as a seminary and offered throughout its first four years formal classes in addition to Torah study on *Shabbat*. Several of the members were designated as teachers and came with rabbinic degrees and considerable Jewish expertise.[5] At Worship and Study, only the founding rabbi brought that level of expertise; Torah study, which was essential to the group from its inception in 1964, has been limited primarily to *Shabbat* morning services.

2. The members of Havurat Shalom in those years were primarily in their twenties and often moved to the Boston area for the purpose of joining the *ḥavurah*. Some were married; few had children. The members of Worship and Study are more varied in age, from single people in their twenties to couples in their sixties. Members join with their children, who grow up in the congregation. Members are residents or students in the Boston area and join as congregants of this *ḥavurah*-style congregation.

3. Membership in Havurat Shalom was attained by application and selection. To be a member entailed a series of communal responsibilities beyond study and worship.[6] Membership in Worship and Study is nonselective and entails no defined responsibilities, though more active members volunteer for both organizational and ritual responsibilities such as leading services or Torah discussion, organizing *Kiddush*, or tutoring someone for bar mitzvah.[7]

4. Becoming a member of Havurat Shalom involved making a major commitment of time and energy. (One could become a regular worship-

---

5 Stephen C. Lerner, "The Havurot," *Conservative Judaism* 24 (Spring 1970): 7.

6 Arthur Green, "Havurat Shalom: A Proposal," in *Contemporary Judaic Fellowship*, 149–54.

7 The nature of responsibilities is spelled out in a booklet prepared by members of Worship and Study entitled "The Worship and Study Congregation of Harvard–Radcliffe Hillel."

per on *Shabbat* and not join as a member.) Few became members without already being in the process of becoming a religiously committed Jew.[8] Becoming a member of Worship and Study entails far less commitment and hence is an option chosen by Jews with far greater variability in terms of religious involvement.[9]

Given these salient differences, why join these two disparate groups in this single study? The reasons are threefold: (1) Both made a serious effort to bring adult Jews with relatively little Jewish background into the circle of *davening* and Torah study by welcoming them into the *Shabbat* morning service; (2) Both relied heavily on the community to encourage and teach newcomers; (3) But each also had a founding rabbi who served as a guide to the group in its collective growing in knowledge of Torah.

These two groups were not selected to be representative of the network of *ḥavurot* that currently exists around the country. While the features of their group life to be analyzed are not unique to these two groups, the groups do have other features, such as their location in a university community, which could be seen as nonrepresentative of the majority of *ḥavurot*. What I present may have limited generalizability, and the broader application of my findings must remain suggestive.

Adult Jewish Learning

Andragogy, the art of teaching adults, is a term introduced into the literature by Malcolm Knowles. Its basic assumptions about adult learning are "that as individuals mature, they become more self-directed, have many experiences that can be used as learning resources, learn for specific purposes and want to apply what they learn immediately."[10]

Adapting andragogy to the *ḥavurah* setting, I am positing that when an adult Jew, for whatever personal motivation, decides to become a regular attendee at the weekly *Shabbat* morning service, despite not having the skill to knowledgeably participate in the *davening* and Torah study, that individual is placing him or herself in a position to become an adult Jewish learner. The learning often also involves taking more formal

---

[8] Arthur Green, "Some Liturgical Notes from Havurat Shalom," in *Contemporary Judaic Fellowship*, 155–60.

[9] In terms of diversity of members and religious practice, Worship and Study more resembles the synagogue *ḥavurot* that Reisman describes than does Havurat Shalom.

[10] Janet R. Moore, "Guidelines Concerning Adult Learing," *Journal of Staff Development* 9 (Summer 1988): 2.

courses in Hebrew and Judaica, but my focus is on what this relatively unlettered Jew may learn in self-directed ways from the experience of regularly attending services.

To place this learning in context, at Havurat Shalom it would have applied either to new members or spouses who were joining the *ḥavurah* with little previous experience in Jewish study and worship, or to the fifty to sixty outsiders who would attend *Shabbat* services.[11] At Worship and Study it would apply to many of the 75 regular worshipers who heard about this service, came in to try it, and decided to make it a regular feature of their week. These include faculty and graduate students, parents looking for a congregation in which to celebrate their child's bar mitzvah, potential converts, and Jews who had not found themselves in other synagogues but were attracted to the *ḥavurah* style of this congregation.[12]

Following Getzels, I am not drawing a sharp line between education and socialization.[13] As the newcomers are socialized into these *ḥavurah* groups, they become educated in how to participate in *davening* and study. They may learn a lot of content from hearing the Torah discussions, but the effect of the socialization process is broader. In becoming group members, they become a certain kind of Jew. To a greater or lesser degree, they acquire a new aspect of identity. Where previously "being Jewish" may only have had a vague and undefined meaning in their lives, in becoming active participants "being Jewish" takes on a greater clarity and salience. As their competence increases and comfort level rises, they feel themselves to be more Jewish in the *ḥavurah* sense of that term. And it is that self-transformation—which is simultaneously a self-education and a socialization to the group—that is the focus of our inquiry.[14]

---

[11] Green, "Some Liturgical Notes," 158.

[12] Members come from all around the Boston area; many live in areas that do not have synagogues. This congregation runs the very large Conservative services on High Holy Days for Harvard University that attract over fifteen hundred people. A small percentage of these join the regular *Shabbat* group.

[13] J.W. Getzels, "Socialization and Education: A Note on Discontinuities," in *The Family as Educator*, ed. Hope Jensen Leichter (New York: Teachers College Press, 1974), 44-51.

[14] See Janet Aviad, *Return to Judaism: Religious Renewal in Israel* (Chicago: University of Chicago Press, 1983), for a similar treatment of *baʿalei teshuvah* in Jerusalem, where adult education in Orthodox Judaism is subsumed under their socialization into yeshiva culture.

The Risks of Being a Beginner

In observing people as they begin to attend *Shabbat* services, what stands out for me is the degree of risk they are taking in joining these groups and readying themselves to encounter Jewish religious activity in this relatively intense context. For beginners new to Judaism or returning after a long hiatus, the participatory nature of the *ḥavurah* service and intellectual level of the Torah study can indeed be intimidating. It is not unusual for newcomers to sit in a back row or corner (which spatially is still not very far from the center), hoping to go unnoticed. That they often do not go unnoticed, but are drawn toward the center of activity by veteran members, is the immediate social risk that a newcomer faces. In a *ḥavurah* group one cannot remain anonymous for long, and where there is a strong group norm toward participation, the newcomer is quickly faced with the question: Will I risk a first step of participation in a ritual context which is unfamiliar to me or prefer a spectator role?

In Worship and Study, it is not unusual for a newcomer to sit quietly for a year before participating verbally in a Torah discussion or accepting an aliyah to the Torah. Leading a *tefillah* or a Torah discussion can take two or more years of observation, acclimation, and learning. In the meanwhile, one can be a spectator in the service but a participant in the social network and in the tasks required to keep the group functioning (such as bringing *Kiddush*). Some use this period to acquire skill in Hebrew and familiarity with the *siddur* and *Chumash*. Others elect to continue in a quieter role, accepting aliyot in English, rarely commenting during discussion, but making their most active contribution in the social realm.

Beyond the social risk of participation stands the personal risk of change of self. These *ḥavurah* groups attract people who often have achieved a high degree of professional competence in their work or student lives. They are accustomed to being in control of their interactions and taking pride in exhibiting their mastery and expertise.

But what happens when as adults they become interested in the area of Jewish practice in which they have little previous knowledge and skill? The very act of venturing into a new area raises questions for an adult which a child might not have to face. Children are expected to be beginners in new areas of knowledge, but adults are not. Thus the newcomer might be asking him or herself: Why is this suddenly important to you? If it is important to you, why are you so relatively ignorant about it? And, if you are who you say you are, how come you are going off and developing this unpredictable interest? That as adults we have developed an identity by which we know ourselves and others know us can make it riskier to pursue new areas of interest.

The literature on adult development is helpful in putting this element of personal risk in perspective. Erikson has made famous the notion of "an identity crisis," typically occurring during one's adolescent years. The resolution of that crisis comes when as a young adult one can put into place some relatively stable decisions about the directions one wishes to pursue and not to pursue.[15]

The work of Levinson, Vaillant, and others in tracing the course of development across people's twenties, thirties, and forties makes clear that the identity one constructs by the end of adolescence will need to be reexamined and reconstructed as one faces the challenges of living as an adult.[16] Decisions that once seemed final—such as, "I have no interest in the Jewish religion"—can come up for reexamination when one is facing the challenges of raising children, dealing with a parent's dying, or facing one's own aging.

But reexamination rarely comes without anxiety and dislocation. Robert Kegan, in *The Evolving Self*, writes lucidly about what he calls "the institutional self," the adult who has come to know himself or herself as a certain person in the world and is fully invested in living that self-conception. The self has become an "institution" with its own autonomy, interests, and needs. The person guards its boundaries carefully but can be thrown off guard by an unanticipated change or crisis. Then, "the experience of losing one's balance consists in feelings of negative self-evaluation, feelings that one's personal organization is about to collapse, fears about losing one's control and one's sense of being distinct."[17]

This is not to suggest that every newcomer to the *ḥavurah* groups is in a state of personal crisis, but that moving from having "an interest in" things Jewish to making the commitment to learn the unfamiliar involves a risky willingness to let go of some control and face the group as some-

---

15 Erik H. Erikson, *Identity Youth and Crisis* (New York: Norton, 1968).

16 Daniel J. Levinson et al., *The Seasons of a Man's Life* (New York: Knopf, 1978); George Vaillant, *Adaptation to Life* (Boston: Little, Brown, 1977). For a treatment of women's development in these decades, see Grace Baruch, Rosalind Barnett, and Caryl Rivers, *Life Prints: New Patterns of Love and Work for Today's Women* (New York: New American Library, 1983).

17 Robert Kegan, *The Evolving Self: Problem and Process in Human Development* (Cambridge: Harvard University Press, 1982), 223.

one who is first learning to read Hebrew, to lift or wrap the Torah, to understand the subtleties of a biblical text.

The personal risk may be magnified when the area of new interest is Jewish religious practice. In forming one's identity, a Jew has to decide how to relate to his or her Jewishness. When one has earlier taken a neutral or negative stand to being Jewish and then during one's adulthood begins to alter that stand, one is reopening a set of difficult personal questions. One may have related to Jewishness as a "stigma," in Goffman's sense of the term,[18] and chosen to stay as far away as possible from identifying with others who were openly Jewish. Now, in joining this group, one has to embrace the "stigma" and admit to oneself and others that one is choosing to be Jewish. Rarely can that be done without facing one's negative feelings about Jewishness.

In addition, family members and close friends are likely to take immediate notice. They sense the implications of the individual's actions for defining the family or friendship and may react defensively: How can you be doing this to us?"[19] The newcomer may be bringing a lot of doubt and ambivalence about not only whether he or she can take on this new learning, but also whether he or she should: Is it right to do the unpredictable, to raise anew hard questions, to cross established lines, to shake up important relationships?

In this regard, there can be no doubt that Havurat Shalom benefited from the relative youthfulness of its members. Single young adults in their twenties are often still forming their identities and can afford to take on a new interest in a way that is far more challenging to a mature adult. Worship and Study attracts new members primarily in their late twenties, thirties and forties. For many of them, the element of personal and interpersonal risk is heightened, as is the difficulty of beginning from *alef–bet*.

Yet some mature as well as younger adults take up the challenge. My question is, how does the *ḥavurah* group work to support their taking this risk? I am not looking at personality factors that might distinguish one newcomer from another, but at the characteristics of these two groups

---

[18] Erving Goffman, *Stigma: Notes on the Management of Spoiled Identity* (Englewood Cliffs, N.J.: Prentice-Hall, 1963).

[19] For one articulation of how from a family system's perspective a change in the life of one family member calls forth resistance from other family members who are maintaining the existing systems, see Salvador Minuchin, *Families and Family Therapy* (Cambridge: Harvard University Press, 1974), 52.

that are supportive to the newcomer in the course of his or her taking the personal risk of joining the group and learning to become a *ḥavurah* Jew.

Group Supports for the Newcomer

There are three elements of the group experience that I would hypothesize as essential supports to the newcomer's taking of risk: the nature of the service, the norms of the peer group and the quality of leadership.

The Nature of the Service

These *ḥavurah* groups have worked hard to establish a service that is simultaneously informal and intense. Informality is established by the design of the room, the clothing worn by participants, the give-and-take among participants, and the looser rules of etiquette that govern behavior. A *ḥavurah* service is meant to be a study in contrasts with that of a large suburban non-Orthodox synagogue. It is meant to re-create something of the atmosphere of a *shtiebel,* an alternative decorum that allows for more freedom of movement and expression.[20] In Havurat Shalom, that included sitting on cushions rather than on chairs, wearing jeans but with a large woolen tallith, and including humor as part of the Torah discussion. At Worship and Study, there are folding chairs, but dress remains casual and there are many young children who wander in and out at different points in the service.

The informality functions as a relaxer, communicating, "Here we retain a sense of humor, down-to-earthness, casualness. Here you are not in your parents' or family's synagogue but among friends like yourself. Here you can be more of yourself; there is less need to dress up, to pretend. We are all in this learning together; there are no official rabbis or cantors to lead the service or make decisions for us."[21]

The informality is meant to be balanced by intensity and seriousness. At Havurat Shalom, the *davening* itself had an unusual degree of intensity, as this quote from a former member indicates:

---

[20] See Prell, *Prayer and Community,* 92-109, for a fuller statement on the *ḥavurah*'s developing a decorum alternative to the practices in suburban non-Orthodox synagogues.

[21] For a possible understanding of how informality functions to lighten the seriousness of religious role performance in a *ḥavurah* context, see Erving Goffman's concept of "role distance" in *Encounters* (Indianapolis: Bobbs-Merrill, 1961), 85–152.

> The first service we went to at Havurat Shalom was a Friday night service. We walked into the house [where Havurat Shalom met] and then the prayer room. And in the prayer room there are no seats, just cushions on the floor. The candles were lit; it was dusk. It was really quiet and serene, people sitting around on cushions. After a while someone began a slow *niggun* (wordless melody); it was incredible. At the ḥavurah there was an incredible consciousness of mood, of what constitutes mood, enhances and detracts from it, and a terrific sense of aesthetics, of Jewish aesthetics. What is appropriate and not appropriate to do; what enhances beauty and what detracts from it. I never understood that Jews could pray like that.[22]

Shabbat morning services retained some of that inner-group intensity but were modified to accommodate the presence of outsiders, as Arthur Green explains:

> A few words about our Shabbat-morning congregation: we generally have seventy-five to a hundred people, mostly of college age. More than half are familiar enough with Hebrew liturgy to follow, if not to understand. Perhaps a third of the *kahal* understands the Hebrew text without translation. The others are encouraged to sing along with the *nigunim*, to *daven* aloud in English, or to use the chant as a background for meditation. Some obviously felt left out by the Hebrew in the service, but we try to make up for that by general informality, friendliness, and encouragement. It is clear that we live with two often competing claims: a liturgy that is authentic to us as a Havurah versus a liturgy planned for the outside people who come. We try to do it somewhere in between, sacrificing neither personal integrity nor friendliness; it's sometimes a tough balance.[23]

At Worship and Study, while the *davening* is less intense, it remains serious and the Torah study session takes on an added intensity. When Worship and Study began, it was essentially a study group in English with some *tefillah* surrounding the study. As the founding members became more comfortable with being a regular *Shabbat* group, they expanded the parameters of the *tefillah* until it grew to include almost the whole traditional liturgy (but with a shortened *musaf*). Yet the Torah study, which now follows the Torah reading, remains the central moment of intensity, with members taking turns leading the discussion and with participants often heatedly discussing the weekly portion in

---

22 Prell, *Prayer and Community*, 103.

23 Green, "Some Liturgical Notes," 158.

relation to their own set of interpretations. Over the years the level of knowledge of the text and commentaries on the *parashah* has steadily increased. It is also not unusual for members to refer back to past discussions, for the group has developed a repository of its own commentaries and interpretations that can be called upon to further their understanding of the weekly *parashah*.

If the informality of decorum communicates a relaxed posture, the intensity communicates, "For all that we are relaxed, we are also intently committed to this undertaking. You have entered a community of real personal involvement—if that is what you are looking for."

This combination of informality and intensity may match the needs of the searching yet ambivalent newcomer. The part of the person that is seeking a new identity is drawn to the intensity and seriousness; the part that is yet ambivalent may be relieved to realize that ambivalence is welcomed and that the newcomer is not alone in his or her uncertainties about choosing this path.

The Peer Group

The *ḥavurah*, in not accepting the traditional, hierarchical role division between clergy and congregation, has elevated the community, or peer group, to a position of dominance. In Havurat Shalom, the emphasis on community was so strong that if any norm was clear, it was that every participant was to treat the other as a *ḥaver*. That meant, as Green makes clear, attempting to get to know every member of the group, and taking some responsibility to help one another grow as humans and as fellow seekers in a religious path.[24]

In Worship and Study, and many other contemporary *ḥavurah* groups, while the communitarian norm has softened, the norms of participation and communal decision-making remain strong. By definition, *ḥavurot* are self-governing, democratic groups that do not rely on appointed professionals but on their own members to carry out the religious and social functions of the group.[25]

For the newcomer's learning, what is essential is the peer group as resource and reinforcer.

ALONENESS is an essential problem for a newcomer. By having stepped away from his or her established identity patterns, the newcomer may feel all alone in the religious quest, not knowing others

---

24 Green, "Havurat Shalom," 152f.

25 See Reisman, *The Chavurah*, 41-50.

who share this interest. To join the group and find peers who are also beginning this quest is a powerful resource and reinforcer for the newcomer. Their presence and accessibility means that he or she need not be alone, that there are others taking similar risks to his or her own.

The norms of the peer group encourage and support RISK-TAKING. It is expected that new members, if interested, will progress in learning Jewish practice. People watch for new steps: the first aliyah, the first active participation in a discussion, the first group function assumed, the first leading of a service or Torah study, the first reading of Torah or Haftarah. There is a sense of excitement and encouragement about a step successfully taken and a sense of tolerance and support for mistakes made along the way.

Peers are available as TEACHERS of different Judaic skills. More advanced peers can tutor you in Hebrew *trup* or *niggun*, or help prepare you to lead a Torah discussion. Peers can invite you home to show you how a *Shabbat* meal is conducted. Or more simply, by their example, peers are available as models for how you take the next step and the ones beyond.

That in these two *ḥavurah* groups it was commonly known that almost all the members, no matter how currently knowledgeable, had come to their Jewish practice not as children, but as adults, may have created a sense that this transformation is achievable without necessarily resulting in creating an unrecognizable self. Yet it is also the case that veterans can be intimidating and that *ḥavurot* are not free of intragroup tensions between oldtimers and newcomers. It is only when the group, being aware of these tensions, takes steps to continue welcoming and educating newcomers that the positive learning effects of the peer group can continue.[26]

The Leadership

In these democratic groups, leadership is spread out by design among many members. There is a rotating *gabbai* or coordinator. Members by rotation are in charge of coordinating given functions: leading a service, reading Torah, organizing *Kiddush*, welcoming newcomers, and so forth. On a more informal level, some particular members may be looked to as sources of Judaic information, as facilitators of the discussions, as innovators in services, as healers of wounds that arise in the group. No one

[26] See Prell, *Prayer and Community*, 143–55, for a treatment of what occurred in another *ḥavurah* group when intragroup tension threatened to disrupt the group's efforts to integrate and educate new members.

person provides leadership in all these areas, and the strength of the group may lie in its containing members who are strong in different areas of group functioning.[27]

However, what characterizes Havurat Shalom and Worship and Study—and differentiates them from many other Havurah groups—is that each had a founder who remained on to serve as a particular type of leader in the group. In Havurat Shalom, this was Arthur Green; in Worship and Study, Ben Zion Gold. Both are ordained Conservative rabbis with a scholarly bent, a charismatic charm, and a strong interest in eastern European Jewry and particularly Hasidism. Their roles were unusual in a *ḥavurah* setting in that, while they eschewed the formal role of rabbi, they exerted a particular influence different from that of any other member of the group. They remained founders.[28]

Leadership in a *ḥavurah* setting is not easy to describe or understand. There is no formal role of founder to be filled. Nor would the group tolerate a *rav* or a *rebbe* to give direction or *pasqen halakhah*. The ideological bent of the group is too egalitarian to favor such set positions, and these rabbis, like other professionals within *ḥavurah* groups, are themselves opposed to being seen as the authorities or leaders within the group. They aspire to be one among many leaders in the group.

Yet it has been observed that there is something within the dynamic of these two groups that resists allowing their founders to become simply one among equals in the group. Some have attributed this to the powers of individuals, as Lerner did in his article on Havurat Shalom:

> While the institution has no true hierarchy, and lines of authority are fluid (all are equal members), there is nevertheless a leader—Rabbi Arthur Green. The force of Green's personality, his primary role in the founding of *ḥavurah*, his devotion to its goals, have made him clearly a sort of *mareh d'atra*, although the term *rebbe* might more properly describe his position.[29]

---

[27] For a clear statement on leadership or executive processes in group life, see Theodore M. Mills, *The Sociology of Small Groups* (Englewood Cliffs, N.J.: Prentice-Hall, 1967), 88-100.

[28] For an incisive analysis of the role of the leader-founder in the formation of a new setting and his or her relationship to the core group, see Seymour B. Sarason, *The Creation of Setting* and *The Future Societies* (San Francisco: Jossey-Bass, 1972), 47-96. Sarason's analysis highlights the tensions and limitations inherent in these roles; my analysis is limited to the teaching function vis-à-vis new members.

[29] Lerner, "The Havurot," 5.

While not denying the force of personality involved in either case, I am asking a different question: Is there in the nature of the *ḥavurah* learning experience some dynamic that may contribute to granting these founders a special leadership role in the group?

Although newcomers have available to them many role-models and teachers from within the peer group, I suggest there are limits to how much peers can contribute to an adult's Jewish learning, and there may be a push from the learners themselves for the founders to informally play an enhanced leadership role.

The greatest risk to the adult learner in this process is the fear of loss of identity. "If I start on this journey and leave behind part of my known self to become more Jewishly and religiously involved, who will I become? How will I know my way? How will I know what is authentically Jewish and what path is right for me?" Given the liberal definition of right and wrong within *ḥavurah* culture and the pluralistic conceptions of truth, a newcomer may be reassured that the group will allow him or her a continued degree of autonomy and yet be quite anxious that the lack of clear direction may lead to an anarchic situation in which he or she will never know for sure what Judaism is really about.

In addressing this deep-seated anxiety, the peer group is of only limited value. As resource and reinforcer, it works well to teach next steps and new skills. But what lies beyond those steps and beyond the *Shabbat* service itself? What is the larger Jewish picture for orienting oneself in finding a personally authentic Jewish identity?[30]

Here the founder-leader can play a unique role. It is not that he takes over the leadership of the group, but through his presence, he symbolizes something for the group. Through his knowledge and spiritual depth, he symbolizes the group's roots in the Jewish past, and through his example, he is the group's guarantor that the journey taken into the future is feasible and worthwhile. He is perceived as being enough steps

30 The anxiety of the newcomer to the *ḥavurah* is comparable in a different setting to the anxiety of a newcomer to the world of professional careers as described by Levinson in *The Seasons of a Man's Life*. Levinson describes newcomers as searching for direction to fulfill their professional dream and, if fortunate, finding a mentor, a more senior person in that field, to guide their next steps and help give shape to a view of a possible future in this field. The *ḥavurah* leader-founder cannot be a mentor to every member of the *ḥavurah* group, though several members may become his mentees by developing a close personal relationship with time. But, I am suggesting, the leader-founder can be a modern-day spiritual guide even to those members of the group with whom he does not have a close personal relationship because the group qua group looks to the leader-founder to play this leadership role.

ahead on this spiritual journey to be an anchor, one who allows passage from here to there to seem achievable.[31]

This is a most delicate leadership role to play. If the *ḥavurah* founder were to assert his authority in the sense of becoming a *rav* or a *rebbe,* he would be betraying the egalitarian ethic of the group.[32] He has to limit himself to the power of presence and example, comment and suggestion. He has to believe in others and in their spiritual journeys, allowing them and the group the autonomy to find their own way, while also knowing that his example, in its nondemanding tone, is yet setting the ground for their evolving lives as Jews.

An example of the exercise of his leadership is the *Tiqqun Leil Shavuot* at Worship and Study. The *tiqqun* is a late-night study session traditionally held at midnight of the first day of Shavuoth to prepare for the receiving of the Torah that is symbolically reenacted the following morning.[33]

A few years ago, Rabbi Gold began the practice of asking four members to each select one *miṣvah* of importance to him or her and to teach it to the group. Each person is given twenty minutes to present followed by ten minutes for group discussion. The *tiqqun* takes place in the regular worship space, but seats are arranged in a circle so everyone is facing the others. Attendance is comparable to that on a *Shabbat* morning.

---

31 See Mills, *Sociology of Small Groups,* 124–26, for his description of two types of a group leadership, Idealistic and Democratic. I am positing that in these *ḥavurah* groups there is a blend of the two types; while the articulated ethos of the group is democratic, and both the group and the leader-founder conciously follow the procedures of democratic governance, there is also a spiritual pull to the idealistic, where the leader is perceived as embodying the ideal to which the group strives. Lerner (see note 29) captures this in describing Green as fulfilling the role of *rebbe.* But neither Green nor the members of Havurat Shalom were comfortable with the leader-disciple model of relationship inherent in idealistic leadership. Hence they, like the Worship and Study group, worked on a blend of models that was functional, but also open to tension, as when the founder might feel called upon to exert influence but find others resisting the influence in the name of democracy and equality.

32 Contrast the egalitarian ethic of the *ḥavurah* groups with the more explicitly idealistic model of the *baʿalei teshuvah* yeshivas described by Aviad, *Return to Judaism,* in which the founder-rabbi, though tolerant of the strains involved in these young adults becoming Orthodox, yet retained the authority to direct their spiritual development in the particular direction of yeshiva Orthodoxy.

33 Michael Strassfeld, *The Jewish Holidays: A Guide and Commentary* (New York: Harper and Row, 1985), 73-74.

In the first year of this practice, four of the most Jewishly knowledgeable members were asked to present. In subsequent years, there has been a mix of more knowledgeable members and members who are recent to Jewish study. The mix insures that while some presentations will be more textually based, others will derive primarily from the presenter's personal experience of the *miṣvah*. *Miṣvot* chosen have ranged from healing the sick and pursuing peace to honoring one's parents and keeping kosher.

What is the founder's role in the *tiqqun*? Rather than assuming the more familiar role of leading the discussion—which, for example, Rabbi Gold does during the High Holy Days for the large university *kahal*—he has chosen to be the organizer and coordinator of the Torah study. But the *tiqqun* is special because the presentations are more personal; they are about each person's own relation to Torah. The presentations involve greater risk, as, for example, a doctor in the group explains how practicing medicine relates to his Jewishness or a mother of grown children explains her understanding of why honoring parents still plays an important part in her relationship to her children. Rabbi Gold's selecting people to present, his being there to listen to their Torah, and his articulating that "these too are commentaries on Torah" have the effect of confirming each of the members—veteran and newcomers—in his or her growing sense of being, in Rosenzweig's terms, not just "children" but also "builders" of the Law.[34]

Conclusions

In presenting these *ḥavurah* groups as contexts for adult Jewish education, I have highlighted their positive features, aspects of their group life that are supportive of newcomers becoming members and learning the practices of *davening* and Torah study. In a more detailed study, inevitably a more balanced picture would emerge in which the groups are not always supportive, the founders do not play their role to perfection, and newcomers feel intimidated or unwelcome and decide to leave.[35]

---

34 Franz Rosenzweig, *On Jewish Learning* (New York: Schocken, 1965), 91; cf. the fifth section of Paul Mendes-Flohr's contribution to this volume.

35 See Prell, *Prayer and Community*, for an ethnographic description of a *ḥavurah* group which, though not having a single leader-founder figure, yet experienced almost all these tensions and worked toward their resolution.

But for all its imperfections, the *ḥavurah* may offer the field of adult Jewish education several significant insights in how to promote certain aspects of adult Jewish learning.

A definite attraction of the *ḥavurah* context is its offering a stable social group to which the newcomer to Judaism can belong. Beginning a journey means leaving behind the familiar, which can leave one feeling alone. To have stable and attractive company who are fellow journeyers can be an antidote to the loneliness of the beginner.

Once a newcomer moves beyond the intellectual focus of learning about Judaism to the more involving focus of how to live as a Jew, the level of personal and social risk greatly increases. People will be far less likely to take this risk if they do not feel the welcome and support of others who care about the self at risk and are invested in the success of the spiritual journey.

To learn how to live as a Jew requires access to models of that lifestyle. Telling about Jewish life is not nearly as effective as inviting someone to behold—first as spectator, then as participant—how it is done. Observation needs to be followed by trying out behavior in an atmosphere that rewards effort, but is tolerant of slow learning and accommodating to the learning needs of the beginner.

The *ḥavurah* offers the learner a mix of informality and intensity that sets high goals but also allows participants to back off from being overly serious. The environment encourages a low-key, set-your-own-pace style of learning that balances wanting to be more learned and observant with an acknowledged realization that change in an adult's life style usually comes gradually.

These *ḥavurah* groups offer a model of teacher-leader who is not the traditional rabbi, but the anchor to the group's journey into unchartered Jewish learning. The leader, whose role it is to set the course and ready the runners, is yet careful not to set the destination. The leader offers encouragement and suggestions about the journey; but he or she is careful not to be placed in the position of the guide or authority, recognizing that these times and contexts may require careful balancing between honoring individual autonomy and offering spiritual direction.

While the numbers of American Jews who will join *ḥavurah* groups such as these described in this paper may be few, the issues raised may have a wider resonance. As soon as adult Jewish education moves beyond the lecture format into preparing adults to live more informed and involved Jewish lives, the needs of the adult learner will arise. Then the judicious use of natural settings such as a worship and study service, the reliance on a group of learners such as the *ḥavurah* community, and the delicate leadership to be provided by teachers such as the leader-founder will take on more general and significant relevance to the enterprise of educating adults in living Judaism.

17

Tradition, Judaism, and the Jewish Religion in Contemporary Israeli Society

CHARLES S. LIEBMAN

This paper argues that whereas Tradition, Judaism, and the Jewish religion existed as distinguishable conceptions in the period of the *yishuv* (The Jewish settlement of Palestine), they no longer do so—or if they do, distinctions are less pronounced and exist among a smaller segment of the population than in the past. On the other hand, Tradition no longer carries the authority over the lives of Jews which it once did.

Tradition, Judaism, and Jewish Religion Defined

I prefer to capitalize the term Tradition because I am referring to a specific tradition. Edward Shils, who has written the most important book on tradition from a social scientific perspective, describes tradition as

> that which has been and is being handed down or transmitted. It is something which was created, was performed or believed in the past, or which is believed to have existed or to have been performed or believed in the past.[1]

But in my use of the term Tradition I do not mean everything transmitted from the past or even everything Jewish transmitted from the past, but

1 Edward Shils, *Tradition* (Chicago: University of Chicago Press, 1981), 13.

rather what Robert Redfield has called a "great tradition" as distinct from a "little tradition." According to Redfield,

> In a civilization there is a great tradition of the reflective few, and there is a little tradition of the largely unreflective many. The great tradition is cultivated in schools or temples; the little tradition works itself out and keeps itself going in the lives of the unlettered in their village communities. The tradition of the philosopher, theologian, and literary man is a tradition consciously cultivated and handed down; that of the little people is for the most part taken for granted and not submitted to much scrutiny or considered refinement and improvement.[2]

The fact that Tradition, or what Redfield calls the great tradition, is cultivated by an elite does not mean that the masses have no part in it. It does mean that any transformation which the Tradition undergoes in their hands is unselfconscious and that they only play an indirect role in its development. This occurs when the custodians of Tradition integrate folk traditions into the great tradition.[3] The masses, regardless of how they behave, defer to the custodians, the religious elite, as authorities in interpreting Tradition.

The Jewish Tradition may be, but need not be, identical to Judaism or even the Jewish religion. It certainly is identical in the minds of the religious elite. They use the terms *masoret* or *masorah* (tradition), and sometimes *Yisra'el sabba* (grandfather Israel), synonymously with Torah (a euphemism for the Jewish religion). They are less likely to refer to Judaism—but when they do, they mean Torah and *masoret*. In other words, all the terms are basically identical although they do evoke somewhat different images. But Tradition, we must recall, is that which is handed down or transmitted from the past or what is believed to have been from the past. Therefore, it is entirely possible that Tradition undergoes change in the process of transmittal and the set of beliefs or practices or symbols which one generation calls Tradition differs from that which a prior generation identified as Tradition. The term Judaism,

---

[2] Robert Redfield, *Peasant Society and Culture* (Chicago: University of Chicago Press, 1956), 41f.

[3] Customs such as reading *Kol Nidre* on the eve of Yom Kippur or reciting *Tashlikh* on the New Year are examples of transformation in the little tradition which the elite ultimately incorporated into the great tradition. For a more dramatic example of the influence of popular behavior and belief, in this case of a very special kind of community, on the custodians of Tradition, see Haym Soloveitchik, "Religious Law and Change: The Medieval Aṣhkenazic Example," *AJS Review* 12 (Fall 1987): 205–21.

on the other hand, may refer to some essence, some basic set of ideas or beliefs or rituals or symbols which remains constant and to which Tradition may be more or less faithful. The distinction is an important one for those who are dissatisfied with Tradition but anxious to declare their fidelity to Judaism. An alternate strategy for such individuals is to deny that Judaism is composed of ideas or beliefs or rituals. Some have argued that Judaism is the label for what Jews or the Jewish community believe and practice. They may acknowledge that there is a Tradition, that is, a set of beliefs or practices that were transmitted from the past, but deny that this Tradition is the essence of Judaism.

Finally, one can conceive of the Jewish religion as distinct from Judaism or Tradition. Some claim that the essence of Judaism is something other than religion—not a core set of beliefs about God and humanity, or a set of rituals which God imposes upon humanity. Instead, they argue, Judaism is concerned with the nature of the Jewish people and the Jewish community. Hence, Judaism is not the same as the Jewish religion. But one can also argue that Judaism and religion are synonymous, that is, the essence of Judaism is a set of beliefs about God and humanity and a set of rituals which God imposes upon humanity, but deny that they are the same thing as the Tradition. The latter, though it may be religious in its parameters, may also be something other than the religious essence of Judaism. All these views were represented in the late nineteenth and early twentieth centuries.

Tradition, Judaism, and Religion in the *Yishuv* Period

The end of the nineteenth and the first few decades of the twentieth centuries are the critical years in the formation of the Jewish national identity. A variety of thinkers sought to formulate the essence of a Jewish nationalism. Whereas the Zionist settlers in the land of Israel often wavered between one formulation and another, I want to identify three important trends of thought which help distinguish between the different poles of Jewish national identity in that period—all characterized by various degrees of unwillingness to accept the Jewish tradition (what I call Tradition) as normative.

Radical Secular Zionism

The stream of thought most antagonistic to Tradition was forcefully articulated by Micha Joseph Berdyczewski (1865-1921). He felt that Tradition had to be destroyed in the process of creating a new Hebrew.

He protested against the "artificial mending of the rift between the old and new."[4] The rabbinic culture "that led us into exile and was built on the ruins of the land cannot live together with the national culture, which wants to break the thread of exile and plant within us new values and a totally new will."[5]

Berdyczewski did not reject Judaism. But as Dan Ben-Amos points out,

> A central theme in his scholarship was the romantic quest for *nefesh ha-umah,* "the national soul," and *ruah ha-ʾam,* "the folk spirit." He wished to explore the psychological, religious and social forces that generated the Jewish national spirit, before the spirit became subjugated by the pressures of normative Judaism and its religious and ethical value system.[6]

In other words, Berdyczewski distinguished between "the national soul" and the "folk spirit," which he sought to identify and affirm, and Tradition, which represented its distortion. But recovering the national spirit did not mean, from Berdyczewski's point of view or that of his followers, that it would now become normative. He remained antitraditionalist and highly individualistic in orientation. "The Jews must come first, before Judaism," he said. As Ehud Luz points out, he was the first Jewish thinker to declare that Judaism is a multiplicity of streams, beliefs, and opinions and not a fixed system of values. "Whatever a Jew does and thinks—this constitutes his Jewishness."[7]

Berdyczewski's individualism was poorly suited to the conditions of the new (Zionist) *yishuv* and the need for collective action in the struggle for national autonomy. But his antagonism to Tradition remained a powerful component in the life of the new *yishuv.* In its most extreme manifestation, it led to what Amnon Rubinstein has called "the mythological sabra" who, as a literary archetype, is without parents.[8] This "new Hebrew," however, may have been more ignorant and indifferent than antagonistic to the Jewish past.

---

4 Ehud Luz, *Parallels Meet: Religion and Nationalism in the Early Zionist Movement, 1882-1904* (Philadelphia: Jewish Publication Society, 1988), 165.

5 Quoted ibid., 166.

6 Dan Ben-Amos, Introduction to *Mimekor Yisrael: Classical Jewish Folktales,* by Micha Joseph Bin Gorion, vol. 1 (Bloomington: Indiana University Press, 1976), xxxii.

7 Luz, *Parallels Meet,* 165.

8 Amnon Rubinstein, *Lʿheyot am hofshi* (To Be A Free People) (Tel-Aviv: Schocken, 1977), 101–39.

Conservative Secular Zionism

Whereas one major school of secular Zionist thought, that of Berdyczewski and his followers, not only rejected Tradition but was antagonistic to the very notion of a normative tradition, the other major school, that of Aḥad Haʿam and his followers, adopted a different strategy. They ostensibly affirmed Tradition but attempted to redefine its parameters. They sought to appropriate Tradition from the hands of its former custodians, the rabbis, reinterpret it in national terms, and transfer custody to Judaic scholars and literary leaders. This program is evident in a series of essays by one of Aḥad Haʿam's most devoted followers, the "national" poet, Hayyim Nahman Bialik. The most important of these essays, for our purposes, is "Ha-sefer Ha-ivri" (On The Hebrew Book), written in 1913. It was Bialik's dream to reproduce a compendium, necessarily selective, of the major texts of the Tradition in order to make them available to the modern Hebrew reader. Increasing numbers of these readers, Bialik felt, were ignorant of Tradition and unable to penetrate its textual sources, even if they wanted to do so. But the problem implied in the essay is even more serious. For, Bialik observes, there are those who think that "all the literary output of the nation in its entirety and its spiritual giants, over the course of thousands of years, has no value in our day."[9]

Bialik proposes what he calls a *kinnus*—a compilation of the major literary works of the Jewish people or selections from such works.[10] He describes this effort as the creation of a new canon, noting explicitly that, as was true of past canonizations, such an effort would also exclude many texts.

The essay invokes terms such as "holy spirit" or "sacred" numerous times, but the referent is not God but the Jewish people. Indeed, the enterprise is steeped in an aura of holiness but, as Bialik observes, differs from previous canonizations since the present one would be in accordance with the "national" rather than the "religious" spirit.

Bialik deals with the question, Who would make the decisions? Who would decide what was to be included in the *kinnus* and what was to be excluded? His general answer is, "The opinion of the people and its

---

9 *Kol Kitvei Ḥ.N. Bialik* (The Collected Work of H.N. Bialik), 9th ed. (Tel-Aviv: Dvir, 1947), 194.

10 Rotenstreich translates the term as "ingathering." See Nathan Rotenstreich, *Tradition and Reality: The Impact of History on Modern Jewish Thought* (New York: Random House, 1972), 97-108.

sentiments, or as the ancient phrase puts it: 'The holy spirit' of the nation. We have no other criteria at the present time."[11]

But this is hardly a practical answer. It turns out that the custodians of the new Tradition, those who determine what will or will not be included in the canon, are to be Judaica scholars—and, Bialik later adds, "the best writers." The scholars, he states, "are nothing but the spiritual representatives of the people, and they have no choice but to defer to the demands of life, sometimes in opposition to their own inclinations."[12]

Bialik uses the term *ḥakhamim* (wise men) for Judaica scholars, and this permits him to juxtapose them with the ancient *ḥakhamim*, the rabbinical sages. Thus, without so much as an apology to the reader, he demonstrates the power of life over the private inclinations of the scholars by quoting texts concerning the desire and subsequent failure of *ḥakhamim* to exclude the books of Ezekiel and Ecclesiastes from the canon.

Bialik warned against efforts to rewrite or distort the content of the texts to be selected. But his own major effort in this direction, his six-volume *Sefer Haggadah*, compiled with Yehoshua Hana Ravnitsky, according to Dan Ben-Amos "expurgated the text of offensive statement . . . [and] omitted those narratives which they found either aesthetically unappealing or educationally inappropriate."[13]

In summary, and at risk of oversimplification, Berdyczewski and his followers were prepared to concede Tradition to the rabbis. Tradition was "rabbinic culture," which was not the same as the spirit of Judaism. Tradition was associated with the old *yishuv*, from which the Zionist settlers were so anxious to disassociate themselves.[14] Aḥad Haʿam and his followers looked to the scholars (often themselves) as the custodians of a reformulated Tradition and identified it with Judaism.

In practice, however, the Tradition, certainly in symbolic form, in terms of ritual, ceremonial, objects, and language, was less and less evident in Israeli society until the 1960s. Bialik's fears about the ignorance and antagonism of the new Hebrew to the Jewish tradition were increasingly realized. The effort of the Aḥad Haʿam school at reconstituting Tradition was largely in vain. Until the end of the 1960s,

[11] Ibid., 196.

[12] Ibid.

[13] Ben-Amos, Introduction, xl.

[14] Yehoshua Kaniel, "The Terms 'Old Yishuv' and 'New Yishuv' in Contemporaneous Usage (1882-1914) and in Historiographical Usage," *Cathedra* 6 (December 1977): 3-19.

Israeli society seemed to be increasingly indifferent if not alienated from Tradition.[15]

Religious Zionism

The third trend within the new *yishuv* that deserves mention is that of religious Zionism. It was a minor influence in the period of the *yishuv* but has become far more influential in contemporary Israeli society. Therefore, its transformation is especially interesting.

Religious Zionist thinkers adopted a rather ambiguous attitude toward Tradition. This was especially true within Torah ve-Avodah, the labor wing of religious Zionism. This is not surprising in view of the fact that the vast majority of rabbis, and the leaders of the rabbinic world in particular, that is the custodians of Tradition, bitterly opposed the Zionist enterprise. Aryei Fishman has shown how the religious Zionists integrated both Zionism and modernity into their religious formulations.[16] They termed their own efforts "a holy revolution" and, in the tradition of Jewish religious reformers, invoked the message of the prophets—that is they ostensibly returned to an original, essential, more pristine Judaism and paid relatively less attention to later rabbinic texts with their emphasis on *halakhah*. Furthermore, as Fishman notes, the religious Zionists attributed a special sanctity to their own community, confident that the special charisma that resided among them would insure their fidelity to the commands of God, even as these appeared contrary to Tradition.

Tradition, Judaism, and Religion Today

Tradition, the Jewish religion, and Judaism are understood today, by the vast majority of Israeli Jews, as meaning more or less the same thing. In the process of reintegrating Tradition, religion, and Judaism, Tradition, in particular has assumed new content—a process which, in

---

15 This topic is treated more fully in Charles S. Liebman and Eliezer Don-Yehiya, *Civil Religion in Israel: Traditional Judaism and Political Culture in the Jewish State* (Berkeley: University of California Press, 1983).

16 Aryei Fishman, "'Torah and Labor': The Radicalization of Religion within a National Framework," *Studies in Zionism* 6 (Autumn 1982): 255–71; idem, "Tradition and Renewal in the Religious-Zionist Experience" (in Hebrew), in *be-shevilei ha-taḥya: meḥkarim ba-ṣionit ha-datit* (In the Paths of Renewal: Studies in Religious Zionism), ed. Abraham Rubinstein (Ramat-Gan: Bar-Ilan University Press, 1983), 127–47; and (Hapoel Hamizrahi 1921-1935 [Documents]), ed. Aryei Fishman (Tel-Aviv: Tel-Aviv University, 1979).

Ivan Marcus's felicitous term, we can label "innovation disguised as tradition."[17]

The first point to note is that the rabbis have reemerged as the custodians of Tradition. Their influence has come at the expense of custom (community practice) and the role of Judaic scholars. This is true among both the *dati* (religious) and the non-*dati* population. Among the *datiim*, for example, decisions of Jewish law, which once accommodated and even deferred to communal and familial custom, no longer do so. The classic anecdote in this regard is the refusal of the grandson of the preeminent rabbinical sage of two generations ago, the Ḥafetz Ḥaim, to offer the benediction over wine in his grandfather's goblet, because its size is inadequate according to criteria established by the Ḥazon Ish, the preeminent rabbinical sage of the last generation.[18] Among non-*datiim*, especially but not exclusively among those of Sephardic descent, one can point to the rising influence of holy men, whose advice as well as blessings are increasingly considered critical in matters ranging from health care, marriage, and accident prevention to the choice of political candidates. These holy men are possessed of charisma; they are not simply custodians of Tradition. But they nevertheless speak in the name of Tradition and never in opposition to it.

One observer traces the growth of rabbinic influence among the nonreligious to the decline of the influence of politicians and generals who "found popular trust being withdrawn from them and reinvested, if anywhere, in rabbis."[19] The growing importance of rabbis as custodians of Tradition is evident in the space offered to them in the general press prior to holidays. Most, perhaps all, Israeli dailies devote at least one article on the eve of a holiday to a description of the nature of that holiday. My impression is that during the last two decades a decreasing number of these articles have been written by Judaic scholars from a scholarly perspective and an increasing number of articles have been written by rabbis from a rabbinic perspective. The noted Judaica scholar Yosef Dan notes the decline in importance of Judaica scholarship and scholars in Israeli society in the present period. He attributes this decline

---

[17] Ivan Marcus, "The Devotional Ideals of Ashkenazic Pietism," in *Jewish Spirituality*, vol. 1, *From the Bible through the Middle Ages*, ed. Arthur Green (New York: Crossroad, 1988), 357.

[18] See the essay by Menachem Friedman in this volume.

[19] Edward Norden, "Behind 'Who Is a Jew': A Letter from Jerusalem," *Commentary* 87 (April 1989): 30.

to the secular public's increasing association of Judaism with its religious, indeed its Ḥaredi, interpretation.[20]

But the Tradition over which the rabbis reign is not, as we noted, the same Tradition over which they held sway in the past. The most important change is its nationalization—a process accompanied by the "traditionalizing" of Zionism.

This is not a historiographical paper so I confine myself to repeating the observation by Immanuel Etkes about recent efforts, from a variety of sources, to blur any major distinction between the *aliyot* of traditional Jews—the Hasidim in the late eighteenth century and the Vilna Gaon's students in the early nineteenth century—with the Zionist *aliyot* beginning in the late nineteenth century.[21] One finds efforts to "Zionize" the early *aliyot* of religious Jews by describing them as messianic in intent and nationalist in activity. And one also finds efforts to traditionalize the Zionist *aliyot* by emphasizing the number of religious Jews present in the first *aliyah*. Etkes's observation is all the more significant because while he points to a tendency among academicians and putative scholars, I believe it is present among political leaders as well—in no less a figure than Ben-Gurion, especially toward the end of his life.

The nationalization of the Tradition takes place at many levels. A necessary condition, perhaps even a catalyst, was the transformation of the Tradition in the hands of the religious Zionists.

Religious Zionism could have legitimated the effort to establish a Jewish state and cooperate with secular Zionists through a number of alternative strategies.[22] It could have argued, as did Rabbi Isaac Jacob Reines (1839-1915) and more recently Yeshayahu Leibowitz, that a Jewish state is vital for the physical well-being of the Jewish people but that the Zionist enterprise has nothing to do with religion. It could have argued, as did Rabbi Moshe Avigdor Amiel (1883-1946), for a rigidly utilitarian program of cooperation with secular Zionists, taking care to stress that on religious issues there is no distinction between religious Zionists and anti-Zionist Ḥaredim. Instead, religious Zionism adopted the ideology of Rabbi Abraham Isaac Hacohen Kook (1865-1935), an ideology which

---

[20] Yosef Dan, "The Hegemony of the Black Hats," *Politika* 29 (November 1989): 12-15.

[21] The observation was made in a paper delivered at a Shorashim conference at the Mount Zion Hotel in Jerusalem, March 1989.

[22] See Charles S. Liebman and Eliezer Don-Yehiya, "Religious Orthodoxy's Attitudes toward Zionism," Ch. 4 in *Religion and Politics in Israel* (Bloomington: Indiana University Press, 1984), 57-78.

sanctified Zionist ideals in religious terminology and even legitimated secular Zionism by explaining it as an instrument of God in the Redemption of the Jewish people.

In retrospect, the victory of Rav Kook's reconceptualization of the Tradition was inevitable. Few religious people will dedicate their lives to a project which is not a matter of religious concern. What I find especially instructive is that this transformation in the content of Tradition took place before most religious Zionists had read Rav Kook's work or heard his ideology expounded. It is only since the 1960s that interpretations of Rav Kook have flourished, that his disciples have founded yeshivas which preach his message, or that study groups have been established all over Israel where Rav Kook's doctrines are taught as normative Judaism. I do not mean to minimize the impact of this effort. But it is important to note that Rav Kook's basic doctrine—a doctrine that pointed to the Zionist enterprise as the signal of divine redemption and to those engaged in that enterprise as fulfilling God's commands, whether they acknowledged it or not—was adopted by religious Zionists because the idea facilitated their acceptance into the new *yishuv* and their alliances with the nonreligious, not because they found the proof texts in this regard overwhelming. But Rav Kook himself appreciated the radical nature of much of what he preached and the difficulty of integrating it into Tradition. Indeed, it has even been argued that he adopted a negative attitude toward "religion" although he construed this term in a very special manner—and at one stage some of his disciples sought to emphasise the distinction between "religion," which carried the negative association of *galut* and house of study, with "faith" and the Jew living a natural life in his own Land.[23] Today his disciples have been at some pains to deny the radical nature of Rav Kook's thought; to the point of editing and censoring some manuscripts and refusing to publish others.[24] Rav Kook, in the eyes of his followers, is no longer a revolutionary voice or the radical innovator he was once reputed to be, but the successor in a line of luminaries that extends from Rabbi Judah HaLevi to Naḥmanides to the Maharal.

The integration of tradition, religion, and Zionism in Israel is nicely illustrated in a recent bulletin of Tehilla, an organization dedicated to

---

[23] Gideon Aran, "From Religious Zionism to a Zionist Religion: The Origin and Culture of *Gush Emunim,* a Messianic Movement in Modern Israel" (Ph.D. diss.,Hebrew University, 1987).

[24] Hagai Segel, "Lights From Dimness" (in Hebrew), *Nekudah* 113 (September 1987).

promoting *aliyah* among religious Jews. The bulletin contains an article by one rabbi and a news story about another. The first rabbi serves a major congregation in Tel Aviv. In the photo accompanying his article he appears in a distinctively rabbinical style—black frock coat, homburg hat, beard, indistinguishable from a Ḥaredi. The article centers on the different message to which each of the four cups of wine which the Jew drinks at the Seder points. The messages are distinguished by their level of spirituality, but all point to the "spiritual centrality of the holy land." The most important or highest level message, the rabbi notes, must be transmitted to religious as well as nonreligious Jews. Eventually they must all appreciate, he says, that the ultimate purpose of *aliyah*, which he compares to the Exodus from Egypt, is the appropriation of the verse "and I shall be your God and you shall know that I am the Lord."[25]

This mingling of religion, tradition, and *aliyah* stands in contrast to a news story about an American rabbi who immigrated to Israel and after a year and a half revisited his native country. He is quoted as telling Orthodox audiences, "There's lots more to being Jewish than religion. . . . Judaism is not just a religion but a nationhood."[26]

The reappropriation of Tradition and its nationalization by religious Zionists was probably a necessary condition in the acceptance of Tradition and the legitimation of religion among the non-*datiim*. I have already made reference to the growing influence of the rabbis in defining the content of Tradition among non-*datiim*. This is especially true of non-*datiim* aligned with the political right. Religious Jews are perceived as their political allies and religion as a powerful instrument to legitimate their political demands. Their conceptions of Judaism may more properly be termed a "mood" or an "identity" rather than an ideology. One reason it lacks clear articulation may be that its proponents are so sympathetic to traditional religion that they are reluctant to pose an alternative to religious conceptions of Tradition. Disproportionate numbers of Sephardi Jews, the bulk of those who define themselves as *masoratiim* (traditional in their religious orientation), share this mood. But they include some who define themselves as *ḥilloni* (secular) as well. Ariel Sharon, the favorite political leader of the ultranationalists, is quoted as saying, "I am proud to be a Jew but sorry that I am not religious."[27]

---

25 Ben-Zion Nesher, "Four Languages of Redemption" (in Hebrew), *Derekh Tehillah*, 22 (April 1989): 9.

26 The story apeared in the *Cleveland Jewish News* (24 February 1989) and was reprinted in *Derekh Tehillah*, 22 (April 1989): 30.

27 *Maᶜariv* Weekend Supplement (10 March 1986): 12.

In the last few years, as divisions between doves and hawks have sharpened, one hears increasingly that fidelity to religion and loyalty to the state are associated. Thus, a circular from the Religious Division within the Ministry of Education to principals of religious schools in 1988 reminded them that Jewish traitors come from the antireligious left and not from within the ranks of the religious. And a columnist for the religious-Zionist daily discusses "the Israeli left, sections of which betrayed the State and associated themselves with the PLO."[28] The writer notes that "leftism" is correlated with disorganized family life, divorce, and "unofficial marriages," marriages not conducted in accordance with Jewish law.

It is not surprising that *dati* spokespersons emphasize the association between religion and patriotism. But non-*dati* leaders do so as well. Thus, for example, Prime Minister Yitzhak Shamir is quoted as saying:

> The left today is not what it once was. In the past, social and economic issues were its major concern. Today, its concern is zealousness for political surrender and, on the other hand, war against religion. It is only natural that someone whose stance is opposed to the Land of Israel will also oppose the Torah of Israel.[29]

The affirmation of nationalist ideals and their integration into the Tradition, in the hands of the rabbis, certainly eased the way for the non-*datiim* to reaffirm their own ties to the Jewish people (no longer Hebrews as distinct from Jews) and to Jewish history (no longer repressing "two thousand years" of *galut* or reducing it to an unfortunate interlude).

Tradition has been nationalized, among non-*datiim* as well as religious Zionists, through a selective interpretation of sacred texts and of Jewish history. Emphasis is given to the sanctity and centrality of *eretz yisraʾel,* the Land of Israel. The Zionists celebrated their radical departure from the Tradition in their efforts to reclaim and settle the Land; Israelis celebrate their continuity with the Tradition in this regard. What is all the more remarkable is that *eretz yisraʾel* has come to symbolize both loyalty to the state of Israel and loyalty to the Tradition. Indeed, as Baruch Kimmerling points out, the term "the land of Israel" has increasingly replaced the term "State of Israel" in the pronouncements of national

---

[28] *Ha-ṣofeh* (27 June 1968): 3.

[29] *Maʿariv* (20 December 1987): 6.

leaders, especially those on the political right.[30] To be a good Jew means to live in the Land of Israel under conditions of Jewish autonomy.

The nationalization of the Tradition means its particularization as well. I do not wish to argue that this is a distortion of the Jewish past. I suspect that the effort to interpret the Tradition as moralistic and universalistic, an effort that is basic to the American Jewish understanding of Tradition, is far less faithful than is the Israeli version to what Jews throughout the ages understood as Tradition.[31] But it merits mention because it does stand in contrast to the Zionist effort to "normalize" Jewish existence. Classical Zionists suggested that anti-Semitism was a consequence of the peculiar condition of the Jews as perennial "guests" or "strangers" in countries not their own. It was not, they claimed, the result of any special animus toward Jews as such. This claim was necessary to bolster Zionist belief that once the Jews had a country of their own, their condition would be normalized and anti-Semitism would disappear. This was among the more nontraditional components of the Zionist credo.

Israeli Jews, for the most part, no longer believe this to be true. Anti-Semitism, they are likely to believe, is endemic. "The world is all against us," as the refrain of a popular song went, suggests that there is nothing that Jews in general or Israelis in particular can do to resolve the problem. The Jew is special because he is hated, and he is hated because he is special. This is the lesson of Jewish history, as my own students are wont to remind me, and it serves to anchor the state of Israel within the currents of Jewish life. In summary, Zionism, the ideology of Jewish nationalism, has been transformed and anchored to the Tradition, and the Tradition, in turn, has been nationalized. Erik Cohen describes this trend as

> a reorientation of the basic principles of legitimation of Israel: a trend away from secular Zionism, especially its pioneering-socialist variety, towards a neo-traditionalist Jewish nationalism which, while it reinforces the primordial links among Jews

---

30 Baruch Kimmerling, "Between the Primordial and the Civil Definition of the Collective Identity: *Eretz Israel* or the State of Israel?" *Comparative Social Dynamics: Essays in Honor of S.N. Eisenstadt, ed.* Erik Cohen, Moshe Lissak and Uri Almagor (Boulder: Westview, 1985), 262-83.

31 I explore this notion in greater detail in "Ritual, Ceremony and the Reconstruction of Judaism in the United States," *Studies in Contemporary Jewry*, 6 (New York: Oxford University Press, 1990), 272–83.

> both within Israel and the diaspora, de-emphasizes the modern, civil character of the state.[32]

The rise of particularism has implications for the interpretation of ethics and morality as well. Emphasis on law (and ritual) means a deemphasis on the centrality of ethics. But, in addition, religious Jews in Israel have redefined "morality" in particularistic rather than universalistic terms. According to the rabbi who pioneered the establishment of extremist education within the religious-Zionist school system, Jews are enjoined to maintain themselves in isolation from other peoples. Foreign culture is a particular anathema when its standards are used to criticize Jews.[33] "Between the Torah of Israel and atheist humanism there is no connection"; there is no place in Judaism for "a humanistic attitude in determining responses to hostile behavior of the Arab population," says another. According to a leader of Jewish settlers on the West Bank, "Jewish national morality is distinct from universal morality. Notions of universal or absolute justice may be good for Finland or Australia but not here, not with us."[34]

This deemphasis on universal standards of morality among rabbis extends to areas other than the Jewish-Arab dispute. The chief rabbi of Ramat-Gan, for example, decries the practice of childless Israeli couples adopting Brazilian children, even though the children undergo conversion procedures. Such children, he says, will be raised as Israelis but not all of them will identify with the Jews. "After all, it is clear that children inherit characteristics from their parents," he says. He then cites rabbinic texts in order to prove that non-Jews are not blessed with the quality of mercy with which Jews are blessed, but on the contrary are cruel by their very nature.[35]

Many non-*dati* Jews may be unhappy with this type of interpretation, but they do not doubt that it is the authentic voice of Tradition.

---

32 Erik Cohen, "Citizenship, Nationality and Religion in Israel and Thailand," in Baruch Kimmerling, The Israeli State and Society: Boundaries and Frontiers (Albany: SUNY Press, 1989), 70.

33 Charles S. Liebman, "Jewish Ultra-Nationalism in Israel: Converging Strands," in *Survey of Jewish Affairs, 1985,* ed. William Frankel (Rutherford, N.J.: Fairleigh Dickinson University Press, 1985), 28-50.

34 Ibid., 46.

35 *Ha-ṣofeh* (20 June 1988): 4.

The Authority of Tradition in Contemporary Israel

There is no question that Tradition has assumed a positive valence in Israeli society today. The initial rejection of Tradition was probably inevitable. Even those Zionists who did not reject religion itself were conscious of the fact that their efforts stood in opposition to central values of the Tradition and the pronouncements of its custodians. But in addition, the very excitement and hope, the revolutionary ardor which the Zionist enterprise generated among many of its followers, youth in particular, undermined a basic sympathy for tradition of any kind. "No more tradition's chains shall bind us . . . the earth shall rise on new foundations" is the anthem of the worker's International but is a sentiment which revolutionaries of all stripes are likely to share. The creation of Israel, the need to consolidate rather than innovate a national consciousness, the mass immigration of traditionally oriented Jews from eastern Europe but especially from north Africa, the decline of secular Zionism, all help explain the reemergence of Tradition, religion and Judaism as important components of Israeli culture.

Of course, not all Israelis have adapted themselves to this change. Important segments of Israeli society demur. A few of these merit attention. Steven Cohen and I have described them in fuller detail elsewhere.[36] First are those whose dissent is an extension of their religious extremism—the antimodernist and anti- or non-Zionist Ḥaredim who understand Tradition in its prenationalist and premodernist form. Second are those who understand the Tradition in less stridently nationalistic, in pan-Jewish and more moralistic terms. They include a segment of religious Zionists, of whom Rabbis Yehuda Amital and Aaron Lichtenstein (yeshiva heads) or Rabbi David Hartman (theologian) are representative, and on the other hand, those secular Zionists who have remained faithful to an older generation's formulation of Judaism. The late Abba Kovner was an exemplary representative of this tendency. Finally, there are those who do not object to the contemporary Israeli interpretation of Tradition but wish to have no part of it. This is probably the dominant strain in the political party Ratz, the Citizens' Rights Movement. Political scientist Ze'ev Sternhall, though himself a member of Mapam, expressed this idea on the pages of *Politika,* a journal sponsored by Ratz. Sternhall bewails the absence of Western-style democracy in Israel, which he defines as a system of government which places the

---

36 Charles S. Liebman and Steven M. Cohen, *Two Worlds of Judaism* (New Haven: Yale University Press, 1990).

individual and not collective goals at the center of its concern. The key problem in Israel, he says, is understanding the essence of democracy, "the rights of humans to be masters of themselves . . . the expression of man's recognition that all sources of political, social, and moral authority in here in man himself."[37]

Israeli political culture, he suggests, rejects the basis of democratic thought—that "society and state exist in order to serve the individual . . . and are never ends in themselves." A major source of Israel's collectivist culture, according to Sternhall, is the Jewish tradition. Even the nonreligious Zionists, he maintains, "never really freed themselves from the tradition of their father's home, and in one form or another they deferred to *Yisraᵓel sabba.*"

Sternhall's sharp critique leads us to a final question: Granted that his description of the Jewish tradition is accurate, to what extent does it carry real authority within Israeli society? Since we defined Tradition in terms of the perception or consciousness of contemporary society, it is reasonable to assume that Israelis would not understand Tradition in the way they do unless it was congenial to them. I am not suggesting that Israeli or any other society defines its Traditions arbitrarily and consciously to suit its preferences. There are two good reasons why it cannot and does not do so. First, because preferences themselves are a product, at least in part, of Tradition. Second, because the conscious manipulation of Tradition, like the conscious manipulation of religion or law, destroys its authority. It ceases to compel deference and obedience once it is viewed as an instrument to satisfy contemporary needs rather than rooted in a transcendent source or a hoary past or the nature of reality. But there still remains an element of subjectivity, of preference, of utility in the manner in which we define our Tradition, in the themes we select for emphasis, in the interpretation we offer to the symbols that compel us. In this respect, therefore, it is never entirely accurate to explain patterns of behavior by Tradition. For, at least in some respects, if such patterns did not suit us, we would behave otherwise.

One must not exaggerate the compelling quality of Tradition in contemporary Israeli society. Clifford Geertz distinguishes between "religiousness" and "religious-mindedness"—the difference between being held by religious conviction and holding such convictions.[38]

---

[37] Ze'ev Sternhall, "The Battle for Intellectual Control," (in Hebrew) *Politika* 18, (December 1987), 2-5.

[38] Clifford Geertz, *Islam Observed: Religious Development in Morocco and Indonesia* (New Haven: Yale University Press, 1968).

Religiousness celebrates the content of the belief, religious-mindedness celebrates the belief. Tradition, in Israeli society, is analogous to religious-mindedness. Israelis are in favor of the idea of Tradition, which is not the same as saying that they submit themselves to Tradition. Tradition in the modern world—because it is self-conscious, because it exists even in the mind of its adherents as something apart from them, because one can imagine non-Tradition—means that one must make choices with respect to it. The necessity to choose Tradition rather than simply live one's life in accordance with its norms and values inspires fanatical devotion among some but leads others to adopt a more permissive, latitudinarian, and less submissive orientation.

Furthermore, despite the deference which Israeli society accords Tradition, it is my impression that many Israelis are ignorant of (not simply mistaken about) its basic tenets. Ritual and ceremony is certainly a source of knowledge about Tradition and a mechanism for socializing its adherents to its norms. In a forthcoming study of a middle-income Tel Aviv neighborhood, sociologist Ephraim Tabory shows how second-generation secular Jewish Israelis, that is, Israelis who define themselves as secular and report that they were raised in secular homes, observe virtually no Jewish ceremony or ritual.[39] The number of such Israelis is increasing far more rapidly than the number of *ḥozrim bitshuva* (non-religious who have chosen to become religious).

Tradition, as we have indicated, is not necessarily the same as religion and is certainly not the same as the observance of religious ritual. But religion, especially in Judaism, is the most important instrument for socializing a population to the norms of Tradition. The fact that less than twenty percent of the Israeli Jewish population defines itself as *dati* suggests that the position of Tradition within Israeli society is not as secure as one might otherwise believe. If the compelling quality of Tradition is so limited with respect to ritual and legal matters, than how compelling can it be in matters of values and general social norms, where it confronts a world of competing and alternative values and norms? Individualism, Sternhall to the contrary notwithstanding, is becoming far more commonplace in Israel. The demand for self-fulfillment and personal gratification is growing. The mass media, foreign travel, and the structure of the economy are enough to insure that. And those who

39 Ephraim Tabory, "Patterns of Living in a Mixed Community," in *Yeḥasim beyn datiim ve-ḥilyonim be-ḥevra ha-yisraʾelit* (Relations Between Religious and Secular In Israeli Society) ed. Yeshayahu [Charles] Liebman (Jerusalem: Keter, 1990).

dissent from Tradition, even if they constitute a small minority, occupy key positions among the economic, political, and cultural elite.

Among such people, generally the better educated and more "enlightened," to use Shils' term, there is a prevailing notion that

> a great many of the beliefs, practices, and institutions . . . [need] to be changed, replaced, or discarded in favor of new ones which would invariably be better ones. . . . The accent of intellectual and political discourse still remains on a movement forward from the recent and remote past. The emphasis is on improvement.[40]

It is difficult to sustain Tradition in a social milieu antagonistic to the norms of the past. We have only to remember that the opposite of utilizing tradition as a basis for decision-making is utilizing reason, and we are reminded of Tradition's inherent weakness.

---

40 Shils, *Tradition,* 2.

18

Constructing the Usable Past: The Idea of Tradition in Twentieth-Century American Judaism

ARNOLD M. EISEN

"Tradition" is perhaps the most pervasive term of authority in contemporary American Jewish thought—and, arguably, the most problematic. At a time when my flannel shirt bears the label "New Traditions" (the title of the journal once published by the *ḥavurah* movement), when the architecture of my newly built California condominium is labeled "traditional" (and market research confirms the name's appeal), when the *New York Times* regularly employs the word "tradition" as a synonym for any state of affairs preceding the one being reported (as in the breakdown, in late 1989, of "traditional cold-war alliances and rivalries"), and when popular culture teems with highly ambivalent visions (e.g., the film *Dead Poets' Society*) of a bygone era ostensibly characterized by "tradition, discipline, and rules"—at such a time it is perhaps not surprising that religion too should invoke the term so regularly.[1] "Tradition" resonates as few words do in the contempo-

[1] See the extended meditation on this theme by Edward Shils in *Tradition* (Chicago: University of Chicago Press, 1981), particularly the introduction and chs. 1, 9, and 10. On contemporary traditional architecture see Carol Vogel, "Clustered for Leisure: The Changing Home," *New York Times Magazine* (28 June 1987), CMS § 16.125). Further testimony to the widespread popularity of the term TRADITION is provided by this recent flier: "Please volunteer at Super Sunday—The Jewish

rary lexicon of faith—certainly more than "faith" or "religion" themselves. It harks back to roots dearly desired without imposing obligation to any particular behavior or creed. Jews, like other Americans, seem to want connection with their ancestors while reserving the right to depart, however radically, from the paths which the ancestors walked. Jewish thinkers, for precisely the same reasons, seek continuity with and legitimacy from past forms of practice and belief, even as they re-form and reconstruct them. Hence the appeal of "tradition," and the problematic character of its use. For how does one locate authority in the past when one is aware of the degree to which that past is a product of one's own construction? How does one simultaneously and with utter self-consciousness both read into and read out of the "sources of Judaism"? The dilemma, I shall argue, is unavoidable in contemporary American Judaism, and insoluble; the invocation of "tradition" that gives rise to it is likewise unavoidable—and in fact goes to the heart of contemporary American Jewish religiosity.

I hope to get at this dilemma by analyzing two "moments" of special consequence in the usage of "tradition" in our century. Mordecai Kaplan's method of "functional revaluation," I believe, constituted a critical turning point in the transition from uncritical participation in a received structure of action and belief to the self-conscious selection (in good faith or bad) from one's inheritance in order to create new patterns of belief and observance. Kaplan was the first American Jewish thinker to confront head-on the issues involved in claiming continuity with tradition even as one introduced wholesale innovation. He was also the first to realize, albeit dimly, that the past which he defined was one of many which existed to be "discovered" and reconstructed. The second "moment" to be examined is the present effort by two thinkers in whose work the approach inaugurated by Kaplan reaches mature (and divergent) fulfillment. Elliot Dorff invokes the form and substance of rabbinic "tradition" to legitimate his redefinition of Conservative Judaism as a movement of "flexible Halakhah." Judith Plaskow appropriates the very same precedents, and others, to legitimate her far more radical attempt to articulate a feminist Judaism. Both thinkers are free of Kaplan's need to disengage from the past which they wish to reconstruct, free too of the need to justify their right to appropriate that past for their own contemporary purposes. Like Kaplan, however, both belong to the American

---

Community Federation's community-wide annual fundraising phonathon, and help to carry on the tradition." In the course of writing this essay I encountered literally hundreds of similarly vague appeals to tradition.

Jewish "center"—running from Kaplan and moderate Reform thinkers on the "left" to Conservative and modern Orthodox thinkers on the "right"—for whom "tradition" (and not, say, "ethics" or "Halakhah") is the authority of choice. Not for nothing does the Reform movement boast of the "return to tradition" evinced by its new prayer book, and the organization of modern Orthodox rabbis titles its journal *Tradition*. No better "god-term" is presently available to such thinkers, given what they do and do not believe, will and will not do, and no term is better calculated to appeal to their congregants.[2] My aim in the present essay is to explain why that authority and that appeal are so widespread and so fraught with dilemmas that cannot be overcome, but only confronted.

We can best get a handle on these late-twentieth-century issues, I think, by recalling the periodization of Jewish history offered by one of the most significant Jewish scholars and theologians of the nineteenth century, Abraham Geiger. The first of Judaism's four eras, in Geiger's account, was that of "Revelation . . . an era of free, creative formation from within." It was followed by the age of Tradition, during which "Judaism took root in the spiritual heritage of the past and at the same time still maintained a certain degree of freedom in its approach to that heritage." Next came the "toilsome" millennium of "rigid Legalism, of casuistry, the era devoted to the summing up of what had been handed down by tradition." Finally came Geiger's own age, that of "liberation . . . marked by an effort to loosen the fetters of the previous era by means of the use of reason and historical research."[3] The passage is remarkable, not least in its prescience. Geiger has adumbrated and even captured the principal motifs, tendencies, distortions, and dilemmas which have characterized modern Jewish preoccupation with tradition ever since.

Three features especially pertinent to the present essay can be picked out at once. First, Geiger is utterly ambivalent about his chosen past. He lauds and even romanticizes (the key encomia are creativity and freedom) part of his past, the more distant from himself. He condemns out of hand more recent generations. The reason for this is apparent. Geiger's efforts at reform are meant to recall—and so derive legitimacy from—the initial creation and "shaping" of the Jewish heritage. He will "revitalize" the honored ancestral dead whom more recent generations had done

[2] See Arnold Eisen, "American Judaism: Changing Patterns in Denominational Self-Definition," *Studies in Contemporary Jewry* 8 (1991).

[3] Abraham Geiger, "A History of Spiritual Achievement," in *Ideas of Jewish History*, ed. Michael A. Meyer (New York: Behrman, 1974), 168–70.

nothing to bring back to life. The latter had in fact made his reforms necessary. The former—ancestors long dead—had made it possible.

Second, Geiger claims his chosen ancestral role models, the rabbis, as precedent, not by defining Judaism as they did but by engaging, as they had, in the process of REdefining Judaism. Geiger takes care not to identify Jewish creativity with pristine moments of divine prophecy. Nor does he describe rabbinic work on the Biblical inheritance as mere legalism. On the contrary: revelation comes "from within"—not only a barely disguised statement of Geiger's disbelief in the doctrine of Torah from Heaven, but testimony to Geiger's belief in the importance of human effort in creating Judaism. He describes the rabbis' early work similarly as creative and receptive. Only later rabbis had fallen into rigidity and imitation, thereby proving unfaithful to their inheritance—by failing to transform it! Geiger would carry on the rabbinic work of "freedom in its approach to [the Jewish] heritage."[4] Earlier innovators had been no less radical than he and had come in time to be regarded as faithful heirs and transmitters of Judaism. In good faith acquired by dint of his scholarship, Geiger could imagine a parallel role for himself.

Third, note the crucial role of that Jewish scholarship in the discovery and renewal of Jewish tradition. "Reason and historical research" do not sever the bond with the past, in Geiger's view, but serve to "revitalize Judaism and to cause the stream of history to flow forth once again." Science and faith could walk hand in hand, as it were, so long as each understood the other properly and respected its own limits. Geiger could envisage such harmony, in part, because he presumed a Kantian notion of universal reason as well as an Idealist vision of Spirit (or an essence) working its way through particular eras and forms. One could know with confidence what Judaism had always been, despite its varieties, and so what it would be in any future. And one could know that one knew. Science might have been the sworn enemy of the old faith, but it would prove the midwife of the new.[5]

Those assumptions—and the confidence which goes with them—are of course not available to contemporary scholars. However, as we shall see, Geiger's use of history in defining and appropriating a usable past remains at the center of Jewish thought. His marriage of scholarship and

---

4 Ibid., 170.

5 Ibid., 170. In this analysis I have also drawn on the fine recent survey of Geiger in Michael A. Meyer, *Response to Modernity: A History of the Reform Movement in Judaism* (New York: Oxford University Press, 1988), 89-99, and on the research of my student Zachary Braiterman, as yet unpublished.

faith, like his reliance on and ambivalence toward his chosen ancestors, are still very much with us. The terms in which Geiger couched the effort to reform and reclaim the past still hold, even if—after Marx and Weber and Freud, Gadamer and Scholem, the hermeneutics of suspicion and the hermeneutics of retrieval—the effort to reform as one conserves has become immensely more difficult.

The Ambiguities of Reconstruction

The use of Geiger as a point of departure for the consideration of Mordecai Kaplan is, upon reflection, not as surprising as it may seem at first blush. It is true that Kaplan, in *Judaism as a Civilization* as elsewhere, singles out Zacharias Frankel and his heirs in the Conservative movement for special praise because they first glimpsed intuitively the changes which he proposes to carry to rational fulfillment. Kaplan states quite clearly that Frankel's (not Geiger's) is the tradition in which he operates.[6] Moreover, one cannot minimize Kaplan's crucial divergence from Reform over the question of Jewish peoplehood, concretized in his day by the issue of Zionism. Geiger, in a now infamous passage, had refused to acknowledge special obligation as a German Jew to other Jews living elsewhere.[7] Kaplan saw classical Reform's opposition to the Zionist project as entirely consistent with the movement's basic premisses—and therefore rejected those premises out of hand.

Once Reform had officially accepted Zionism in the Columbus Platform of 1937, however, its approach to tradition came to parallel Kaplan's rather closely—which could explain why, to the end of his days, Kaplan refused to recognize that any such transformation had occurred. A Reform movement committed to Jewish peoplehood, Jewish civilization, and the Jewish homeland obviated the clear need for a second movement that, in Geiger's words, "felt authorized to reconstruct" and "develop further" its "spiritual heritage." That was all the more true because in most essentials Kaplan's approach was far closer to Geiger than he ever allowed. Like Geiger, Kaplan pressed a nineteenth-century notion of *Wissenschaft* into the service of religious reconstruction. Like him, too, he presumed a constant, universal human nature—in

---

6 Mordecai M. Kaplan, *Judaism as a Civilization: Towards a Reconstruction of American-Jewish Life* (New York: Macmillan, 1934; repr. New York: Schocken, 1967), 386–88.

7 See Max Wiener, ed., *Abraham Geiger and Liberal Judaism* (Philadelphia: Jewish Publication Society, 1962), 89f.

essence rational—at work through all human history, undergirded by a divine force—in essence ethical—uniquely evident in the workings of a unique Jewish "spirit." Like Geiger, finally, Kaplan found "halfway" measures such as Frankel's woefully inadequate. But whereas Geiger and the Reformers sought to pivot Judaism around an unchanging essence, ethical monotheism, Kaplan (in the wake of Aḥad Haʿam, Solomon Schechter, and the "science" of Emile Durkheim) sought continuity precisely in the "forms" of Judaism, demanding the radical reformulation of belief. The two approaches mirrored each other rather precisely and in the end came together. Kaplan (in *The Future of the American Jew*, 1948) accepted the uniqueness and primacy of the Jewish "vocation" among the nations, and Reform came (with the Columbus Platform) to accept Jewish peoplehood and the definition of Judaism as a "religious civilization." Geiger was not as distant from Frankel and his heirs as partisans of the latter would have us believe. Kaplan drew heavily from both.[8]

The concept of tradition figured crucially in Kaplan's effort of redefinition in two contradictory ways. In the first 25 chapters of *Judaism as a Civilization* (1934), the word appears almost entirely in negative contexts. Tradition is associated with primitive superstition, describes a supernatural notion of God that Kaplan dismisses, is contrasted pejoratively with scientific truth, is identified repeatedly with Orthodoxy and its mistaken view that Judaism had not evolved over the centuries, and is linked to otherworldliness as opposed to the (modern, rational) focus upon this world—the only world, Kaplan believed, in which human beings could hope to experience salvation.[9] Kaplan's view of the Jewish past was in this sense far less charitable than Geiger's. His own fourfold periodization began with the "henotheistic" stage of early Israelite religion (rather than "Revelation"), proceeded to a "theocratic" period corresponding to the centuries of the Second Temple, continued with an "otherworldly stage" encompassing all of rabbinic and medieval Judaism, and, finally, came to the period driven by "modern man's demand for historic truth."[10] He held the ENTIRETY of the Jewish past as inappropriate in its current form to modernity's new realities. Kaplan's break with that past,

---

[8] For more on Kaplan, and particularly his debt to classical Reform, see Arnold Eisen, *The Chosen People in America* (Bloomington: Indiana University Press, 1983), ch. 4.

[9] Kaplan, *Judaism as a Civilization.* See for example the usages on 38, 164, 182, 197, 313, 327, 351f.

[10] Ibid., ch. 25; the quotation is found on 383.

including his immediate modern predecessors, would therefore have to be complete. "An entirely different method must be evolved," he writes,

> to achieve religious continuity with the past, a method compatible with the evolutionary and historical conception of religion, and based upon needs of the human spirit which cannot be disregarded without danger to man's moral and spiritual health.[11]

At this point in the argument, however, Kaplan's attitude to tradition takes—must take—a decisive turn. He seeks "continuity" after all. Where before Kaplan had referred to tradition but sparingly, and always in denigration, he now must appeal to tradition in order to legitimize his project of wholesale reconstruction. The word itself begins to appear in this new light with astonishingly regularity. Kaplan begins the crucial chapter on "the functional method of interpretation" by arguing that "the Jewish quality of the religion of the Jews . . . will consist chiefly in the fact that it will be lived by Jews." However, he apparently realizes at once that this is not sufficient.

> The religion lived by Jews can be given character and individuality by utilizing the vast storehouse of spiritual values that are implicit in its traditions. If the recorded experiences of Jewish prophet and sage, poet and saint will occupy a predominant place in the Jewish consciousness as it strives to adjust itself to life, the resulting adjustment will constitute Jewish religious behavior.[12]

Kaplan seems to intend this claim in two senses. The "resulting adjustment" will be Jewish because Jewishly informed Jews created it (a variation on his initial claim that Jewish is what Jews do), but it will also be Jewish because a group of human beings, having decided to make a particular tradition "predominant" in their "consciousness," cannot but generate beliefs and behavior continuous with that tradition and in fact "implicit" in it.

Kaplan's attention henceforth is devoted to the latter meaning of his claim. "If the traditional Jewish religion is inherently capable of engendering the most significant human attitudes"—and Kaplan assumes that it is, despite previous wholesale condemnation; if "the advantage of utilizing traditional concepts is that they carry with them the accumulated momentum and emotional drive of man's previous efforts to attain

---

[11] Ibid., 384.
[12] Ibid., 385.

greater spiritual power"—no small thing for a convinced evolutionist; then it was imperative "to develop a method of discovering in traditional Jewish religion adumbrations of what we consider an adequate spiritual adjustment to life." His method offered a means of revealing and developing "the pragmatic implications of the traditional teachings."[13] Note that in these four usages—all from a single page—tradition is a resource to be used. Not at all coincidentally, Kaplan proceeds in the following pages to link himself to his own particular intellectual and institutional tradition, the Historical School, and Frankel more particularly, and to fault it for not going far enough in putting to good use its discovery of the "spirit that groped after self-expression in the traditional teaching."[14]

Kaplan's methodology is fascinating to observe from a distance of nearly sixty years because it is at once highly self-conscious and fraught with insuperable difficulties. He begins, for example, with a recognition that "the task of reinterpretation consists first in selecting," a staple of contemporary hermeneutics. One selects, however, "from among the ideational and practical consequences of the traditional values those which are spiritually significant for our day." This crucial statement requires unpacking. We recall that Kaplan claims on the basis of science to possess CERTAIN "knowledge of human nature as it functions in society and in the individual." Moreover, he believes (on the basis of philosophical pragmatism and of social science, especially Durkheim) that human nature does not change. Human needs are accordingly constant. Religious doctrines (like other aspects of culture) are formulated in order to satisfy those needs. Kaplan can therefore hope to reason back from particular ideas and institutions to the permanent needs or desiderata ("values") which they were meant to supply, and then act to supply these in the present with other ideas and institutions. His substitutions can be considered "equivalent" in functional terms to the originals. Reinterpretation is not the assignment of new meaning to existing ideology and symbols, but "the process of finding equivalents in the civilization to which we belong for values of a past stage," values which are admittedly qualitatively different but "possess equivalence" when "considered morphologically"—that is, in relation to their use.[15]

Kaplan, of course, must understand the thinking of previous generations well enough to know how they hoped to advance unchanging

[13] Ibid., 386.
[14] Ibid., 388.
[15] Ibid., 389. See also, e.g., 336.

human values by adopting particular beliefs and practices suited to the needs of their own day. He must "reconstruct mentally the aspirations implied" in particular teachings and institutions, "disengaging from the mass of traditional lore and custom the psychological aspect which testifies to the presence of ethical and spiritual strivings." In this way the tradition ceases to be regarded as something to be accepted or rejected, becoming instead a "symbol for a spiritual desideratum in the present."[16] The word "tradition" appears five times in a dozen lines at this point, shouting down, as it were, the doubts concerning continuity which Kaplan's complex methodology must overcome. He then applies revaluation to the God-idea ("as handed down" it meant one thing, but it would now signify something very different) and, in the following chapter, to the idea of Torah. The "traditional Torah" was no longer acceptable, Kaplan avers, and he will now tell us what "Torah should mean"—Jewish civilization as envisioned by Reconstructionism.[17]

Before turning to the fuller treatment accorded these issues in *The Meaning of God in Modern Jewish Religion* (1937), I want to note that Kaplan's approach was in two respects fully as unprecedented as he claimed it to be. First, his view of the commandments was quite radical. He agreed with Geiger and other reformers that "should our spiritual well-being . . . require the change or abrogation of any of those practices, the fact that they are designated *miswot* [sic] ought not to exercise any inhibitive influence."[18] But where the Reformers retained belief in some sort of "progressive revelation," Kaplan allowed no other author (or authority) for the commandments than the Jewish people itself. Like Spinoza, he argued that "traditional practices," no longer regarded as divine commands, might nonetheless be called *miṣvot* if the term were used "in the sense that they arouse in us the religious mood."[19] The adjective "divine" referred to the EFFECT of an action rather than its SOURCE. Kaplan faulted Mendelssohn's reconception of the *miṣvot* as ceremonies for stopping "halfway between traditionalism and modernism." He criticized Hirsch's attempt to account for the mitzvot in symbolic terms for failing to make a compelling case either for observance or for its own interpretations.[20] Interestingly, Kaplan derived his

---

16 Ibid., 390.

17 Ibid., 393-415.

18 Ibid., 431.

19 Ibid.

20 Ibid., 432. Kaplan's attitude to Hirsch is generally positive. See, e.g., ch. 11, p. 354, n. 2..

term for *miṣvot*, "folkways," from the use of *minhag* in "the traditional literature" to denote certain ritual practices not sanctioned with the full weight of Halakhah. William Graham Sumner, undoubtedly Kaplan's source for the term (and the concept) of folkways, is mentioned elsewhere in *Judaism as a Civilization*—but not here.[21] Apparently Kaplan was alert to the need to clothe modern Jewish conceptions in traditional Jewish language, a step which the method of functional revaluation not only legitimates but compels.

That method, secondly, is truly far-reaching in its implications. Mendelssohn, hoping to persuade his readers to observe voluntarily what could no longer be elicited by communal coercion, urged them to endow the *miṣvot* with new and even individual meaning. Practice, he wrote, not beliefs, links Jews to one another—a lesson not lost on Kaplan. But Mendelssohn allowed only the degree of flexibility that enters into Jewish practice through transmission, preferably oral, of the law. He apparently rested confident that the means attached to such practice, while varied, would remain within a range compatible with the teaching of "eternal" and "historical" truth as he perceived them. Hirsch, who likewise urged readers to find new meaning in traditional practices and beliefs, claimed a monopoly on the supply of correct new meaning, and of course insisted that the commandments themselves remain largely unchanged. Kaplan once again was far closer to Reform thinkers who felt authorized to change or discard any element in their inheritance that was not essential to the "spirit" or heart of Jewish religion: the teaching of ethical monotheism. While Kaplan by and large took an opposite tack—endowing existing practice with new meaning, rather than discarding practices which did not suit a meaning held to be eternal—the effect of his method was still more far-reaching. For Kaplan's understanding of Judaism as a civilization meant that all of Jewish culture stood at the disposal of his reconstructions. Every aspect of life could and should be transformed to better serve the needs which, he believed, every religious tradition in every age existed in order to meet.

---

[21] Ibid., 431. Kaplan's definition of "civilization," the linchpin of his reconception of Judaism, is (he tells us in n. 2 to ch. 14, on p. 535), "a paraphrase of the definition of ethos" offered in Sumner's book *Folkways* (Boston: Ginn, 1906), 36. He does not tell us that Sumner there derives positive law from folk custom—the conception undergirding Kaplan's crucial translation of *miṣvot* as "folkways". Sumner also appears (ch. 19, p. 539, n. 4) in connection with Kaplan's critique of the "chosen people" idea. We should note that other non-Jewish sources, such as Dewey and Durkheim, appear in the body of Kaplan's text itself.

In *The Meaning of God,* Kaplan rehearsed his dissatisfactions with existing versions of Judaism and then proceeded to apply the method of functional revaluation to the yearly cycle of Jewish holidays. Where past generations had practiced "transvaluation . . . ascribing meanings to the traditional content of a religion or social heritage, which could neither have been contemplated nor implied by the authors of that content," his method would exhibit a very different relation to tradition.[22] I will consider Kaplan's revaluation of the Sabbath, a virtual tour de force, in some detail. The beauty of the example, once more, is the self-consciousness which Kaplan brought to his task of retaining continuity with the tradition that he overhauled.

Note the progression of the argument.[23]

1. "From the point of view of tradition, the Sabbath enjoys a measure of sanctity beyond that of any other occasion in the year, with the single exception, perhaps, of the Day of Atonement." Kaplan reasonably infers this from the strict prohibitions on labor enforced on the Sabbath; his reification and virtual personification of "tradition" is far from unusual in Jewish thought and even Jewish scholarship. Somewhat less convincingly, he concludes from a rabbinic statement mentioning the Sabbath in one clause and all other commandments in another that "the Sabbath is thus made coordinate with [viz., equal in weight to] the whole system of Mosaic Law."[24]

2. The holiday invested with most sanctity must come to fulfill the most central human need or desideratum. "What more comprehensive purpose can there be to human life than the complete and harmonious fulfillment of all the physical, mental and moral powers with which the human self as a social being is endowed?"[25] Kaplan, we recall, rests confident that human nature is unchanging and that he, thanks to modern science, is equipped to understand it.

3. Self-fulfillment is the "equivalent of what in general life is expressed by the term 'salvation' and in traditional Jewish life by the phrase 'having a share in the world to come.'"[26] The locution "general

---

[22] Mordecai M. Kaplan, *The Meaning of God in Modern Jewish Religion* (New York: Reconstructionist Press, 1962), 1-14. Kaplan takes special pains to point out that the ambiguity of Conservative Jewish theology is a function of its "refusal to recognize the chasm between the traditional and the modern world-view" (9).

[23] Ibid., 40-43.

[24] Ibid., Kaplan, 41; Source: Jer. Nedarim III, 14 (386).

[25] Ibid., Kaplan, 41.

[26] Ibid., Kaplan, 41.

life" is obviously out of place; the context calls for a reference to something like "traditional religion." One wonders if the odd usage is coincidental. Kaplan's entire "revaluation," his claim to continuity with tradition despite radical innovation, of course stands or falls on the "equivalence" of function and meaning which he asserts. His slip comes precisely where his footing needs to be most sure.

4. Reinforcing this purported "equivalence," Kaplan argues that the tradition too regarded holidays as tools to be used for the achievement of Jewish needs. It too practiced functionalism! The Sabbath "was designed to make the Jew aware" that meaning and purpose were at hand. It was "calculated to impress the Jew" that salvation was attainable, and it had in fact "function[ed] . . . as the symbol of salvation."[27] True to his contrast between transvaluation and revaluation, then, Kaplan is not imposing a foreign methodology on the tradition but bringing to light what had been present, albeit latently so, all along.

5. Revaluation of the Sabbath, therefore, consists in reworking the notion of salvation linked by tradition to the Sabbath. Kaplan aims to find a modern equivalent for each of the idea's component parts: creativity, holiness, and covenant.[28] He devotes twenty pages to his well-known vision of "God as the creative life of the universe" and thus "the antithesis of irrevocable fate and absolute evil."[29] He dedicates ten pages to the translation of "holiness" as "transcendent importance" and the argument that human beings and their world are both holy in this sense, that is, possessed of ultimate meaning and purpose. Finally, he spends some thirteen pages on a reading of covenant as "commitment to Judaism," that is, loyalty to the Jewish people and its civilization.

The complicated (and unsatisfactory) notion of functional equivalence is certainly present as Kaplan proceeds through the Jewish holidays, but it proves less important than the related act of TRANSLATION. We have already seen several examples of this: salvation translates as self-fulfillment, holiness as importance, divine creation as the potential for human creativity. *The Meaning of God* is as good and as bad as these translations; more precisely, the holidays are only as compelling as the meanings with which Kaplan invests them and his success in linking those meanings to the rituals and texts associated with a given festival. (Kaplan rarely proposes new rituals. The link between generations, as we have seen, is supplied by the preservation of EXISTING rituals and their investment

27 Ibid., Kaplan, 42.

28 Ibid., 57-61. My summary of his position concerns the remainder of ch. 2.

29 Ibid., 61–81.

with new meaning.)[30] We will find profundity in Passover as the holiday of freedom—a very ancient linkage, of course—if Kaplan's vision of human freedom inspires us. Some chapters, in the nature of the case, are more compelling than others. Shavuoth is rendered as the festival that reminds us of God's role as the "power that makes for righteousness-not ourselves" (a phrase borrowed from Matthew Arnold) far more convincingly, in my view, than Sukkoth, the symbol for "God as the power that makes for cooperation." Herein lies the problem. Kaplan must convince us at every turn not only that he "translates" accurately, but that his version represents an improvement on the original. So he must join his embrace of "the tradition," his paeans to the "Jewish spirit," with the argument that our appreciation for our cultural heritage often "blinds us to new insights based on broader experience." Loyalty to tradition in that case leads us to reject new truth and makes us "faithful to an idol, not to God."[31]

But why should we remain loyal to tradition at all? Why are needs shared with all humankind best served by particularist observances set thousands of years ago? In what way does "Jewish tradition" obligate the Jew? Kaplan wavers on this point. At times (as in the section on covenant) it seems that no obligation is involved. One simply makes a rational choice. Having experienced the meaning and purpose conferred by observance of Jewish holidays, the Jew comes to participate in "the feeling which was universal among the Jewish people before the so-called Emancipation, that it was a privilege to be a Jew."[32] Here modernity is denigrated; the "so-called" points to deracination, alienation, spiritual impoverishment. It would be folly not to seize an opportunity for wholeness, particularly if one is convinced by Kaplan's argument that no other existing tradition is comparably equipped to offer self-fulfillment to modern individuals. Kaplan assumes that modern Jews, like everyone else in a rational age, operate according to a utilitarian calculus. Having experienced the benefits of Judaism, they will return for more. Having felt a need and its satisfaction, the source of that satisfaction will command their attention and their loyalty.

---

30 The exception is his ecumenical effort to define a new civil religion for Americans. See Mordecai Kaplan, J. Paul Williams, and Eugene Kohn, *The Faith of America* (New York: Schuman, 1951). I discuss this effort in my *Chosen People*, 87.

31 Kaplan, *Meaning of God*, 147.

32 Ibid., 92. The discussion comes in the context of Kaplan's translation of "covenant" as Jewish commitment.

He then adds a second source of obligation to Jewish tradition: the self's demand for authenticity and integrity. Orthodoxy gave Jews adequate reason for rejecting Judaism. One could not in good faith believe what it asserted. But Reconstructionism would enable the Jew to be "as critical of Jewish tradition as he may be, provided he tries not only to criticize Jewish tradition but to correct it." The latter, for Kaplan, was a moral imperative. The Jew could not permit himself "the indulgence of aloofness. 'Separate not thyself from the community' is an implication of covenantship on which we must insist." Kaplan is relentless in his criticism of status-seekers who abandoned their people in pursuit of social acceptance or in flight from anti-Semitism. He implicitly makes the argument (quite common after the Holocaust) that Jews are bound together in a common fate and are therefore obligated to cooperate in forging their common destiny. "If the Jewish people succeed in establishing a Jewish community life, committed to the maintenance of Jewish tradition in the sense here formulated, there is no reason why Jewish civilization cannot again function as a way of salvation."[33] The possibility of that outcome, in Kaplan's eyes, mandated the attempt to achieve it. How could a Jew refuse such a gift, particularly when refusal involved turning one's back upon both fellow Jews and one's own authentic self-realization?

There was, finally, a third source of obligation: the ancestors. Note Kaplan's formulation of what is involved in attachment to tradition. "Loyalty to tradition" does not mean closing our minds to present experience or having our "ancestors" tell us what we ought to think. Responsibility for our belief and our behavior rests squarely with us. "Our responsibility to our forefathers is only to consult them, not to obey them. Our responsibility to our descendants is only to impart our most cherished experiences to them, but not to command them."[34] We observe

---

33 Ibid., 99. Kaplan knows that in presuming lines of authority binding past to future and individual Jews to the Jewish people he is going against the grain of modern individualism—the one aspect of modernity which he persistently attacks. Note too that "tradition" and "the fathers" are virtually synonymous throughout the chapter.

34 Ibid., 96-98. Kaplan makes two critical assumptions in this discussion, both of them to my mind correct. First, Jews must be persuaded that identification with their people and culture is worthwhile before they set about reconstructing Judaism. Second, this identification comes about through experiences of meaning or fulfillment rather than through assent to truth claims. For one recent empirical confirmation of this argument, see Jonathan Woocher, *Sacred Survival: The Civil Religion of American Jews* (Bloomington: Indiana University Press, 1986).

that this repudiation of obligation comes at the very moment when Kaplan links tradition to the most primal source of obligation known to human beings: the ties binding parents to children and children to their parents.

On the face of it, this is a highly paradoxical point for Kaplan to make. It is one thing for the rabbis of old to invoke "our forefathers" and their "merits," as in pleading the case for another year of life before the Supreme Judge of the Universe on Yom Kippur. It is another for a modern, "scientific" figure—who no longer believes in the existence of that Judge, and believes quite firmly that his ancestors were mistaken in so believing—to do the same. Yet obligations to ancestors and descendants are such an obvious matter to Kaplan that he mentions them in passing, without argument. Geiger, too, we recall, had sought out "fathers" whom he could imitate and reject. Kaplan invokes the ancestors so regularly that one is driven to speculate (despite and because of his failure to address the subject) on what the implications of that invocation might be.

Two suggestions seem particularly relevant to our discussion. First, the substitution of "fathers" for "tradition" would help to account for the depth of Kaplan's ambivalence to the latter, and perhaps for the fact the he is most solicitous of tradition, most anxious to prove his fidelity, when he most departs from its instruction.[35] "Fathers" are more than a metaphor for tradition; they are the immediate transmitters of tradition. One's deepest feelings and attitudes toward the latter are inevitably bound up in one's highly charged and deeply ambivalent attitudes toward the parents with whom tradition is identified.[36]

Kaplan's linkage of tradition to the fathers, secondly, may help us to understand why religious American Jews, like Kaplan himself, have been willing to attenuate their links with "the chain of tradition" but unwilling to break the chain entirely. Indeed, as Charles Liebman has pointed out, Kaplan's open disbelief in our "Father in Heaven" has not proved popular among American Jews, nor has his translation of "holiness" to

---

[35] I rely here on the well-known and (at this level of generality) commonly accepted theory of ambivalence put forth in Sigmund Freud, *Totem and Taboo* (New York: Norton, 1950).

[36] Compare Kaplan's highly ambivalent relation to his fathers with the highly positive, even idealized, treatment of the "mothers" in much recent Jewish feminist writing.

"importance" or "commandments" to "folkways."[37] Jews far less traditional than Kaplan in their observance have found it all the more necessary to cleave to the vestiges of traditional belief and language. The very loyalty to ancestors which Kaplan invoked and hoped to revalue, then, may have precluded potential adherents from following him in the AVOWED reconstruction of the ancestors' legacy. The line between consulting the ancestors, which he urged, and obeying them, which he rejected, is not easily drawn—as Kaplan's own example demonstrates.

In sum, Kaplan, like Geiger, chose his ancestors carefully. He divided his patrimony into parts he could and could not use, denied God direct authorship of that patrimony, and assumed the mantle of the rabbis who, he believed, had first carried forward a Judaism inherited from THEIR fathers and transformed it through "revaluation." Like Geiger, too, he invoked science as his chosen instrument of selection and renewal. Functionalism and pragmatism in fact afforded Kaplan a flexibility of interpretation denied to Geiger, who had to make the difficult case that all he discarded was mere "vessel" and all he retained was fundamental "essence." Kaplan could retain more of traditional practice than Geiger while more radically altering the meanings associated with that practice. Freed of the "essence" discourse, he was able to acknowledge that no Invisible Hand guided the generations in their negotiation of a Jewish way. No necessity underlay the repeated transformation of Jewish belief, but only a people responding, like others, to unchanging human needs according to unchanging human patterns discernible to the eyes of objective modern science.

Children had always responded to the demands and legacies of their parents in this fashion, but they had generally not admitted it. Kaplan, with the help of science, could for the first time openly "revalue" and "reconstruct" the very tradition in whose name he performed the task of revaluation and reconstruction. His successors in our own day, robbed of Kaplan's positivistic faith in objective science and his claim to understand and meet the demands of "modernity," have found the effort to legitimate change in the name of the tradition that one changes no less necessary but a good deal more problematic.

---

37 Charles Liebman, "Reconstructionism in American Jewish Life," *American Jewish Yearbook* (1970): 3-99. I think it fair to say that Kaplan's theory of "revaluation" did not change in subsequent works, and that his effort to infuse new meaning into existing rituals, rather than dropping or adding rituals to suit existing beliefs, has become the dominant mode of religious adaptation among American Jews.

The Reappropriation of Tradition

Judith Plaskow's alertness to the dilemmas at issue here is exemplary. In fact, the impossibility of objectively locating the "tradition" or its putative essence is crucial to her project of constructing a feminist Judaism radically different from any Judaism that has existed heretofore. As a feminist, Plaskow must reject the notion that Judaism is "a given that I could fit myself into or decide to reject." She must insist that it is "a complex and pluralistic tradition involved in a continual process of adaptation and change." For she wishes to "remain within a patriarchal tradition" and yet alter it so that she can be a Jew not despite but as part of her feminism. Her work, very much like Kaplan's, is avowedly intended not only to change the tradition but to save it. "I am convinced that a feminist Judaism can restore the viability of God-talk within Judaism, providing the tradition with a language it has lost and sorely needs."[38]

Neither Plaskow's argument nor her method can be treated adequately here, but I do want to highlight several features which illustrate her relation to Kaplan and to more contemporary understandings of tradition.[39] Note, first, that she begins with a "heavy silence." Women rarely appear in historical accounts of the Jews, and appear even more rarely as authors (or even subjects) of sacred texts. Their experiences are not part of what has been considered tradition. Plaskow must assume that what has been handed down is not a complete record of what was. It is rather a partial, biased record in need of correction. "Tradition" must be studied, therefore, and studied suspiciously, so that it can be rewritten.

Plaskow's blueprint for doing so—a chapter on "Torah: Reshaping Jewish Memory"—draws heavily on Kaplan, on Buber's understanding of the Biblical text as a partial record of God's encounter with ancient Israelites, and on Scholem's reading of the kabbalistic notion of the hidden versus the manifest Torah. Her own chain of inheritance is clear. Moreover, she claims at more than one point that her own reconstruction of Judaism follows in the footsteps of the rabbis, who like her were not engaged in "discovering what 'really happened' but [in] projecting later

---

38 Judith Plaskow, *Standing Again at Sinai: Judaism from a Feminist Perspective* (San Francisco: Harper and Row, 1990), ix-xviii; quotations from x and xviii.

39 For a briefer statement in which these relationships are no less apparent, see Judith Plaskow, "Standing Again at Sinai: Jewish Memory from a Feminist Perspective," *Tikkun* 1/2 (1986): 28-34.

developments back onto the eternal present of Sinai, and in this way augmenting and reworking Torah." The rabbis too "brought to the Bible their own questions and found answers that showed the eternal relevance of biblical truth." Her continuity with that effort is further highlighted by the division of her text into chapters on Torah, Israel, and God.[40]

The "traditional" triad points to her divergence from the rabbis as well. I do not agree with her that placing God AFTER discussion of Torah and Israel represents discontinuity; one simply can't say that "Jewish thinking traditionally begins with God," let alone that this was so "because God is the beginning, the sine qua non of Jewish existence and experience."[41] In this instance Plaskow (again like Kaplan) has rendered the tradition more unitary than she knows it to be, in order to exaggerate the extent of her own departure from its dictates. More importantly, however, she feels the need to radically transform the "metaphors" which have dominated Jewish self-understanding until now. All previous understandings of God, Torah, and Israel are unacceptable. Aware that the very extent of her innovation jeopardizes her claim to continuity with Judaism's past, Plaskow takes pains, as Kaplan did, to argue that all description of God is metaphor and that the superiority of one metaphor to another is not a function of its truth value but of its use.

"The experience of God in community is both the measure of the adequacy of traditional language and the norm in terms of which new images must be fashioned and evaluated."[42] The novelty here is that whereas Kaplan too would have regarded religious language as a cultural product to be judged by its pragmatic adequacy, he believed that language described REALITY, with greater and lesser accuracy that science had enabled us to gauge. For Plaskow the only standard is communal experience. As she puts it elsewhere in the book, authority must rest somewhere and

> from a feminist perspective, . . . human beings are fundamentally communal; our individuality is a product of community, and our choices are shaped by our being with others. Scripture itself is a product of community. . . . My most important experiences of God have come through this community [of Jewish feminists], and . . . it has given me the language with which to

---

[40] Plaskow, *Standing Again,* chs. 1 and 2. For Plaskow's explicit linkage of her own innovations to the rabbis, see 35, 53.

[41] Ibid., 121.

[42] Ibid., 122.

> express them . . . without it [Jewish feminism] I could not see the things that I see.[43]

Having decided to remain within the "tradition" of Judaism, Plaskow takes care to describe these experiences, if at all possible, in terms derived from Jewish sources and highlights Jewish feminist liturgies which do the same.

The problem of authority thus resolves itself into the question of "whether the primary community to which I am accountable" finds her images of God or Torah, or Israel compelling. Plaskow can reasonably assume that communities of faith coalesce and disintegrate over time in relation to visions and metaphors which do or do not prove adequate to their needs and experience. Her tentative feminist theology of Judaism will prove of lasting import if it nurtures future growth. A community might actually define itself around that vision while other readers will incorporate what they find useful in her vision into their own communities, ignoring elements (for example, the "theology of sexuality" added to the "traditional" triad of God, Torah and Israel) which do not speak with "inner power." Plaskow's readers, like the author herself, must take the desire to remain continuous with Jewish tradition as a given. The only question is whether her vision proves compelling to them. Unlike Geiger, she need not establish continuity with an essence of Judaism. Unlike Kaplan, she need not presume a particular and unchanging conception of human nature and need not engage in the complicated work of locating "functional equivalents" to human needs and desiderata. All she needs to locate are readers. Her task is in that sense far simpler, even if, given the total lack of any authority for her Judaism except the consensus of her community, the power of the tradition which she mediates to hold and shape Jewish lives has been severely truncated.

Many of the same assumptions underlie Elliot Dorff's quite different effort to articulate a Conservative Jewish ideology, and many of the same dilemmas result. Like Plaskow, Dorff seeks to turn the historical variety of Jewish belief and practice—a variety that, given historical consciousness, he cannot deny—to advantage. Conservative Judaism and only Conservative Judaism, he argues, seeks to carry on the whole of Jewish tradition rather than one element of it ("ethics" in the case of Reform, "Halakhah" in that of Orthodoxy). Like Plaskow, Dorff claims the mantle of the rabbis. Conservative Judaism was devoted to "tradition" and change. For the rabbis too "it was clearly a matter of 'tradition and

---

43 Ibid., 19.

change'"; for other movements, one or the other of these ideals prevailed.[44] Dorff's presentation of Jewish tradition gives prominence to the two aggadot which feature centrally in Scholem's influential essay "Revelation and Tradition as Religious Categories in Judaism" (1962)[45] and are almost universally cited in recent centrist discussion of the issue. Like Rabbi Joshua in the Oven of Akhnai story, Dorff wishes to emphasize that authority to alter the law is "not in heaven" but vested in the students of Torah.[46] And in keeping with the depiction of a Moses perplexed because he is set down in the academy of Rabbi Akiva and cannot follow the discussion, Dorff urges the inevitability of halakhic and aggadic transformation. He insists that we follow the example of what the rabbis did as well as what they said. As he puts it elsewhere, just as the rabbis saw the judges of each generation as on a par with Moses and Aaron, so we should not see ourselves as inferior to them. If Reform's credo could be stated as "back to the ethics of the prophets," Conservatism should declare "back to the method of the Talmud."[47]

That method is both formal AND substantive. Dorff insists, as Plaskow does not, that we follow the rabbis in making Halakhah central to Jewish life. He also rejects the democratization of authority involved in Plaskow's reliance upon a plurality of communities, each with its own normative consensus as to what tradition means and shall be. Dorff, in the name of his models the rabbis, argues that "traditionally, Judaism has always been an aristocracy of the learned; laymen have not been considered able to weigh the importance of tradition accurately." In retaining this elitism, "we are simply following the Tradition." Thus, when a question of law arises, "we first must examine the traditional Jewish Codes." The ancestors need not be obeyed but they must be consulted. If a law with deep roots in Jewish legal history is out of keeping with contemporary needs and sensitivities, "we should not engage in overdoses of legal fictions, as we have been wont to do in the past . . . We should instead state the traditional law, our reasons for abrogating it, and the new

---

44 Elliot Dorff, *Conservative Judaism: Our Ancestors to Our Descendants* (New York: United Synagogue of America, 1977), 59, 103.

45 The essay appears in Gershom Scholem, *The Messianic Idea in Judaism* (New York: Schocken, 1971), 282-303.

46 Dorff, *Conservative Judaism*, 79-157.

47 Elliot Dorff, "Towards a Legal Theory of the Conservative Movement," *Conservative Judaism* 27/3 (Summer 1973): 65.

position that we are taking. That is a perfectly legitimate move to make in Jewish Law, as I have demonstrated above."[48]

Dorff is walking a fine line here, and its delicacy is further evidence for his claim that the path he urges is not one which very many Jews are competent to chart. His awarding of "a vote but not a veto" to the past is of course consonant with Kaplan. His conception of commandment, however, is far more traditional and far more complicated—a further working out of the line begun with Frankel's reliance on the popular will of the Jewish people, Schechter's turn to the will of "Catholic Israel," and Robert Gordis's narrowing of that population to the Jewishly learned and observant among them. Differentiating his position from those of both Kaplan and Gordis, Dorff writes that he conceives the Torah as written by human beings but constituting "the human record of the encounter between God and the People Israel at Sinai." Its authority thus rests not on God's will (Gordis) or the will of the Jewish people (Kaplan), but on the will of God as mediated by an elite of God's covenant people. "It is the rabbis, representing the community, and not every individual on his own, who must determine the content of Jewish law in our day."[49]

Dorff is aware that his own identification with the rabbis and their texts, rather than with the authors of the Codes or the Kabbalah, is in part a function of the fact that "two generations of Conservative rabbis have been raised on a Seminary program in which Talmud has been emphasized each year, while the Codes have been given only perfunctory treatment."[50] He also seems aware (although this consideration is not voiced explicitly in writings with which I am familiar) that in deciding to take the Judaism of the rabbis as normative, a Jew like himself votes to "privilege" one portion of the tradition over others and to count certain readings of and within that portion as authoritative while ignoring or discounting others. This choice, while not unreasoned, cannot be defended by appeal to "the tradition" or its putative essence. Dorff has not yet addressed the issue of selective inheritance directly. It will not do to say that "discovering the psychological reasons as to why we take the position that we do is far beyond the scope of this paper."[51] In general, however, he like Plaskow is aware of the difficulties in working with a constructed "tradition" rather than a given tradition—this without the benefit of a method of "certain" translation such as the one

---

48 Ibid., 75f.

49 Dorff, *Conservative Judaism*, 115.

50 Dorff, "Towards a Legal Theory," 76f.

51 Ibid.

which Kaplan employed. "The point is that we maintain that we have both the right and the duty to make changes in the law when necessary, even when these changes do not follow directly from precedents."[52]

Dorff has the right, because rabbinic innovations which he has decided to take as normative, according to certain texts which he has opted to "privilege," declare that precedent. He has the right, too, because scholarship, far from discerning an eternal essence or an unchanging human nature, has pointed up historical variation no more radical than his own. He knows, moreover (as Plaskow does), that the choices he makes in this regard—his selections from the past, the authorities to which he appeals—may over time come to constitute a community composed of those who assent to the same definition of tradition and identify in the same manner with the ancient rabbis. Thus, "I firmly believe that we are doing exactly what the Tradition would have us do, if only we can muster the personal qualities necessary to carry out our program wisely."[53] The Tradition can be personified in good faith, ascribed an overarching intention, and be invoked as ground for contemporary behavior—all this despite a degree of awareness that it is not unitary but variegated, and despite the explicit avowal that it has no essence. Dorff follows in footsteps which he has discovered through selective reading, and even marked out.

The theoretical contribution which more than any other has made this move possible, or at least has validated it most explicitly, is the essay by Scholem to which I referred earlier. Scholem's scholarship as a whole avowedly aimed at the overturning of long-held assumptions about what was essential to or dominant in Judaism. No longer could one doubt the role of Jewish mysticism in the belief and practice of Jews over the centuries. No longer could one credibly claim that Judaism developed in one and only one "necessary" direction.[54] In "Revelation and Tradition," Scholem announced a clear break with that view, which is held by many scholars as well as by many Jewish believers. The faithful in the nature of the case are unconcerned with the origins of their tradition, he wrote. The historian, by contrast, must understand how tradition came to be and came to define the revelation from which its authority is derived. Scholem, attempting to describe this process as it occurred in Judaism,

---

[52] Ibid.

[53] Ibid. See also Elliot N. Dorff and Arthur Rosett, *A Living Tree: The Roots and Growth of Jewish Law* (Albany: SUNY Press, 1988), 5, 187, 246, 303, 340–42.

[54] See David Biale, *Gershom Scholem: Kabbalah and Counter-History* (Cambridge: Harvard University Press, 1979).

calls his investigation into rabbis and kabbalists a case study of what "in general human terms" could be called "the function of creativity and spontaneity in relation to that which is given."[55]

This description of tradition as essentially creative and spontaneous is determinative for the essay. The stories of the Oven of Akhnai and of Moses in Akiva's academy,[56] both quoted in full by Scholem, drive home the point that the "given," whether of revelation or tradition, is never merely a "given." It must be received and then transmitted. Interpretation and change inevitably intervene. The details of the process as Scholem explicates it need not concern us here. What is essential is the picture of tradition as an innovative activity, not the frozen preservation of the dead letter—a rejection by Scholem of "all or nothing" accounts offered by believers, nonbelievers, and classical social scientists alike. One has only to compare Scholem's dynamic description of tradition with Durkheim's dichotomy of primitive and modern, or Weber's ideal-type of tradition as ritualistic, habitual action—the authority of the "eternal yesterday," sanctified "through the unimaginably ancient recognition and habitual orientation to conform"[57]—to appreciate just how radically Scholem wishes to alter our perception. The appeal of that vision for partisans of the Jewish center, whether Kaplanian, Conservative, right-wing Reform, or left-wing Orthodox, should also be apparent.

Beyond the impact of Scholem, who is directly cited by Plaskow and Dorff, one can only guess at the particular sources which have made the conceptualization of tradition in the current generation very different from what it was in Kaplan's day. Two instances of the reigning *Zeitgeist*

---

55 Scholem, "Revelation and Tradition," 282.

56 *b. B. Meṣ* 59b and *b. Menaḥ* 29b respectively.

57 The passage comes from Max Weber, "Politics as a Vocation," in *From Max Weber: Essays in Sociology*, ed. Hans Gerth and C. Wright Mills (New York: Oxford University Press, 1969), 78f. Weber adds at once that his three types of authority (rational, traditional, charismatic) are ideal types only, but he repeatedly finds instances of each and consistently adopts the same value-standpoint toward them. He is ambivalent toward rational authority but identified with it; fearful of charisma but drawn to it as the only hope of salvation from modernity's "iron cage"; and respectful of but hostile to frozen, ritualistic tradition—the barrier to the rational activity on which he focuses and the methodical, self-directed personality types whom he most values. The categorizaton of social action near the start of *Economy and Society* (Berkeley: University of California Press, 1978), 1:25, is striking in its bias. Action can be instrumentally rational, value-rational, affectual, or "traditional, that is, determined by ingrained habituation." For other strking usages see Max Weber, *Ancient Judaism*, trans. Hans Gerth and Don Martindale (New York: Free Press, 1952), 12, 253, 393.

may be cited as illustrative. On the one hand, sociologists such as Edward Shils and Shmuel Eisenstadt have disavowed Weber's bias against tradition, his use of "tradition" as a foil for the rational, systematic, calculated behavior characteristic of "modernity." They have urged a more nuanced view of both. Eisenstadt begins his conceptual essay on "Post-Traditional Societies" (1973) by arguing that one simply could not explain the process of modernization without first dissolving stereotypical notions of "tradition" and "traditional societies" into historical particulars and then inspecting each society at each point in time to see what proved enduring and what was altered—or, better, what proved enduring BECAUSE it was altered.[58] Zwi Werblowsky, seeking in 1976 to take scholarly discussion *Beyond Tradition and Modernity*, emphasized that the latter has itself become a tradition in many respects, while the former has exhibited significant plasticity.[59] Shils, the author of a sustained meditation on the concept of tradition, speculates that the concept has failed to function significantly in social science in the way that other Weberian concepts such as "charisma" or "bureaucracy" have functioned precisely because it was so heavily laden with Weber's biases and served as a sort of catch-all foil, an undifferentiated background, for what really interested Weber: rationality, modernization, and (to a lesser extent) charisma.[60]

A rather exact parallel to this line of thought can be found in recent work in hermeneutics, for example the writings of Hans-Georg Gadamer. Consider the well-known section in *Truth and Method* in which Gadamer offers an incisive critique of the attempt by Enlightenment thinkers to "discredit prejudice," by which they meant primarily "the religious tradition of Christianity," and to replace it with the light of reason. Gadamer wants to expose this viewpoint as no less a prejudice than the view it supplanted or than the Romantic attempt (which followed) to "establish the old, simply because it is old."[61] He then traces the way in which the two tendencies of enlightenment and romanticism combined in the founding of the historical sciences in the nineteenth century.

---

[58] Shmuel Eisenstadt, "Post-Traditional Societies and the Continuity and Reconstruction of Tradition," *Daedalus*, 102/1 (Winter 1973): 1-25.

[59] R. J. Zwi Werblowsky, *Beyond Tradition and Modernity* (London: Athlone, 1976), 17-19, 102-114.

[60] Shils, *Tradition*, 19f., 86-88.

[61] Hans-Georg Gadamer, *Truth and Method* (New York: Crossroad, 1975), 241–74; quotations from pp. 241f.

Gadamer's project—in need of no rehearsal here—is to argue the "indispensability of tradition," its importance and indeed its necessity for the reading of anything. Having become aware of our own "horizon" of understanding and its limits, we can approach the "horizon" of the text or subject under study, knowing full well that we will never capture it as it was but only as the limits of our culture permit us to bring it into focus. Such a "fusion of horizons" is the best we can attain. If we pretend to objectivity, ignore the tradition from which we come, "disregard ourselves . . . we have no historical horizon," no approach whatever to the past.[62]

Given the interrelationship between Jewish religious thought and Jewish scholarship from Geiger's day until our own, we should note that the dilemma which the view of tradition just enunciated presents for Jewish theology plagues contemporary Jewish scholarship as well. No subject matter can any longer be taken as a given, independent of the definition given it by the scholar. And when one moves from monographic works on particular authors or texts to generalized treatments of "the rabbis" or "the kabbalists" or—most difficult of all—"Judaism," the methodological difficulties are truly immense. The problem is generally overcome in one of two ways.

In some cases, lip service is paid to the need for historical variation, but then—given the necessity of saying something meaningful about "Judaism," the "Jewish tradition" as opposed to others—resort is had to language which could easily be mistaken for the sort which prevailed a generation ago. The British scholar Nicholas de Lange, for example, begins his recent short introduction to Judaism by explaining that the term connotes a "family relationship" among differing but related forms. At once, however, there are problems. Judaism cannot be reduced to a system of beliefs, and if one focuses instead on "observable phenomena such as worship and ritual" (the "sociological" approach), we "may well end up by wondering whether we are studying a single phenomenon or an apparently infinite variety of different 'Judaisms'." Judaism has taken different forms, but "it is also strongly felt" (note the passive voice here, indicating appeal to an undocumented consensus) "that there is a single thing called 'Judaism'." Similarly, while de Lange warns against imposing foreign categories on Judaism, and for that reason opts for a "historical approach," he also assumes that "from a sociological viewpoint, Jewish society is profoundly traditional. A historical approach

62 Ibid., 269–74.

gives full value to tradition. In what follows we shall investigate the different traditions which have contributed to contemporary Judaism." These, it turns out, are not so much competing strands, roads not taken, victorious and silenced voices, as reified members of the "traditional" family: "Torah and Tradition," "The Tradition of Worship," The Biblical Tradition," "The Legal Tradition," etc.[63] The definite articles, the inability (if only in such an introductory text) to countenance the idea that there might well be "objectively" an "apparently infinite variety of different Judaisms" is conclusive.

The alternative method is explored by Michael Fishbane in his own introductory text, entitled *Judaism: Revelation and Traditions*. Scholem's influence is pronounced. The first chapter begins with Judaism's "myth of origins," revelation at Sinai, which is couched in terms of the Moses in Akiva's Academy story. The word "myth" at once separates the reader/scholar from the Orthodox believer, for whom the "myth" is of course true in every sense, historically first of all. Fishbane then passes on to TRADITION, dealing at once with the problem of heterogeneity. To speak of an essence would be as misleading as to argue that Judaism is merely "a disconnected miscellany of beliefs and behaviors. The fact is that a fairly stable pattern of behaviors and beliefs has marked the expressions of traditional Judaism from classical times . . . to the present day." One can speak of essential features even if not of essence. Fishbane proceeds to do so, first summarizing the "converging authority structures" of "the Jews," "God," and "Torah and Interpretation" (the "traditional" triad, of course), and then (after reference to the Oven of Akhnai story) arguing that "the cumulative result of the converging authority structures of God, Torah, and interpretation is *tradition*—itself an authority structure and religious reality of major significance in Judaism."[64]

No better "finesse" of the problems facing the historian may be available. What constitutes a "stable pattern" is of course subject to dispute; what counts as an "essential feature" will occasion still further argument. So long as one articulates the methodological difficulties, as Fishbane does, keeps all characterizations of "Judaism" on a high level of generality, and makes the reader aware of evidence which does not fit the categories which one proposes, one may have done all that one CAN do. The

---

63 Nicholas de Lange, *Judaism* (Oxford: Oxford University Press, 1987), 1-8; quotations from pp. 1, 5, 8. See also the table of contents.

64 Michael Fishbane, *Judaism: Revelation and Traditions* (San Francisco: Harper and Row, 1987), 11-24; quotations from pp. 18 and 23..

reader must then beware when she encounters a rather bald summary of "Judaism as a Ritual System," its unity and stability taken as a given until the disruptions of modernity.[65] She might be still more suspicious when she encounters the claim that "the massive scope of the Jewish tradition and its fluid extension into every aspect of life constitute for the traditionalist nothing short of the immediate covenantal Presence of God at all times."[66] Who is this "traditionalist," anyway? What "fusion of horizons" has occurred here? Such are the contemporary dilemmas of anyone who would claim to speak for—or about—"Jewish tradition." They are likely to be with us for some time to come, bedeviling and enriching the attempt to take that tradition, as Rosenzweig put it, "from path to pathlessness."

Tradition, "Tradition," and "Traditioning"

Rosenzweig is a good starting point for consideration of the implications for American Jewish thought of the developments we have been charting: not only because he has influenced both Scholem and the American thinkers on whom Scholem too has had enormous impact, but because his approach to the redefinition of tradition gives poignant expression to the problematic that has beset his successors. The context for Rosenzweig's remarks concerning the move from "path to pathlessness," we recall, was a dispute with Martin Buber. Like Buber, Rosenzweig rejected the notion of any given Judaism to which one must conform and rejected no less the notion of eternal "essentials" which would enable one to choose among the elements of the given with the certainty that one thereby carried on the heart and soul of the tradition, leaving nothing significant behind. Buber had pointed to a new principle of selection, "the concept of inner power, . . . what you demand when you ask him who learns to stake his whole being for the learning." Rosenzweig endorsed this principle, insisting only that not only "the teaching" but "the law" too must be carried on and transformed in this way. And here too, as with the teaching, no guide to future practice existed. It had to be charted. "We can reach both the teachings and the

---

65 Ibid., ch. 3.

66 Ibid., 23. Fishbane has elsewhere warned eloquently about "introductory survey courses [in Judaism which] often present Judaism in terms of standard or recurrent patterns in Jewish life and culture and rarely emphasize its diversity, variety and unexpected developments" (Michael Fishbane, "The Academy and the Community," *Judaism* [Spring 1986]: 148).

Law only by realizing that we are still on the first lap of the way, and by taking every step on it, ourselves. But what is this way to the Law?"[67]

Briefly put, the way leads "through the entire realm of the knowable, but really through it." One takes the tradition in all its varieties into oneself, wrestles with its decisions, and then goes forward. But, asks Rosenzweig, given that one must leap "from path to pathlessness" in any case, from map to terra incognita, "what advantage has he who has gone the way over him who right at the outset ventured the leap, which must come in the end in any case?" His answer is crucial: "Only this laborious and aimless detour through knowable Judaism gives us the certainty that the ultimate leap, from that which we know to that which we need to know at any price, the leap to the teachings, leads to *Jewish* teachings."[68] Put another way: Jewishly informed Jews, in serious dialogue with their tradition, living in a Jewish community, will carry their tradition forward in a way continuous with its past. One must have this trust in the process. There is simply no other choice.

Scholem's model of the relation between "revelation and tradition" seems a working out of Rosenzweig's conception, and together the two have shaped a principal contemporary strategy for the maintenance of Jewish faith in the face of historical consciousness.[69] To wit: one changes the question at issue from the nature of faith or belief to how one can appropriate, and so carry on, a tradition. The criteria for judging the continuity or discontinuity with the past of any proposed innovation likewise change. One does not line up putative elements in two columns, past and present, to see how many are retained. Nor does one count some as essential and deem their presence in column B a necessary and sufficient condition of conformity to column A. One rather inquires into the FORMAL requirements for transmission of any tradition: knowledge of the tradition in all its varieties, along with the presence of relevant sociological factors such as community, language, symbol, calendar. Kaplan and Geiger, Plaskow and Dorff all take pains to demonstrate their grounding in traditional sources, and all emphasize the continuity of their enterprise with the process of perpetual "spontaneity" and

---

[67] Franz Rosenzweig, "Teaching and Law," in *Franz Rosenzweig: His Life and Thought,* ed. Nahum Glatzer (New York: Schocken, 1953), 234–42; quotations from pp. 236, 240f.

[68] Ibid., 234–42.

[69] For more on this strategy see Arnold Eisen, "Secularization, `Spirit', and the Strategies of Modern Jewish Faith," in *History of Jewish Spirituality,* ed. Arthur Green (Philadelphia: Crossroad, 1987), 2:283–91, 313–15.

"receptivity" which Scholem describes. All, finally, point to SUBSTANTIVE continuity—for the leap from path to pathlessness will never be convincing in the total absence of such overlap—but, unlike Geiger, none of the twentieth-century thinkers make this claim decisive. For they are aware that the "path" from which they leap is only one of many which Jews in the past had walked.

Critical problems threaten the success of this strategy, I believe, even as they make it inevitable. The most important problem is continuing popular ambivalence toward "tradition" (and the fathers!), related to widespread resistance to allowing tradition to function as a commanding authority in one's life.[70] For religious thinkers, even the liberals among them, tradition continues to OBLIGATE, in a way that choices of STYLE ("traditional" architecture, furniture, clothing) do not. Religion may be a leisure time activity for many American Jews and may transpire in private rather than public space, but the sources of obligation to which Kaplan too responded remain compelling for the believer. One seeks rightness and authenticity, one feels obligations to ancestors and descendants, one assumes obligations to fellow Jews. "Community" is a powerful locus of authority to Kaplan, Dorff, and Plaskow. It offers the self anchor—all the more necessary when "God" and the "eternal yesterday" can no longer provide that mooring. Whether the average Jew will submit to the authority of tradition, however, is a matter of serious doubt.

Walter Benjamin's marvelous essay, "The Work of Art in the Age of Mechanical Reproduction," reminds us that these developments regarding tradition are not unique to religion, let alone to Judaism. His argument is that the nature and function of works of art have changed dramatically with the social (and even more the technological) changes in the way modern art is produced and received. Most crucially for our purposes, the modern "technique of reproduction" (photography first of all, and then film)

> detaches the reproduced object from the domain of tradition. By making many reproductions, it substitutes a plurality of copies for a unique existence. . . . Its social significance, particularly in its most positive form is inconceivable without its destructive, cathartic aspect, that is, the liquidation of the traditional value of the cultural heritage.

---

70 Compare Shils, *Tradition*, chs. 9 and 10.

Benjamin gives the example of a statue of Venus which stood in one "traditional context" among the Greeks (worship), and in quite another among iconoclastic Christians; in our time, the traditional accent on the "cult value" of the work of art has given way to emphasis on its "exhibition value." We see the work neutrally, and, if mechanically reproduced, we (and many others) can see it simultaneously, many times over, thereby depriving the work of its "aura."[71]

The point seems to be twofold. First, the modern work of art, even if not produced mechanically, sits in a museum alongside countless others from countless cultures. It is detached from its original context of creation and reception. It signifies only in OUR contexts, adding one more fragment to our assorted cultural collection. It figures in no ritual but the ritual of museum-going. We may even glance at it as we sit in an office or make our way down a corridor. If the work of art is a film or photograph, it is in principle universally available, denied any context whatever.

Second, Benjamin traces the preference for film over nonmechanically produced forms of art in popular culture to "the desire of contemporary masses to bring things 'closer' spatially and humanly, which is just as ardent as their bent toward overcoming the uniqueness of every reality by accepting its reproduction." That which is high must be brought low. That which is far away must be brought close. In fact, "The distinction between author and public is about to lose its basic character." Perception itself is altered as a result, Benjamin argues. Film in particular causes us to see differently, because "the camera that presents the performance of the film's actors to the public need not respect the performance as an integral whole. Guided by the cameraman, the camera continually changes its position with respect to the performance."[72] One does not stand, even in a museum, and see a stable, unitary work of art at length and from several perspectives; nor does one see it from a perspective determined by one's own stance. Instead, one sits alongside others in a darkened theater and sees a procession of quickly moving images constructed by the filmmaker—exactly the same procession that everyone else sees. In both cases, of course—movie theater and museum—one then integrates the work of art into the larger, virtually infinite collection of images which furnishes our minds in a modern, fragmentary culture.

---

71 Walter Benjamin, "The Work of Art in the Age of Mechanical Reproduction," in *Illuminations*, ed. Hannah Arendt (London: Fontana, 1973), 219–27.

72 Ibid., 223–44.

Jewish thinkers since Mendelssohn have been wrestling with an analogous problem: the transformed character of Jewish observance in the modern social order. Ritual observance is of course more like the performance of a play or a piece of music—the realization of the script or score varying somewhat with each individual performance—than it is like a work or art or a film which stand independently of their audience. Nonetheless, Benjamin's observations are highly relevant.

Consider first the transformed context for ritual behavior. Most anthropological descriptions of ritual enactment presume a stable, distinct, and highly integrated society which receives symbolic expression in ritual performance and is in turn reinforced by that performance. That picture of "traditional" society is overstated, but it is certainly true that Jews in the modern period live and work primarily with Gentiles, which means that their distinctive rituals no longer mark the boundaries of their world. Moreover, Jews now vary greatly in their observance, from Reform to "Traditionalist Orthodox" and even within such groupings. The normal pattern at the end of the twentieth century—certainly outside Orthodoxy—is for individuals or individual families to chart their own patterns of observance, selecting as they go from the array of options available, and often changing patterns rather frequently. This means, regardless of the theology of commandment that one holds or the concept of tradition, that observance is highly voluntarist. Its character as what the anthropologist Victor Turner calls "play" rather than "work" is reinforced by the prevalent restriction of ritual activity to private space and leisure time.[73] "Traditionally"—even allowing for significant variation, as between Spanish Jewry in the Golden Age and Polish Jewry in the eighteenth century—that was not the case.

Benjamin's point about the democratization of art—the tension between genius, necessarily elitist, and the desire to bring everything close—is no less relevant to our concerns. Mendelssohn's tortuous explanation of the *miṣvot* as a symbolic script can be read as an attempt to preserve the commanded and near-universal character of observance while allowing individuals to impose their own meaning on these shared observances.[74] The traditional character of their Jewish lives, we might say—the features which "link the generations one to another"[75]—lay in

73 See Turner.

74 See Arnold Eisen, "'Divine Legislation' as 'Ceremonial Script': Mendelssohn on the Commandments," *AJS Review*, 15/2 (Fall 1990), 239–67.

75 I quote the reading which precedes recitation of the *Mourner's Kaddish* in the Conservative *siddur*.

what they did, and not in the particular significance which they attached to what they did. He would also have argued that this variation had always been present—it too was thus thoroughly traditional! Solomon Schechter made a similar argument when he sought to define the commonalties of Judaism throughout the ages despite the variations which, as a result of *Wissenschaft*, he could not deny. Maimonides and Akiva disagreed on a great deal, but "they both observed the same fasts and feasts, . . . revered the same sacred symbols, though they put different interpretations on them, . . . prayed in the same language, . . . were devoted students of the same Torah, . . . looked back to Israel's past with admiration and reverence. . . . And they both became rocks and pillars of Judaism."[76] These commonalties correspond almost exactly to the "formal" elements of tradition which we identified when considering Scholem's essay. Not surprisingly, given Schechter's relation to Kaplan, the vision which he shared with Mendelssohn is close to that of Reconstructionism as well. For Kaplan too, after all, symbols and observances are the givens; interpretation can and must vary. Benjamin's essay teaches us to see this as in part a consequence of the democratic ethos, in which all must have a share in "creativity," all must be authors and not merely audience, authority must be sought (as it is in Plaskow and to a degree in Dorff) horizontally, among one's community, rather than vertically, in Revelation from God.

I take it that this selective, self-conscious, reconstructive or reformist approach to "tradition" is not only characteristic of many Jews at present, but constitutes a principal strategy by which Jews, "elite" and "folk," have gotten around the problems which modern scientific and historical consciousness, along with our highly individualist notion of self, have posed to Jewish commitment.[77] I think we can also say, on the basis of contemporary behavior, that more and more Jews have become practitioners of what anthropologist Samuel Heilman has dubbed "traditioning," the movement into and out of "tradition" as demanded by one's "lifestyle" and one's commitments of the moment.[78] One drapes a tallith lightly over the shoulders for a couple of hours, as it were, rather than wearing it all day, or head to toe. One fully participates neither in TRADITION—a given, all-embracing pattern of belief and observance, held

---

76 Solomon Schechter, "The Seminary as a Witness," in *Seminary Addresses and Other Papers* (New York: Burning Bush, 1959), 41-52; quotation from p. 51.

77 See n. 69.

78 Samuel Heilman, *The People of the Book: Drama, Fellowship, and Religion* (Chicago: University of Chicago Press, 1983), 62-65.

to be THE way of being Jewish as determined by God and by age-old authorities—nor in what we might now call "TRADITION": a self-consciously selective pattern of observance, the "traditionality" of which is measured primarily by the formal criteria (learning, language, symbol, community) set forth in our discussion of Scholem and Rosenzweig. Rather, at the very moment that self-conscious, selective "tradition" assumes more and more importance among Reform, Reconstructionist, and Conservative elites, their "folk" seem increasingly inclined to practice a fragmentary, variable, and individualized form of TRADITIONING. Geiger and Kaplan, Plaskow and Dorff all display great ambivalence toward their inheritance, enact their innovations in the name of earlier authorities, and regard history as both ally and enemy of their Jewish commitment. But that commitment stands. Obligation to the past, however altered, is maintained. The ancestors continue, to some degree, to command. The voice of the fathers—and more recently the mothers—is decisive. For the average Jew—largely ignorant of Jewish history, not part of an integral community such as those presumed by Dorff and Plaskow, and therefore far more responsive to contemporary cultural and societal pressures than to the demands of a God they no longer experience as commanding in any sense—the strategy of "tradition" cannot work to the same degree. They will likely not utterly ignore the wishes of the ancestors, as they perceive them, but neither will they accord those wishes central significance in their lives. More important, armed with popular notions of tradition such as those proclaimed by *Fiddler on the Roof* and the label of my flannel shirt, they may well regard their stance as the only authentic response to the past. "Sunrise, sunset, quickly flow the years." Times change. Children leave their parents behind. Life is in the future.

Time will tell whether the "tradition" as understood by the elites of the center can survive the popular tendency to traditioning or the elites' own doubts as to the authority underlying their selections. "Spontaneity in relation to that which is given" may well demand a greater restraint of spontaneity, a greater submission to the given, and a greater awareness of the choices involved in innovation and transmission, than are available to the vast majority of Jews in late-twentieth-century America.

CONCLUSION

When Modern Jews Appropriate From the Tradition: A Symposium

This book of essays concludes with statements by three leading scholars, Michael A. Meyer, Charles S. Liebman, and Ivan G. Marcus, on the problematic aspects of appropriating from the tradition. To what extent does selective appropriation betray the tradition? Who wields the authority to select? And is there a Jewish tradition of selective appropriation?

The authors agree on three vital issues: First, that modern Jews by definition are not traditional even when they retrieve from the tradition; that living in the grip of a traditional society differs from living in a modern society and choosing to behave traditionally. Second, Jewish tradition is not a fixed body of beliefs and observances, but has changed over time. And third, it is not the act of selective appropriation that separates modern from traditional Jews, but self-awareness about one's selectivity: the historical self-consciousness of moderns about their selective reappropriation irretrievably sets them apart from traditional Jews of earlier eras.

Our authors disagree over questions of authority and limits. There is no concensus on who has the right to reappropriate and how such a retrieval can legitimately take place. It is fitting that we conclude with the statements of engaged scholars who reflect contemporary debates within Jewish society over the proper uses of tradition.

Tradition and Modernity Reconsidered

MICHAEL A. MEYER

If we are to reconsider the relation between TRADITION and MODERNITY, it is essential that we be clear about the two terms in question. By "tradition," or *masoret* in Hebrew, I mean not only to point to the collective body of laws and customs as well as the individual components that constitute Judaism, but also—and more basically—to the fact of their continuous transmission from generation to generation. *Masoret*, after all, like the Latin *traditio*, comes from the root to transmit. It can refer either to the entire corpus that has been passed on, as *Pirke Avot* tells us, from Sinai onward, through the generations, in a chain of tradition, a *shalshelet ha-qabbalah*, or to a single element, as in the phrase *masoret beyadam me᾽avotehem* (they possess a tradition from their ancestors).

"Modernity" is a term that can be used either for the most recent period of time, including our own, regardless of content—in which case there can by definition be no "postmodernity." Or it can be understood to possess a particular content—variously defined according to predilection—in which case we may have gone beyond it, investing our age with a different content from that which characterized the past two hundred years or so. My own predilection in this presentation is to regard modernity as especially characterized by two elements: by independent critical thought, what Kant saw as the imperative of all enlightenment: *sapere aude*—"Dare to know!" and by the internal authority of the individual in matters of religion, morality, and art. It is my argument that, thus defined, tradition and modernity have been at odds in Judaism since at least the eighteenth century and that, despite all the relevant and significant developments that have taken place from then until the present, they continue to represent polar opposites.

As I have argued elsewhere, at the beginning of the confrontation between tradition and modernity the latter was widely perceived as presenting a crisis for the Jews. Whereas Christians in central and western Europe had had about two hundred years to come to grips with critical thought and individual authority, Jews were thrust into the modern world within two generations. Judaism lacked the armor to fend off first the rationalistic and then the historical critique launched against it, and some of its leading figures questioned whether it could successfully resist. Christians argued that only their faith was compatible with modernity, that Judaism was so traditionalist as to be incapable of adaptation. Those Jews who agreed drew the consequences and joined that religion which, they were told and came to believe, could alone survive in modernity.

But other Jews, no less touched by modernity, chose not to abandon the Jewish camp. Instead, they took the daring step of bringing the ravenous beast of modernity inside the pale of Judaism. That is precisely what the *Wissenschaft des Judentums* movement did, with the result that modernity ate away much of tradition. Its sharp teeth cut through the links in the chain—between Torah and Talmud, between Mishnah and Gemara, for example—showing that at each stage profound changes had taken place. Everywhere historical study found development and variety, no simple passing on of an unchanging, "eternal" Judaism. Criticism left tradition desiccated. If it was to survive in harmony with modernity, it would need to be reconceived in a manner that did not violate its canons.

But critical historical study was only one way in which modernity affected tradition. Another of equal significance was the confrontation between tradition and contemporary conscience and sensibility. Religious authority was claimed for the present generation over against generations past. Whereas earlier conflicts between traditional requirements and customs, on the one hand, and individual intellectual and moral concerns on the other, had been nonexistent or muted, newly modernizing Jews began to feel a sense of conflict between them. As *Wissenschaft des Judentums* sought to do with historical criticism, so did religious reform attempt to bring the individual authority characteristic of modernity within the bounds of Judaism. The nature of the worship service now ceased to be influenced by tradition alone. Subjective criteria were given a voice as well. The hope for the rebuilding of the Temple and the consequent reinstitution of the sacrificial service, for example, was a tradition of central importance, but it fell before the subjective criterion of intellectual honesty. How could one pray for what one did not, in fact, desire? Whereas at first distinctions between mere customs (*minhagim*) and authoritative laws (*halakhot*) were scrupulously observed, even these fell away more and more, especially in individual practice (kashruth, for example), but also—notably among Reform Jews in the United States—in communal matters as well.

Thus both *Wissenschaft des Judentums* and religious reform dissolved the chain of tradition in the acid of modernity. But they did not entirely destroy its elements. Nor did they preclude the possibility of forging the chain anew. On the contrary, in various ways scholar/reformers (for they were often the same men) sought to reconceive the tradition in such a way that it became invulnerable to modernity: by humanizing it to varying degrees, by building change and variety into it, or by altering its substance from law to a set of religious ideas. By these means they hoped to preserve continuity and prevent rupture.

Yet, in fact, the prospect of rupture loomed ever larger as criticism and subjectivism (the former more for the intellectual, the latter more for the average Jew) produced diminishing faith and neglect of ritual acts. Increasingly, it seemed, there was neither chain nor even broken links. At most there was a treasure trove of customs and ceremonies from which individuals might select whichever ones served a purpose in their religious lives. But that meant there was no longer a collective tradition, only particular ritual acts freely and personally chosen. The result, to use Leo Baeck's image, was many paths variously traversing a single landscape.

As for more and more Jews observances were drained of their divine authority and thus they more easily gave way before competing concerns, the number of traditions that children received from their parents diminished ever more. Modernity clearly had the upper hand. And then, beginning about the end of the nineteenth century in the United States, the process that seemed irreversible began to reverse itself, certainly not for all Jews, but for some. Modernity and tradition now began to appear as poles in a magnetic field. Seen as operating within a dialectical process, modernity had initially drawn Jews sharply away from tradition; now tradition seemed to be regaining force and a process of "reappropriation" to begin.

I put the word "reappropriation" in quotation marks since traditions, as I strictly defined the term, cannot be reappropriated or reclaimed. Once the link is broken, there is no tradition. Instead there is the self-chosen recovery of a custom or practice to which the individual is no longer linked, a new practice for that person, which may once again become tradition if he or she succeeds in passing it on within the family to the next generation.

Why has there been this desire to reinstitute customs and ceremonies, which has manifested itself collectively in American Judaism and among individual Jews? Let me begin with the collective. The best example is, of course, American Reform Judaism. A hundred years ago, in its classical form, it gave great weight to modernity and relatively little to tradition. Again and again it broke the chain of tradition with regard to one observance after another. But by the turn of the century some of its rabbinical leadership was beginning to feel uneasy on account of a sense of rupture with the past and was beginning to doubt the viability of a religion so bereft of traditional elements. The following generations witnessed the reinstitution of numerous once-abandoned rituals, from the *shofar* to the *sukkah* to the *havdalah* and *seliḥot* services. The result was, and often still is, conflict. Ironically, it is a conflict between adherents of the "traditions" of Reform, received from classically Reform parents and grandparents, on the one side; and a coalition composed of new Reform Jews, who have these customs as traditions from their Orthodox or Conservative upbringing, and born Reform Jews for whom the customs are not tradition at all, but a desired novelty. Within the Reform movement as a whole such newly reinstituted customs and ceremonies are only gradually becoming traditions.

Among most individual Jews, I would like to argue, the resulting so-called "return to tradition" in Judaism is not motivated by a resurgence of religious faith nor by a desire to engage in a fuller and richer life of religious practice. It is instead prompted, I believe, precisely by a felt need for tradition in the narrower sense in which I have defined it: a generational link with the Jewish past. Why do synagogues, of any denomination within Judaism, fill up for *benei miṣvah* celebrations, and why do those who participate in them almost invariably find themselves moved by the ceremony? Is it not because this ceremony, more than any other, points to a link between the generations, a dramatic communal testimony following the Holocaust that the chain of transmission has not ceased? In many Reform synagogues a custom has relatively recently gained immense popularity. During the bar or bat mitzvah, grandparents and parents are called to the bimah and the Torah scroll is passed from one generation to the next. In most cases none of the three generations involved has more than passing familiarity with the contents of the scroll nor has or will practice most of its specific precepts. But the scroll is the visible symbol of Jewish identity and of Jewish survival. To pass it on is foremost passing on the commitment to remain Jewish in some manner. In time this new custom that somewhat artificially creates tradition will itself become tradition.

I said at the beginning that modernity and tradition remain in a polar relationship. Despite the various attempts to harmonize them, I believe they continue to pull in opposite directions, the one toward individual authority, exercised in thought and practice, the other toward the authority of a transmitted heritage. Although the dialectical process will continue to play itself out in organized Judaism and within individual Jews—perhaps in ways we cannot yet imagine—it seems clear that each element has retained its force. To be a modern traditional Jew is not an oxymoron, but it is a perpetual challenge.

The Reappropriation of Jewish Tradition in the Modern Era

CHARLES S. LIEBMAN

One might argue that the "reappropriation of tradition" is a process that takes place in a particular period. Just as there are identifiable periods in which societies or dominant groups within societies reject tradition, there are periods in which societies or dominant groups in societies reaffirm their ties to tradition. The French Revolution is characterized by the rejection of tradition.[1] The revolution proclaimed a new world; one so new, so dramatically different from the old, that even the order of time and space had to be revised. The American Revolution represented a far less radical break with the past. But as the story of George Washington's chopping down the cherry tree (symbol of cultivated England and its old world culture) reminds us, American society emphasized its distance from rather than its linkages with the English tradition out of which it self-consciously emerged.[2] The International Workers of the World proclaimed, "no more tradition's chains shall bind us ... the earth shall rise on new foundations," and Vladimir Mayakovsky wrote how

---

[1] For a persuasive discussion of this point see Robert Darnton, "What Was Revolutionary about the French Revolution?" *The New York Review* (19 January 1989): 3–10.

[2] James Robertson, *American Myth, American Reality* (New York: Hill and Wang, 1980).

The laws of creation we'll cancel
Uproot what remains of the past
End the carcass called history.

Within the Zionist movement, a prominent segment, with special appeal for the pioneer settlers, rejected historical Judaism and the importance of cultural continuity. The outstanding spokesman of this ideal, Micha Joseph Berdyczewski, protested against the "artificial mending of the rift between the old and new."[3]

Just as some groups and some societies in some periods have rejected tradition, so other dominant groups in other societies in other periods have affirmed it. And it is in this respect that one can meaningfully talk about the reappropriation of tradition. It is widely acknowledged that Israel has experienced a reappropriation of the Jewish tradition following the Six Day War. Some observers have argued that since the 1960s we have experienced a reappropriation of the Jewish tradition by Jewish organizations in the United States. If we compare American Jewish life today with that of two or three decades ago, we find, for example, a far greater concern with Jewish ceremonial.

On the other hand, the rejection and affirmation of tradition may be figments of the observer's conceptualizations. Tradition, it may be argued, is essential to the functioning of any society. Even the most revolutionary of societies, in the most revolutionary periods, looks backward to some prior era in which man, the structure of social relations, and the nature of society provide the image of what the revolutionary society strives to achieve. Otherwise, as Mona Ozouf indicates in her study of the French Revolution, there is no assurance that the dream of a new man and a new society is capable of realization.[4] Even utopians, in other words, require a golden age. A society may reject the "idea" of tradition, and the tradition which any given society projects as its own may change from one period to another, but there is always some tradition which is

---

[3] Ehud Luz, *Parallels Meet: Religion and Nationalism in the Early Zionist Movement, 1882-1904* (Philadelphia: Jewish Publication Society, 1988), 165.

[4] Mona Ozouf, *Festivals and the French Revolution,* trans. Alan Sheridan (Cambridge: Harvard University Press, 1988). My colleague Ella Belfer, whose field of expertise includes Russian studies, tells me that this is not true of the Bolshevik revolutionaries, and she has suggested why that revolution may be *sui generis.* This may explain why the Bolsheviks were so quick to traditionalize their own immediate past. For example, Shils quotes the following passage from a letter written by Leon Trotsky in 1927: "And we never felt as deeply and unmistakably our ties with the entire tradition of Bolshevism as we do now in these difficult days" (Edward Shils, *Tradition* [Chicago: University of Chicago Press, 1981], 3).

invoked to defend a particular way of life, particular policies, or a particular set of values. Regardless of what revolutionaries may say, they do not reject ALL tradition (at least not for more than a brief period), but replace one tradition with another. On the other hand, even archconservatives do not affirm ALL tradition. No one values everything from the past. In the process of living with tradition, and certainly if one tradition is replaced by another, that tradition is modified or transformed. Therefore, it might be argued, the "reappropriation of tradition" should not be understood as referring to some discrete period or event in which a tradition becomes sanctified, but rather to the continual process wherein the tradition is reappropriated so that it may retain its relevance for contemporary society.

The Jewish tradition is always valued by the Jewish people and Jewish society. If they have no positive sense of Jewish tradition, then they have no sense of being Jewish. The question raised by "reappropriation of the Jewish tradition" is, how do Jews continually reformulate that tradition, and what is the relationship between the reformulation of tradition and the manner in which Jews conduct their lives?

I understand the term "tradition" as the set of norms and values and beliefs which an individual or society attributes to its own past and which are of some relevance, positive or negative, for the present.[5] Tradition, therefore, however compelling it may be for the individual or for society—regardless of how sympathetic, committed, and even submissive one may feel toward its norms and values—is something apart from and in some sense alien to the individual and/or society. Tradition is not simply LIVED, but is an object of UNDERSTANDING. It is something to be learned. The Jewish tradition is not the culture of the past, but rather that which the modern Jews PERCEIVE as the culture of their past. Tradition, therefore, changes as perceptions of the past change.

In accordance with this definition, tradition becomes a peculiarly modern notion. We have a conception of tradition because we have a conception of ourselves as distinct from tradition. Traditional society takes its rhythms of life, including its changes, for granted. It is guided both emotionally and intellectually, in judgment and activity, by unexamined prejudices.[6] If the sociologists and historians who distinguish the

---

5 This is a refinement of a definition I first offered in my *Attitudes toward Jewish–Gentile Relations in the Jewish Tradition and Contemporary Israel* (Cape Town: University of Cape Town, Kaplan Centre, 1983).

6 Clifford Geertz, "Ideology as a Cultural System," in *The Interpretation of Cultures* (N.Y.: Basic Books, 1973), 218.

modern era and modern man from the premodern era and premodern man are correct,[7] then man and society may in the past have lived their lives in total harmony with tradition. But if they did so, then they were unaware of tradition. The idea of tradition, according to Edward Shils, took form in the eighteenth and nineteenth centuries.[8] It is preceded by historical self-consciousness, which arises, as a distinct mode of thought, in seventeenth-century Europe. As Elie Kedourie observes, the modern attitude is that history "gives coherence and significance to actions, documents, institutions which had hitherto been accepted as forming an uncomplicated and perhaps timeless tradition."[9] Yosef Yerushalmi's comment that "the modern effort to reconstruct the Jewish past begins at a time that witnesses a sharp break in the continuity of Jewish living,"[10] helps us understand why tradition is a peculiarly modern notion. It seems fair to conclude, therefore, that no matter how faithful any modern society may claim to be toward tradition, it is, by definition, nontraditional.

The distinction between "reappropriation" in the modern and premodern periods rests on the degree to which those who do the reappropriating are self-conscious about their activity. We may assume that the modern reappropriation is carried out by those who are conscious of what they are doing—striving to fit the past to the needs of the present. This does not mean that they are manipulative charlatans. I do not think that would be a fair characterization of Joseph Klausner, who wrote a history of the Second Temple period in light of his Revisionist-Zionist ideology, or of such distinguished historians as Ben Zion Dinur or Yitzhak Baer, whose contributions to Jewish history have been criticized as reflecting their Zionist prejudices. It is not even true of Yonathan

---

7 The differences have probably been exaggerated, but this is not the place to challenge the scholarly consensus, nor am I learned enough to engage in that challenge. A great deal has been written on the nature of traditional societies. I have found the work of Clifford Geertz instructive in this regard. Peter Berger, *The Heretical Imperative* (New York: Doubleday, 1979), is especially helpful in defining modernity and modern man in contrast to traditional man. But I know of no single essay that outlines the nature of traditional society in more concise a manner than Jacob Katz, "Traditional Society and Modern Society," first published in 1960 and most recently reprinted (in Hebrew) in his *Jewish Nationalism: Essays and Studies* (Jerusalem: The Zionist Library of the World Zionist Organization, 1979), 155–66.

8 Shils, *Tradition*, 18.

9 *Nationalism in Asia and Africa*, (London: Cass, 1979), 36.

10 Yosef Hayim Yerushalmi, *Zakhor: Jewish History and Jewish Memory* (Seattle: University of Washington Press, 1982), 85.

Ratosh, father of the Canaanite movement, whose image of the Hebrew past is far-fetched to say the least.[11] Klausner, Dinur, Baer, Ratosh, and others like them believed that what they said about the past was true. But they were aware of the fact that what they said was very different from what others had to say, and that what they said served the needs (as they perceived them) of the society in which they lived. I suspect that those who reappropriated traditions in the premodern period were less self-conscious about what they were doing. I suspect that their major effort was in demonstrating that what they were saying was in essence no different from what others had said, and that apparent differences could be accounted for by extraneous factors. I do not believe this means they were simpletons any more than I believe that the contemporary reappropriators are charlatans. I do think that religious faith, deeply pious sentiments toward the past, and the belief that the tradition (Torah in the case of the Jews) always speaks to man's contemporary condition contribute to the process whereby those responsible for reappropriating the tradition become unselfconscious about its transformation.

This is certainly the process by which the rabbis reappropriated the tradition. Now one may want to argue that this is still the process which the rabbis invoke. This leads us to the observation that the rabbis played a more significant role in the past, whereas organizational or political leaders (governments in the case of Israel) play a more significant role today. But this is hardly the whole story.

I suspect that the forms of reappropriation remain basically unchanged The three major forms that I can think of are selectivity, transformation, and transvaluation. These forms are not mutually exclusive.

SELECTIVITY means the selection or emphasis of certain themes and the deemphasis or ignoring of others. This is the process through which Rav Kook's followers reappropriated Judaism in an ultranationalist, xenophobic form, and an important mode through which Reform and contemporary Conservative Judaism reappropriated it in universalistic, politically liberal form.[12] TRANSFORMATION refers to the retention of structurally recognizable features of traditional symbols, while changing certain aspects of its form. For example, Jewish communities may continue to commemorate the fast of Tishah b'Av but add references to

---

[11] Yehoshua Porath, *Shelak ve-ate be-yado: sipur ḥayav shel uriel shelaḥ* (The Life of Uriel Shelah [Yonathan Ratosh]) (Jerusalem: Machbarot Lesifrut, Zmora Ltd., 1989).

[12] The point is expounded in detail in Charles S. Liebman and Steven M. Cohen, *Two Worlds of Judaism: The Israeli and American Jewish Experience* (New Haven: Yale University Press, 1990).

the Holocaust or other contemporary tragedies. TRANSVALUATION refers to the retention of the forms of traditional symbols while imposing new meanings on the traditional symbol—the transvaluation of Hanukkah from a holiday commemorating God's miracles to a holiday commemorating Jewish courage is one of the clearest examples we have of the modern transvaluation of a Jewish holiday.[13]

This raises the question of who defines, selects, transforms and transvalues tradition. In one respect, it is the community itself, in its perceptions of the past and in its behavior, insofar as the community believes that its behavior is linked to the past. Nathan Rotenstreich observes that "tradition in its theoretical formulation appears in fact as the historical consciousness of the Jewish community, a consciousness that creates and reflects the history of that community."[14] But we have defined tradition as a modern conception in which that entity described as tradition is distinct from the life of an individual or society. Tradition is not only set apart from the society which affirms it, the members of that society are aware of their own ignorance of the tradition. What sustains the credibility of tradition, therefore, is the belief by large numbers of people that whereas they have only a general, rather hazy knowledge about the details of tradition, someone else, some cultural elite, does understand it fully and can, therefore, speak authoritatively about its content. In this sense, therefore, tradition is not only a text or a way of life, it is a special group of people, or sometimes one person in particular. In the case of observant Jews, the reference is to talmudic sages,and in the specific case of Hasidim, their *rebbe*. In the case of nonobservant Jews, the problem is more complicated—especially if they themselves have some familiarity with Jewish scholarship, that is, are self-conscious about the reappropriation of the tradition.[15]

---

[13] These terms are described and illustrated in much greater detail in Charles S. Liebman and Eliezer Don-Yehiya, *Civil Religion in Israel: Traditional Judaism and Political Culture in the Jewish State* (Berkeley: University of California Press, 1983).

[14] Nathan Rotenstreich, *Tradition and Reality: The Impact of History on Modern Jewish Thought* (New York: Random House, 1972).

[15] Observing non-Orthodox professors of Jewish studies in "traditional" settings, for example during synagogue services in congregations in which they are members, I am struck by their effort to maintain what might be called detached involvement. They seek to both participate as well as distance themselves from tradition and ritual at one and the same time. The traditional synagogue setting allows them to participate in a self-consciously ambivalent manner, and this is probably more satisfactory to many of them than the *ḥavurah*. The *ḥavurah* with its deliberately innovative procedures, makes demands for total commitment with which few intellectuals are com-

This view of tradition introduces a number of additional questions. For example, a society might believe itself to be acting in accordance with tradition, whereas an outsider, for example a historian, might argue that society has misunderstood or is mistaken about the norms, values, and beliefs of the past. The answer, I believe, depends on the "good faith" of the society in question. Does it really believe it is behaving in accordance with Tradition, or is it manipulating the Tradition? This answer, in turn, raises two more questions. First, how do we determine "good faith"? Second, what if one group, say a cultural elite, is deliberately manipulating a Tradition but the masses believe in good faith that they are living in accordance with it?[16]

---

fortable. The Orthodox exhibit different modes of detached participation, and among them the scholarly conference rather than the synagogue may become the forum in which they express their ambivalences. On this point see Steven T. Zipperstein, "Response to Bernard Cooperman," in *Jewish Identity in America,* ed. David Gordis and Yoav Ben-Horin (Los Angeles: University of Judaism, Wilstein Institute, 1991), 211-14.

[16] Haym Soloveitchik, "Religious Law and Change: The Medieval Ashkenazic Example," *AJS Review* 12 (Fall 1987), 205-21, is most instructive in this regard because he demonstrates that precedents in the manipulation of tradition do exist in the most traditional of societies. However, the example Soloveitchik uses, suicide as an instance of sanctifying God's name, invites the objection that it may be *sui generis.* On the other hand, Soloveitchik's article invites the further observation that the incorporation of tradition in sacred text which characterizes the Jewish tradition makes radical manipulation a necessity, since there is always some disjunction between life and sacred text. Where the tradition is articulated in nontextual form, its transformation or reappropriation may appear less obvious.

Postmodern or Neo-Medieval Times?

IVAN G. MARCUS

A quarter of a century ago, when I began my graduate studies, it was still commonplace to divide Western history into three periods: ancient, medieval and modern, and there was little doubt that one was living then in the Modern period. As we approach the end of the century, that is no longer the case. Modern times are now frequently divided into at least three periods: early modern, modern, and postmodern, and with the emergence of the last, there is considerable doubt as to which period or periods one lives in today.

Jewish historians have followed suit. *Mutatis mutandis*, we too have our early modernists, although historical demographics force us to focus, as far as Western Europe is concerned, more on Italy, the Netherlands, and Central Europe, or on the *conversos* in those lands from which Jews, as Jews, had been expelled in the late medieval years. Modern history per se is a growth industry. Its practitioners in North America and Israel outnumber by far those working on all earlier periods combined. And lately, we too have been pondering the implications of the term "postmodern."

As a medievalist, who tends to be held accountable for what came before as well as what came after the so-called medieval centuries, some of the characteristics attributed to "postmodern" strike me as appropriately referred to as the Neo-Medieval. Like other neo-periods, such as Neo-Classical of the eighteenth century or Neo-Gothic of the late nineteenth, the notion of postmodern as Neo-Medieval suggests that some features that modernists claim ended with modern times have reemerged, albeit in a transformed way. The Neo-Medieval is not a return to the Middle Ages, for no institutions or values or patterns of behavior that are demonstrably premodern can mean the same thing they once did in a world that has known modernity. With Thomas Wolfe the medievalist knows that you can't go home again.

Yet, several central issues that originate in premodern times seem to be reemerging, even if transformed or subverted, and I would like to comment briefly on four of them. They are: 1) the Jewish political tradition; 2) the place of the Jews in a Christian (or Muslim) society; 3) the Jewish self-image of superiority or inferiority vis-à-vis the Christian or Muslim majority; and 4) the existence of variety in elite Judaisms.

From post-Israelite antiquity through the premodern, that is, preemancipation era, Jews organized themselves and were expected by gentile authorities to constitute self-governing religious polities. Jewish leaders sometimes shared overlapping political and religious roles and sometimes were more clearly one or the other, but at all times, these leaders were responsible for dealing with the Jewish community and with the gentile authorities. They collected taxes for both, provided social services to the former, and interceded at times of crisis with bribes and influence-peddling with the latter. In typical medieval fashion, Jewish bankers, courtiers, and *stadlanim* played a role in a gentile government and often as not used the power they had gained there to exert influence on the inside workings of a Jewish community. This was true of the Netira banking family in Baghdad and of Maimonides in Fustat; and it was true of Jewish courtiers and other members of the power elite in modern states.

Shaping Jewish political practice was a theory. It held that the greatest source of Jewish security lay with the protection offered by central gentile political and religious authorities; danger, in turn, lay with the undisciplined gentile rabble. Hence, the Jewish political tradition until modernity, tended to serve and support central political authorities in return for at least the promise of protection and religio-political toleration. This often worked. The legally organized Jewish communities generally fared well from Persian times in the sixth century B.C.E. throughout the preemancipation era. The breakup of collective Jewish political identity in parts of the Jewish world that experienced modernity brought with it the problem of facing political problems on a more or less equal footing with Christian or Muslim majorities. Modernity also saw the Jewish political tradition broaden dramatically to include Jewish participation in revolutionary politics.

With the growth of political Zionism in the late nineteenth century and of greater ethnicity in the late twentieth, some of the centuries-old experience of Jewish collective political behavior and theory, grounded in part in self-interest, reemerged and came into conflict with modernist ideologies, such as political liberalism. Thus, even when Jews behave politically as a nation-state motivated by their national interest, on the one hand, as in Israel, or as a political action group in the United States, on the other, Jews are in some ways adapting Neo-Medieval modes of political behavior to modern problems. To be sure, the very ideas of nationalism and of political lobbies are modern ones, but their appropriation by Jews is as much a transformation of a persisting tradition of collective Jewish political behavior as it is an accommodation to modernity.

Second, since late biblical times, Jewish religious culture has dwelt on the dichotomy between Israel and the other nations. From rabbinic times the polarity between Israel and the Nations of the World has existed. It provided that all peoples can achieve religious salvation, under different covenants and sets of demands—the Noachide Laws for one, the full gamut of the commandments for the other. Until the Christianization of the Roman Empire, the Jewish religious polity was generally regarded as just one more ethnic community. If it kept the laws and paid its taxes, it was allowed to practice its ancestral customs and was not put into an ideologically inferior status.

With the advent to power of the exclusivist ideologies of Christianity and Islam, this changed, and the problem of the place of the Jews emerged. Hierarchical condescension characterized both Christian and Muslim views of Judaism and contemporary Jews. True, pragmatically, Jews were tolerated for the most part, but it was in return for their subservience to the majority.

This problem of the place of the Jews was a lasting legacy of the Middle Ages. With the promise of equality of citizenship, this problem should have disappeared. We know it did not. In part, this was because the Christian character of Western societies did not disappear or was not held in check by liberal values. In part it did not disappear because modern forms of anti-Semitism found new reasons for reinforcing or perpetuating traditional Christian anti-Judaism and anti-Semitism. Neither the collective attempt to dissolve this through the assimilation of the Jews as one nation state among other nations, in political Zionism, nor the assimilation of individual Jews as citizens of the same nation could collapse the hierarchically invidious condescension with which the gentiles regarded the Jew. This persistence is reflected not only in such symbolic examples as the Vatican's not recognizing the state of Israel, but also in the tensions that exist in the divided Jewish and Christian American communities between more libertarian and more traditionalist religious camps on Christmas symbols in public places, prayer in the public schools, and abortion, among others. Even if significant numbers of Jews and other Americans support the notion of separation of church and state, others view America as a Christian country.

A third and complementary issue that characterizes Neo-Medieval times is the Jewish self-image in relation to the Christian or Muslim majority. Played down largely for apologetic reasons is the fact that until the emancipation process, Jews who wrote about the subject saw Judaism and being Jewish as superior to being Christian or Muslim. Most Jewish thinkers had no doubt as to the absolute truth of the Torah revelation and the falsehood of Christianity and Islam. The only issue over which they disagreed was whether Christianity or Islam was worse. Most Ashkenazic writers, for example, dismissed Christianity as paganism, whereas Islam was viewed as a monotheistic but distorted version of Judaism. In the minority was Maimonides, who hated Islam more, possibly because he and his family suffered persecution from Muslim fundamentalists, and Christians were known to him mainly from the docile Coptic minority community in Egypt.

One of the signs of modernity is the trend for the Jews to view the gentile as superior, more cultured, or just plain cultured, and the Jew as backward and inferior. Jewish self-hatred is modern and ironically represents Jews' belated internalization of the medieval Christian or Muslim majorities' view of the Jews, whom they regarded as inferior. In other ways, of course, it is something else.

More recently, the appearance of Jewish triumphalism, as in Gush Emunim, for example, suggests that there are instances of a return to a medieval Jewish view of their superiority in relation to gentiles. There are even occasional statements about the superior value of a Jewish life compared to a gentile life, statements, by the way, that find explicit confirmation in Talmudic sources but that the more liberal, modernist mainstream tends to play down or ignore. Are contemporary gentiles pagans, or other traditional Jewish categories that distinguish between Israel and the Other? To what degree do the old boundaries clash with the modernist values of equality? How much equality before Jewish collective identity disappears? The Meir Kahane rhetoric that pits democracy against Judaism is a sign of the Neo-Medieval today no less than Muslim Fundamentalism or certain conservative Roman Catholic trends.

And fourth, the modernist's tendency to see diversity in the religious, political, and social movements that characterize the emancipation and Zionist era sometimes act as though what came before was an uninterrupted, homogeneous stretch of centuries of rabbinic Judaism cut of the same cloth. The historical record, however, indicates otherwise. Kabbalists, religious philosophers, Talmudists, biblical commentators, Karaites, Hasidim are but a few groups who advocated a special tradition in addition to taking for granted the centrality of a halakhic tradition, and that includes the Karaites, who had their own. Each group developed an ideology, sometimes rejecting the importance of the others. Each sought to educate their children and fellow adults to follow a curriculum that stressed their set of values over the others. In addition, Jewish elites differed over the need and importance of studying science and mathematics, foreign languages, and the like. These are all premodern clashes.

Thus, variety, polemics, disagreements, prioritization of values, and educational reform movements are not per se modern. What does constitute a modern twist on ancient and medieval disagreements about Judaism is the loss of a religious polity which formed the political basis of a traditional Jewish way of living and in which these elites disagreed. The rejection of central features of collective political Judaism as a minority is a hallmark of modernity, even though it threatens to reemerge in Israel. Similarly, the reappearance of religious standards as political issues, in Israel and in the American Jewish and Christian communities, is yet another sign of the Neo-Medieval.

I would like to close with some comments on the mechanism of some of these changes in the Middle Ages and in modern and more recent times. The way a traditional culture adapts to new circumstances or breakthrough ideas is often by reverting back to an earlier tradition and reinstating it in the present. Michael Hill referred to this pattern as "the revolution by tradition."[1] There are many examples of this from earlier Judaism: the Karaite al-Qirqasani claimed that his customs were the original Mosaic revelation and that the Rabbanites were descendants of Jereboam, the archrebel responsible for the divided monarchy. So, too, the early rabbinic movement, as reflected in *m. Avot*, claimed that their

---

1 Michael Hill, *The Religious Order* (London: Heinemann Educational, 1973).

interpretations of Jewish law and values were all derived from Sinai along with the written Torah. And the Zohar claimed to be a tannaitic work no less pristine than the Mishnah.

The pattern of developing religious creativity within Judaism by reaching back to an earlier time influenced modern religious movements as well. Thus classical Reform looked back to the biblical Prophets as the essence, thereby skipping over talmudic Judaism as time-bound and less essential. Modern Orthodoxy generally continued to look to the long line of halakhic authorities down to modern times—the medieval and late medieval sages. The Conservative movement, too, looked back, but this time to the sages of the rabbinic era, to ethical heroes like Rabbi Akiva. Maimonides could serve as everyone's idol at one time or another, thereby symbolizing a hero who combined, so it seemed, authentic Jewish loyalties with worldliness.

More recently, egalitarian trends in Conservatism that pointed to the book of Genesis for a charter of gender equality are challenged by a traditional wing that resists such moves. At the same time, more tradition-minded Reform Jews are dealing with the weight of Halakhah and the Talmud in a postmodern, if not Neo-Medieval, mode. And the increasingly antimodern wings of Orthodoxy may no longer consider Maimonides an appropriate model.

Despite the similarities of the mechanism, whenever it is employed, there is a basic difference between its use in a tradition-bound medieval Jewish society and in postmodern times. The former were of the opinion that there was no qualitative difference between their own times and the anterior past which they adopted themselves. They did not think of themselves as moderns who were traditional. Postmoderns or Neo-Medievals are conscious of being moderns in search of a more meaningful way of life. Neo-Medievalism, in other words, reflects not only an affinity for tradition but also discontent with being modern.

This leads me to a final point. The medievals and we moderns, at least until recently, sought, and by and large succeeded at the creation of a coherent synthesis between conflicting values. One of the challenges of the postmodern is that it may no longer be desirable or possible to do so. Rather, it may be necessary to consciously entertain conflicting values: some aspects of traditional rabbinic culture on the one hand, and gender equality or a woman's right to choose to have an abortion, on the other; Jewish political self-interest on the one hand, and concern for the body politic as a whole on the other.

Indeed, the very ideal of a coherent, consistent synthesis may need to be reexamined, for I submit that it is itself a construct that is conditioned by the modern. In a postmodern or Neo-Medieval era, we may have to learn to live in more than one world, alternatively at times, to play off one against the other, and to choose which values, which patterns of behavior, which loyalties to follow, each year, each day, each moment. In point of fact, we tend to do this, but we are embarrassed about it and vigorously deny it. It is about time postmodern or Neo-Medieval Jews came out of the closet.

Index

Page numbers of illustrations appear in italics.

— I —

—M—

Lithuanian Mitnaggedism and, 150, 162-63
Metz essay contest and European Jewry, 121-120
Musar movement and, 3, 150
North African Jewry and, 119, 120, 122-27, 128-37
popularity of, 467
religious Zionists and, 417
secularization and, 7, 9, 11
Talmud study and, 3
tradition
as foil for/polar opposite, 452, 465-69
ultra-orthodoxy and, 24, 55
women and, 317, 336
See also Ansky, S.; Kaplan, Mordecai; Law, Jewish, *miṣvot*; Reform movement; specific communities
mohelim, 86, 104
Monish (Peretz), 254
Montefiore, Moses, *217*
Moravia, Jews of, 192
Morocco, Jews of, 2, 120, 124*n*, 128, 135, 135*n*, 136, 138, 139, 140, 142-43
See also North African Jewry
Moscow Jewry, 91, 98, 101
Moses
in the academy of Rabbi Akiva (aggadah), 448, 451, 454
See also Law, Jewish
Moskolik, Yaakov, 94, 94*n*
Mosse, George, 286
Musar movement. *See* Lithuanian Jewry
museums
creation of Jewish, 205, 209, 215, 218*n*, 219, 220*n*, 221, 222, 224, 225, 228-29, 231, 231*n*, 232, 233, 233*n*, 234, 238-40
creation of public, 207
definition/concept of, 206, 215, 225, 230, 232, 238, 240
See also Bezalel museum; specific museums
Mussolini, Benito, 126
Myerhoff, Barbara, 342, 343
mysticism, Jewish. *See* Kabbalah

— N —

*Na*ʿ*ar* ʿ*Ivri* (Schlesinger), 62
Naḥmanides (Moses ben Nachman), 265, 266, 266*n*, 270, 271, 273, 274, 420
Nahoum, Haim, 124*n*
names, Hebrew, use of, 57, 66, 68, 69, 70
Navot, Jeroboam ben, 68*n*
neo-Orthodoxy
defined, 26*n*
emergence of, 25, 66-67
Ḥaredi Judaism and, 177
See also German Orthodox Judaism; Hildesheimer, Rabbi Esriel; Hirsch, Rabbi Samson Raphael; Hungarian neo-Orthodoxy
Netira family, 480
Neturei Karta, 24, 79*n*, 83, 83*n*
Neusner, Jacob, 336, 378
New Moon celebrations, x, 328
Nobel, Nehemia Anton, 21, 22*n*
North African Jewry (Jews of the Maghrib), 2, 3
cemetery visits, 138
community as repository of tradition, 134-36
contrast with European Jewry, 122-23
dress, 132, 135
education
Alliance Israélite Universelle schools, 120, 123-24, 136
reform (Hazzon's school), 129-30, 136
secular schooling, 131, 137
women and, 131, 135-36
European influence, 123-24, 134, 135, 137
French presence, 120, 123, 124*n*, 125-26
Hasidim in, 141
in Israel, 3, 120, 143, 144*n*, 418, 421, 425
Italian influence, 124*n*
mellaḥ/ḥara, Jews of, 135, 135*n*
and Muslims, 122, 123, 128-29, 137, 138, 139
orthodox reaction to modernity, 121, 126, 126*n*, 127, 136-37
rabbinic authority in, 127-31, 143
selective maintenance of tradition, 121, 129, 131-36
synagogues
community life and, 134-35
Dar Burta, 137
European architecture of, 125-26
pilgrimages to, 142
Tunisia, building of, 125
veneration of saints (*ṣaddiqim*), 121, 138-43
meal for (*se*ʿ*udah*), 138
pilgrimages (*hillulot*), 121, 138-42, 144

— R —

— S —

— U —